Baseball America
2023 DIRECTORY

©2023 by Baseball America Enterprises, LLC. All Rights Reserved.

Baseball America
2023 DIRECTORY

Editors
J.J. Cooper, Josh Norris,
Chris Hilburn-Trenkle

Assistant Editors
Matt Eddy, Carlos Collazo,
Teddy Cahill, Kyle Glaser,
Ben Badler

Design & Production
Seth Mates, Neville Harvey

Cover Illustration
Dmytro Aksonov

Schedules Assistance
Brent Lewis

Contributing
Paul Trap

No portion of this book may be reprinted or reproduced without the written consent of the publisher.
For additional copies, visit our Website at **BaseballAmerica.com** or call **1-800-845-2726** to order.
Cost is US $36.95, plus shipping and handling per order. Expedited shipping available.

Distributed by: Simon & Schuster **ISBN-13:** 979-8-9869573-1-9

Baseball America

PRESIDENT Tom Dondero
EDITOR IN CHIEF J.J. Cooper @jjcoop36
EXECUTIVE EDITOR Matt Eddy @MattEddyBA
CHIEF INNOVATION OFFICER Ben Badler @benbadler
VICE PRESIDENT, DESIGN & STRATEGY Seth Mates @sethmates

EDITORIAL
SENIOR EDITOR Josh Norris @jnorris427
SENIOR WRITER Kyle Glaser @KyleAGlaser
NATIONAL WRITERS Teddy Cahill @tedcahill,
Carlos Collazo @CarlosACollazo, Peter Flaherty @PeterGFlaherty
PROSPECT WRITER Geoff Pontes @GeoffPontesBA
ASSOCIATE EDITOR Chris Hilburn-Trenkle @ChrisTrenkle
WEB EDITOR Kayla Lombardo @KaylaLombardo11
CONTENT PRODUCER Savannah McCann @savjaye
SPECIAL CONTRIBUTOR Tim Newcomb @tdnewcomb

BUSINESS
CHIEF TECHNOLOGY OFFICER Mark Taylor
MARKETING/OPERATIONS COORDINATOR Angela Lewis
CUSTOMER SERVICE Melissa Sunderman

STATISTICAL SERVICE
Major League Baseball Advanced Media

BASEBALL AMERICA ENTERPRISES
CHAIRMAN & CEO Gary Green
PRESIDENT Larry Botel
GENERAL COUNSEL Matthew Pace
DIRECTOR OF OPERATIONS Joan Disalvo
PARTNERS Stephen Alepa, Jon Ashley, Martie Cordaro,
David Geaslen, Glenn Isaacson, Sonny Kalsi, Peter G. Riguardi,
Ian Ritchie, Brian Rothschild, Beryl Snyder, Tom Steiglehner

©2023 by Baseball America Enterprises, LLC. All Rights Reserved.

TABLE OF CONTENTS

MAJOR LEAGUES

Major League Baseball	11
American League	13
National League	13

Arizona	14	Milwaukee	44
Atlanta	16	Minnesota	46
Baltimore	18	New York (NL)	48
Boston	20	New York (AL)	50
Chicago (NL)	22	Oakland	52
Chicago (AL)	24	Philadelphia	54
Cincinnati	26	Pittsburgh	56
Cleveland	28	St. Louis	58
Colorado	30	San Diego	60
Detroit	32	San Francisco	62
Houston	34	Seattle	64
Kansas City	36	Tampa Bay	66
Los Angeles (AL)	38	Texas	68
Los Angeles (NL)	40	Toronto	70
Miami	42	Washington	72

Media	75
General Information	77
Spring Training	80

MINOR LEAGUES

Minor League Baseball	84

International	85	South Atlantic	122
Pacific Coast	95	Northwest	127
Eastern	101	California	130
Southern	107	Carolina	134
Texas	111	Florida State	139
Midwest	116		

MLB PARTNER LEAGUES

American Assoc.	176	Pecos	192
Atlantic	180	United Shore	192
Frontier	184		
Pioneer	189		

OTHER LEAGUES & ORGANIZATIONS

International	193	Summer College	232
College	199	Youth	248
Am. International	230	Senior	249
National	231		

WHAT'S NEW IN 2023

The minor leagues saw the biggest shakeup in decades coming into the 2021 season. Major League Baseball took over governance and responsibility for administering the minor leagues, and minor league teams signed 10-year licenses directly with MLB. The 2023 season is the third under the current agreement.

Because of that, there is very little movement and/or changes in professional baseball for 2023. There has been talk of some potential franchise movement in the minors going forward, as facility standards come into effect in 2025, but for now, all 120 minor league teams that began the new Professional Development License era in 2021 remain in place for 2023.

LEAGUE MOVEMENT

ATLANTIC LEAGUE
Added: Frederick Keys

PIONEER LEAGUE
Added: Northern Colorado Owlz
New Nickname: The Pioneer League's Grand Junction Rockies became the Grand Junction Jackalopes.

TRAVEL GUIDE / WEST

Map illustrations by Paul Trap

Vancouver (A)
Everett (A)
Spokane (A)
(AAA) Tacoma
Tri-City (A)
(A) Hillsboro
(A) Eugene

Sacramento (AAA)
(AAA) Reno
A's (a) Stockton
(a) Modesto
(a) Fresno
San Jose (a)
(a) Visalia
Rancho Cucamonga
(AAA) Salt Lake
(AAA) Las Vegas
(a) (a) Inland Empire
(a) Lake Elsinore
(AAA) Albuquerque
(AAA) El Paso

TRIPLE-A
(AAA) West

HIGH-A
(A) West

LOW-A
(a) West

6 • Baseball America 2023 Directory   BaseballAmerica.com

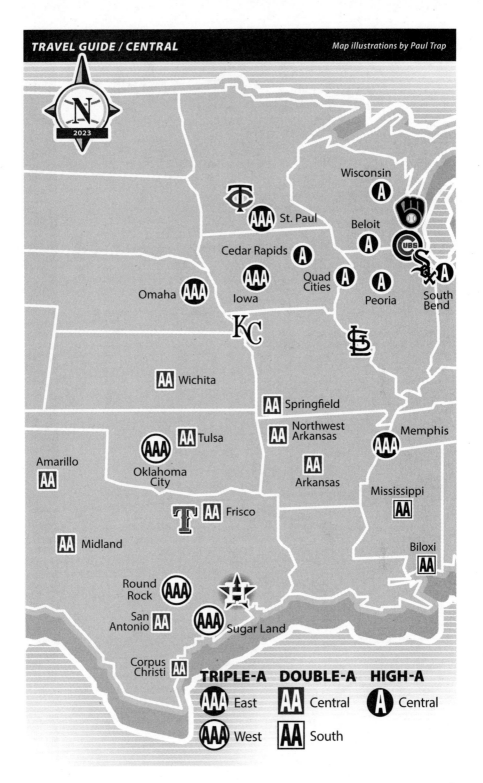

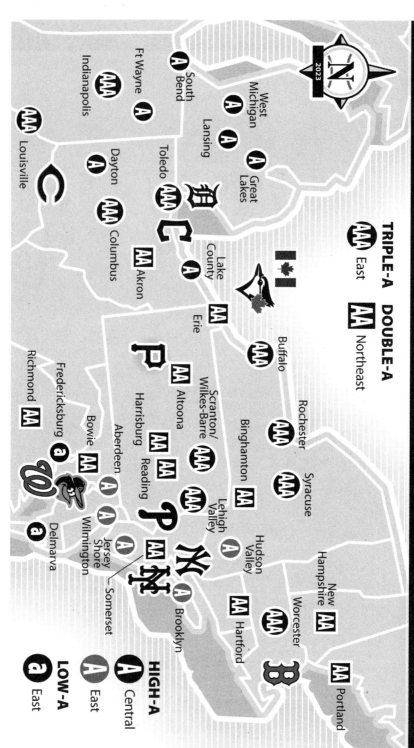

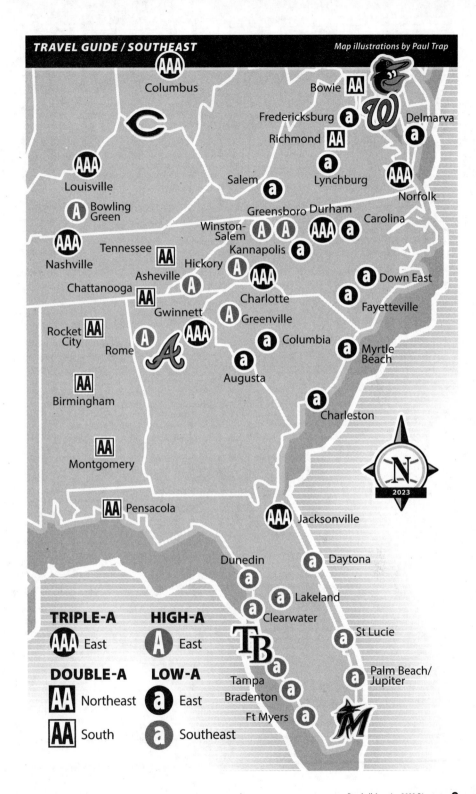

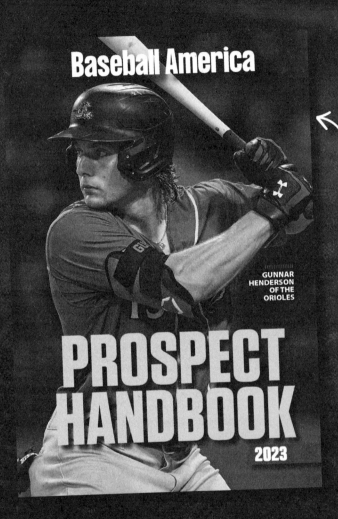

PROSPECT HANDBOOK

The **2023 Prospect Handbook** is a must-have for superfans and fantasy players. You will find yourself returning to the book—now in its 23nd edition—all year to see what we wrote. Get the scoop on big league callups, trade acquisitions or even prospective additions to your dynasty team.

GET YOURS AT:
BaseballAmerica.com/books

MAJOR LEAGUES

MAJOR LEAGUES

MAJOR LEAGUE BASEBALL

Mailing Address: 1271 Avenue of the Americas, New York, NY 10020.
Telephone: (212) 931-7800. **Website:** www.mlb.com.
Commissioner of Baseball: Rob Manfred.
Deputy Commissioner, Baseball Administration and Chief Legal Officer: Dan Halem.
Chief Communications Officer: Pat Courtney. **Chief Revenue Officer:** Noah Garden. **Chief Operations & Strategy Officer:** Chris Marinak. **Chief Baseball Development Officer:** Tony Reagins. **Chief Financial Officer/Sr. Advisor:** Bob Starkey. **Executive Vice President, Chief Marketing Officer:** Karin Timpone. **Executive Vice President & General Counsel:** Lara Pitaro Wisch.

Rob Manfred

ON-FIELD OPERATIONS

Executive VP, Baseball Operations: Morgan Sword. **SVP, Amateur & Medical:** John D'Angelo. **SVP, Baseball Economics:** Reed MacPhail. **SVP, Minor League Operations & Development:** Peter Woodfork. **SVP, On-Field Operations:** Michael Hill. **SVP, On-Field Operations:** Raul Ibañez. **Special Assistant, Baseball Operations:** Glen Caplin. **VP, Baseball Operations:** Jeff Pfeifer. **VP, Head Baseball Operations Counsel:** Paul Mifsud. **VP, Instant Replay Operations:** Justin Klemm. **VP, International Operations:** Rebecca Seesel. **VP, On-Field Strategy:** Joe Martinez. **VP, Umpiring Operations:** Matt McKendry. **Sr. Director, Draft Operations:** Bill Francis. **Sr. Director, Front Office & Field Staff Diversity:** Tyrone Brooks. **Sr. Director, Minor League Operations & Affairs:** Freddie Seymour. **Sr. Directors, On-Field Operations:** Dan Otero, Gregor Blanco, Rajai Davis. **Sr. Director, Player Development:** Mike LaCassa. **Sr. Director, Player Programs:** Yenifer Fauche. **Director, Baseball Economics:** Kyle Macri. **Director, Sports Medicine:** Scott Sheridan. **Director, Umpire Development:** Rich Rieker. **Sr. Manager, Baseball Economics:** Travis Buck. **Sr. Manager, Baseball Operations:** Garrett Horan. **Sr. Manager, Medical & Equipment:** Kevin Ma. **Sr. Manager, On-Field Operations:** Chris Knettel. **Sr. Manager, Umpiring Operations:** Juliette Verrengia. **Sr. Manager, Umpiring Administration:** Dusty Dellinger. **Sr. Manager, Umpiring Operations:** Raquel Wagner. **Manager, Instant Replay:** Jeff Moody. **Manager, On-Field Strategy:** Sean Wheatley. **Manager, Sports Medicine & Performance:** Shawn Fcasni. **Manager, Timing Operations:** Eric Feibusch. **Manager, Umpire Operations:** Thomas Honec. **Sr. Coordinator, Baseball Operations:** Gina Liento-Binder. **Sr. Coordinators, Draft Operations:** Diego Delgado, Mark Nader. **Sr. Coordinator, Medical Operations:** Liz Hebert. **Sr. Coordinator, Minor League Operations:** Sabrina Warren. **Sr. Coordinator, On-Field Operations:** Danielle Monday. **Sr. Coordinator, Player Programs:** Carla Chalas. **Sr. Coordinator, Umpire Operations:** Chris Romanello. **Sr. Coordinator, Umpiring Operations:** Alejandro Bermudez. **Sr. Coordinator, Video:** Freddie Hernandez. **Sr. Administrative Assistants:** Claudia Aristizabal, Llubia Reyes-Bussey. **Sr. Coordinator, International Operations:** Ramon Luciano. **Analyst, Baseball Operations:** Josh Keen. **Coordinators, Baseball Economics:** Isaac Silber, Mallory Williamson. **Coordinator, Baseball Operations:** Anthony Montes. **Coordinator, Draft Operations:** Conor Furey. **Coordinator, International Operations:** Maritza Grillo. **Coordinator, Medical Operations:** Helen Casey. **Coordinator, Minor League Operations:** Gianna Finz. **Coordinator, On-Field Operations:** Julia Hernandez. **Coordinator, On-Field Operations & Strategy:** Sam Therrien. **Coordinator, Scouting Video:** Jack Clark. **Fellows, Baseball Operations:** Daniel Barrueco, James Proctor.

LABOR RELATIONS

SVP & Deputy General Counsel: Patrick Houlihan. **VP & Deputy General Counsel:** Kasey Sanossian. **VP, Drug, Health & Safety Programs:** Jon Coyles. **Senior Counsel:** Vanish Grover. **Senior Counsel:** Justin Wiley. **Director, Drug, Health & Safety Programs:** Lindsey Ingraham. **Sr. Coordinator, Mental Health & Safety Programs:** Isabel Caro. **Coordinator, Drug, Health & Safety Programs:** Mary Ney. **EAP, Latin America:** Francisco Cedano.

BASEBALL AND SOFTBALL DEVELOPMENT

Chief Baseball Development Officer: Tony Reagins. **VP, Baseball & Softball Development:** David James. **VP, Youth & Facility Development:** Darrell Miller. **VP, Baseball Development:** Del Matthews. **Sr. Directors, Baseball & Softball Development:** Chris Haydock, Chuck Fox. **Youth Protection Compliance Officer:** Katherine Anderson. **Director, New Orleans Youth Academy:** Eddie Davis. **Sr. Manager, Play Ball & RBI:** Bennett Shields. **General Manager Baseball Development, Asia:** Rick Dell. **Manager, Baseball and Softball Development and Legal:** Sarah Padove. **Sr. Coordinator, Baseball Development, RBI:** Steven Smiegocki. **Sr. Coordinator, International Baseball Development, RBI:** Chris Madden. **Sr. Coordinator, Baseball Development:** Kindu Jones. **Coordinators, Softball Development:** Rachel Hubertus, Natalia Reynoso. **Coordinator, Baseball & Softball Development:** Cameron Scott. **Managing Director, Jackie Robinson Training Complex:** Rachelle Madrigal. **Coordinator, MLB Compton Youth Academy:** Kenneth Landreaux. **Coordinator, MLB Compton Youth Academy Softball:** Eliza Crawford. **Sr. Administrative Assistant:** Grace Carrasco.

COMMUNICATIONS

Telephone: (212) 931-7878. **Fax:** (212) 949-5654.
Chief Communications Officer: Pat Courtney. **SVP, Communications:** Matt Bourne. **VP, Corporate Communications:** Steve Arocho. **VP, Communication:** John Blundell. **VP, Communication:** Mike Teevan. **Sr. Director, Business Communications:** Ileana Peña. **Director, Communications:** Donald Muller. **Director, Business & Technology Communications:** David Hochman. **Sr. Manager, Communications:** Yolayna Alvarez. **Sr. Manager, Communications, Minor League Baseball:** Jeff Lantz. **Sr. Coordinator, Corporate Communications:** Abigayle Goodman. **Sr. Coordinator, Communications:** Julie Lopez. **Executive Assistant, Communications:** Ginger Dillon. **Official Historian:** John Thorn.

MAJOR LEAGUES

AMERICAN LEAGUE

Year League Founded: 1901.
2023 Opening Date: March 30. **Closing Date:** Oct. 1. **Regular Season:** 162 games.
Division Structure: East—Baltimore, Boston, New York, Tampa Bay, Toronto. **Central**—Chicago, Cleveland, Detroit, Kansas City, Minnesota. **West**—Houston, Los Angeles, Oakland, Seattle, Texas.
Playoff Format: The Nos. 3 and 6 and 4 and 5 seeds play in three-game wild card series. The Nos. 1 and 2 seeds receive byes to the divisional round, where they meet the winners of the wild card round in a five-game series. The divisional winners advance to a seven-game championship series to determine a World Series team.
All-Star Game: July 11, T-Mobile Park, Seattle (American League vs. National League).
Roster Limit: 26, through Sept. 1, when rosters expand to 28. **Brand of Baseball:** Rawlings.
Statistician: MLB Advanced Media, 1271 Avenue of the Americas, New York, NY, 10020.

STADIUM INFORMATION

Team	Stadium	LF	CF	RF	Capacity	2022 Att.
Baltimore	Oriole Park at Camden Yards	333	410	318	45,971	1,368,367
Boston	Fenway Park	310	390	302	37,673	2,625,089
Chicago	Guaranteed Rate Field	330	400	335	40,615	2,009,359
Cleveland	Progressive Field	325	405	325	37,675	1,295,870
Detroit	Comerica Park	345	420	330	41,782	1,575,544
Houston	Minute Maid Park	315	435	326	40,976	2,688,998
Kansas City	Kauffman Stadium	330	410	330	37,903	1,277,686
Los Angeles	Angel Stadium	333	404	333	45,050	2,457,461
Minnesota	Target Field	339	404	328	39,504	1,801,128
New York	Yankee Stadium	318	408	314	50,291	3,136,207
Oakland	RingCentral Coliseum	330	400	367	35,067	787,902
Seattle	T-Mobile Park	331	401	326	47,447	2,287,267
Tampa Bay	Tropicana Field	315	404	322	41,315	1,128,127
Texas	Globe Life Field	332	400	325	48,114	2,011,361
Toronto	Rogers Centre	328	400	328	50,598	2,653,830

NATIONAL LEAGUE

Year League Founded: 1901.
2023 Opening Date: March 30. **Closing Date:** Oct. 1. **Regular Season:** 162 games.
Division Structure: East—Atlanta, Miami, New York, Philadelphia, Washington. **Central**—Chicago, Cincinnati, Milwaukee, Pittsburgh, St. Louis. **West**—Arizona, Colorado, Los Angeles, San Diego, San Francisco.
Playoff Format: The Nos. 3 and 6 and 4 and 5 seeds play in three-game wild card series. The Nos. 1 and 2 seeds receive byes to the divisional round, where they meet the winners of the wild card round in a five-game series. The divisional winners advance to a seven-game championship series to determine a World Series team.
All-Star Game: July 11, T-Mobile Park, Seattle (American League vs. National League).
Roster Limit: 26, through Sept. 1, when rosters expand to 28. **Brand of Baseball:** Rawlings.
Statistician: MLB Advanced Media, 1271 Avenue of the Americas, New York, NY, 10020.

STADIUM INFORMATION

Team	Stadium	LF	CF	RF	Capacity	2022 Att.
Arizona	Chase Field	330	407	334	49,033	1,605,199
Atlanta	Truist Park	335	400	325	41,500	3,129,931
Chicago	Wrigley Field	355	400	353	41,160	2,616,780
Cincinnati	Great American Ball Park	328	404	325	42,319	1,395,770
Colorado	Coors Field	347	415	350	50,499	2,597,428
Los Angeles	Dodger Stadium	330	395	330	56,000	3,861,408
Miami	loanDepot Park	344	407	335	36,742	907,487
Milwaukee	American Family Field	344	400	345	41,900	2,422,420
New York	Citi Field	335	408	330	42,200	2,564,737
Philadelphia	Citizens Bank Park	329	401	330	43,647	2,276,736
Pittsburgh	PNC Park	325	399	320	38,496	1,257,458
St. Louis	Busch Stadium	336	400	335	46,681	3,320,551
San Diego	Petco Park	336	396	322	42,685	2,987,470
San Francisco	Oracle Park	339	399	309	41,503	2,482,686
Washington	Nationals Park	336	402	335	41,888	2,026,401

MAJOR LEAGUES

ARIZONA DIAMONDBACKS

Office Address: Chase Field, 401 E. Jefferson St, Phoenix, AZ 85004.
Mailing Address: P.O. Box 2095, Phoenix, AZ 85001.
Telephone: (602) 462-6500. **Website:** www.dbacks.com

OWNERSHIP
Managing General Partner: Ken Kendrick. **General Partners:** Mike Chipman, Jeff Royer.

BUSINESS OPERATIONS
President & CEO: Derrick Hall. **Executive Vice President & Chief Financial Officer:** Tom Harris. **Executive Vice President & General Manager:** Mike Hazen. **Executive Vice President, Business Operations & Chief Revenue Officer:** Cullen Maxey.

Ken Kendrick

COMMUNITY IMPACT
Senior Vice President, Corporate/Community Impact: Debbie Castaldo. **Senior Director, Foundation Operations & Grants:** Tara Trzinski. **Senior Director, Strategic Community Partnerships & Programs:** Dustin Payne.

CONTENT & COMMUNICATIONS
Senior Vice President, Content & Communications: Jaci Brown. **Vice President, DBTV Productions & Game Ops:** Rob Weinheimer. **Vice President, Communications:** Casey Wilcox.

CORPORATE PARTNERSHIPS, MEDIA & EVENTS
Senior Vice President, Corporate Partnerships, Media & Events: Steve Mullins. **Vice President, Broadcasting:** Scott Geyer. **Vice President, Event Development & Operations:** Michael Hilburn. **Senior Director, Corporate Partnerships:** Julie Romero. **Director, Corporate Partnerships:** Dan Lentz.

FINANCE
Vice President, Finance: Craig Bradley. **Vice President, Project Management:** Jeff Jacobs. **Director, Accounting:** Jeff Barnes.

INFORMATION TECHNOLOGY
Senior Vice President & Chief Technology Officer: Bob Zweig. **Senior Director, Technology Infrastructure & Services:** Jay Gaskin. **Director, Networking, Telecom & InfoSec:** Manuel Sanchez. **Director, Software Development:** Jacob Sloan.

LEGAL
Vice President & General Counsel: Caleb Jay.

MARKETING & BUSINESS ANALYTICS
Senior Vice President, Marketing & Analytics: Kenny Farrell. **Senior Director, Ticket Operations:** Josh Simon. **Director, Business Development:** Carsten Bocchi. **Director, Clubhouse Creative:** Zachary Alvarez.

TICKETING
Telephone: (602) 514-8400. **Senior Vice President, Ticket Sales & Marketing:** John Fisher. **Vice President, Season Sales & Service:** Mike Dellosa. **Director, Season Ticket Experience:** Jamie Roberts. **Director, Group Events & Hospitality:** Alexis Espinosa. **Director, Suites & Premium Hospitality:** Jeremy Eisler.

BASEBALL OPERATIONS
Executive Vice President, General Manager: Mike Hazen. **Senior Vice President, Assistant GM:** Amiel Sawdaye. **Vice President, Assistant GM:** Michael Fitzgerald. **Vice President, Latin Operations:** Junior Noboa. **Special Assistant to the General Manager:** Allard Baird. **Special Assistant to the General Manager:** Deric Ladnier. **Special Assistant to the General Manager:** Jason McLeod. **Special Assistant to the General Manager:** Craig Shipley. **Special Assistant to the General Manager/Pitching Performance:** Burke Badenhop. **Special Assistant to the General Manager/Pitching Strategist:** Dan Haren. **Assistant to Baseball Operations:** Daniel Descalso. **Senior Director of Team Travel:** Roger Riley. **Director, Baseball Administration:** Kristyn Pierce. **Director, Baseball Research & Development:** Max Glick. **Director, Baseball Systems:** John Krazit. **Manager, Baseball Developmental Technology:** Cory Swope. **Assistant Director, Baseball Operations:** Max Phillips. **Assistant Director, Player Personnel:** Connor Shannon. **Coordinator, Baseball Research & Development:** Cody Callahan. **Assistant, Baseball Operations:** Arianna Medina. **Senior Analyst, Research & Development:** Taylor Choe. **Senior Analyst, Research & Development:** Micah Daley-Harris. **Senior Baseball Systems Developer:** Thomas Johnson. **Analyst, Player Personnel:** Chris Slivka. **Analyst, Player Personnel:** Jake Greenberg.

GENERAL INFORMATION
Stadium (year opened): Chase Field (1998). **Home Dugout:** Third Base.
Team Colors: Sedona Red, Sonoran Sand and Black. **Playing Surface:** Grass.

MAJOR LEAGUES

MAJOR LEAGUE STAFF
Manager: Torey Lovullo. **Bench Coach:** Jeff Banister. **Hitting Coach:** Joe Mather. **First Base Coach:** Dave McKay. **Third Base Coach:** Tony Perezchica. **Assistant Hitting Coach:** Damion Easley. **Pitching Coach:** Brent Strom. **Bullpen Coach:** Mike Fetters. **Major League Video Coordinator:** Allen Campbell. **Run Prevention Coordinator:** Sharif Othman. **Run Prevention Assistant:** Rolando Valles. **Bullpen Catcher:** Jose Queliz. **Bullpen Catcher:** Jhonatan Solano

MEDICAL/TRAINING
Club Physician: Dr. Gary Waslewski. **Club Physician:** Roger McCoy. **Club Physician:** Kareem Shaarawy. **Director, Sports Medicine & Performance:** Ken Crenshaw. **Head Athletic Trainer:** Ryan DiPanfilo. **Assistant Athletic Trainer:** Max Esposito. **Strength & Conditioning Coordinator:** Nate Shaw. **Assistant Strength & Conditioning:** Scott Cline. **Manual Therapist:** Ben Hagar. **Physical Therapist:** Merritt Walker. **Manual Therapist/Athletic Trainer:** Junko Yazawa. **Senior Analyst, Sports Medicine & Performance:** Patrick Sellas. **Coordinator, Sports Nutrition:** Joe Scire

Mike Hazen

PLAYER DEVELOPMENT
Director, Player Development: Josh Barfield. **Assistant Director, Minor League Administration:** Shawn Marette. **Assistant Director, Player Development:** Matt Grabowski. **Field Coordinator:** Blake Lalli. **Pitching Coordinator / Assistant ML Pitching Coach:** Dan Carlson. **Pitching Coordinator / Assistant ML Pitching Coach:** Barry Enright. **Director of Minor League Hitting/ Assistant ML Hitting Coach:** Drew Hedman. **Minor League Hitting Coordinator/ Assistant ML Hitting Coach:** Rick Short. **Infield Coordinator:** Gil Velazquez. **Outfield/Baserunning Coordinator:** Peter Bourjos. **Catching Coordinator:** Mark Reed. **Quality Control Coordinator:** Jeff Gardner. **Assistant Hitting Coordinator:** Nick Evans. **Rehab and Complex Pitching Coordinator:** Matt Herges. **Rehab Pitching Coordinator:** Brad Arnsberg. **Special Assistant, Player Development:** Miguel Montero. **Player Development Assistant:** Orlando Hudson. **Short-Season Pitching Coordinator:** Manny Garcia. **Short- Season Hitting Coordinator:** Juan Francia. **Short- Season Hitting Coordinator:** Josue Perez. **Arizona Complex Coordinator:** Jaime Del Valle. **DR Complex Coordinator:** Luis Silverio. **Director, Skills Development/Strength & Conditioning Coordinator:** Vaughn Robinson. **Minor League Medical Coordinator:** Kelly Boyce. **Assistant Minor League Medical Coordinator:** Mike Powell. **Major League & Minor League Medical Administrator/Trainer:** Jon Herzner. **Strength and Conditioning Coordinator:** Derek Somerville.

FARM SYSTEM

Class	Club (League)	Manager	Hitting Coach	Pitching Coach
Triple-A	Reno (PCL)	Blake Lalli	M. Reed/T. Denker	D. Drabek/J. Bajenaru
Double-A	Amarillo (TL)	Shawn Roof	Terrmel Sledge	Tom Gorzelanny
High-A	Hillsboro (NWL)	Ronnie Gajownik	Ty Wright	Gabriel Hernandez
Low-A	Visalia (CAL)	Dee Garner	Kyle MacKinnon	Tyler Mark
Rookie	Diamondbacks Black (ACL)	Jorge Cortes	Xen Penny	Manny Garcia
Rookie	Diamondbacks Red (ACL)	Jaime Del Valle	H. Quattlebaum/K. Judge	Hatuey Mendoza
Rookie	Diamondbacks Black (DSL)	Izzy Alcantara	Luis Sumoza	Josue Matos
Rookie	Diamondbacks Red (DSL)	Luis Alen	Jean Carlos Rodriguez	Manuel Soliman

SCOUTING
Telephone: (602) 462-6500. **Fax:** (602) 462-6425.
Director, Amateur Scouting: Ian Rebhan. **Assistant Director, Amateur Scouting:** Kerry Jenkins. **Assistant, Amateur Scouting & Latin American Assimilation:** Chloe Medina. **Director, Pro Scouting:** Jason Parks. **Assistant Director, Pro Scouting:** Cory Hahn. **Vice President, Latin American Scouting & Player Development:** Cesar Geronimo. **Director, International Scouting:** Peter Wardell. **Manager, International Baseball Operations & Scouting:** Mariana Patraca. **National Scouting Supervisor:** Greg Lonigro (Connellsville, PA). **National Scouting Supervisor:** James Merriweather III (Glendale, AZ). **National Pitching Supervisor:** Jeff Mousser (Gilbert, AZ). **Amateur Scouting Supervisor:** Steve Connelly (Hubert, NC). **Amateur Scouting Supervisor:** Frank Damas (Miami Lakes, FL). **Amateur Scouting Supervisor:** Rick Matsko (Davidsville, PA). **Amateur Scouting Supervisor:** Steve McAllister (Chillicothe, IL). **Amateur Scouting Supervisor:** Doyle Wilson (Queen Creek, AZ). **Area Scouts:** Andrew Allen (Sacramento, CA), Stephen Baker (Navarre, FL), Nathan Birtwell (St. Louis, MO), Eric Cruz (Pembroke Pines, FL), Jason Gallagher (Downingtown, PA), Pedro Hernandez (Vega Baja, PR), Jeremy Kehrt (Avon, IN), Jeremiah Luster (Long Beach, CA), Rick Matsko (Davidsville, PA), Matt Mercurio (Indian Harbour Beach, FL), Mike Meyers (Houston, TX), Dan Ramsay (Spokane, WA), Mark Ross (Tucson, AZ), JR Salinas (Roanoke, TX), George Swain (Wilmington, NC), Garry Templeton (Menifee, CA), Derrick Tucker (Atlanta, GA), Jake Williams (Kansas City, MO). **Special Assignment Scouts:** Todd Greene (Alpharetta, GA), Danny Haas (Madeira, OH). **Major League Scouts:** Bill Gayton (San Diego, CA), Mike Piatnik (Winter Haven, FL). **Professional Scouts:** Tucker Blair (Tampa, FL), Alex Cultice, Chris Carminucci (Scottsdale, AZ), Jacob Frisaro (Scottsdale, AZ), Matthew Hahn (Tampa, FL), Rob Leary (Melbourne, FL), Alex Lorenzo (Miami, FL), Aaron Thorn (Scottsdale, AZ), Brett West (Palm Harbor, FL). **Professional/International Scout:** Mack Hayashi. **Professional Scout, Japan:** Kelvin Kondo. **International Crosschecker:** Jon Lukens (Dana Point, CA). **International Crosschecker:** Hector Otero (Miami, FL). **Crosschecker, Latin America:** Francisco Cartaya (Collierville, TN). **Crosschecker, Dominican Republic:** Omar Rogers. **Supervisor, Dominican Republic:** Ronald Rivas. **Special Assignment Scout:** Mark Snipp (Magnolia, TX). **Coordinator, Venezuela:** Gregory Blanco. **Crosschecker, Venezuela:** Didimo Bracho. **International Scouts:** Luis Gonzalez Arteaga (Colombia), Pablo Arias (Dominican Republic), Diego Bordas (Santo Domingo, DR), David Felida (Dominican Republic), Kyle Lee (Korea), Limberth Marin (Venezuela), Pedro Meyer (Dominican Republic), Alejandro Nunez (Venezuela), Jose Ortiz (Dominican Republic), Ray Padilla (Mexico), Luis Pena (Mexico), Ronald Salazar (Venezuela), Julio Sanchez (Nicaragua), Jose Luis Santos (Panama), Wilfredo Tejada (Dominican Republic), TY Wei (Taiwan).

MAJOR LEAGUES

ATLANTA BRAVES

Office Address: 755 Battery Avenue, SE Atlanta, GA 30339-3017.
Mailing Address: PO Box 723009, Atlanta, GA 31139-2704.
Telephone: (404) 522-7630. **Website:** www.braves.com.

OWNERSHIP
Operated/Owned By: Liberty Media. **Chairman:** Terry McGuirk. **Vice Chairman, Emeritus:** John Schuerholz.

BUSINESS OPERATIONS
President/CEO, Atlanta Braves: Derek Schiller. **President/CEO, Braves Development Company:** Mike Plant. **Executive VP/Chief Legal Officer:** Greg Heller.

Terry McGuirk

MARKETING/SALES
Senior VP, Marketing and Content: Adam Zimmerman. **Senior VP, Ticket Sales:** Paul Adams. **Senior VP, Corporate & Premium Partnerships:** Jim Allen. **Executive VP, Chief Culture Officer:** DeRetta Rhodes, PhD.

FINANCE
Executive VP, Chief Financial Officer: Jill Robinson.

COMMUNICATIONS
Telephone: (404) 522-7630.
Senior Vice President, Communications: Beth Marshall. **Director, Baseball Communications:** Jonathan Kerber. **Manager, Baseball Communications:** Jared Burleyson. **Manager, Player Relations:** Franco García. **Coordinator, Baseball Communications:** Mitch George. **Director, Corporate Communications:** Sarit Babboni. **Senior Coordinator, Corporate Communications:** Kara Zoellner.

STADIUM OPERATIONS
Senior Vice President, Facility Operations: Eric Perestuk. **Senior Director, Field Operations:** Ed Mangan. **VP, Fan Experience:** Scott Cunningham. **PA Announcer:** TBD. **Official Scorers:** Guy Curtright, Richard Musterer, Mike Stamus.

TICKETING
Telephone: (404) 577-9100. **Email:** ticketsales@braves.com.
Senior VP, Ticket Operations: Anthony Esposito.

TRAVEL/CLUBHOUSE
Director of Team Travel: Jim Lovell. **Director, Equipment & Clubhouse Service:** Calvin Minasian. **Visiting Clubhouse Manager:** Fred Stone. **Assistant Equipment and Clubhouse Service Managers:** Eric Durban and Chris Hunter.

BASEBALL OPERATIONS
Telephone: (404) 522-7630. **Fax:** (404) 614-3308.
President, Baseball Operations & General Manager: Alex Anthopoulos. **VP, Baseball Development:** Mike Fast. **Assistant GM/Research & Development:** Jason Paré. **Special Assistant to GM:** Bobby Cox. **Senior Director, Baseball Administration:** Dixie Keller. **Executive Assistant to the President, Baseball Operations & General Manager:** Elizabeth Terán. **Director, Baseball Operations:** Adam Sonabend. **Assistant Director, Major League Operations:** Doug Wachter. **Manager, Baseball Video Operations:** Rob Smith. **Advance Scout:** Jonathan Schuerholz. **Replay Coordinator:** Braeden Schlehuber. **Special Assistants, Major League Operations:** Tyler Flowers and Josh Tomlin. **Managers, Major League Operations:** Caelan Collins and Tom O'Donnell. **Coordinator, Major League Operations:** Will Siskell. **Analysts, Major League Operations:** Jack Byrne, Casey Ciucci, Jeremy Dorsey, Robert Sanders and Matt Winn. **Assistant Director, Baseball Systems:** Garrett Wilson. **Lead Developer, Baseball Systems:** Mike Copeland. **Senior Developer, Baseball Systems:** Isaac Lee. **Developer, Baseball Systems:** Isaac Dinsky. **Director, Research & Development:** Josh Malek. **Coordinator, Research & Development:** Kyle Sargent. **Analysts, Research & Development:** Ryan Corkrean (Data Quality), Stephen Loftus, PhD, Evan Olawsky. **Data Scientist Specialist:** Evan Tucker, PhD. **Manager, Family Relations:** Rafael Becerra. **Coordinator, Family Relations:** Seth Heizer. **Bill Lucas Fellowship:** Terrence Pinkston. **The Diamond Fellowship:** Chloe Tjogas.

MAJOR LEAGUE STAFF
Manager: Brian Snitker. **Coaches: Bench**—Walt Weiss, **Pitching**—Rick Kranitz, **Hitting**—Kevin Seitzer, **Assistant Hitting Coach**—Bobby Magallanes, **First Base**—Eric Young Sr., **Third Base**—Ron Washington, **Catching:** Sal Fasano, **Bullpen:** Drew French, **Coach:** Eddie Pérez, **Special Assistant to Baseball Operations:** Chipper Jones, **Bullpen Catchers:** Jimmy Leo & José Yépez.

GENERAL INFORMATION
Stadium (year opened): Truist Park (2017).
Team Colors: Red, white and blue.
Home Dugout: First Base.
Playing Surface: Grass.

MAJOR LEAGUES

MEDICAL/TRAINING
Director, Player Health/Head Athletic Trainer: George C. Poulis. **Head Team Physician:** Tim Griffith. **Assistant Athletic Trainer:** Jeff Stevenson and Nick Flynn. **Head Strength & Conditioning Coach:** Brad Scott. **Assistant Strength & Conditioning Coach:** Jordan Wolf. **Assistant Strength Coach:** Paul Howey. **Assistant Director, Player Health/Head Physical Therapist:** Nick Valencia. **Assistant Physical Therapist:** Marcus Ahrens. **Massage Therapist:** Nate Leet. **Nutritionist:** Patrick O'Brien.

Alex Anthopoulos

PLAYER DEVELOPMENT
Telephone: (404) 522-7630.
Assistant GM/Player Development: Ben Sestanovich. **Director, Minor League Operations:** Ron Knight. **Coordinator, Minor League Operations:** Dylan Quantz. **Manager, Video & Technology:** Kyle Clements. **Assistants:** Sean Reagan (Video), Ryan Taylor (International) and Tucker Meredith (Technology). **Special Assistant, Player Development:** Terry Pendleton. **Senior Advisor:** Doug Mansolino. **Director, Player Development:** Kevin Hooper. **Director, Pitching Development:** Paul Davis. **Field Coordinator:** Chris Swauger. **Instructors:** Devon Travis & Tom Goodwin. **Roving Coordinators:** Chris Antariksa (hitting) Jay Pryor (infield), Matt Taylor (assistant pitching), Michael Saunders (outfield/baserunning), Greg Walker (assistant hitting), JD Closser (catching), Eric Hrycko (medical), Toby Williams (assistant medical), Jordan Sidwell (strength & conditioning), Ryan Meehan (assistant strength & conditioning), Fernando Piñeres (cultural development), Austin Merrill & Zach Sorensen (mental skills) and Eric Tucker (performance dietician). **Coordinator, Florida Operations:** Matt Forbes. **Physical Therapist:** Johnny Passarelli. **Assistant Director, Baseball Development Analytics:** Colin Wyers. **Data Scientist:** Christina Zaccardi. **Assistant, Baseball Development:** David Lee.

FARM SYSTEM

Class	Club (League)	Manager	Hitting Coach	Pitching Coach
Triple-A	Gwinnett (IL)	Matt Tuiasosopo	Carlos Mendez	Craig Bjornson
Double-A	Mississippi (SL)	Kaneoka Texeira	Danny Santiesteban	Bo Henning
High-A	Rome (SAL)	Angel Flores	Garrett Wilkinson	Wes McGuire
Low-A	Augusta (CAR)	Nestor Perez Jr.	Connor Narron	Michael Steed
Rookie	Braves (FCL)	Cody Gabella	Einar Diaz	E. Nina/ L. Carter
Rookie	Braves (DSL)	Maikol Gonzalez	Adam Wood	Francisco Martinez

SCOUTING
Telephone: (404) 522-7630. **Fax:** (404) 614-1350.
Assistant Director, Amateur Scouting Operations: Ronit Shah. **Special Assignment Scout:** Fred McGriff. **National Crosscheckers:** Gary Rajsich. **Regional Crosscheckers: West/Southwest**—Joey Davis, **East Coast**—Reed Dunn, **Pacific Northwest**—Alan Hull, **Midwest**—Ron Marigny, Terry Tripp Jr. **Southeast Scout:** Chris Roque (Pembroke Pines, FL). **Area Scouting Supervisors:** Billy Best (Holly Springs, NC), Jon Bunnell (Tampa, FL), Alan Butts (Newnan, GA), Travis Coleman (Trail Hoover, AL), Ryan Dobson (Culver City, CA), Anthony Flora (Phoenix, AZ), Dillon Forsythe (West Milford, NJ), JD French (Kennett, MO), Jeremy Gordon (Clinton Township, MI), Albert Skorupa (Sacramento, CA), Cody Martin (Vancouver, WA), Kevin Martin (Los Angeles, CA), Trey McNickle (Dallas, TX), Will Rich (Nashville, TN), Lou Sanchez (Miami, FL), Alan Sandberg (Hopatcong, NJ), and Brian Sankey (Newburyport, MA. **Manager, Amateur Scouting Video:** Alex Burritt (St. Petersburg, FL). **Video Coordinators:** Trevor Andresen (Solana Beach, CA), Alex Leach (Waterford, CA) and Ryan Egdes (Naples, FL). **Director Latin American Scouting:** Jonathan Cruz. **Manager, International Scouting Administration:** Gerald Milanes. **Manager, Dominican Republic Administration & Operations:** Lothar Schott. **Scouting Supervisors:** Orlando Covo (South America), Raul Gonzalez (Dominican Republic & Mexico), and Carlos Sequera (Venezuela). **International Scouts: Dominican Republic**—Reymond Nunez, Carlos Perez, Miguel Prestol, and Victor Torres. **Venezuela**—Richard Castillo, Raphachel Colatosti, Rafael Marcano, Edison Sanchez, and Jesus Simancas. **Video Coordinator:** Marvin Valderrama (Venezuela). **Scouting Analyst:** Alejandro Roman (Dominican Republic).

MAJOR LEAGUES

BALTIMORE ORIOLES

Office Address: 333 W Camden St., Baltimore, MD 21201.
Telephone: (888) 848-BIRD. **Fax:** (410) 547-6272.
E-mail Address: birdmail@orioles.com. **Website:** www.orioles.com.

OWNERSHIP
Operated By: The Baltimore Orioles Limited Partnership Inc.
Chairman/CEO: John Angelos.

BUSINESS OPERATIONS

SENIOR LEADERSHIP TEAM
Executive Vice President and General Manager: Mike Elias. **Senior Vice President, Administration & Experience:** Greg Bader. **Senior Vice President, Chief Revenue Officer:** T.J. Brightman. **Senior Vice President, Community Development & Communications:** Jennifer Grondahl. **Senior Vice President, CFO:** Michael D. Hoppes, CPA. **Senior Vice President, Chief Content Officer:** Cal Perry. **Senior Vice President, Human Resources:** Lisa Tolson.

EXECUTIVE BUSINESS ADMINISTRATION
Vice President, Ticket Partnerships: Neil Aloise. **Vice President, Finance:** Carole Bohon. **Vice President, Creative Content:** Tyler Hoffberger. **Vice President/Special Liaison to the Chairman:** Lou Kousouris. **Vice President, Ballpark Experience & Operations:** Troy Scott. **Vice President, Ballpark Experience & Product Development:** Jason Snapkoski. **Vice President, Corporate Partnerships:** Anthony Verni. **Executive Administrative Assistant, Partnership Relations:** Colleen Gellatly.

John Angelos

TICKET OPERATIONS & FAN SERVICES
Telephone: (888) 848-BIRD. **Fax:** (410) 547-6270.
Senior Director, Ticket Operations and Fan Services: Scott Rosier. **Senior Manager, Systems Inventory and Reporting:** Steve Kowalski. **Senior Manager, Fan Services and Engagement:** Tracy Silwick. **Manager, Box Office:** Eric Wickenheiser. **Coordinator, Box Office:** Ryan D. Fox. **Coordinator, Processing:** Chrissie Werzynsky. **Main Receptionist:** Debbie Cole.

BALLPARK OPERATIONS & EXPERIENCE
Vice President, Ballpark Experience & Operations: Troy Scott. **Senior Director, Ballpark Operations:** Kevin Cummings. **Senior Director, Field Operations:** Nicole Sherry. **Director, Ballpark Experience:** Kristen Schultz. **Director, Hospitality:** Tom Orszulak. **Senior Manager, Field Operations:** Andrew Lawing. **Manager, Ballpark Operations:** Jack Webb. **Manager, Event Operations:** Ben Ginsberg. **Assistant Manager, Field Operations:** Clint Belau. **Coordinator, Ballpark Operations:** Jessie Praley. **Coordinator, Event Operations:** Kira Sebastianelli. **Coordinator, Authentics and Hospitality:** Brendan Smith. **Manager, Mailroom and Office Services:** Dmitri Carter. **Mailroom and Office Services Assistant:** Ayana Phillips. **Authentics Associate:** Xander Tralins.

INFORMATION TECHNOLOGY
Director, Information Systems: Chad Harvey. **Manager, Business Applications:** Sharon Daniels. **Manager, AV & Technology:** Mike Stashik. **Manager, Service Operations:** Tyrell Jones.

FLORIDA OPERATIONS
Senior Director, Florida Operations: Trevor Markham. **Senior Manager, Florida Operations:** Linda T. Jones. **Senior Manager, Ticket and Sales Operations:** Scott Moudry. **Senior Manager, Grounds & Field Operations:** Drew Wolcott. **Manager, Facility Operations:** Dane Bragg. **Coordinator, Baseball Facilities:** Joe DiPuma. **Maintenance Assistant:** Conlan Murphy. **Supervisor, Ticket Operations:** Charles Held

COMMUNICATIONS/ALUMNI
Telephone: (410) 547-6150. **Fax:** (410) 547-6272.
Senior Vice President, Community Development & Communications: Jennifer Grondahl. **Director, Public Relations:** Jackie Harig. **Senior Coordinator, Baseball Communications:** Nate Rowan. **Coordinator, Baseball Communications:** Liam Davis. **Public Relations Assistant:** Tessa Sayers. **Team Translator and Baseball Communications Assistant:** Brandon Quinones. **Director, Orioles Alumni**, **Team Historian:** Bill Stetka. **Official Scorers:** Marc Jacobson, Ryan Eigenbrode, Dennis Hetrick, Jason Lee.

GENERAL INFORMATION
Stadium (year opened): Oriole Park at Camden Yards (1992).
Team Colors: Orange, black and white.
Home Dugout: First Base.
Playing Surface: Grass.

MAJOR LEAGUES

BASEBALL OPERATIONS
Telephone: (410) 547-6107. **Fax:** (410) 547-6271.
Executive Vice President and General Manager: Mike Elias. **Vice President and Assistant General Manager, Analytics:** Sig Mejdal. **Assistant General Manager, Baseball Operations:** Eve Rosenbaum.

Mike Elias

ADVANCE SCOUTING AND STRATEGY
Manager, Major League Strategy: Bill Wilkes. **Manager, Major League Video/Run Creation Strategist:** Ben Sussman-Hyde.

BASEBALL ANALYTICS
Vice President and Assistant General Manager, Analytics: Sig Mejdal. **Director, Baseball Systems:** Di Zou. **Director, Baseball Strategy:** Brendan Fournie. **Senior Software Engineer:** Peter Ash. **Senior Software Engineer:** Jim Daniels. **Senior Software Engineer:** Glenn Dierkes. **Senior Data Scientist, Pro Player Evaluation:** Ryan Hardin. **Senior Data Scientist:** Daniel Martin. **Senior Data Scientist:** Michael Weis. **Data Scientist:** James Hull. **Developer, Special Projects:** Ryan Hallahan. **Junior Software Engineer:** Gannon Traynor. **Analytics Fellow:** Julia Wapner.

MAJOR LEAGUE STAFF
Manager: Brandon Hyde.
Offensive Strategy Coach: Cody Asche. **Co-Hitting Coach:** Matt Borgschulte. **Major League Field Coordinator/Catching Instructor:** Tim Cossins. **Co-Hitting Coach:** Ryan Fuller. **Bench Coach:** Fredi González. **Major League Coach:** José Hernández. **Assistant Pitching Coach:** Darren Holmes. **Pitching Coach/Director of Pitching:** Chris Holt. **Third Base Coach:** Tony Mansolino. **First Base Coach:** Anthony Sanders. **Manager, Pitching Strategy:** Ryan Klimek. **Home Clubhouse and Equipment Manager:** Fred Tyler. **Visiting Clubhouse Manager:** Andrew Guinart. **Umpire Room Manager:** James W. Tyler. **Assistant Equipment Managers:** Irving "Bunny" German and Patrick Thomas.

MEDICAL/TRAINING
Head Team Physician: Dr. Sean Curtin.
Athletic Trainer: Brian Ebel. **Assistant Athletic Trainers:** Mark Shires, Pat Wesley. **Assistant to Head Athletic Trainer:** Chris Poole. **Strength and Conditioning Coach:** Trey Wiedman. **Assistant Strength and Conditioning Coach:** Carlos Gonzalez. **Massage Therapist:** Aquiles Torrealba. **Major League Physical Therapist:** Kyle Corrick. **Mental Skills Coordinator:** Kathryn Rowe.

PLAYER DEVELOPMENT
Director, Player Development: Matt Blood.
Director, Minor League Operations: Kent Qualls. **Coordinator, Minor League Operations:** Ramón Alarcón. **Coordinator, Technology:** Joe Botelho. **Coordinator, Intercultural Education:** Anaima Garcia. **Coordinator of Instruction:** Jeff Kunkel. **Complex Coordinator of Instruction:** Matt Packer. **Minor League Hitting Coordinator:** Anthony Villa. **Minor League Pitching Coordinator:** Mitch Plassmeyer. **Upper-Level Pitching Coordinator and Triple-A Pitching Coach:** Justin Ramsey. **Latin American Pitching Coordinator:** Anderson Tavarez. **Latin American Field Coordinator:** Samuel Vega. **Complex Pitching and Rehab Coordinator:** Dave Schmidt. **Analyst, Hitting:** Dave Barry. **Analyst, Pitching:** Adam Schuck. **Biomechanist:** Joey Mylott. **Player Development Assistant, Complexes:** Jackson McDonnell. **Dominican Republic Academy Administrator:** Rancel Jose Rosado.

FARM SYSTEM

Class	Club	Manager	Hitting Coach	Pitching Coach
Triple-A	Norfolk (IL)	Buck Britton	Brink Ambler	Justin Ramsey
Double-A	Bowie (EL)	Kyle Moore	Sherman Johnson	Forrest Herrmann
High-A	Aberdeen (SAL)	Roberto Mercado	Zach Cole	Austin Meine
Low-A	Delmarva (CAR)	Felipe Rojas Alou, Jr.	Josh Bunselmeyer	Adam Bleday
Rookie	Orioles (FCL)	Christian Frias	Ferguson/Poulsen	Henry/Sadoski
Rookie	Orioles 1 (DSL)	Chris Madera	Julian Gonzalez	Dioni Pascual
Rookie	Orioles 2 (DSL)	Elbis Morel	Jake Ratz	TBD

SCOUTING
Telephone: 410-547-6107. **Fax:** 410-547-6928.
Senior Director, International Scouting: Koby Perez. **Director, Draft Operations:** Brad Ciolek. **Director, Pro Scouting:** Mike Snyder. **Senior Manager, International Administration and Operations:** Maria Arellano. **Senior Analyst, Scouting:** Hendrik Herz. **Senior Analyst, Scouting:** Chad Tatum. **Analyst, Scouting:** Alex Tarandek. **Senior Analyst, Pro Scouting:** Kevin Carter. **Senior Analyst, Pro Scouting:** Will Robertson. **Analyst, Pro Scouting:** Ben MacLean. **Analyst, Pro Scouting:** Ben Reed. **Scouting Analyst Consultant:** Luke Siler. **International Scouting Analyst Fellow:** Connor Pierce. **Pro Scouting Analyst Fellow:** Jarod Bacon. **Amateur Scouts:** Rich Amaral (Huntington Beach, CA), David Blume (Elk Grove, CA), Quincy Boyd (Harrisburg, NC), Ryan Carlson (Chicago, IL), Thom Dreier (The Woodlands, TX), Dan Drulinger (Brenham, TX), Trent Friedrich (Louisville, KY), Ken Guthrie (Sanger, TX), David Jennings (Spanish Fort, AL), Donovon O'Dowd (Arnold, MD), Jim Richardson (Marlow, OK), Eric Robinson (Acworth, GA), Logan Schuemann (Scottsdale, AZ), Brandon Verley (Stuart, FL), Scott Walter (Manhattan Beach, CA). **Pro Scouting Consultants:** Joe Drake (Fort Myers, FL), John Pierson (Phoenix, AZ), Jake Tillinghast (Phoenix, AZ). **Scouting Consultant:** Anibal Zavas (Puerto Rico). **Dominican Republic—Latin American Supervisor:** Gerardo Cabrera (Santo Domingo). **Scouts:** Michael Cruz (Santo Domingo), Rafael Belén (Santo Domingo), Luis Noel (San Pedro de Macorís), Francisco Rosario (Santiago). **Venezuela—Scouts:** Oscar Alvarado (Valencia), Christian Casanova (Caracas), Yfrain Linares (Maracaibo). **Scouting Assistant, Dominican Republic:** Riliani Familia. **Administrative Consultant:** Scarlett Blanco (Caracas).

MAJOR LEAGUES

BOSTON RED SOX

Office Address: Fenway Park, 4 Yawkey Way, Boston, MA 02215.
Telephone: (617) 226-6000. **Fax:** (617) 226-6416. **Website:** www.redsox.com

OWNERSHIP
Principal Owner: John Henry. **Chairman:** Thomas C. Werner. **President/CEO:** Sam Kennedy. **President/CEO Emeritus:** Larry Lucchino.

BUSINESS OPERATIONS
EVP, COO: Jonathan Gilula. **SVP, Ballpark Operations:** Peter Nesbit. **SVP, Fan Services & Entertainment:** Sarah McKenna. **VP, Red Sox Productions:** John Carter. **VP, Fenway Park Tours:** Marcita Thompson. **VP, Facilities Management:** Jonathan Lister.

STRATEGY & BUSINESS DEVELOPMENT / FINANCE & ANALYTICS
EVP, Chief Strategy Officer: Dave Beeston. **EVP, Chief Financial Officer:** Tim Zue. **SVP, Finance:** Ryan Oremus. **VP, Strategy & Growth:** Samantha Barkowski. **VP, Financial Planning & Operations:** Ryan Scafidi. **VP, Data, Intelligence & Analytics:** Jonathan Hay.

PEOPLE & CULTURE / INFORMATION TECHNOLOGY
EVP, Chief People & Culture Officer: Amy Waryas. **VP, Talent & Employee Experience:** Juan Ruiz-Hau. **SVP, Information Technology:** Brian Shield. **VP, IT Operations:** Randy George. **VP, Software Engineering:** Dan White.

Sam Kennedy

LEGAL
EVP, FSG Corporate Strategy and General Counsel: Ed Weiss. **EVP, Legal & Gov. Affairs Chief Compliance Officer:** David Friedman. **VP, Senior Club Counsel:** Elaine Weddington Steward.

MARKETING/COMMUNICATIONS
EVP, Chief Marketing Officer: Adam Grossman. **SVP, Chief Communications Officer:** Zineb Curran. **SVP, Marketing & Broadcasting:** Colin Burch. **VP, Creative Services & Content:** Tim Heintzelman.

PARTNERSHIPS / CLIENT SERVICES
EVP, Partnerships: Troup Parkinson. **SVP, Client & Sponsor Services:** Marcell Bhangoo. **SVP, Community, Alumni & Player Relations:** Pam Kenn.

TICKETING / SALES / EVENTS
EVP, Ticketing, Concerts, & Events: Ron Bumgarner. **SVP, Fenway Concerts & Entertainment:** Larry Cancro. **SVP, Ticketing:** Richard Beaton. **SVP, Ticket Services & Operations:** Naomi Calder. **SVP, Ticket Sales:** William Droste. **SVP, Fenway Park Events:** Carrie Campbell.

RED SOX FOUNDATION
EVP, Social Impact & Executive Director, Red Sox Foundation: Rebekah Salwasser. **Honorary Chairman:** Tim Wakefield.

SPORTS MEDICINE AND PERFORMANCE
VP, Sports Medicine and Performance: Brad Pearson. **Medical Director, Head Team Internist:** Dr. Larry Ronan. **Head Team Orthopedist:** Dr. Peter Asnis. **Head Athletic Trainer:** Brandon Henry. **Sr. Physical Therapist, Clinical Specialist:** Jamie Creps. **Major League Assistant Athletic Trainers:** Masai Takahashi, Anthony Cerundolo, David Herrera. **Athletic Trainer/Major League Rehab Coordinator:** Jon Jochim. **Strength & Conditioning Coach:** Kiyoshi Momose, Chris Messina. **Massage Therapists:** Russell Nua, Shinichiro Uchikubo. **Mental Skills Coordinator:** Rey Fuentes. **Team Nutritionist:** Allen Tran. **Performance Chef:** Ben Piotrowski. **Head Minor League Physician:** Dr. Brian Busconi. **Manager, Performance Development:** Scott Riewald. **Coordinator, Minor League S&C:** Kirby Retzer. **Minor League Rehab Strength & Conditioning Coach:** Jeffrey Dolan. **Minor League AT Coordinator:** Joel Harris. **Minor League Rehab Coordinator:** Kevin Avilla. **Minor League Assistant AT Coordinator:** Phil Milan. **Sports Scientist:** Shaun Owen. **Sport Science Assistants:** Corby Sidebottom, Amanda Gordon, Ruben Izarra. **Biomechanist:** Donna Scarborough. **Motion Analysis Assistant:** Caleigh Hall. **Minor League Rehab Strength and Conditioning Coach:** BJ Foley. **Director, Behavioral Health Program:** Dr. Richard Ginsburg. **Mental Skills Coordinators:** Adan Severino, Dan Abroms, Jake Chaplin, Oscar Gutierrez. **Minor League Sports Dietitian:** Gabriela Alfonso. **Minor League Dietitian Assistant:** Mike Persichilli. **Sports Medicine Administrative Manager:** Elana Webb.

GENERAL INFORMATION
Stadium (year opened): Fenway Park (1912).
Team Colors: Navy blue, red and white.
Home Dugout: First Base.
Playing Surface: Grass.

MAJOR LEAGUES

BASEBALL OPERATIONS

Chaim Bloom

Chief Baseball Officer: Chaim Bloom **General Manager:** Brian O'Halloran. **EVP, Assistant GM:** Raquel Ferreira, Eddie Romero. **SVP, Assistant GM:** Michael Groopman. **SVP, Baseball Operations:** Ben Crockett. **VP, Amateur Scouting & Player Development:** Paul Toboni. **Director, Team Travel:** Mark Cacciatore. **Director, Major League Operations:** Mike Regan. **Manager, Major League Operations & Pro Scouting:** Alex Gimenez. **Executive Assistant/Manager, Staff Support:** Erin Cox. **Director, Baseball Analytics:** Joe McDonald. **Director, Education & Process Analysis:** Greg Rybarczyk. **Assistant Director, Baseball Analytics/Development Research:** Spencer Bingol. **Assistant Director, Baseball Analytics/Player Evaluation:** Dan Meyer. **Manager, Major League Strategic Information:** Dave Miller. **Manager, Baseball Analytics:** Brad Alberts. **Analysts, Baseball Analytics:** Lily Amadeo, Tyler Burch, Jeb Clarke, Nate Hawkins, Sam Larson, Katy McKeough, Kayla Mei, Jimmy O'Donnell, Jonathan Waring. **Assistants, Baseball Analytics:** Joshua Mould, Coby Schneider, Scott Steinberg. **Clubhouse Analyst, ML Strategic Information:** Joe Cronin, Devin Rose. **Biomechanical Engineer:** Stacy Loushin. **Director, Baseball Systems:** Mike Ganley. **Sr. Developer & Team Lead:** Connor McCann. **Sr. Developer, Baseball Systems:** Fred Hubert, Kim Eskew. **Developers, Baseball Systems:** Deven Swiergiel, Eric Last. **Sr. Data Engineer, Baseball Systems:** John Smith. **Data Engineer, Baseball Systems:** Kameron Wells. Drew Paszek, Vince Fitzpatrick. **Tech Specialist, Baseball Systems:** Javin Vincelette. **Major League Assistant, Baseball Systems:** Tyler Forgione. **Minor League Assistant, Baseball Systems:** Sam Denomme. **Special Assistants:** Pedro Martinez, David Ortiz, Tim Wakefield.

MAJOR LEAGUE STAFF
Manager: Alex Cora. **Coaches: Bench**— Ramon Vazquez; **Pitching**—Dave Bush; **Hitting**—Peter Fatse; **Assistant Hitting**—Luis Ortiz, Ben Rosenthal; **Bullpen Coach**—Kevin Walker; **First Base**—Kyle Hudson; **Third Base**—Carlos Febles; **Game Planning Coordinator:** Jason Varitek; **Field Coordinator:** Andy Fox. **Staff Assistant, Replay/Game Planning:** Michael Brenly; **Bullpen Catcher:** Mani Martinez; Charlie Madden; **BP Pitcher:** Matt Noone; **Interpreter:** Keiichiro Wakabayashi.

PLAYER DEVELOPMENT
Director, Player Development: Brian Abraham. **Assistant Director, Player Development:** Chris Stasio. **Manager, Minor League Operations:** Patrick McLaughlin. **Coordinator, Player Development:** David Besky. **Assistant, Florida Baseball Operations:** Stephen Aluko. **Minor League Field Coordinator:** Andrew Wright. **Special Assistant PD:** Ryan Jackson. **Minor League Rehab Pitching Coach:** Dan DeLucia. **Infield Coordinator:** Darren Fenster. **Outfield/Baserunning Coordinator:** Corey Wimberly. **Catching Coordinator:** Tyson Blaser. **Director, Pitching Development:** Shawn Haviland. **Pitching Coordinator:** Chris Mears. **Pitching Coordinator:** Nick Otte. **Director, Hitting Development & Program Design:** Jason Ochart. **Hitting Coordinators:** Lance Zawadzki, Harry Roberson. **Roving Complex Hitting Coach:** John Soteropulos. **Latin American Pitching Coordinator:** Walter Miranda. **Latin American Field Coordinator:** Jose Zapata. **PD Pitching Advisor:** Goose Gregson, Ralph Treuel. **Coordinator, Baseball Development:** Jordan Elkary. **Minor League Equipment Manager:** Mike Stelmach.

FARM SYSTEM

Class	Club (League)	Manager	Hitting Coach	Pitching Coach
Triple-A	Pawtucket (IL)	Chad Tracy	Rich Gedman	Paul Abbott
Double-A	Portland (EL)	Chad Epperson	Doug Clark	Sean Isaac
High-A	Greenville (SAL)	Iggy Suarez	Chris Hess	Bob Kipper
Low-A	Salem (CAR)	Liam Carroll	Nelson Paulino	Jason Blanton
Rookie	Red Sox (FCL)	T. Kotchman/J. Gonzalez	J. Prince/J. Zamora	B. Merritt/A. Rodriguez
Rookie	Red Sox 1 (DSL)	Sandy Madera	Oscar Lira	Eider Torres
Rookie	Red Sox 2 (DSL)	Amaury Garcia	TBD	TBD

SCOUTING
VP, Scouting Development & Integration: Gus Quattlebaum. **VP, Scouting:** Mike Rikard. **Director, Professional Scouting:** Harrison Slutsky. **Director, Amateur Scouting:** Devin Pearson. **Assistant Director, Professional Scouting:** Mark Heil. **Director, Latin American Operations:** Alberto Mejia. **Special Assistant, Amateur Scouting:** Justin Horowitz. **Manager, International Scouting:** Marcus Cuellar. **Coordinator, Amateur Scouting:** Jake Bruml. **Assistant, Amateur Scouting:** Mark Sluys. **Special Assignment Scout:** Steve Peck. **Special Assistant, Player Personnel:** Mark Wasinger. **Professional Scouts:** Chris Calciano, Joseph Curtis, Nate Field, Blair Henry, Mark Kiefer, Steve Langone, Dana LeVangie, Matt Mahoney, Donovan May, Josh Tobias, Anthony Turco, Kyri Washington. **Professional/Advance Scout:** James Cuthbert. **Crosscheckers:** Chris Becerra, Dan Madsen (National), John Booher (Hitting), Paul Fryer (Hitting), Fred Petersen, Jim Robinson, Tom Kotchman (Florida), Stephen Hargett. Todd Gold. **Area Scouts:** JJ Altobelli, Lee Bryant, Matt Davis, Raymond Fagnant, Kirk Fredriksson, Josh Labandeira, Carl Moesche, Wallace Rios, Chris Reilly, Dante Ricciardi, Willie Romay, Danny Watkins, Vaughn Williams, Alonzo Wright. **Amateur Scout:** Spencer Brown. **Part Time Scouts:** Rob English, Tim Martin, David Scrivines, Dick Sorkin, Terry Sullivan. **Assistants, Professional Scouting:** Michael Vetter, Margaret Zimmer. **Co-Directors, International Scouting:** Todd Claus, Ronaldo Pino. **International Crosscheckers:** Jason Karegeannes, Greg Schilz. **Latin American Crosschecker:** Hector Rincones. **Coordinator, Pacific Rim Operations:** Brett Ward. **Manager, DR Academy:** Javier Hernandez. **Coordinator, DR Academy:** Martin Rodriguez. **Scouting Supervisor, Dominican Republic:** Manny Nanita. **Assistant Supervisor, Dominican Republic:** Jonathan Cruz. **International Scouts:** Juan Carlos Calderon, Alfredo Castellon, Luis Cordoba, Cris Garibaldo, Ernesto Gomez, John Kim, Matias Laureano, Louie Lin, Wilder Lobo, Esau Medina, Rafael Mendoza, Ramon Mora, Jorge Moreno, Cesar Morillo, Rafael Motooka, Dennis Neuman, Carlos Ocando, Alex Requena, Edwin Rodriguez, Rene Saggiaho, Sotero Torres, Carlos Vasquez. **International Pro Scouts:** Won Lee (Korea), Kento Matsumoto (Japan).

MAJOR LEAGUES

CHICAGO CUBS

Office Address: Wrigley Field, 1060 W. Addison St., Chicago, IL 60613.
Telephone: (773) 404-2827. Website: www.cubs.com.

OWNERSHIP
Executive Chairman: Tom Ricketts. Board of Directors: Laura Ricketts, Todd Ricketts.

BUSINESS OPERATIONS
President, Business Operations: Crane Kenney. Executive Assistant to Chairman: Lorraine Swiatly. EVP, Business Operations and Chief Strategy Officer: Alex Sugarman. EVP and CFO: Jon Greifenkamp.

Tom Ricketts

BALLPARK/EVENT OPERATIONS
Senior Vice President, Operations: David Cromwell. Senior Director, Operations and Guest Experience: Morgan Bucciferro. Vice President, Operations: Patrick Meenan. Director, Facilities: Ryan Egan.

LEGAL
EVP, Community & Gov't Affairs, Chief Legal Officer: Michael Lufrano. Senior Vice President, General Counsel: Brett Scharback. Associate General Counsel: Amy Timm. Senior Director, DEI/ Associate General Counsel: Shameeka Quallo. Executive Director, Charities and Community Affairs: Alicia Gonzalez

TICKET SALES/SALES & PARTNERSHIPS
Executive Vice President, Sales & Marketing: Colin Faulkner. Senior Vice President, Marquee 360: Cale Vennum. Vice President, Partnerships, Marquee 360: Alex Seyferth. Vice President, Partnership Development: Andy Blackburn.

COMMUNICATIONS
Senior Vice President, Communications: Julian Green.

MEDIA RELATIONS
Director, Media Relations: Jason Carr. Media Relations Manager: Joanna Schimmel.

BASEBALL OPERATIONS
Telephone: (773) 404-2827. Fax: (773) 404-4147.
President, Baseball Operations: Jed Hoyer. General Manager: Carter Hawkins. Assistant GM/Vice President, Pitching: Craig Breslow. Assistant GM: Ehsan Bokhari. Vice President, Player Personnel: Matt Dorey. Vice President, Baseball Operations: Greg Davey. Vice President, Research & Development: Chris Moore. Senior Advisor: Randy Bush, Billy Williams. Senior Director, Research and Development: Chris Jones. Director, Team Travel and Clubhouse Operations: Vijay Tekchandani. Director, Baseball Operations, Administration and Strategy: Meghan Jones. Director, Baseball Innovation: Bobby Basham. Director, Baseball Sciences: Jacob Eisenberg. Director, Baseball Systems: John Goode. Assistant Director, Baseball Systems: Eli Shayer. Assistant Director, Baseball Technology: Kyle Chin. Lead Architect, Baseball Systems: Jay Aichelman. Head of Mechanical Sciences, Baseball Innovation: Jeff Kensrud. Manager, Baseball Operations: Jasmine Horan. Senior Analyst, Baseball Analytics: Troy Mulholland. Senior Analyst, Baseball Sciences: Bryan Cole. Senior Software Engineer, Baseball Systems: Shingo Murata. Analysts, Baseball Analytics: Tyler Brandt, Jennifer Gossels, Connor Rosenberg, Stephen Whetzel. Analysts, Baseball Sciences: Kyle Blum. Baseball Scientists: John Abbott, Mike Sonne. Software Engineers, Baseball Systems: Brian Guo, Jack Wahlig, Sami Williams. Assistant Software Engineer, Baseball Systems: Michael Kim. Special Assistants: Ryan Dempster, Ted Lilly, Kerry Wood. Coordinator, Family Relations: Terri Osters. Assistant, Baseball Operations Administration and Strategic Initiatives: Eliese Hornberger. Assistant, Baseball Operations: Duncan Wallis. Fellow, Baseball Operations: Cal Christofori.

MAJOR LEAGUE STAFF
Manager: David Ross. Coaches: Bench—Andy Green, Pitching—Tommy Hottovy, Hitting—Dustin Kelly, Assistant Pitching—Daniel Moskos, Assistant Hitting—Johnny Washington, Third Base—Willie Harris, Game Strategist/Catching—Craig Driver, First Base/Baserunning—Mike Napoli, Bullpen—Chris Young, Assistant Hitting—Juan Cabreja, Infield Defense—Jonathan Mota. Major League Coach, Data, Development, and Process: Alex Smith. Assistant Hitting Coach, Game Planning: Jim Adduci. Major League Pitching Strategist: Danny Hultzen. Bullpen Catcher: Garrett Lloyd. Coordinator, Major League Video/Pacific Rim Liaison: Nao Masamoto. Intepreter: Tooi Matsushita.

GENERAL INFORMATION
Stadium (year opened): Wrigley Field (1914).
Team Colors: Royal blue, red and white.
Home Dugout: Third Base.
Playing Surface: Grass.

MAJOR LEAGUES

MEDICAL/TRAINING

Team Physician: Dr. Stephen Adams. **Team Orthopedist:** Dr. Stephen Gryzlo. **Assistant Team Physician:** Dr. Chris Hogrefe. **Orthopedic Consultant:** Dr. Michael Schafer. **Director of Medical Services:** P.J. Mainville. **Director, Strength and Conditioning and Performance Nutrition:** Blaine Kinsley. **Major League Head Athletic Trainer:** Nick Frangella. **Major League Assistant Athletic Trainers:** Neil Rampe, German Suncin, Satoshi Kajiyama. **Manager, Medical Administration:** Chuck Baughman. **Major League S&C Coaches:** Keegan Knoll, Esteban Doria. **Major League Lead Physical Therapist:** Nate Whitney. **Major League Massage Therapist:** Aaron Witz. **Major League Performance Nutritionist and Food Service Manager:** Brittany Jones.

PLAYER DEVELOPMENT

Telephone: (773) 404-2827. **Fax:** (773) 404-4147.

Jed Hoyer

Vice President, Player Development: Jared Banner. **Senior Director, International Player Development:** Alex Suarez. **Director, Hitting:** Justin Stone. **Director, Minor League Operations:** Kevin Walsh. **Assistant Director, Pitching:** Ryan Otero. **Special Assistant to President/GM, Hitting:** Greg Brown. **Equipment Manager:** Dana Noeltner. **Minor League Coordinators:** Kevin Graber (Field), Mark Johnson (Catching/Assistant Field), Casey Jacobson (Pitching Development), James Ogden (Pitching Performance), Rachel Folden (Hitting), Steven Pollakov (Hitting), Doug Dascenzo (Outfield), Dave Keller (Latin America Field), Dai Dai Otaka (Infield), Carlos Chantres (Assistant Pitching), Tony Cougole (Arizona Complex Pitching), George Thanopoulos (Rehab Pitching), Desi Wilson (Rehab Hitting/Development List), Jose Menendez (Education). **Senior Advisor, Hitting:** Tom Beyers. **Advisor to Pitching Development:** Mike Mason. **Mental Skills Coordinators:** Dave DaSilva, Javier Guerrero. **Minor League Medical Coordinator:** James Edwards. **Minor League Assistant Medical Coordinator:** Sean Folan. **Minor League Medical Administrator:** Jeremy Clipperton. **Minor League Physical Therapist:** Logan Nordquist. **Head of Minor League Nutrition:** Yimi Rodriguez. **Minor League S&C Coordinator:** Ryan Clausen. **S&C Specialist, Pitching:** Kevin Poppe. **S&C Specialist, Hitting:** Steffen Simmons. **ACL Complex S&C Coordinator:** Dallas Lopez. **Manager, International Operations:** Manuel Rodriguez. **Latin American Assimilation Coach:** Edgar Perez. **Athletic Trainers:** Aaron Clapp, Tanner Costine, Arnoldo Goite, Amaury Gonzalez, Ed Halbur, Leslie Jimenez, Maggie Lowenhar, Leroy Martinez, Nick Roberts, Logan Severson. **Strength Coaches:** Jesus De La Sancha, Phillip Garcia-Herrera, Nathan Garza, Luis Gutierrez, Kelcey Mosley, Conner Rooney, Mark Weisman. **Manager, Hitting Development:** Will Remillard. **Coordinator, Baseball Technology:** Sam Chinitz. **Assistant, Pitching Performance:** Thomas Boucher. **Assistant, Pitching Development:** Henry Haack. **Assistant, Minor League Operations:** Sarah Ketring. **Assistant, Player Development:** Bryan Guo. **Assistant, Arizona Operations:** Norberto Ramos. **Assistant, Arizona Operations and Equipment:** Nick Bray. **Development Coaches:** Collin Andrews, Andrew Betcher, Andrew Craig, Derron Davis, Marco Romero, Andrew Rueter. **Apprentice, Baseball Technology:** Camden Bauman. Fellows: Jeancarlos Bonilla (DR Pitching), Luis Gutierrez (S&C), Tyler Ladendorf (Hitting).

FARM SYSTEM

Class	Club (League)	Manager	Hitting Coach	Pitching Coach
Triple-A	Iowa (IL)	Marty Pevey	John Mallee	Ron Villone
Double-A	Tennessee (SL)	Michael Ryan	Rick Strickland	Jamie Vermilyea
High-A	South Bend (MWL)	Lance Rymel	Dan Puente	Clayton Mortensen
Low-A	Myrtle Beach (CAR)	Buddy Bailey	Roberto Vaz	Bruce Billings
Rookie	Cubs (ACL)	TBD	C. Pieters/B. Martin	A. Gabino/J. Zapata
Rookie	Cubs 1 (DSL)	Carlos Ramirez	Y. Cuevas/R. Pena	Luis Hernandez
Rookie	Cubs 2 (DSL)	Enrique Wilson	Jhonny Bethencourt	Jordal Williams

SCOUTING

Director, Pro Scouting/Special Assistant to President & GM: Andrew Bassett. **Director, Pro Strategy:** Garrett Chiado. **Coordinator, Pro Scouting:** Sam Abrams. **Senior Pro Personnel Specialist:** Steve Boros. **Senior Pro Personnel Specialist/Supervisor, Pacific Rim Scouting:** Jason Cooper. **Special Assignment Scouts:** Jake Ciarrachi, Kyle Phillips, Mitchell Webb. **Pro Personnel Specialists:** Nate Halm, Thad Weber. **Pro Scouts:** Matt Morales, Steve Nagy, Andrew Ahn. **Pro Scout/Assistant, PD:** Alex McClure. **Pro Scouting Analysts:** Max Brill, Noah Cronbaugh, Andrew Gold. **Part-Time Pro Scout:** Robert Lofrano. **Pacific Rim Scouting Advisor:** Shinsuke Yokote. **Vice President, Scouting:** Dan Kantrovitz. **Coordinator, Amateur Scouting:** Scottie Munson. **Assistant, Amateur Scouting:** Ben Kullavanijaya. **National Supervisors:** Ron Tostenson, Jaron Madison, Marti Wolever. **Crosscheckers: West** — Alex Lontayo (Sun City, AZ), **Central** — Trey Forkerway (Katy, TX), **Southeast** — Bobby Filotei (Mobile, AL), **Northeast** — Matt Sherman (Duxbury, MA). **Area Scouts:** Steve Ames (Vancouver, WA), Ike Ballou (Tampa, FL), M'Lynn Dease (Greenville, SC), Todd George (Temple, TX), Greg Gerard (Athens, GA), Edwards Guzman (Toa Baja, PR), Evan Kauffman (Irvine, CA), Steve McFarland (Scottsdale, AZ), Ty Nichols (Broken Arrow, OK), James Parker (Nashville, TN), John Pedrotty (Portsmouth, RI), Ralph Reyes (Jupiter, FL), Billy Swoope (Norfolk, VA), Will Swoope (Houston, TX), Jacob Williams (Pittsburgh, PA), Jim Woodward (Claremont, CA), Gabe Zappin (Walnut Creek, CA), Zach Zielinski (Warrenville, IL). **Amateur Video Scout:** Garrett Tolivar (Baton Rouge, LA). **Part-Time Area Scout:** Keronn Walker (Chicago, IL). **Vice President, International Scouting:** Louie Eljaua. **Coordinator, International Scouting:** Kenny Socorro. **Director, D.R. Scouting Operations/International Crosschecker:** Gian Guzman. **International/Global Crosschecker:** Pete Vuckovich Jr. **Coordinator, D.R. Scouting:** Miguel Diaz. **Coordinator, Colombian Operations:** Manny Esquivia. **Scouting Supervisor, Central and South America:** Cirilo Cumberbatch. **Scouting Supervisor, Mexico:** Sergio Hernandez. **Scouting Supervisor, Venezuela:** Luis Rondon. **International Scouts:** Hansel Izquierdo, Jaime McFarland, Brent Phelan. **Latin America Scouts: D.R.**—Alejandro Pena, Valerio Heredia, Victor Figuereo, Alfredo Souffront, **Venezuela**— Gioskar Amaya, Julio Figueroa, Carlos Figueroa, Alfonzo Mora, Marco Prieto, **Mexico**—Salvador Hernandez. **Pacific Rim Scout:** Po-Chun Chang.

MAJOR LEAGUES

CHICAGO WHITE SOX

Office Address: Guaranteed Rate Field, 333 W. 35th St., Chicago, IL 60616.
Telephone: (312) 674-1000. **Fax:** (312) 674-5116.
Website: whitesox.com, loswhitesox.com.

OWNERSHIP
Chairman: Jerry Reinsdorf.
Board of Directors: Robert Judelson, Judd Malkin, Allan Muchin, Jay Pinsky, Lee Stern, Burton Ury, Charles Walsh. **Special Assistant to Chairman:** Dennis Gilbert. **Assistant to Chairman:** Katie Hermle. **Coordinator, Administration/Investor Relations:** Elizabeth Anderson.

BUSINESS OPERATIONS
Senior Executive Vice President: Howard Pizer. **Senior Director, IT:** Mark Campbell. **Vice President, Human Resources:** Moira Foy. **Senior Coordinator, Human Resources:** Leslie Gaggiano.

FINANCE
Senior VP, Administration/Finance: Tim Buzard. **VP, Finance:** Bill Waters. **Director of Accounting:** Mallory Penn.

MARKETING/SALES
Senior VP, Chief Revenue and Marketing Officer: Brooks Boyer. **Senior Director, Broadcasting:** Cris Quintana. **Director, Game Operations:** Dan Mielke. **Director, Scoreboard Operations/Production:** Jeff Szynal. **Sr. Manager, Game Presentation:** Michael Gomez. **Sr. Director, Corporate Partnerships Sales Development:** George McDoniel. **Sr. Director, Corporate Partnerships Activation:** Gail Tucker. **Sr. Manager, Corporate Partnerships Development:** Jeff Floerke. **Coordinators/Managers, Corporate Partnership:** Krista Pulcini, Elizabeth Boeder, Kevin Burns, Whitney Holloway, Tristan Elmore, Genny Johnson, Erika Morges. **VP of Sales and Service:** Jim Willits. **Director,Ticket Sales:** John Markiewicz.

Jerry Reinsdorf

MEDIA RELATIONS/PUBLIC RELATIONS
Telephone: (312) 674-5300.
Senior VP, Communications: Scott Reifert. **Senior Director, Media Relations:** Bob Beghtol. **Senior Director, Public Relations:** Sheena Quinn. **Assistant Director, Media Relations:** Ray Garcia. **Coordinator, Public Relations:** Colin McGauley. **Manager, Media Relations/Interpreter:** Billy Russo. **Senior Coordinator, Media Relations:** Joe Roti. **VP, Community Relations/Executive Director/CWS Charities:** Christine O'Reilly. **Director, Community Relations:** Sarah Marten. **Director, Community Baseball Programs:** Anthony Olivo. **Director, Digital Communications:** Tim Brogdon. **Director, Design Services:** Toby Ramos. **Senior Manager, Social Media:** Jordan Doyle.

STADIUM OPERATIONS
Senior VP, Stadium Operations: Terry Savarise. **Senior Director, Park Operations:** Jonathan Vasquez. **Senior Director, Guest Services/Diamond Suite Operations:** Julie Taylor. **Head Groundskeeper:** Roger Bossard. **PA Announcer:** Gene Honda. **Official Scorers:** Don Friske, Randy Liss, Allan Spear, Bill Sieple.

TICKETING
Senior Director, Ticket Operations: Mike Mazza. **Manager, Ticket Operations:** Pete Catizone.

TRAVEL/CLUBHOUSE
Director, Team Travel: Ed Cassin. **Manager, White Sox Clubhouse:** Rob Warren. **Manager, Visiting Clubhouse:** Jason Gilliam. **Manager, Umpires Clubhouse:** Joe McNamara Jr.

GENERAL INFORMATION
Stadium (year opened): Guaranteed Rate Field (1991).
Team Colors: Black, white and silver.
Home Dugout: Third Base.
Playing Surface: Grass.

MAJOR LEAGUES

BASEBALL OPERATIONS
Executive Vice President: Ken Williams.
Senior VP/General Manager: Rick Hahn. **Assistant General Manager:** Jeremy Haber. **Special Assistants:** Bill Scherrer, Marco Paddy, Jim Thome, Nick Hostetler, Jose Contreras, Todd Steverson. **Executive Assistant to GM:** Nancy Nesnidal. **Senior Director, Baseball Operations:** Dan Fabian. **Director, Baseball Analytics:** Matt Koenig **Director, Baseball Operations:** Daniel Zien. **Assistant Director, Baseball Operations:** Rod Larson. **Manager, Baseball Operations:** Zach Jones. **Manager, Analytics Coordinator:** Sam Mondry-Cohen

MAJOR LEAGUE STAFF
Manager: Pedro Grifol. **Coaches: Bench**—Charlie Montoyo; **Pitching**—Ethan Katz; **Hitting**—Jose Castro; **Assistant Hitting Coach**—Chris Johnson; **First Base**—Daryl Boston; **Third Base**—Eddie Rodriguez; **Bullpen**—Curt Hasler. **Bullpen Catcher:** Miguel Gonzalez, Luis Sierra. **Field Coordinator:** Mike Tosar. **Pregame Instructor:** Mike Kashirsky

Rick Hahn

MEDICAL/TRAINING
Senior Team Physician: Dr. Nikhil Verma. **Head Athletic Trainer Emeritus:** Herm Schneider. **Senior Director, Sports Performance:** Geoff Head. **Head Athletic Trainer:** James Kruk. **Director of Rehabilitation:** Brett Walker. **Assistant Athletic Trainer:** Josh Fallin. **Director, Strength & Conditioning:** Goldy Simmons. **Assistant Director, Strength & Conditioning:** Ibrahim Rivera. **Manager of Sports Science:** Todd Kubacki.

PLAYER DEVELOPMENT
Assistant General Manager/Player Development: Chris Getz. **Director, Minor League Administration:** Kathy Potoski. **Assistant Director, Player Development:** Kenny Williams, Jr. **Assistant Director, Baseball Operations:** Graham Harboe. **Manager, PD/International Operations:** Grant Flick. **Assistant, PD/Video:** Jack Larimer. **Biomechanical Analyst:** C.J. Gearhart. **Manager, PD Latin American Operations:** Louis Silverio. **Manager, International PD/Education:** Erin Santana. **Field Coordinator:** Doug Sisson. **Pitching Coordinator:** Everett Teaford. **Assistant Pitching Coordinators:** Matt Zaleski, Donnie Veal. **Pitching Advisor:** J.R. Perdew. **Hitting Coordinator:** Andy Barkett. **Assistant Hitting Coordinator:** Danny Santin. **Infield Coordinator/Coach Development:** Ryan Newman. **Catching Coordinator:** Julio Mosquera. **Assistant Outfield/Baserunning Coordinator:** Mike Daniel. **Rehab Pitching Coach:** Michael Bradshaw. **Hitting Initiatives:** Devin DeYoung. **Minor League Performance Coordinator:** Gage Cosgrove. **Assistant Minor League Performance Coordinator:** Sergio Rojas. **Medical Coordinator:** Scott Takao. **Physical Therapist Coordinator:** Brooks Klein. **Minor League Physical Therapist:** Katie Stone. **Minor League Physical Therapist:** Evan Jurjevic. **Sports Psychologist:** Dr. Rob Seifer. **Nutritionists:** Danielle Mach, Christine Jordhamo. **Arizona Facility Manager:** Joe Lachcik. **Arizona Minor League Clubhouse and Equipment Manager:** Dan Flood. **Arizona Assistant Minor League Clubhouse Manager:** Bryant Biasotti.

FARM SYSTEM

Class	Club (League)	Manager	Hitting Coach	Pitching Coach
Triple-A	Charlotte (IL)	Justin Jirschele	Cameron Seitzer	Matt Zaleski
Double-A	Birmingham (SL)	Lorenzo Bundy	Nicky Delmonico	Danny Farquhar
High-A	Winston-Salem (SAL)	Guillermo Quiroz	Jason Krizan	John Ely
Low-A	Kannapolis (CAR)	Patrick Leyland	Charlie Romero	Blake Hickman
Rookie	White Sox (ACL)	Danny Gonzalez	Gerardo Olivares	Drew Hasler
Rookie	White Sox (DSL)	Anthony Nunez	Julio Bruno	Jose Brito

SCOUTING
Telephone: (312) 674-1000. **Fax:** (312) 674-5105.
Pro Scouts: Bruce Benedict (Eatonton, GA), Joe Butler (Temecula, CA), Nathan Durst (Sycamore, IL), Toney Howell (Darien, IL), Daraka Shaheed (Vallejo, CA), Joe Siers (Dade City, FL), Keith Staab (College Station, TX), Chris Walker (Suwanee, GA), Bill Young (Scottsdale, AZ). **Director, Amateur Scouting:** Mike Shirley. **Assistant Director, Amateur Scouting:** Garrett Guest. **Crosscheckers: West**—Derek Valenzuela (Temecula, CA), **East**—Juan Alvarez (Miami, FL). **Regional Supervisors: East**—Steffan Segui (St. Petersburg, FL), **Southwest**—Ryan Dorsey (Dallas, TX)— **Mid-South**—Rob Cummings (Chicago, IL) **Area Scouts:** Mike Baker (Santa Ana, CA), Dan Budreika (Kansas City, KS), Kevin Burrell (Sharpsburg, GA), Abe Fernandez (Miami, FL), Phil Gulley (Union, KY), Warren Hughes (Mobile, AL), Josh Krustulovich (Seattle, WA), JJ Lally (Orland Park, IL), John Kazanas (Phoenix, AZ), Carlos Muniz (Harbor City, CA), Stephen Octave (New Windsor, NY), John Stott (Charlotte, NC), Adam Virchis (Modesto, CA), Justin Wechsler (McCordsville, IN), Tyler Wilt (Willis, TX), Torreon Woods (Dallas, TX). **International Scouts: Venezuela Supervisor**—Amador Arias (Maracay, Venezuela), Jose Ariza (Santo Domingo, Dominican Republic), Marino DeLeon (Yamasa, Dominican Republic), Tomas Herrera (Saltillo, Mexico), Reydel Hernandez (Puerto La Cruz, Venezuela), Luis Moncada (Valencia, Venezuela), **Latin America Supervisor**—Ruddy Moreta (Santo Domingo, Dominican Republic), Miguel Peguero (Santo Domingo, Dominican Republic), Guillermo Peralta (Santiago, Dominican Republic), Fermin Ubri (Bani, Dominican Republic), Ricardo Ortiz (Colon, Panama).

MAJOR LEAGUES

CINCINNATI REDS

Office Address: 100 Joe Nuxhall Way, Cincinnati, OH 45202.
Telephone: (513) 765-7000. **Fax:** (513) 765-7342. **Website:** www.reds.com.

OWNERSHIP
Operated by: The Cincinnati Reds LLC. **Chief Executive Officer:** Robert H. Castellini. **Chairman:** W. Joseph Williams Jr. **Vice Chairman:** Thomas L. Williams. **President & Chief Operating Officer:** Phillip J. Castellini. **Executive Operations Manager:** Shellie Petrey. **Secretary & Treasurer:** Christopher L. Fister. **Senior Vice President, Finance & CFO:** Doug Healy.

BUSINESS OPERATIONS
Senior Vice President, Business Operations: Karen Forgus. **Business Operations Assistant:** Emily Mahle.

FINANCE/ADMINISTRATION
Sr. Vice President of Finance and CFO: Doug Healy. **Chief Legal Counsel:** James A. Marx. **Executive Assistant to CFO/CLO:** Teena Schweier. **Accounting Manager:** Jill Niemeyer. **Sr. Accountants:** Cathy Brakers, Leah Brandenburg.

TICKETING/BUSINESS DEVELOPMENT
VP, Ticketing & Business Development: Aaron Eisel. **Sr. Director, Ticket Sales & Service:** Mark Schueler. **Director, Ticketing New Business:** Patrick Motague.

MEDIA RELATIONS
Vice President, Media Relations: Rob Butcher. **Director, Media Relations:** Larry Herms. **Director, Media Relations/Digital Content:** Jamie Ramsey.

Bob Castellini

COMMUNICATIONS/MARKETING
Vice President of Communications & Marketing: Ralph Mitchell. **Sr. Director, Social Media & Content Strategy:** Lisa Braun. **Senior Director of Communications:** Jarrod Rollins. **Director of PR & Photography:** Michael Anderson.

COMMUNITY RELATIONS
Sr. Dir, Community Relations & Ops: Lindsey Dingeldein. **Diversity & Community Relations Coord:** Adriana Pons. **Executive Director, Community Fund:** Charley Frank. **Director of Finance & Administration:** Matthew Wagner.

BALLPARK OPERATIONS
Sr. Vice President of Facilities & Operations: Tim O'Connell. **Vice President of Ballpark Operations:** Sean Brown.

BASEBALL OPERATIONS
Vice President and General Manager: Nick Krall. **Executive Assistant to VP & GM:** Sarah Vedder. **Vice President, Assistant General Manager:** Sam Grossman. **VP/Assistant GM, Scouting & Player Dev.:** Brad Meador. **Vice President, Player Personnel:** Chris Buckley. **Vice President, Player Acquisition & Strategy:** Jeff Graupe. **Vice President, Senior Advisor to GM:** Buddy Bell. **Director, Baseball Operations:** Mark Edwards. **Baseball Operations Analyst:** Cameron LeBlanc. **Baseball Operations Analyst:** Nick Perez. **Director, Integrated Baseball Info & Video:** Bo Thompson. **Coordinator, Major League Video & Tech:** Edgar Ferreira. **Director, Baseball Analytics:** Nick Wan. **Senior Data Scientist:** Chris Jackson. **Data Scientist:** Sean Fischer. **Junior Data Scientist:** Matt Boyd, Sam Gasell, Andrew Helmreich, Matthew Lehman, Sydney Newman. **Player Development Analyst:** Sam Rizzuto. **Coordinator of Player Dev. Analytics:** Jordan Wergiles. **Senior Director, Clubhouse Operations:** Rick Stowe. **Visiting Clubhouse Manager:** Josh Stewart. **Reds Clubhouse Assistant:** Mark Stowe

HEALTH & PERFORMANCE
Director of Applied Sports Science: Aaron Cunanan. **Applied Sports Science Coordinator:** Jason Stone. **Director of Minor League Athletic Training:** Patrick Serbus. **Athletic Training Manager:** Clete Sigwart. **Latin America Medical Coordinator:** Manuel Lopez. **Director of Mental Skills:** Dr. Vanessa Shannon. **Mental Performance Coach:** Connor Ryan. **Mental Performance Coach:** Rafael Dubois. **Minor League Dietician:** Rachel Sharley. **Strength & Conditioning Coordinator:** Danny Escobar. **Asst. S&C Coordinator/Rehab Coach:** Kenny Matanane. **Manager of Wellness & Education:** Becky Schnakenberg. **Education Coordinator:** Kaitlin Beltre. **Life Skills Supervisor:** Tim Rosenbaum. **Wellness Coach:** Rafael Castillo. **Director, Rehabilitation & Physical Therapy:** Eric Gonzalez. **Coordinator, Rehabilitation & Physical Therapy:** Garrett Valls. **Physical Therapist, Goodyear:** Zach Mason. **Physical Therapist, Dominican Republic:** Ariana Calderon.

MAJOR LEAGUE STAFF
Manager: David Bell. **Pitching coach:** Derek Johnson. **Bench coach:** Freddie Benavides. **Hitting coach:** Joel

GENERAL INFORMATION
Stadium (year opened): Great American Ball Park (2003).
Home Dugout: First Base.
Playing Surface: Grass.
Team Colors: Red, white and black.

26 • Baseball America 2023 Directory

MAJOR LEAGUES

McKeithan. **Assistant Hitting Coach:** Terry Bradshaw. **Assistant Hitting Coach, Integrated Performance:** Tim LaMonte. **First Base Coach:** Collin Cowgill. **Third Base Coach:** J.R. House. **Bullpen Coach:** Matt Tracy. **Major League Coach/Coordinator of Advance Scouting:** Kyle Arnsberg. **Bullpen Catcher:** Joseph Singley

PLAYER DEVELOPMENT

Vice President, Player Development: Shawn Pender. **Senior Director, Player Development:** Jeremy Farrell. **Asst. Dir. of Player Development/Intl Scouting:** Greg McMillin. **Special Assistant, Player Performance:** Eric Davis. **Special Assistant, Player Performance:** Bill Doran. **Special Assistant, Business & Baseball Ops:** Barry Larkin. **Special Assistant, Player Performance:** Mario Soto. **Baseball Administration Coordinator:** Melissa Hill. **Minor League Video Coordinator:** Mitchell Bonds. **Minor League Video & Technology Specialist:** Chris Gabriel. **Arizona Operations Manager:** Mike Saverino. **Coordinator, Arizona Operations:** Branden Croteau. **Minor League Equipment Manager:** Jonathan Snyder. **Minor League Clubhouse Assistant:** John Bryk. **Field Coordinator:** Chris Tremie. **Academies Coordinator:** Luis Bolívar. **Latin America Field Coordinator:** Joel Noboa. **Hitting Coordinator:** Dave Hansen. **Hitting Coordinator:** Jim Rickon. **Pitching Coordinator:** Bryan Conger. **Pitching Coordinator:** Casey Weathers. **Catching Coordinator:** Corky Miller. **Infield Coordinator:** Jose Nieves. **Outfield/Baserunning Coordinator:** Kevin Mahar. **Asst. Coordinator, Rehab/Pitching Initiatives:** Simon Mathews. **Rehabilitation Coach:** Aaron Bond. **Academy Director, Latin America Operations:** Juan Peralta.

Nick Krall

FARM SYSTEM

Class	Club (League)	Manager	Hitting Coach	Pitching Coach
Triple-A	Louisville (IL)	Pat Kelly	Alex Pelaez	Virgil Vasquez
Double-A	Chattanooga (SL)	Jose Moreno	Daryle Ward	Brian Garman
High-A	Dayton (MWL)	Bryan LaHair	Eric Richardson	Todd Naskedov
Low-A	Daytona (FSL)	Julio Morillo	Jason Broussard	TBA
Rookie	Reds (ACL)	Gustavo Molina	N. Irving/J. Leon	F. Corral/R. Oliveros
Rookie	Reds (DSL)	Juan Ballara	Luis Terrero	C. Garcia/D. Rosario

SCOUTING

Senior Director, Professional Scouting: Rob Coughlin. **Coordinator, Professional Scouting:** Daniel Beattie. **Special Assistant to GM, Player Personnel:** Cam Bonifay. **Special Assistants to the GM:** "J" Harrison, John Morris, Jeff Schugel. **Professional Scouts:** Greg Baker, Gary Glover, Joe Jocketty, Ben Jones, Mick Mattaliano, Jeff Morris, Terry Reynolds, Steve Roadcap. **Manager, Pacific Rim Scouting:** Rob Fidler. **Scout, South Korea:** Dan Kim. **Scout, Pacific Rim:** Jamey Storvick. **Consultant, Japan:** Ryo Shinkawa. **Director, Amateur Scouting:** Joe Katuska. **Assistant Director/Midwest Crosschecker:** Paul Pierson. **East Coast Crosschecker:** Bill Byckowski. **Coordinator, Pitching Acquisition & Development:** Nick Christiani. **West Coast Crosschecker:** Rex De La Nuez. **National Crosscheckers:** Jerry Flowers, Will Harford, Mark McKnight. **Southeast Crosschecker:** Greg Zunino. **Carolinas Supervisor:** Charlie Aliano. **Central California Supervisor:** Rick Allen. **Northern California Supervisor:** Rich Bordi. **Central Florida Supervisor:** Sean Buckley. **Northeast Supervisor:** John Ceprini. **Four Corners Supervisor:** Dan Cholowsky. **South Florida Supervisor:** Andrew Fabian. **Great Lakes Supervisor:** Tyler Gibbons. **Georga Supervisor:** Jerel Johnson. **Midwest Supervisor:** Mike Keenan. **Atlantic Supervisor & Analyst:** Eddie Lehr. **Northwest Supervisor:** Brandon Marr. **Southern California Supervisor:** Mike Misuraca. **South Texas/Louisiana Supervisor:** Mike Partida. **South Supervisor:** Jonathan Reynolds. **North Texas/Arkansas Supervisor:** Paul Scott. **Puerto Rico Scout:** Juan Silva. **Upper Midwest Supervisor:** Andy Stack. **Senior Director, International Scouting:** Trey Hendricks. **Assistant Director, Player Develop & Intl Scouting:** Greg McMillin. **Director, South America Scouting:** Hernán Albornoz. **Director, Caribbean Scouting:** Enmanuel Cartagena. **International Crosscheckers:** Matt Gaski, Boomer Prinstein, Phil Stringer. **Caribbean Crosschecker:** Dargello Lodowica. **Supervisor, Venezuela:** Ricardo Quintero. **Coordinator, Dominican Republic:** Jose Diaz. **International Scouting Analyst:** Grayson Skweres. **Scouts, Australia:** Mat Everingham, Donald Lutz. **Scout, Bahamas:** Brian Armbrister. **Scout, Brazil:** Jean Tome. **Scout, Colombia:** Jose Valdelamar. **Video Scout, Dominican Republic:** Luis Aguero. **Scouts, Dominican Republic:** Victor Nova, Jenfry Del Rosario, Edgar Melo. **Scouting Assistant, Dominican Republic:** Manuel Nunez. **Scout, Europe:** Mauro Mazzotti. **Scout, Mexico:** Alex Ahumada. **Scout, Netherlands:** Evert-Jan 't Hoen. **Scout, Nicaragua:** Gustavo Martinez. **Scout, Panama:** Concepción Rodriguez. **Scouts, Venezuela:** Ivan Mora, Victor Serrano, Aguido Gonzalez. **Scouting Assistant, Venezuela:** German Arteaga. **Video Scout, Venezuela:** Miguel Montero. **Amateur Baseball Liaisons:** Cincinnati, Ohio: Miguel Montero. Greer, S.C.: Lee Seras. Yobucoa, Puerto Rico: Juan Silva. **Video Scouts:** Alec Benavides, Kevin Buckley

MAJOR LEAGUES

CLEVELAND GUARDIANS

Office Address: Progressive Field, 2401 Ontario St., Cleveland, OH 44115.
Telephone: (216) 420-4200. **Fax:** (216) 420-4396. **Website:** mlb.com/guardians.

OWNERSHIP
Owner: Larry Dolan. **Chairman/Chief Executive Officer:** Paul Dolan.

BUSINESS OPERATIONS
President, Business Operations: Brian Barren. **Senior Vice President, Marketing/Strategy:** Alex King. **Executive Assistant, Ownership & Business Operations:** Dana Luci. **Administrative Assistant:** Kim Scott.

CORPORATE PARTNERSHIPS/FINANCE
Vice President, Corporate Partnership: Ted Baugh. **Senior Director, Corporate Partnership & Premium Hospitality:** Kevin Murphy. **Senior Sales Manager, Corporate Partnerships:** Bryan Hoffart. **Sr. Account Manager, Corporate Partnerships & Premium Hospitality:** Julie Weaver. **Director, Corporate Partnership & Premium Hospitality:** Wincy Wong. **Manager, Corporate Partnerships & Premium Hospitality:** Joe Janoviak. **VP/Legal & Strategic Planning:** Joe Znidarsic. **VP/General Counsel:** Max Kosman. **Vice President, Finance & Chief Financial Officer:** Rich Dorffer. **Controller:** Erica Chambers. **Manager, Accounting:** Sue Yates. **Assistant Director, Payroll and Payables Accounting:** Mary Forkapa. **Manager, Financial Planning, Analysis & Reporting:** Fredy Feghali. **Manager, Revenue Accounting:** Sam Reed. **Senior Staff Accountant:** Kim Haist.

Larry Dolan

HUMAN RESOURCES
VP, Human Resources/Chief Diversity Officer: Sara Lehrke. **Head of Diversity, Equity & Inclusion:** Matt Grimes. **Senior Director, Human Resources Operations:** Jennifer Gibson. **Director, Talent Acquisition:** Mailynh Vu Nguyen. **Manager, Talent Acquisition:** Colleen Lynch. **Asst. Director, Organizational Development:** Nate Daymut. **Coordinator, Benefits:** Andrea Jirousek. **Coordinator, Training & Development:** George Hill.

MARKETING
VP, Marketing/Brand Management: Nicole Schmidt. **Director, Brand Management:** Jason Wiedemann. **Manager, Advertising/Promotions:** Anne Madzelan.

COMMUNICATIONS/BASEBALL INFORMATION
Telephone: (216) 420-4380. **Fax:** (216) 420-4430.
Senior VP, Public Affairs: Bob DiBiasio. **Vice President, Communications and Community Impact:** Curtis Danburg. **Director, Baseball Information & Player Relations:** Bart Swain. **Director, Communications & Player Relations:** Court Berry-Tripp. **Asst. Director, Communications:** Austin Controulis. **Coordinator, Player Engagement & Family Relations:** Megan Ganser. **Coordinator, Communications & Team Historian:** Jeremy Feador. **Content Creation Specialist:** Brian Havrilla.

BALLPARK OPERATIONS
VP, Ballpark Improvements: Jim Folk. **Senior Director, Ballpark Operations:** Jerry Crabb. **Senior Director, Security:** Jonathan Wilham. **Head Groundskeeper:** Brandon Koehnke. **Asst. Director, Facility Maintenance:** Rosalie Morrison. **Manager, Ballpark Operations:** Steve Walters. **Manager, Security Systems & Analysis:** Tyler Cochran. **Manager, Facility Security:** David Bonacci. **Manager, Gameday Staff:** Anna Powell.

GENERAL INFORMATION
Stadium (year opened): Progressive Field (1994).
Team Colors: Navy blue, red and silver.
Home Dugout: Third Base.
Playing Surface: Grass.

MAJOR LEAGUES

BASEBALL OPERATIONS

President, Baseball Operations: Chris Antonetti. **General Manager:** Mike Chernoff. **Executive Vice President & Assistant General Manager:** Matt Forman. **Assistant General Managers:** Sky Andrecheck, Eric Binder, James Harris. **Senior Vice President, Scouting:** Paul Gillispie. **Senior Vice President, Player Acquisitions:** Victor Wang. **Vice President, Baseball Operations—Development:** Alex Merberg. **Vice President, Baseball Operations/Strategy & Administration:** Brad Grant. **Vice President, Baseball Learning & Development:** Jay Hennessey. **Vice President, Baseball Learning & Development:** Josh Gibson. **Vice President, Hitting:** Alex Eckelman. **Director, Research and Development:** Kevin Tenenbaum. **Director, Baseball Operations—Technology:** Sam Giller. **Director, Baseball Operations—Systems:** Will Landess.

MAJOR LEAGUE STAFF

Manager: Terry Francona. **Coaches: Bench**—DeMarlo Hale. **Pitching**—Carl Willis. **Hitting**—Chris Valaika. **First Base**—Sandy Alomar Jr. **Third Base**—Mike Sarbaugh. **Bullpen**—Rigo Beltrán. **Assistant Hitting Coach**—Victor Rodriguez. **Assistant Pitching Coach**—Joe Torres. **Assistants, Major League Staff:** Mike Barnett, Armando Camacaro, JT Maguire, Jason Esposito, Ricky Pacione.

MEDICAL/TRAINING

Senior Vice President, Medical Services: Lonnie Soloff. **Head Team Physician:** Dr. Mark Schickendantz. **Head Athletic Trainer:** James Quinlan. **Assistant Athletic Trainers:** Jeff Desjardins, Chad Wolfe. **Performance Coach (Triple-A/Major League):** Brian Miles. **Director of Sport Science:** Jonathan Freeston. **Director of Sport Psychology:** Dr. Lindsay Shaw.

PLAYER DEVELOPMENT

Assistant General Manager: James Harris. **Director, Player Development:** Rob Cerfolio. **Vice President, Hitting:** Alex Eckelman. **Director, Hitting Development:** Nate Freiman. **Director, Pitching Development:** Stephen Osterer. **Director, Physical Development:** Andrew Bahnert. **Asst. Director, Player Development:** Ilana Mishkin. **Asst. Director, Pitching Development:** Ben Johnson. **Asst. Director, Player Development—Education:** Anna Bolton. **Asst. Director, Player Development—Life Skills:** Jen Wolf. **Asst. Director, Player Development and Scouting:** Nilda Taffanelli. **Special Asst. to the President of Baseball Operations:** Tom Wiedenbauer. **Field Coordinator:** John McDonald. **Asst. Field Coordinators:** Anthony Medrano, Larry Day. **Pitching Coordinators:** Joel Mangrum, Caleb Longshore. **Catching Coordinator:** Luke Carlin. **D.R. Academy Coordinator:** Jose Mejia. **Infield Coordinator:** JB Eary. **Hitting Coordinator:** Grant Fink. **Hitting Resource Coordinator:** Josh Tubbs. **Strength and Conditioning Coordinator:** Matt Eiden. **Special Assistants:** Travis Hafner, Travis Fryman, Johnny Goryl, Minnie Mendoza. **Mental Performance Consultant:** Martin Rasumoff. **Manager, Latin American Operations:** Ismael Jansen. **Asst. Manager, Latin American Operations:** Ricardo Garcia. **Administration, Dominican Operations:** Cristina Almonte. **DR Complex Maintenance:** Eduardo Urdaneta. **DR Clubhouse Assistants:** Jose Luciano, Abel Ortiz, Nathaniel Perez. **English Teacher:** Allie Eyers.

ARIZONA COMPLEX STAFF

Academy Development Team Manager: Dennis Malave. **Hitting Development Coaches:** Raul Gonzalez, Amanda Kamekona. **Pitching Development Coach:** Michael Poole. **Pitching Rehab Coach:** Dan Mahoney. **Academy Defensive Coach/Fellow:** Jonathan Lopez. **Strength and Conditioning Coach:** Brian Walker. **Athletic Trainer:** Yuka Ogata. **Complex Manager:** Amiro Santana. **Asst. Complex Manager:** Madeline Craft. **Clubhouse Manager:** Fletcher Wilkes. **Asst. Clubhouse Manager:** Mason Wilbanks. **Clubhouse Assistants:** Nate Sandler, Brandon Gilman. **Goodyear Sous Chef:** Katrina Antles. **Front of House Food Service:** Denise Helenes. **Arizona Utility Cook:** Gloria Quiroz. **Lead Teacher:** Paty De La Rosa-Acosta.

Chris Antonetti

FARM SYSTEM

Class	Club	Manager	Hitting Coach	Pitching Coach
Triple-A	Columbus (IL)	Andy Tracy	Junior Betances	Owen Dew
Double-A	Akron (EL)	Rouglas Odor	Mike Mergenthaler	Brad Goldberg
High-A	Lake County (MWL)	Omir Santos	Jordan Becker	Kevin Erminio
Low-A	Lynchburg (CAR)	Jordan Smith	Ordomar Valdez	Tony Arnold
Rookie	Guardians (ACL)	TJ Rivera	Anderson Polanco	Craig Massoni
Rookie	Guardians Blue (DSL)	Jesus Tavarez	Cole Nieto	Carlos Jan
Rookie	Guardians Red (DSL)	Juan De La Cruz	TBD	Jesus Sanchez

SCOUTING

Amateur Scouting Director: Scott Barnsby. **Assistant Director, Amateur Scouting:** Ethan Purser. **Assistant, Amateur Scouting:** Matthew Czechanski. **Amateur Scouting Coordinators:** Jonathan Heuerman, David Compton, Andrew Krause. **Area Scouts:** Kyle Bamberger, Gustavo Benzan, Alexander Botts, Garrick Chaffee, Michael Cuva, Aaron Etchison, Conor Glassey, Andrew Kelly, Matthew Linder, Chirag Nanavati.
International Scouting Director: Richard Conway. **Director, Latin American Player Personnel:** Alex DeMoya. **International Scouting Coordinator:** Eugenio Melendez. **Senior Vice President, Scouting:** Paul Gillispie. **Director of Acquisitions:** Clint Longenecker. **Special Assistants to the Vice President and General Manager:** David Malpass, Steve Lubratich. **Director, Player Evaluations:** Chris Gale. **Special Assignment Scouts:** David Miller, Scott Meaney, Doug Carpenter. **Sr. Player Acquisition Scouts:** Lukas McKnight, Kevin Cullen. **Player Acquisition Scout:** Ryan Perry.

MAJOR LEAGUES

COLORADO ROCKIES

Office Address: 2001 Blake St., Denver, CO 80205.
Telephone: (303) 292-0200. **Fax:** (303) 312-2116.
Website: www.Rockies.com.

OWNERSHIP
Operated by: Colorado Rockies Baseball Club Ltd.
Owner/Chairman & Chief Executive Officer: Richard L. Monfort. **Executive Assistant to the Owner/Chairman & Chief Executive Officer:** Terry Douglass. **Owner/General Partner:** Charles K. Monfort.

BUSINESS OPERATIONS
President/Chief Operating Officer: Greg Feasel. **Assistant to President/Chief Operating Officer:** Kim Olson. **VP, Human Resources:** Kimberly Molina. **Director, Diversity, Equity, Inclusion & Recruiting, Human Resources:** Dallas Davis.

FINANCE
Assistant to the Executive Vice President: Tammy Vergara. **VP/CFO:** Michael Kent. **VP/General Counsel:** Brian Gaffney. **Payroll Manager:** Juli Daedelow. **Payroll Administrator:** Jillaine Martinez. **Senior Director, Accounting:** Phil Emerson. **Accountants:** Laine Campbell, Cameryn Fox. **Senior Director, Procurement:** Gary Lawrence. **Coordinator, Purchasing:** Robert Wilkinson.

Richard Monfort

CORPORATE PARTNERSHIPS
VP, Corporate Partnerships: Walker Monfort. **Assistant to VP, Corporate Partnerships:** Nicole Scheller. **Senior Director, Client Services & Promotions:** Kari Anderson. **Director, Corporate Partnerships:** Nate VanderWal. **Assistant Director, Corporate Partnerships:** Christopher Zumbrennen. **Senior Director, In-Game Entertainment & Event Operations:** Kent Krosbakken. **Public Address Announcer:** Reed Saunders.

COMMUNITY/RETAIL OPERATIONS
VP, Community & Retail Operations: James P. Kellogg. **Assistant to the VP, Community & Retail Operations:** Kelly Hall. **Senior Director, Retail Operations:** Aaron Heinrich.

MARKETING/COMMUNICATIONS
Senior Director, Communications: Cory Little. **Manager: Communications:** Shelby Cravens. **Coordinators, Communications:** Kevin Collins, Robert Livingston. **Manager, Digital Communications/Social Media:** Nora Farrell. **Coordinator, Social Media:** Madison Casiano. **Team Photographer:** Kyle Cooper.

BALLPARK OPERATIONS
VP/Chief Customer Officer, Ballpark Operations: Kevin Kahn. **Assistant to the VP/Chief Customer Officer, Ballpark Operations:** Lenus Lucero. **Senior Director, Food Service Operations/Development:** John McKay. **Senior Director, Guest Services:** Steven Burke. **Head Groundskeeper:** Mark Razum. **Assistant Head Groundskeeper:** Doug Zabinsky. **Senior Director, Engineering & Facilities:** Allyson Gutierrez.

TICKETING
Telephone: (303) 762-5337, (800) 388-7625. **Fax:** (303) 312-2115. **VP, Ticket Operations, Sales & Services:** Sue Ann McClaren.

TRAVEL/CLUBHOUSE
Senior Director, Major League Operations: Paul Egins. **Manager, Major League Clubhouse:** Mike Pontarelli. **Manager, Clubhouse Purchasing/Visiting Clubhouse:** Alan Bossart.

BASEBALL OPERATIONS
Senior VP/General Manager: Bill Schmidt. **Assistant to Senior VP/GM:** Irma Castañeda. **VP, Asst GM/BB Ops and Assistant General Counsel:** Zack Rosenthal. **Senior Director, ML Operations:** Paul Egins. **Director, Baseball Operations:** Al Gilbert. **Analyst, Baseball Operations:** Amir Mamdani. **Coordinator, Baseball Operations:** Julianna Rubin. **Director: Research & Development:** Brian Jones. **Manager, Baseball Research:** Brittany Haby. **Manager, Baseball Systems:** Isaac Gerhart-Hines. **Data Engineer:** Declan Costello. **R&D Analyst, Player Development:** Chris Bonk. **Full Stack Developer, R&D:** Michael Brandt. **Analyst, R&D:** Jack Voigt. **Baseball Operations Fellow:** Allison Florian.

MAJOR LEAGUE STAFF
Manager: Bud Black. **Coaches: Bench**—Mike Redmond, **Pitching**—Darryl Scott, **Hitting**— Hensley Meulens.

GENERAL INFORMATION
Stadium (year opened): Coors Field (1995). **Playing Surface:** Grass.
Team Colors: Purple, black and silver.
Home Dugout: First Base.

MAJOR LEAGUES

Assistant Hitting Coaches—Andy Gonzalez, P.J. Pilittere. **First Base**—Ron Gideon, **Third Base**—Warren Schaeffer, **Bullpen**—Reid Cornelius, **Bullpen Catchers**—Kyle Cunningham, Aaron Munoz, **Director, Physical Performance**—Gabe Bauer. **Coordinator, ML Performance:** Mike Jasperson. **Video**—Jimmy Hartley.

MEDICAL/TRAINING
Director of Medical Operations/Major League head Athletic Trainer: Keith Dugger. **Medical Director:** Dr. Thomas Noonan. **Club Physicians:** Dr. Allen Schreiber, Dr. Douglas Wyland. **Assistant Head Athletic Trainer:** Heath Townsend. **ML Assistant Athletic Trainer:** Andy Stover. **ML Athletic Training/Rehab Coordinator:** Scott Murayama.

PLAYER DEVELOPMENT
Director: Chris Forbes. **Assistant Director:** Jesse Stender. **Coordinator:** Tim Batesole. **PD & Pro Scouting Assistant:** Avery Griggs. **Director Pitching Operations:** Steve Foster. **Coordinator of Pitching Strategies:** Flint Wallace. **Pitching Coordinator:** Doug Linton. **Latin American Hitting Coordinator:** Michael Ramirez. **Field & Catching Coordinator:** Mark Strittmatter. **Defensive Coordinator:** Doug Bernier. **Latin America Field & Pitching Coordinator:** Edison Lora. **Physical Performance Coordinator:** Trevor Swartz. **Cultural Development Coordinator:** Arnaldo Gomez. **Director, Mental Skills Development:** Doug Chadwick. **Coordinators, Mental Skills:** Jerry Amador, Colt Olson. **Coordinator, Cultural Development:** Angel Amparo. **Minor League Clubhouse & Equipment Manager/Manager Salt River Fields:** Daniel Kleinholz. **Dominican Republic Complex Administrator:** Ana Espiñal. **Special Assistants:** Todd Helton, Clint Hurdle, Marcel Lachemann, Rick Mathews, Scott Oberg, Rick Mathews, Jerry Weinstein.

Bill Schmidt

FARM SYSTEM

Class	Club (League)	Manager	Hitting Coach	Pitching Coach
Triple-A	Albuquerque (PCL)	Pedro Lopez	Jordan Pacheco	Chris Michalak
Double-A	Hartford (EL)	Chris Denorfia	Tom Sutaris	Blaine Beatty
High-A	Spokane (NWL)	Robinson Cancel	Zach Osborne	Ryan Kibler
Low-A	Fresno (CAL)	Steve Soliz	Trevor Burmeister	Mark Brewer
Rookie	Rockies (ACL)	Fred Ocasio	TBA	D. Burba/H. Rodriguez
Rookie	Rockies (DSL)	M. Gonzalez/E. Jose	F. Rosario/F. Nunez	Sam Deduno

SCOUTING
VP / Assistant General Manager Scouting: Danny Montgomery. **Sr. Director, Scouting Operations:** Marc Gustafson. **Scout/Scouting Ops Administrator:** Emily Glass. **Assistant Scouting Director:** Damon Iannelli. **Advance Scouts:** Joe Little (Arvada, CO), Alan Regier (Gilbert, AZ). **Director, Pro Scouting:** Sterling Monfort. **Special Assistant, Player Personnel:** Ty Coslow (Louisville, KY). **Major League Scouts:** Kevin Bootay (Elk Grove, CA), Steve Fleming (Louisa, VA), Max George (Denver, CO), Will George (Milford, DE), Jack Gillis (Sarasota, FL), Mark Germann (Denver, CO), Joe Housey (Hollywood, FL), John Corbin (Savannah, GA). **National Crosscheckers:** Mike Ericson (Phoenix, AZ), Jay Matthews (Concord, NC). **Area Scouts:** Scott Alves (Phoenix, AZ), Brett Baldwin (Kansas City, MO), Julio Campos (Guaynabo, PR) John Cedarburg (Fort Myers, FL), Garrick Chaffee (Dallas, TX) Jermaine Clark (Fresno, CA) Scott Corman (Lexington, KY), Jordan Czarniecki (Greenville, SC), Sean Gamble (Atlanta, GA), Mike Garlatti (Edison, NJ), Matt Hattabaugh (Westminster, CA), Tim McDonnell (Olinda, CA) Matt Pignataro (Seattle, WA), Jesse Retzlaff (Dallas, TX), Rafael Reyes (Miami, FL), Ed Santa (Powell, OH), Zack Zulli (Ocean Springs, MS). **Part-Time Scout:** Greg Pullia (Plymouth, MA). **VP, International Scouting/Player Development:** Rolando Fernandez. **International Crosscheckers:** Alving Mejias, Marc Russo. **Supervisor, Latin America Scouting:** Orlando Medina. **Scouting Operations Coordinator:** Enmanuel Frias (Dominican Republic), **Scouting Coordinator:** Omar Frias (Dominican Republic),Martin Cabrera (Dominican Republic), Joel Diaz (Venezuela), Rogers Figueroa (Colombia), Carlos Gomez (Venezuela), Alberto Plascencia (Mexico), Frank Roa (Dominican Republic).

MAJOR LEAGUES

DETROIT TIGERS

Office Address: 2100 Woodward Ave, Detroit, MI 48201.
Telephone: (313) 471-2000. **Fax:** (313) 471-2138. **Website:** www.tigers.com

OWNERSHIP
Operated By: Detroit Tigers Inc. **Chairman & CEO, Detroit Tigers:** Christopher Ilitch.

BUSINESS OPERATIONS

BUSINESS OPERATIONS LEADERSHIP
President & CEO, Ilitch Sports and Entertainment: Chris McGowan. **Senior Vice President, Ticket Sales & Service:** Spencer Ambrosius. **Senior Vice President, Human Resources:** Michele Bartos. **Senior Vice President, Finance:** Russ Borrows. **Senior Vice President, Operations and Development:** Keith Bradford. **Senior Vice President, Legal Affairs:** Robert E. Carr. **Senior Vice President, Corporate Sales:** Chris Coffman. **Senior Vice President, Communications & Broadcasting:** Ron Colangelo. **Senior Vice President, Business Operations Strategy:** Ryan Gustafson. **Senior Vice President & Chief Marketing Officer:** Alexis Lee. **Vice President, Corporate Partnership Sales:** Melissa Brennan. **Vice President, Lakeland Business Operations:** Josh Bullock. **Vice President, Venue Security:** Mike Hartnett. **Vice President, Finance:** Bobby Hoekstra. **Vice President, Park Operations:** Chris Lawrence. **Vice President, Premium Sales & Private Events:** Michael Lienert. **Vice President, Ticket Sales & Service:** Joe Schiavi. **Vice President, Corporate Partnerships Business Strategy & Solutions:** Mike Singer. **Vice President, Marketing:** Ellen Hill Zeringue.

Chris Ilitch

FINANCE/HUMAN RESOURCES
Director, Finance: Katelyn Haas. **Director, Purchasing:** McKenzie Reeves. **Director, Talent Acquisition:** Rich Balow. **Accounting Manager & Treasury Analyst:** Sheila Robine. **Accounting Manager:** Mark Renshaw. **Manager, Payroll:** Mark Cebelak.

CORPORATE PARTNERSHIPS/TICKET SALES & SERVICES
Director, Corporate Partnership Activation: Tiffany Harrington. **Activation Managers, Corporate Partnerships:** Ian Fontenot, Michael Holley, Riley McCord, Cullen Munz. **Agency Activation Manager, Corporate Partnerships:** Bean O'Malley. **Activation Project Manager, Corporate Partnerships:** Tina Genitti. **Radio Sales Manager, Corporate Partnerships:** Christine Galasso. **Solutions Managers, Corporate Partnerships:** Madison Curl, Max Klepper, Jacob Pnakovich. **Sales Managers, Corporate Partnerships:** Cameron Close, Megan Garlow, Matt Gay, Stephen Girard, Dave Nietzer, Donovan Powell, John Wolski.

TICKET SALES & SERVICES
Senior Director, Ticket Services: Grant Anderson. **Senior Director, Ticket Sales:** Allen Jabero. **Senior Director, Client Services:** Brian Jemison. **Director, Ticket Sales & Service Operations:** Liz Karolak. **Director, Ticket Services:** Adam Klein. **Director, Inside Sales:** Hayden Dotson. **Director, Business Analytics:** Jeff Lutz. **Manager, Ticket Services:** Andrew Burnham. **Manager, Inside Sales:** Aaron Ryley. **Manager, Group Sales:** Marc Lopez. **Manager, Private Events:** Emily Brandt. **Manager, Premium Sales:** Kevin McConnell. **Manager, Premium Service:** Stacy Winters.

MARKETING/COMMUNICATIONS/COMMUNITY IMPACT
Director, Community Impact: Kevin Brown. **Director, Communications:** Chad Crunk. **Director, Communications & Broadcasting:** Ben Fidelman. **Director, Player Relations & Authentics:** Jordan Field. **Director, Broadcasting & In-Game Entertainment:** Stan Fracker. **Director, Promotions & Special Events:** Haley Kolff. **Director, Fundraising & Development:** Shannon Lapsley. **Manager, Digital Marketing:** Blaze Chastain. **Manager, Social Media:** Greg Garno. **Manager, Promotions & Special Events:** Evan Novak. **Manager, Marketing:** Taylor Olson. **Manager, Outreach & Engagement:** Jonathon Perry. **Manager, Fantasy Camp, Player & Alumni Engagement:** Ashley Robinson. **Manager, Fundraising & Development:** Kelsey Stewart. **Manager, Sport Participation & Growth:** Matthew Williams. **Senior Producer & Scoreboard Production Manager:** Alex Lovachis.

PARK OPERATIONS/SECURITY
Director, Event Operations: Mike Bauer. **Director, Facilities:** Shaun O'Brien. **Director, Security:** Lori Dillon. **Head Groundskeeper:** Heather Nabozny. **Manager, Event Operations:** Caitlin Kelly. **Manager, Guest Experience:** Alex Santisteban. **Manager, Event Services:** Dana Moore. **Engineering Services Manager:** Richard Klemm. **Managers, Operations:** Steve Burrows, Austin Doherty, Mike Kiefer. **Manager, Security:** Andy Torok.

GENERAL INFORMATION
Stadium (year opened): Comerica Park (2000).
Team Colors: Navy blue, orange and white.
Home Dugout: Third Base.
Playing Surface: Grass.

MAJOR LEAGUES

BASEBALL OPERATIONS

Telephone: (313) 471-2000. **Fax:** (313) 471-2099.
President, Baseball Operations: Scott Harris. **Vice President/Assistant General Managers:** Sam Menzler, Rob Metzler, Jay Sartori. **Vice President, Player Personnel:** Scott Bream. **Vice President, Player Development:** Ryan Garko. **Special Assistants to the GM:** Kirk Gibson, Willie Horton, Jim Leyland, Lance Parrish, Mike Russell, Alan Trammell. **Director, Baseball Research & Development:** Jim Logue. **Director, Team Travel:** Brian Britten. **Executive Assistant to the President, Baseball Operations:** Marty Lyon.

Scott Harris

MAJOR LEAGUE STAFF

Manager: A.J. Hinch. **Coaches: Pitching**—Chris Fetter, **Hitting**—Keith Beauregard, Michael Brdar, **First Base**—Alfredo Amezaga, **Third Base**—Gary Jones, **Assistant Pitching**—Robin Lund, Juan Nieves, **Bench**—George Lombard, **Assisting Hitting**—James Rowson, **Catching**—Tim Federowicz.

MEDICAL/TRAINING

Head Athletic Trainer: Ryne Eubanks. **Director, Medical Administration & Lakeland Operations:** Doug Teter. **Assistant Athletic Trainers:** Matt Rankin, Chris McDonald. **Physical Therapist:** Duncan Evans. **Major League Nutrition Coordinator:** Maureen Stoecklein, RD. **Major League Strength & Conditioning Coach:** Nelson Perez. **Major League Performance Coach:** Shane Wallen.

PLAYER DEVELOPMENT

Vice President, Player Development: Ryan Garko. **Director, Minor League Operations:** Dan Lunetta. **Director, Hitting:** Kenny Graham. **Director, Pitching:** Gabe Ribas. **Director, Coaching & Field Coordinator:** Ryan Sienko. **Director, Performance Science:** Dr. Georgia Giblin. **Director, Minor League & Scouting Administration:** Cheryl Evans. **Director, International Operations:** Tom Moore. **Director, Latin American Operations:** Miguel Garcia. **Director, Latin American Player Development:** Euclides Rojas. **Administrators, Dominican Academy:** Wilfredo Crespo, Jimmy Ortiz. **Assistant Director, Player Development:** Peter Bransfield. **Manager, Player Development:** David Allende. **Manager, International Operations:** Rafael Gonzalez. **Coordinators, Player Development:** Daniel Crago, Jose Sajour. **Coordinator, Minor League Complex:** Kevin Guthrie. **Minor League Medical Coordinator:** Corey Tremble. **Minor League Strength & Conditioning Coordinators:** Ryan Maedel, Francisco Rivas. **Medical Coordinator—International:** Manny Pena. **Minor League Nutrition Coordinator:** Susana Melendez. **Minor League Video Coordinators:** Correy Erickson, Zach Monash. **Minor League Clubhouse Manager:** Patrick Saenz. **Minor League Clubhouse Assistant Manager:** Pete Mancuso. **Coordinators:** Jeff Branson (hitting), Max Gordon (hitting), Steve Smith (pitching), Stephanos Stroop (pitching), Jorge Cordova (assistant pitching), John DeRouin (rehab pitching), Ramon Santiago (infield), Angel Berroa (Latin American infield), Arnie Beyeler (base running/outfield), Brian Taggett (professional development coach).

FARM SYSTEM

Class	Club	Manager	Hitting Coach	Pitching Coach
Triple-A	Toledo (IL)	Anthony Iapoce	Mike Hessman	Doug Bochtler
Double-A	Erie (EL)	Gabe Alvarez	John Murrian	Juan Pimentel
High-A	Lakeland (MWL)	Brayan Pena	Francisco Contreras	Dan Ricabal
Low-A	West Michigan (FSL)	Andrew Graham	CJ Wamsley	Dean Stiles
Rookie	Tigers (FCL)	Mike Alvarez	Nick Bredeson	Gabe Luckert
Rookie	DSL Tigers (DSL)	TBA	TBA	TBA
Rookie	DSL Tigers 2 (DSL)	TBA	TBA	TBA

SCOUTING

Vice President, Assistant General Manager: Sam Menzin, Rob Metzler. **Vice President, Player Personnel:** Scott Bream. **Special Assistant to the GM:** Mike Russell. **Director, Amateur Scouting:** Mark Conner. **Director, Minor League & Scouting Administration:** Cheryl Evans. **Assistant Director, Amateur Scouting:** Eric Nieto. **Amateur Scouting Video Coordinator:** Greg Bundrage. **Pro Scouting Coordinator:** P.J. Jones. **Major League Scouts:** Ray Crone, Jim Elliott, Kevin Ellis, Joe Ferrone, Dave Littlefield, Paul Mirocke, Jim Olander, Jim Rough, John Stockstill, Bruce Tanner, Josh Wilson. **National Crosscheckers:** Justin Henry, Steve Hinton, James Orr. **Regional Crosscheckers: East**—Taylor Black, **Midwest**—Tim Grieve, **Central**—Bryson Barber, **West**—Dave Lottsfeldt. **Crosschecker:** Matt Haas. **Area Scouts:** Nick Avila, Jim Bretz, Donald Brown, RJ Burgess, Ryan Johnson, Joey Lothrop, Tim McWilliam, Steve Pack, Daniel Sabatino, George Schaefer, Mike Smith, Steve Taylor, Cal Towey, Matt Zmuda, Harold Zonder. **Part-Time Scouts:** German Geigel, Deryl Horton, Mark Monahan, Clyde Weir. **Director, International Operations:** Tom Moore. **Director, Latin American Operations:** Miguel Garcia. **Manager, International Operations:** Rafael Gonzalez. **Coordinator, Pacific Rim Scouting:** Kevin Hooker. **International Crosscheckers:** Alejandro Rodriguez, Jeff Wetherby. **Dominican Republic Special Assignment Scout:** Oliver Arias. **Venezuelan Scouting Supervisor:** Jesus Mendoza. **Venezuelan Academy Administrator/Area Scout:** Oscar Garcia. **International Area Scouts:** Rodolfo Penalo, Aldo Perez, Miguel Rodriguez, Carlos Santana, Rudy Garcia, Raul Leiva, Jose Zambrano, Pedro Vivas, Pedro Castellano, Luis Molina, Michael Hsieh, Kan Ikeda, Ho-Kyun Im.

MAJOR LEAGUES

HOUSTON ASTROS

Office Address: Minute Maid Park, Union Station, 501 Crawford, Suite 400, Houston, TX 77002. **Mailing Address:** PO Box 288, Houston, TX 77001. **Telephone:** (713) 259-8000. **Fax:** (713) 259-8981. **Email Address:** fanfeedback@astros.mlb.com. **Website:** www.astros.com.

OWNERSHIP
Owner and Chairman: Jim Crane.

BUSINESS OPERATIONS
Senior Vice President, Business Operations: Marcel Braithwaite. **Senior Vice President, Community Affairs and Executive Director, Astros Foundation:** Paula Harris. **Senior Vice President, Corporate Partnerships:** Matt Brand. **Senior Vice President, Affiliate Business Operations:** Creighton Kahoalii. **Senior Vice President, General Counsel & President of Astros Golf Foundation:** Giles Kibbe. **Senior Vice President, Marketing and Communications:** Anita Sehgal. **Senior Vice President, Chief Financial Officer:** Michael Slaughter. **Vice President, Affiliate Operations:** Thomas Bell. **Vice President, Accounting:** Abby Brantley. **Vice President, Tax:** Vito Ciminello. **Vice President, Communications:** Gene Dias. **Vice President, Stadium Operations:** Bobby Forrest. **Vice President, Information Technology:** Chris Hanz. **Vice President, Foundation Development:** Marian Harper. **Vice President, Merchandising and Retail Operations:** Tom Jennings. **Vice President, Ticket Sales & Services:** P.J. Keene. **Vice President, Finance:** Doug Seckel. **Vice President, Human Resources:** Jennifer Springs. **Vice President, Event Sales and Operations:** Stephanie Stegall. **Vice President, Corporate Partnerships:** Jeff Stewart. **Vice President, Business Strategy and Analytics:** Jay Verrill. **Vice President, Marketing:** Jason Wooden. **Paralegal:** Jessi Merlo. **Business Analyst:** Connor Huff. **Executive Assistants:** Eileen Colgin, Mary Kate Hail. **Administrative Assistant:** Brittany Redeaux.

COMMUNICATIONS/COMMUNITY RELATIONS
Director, Communications: Steve Grande. **Manager, Business Communications:** Rachel Caton. **Senior Coordinator, Communications:** Meshach Sullivan. **Director, Youth Academy:** Daryl Wade. **Manager, Youth Academy:** Duane Stelly. **Program Manager, Community Relations and Astros Foundation:** Hugo Mojica. **Coordinator, Community Relations and Astros Foundation:** Andrew McMullin. **Coordinator, Youth Academy:** Megan Hays.

MARKETING/ANALYTICS
Senior Director, Fan Experience: Chris Garcia. **Director, Advertising and Digital Marketing:** Daniel Klimpel. **Director, Content:** Alex Herko. **Senior Manager, Marketing Entertainment:** Kyle Hamsher, Richard Tapia. **Senior Manager, Graphics and Marketing Projects:** Larry Provitt. **Senior Manager, Production Producer:** Garret Young. **Manager, Digital Marketing:** Catie Willis Guidry. **Graphic and Digital Media Designer:** Clint Self, Ruben Valdez. **Content Graphic Designer:** Jake Chambers. **Team Photographer:** Evan Triplett. **Senior Coordinator, Promotions and Events:** Carolyn Scherpe. **Coordinator, Grassroots Marketing:** Meehee Kim. **Coordinator, Production:** Logan Lozano. **Coordinator, Promotions and Events:** Dusti Loreant. **Coordinator, Social Media:** Harrison Zhang. **Coordinator, Trophy Tour:** Armando Lugo. **Producer, Content:** Matt Blum, Matt Rewis, Michael Eng.

CORPORATE PARTNERSHIPS
Senior Director, Corporate Partnership Sales: Matt Richardson. **Director, Corporate Partnerships:** Jimmy Comerota, Melissa Hahn, Keisha Henderson. **Senior Strategic Account Manager, Corporate Partnerships:** Craig Bristow. **Senior Account Manager, Corporate Partnerships:** Chris Leahy. **Account Manager, Corporate Partnerships:** Lauren Hill, Cam Copeland, Brittany Bivens, Jake Sims. **Manager, Corporate Partnership Sales:** Kyle McLaughlin. **Partnership Lead:** Alexis Phillips, Justin Carter.

STADIUM OPERATIONS
Director, Security: Freddrick Richardson. **Senior Manager, Stadium Operations:** William Connaught. **Senior Manager, Parking:** Gary Rowberry. **Manager, Engineering:** Orlando Mendenhall. **Manager, Security:** Roy Pippin. **Engineering Supervisor:** Johnny Burton. **Supervisor, HVAC:** Cesar Ramirez **Sr. Electrician:** Eric King. **Specialist, A/V:** Chad Carden. **Specialist, Carpentry:** Kevin Chap. **Specialists, Painting:** Juan Gonzalez, Marset Mitchner, Miguel 'Angel' Hernandez. **Technicians, Engineering:** Seth Foreman, Keanu Hernandez, James Pierce, Jamal Green.

TICKETING
Director, Ticket Operations: Mark Cole. **Senior Manager, Ticket Technology and Solutions:** Trevor Purvis. **Senior Manager, Box Office and Ticket Services:** Marcus Barefield II. **Representative, Ticket Operations:** Ray Cervenka. **Account Executives, Ticket Sales:** Amanda Roggeman, Ashli Henk, Jacob Padelski, Juwan Hill, Austin Moore, Hugo Cortes Batista, Pablo Ortiz, Shaki Wilson. **Business Development Assistant:** Colleen H. Westwood. **Business Strategy & Analytics Analyst:** Joshua Pieniazek.

BASEBALL OPERATIONS
General Manager: Dana Brown. **Assistant General Managers:** Andrew Ball, Bill Firkus, Charles Cook. **Special**

GENERAL INFORMATION
Stadium (year opened): Minute Maid Park (2000).
Team Colors: Navy and orange.
Home Dugout: First Base.
Playing Surface: Grass.

MAJOR LEAGUES

Assistant to the General Manager: Craig Biggio. **Special Advisor to Baseball Operations:** Will Sharp. **Director, Latin American Operations:** Caridad Cabrera. **Director, Minor League Operations:** Derrick Fong. **Director, Player Development:** Sara Goodrum. **Director, Player Personnel:** Matt Hogan. **Director, Research and Development:** Sarah Gelles. **Director, Amateur Scouting:** Kris Gross. **Director, International Scouting:** Brian Rodgers. **Manager, Travel:** Juan Huitron. **Major League Game Planning Coach:** Tommy Kawamura. **Manager, Baseball Operations:** Anthony Cacchione. **Manager, Baseball Technology:** Sam Visser. **Manager Player Development:** Cristian Perez. **Manager, Player Personnel:** Aaron Del Giudice. **Senior Advisor, Latin American Development:** Julio Linares. **Coordinator, Baseball Operations:** Natan Cristol-Deman. **Coordinator, Dominican Academy Operations:** Jessica Ben. **Coordinator, Minor League Operations:** Rafael Soto. **Assistant, Latin American Operations:** Elizabeth Nunez. **Analyst/Coordinator, Player Evaluation:** Cam Pendino. **Amateur Scouting Coordinator:** T.J. Tullis.

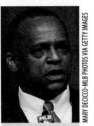
Dana Brown

MAJOR LEAGUE STAFF
Manager: Dusty Baker. **Coaches: Bench**—Joe Espada, **Pitching**—Josh Miller. **Pitching**—Bill Murphy. **Hitting**— Alex Cintron. **Second Hitting**—Troy Snitker. **First Base**—Omar Lopez. **Third Base**—Gary Pettis. **Quality Control**—Dan Firova. **Major League Coach**—Jason Kanzler. **Coach**—Michael Collins. **Major League Game Planning Coach**—Tommy Kawamura

TEAM OPERATIONS/CLUBHOUSE
Manager, Team Travel: Juan Huitron. **Clubhouse Manager:** Carl Schneider. **Visiting Clubhouse Manager:** Steve Perry.

MEDICAL/TRAINING
Head Team Physician: Dr. David Lintner. **Team Physicians:** Dr. Thomas Mehlhoff, Dr. James Muntz, Dr. Michael Hopson, Dr. Vijay Jotwani. **Team Chiropractor:** Dana Harper. **Head Athletic Trainer and Head Physical Therapist:** Jeremiah Randall. **Massage Therapist:** Katsumi Oka. **Major League Strength/Conditioning Coach:** Taylor Rhoades.

PLAYER DEVELOPMENT
Director, Player Development: Sara Goodrum. **Director, Minor League Operations:** Derrick Fong. **Minor League Coordinators:** Jason Bell (Assistant Director, Player Development/Field Coordinator), Rafael Pena (Hitting), Eric Nielsen (Pitching), Michael Thomas (Catching/Outfield), Mike Ramazzotti (Infield/Base running), Rene Rojas (Assistant Hitting), Thomas Whitsett (Assistant Pitching), John Gregorich (Medical), Brian Faller (Rehabilitation Medical), Taylor Lile (Head Dietitian), Nick Shedd (Head Strength and Conditioning), Chris Martin (Strength and Conditioning Rehab Coordinator), Eric Pimentel (Dominican Medical Coordinator), Laura Ramos (Mental Health and Performance)

FARM SYSTEM
Class	Club	Manager	Hitting Coach	Pitching Coach
Triple-A	Sugar Land (PCL)	Mickey Storey	Aaron Westlake	Erick Abreu
Double-A	Corpus Christi (TL)	Joe Thon	TBD	John Kovalik
High-A	Asheville (SAL)	Nate Shaver	Bryan Muniz	Sean Buchanan
Low-A	Fayetteville (CAR)	Ricardo Rivera	Luis Reynoso	Zach Wilkins
Rookie	Astros (FCL)	Carlos Lugo	Andrew Cresci	A. des Carminero
Rookie	Astros 1 (DSL)	Manuel Martinez	TBD	Rick Aponte
Rookie	Astros 2 (DSL)	Marcelo Alfonsin	Brauly Mejia	Starlyng Sanchez

SCOUTING
Director, Amateur Scouting: Kris Gross. **Assistant Director, Scouting:** Evan Brannon. **Special Assistants, Scouts:** Gavin Dickey and Charlie Gonzalez. **Manager, Amateur Scouting:** Ryan Courville, **Domestic Crosschecker:** Ryan Leake. **Domestic Scouts:** Tim Costic (Los Angeles, CA), Brian Sheffler (Houston, TX), Steven DiPuglia (Bradenton, FL), Joe Dunigan (Phoenix, AZ), Andrew Johnson (Raleigh, NC), Kevin Mello (Richmond, CA), Scott Oberhelman (Columbus, OH), Steve Payne (Barrington, RI), Drew Pearson (Milwaukee, WI), Freddy Perez (Nashville, TN), Bobby St. Pierre (Atlanta, GA), Jim Stevenson (Tulsa, OK), Landon Townsley (Baton Rouge, LA), Eli Tupuola (San Diego, CA).
Amateur Scouting Analyst: Cam Pendino. **Amateur Scouting Coordinator:** TJ Tulis. **Scouting Information Coordinator:** Kyle Connell, **International Scouting Director:** Brian Rodgers. **Assistant Director, International Scouting:** Raymon Sanchez. **Supervisors:** Alfredo Ulloa (Dominican Republic), Jose Palacios (Venezuela), Miguel Pintor (Mexico). **Scouts, Dominican Republic:** Leocadio Guevara, Jose Lima, Hassan Wessin, Jose Torres, Alfred Ramirez. **Venezuela:** Enrique Brito. **Assistant Scouts, Dominican Republic:** Omar Frias and Oriana Gonzalez. **International Scouting Analyst:** Camron Shipley. **International Scouting Coordinator:** Ricardo Lizarraga. **Dominican Republic Scouting Coordinator:** Francisco Navarro. **Venezuela Scouting Coordinator:** Carlos Freites

MAJOR LEAGUES

KANSAS CITY ROYALS

Office Address: One Royal Way, Kansas City, MO 64129.
Mailing Address: PO Box 419969, Kansas City, MO 64141.
Telephone: (816) 921-8000. **Fax:** (816) 924-0347. **Website:** www.royals.com.

OWNERSHIP
Operated By: Kansas City Royals Baseball Club, LLC. **Chairman & CEO:** John Sherman.

EXECUTIVE LEADERSHIP
Exec. VP/General Manager: J.J. Picollo. **President-Business Operations:** Brooks Sherman. **Exec. VP/Chief Commercial Officer:** Sarah Tourville. **Sr. Vice President/Chief Legal Officer:** Adam Sachs.

BUSINESS OPERATIONS

FINANCE/ADMINISTRATION
VP, Chief Financial Officer: Whitney Beaver. **VP, People & Culture:** Iris Edelen. **Director, Finance:** Sarah Kongs. **Controller:** Luke Franken. **VP, Ticket Operations:** Anthony Blue. **Director, Ticket Ops:** Chris Darr. **Director, Authentic & Aramark:** Ashley Ficken. **Director, Risk Management:** Patrick Fleischmann. **Sr. Director, Payroll:** Jodi Parsons.

TECHNOLOGY
VP, Technology & Business Analytics: Brian Himstedt. **Director, Business Analytics:** Daniel Sommerhauser. **Director, Business Data Architecture:** Collin Brody. **Director, Technology Infra/Ops:** Mitchell McDaniel. **Director, Business Solutions:** Brian Desch

John Sherman
GITTINGS PHOTOGRAPHY

TICKET SALES
Sr. Director, Ticket Sales & Service: Kayla Shively. **Director, New Sales & Development:** Adam Cain. **Director, Premium Sales & Service:** Jeff Close.

COMMUNICATIONS
VP, Communications: Sam Mellinger. **Sr. Director, Communication Strategy:** Sharita Hutton. **Director, Media Relations:** Nick Kappel. **Assistant Director, Media Relations:** Ian Kraft. **Manager, Communications:** Logan Jones.

COMMUNITY IMPACT & URBAN YOUTH ACADEMY
VP, Community Impact: Luis Maes. **Sr. Director, Community Investments & Exec. Director, Royals Charities:** Amanda Grosdidier. **Director, Community Partnerships & Events:** Chris Major. **Director, Community Investments/Alumni:** Dina Blevins. **Sr. Director, Royals Hall of Fame:** Curt Nelson. **Sr. Manager, Urban Youth Academy:** Philip Hannon.

BALLPARK OPERATIONS
VP, Ballpark Operations: Isaac Riffel. **Sr. Director, Landscaping:** Trevor Vance. **Sr. Director, Stadium Engineering:** Todd Burrow. **Director, Ballpark Services:** Johnny Williams. **Director, Guest Experience:** Nick Pieroni. **Director, Event Operations:** Bryan Ross.

PINE TAR COLLECTIVE
VP, Pine Tar Collective: Tony Snethen. **Group Director, Branded Content & Innovation:** Scott Lichtenauer. **Sr. Director, Content Strategy & Emerging Tech:** Erin Sleddens. **Sr. Director, Scoreboard Operations:** Steven Funke. **Director, Event Presentation:** Nicole Averso. **Creative Director, Brand & Marketing:** Caitlin Wienck

CORPORATE PARTNERSHIPS
VP, Corporate Partnerships: Alex Schulte. **Sr. Director, Partnership Development:** David Adams. **Director, Partnership Solutions:** Steve Garvey.

BASEBALL OPERATIONS
Telephone: (816) 921-8000. **Fax:** (816) 924-0347.
Exec. VP/General Manager: J.J. Picollo. **Executive Asst. to the GM:** Emily Penning. **SVP/Asst., GM: Major League/International Operations:** Rene Francisco. **Major League Operations:** Scott Sharp. **VP, Asst. GM: Baseball Administration:** Jin Wong. **Research & Development:** Dr. Daniel Mack. **Major League Scouting:** Gene Watson. **VP, Player Personnel:** Lonnie Goldberg. **Special Asst. to Baseball Ops/Leadership:** Willie Aikens, Blaine Boyer, Reggie Sanders, Mike Sweeney. **Sr. Directors: Leadership & Cultural Dev:** Matt Marasco. **Performance Science:** Austin Driggers. **Behavioral Science:** Dr. Ryan Maid. **Director, Professional & Cultural Dev:** Jeff Diskin. **Lead Developer:** Paul Turner. **Sr. Developer:** Joseph San Diego. **Developer:** Jenny Segelke. **Analysts:** Alan Kohler, Brandon Nelson, Grace Rieger, Rob Sorge, Robyn Wampler, Hailey Yabroudy. **Baseball Operations Asst.:** Jared Hinton.

GENERAL INFORMATION
Stadium (year opened): Ewing M. Kauffman Stadium (1973).
Home Dugout: First Base.
Playing Surface: Grass.
Team Colors: Royal blue and white.

MAJOR LEAGUES

JJ Picollo

TRAVEL/CLUBHOUSE
Vice President, Major League Team Operations: Jeff Davenport. **Sr. Advisor, Visiting Clubhouse:** Chuck Hawke. **Director, Equipment:** Patrick Gorman. **Managers, Visiting Clubhouse:** Levi Noble. **Culinary Service:** T.J. Stack. **Clubhouse & Umpire Services:** Tom Walsh.

MAJOR LEAGUE STAFF
Manager: Matt Quatraro. **Coaches: Bench**—Paul Hoover, **Pitching**—Brian Sweeney, **Sr. Director, Hitting Performance/Hitting Coach**—Alec Zumwalt, **Asst. Hitting**—Keoni DeRenne, **First Base**—Damon Hollins, **Field Coordinator/Third Base**—Vance Wilson, **Infield**—Jose Alguacil. **Bullpen**—Mitch Stetter. **Director, Pitching Strategy/Asst. Pitching Coach:** Zach Bove. **Replay/Advance Scouting Coordinator:** Bill Duplissea. **Bullpen Catchers:** Parker Morin, Allan de San Miguel. **Video:** Jason Nicols. **Asst. Video:** Ethan Blouin. **Pitching Strategist:** Andy Ferguson. **Major League Coach:** Miguel Garcia. **Rehab:** Ryan Eigsti.

MEDICAL/TRAINING
Team Physician: Dr. Vincent Key. **Director Medical Services:** Nick Kenney. **Head Athletic Trainer:** Kyle Turner. **Asst. Athletic Trainers:** Chris Delucia, Dave Iannicca. **Strength & Conditioning:** Ryan Stoneberg, Luis Perez. **Physical Therapist:** Jeff Blum. **Director, Sports Nutrition:** Erika Wincheski. **Director, Behavioral Science, Major League Mental Performance:** Melissa Lambert.

PLAYER DEVELOPMENT
Sr. Director: Pitching Performance: Paul Gibson. **Directors: Player Development:** Mitch Maier. **Minor League Ops:** Nick Leto. **Arizona Ops:** Will Simon. **Hitting Performance:** Drew Saylor. **Medical Services/Physical Therapist:** Justin Hahn. **Asst. Directors, Player Development:** Malcom Culver. **Minor League/International Ops:** Kristin Lock. **Pitching Performance/Scouting:** Nate Adcock. **Special Asst. to the GM/Player Development:** Rafael Belliard, Chino Cadahia. **Field Coordinators:** Scott Thorman, Omar Ramirez (AZ), Victor Baez (DSL). **Special Asst., Player Development:** Harry Spilman. **Pitching Advisor:** Paul Menhart. **Asst. Manager, Pitching Performance/Strategist:** Justin Friedman. **Coordinators:** J.C. Boscan (Catching), Logan Gudde (Physical Therapy), Justin Kemp (Medical), Jarret Abell (Strength/Conditioning), Brittany Bozzini (Performance Science), Sebastian Cambo (Behavioral Science), Bryce Allison (Sports Nutrition), Brendan Sexton (Video). **Assistant Coordinators:** Nic Jackson (hitting), Abraham Nunez (hitting/Latin America), Tony Medina (Medical/Latin America), Phil Falco (Strength/Conditioning), Joey Manana (Strength & Conditioning/Latin America) Zack O'Reilly (Video), Eddy Abad (DSL Video). **Support Staff:** Monica Ramirez (Ed/ESL & Latin American Initiatives), Obnerys Dominguez (DSL Lead Educator), Jorge Guzman (AZ Complex/Life Skills), Massiel Rodriguez (Asst. Dominican Operations), Randy Fernandez (Asst. Dominican Operations), Susana Richardson (Dominican Admin Asst.).

FARM SYSTEM

Class	Club (League)	Manager	Hitting Coach	Pitching Coach
Triple-A	Omaha (PCL)	Mike Jirschele	Bijan Rademacher	Dane Johnson
Double-A	Northwest Arkansas (TL)	Tommy Shields	Andy LaRoche	Larry Carter
High-A	Quad Cities (MWL)	Brooks Conrad	Ryan Powers	Derrick Lewis
Low-A	Columbia (CAR)	Tony Pena Jr	Ari Adut	John Habyan
Rookie	Royals (ACL)	Jesus Azuaje	Ramon Castro	J. Pimentel/J. Delgado
Rookie	Royals 1 (DSL)	Ramon Martinez	Wilson Betemit	Christopher Marte
Rookie	Royals 2 (DSL)	Sergio de Luna	Fernando Martinez	Jose Veras

SCOUTING
Telephone: (816) 921-8000. **Fax:** (816) 924-0347.
Director, Amateur Scouting: Danny Ontiveros. **Baseball Ops—Amateur Scouting:** Jack Monahan. **Sr. Advisors:** Mike Arbuckle, Roy Clark. **Special Assts to the GM:** Tim Conroy, Tom McNamara, Louie Medina, Don Poplin. **Special Assignment Scouts:** Mitch Webster. **Pro Scouts:** Dennis Cardoza, Orlando Estevez, Brad Kelley, Mark Leavitt, John McMichen, Terry Wetzel. **Advance Scout:** Tony Tijerina. **Special Assignment Scout:** Darwin Pennye. **National Pitching Supervisor:** Gary Wilson. **Regional Supervisors: Midwest**—Gregg Miller, **Northeast**—Keith Connolly, **Southeast**—Sean Gibbs, **West**— Colin Gonzales. **Area Supervisors:** Joe Barbera, Tim Bavester, Tim Bittner, Cody Clark, Mike Farrell, Buddy Gouldsmith, Todd Guggiana, Josh Hallgren, Nick Hamilton, Will Howard, Scott Melvin, Ken Munoz, Matt Price, Nick Presto, Joe Ross, Bobby Shore. **Underclass Scouts:** Vance Vizcaino. **Part-Time Scouts:** Brett Bailey, Rick Clendenin, Louis Collier, Jason Gill, Jeremy Jones, Howard McCullough, Johnny Ramos, Mike Ranson, Chris Reitsma, Lloyd Simmons, Adam Stern.
International Coordinators: International Scouting: Daniel Guerrero. **Latin America:** Richard Castro. **Pacific Rim:** Phil Dale. **Manager, International Ops:** Fabio Herrera. **International Supervisor:** Luis Ortiz. **International Scouts:** Michael Acevedo (D.R.), Roberto Aquino (D.R.) Nicolas Bautista (D.R.), Neil Burke (Australia), Elias Despardel (D.R.), Francis Feliciano (D.R.), Alberto Garcia (VZ), Joelvis Gonzalez (VZ), Jose Gualdron (VZ), Edson Kelly (Aruba), Hyunsung Kim (S. Korea), Nathan Miller (Taiwan), Rafael Miranda (Colombia), Fausto Morel (D.R.), Hiroyuki Oya (Japan), Manuel Samaniego (Mexico), Rafael Vasquez (D.R.).

MAJOR LEAGUES

LOS ANGELES ANGELS

Office Address: 2000 Gene Autry Way, Anaheim, CA 92806.
Mailing Address: 2000 Gene Autry Way, Anaheim, CA 92803.
Telephone: (714) 940-2000. **Fax:** (714) 940-2205. **Website:** www.angels.com.

OWNERSHIP
Owners: Arte & Carole Moreno. **Chairman:** Dennis Kuhl. **President:** John Carpino. **Executive VP:** Dana Wells.

BUSINESS OPERATIONS
Senior Vice President, Finance/Administration: Molly Jolly. **Senior Director, Finance:** Doug Mylowe. **Controller:** Sue Bassett. **Assistant Controller:** Jennifer Whynott. **Financial Operations Manager:** Jennifer Jeanblanc. **Payroll Manager:** Lorelei Schlitz. **Accountants:** Kylie McManus and Sarah Talamonte. **Accounts Payable Specialist:** Rosie Alvarez. **Vice President, Human Resources:** Deborah Johnston. **Director, Human Resources:** Mayra Castro. **Senior Manager, Benefits:** Cecilia Schneider. **Human Resources and Payroll Coordinator:** Reyna Mancilla. **Human Resources Assistant:** Julissa Julio. **Senior Director, Information Services:** Al Castro. **Director, Network Infrastructure:** Neil Fariss. **Senior Network Engineer:** James Sheu. **Technical Services Manager:** Josh Schnoor. **Desktop Support Analyst:** Dennis De Jesus, Jr. **Information Services Support Analyst:** Scott Tuttle.

Arte and Carole Moreno

CORPORATE SALES
Vice President, Corporate Partnerships: Mike Fach. **Senior Director, Partnership Services:** Bobby Kowan. **Director, Corporate & Community Partnerships:** Nicole Provansal. **Senior Corporate Account Executive:** Drew Zinser. **Account Executives, Corporate Partnerships:** Jonathan Chodzko and Jared Florin. **Sr. Manager, Partnership Services:** Andie Mitsuda. **Account Managers, Partnership Services:** Vanessa Gilles, Gabi Cipolletti and Kira Czyrklis. **Authentication & Fulfillment Supervisor:** Tyler Ogawa.

ENTERTAINMENT
Director, Entertainment & Production: Davin Maske. **Manager, Video Production:** Lizette Cabrera. **Production Manager:** Cole Dragon. **Engineer:** Zac Applegate. **Marketing and Entertainment Manager:** Mandi Ortiz.

MARKETING
Director, Ticket Marketing and Business Analytics: Ryan Vance. **Senior Director, Brand and Product Marketing:** Alex Tinyo. **Marketing and Promotions Coordinator:** Riley Ersek. **Senior Manager, Business Analytics:** JJ Evans. **Application Integration Manager:** Nicole Yamasaki. **Senior Graphic Designer:** Rich Esteban. **Graphic Designer:** Danny LeClaire.

PUBLIC/MEDIA RELATIONS/COMMUNICATIONS
Telephone: (714) 940-2014.
Senior Director, Communications: Adam Chodzko. **Senior Manager, Communications:** Matt Birch. **Communications Manager:** Grace McNamee. **Communications Rep:** Marco Peralta. **Senior Manager, Digital Communications:** Hannah Stange. **Manager, Digital Communications:** Ricardo Zapata. **Team Photographer:** Blaine Ohigashi.

COMMUNITY RELATIONS
Director, Corporate & Community Partnerships: Nicole Provansal. **Manager, Foundation and Community Initiatives:** Adam Cali. **Scholarship Programs Manager:** Lillea Acasio. **Scholarship Program & Community Coordinator:** Peggy Berroa-Morales.

BALLPARK OPERATIONS/FACILITIES
Vice President, Ballpark Operations: Brian Sanders. **Director, Ballpark Operations and Development:** Nathan Bautista. **Director, Stadium Operations:** Calvin Ching. **Director, Special Events:** Courtney Wallace. **Director, Fan Hospitality:** Eric Ursua. **Director, Stadium Operations and Security:** Carlos Campos. **Senior Manager, Facilities & Housekeeping:** Jose Padilla. **Managers, Ballpark Operations:** Shanelle Stephens and Jacqueline Urbanus. **Security Manager:** Mark Macias. **Security Assistant Manager:** JB Jaso. **Managers, Special Events:** An Pham and Brett Halstead. **Coordinator, Special Events:** Mallory Mathis. **Custodial Supervisors:** Robert Iglesias and Ray Nells. **Purchasing Manager:** Suzanne Peters. **Purchasing Assistant:** Lincoln Bath. **Purchasing and Facilities Assistant:** Rene Escarcega Manager, Stadium Facilities:** Pedro Del Castillo. **Wardrobe Supervisor:** Genero Luna.

TICKETING
Senior Director, Ticket Sales & Service: Jim Panetta. **Director, Business Development, Premium Sales &

GENERAL INFORMATION
Stadium (year opened): Angel Stadium of Anaheim (1966). **Playing Surface:** Grass.
Team Colors: Red, dark red, blue and silver.
Home Dugout: Third Base.

38 • Baseball America 2023 Directory

Service: Aaron Dragomir. **Senior Director, Ticket Operations & Services:** Tom DeTemple. **Senior Manager, Ticket Sales:** David Neumann. **Senior Manager, Ticket Operations:** Sheila Brazelton.

TRAVEL/CLUBHOUSE
Traveling Secretary: Tom Taylor. **Director, Equipment and Clubhouse Operations:** Guy Gallagher. **Visiting Clubhouse Manager:** Brett Crane. **Assistant Clubhouse Manager:** Shane Demmitt. **Assistant Clubhouse Manager:** Aaron Wiedeman. **Home Clubhouse Supervisor:** Jim Greer. **Manager, Major League Video:** Ryan Dundee

BASEBALL OPERATIONS
General Manager: Perry Minasian. **Assistant GM:** Alex Tamin. **Special Advisor Assistant to GM:** Bill Stoneman. **Director, Player Procurement:** David Haynes. **Senior Director, Research & Development:** Michael Lord. **Director, Advance Scouting:** John Pratt. **Assistant Director, Research & Development:** Connor Moffatt. **Senior Coordinator, Baseball Administration:** Amanda Kropp. **Coordinator, Pitching Analysis:** Jared Hughes. **Sr. Analyst, Research and Development:** Chet Gutwein. **Analyst, Research and Development:** Matt Johnson and Cam Rogers. **Analyst, Baseball Operations:** Joe Chernak, Austin Marchesani, Dylan Mortimer, Jake Sauberman and Andrew Zenner. **Pitching Analyst, Baseball Operations:** Connor Hinchliffe. **Sr. Developer, Baseball Systems:** Josh Krowiorz. **Baseball Systems Developer:** Mitchell Glazier, Patrick Seminatore, Nick Usoff and Max Werner. **MLB Advance Scout:** Ben Rowen.

Perry Minasian

MAJOR LEAGUE STAFF
Manager: Phil Nevin. **Bench Coach:** Ray Montgomery. **Field Coordinator:** Benji Gil. **Pitching Coach:** Matt Wise. **Hitting Coach:** Marcus Thames. **Assistant Pitching Coach:** Bill Hezel. **Assistant Hitting Coach:** Phil Plantier. **First Base Coach:** Damon Mashore. **Third Base Coach:** Bill Haselman. **Catching Coach:** Drew Butera. **Batting Practice Pitcher:** Mike Ashman. **Staff Assistants:** Jason Brown, Tim Buss and Ali Modami. **Bullpen Catcher/Interpreter:** Manny Del Campo. **Interpreter:** Ippei Mizuhara.

MEDICAL/TRAINING
Team Physician: Dr. Craig Milhouse. **Team Orthopedic Physicians:** Dr. Brian Schulz, Dr. Steve Yoon, Dr. John Itamura and Dr. Carlos Uquillas. **Director, Sports Medicine & Head Athletic Trainer:** Mike Frostad. **Assistant Athletic Trainers:** Eric Munson and Matt Biancuzzo. **Athletic Training Services Coordinator:** Rick Smith. **Head Strength/Conditioning Coach:** Matt Tenney. **Assistant Strength and Conditioning Coach:** Adam Auer. **Head Physical Therapist:** Marc Oceguera. **Assistant Physical Therapist:** Robbie Williams. **Massage Therapist:** Yoichi Terada. **Registered Dietician:** Rebecca Twombley.

PLAYER DEVELOPMENT
Director, Player Development: Joey Prebynski. **Assistant Director, Player Development:** Tony Ferreira. **Assistant, Player Development:** Luis Barranco. **Field Coordinator:** Joe Kruzel. **Assistant Field Coordinator:** Jayson Nix. **Arizona & Latin American Field Coordinator:** Erick Salcedo. **Manager, Minor League Equipment:** Louie Raya. **Minor League Video Coordinator:** Alexandria Woody. **Roving Instructors:** Tony Jaramillo (Hitting Coordinator), Jobel Jimenez (Assistant Hitting Coordinator), Buddy Carlyle (Pitching Coordinator), Dylan Axelrod (Pitching Performance Coordinator), Chris Carpenter (Pitching Consultant), Eddie Guardado (Special Assistant, Player Development), Ben Francisco (Outfield/Baserunning Coordinator), Hainley Statia (Infield Coordinator), Jerry Narron (Catching Coordinator), Mike Gallego (Player Development Staff Coach). **Medical Coordinator:** Matt Morrell. **Strength & Conditioning Coordinator:** Dylan Cintula. **Minor League Rehab Coordinator:** Joseph Skrzypek. **Rehab Coach:** Kernan Ronan. **Physical Therapist:** Keith Kocher. **Assistant, Strength & Conditioning/Return to Performance Coordinator:** Adam Smith. **Coordinator, Minor League Medical Administration:** Geoff Hostetter. **Coordinator, Latin America Operations:** Michael Noboa. **Coordinator, DR Academy Administration:** Fausto Betances. **Asst., DR Academy Administration:** Pietro Oliva.

FARM SYSTEM

Class	Club	Manager	Hitting Coach	Pitching Coach
Triple-A	Salt Lake (PCL)	Keith Johnson	Joel Chimelis	Derrin Ebert
Double-A	Rocket City (SL)	Andy Schatzley	Sean Kazmar	Michael Wuertz
High-A	Tri-City (NWL)	Jack Howell	Ryan Sebra	Doug Henry
Low-A	Inland Empire (CAR)	Dave Stapleton	Willie Romero	Elmer Dessens
Rookie	Angels (ACL)	Ever Magallanes	Raywilly Gomez	Gil Heredia/Bo Martino
Rookie	Angels (DSL)	Hector De La Cruz	A. De los Santos	J. Marte/E. Gonzalez

SCOUTING
Senior Advisor, Scouting & Player Personnel: Matt Swanson. **Director, Pro Scouting:** Derek Watson. **Coordinator, Pro Scouting:** Charles St. Clair. **Special Assignment Scout:** Ric Wilson. **Professional Scouts:** Jared Barnes, Jim Miller, Andrew Schmidt, Bobby Williams and Rick Williams. **Director, Amateur Scouting:** Timothy McIlvaine. **Assistant Director, Amateur Scouting:** Jeremy Schied. **Assistant, Amateur Scouting:** Drew Plant. **National Crosschecker:** Steffan Wilson. **Cross-Checkers:** Jason Baker, Jayson Durocher, Scott Richardson, Nick Gorneault, Brandon McArthur and Doug Witt. **Area Supervisors:** Drew Dominguez, Abe Flores, Brian Gordon, KJ Hendricks, Bo Hughes, Billy Lipari, Chris McAlpin, Dennis Moeller, Joel Murrie and Ross Vecchio. **Senior Director, International Scouting:** Brian Parker. **Asst. Director, International Scouting:** Brian Cruz. **Administrator, International Scouting:** Grace Mercedes. **Amateur & International Crosschecker:** Matt Bishoff. **Latin American Crosschecker:** Jean Carlos Alvarez. **DR Supervisor:** Felix Feliz. **VZ Supervisor:** Marlon Urdaneta. **DR Area Scouts:** Jochy Cabrera, Rusbell Cabrera, Domingo Garcia, Jonathan Genao and Frank Tejeda. **VZ Area Scouts:** Joel Chicarelli, Melvin Dorta, Ender Gonzalez and Vicente Lupo. **Panama Area Scout:** Raul Gonzalez. **Mexico Area Scout:** Cosme Valle. **Curacao Area Scout:** Rubylin Nicasia. **Video Scout:** Jesus Colina (VZ) and Rafael Reyes (DR).

MAJOR LEAGUES

LOS ANGELES DODGERS

Office Address: 1000 Vin Scully Ave., Los Angeles, CA 90012.
Telephone: (323) 224-1500. **Fax:** (323) 224-1269. **Website:** www.dodgers.com.

OWNERSHIP/EXECUTIVE OFFICE
Chairman: Mark Walter. **Partners:** Earvin 'Magic' Johnson, Peter Guber, Todd Boehly, Robert 'Bobby' Patton, Jr, Billie Jean King, Ilana Kloss, Robert L. Plummer, Alan Smolinisky. **President/CEO:** Stan Kasten.

BUSINESS OPERATIONS
Executive Vice President/COO: Bob Wolfe. **Executive VP/Chief Marketing Officer:** Lon Rosen. **Executive Director, Business Enterprises:** Chris Koenig. **Senior Vice President and General Counsel:** Daniel Martens. **Vice President and Deputy General Counsel:** Chad Gunderson. **Senior VP, Marketing, Communications and Broadcaster:** Erik Braverman. **Senior VP, Stadium Operations:** Joe Crowley. **Senior VP, Ticket and Premium Sales & Service:** Antonio Morici. **Executive VP, Planning/ Development:** Janet Marie Smith.

Mark Walter

FINANCE AND BUSINESS ANALYTICS
VP, Finance: Eric Hernandez. **Sr. Director, Financial Planning/Analysis:** Gregory Buonaccorsi. **Director, Purchasing:** Lisa McShane. **Controller:** Sara Curran. **Senior VP, Business Strategy:** Royce Cohen. **Director, Business Analytics:** Michael Spetner.

GLOBAL PARTNERSHIPS
Senior VP, Global Partnerships: Corey Norkin. **Sr. Director, Global Partnership Administration & Services:** Jenny Oh. **Sr. Director, Marketing Solutions:** Matt Grable. **Directors, Global Partnership Services:** Kristen Jareck, Kali Hengsteler, Karen Luciano.

MARKETING/BROADCASTING AND COMMUNICATIONS
Sr. VP, Marketing/Broadcasting Communications: Erik Braverman. **Sr. Director, Public Relations:** Joe Jareck. **Executive Producer, Production:** Greg Taylor. **Sr. Director, Graphic Design:** Ross Yoshida. **Sr. Director, Broadcast Engineering:** Tom Darin.

HUMAN RESOURCES/LEGAL
VP, Human Resources: Marilyn Davis. **Sr. Manager, Human Resources:** Mayra Salazar. **Senior Vice President and General Counsel:** Daniel Martens. **Vice President and Deputy General Counsel:** Chad Gunderson

LOS ANGELES DODGERS FOUNDATION AND COMMUNITY AFFAIRS
Chief Executive Officer, Los Angeles Dodgers Foundation: Nichol Whiteman. **Chief Program Officer:** Manny Aceves. **COO, Los Angeles Dodgers Foundation:** Chaitali Gala Mehta.

TICKETING
Telephone: (323) 224-1471. **Fax:** (323) 224-2609.
VP, Ticket Operations: Seth Bluman. **VP, Premium Sales & Services:** Craig Sindici. **Director, Premium Sales & Services:** Justine Treibel.

BASEBALL OPERATIONS
Telephone: (323) 224-1500. **Fax:** (323) 224-1463.
President: Andrew Friedman. **Executive Vice President & General Manager:** Brandon Gomes. **Vice President & Assistant General Managers:** Jeffrey Kingston, Alex Slater, Damon Jones. **Senior Vice President:** Josh Byrnes. **Vice Presidents:** Dave Finley (Amateur & International Scouting), Galen Carr (Player Personnel), Ismael Cruz (International Scouting), Billy Gasparino (Amateur Scouting). **Senior Directors:** Ellen Harrigan (Baseball Administration); Scott Akasaki (Team Travel), Duncan Webb (Baseball Resources). **Directors:** Brian Stoneberg (Minor League Player Performance); Michael Voltmer (Strategy and Information); Megan Schroeder (Performance Science); John Focht & Brian McBurney (Baseball Systems). **Senior Advisors & Special Assistants:** Chase Utley, Pat Corrales, Ron Roenicke, Rick Honeycutt, Jose Vizcaino, John Sears.

MAJOR LEAGUE STAFF
Manager: Dave Roberts. **Bench Coach:** Danny Lehmann. **Major League Field Coordinator:** Bob Geren. **Pitching Coach:** Mark Prior. **Bullpen Coach:** Josh Bard. **Hitting Coach:** Robert Van Scoyoc. **Hitting Coach:** Aaron Bates. **First Base Coach:** Clayton McCullough. **Third Base Coach:** Dino Ebel. **Assistant Pitching Coach:** Connor McGuiness.

PLAYER DEVELOPMENT
Telephone: (323) 224-1500. **Fax:** (323) 224-1359.
Director: Will Rhymes. **Assistant Director:** Matt McGrath. **Manager, Minor League Administration:** Juliana Ortega.

GENERAL INFORMATION
Stadium (year opened): Dodger Stadium (1962).
Team Colors: Dodger blue and white.
Home Dugout: Third Base.
Playing Surface: Grass

MAJOR LEAGUES

Andrew Friedman

Field Coordinator: Bob Geren. **Manager, Arizona Operations:** Matt Peabody. **Manager, Player Development:** Andrea La Pointe. **Assistant, Player Development:** James Weilbrenner. **Assistant, Baseball Operations:** Mark Kozhaya. **Directors:** Rob Hill (Minor League Pitching), Brian Stoneberg (MiLB Player Performance), Leo Ruiz (Strong Mind Cultural Development). **Coordinators:** Don Alexander (Pitching, Logistics), Brent Minta (Pitching, Analytics), Ian Walsh (Minor League Pitching Development Assistant), Rocky Gale (Catching), Louis Iannotti (Hitting Analytics), Tim Laker (Hitting), Jeff Salazar (Hitting), Mark Kertenian (Strategy and Communication), AJ LaLonde (Strong Mind), Charles Wagner (Video), Cole Finnegan (Assistant Video). **Minor League Medical Coordinator:** Victor Scarpone. **Assistant Minor League Medical Coordinator:** James Southard. **MiLB Strength and Conditioning Coordinator:** Carl Kochan. **International Athletics Coordinator:** Chris Dunaway. **Return-to-Competition Coordinator:** Jeff Taylor.

CAMPO LOS PALMAS

Senior Facility Manager: Jesus Negrette. **Manager:** Marian Vasquez. **Operations Coordinator:** Jose Vargas. **Manager, Clubhouse:** Julio Martinez

CAMELBACK RANCH

Manager, Arizona Operations: Matt Peabody. **Minor League Equipment Manager:** Troy Timney.

FARM SYSTEM

Class	Club (League)	Manager	Hitting Coach	Pitching Coach
Triple-A	Oklahoma City (PCL)	Travis Barbary	Manny Burriss	Doug Mathis
Double-A	Tulsa (TL)	Scott Hennessey	Lou Iannotti	R. Dennick/ D. O'Linger
High-A	Great Lakes (MWL)	Daniel Nava	O'Koyea Dickson	David Anderson
Low-A	Rancho Cucamonga (CAL)	TBD	TBD	TBD
Rookie	Dodgers (ACL)	TBD	TBD	TBD
Rookie	Dodgers Mega (DSL)	TBD	TBD	TBD
Rookie	Dodgers Bautista (DSL)	TBD	TBD	TBD

SCOUTING

VP, Amateur/International Scouting: David Finley. **VP, Director, Amateur Scouting:** Billy Gasparino. **VP, International Scouting:** Ismael Cruz. **Assistant Director, Amateur Scouting:** Zach Fitzpatrick. **Assistant Director, International Scouting:** Matthew Doppelt. **Manager, Amateur Scouting:** Jalen Phillips. **Manager, International Scouting:** Javier Camps. **Special Advisor:** Paul Cogan. **Athleticism Development Coordinator:** Tyler Norton. **Global Crosschecker:** John Green. **National Crosscheckers:** Brian Stephenson, Rob St. Julien. **National Pitching Crosschecker:** Jack Cressend. **Regional Crosscheckers:** Jon Adkins, Brian Compton, Stephen Head, Brian Kraft, Alan Matthews. **Area Scouts:** Tim Adkins, Garrett Ball, Clint Bowers, Tom Kunis, Marty Lamb, Benny Latino, Brent Mayne, Paul Murphy, Tom Myers, John Pyle, Jonah Rosenthal, Wes Sargent, Mitch Schulewitz, Jeffrey Stevens. **Junior Area Scouts:** Logan Crook, Dean Kim. **Part-Time Scout:** Luis Faccio. **VP, Player Personnel:** Galen Carr. **Manager, Pro Scouting:** Luke Geoghegan. **Special Assistant to Pro Scouting:** Jeff McAvoy. **Special Assignment Scouts:** Vance Lovelace, Matt Smith. **Professional Scouts:** Tydus Meadows, Scott Groot, Peter Bergeron, Jason Lynn, Franco Frias, Lee Tackett, Jack Murphy, Greg Golson, Stephen Lyons, Sam Ray, Carlos Jose Lugo, Tim Schmidt. **Advisor, Pacific Rim:** Yogo Suzuki.

MAJOR LEAGUES

MIAMI MARLINS

Office Address: Marlins Park, 501 Marlins Way, Miami, FL 33125
Telephone: (305) 480-1300. **Fax:** (305) 480-3012.
Website: www.marlins.com.

OWNERSHIP
Chairman & Principal Owner: Bruce Sherman.

BUSINESS OPERATIONS
Chief of Staff: Thomas Stolarski. **Chief Operating Officer:** Caroline O'Connor.

FINANCE
Chief Financial Officer: Fred Koczwara. **Administrator, Payroll:** Carolina Calderon. **Assistant Payroll Administrator:** Edgar Perez. **Supervisor, Accounts Payable:** Anthony Paneque. **Associate, Accounting:** William Heiberger. **Manager, Finance:** Veronica Vega.

MARKETING
Senior Director, Experience/Promotions: Juan Martinez. **Vice President, Digital Marketing:** Tiago Pinto. **Manager, Marketing:** Nathania Maldonado.

LEGAL & RISK MANAGEMENT
Senior Counsel: Benjamin Lash. **Staff Counsel:** Aaron Caputo. **Manager, Risk Management:** Will Moy. **Coordinator, Worker's Compensation:** Selina Brown.

Bruce Sherman

SALES/TICKETING
Vice President, Ticket Sales & Service: Andre Luck. **Senior Director, Ticket Sales & Service:** Jason Liss. **Director, Membership Sales:** Jason Arellano. **Manager, Membership Experience:** Eric Sutcliffe. **Manager, Premium Experience:** Samantha MacIntosh. **Manager, Business Development:** Chema Sanchez. **Manager, Business Development:** Isaac Paladino. **Manager, Business Development:** Antonio Diz. **Manager, Business Development:** Matthew Ellias. **Manager, Business Development:** Samir Mekrami. **Manager, Business Development:** John Michos. **Coordinator, Ticket Sales & Service:** Amanda Hoyos. **Coordinator, Group Sales:** Nicole Sheehan. **Membership Experience Executive:** Timothy Jenkins. **Membership Experience Executive:** Cassidy Ricci. **Membership Experience Executive:** Kaleigh Fowler. **Membership Experience Executive:** Kelly Rico. **Membership Sales Executive:** Jake Cohen. **Membership Sales Executive:** Bryan Nunez. **Membership Sales Executive:** Andrea Van Den Berg. **Membership Sales Executive:** Jaime Busch. **Membership Sales Executive:** Nate Ball. **Senior Manager, Ticket Operations:** Ossie Alvarez. **Manager, Ticket Operations:** Gerry Fernandez. **Manager, Ticket Operations:** Jose Braojos. **Coordinator, Ticket Operations:** Laura Ramirez. **Coordinator, Ticket Operations:** Yanelis Fundora.

COMMUNICATIONS/MEDIA RELATIONS
Senior Vice President, Communications & Outreach: Jason Latimer. **Director, Communications:** Jon Erik Alvarez. **Broadcaster:** Kyle Sielaff. **Manager, Fan Services:** John-Albert Rodriguez. **Player Relations & Spanish Media Liaison:** Luis Dorante. **Coordinator, Media Relations:** Gali Sharoni.

TRAVEL/CLUBHOUSE
Director, Team Travel: Max Thomas. **Equipment Manager:** John Silverman. **Visiting Clubhouse Manager:** Rock Hughes. **Assistant Clubhouse Manager:** Michael Diaz.

BASEBALL OPERATIONS
Telephone: (305) 480-1300. **Fax:** (305) 480-3032.
General Manager: Kim Ng. **Assistant General Manager:** Brian Chattin. **Assistant General Manager:** Daniel Greenlee. **Assistant General Manager:** Oz Ocampo. **Director, Team Travel & Clubhouse Operations:** Max Thomas. **Assistant Director, Baseball Operations:** Matthew Marks. **Manager, Baseball Operations:** Jordan Jackson. **Executive Assistant, Baseball Operations:** Carolina Zapata. **Director, Analytics:** Myles Lewis. **Coordinator of Baseball Information Services:** Bradley Woodrum. **Coordinator, Major League Analytics:** Neil Gahart. **Coordinator, Baseball Data:** Justin Littman. **Senior Analyst:** Robert Knopf. **Senior Analyst:** Tim Pugh. **Senior Data Engineer:** Benjamin Wong. **Analyst:** Jennifer Brann. **Analyst:** Claire Wilson. **Senior Director, International Operations:** Adrian Lorenzo. **Senior Director, Amateur Scouting:** DJ Svihlik. **Director, Minor League Operations:** Hector Crespo. **Director, International Scouting:** Roman Ocumarez. **Assistant Director, Minor League Operations:** Danny M. Henriquez. **Assistant Director, Pro Scouting:** Alexandria Rigoli. **Assistant Director, International Scouting:** David Hernandez-Beayne. **Manager, Amateur Scouting:** Joshua Kapiloff. **Coordinator, Minor League Video:** Timothy Sylvester. **Analyst, Amateur Scouting:** Justin Brands.

MAJOR LEAGUE STAFF
Manager: Skip Schumaker. **Hitting Coach:** Brant Brown. **Pitching Coach:** Mel Stottlemyre Jr. **First Base/Outfield**

GENERAL INFORMATION
Stadium (year opened): Marlins Park (2012). **Playing Surface:** Grass.
Team Colors: Caliente Red, Miami Blue, Midnight Black and Slate Grey.
Home Dugout: Third Base.

MAJOR LEAGUES

Coach: Jon Jay. **Third Base/Infield Coach:** Jody Reed. **Bullpen Coach:** Wellington Cepeda. **Bullpen Coordinator:** Rob Flippo. **Field Coordinator:** Rod Barajas. **Quality Assurance Coach:** Griffin Benedict. **Bench Coach:** Luis Urueta. **Assistant Hitting Coach:** John Mabry.

MEDICAL/TRAINING

Senior Director, Medical Services: Stan Conte. **Medical Director:** Lee Kaplan, M.D. **Head Athletic Trainer:** Lee Meyer. **Assistant Athletic Trainer:** Richard Lembo. **Assistant Athletic Trainer:** Ben Potenziano. **Major League Physical Therapist:** Andrew Turpin. **Massage Therapist:** Koji Tanaka. **Major League Equipment Manager:** John Silverman. **Visiting Clubhouse Manager:** Rock Hughes. **Assistant Home Clubhouse Manager:** Michael Diaz. **Major League Strength & Conditioning Coach:** Brendan Verner. **Minor League Strength & Conditioning Coordinator:** Brad Hyde.

PLAYER DEVELOPMENT

Kim Ng

Director, Minor League Operations: Hector Crespo. **Senior Advisor, Player Development:** Jim Riggleman. **Assistant Director, Minor League Ops:** Danny Henriquez. **Intern, Player Development:** Alan Santiago. **Field Coordinator:** Patrick Osborn. **Pitching Coordinator:** Scott Aldred. **Pitching Coordinator:** Tommy Phelps. **Hitting Coordinator:** Tom Slater. **Hitting / Catching Coordinator:** Jeff Livesey. **Infield Coordinator:** Jorge Hernandez. **Player Performance Coordinator:** Angel Espada. **Player Performance Coordinator:** Frank Moore. **Player Performance Coordinator:** Esmerling De La Rosa. **International Pitching Coordinator:** Elvys Quezada. **Rehab Coordinator and Physical Therapist:** JT Taylor. **Rehab Athletic Trainer:** Christine Padilla. **Minor League Physical Therapist:** Deanna DeNapoli. **Rehab S&C Coordinator:** Alexander Pons. **Strength & Conditioning Coordinator:** Brad Hyde. **Video Coordinator:** Tim Sylvester. **Mental Skills Coordinator:** Jim Soda. **Clubhouse Coordinator:** Simon Beloff. **Jupiter Lead Teacher:** Pamela Mejia. **Specialist, Education & Community Service:** Colleen Mitchell. **Education Initiatives Assistant:** TBD. **Player Development Nutritionist:** TBD. **Rehab Pitching Coach:** Jeff Schwarz. **Rehab Position Player Coach:** Tom Lawless. **Manager, Dominican Republic Operations:** Ismael Granadillo. **Latin American PD Coordinator:** Ivan Arteaga. **LA Athletic Training Coordinator:** Jose Alvarez. **DR Physical Therapist:** Ken Hoefs. **LA Mental Skills Coordinator:** David Soto. **D.R. Academy Maintenance Supervisor:** Rene Castro.

FARM SYSTEM

Class	Club (League)	Manager	Hitting Coach	Pitching Coach
Triple-A	Jacksonville (IL)	Daren Brown	Greg Colbrunn	Jeremy Powell
Double-A	Pensacola (SL)	Kevin Randel	Matt Snyder	Dave Eiland
High-A	Beloit (MWL)	Billy Gardner Jr.	Dan Radison	Jason Erickson
Low-A	Jupiter (FSL)	Nelson Prada	Ty Hawkins	Glenn Dishman
Rookie	Marlins (FCL)	Luis Dorante Sr.	Jesus Merchan	Justin Pope
Rookie	Marlins 1 (DSL)	TBD	Rigo Silverio	Cesar Jimenez
Rookie	Marlins 2 (DSL)	Oscar Escobar	Emilio Linares	Yohan Pino

SCOUTING

Senior Director, Amateur Scouting: DJ Svihlik. **Manager, Amateur Scouting:** Josh Kapiloff. **National Crosschecker:** Eric Valent. **Amateur Scouting Analyst:** Justin Brands. **Amateur Scouting Assistant:** Jordan Klinge. **Crosscheckers:** Scott Goldby, Ryan Wardinsky, Carmen Carcone, Mike Soper, T.R. Lewis. **Area Scouts:** Eric Brock, Hunter Jarmon, Scott Stanley, Scott Fairbanks, Eric Wordekemper, Ryan Cisterna, Chris Joblin, Brett Bittiger, JT Zink, Davis Knapp, Shaeffer Hall, Blake Newsome, Alex Smith. **Part-Time Scouts:** Bob Oldis, Omar Rosado. **Assistant Director, Professional Scouting:** Alexandria Rigoli. **Special Assignment Scout:** Joe Caro. **Professional Scouting Supervisors:** Chris Pelekoudas, Johnny Almaraz, Joe Lisewski. **Professional Scouts:** Jim Howard, Jose Almonte, Jordan Bley, John Eshleman, Eddie Almonte, Alexander Noel, Alvin Rittman, Phil Rossi. **Part-Time Scouts:** Paul Ricciarini. **Senior Director, International Operations:** Adrian Lorenzo. **Director, International Scouting:** Roman Ocumarez. **Assistant Director, International Scouting:** David Hernandez Beayne. **International Crosschecker:** Manny Padron. **International Crosschecker:** Adrian Puig. **Scouts, Dominican Republic:** Angel Izquierdo, Sahir Fersobe, Miguel Beltre. **Venezuela Administration Coordinator:** Clifford Nuitter. **Scouts, Venezuela:** Tibaldo Hernandez, Nestor Moreno, Aly Gonzalez. **Scout, Mexico:** Andres Guzman. **Video Coordinator, Dominican Republic:** Edward Artiles. **Manager, Dominican Operations:** Ismael Granadillo.

MAJOR LEAGUES

MILWAUKEE BREWERS

Office Address: Miller Park, One Brewers Way, Milwaukee, WI 53214.
Telephone: (414) 902-4400. **Fax:** (414) 902-4053. **Website:** www.brewers.com.

OWNERSHIP
Operated By: Milwaukee Brewers Baseball Club.
Chairman/Principal Owner: Mark Attanasio.

BUSINESS OPERATIONS
President, Business Operations: Rick Schlesinger. **SVP/GM:** Matt Arnold. **Executive Vice Presidedent, Chief Commercial Officer:** Jason Hartlund. **Chief Financial Officer:** Daniel Fumai. **Chief Operating Officer:** Marti Wronski. **Senior Vice President, Communications & Affiliate Operations:** Tyler Barnes. **Senior Vice President, Stadium Operations:** Steve Ethier. **Executive Assistant, Revenue:** Lisa Brzeski. **Executive Assistant, Ownership Group:** Samantha Ernest. **Executive Assistant, General Manager:** Nichole Kinateder. **Executive Assistant, Paralegal:** Kate Rock. **Executive Assistant:** Adela Reeve. **Executive Assistant:** Kate Stempski. **Consultant:** Bob Quinn.

Mark Attanasio

FINANCE/ACCOUNTING
Director, Accounting: Vicki Wise. **Director, Disbursements:** Erica Umbach. **Manager, Risk Management:** Darius Anderson. **Manager, Workday Systems:** Tara Ali. **Senior Financial Analysts:** Cory Loppnow, Mike Anheuser, Kristin Hahn, Pat Fennell. **Payroll Administrator:** Sandra Halvorsen. **Senior Accounts Payable and Payroll Specialist:** Ryan Barnard. **Workday HRIS Analyst:** Rebecca Hartley. **Treasury Accountant:** Jake Lindmair. **Accounts Payable Clerk:** Jim Woelfel.

MARKETING
VP, Marketing: Sharon McNally. **Senior Coordinator, Marketing:** Gina Moretti. **Marketing Administrator:** Brittany Luznicky. **Director, Design Services:** Jeff Harding. **Senior Graphic Designer:** Brandon Frederickson. **Graphic Designer:** Alex Pera. **Director, Video Production:** Matt Gompper. **Productions Manager:** Caitlin Walter.

BUSINESS ANALYTICS
Senior Director, Consumer Insights: Marla Grossberg. **Director, Business Analytics:** Danny Henken. **Business Analyst:** Ryan Hinchcliffe.

MEDIA RELATIONS
Senior Director, Media Relations: Mike Vassallo. **Senior Director, Business Communications:** Leslie Stachowiak. **Manager, Media Relations:** Andrew Gruman.

MILLER PARK OPERATIONS
VP Facilities and Projects: Mike Brockman. **Senior Director, Event Services:** Matt Lehmann. **Senior Director, Security:** Randy Olewinski. **Senior Director, Grounds:** Ryan Woodley. **Senior Manager, Security:** Dennis Angle. **Senior Manager, Event Services:** Scott Quade. **Senior Manager, Warehouse:** John Weyer. **Manager, Warehouse:** Matt Bischoff. **Manager, Guest Experience:** Sarah Olewinski. **Manager, Grounds:** Grant Roth. **Manager, Fields:** Tyler Tschetter.

TICKET SALES
Telephone: (414) 902-4000. **Fax:** (414) 902-4056.
VP, Ticket Sales: Jim Bathey. **Sr. Director, Ticket Sales:** Billy Friess. **VP, Ticket Technology & Booking:** Jess Brown. **Director, Group Sales:** Chris Kimball. **Senior Director, Partnership and Premium Sales:** Chris Rothwell.

BASEBALL OPERATIONS
Telephone: (414) 902-4400. **Fax:** (414) 902-4515.
Assistant to Ownership and Baseball Operations: David Stearns. **Special Asst. to GM:** Doug Melvin. **SVP, Player Personnel:** Karl Mueller. **VP, Baseball Projects:** Gord Ash. **VP, Minor League Operations:** Tom Flanagan. **VP, Domestic Scouting:** Tod Johnson. **VP, Baseball Operations:** Matt Kleine. **Special Asst. to GM:** Matt Klentak. **VP and Special Asst. to GM and Baseball Operations:** Eduardo Brizuela. **VP, Baseball Systems and High Performance:** Will Hudgins. **VP, Baseball Research and Innovation:** Dan Turkenkopf. **Special Asst., Baseball Operations and Player Development:** Quinton McCracken. **Special Asst. to GM, Player Development:** Carlos Villanueva. **Special Assignment Scout:** Scott Campbell. **Special Asst. Baseball R&D:** Nick Davis. **Director, Baseball Ops.:** Eric Babitz. **Director, Baseball Systems:** Matt Culhane. **Director, Technology Operations:** Matt Kerls. **Senior Manager, Baseball Administration:** Mark Meuller. **Lead Analyst, Player Personnel:** Ethan Bein. **Manager, International Scouting and Player Personnel:** James Armstrong. **Manager, Advance Scouting:** Brian Powalish. **Senior Engineer Analyst,

GENERAL INFORMATION
Stadium (year opened): American Family Field (2001).
Team Colors: Navy blue, gold and white.
Home Dugout: First Base.
Playing Surface: Grass.

MAJOR LEAGUES

Baseball Ops.: Andrew Fox. **Senior Data Quality Engineer:** Josh Schaffer. **Senior Analysts, Baseball R&D:** Dan Kutner, Scott Van Lenten. **Senior Software Engineers:** James Beaudoin, DJ Michalski, Scott Molling. **Senior Data Engineer:** Charles Clark. **Senior Coordinator, Major League Video and Technology:** August Sandri. **Analysts, Baseball R&D:** Eric Albers, Everett Johnson, Austin Leonard. **Data Architect:** Phil Hauser. **Software Engineer:** Daniel Oh. **Data Engineer:** Harrison Jacobs. **Assistant, Major League Video and Spanish Translator:** Carlos Brizuela. **Coordinator, Technology Ops.:** Ronnie Bedrosian. **Coordinator, Player Development Information:** Matt Ducondi. **Coordinator, Scouting:** Oscar Garcia. **Coordinator, Data Quality Assurance and Technology Ops.:** Kevin Ottsen. **Coordinator, Scouting Ops.:** Matt Roffe. **Coordinators, Technology Ops.:** Daniel Sarna, Tyler Spicer. **Assistant, International Scouting:** Zorian Schiffman. **Assistant, Baseball Ops.:** Michael Silber. **Assistant Technology Ops.:** Ethan Stern.

MAJOR LEAGUE STAFF

David Stearns

Manager: Craig Counsell. **Coaches: Bench**—Pat Murphy, **Pitching**—Chris Hook, **Hitting**—Connor Dawson, Ozzie Timmons, **First Base**—Quintin Berry, **Third Base**—Jason Lane, **Bullpen**—Jim Henderson, **Coach**— Néstor Corredor, **Bullpen Catchers**— Daniel de Mondesert, Adam Weisenburger, **Associate Pitching, Catching and Strategy Coach**—Walker McKinven.

MEDICAL/TRAINING

Head Team Physician: Dr. William Raasch. **Team Physicians:** Dr. Mark Niedfeldt, Dr. Craig Young. **Director, Player Health:** Blair Bundy. **Assistant Director, Player Health:** Frank Neville. **Assistant Director, Performance Psychology:** Blake Pindyck. **Head Athletic Trainer:** Scott Barringer. **Assistant Athletic Trainer:** Dave Yeager. **Assistant Athletic Trainer/Physical Therapist:** Theresa Lau. **Strength and Conditioning Specialist:** Jason Meredith. **Assistant Strength and Conditioning Specialist:** Daniel Vega. **Coordinator, Minor League Medical Administration:** Matt Deal. **Rehab Coordinator:** Bryn Hester. **Coordinator, Minor League Medical:** Nick Jensen. **Coordinator, Performance Psychology:** Alex Raske. **Physical Therapists:** Bridget Graff, Reese Wilmoth. **Consulting Orthopedic Physician, Phoenix:** Dr. Evan Lederman. **Consulting Team Physician, Phoenix:** Dr. Carlton Richie.

PLAYER DEVELOPMENT

VP, Player Development: Cam Castro. **Director, Player Development Information:** August Fagerstrom. **Assistant Director, Player Development:** Charlie Greene. **Lead Strategist, Pitching Development:** Bryan Leslie. **Senior Coordinator, Player Personnel:** Zack Sorensen. **Minor League Field Coordinator:** Spencer Allen. **Assistant Field Coordinator:** Rafael Neda. **Coordinator, Minor League Pitching:** Nick Childs. **Coordinator, Minor League Hitting:** Brenton Del Chiaro. **Coordinator, Player Development Information:** Ben Harris. **Coordinator, Baseball Diversity Initiatives:** Junior Spivey. **Infield Coordinator:** Bob Miscik. **Roving Field Instructor:** Matt Erickson. **Assistant Coordinator, Minor League Hitting:** Eric Theisen. **Rehabilitation Coach:** Avery Sullivan. **Latin America Strength and Conditioning Liaison:** Luis Rios Reyes. **Coordinator, Latin America Operations:** Manuel Vargas. **Assistant Coordinator, Administration and Video:** Juan De Leon. **Assistant, Baseball Operations and Player Development:** Pedro Álvarez. **Assistants, Player Development:** Adam Harband, Josh Lindblom, Rickie Weeks. **Minor League Clubhouse Manager:** Adam Gutierrez. **Assistant Minor League Clubhouse Manager:** Joey Hickey. **Education Coordinator:** Adela Marquez.

FARM SYSTEM

Class	Club (League)	Manager	Hitting Coach	Pitching Coach
Triple-A	Nashville (IL)	Rick Sweet	Al LeBoeuf	Jeremy Accardo
Double-A	Biloxi (SL)	Mike Guerrero	Chuckie Caufield	Will Schierholz
High-A	Wisconsin (MWL)	Joe Ayrault	Ken Joyce	Drew Thomas
Low-A	Carolina (CAR)	Victor Estevez	J.J. Reimer	Michael O'Neal
Rookie	Brewers (ACL)	Rafael Neda	C. Retherford/M. Habas	P. Moeller/ H. Burgos
Rookie	Brewers Blue (DSL)	Fidel Pena	José García	Juan Sandoval
Rookie	Brewers Gold (DSL)	Natanael Mejia	Austin Turner	Jesús Hernández

SCOUTING

Telephone: (414) 902-4400. **Fax:** (414) 902-4059.

Special Assistants, Scouting: Mike Berger, Bryan Gale, Chip Lawrence. **Assistant Director, Scouting/International Player Development:** Taylor Green. **Assistant Director, International Scouting:** Luis Pérez. **National Supervisor, Scouting:** Doug Reynolds. **Supervisor, Scout Teams/West Coast Special Assignment Scout:** Corey Rodriguez. **Regional Supervisors, Scouting:** Drew Anderson, Dan Nellum, Wynn Pelzer, Mike Serbalik. **Domestic/International Scout:** Bryan Bullington. **Area Scouts:** Riley Bandelow, Daniel Cho, Steve Ditrolio, James Fisher, Taylor Frederick, Joe Graham, Adam Hayes, Lazaro Llanes, Ketchum Marsh, Scott Nichols, Pete Orr, Kevin O'Sullivan, Ginger Poulson, Jeff Simpson, Craig Smajstrla, Steve Smith, Shawn Whalen. **Developmental scouts:** Hashim Cole, Joseph Rivera, Jacob Vollen. **Latin America Crosschecker/Venezuela Operations:** Fernando Veracierto. **Supervisor, Dominican Republic:** Gary Peralta. **Supervisor, Venezuela:** José Rodríguez. **Regional Crosscheckers, Dominican Republic:** Esteban Castillo, Rodolfo Rosario. **Coordinator, Dominican Republic:** Pedro Robles. **Coordinator, International Scouting Administration and Technology:** Diego Flores. **Scouts:** Trino Aguilar, Salvador Ayestas, José Barraza, Javier Castillo, Julio De La Cruz, Kenji Galavis, Jesús Garces, Jose Gomez, Teofilo Gutierrez, Jonas Lantigua, Fabian Mendez, Mario Mendoza, Javier Meza, José Morales, Kevin Ramos, Jean Carlos Reynoso, Luis Rosario, Samuel Uribe, Miguel Vásquez.

MAJOR LEAGUES

MINNESOTA TWINS

Office Address: Target Field, 1 Twins Way, Minneapolis, MN 55403.
Telephone: (612) 659-3400. **Fax:** 612-659-4025. **Website:** www.twins.com.

OWNERSHIP
Operated By: The Minnesota Twins. **Controlling Owner:** Jim Pohlad. **Executive Chair:** Joe Pohlad. **Executive Board:** Jim Pohlad, Joe Pohlad, Bob Pohlad, Bill Pohlad, Dave St. Peter.

BUSINESS OPERATIONS
President/Chief Executive Officer, Minnesota Twins: Dave St. Peter. **Executive Vice President/Chief Business Officer:** Meka Morris. **Executive Vice President/Chief Administrative Officer/Chief Financial Officer:** Kip Elliott. **Senior Vice President/Chief Technology Officer:** John Avenson. **Senior Vice President, Consumer Revenue:** Mike Clough. **Senior Vice President, General Counsel:** Mary Giesler. **Senior Vice President, Operations:** Matt Hoy. **Senior Vice President/Chief Strategy Officer:** Jason Lee. **Senior Vice President, Human Resources:** Leticia Silva. **Vice President, Finance:** Andy Weinstein. **Deputy General Counsel:** Mari Guttman. **Senior Associate Counsel:** Wyatt Little. **Senior Executive Assistant:** Danielle Berg. **Executive Assistants:** Rachel Snyder, Tina Flowers.

Jim Pohlad

HUMAN RESOURCES/FINANCE/TECHNOLOGY
Senior Director, Compensation & Benefits: Lori Beasley. **Senior Director, Business Systems:** Wade Navratil. **Senior Director, Procurement:** Bud Hanley. **Director, Accounting:** Lori Windschitl. **Director, Information Security:** Robert Jacoby. **Director, Technology Infrastructure:** Tony Persio. **Director, Inclusion and People Development:** Cecilia Lettner.

BRAND MARKETING
Vice President, Brand Marketing: Heather Hinkel. **Director, Broadcast:** Andrew Halverson. **Director, Brand Marketing:** Becky Holten.

BRAND PARTNERSHIPS
Vice President, Brand Partnerships: Sean Moore. **Director, Partnership Activation:** Amelia Johnson. **Director, Research & Strategy:** Will Clayton. **Director, Brand Partnerships Sales:** Philicia Douglas.

BUSINESS STRATEGY & ANALYTICS
Senior Director, Brand Experience & Innovation: Chris Iles. **Senior Director, Business Strategy & Analytics:** Brandon Johnson. **Director, Business Intelligence & Analytics:** Lisa Moschkau.

COMMUNICATIONS & CONTENT
Vice President, Communications & Content: Dustin Morse. **Director, Game Day Experience:** Sam Henschen. **Director, Business Communications:** Matt Hodson.

COMMUNITY ENGAGEMENT
Vice President, Community Engagement: Nancy O'Brien. **Senior Director, Community Engagement & Executive Director, Minnesota Twins Community Fund:** Kristen Rortvedt. **Director, Community Engagement & Events:** Julie Vavruska.

TICKETING
Vice President, Ticket Sales & Strategy: Eddie Eixenberger. **Vice President, Ticket Operations:** Paul Froehle. **Senior Director, Ticket Service & Retention:** Eric Hudson. **Senior Director, Ticket Strategy & New Business:** Rob Malec. **Senior Director, Ticket Operations/Technology:** Mike Stiles. **Senior Director, Suites & Premium Seating:** P.J. Williams. **Director of Season Memberships & Retention:** Craig Gumz. **Director of Group Sales and Service:** Phil McMullen. **Director, Florida Business Operations:** Mark Weber. **Director of New Business Development:** Bryan Van Den Bosch.

BALLPARK OPERATIONS
Vice President, Ballpark Operations: Dave Horsman. **Senior Director, Ballpark Development & Planning:** Dan Starkey. **Senior Director, Facilities:** Gary Glawe. **Senior Director, Guest Experience:** Patrick Forsland. **Senior Director, Security:** Jeff Beahen. **Director, Team Security:** Charles Adams III. **Director, Ballpark Maintenance:** Dana Minion. **Head Groundskeeper:** Larry DiVito. **Director, Target Field Events:** Quinn Handahl.

GENERAL INFORMATION
Stadium (year opened): Target Field (2010). **Playing Surface:** Grass.
Team Colors: Red, navy blue and white.
Home Dugout: First Base.

MAJOR LEAGUES

BASEBALL OPERATIONS
President, Baseball Operations: Derek Falvey. **Senior Vice President/General Manager:** Thad Levine. **Vice President/Special Assistant to Baseball Operations:** Rob Antony. **Vice President, Assistant GM:** Daniel Adler. **Vice President, Assistant GM:** Jeremy Zoll. **Vice President, Baseball Operations Strategy & Innovation:** Josh Kalk. **Senior Director, Team Travel:** Mike Herman. **Senior Director, Baseball Systems:** Jeremy Raadt. **Director, Baseball Research:** Dane Sorensen. **Director, Baseball Technology:** Sean Harlin. **Assistant Director, Baseball Operations:** Nick Beauchamp. **Assistant Director, Baseball Research:** Kevin Wright. **Special Assistants:** Michael Cuddyer, LaTroy Hawkins, Torii Hunter, Justin Morneau.

MAJOR LEAGUE STAFF
Manager: Rocco Baldelli. **Coaches: Bench**—Jayce Tingler, **Assistant Bench/Infield**—Tony Diaz, **Pitching**—Pete Maki, **Hitting**—Rudy Hernandez, **Hitting**—David Popkins, **Assistant Hitting**—Derek Shomon, **First Base/Catching**—Hank Conger, **Third Base/Outfield**—Tommy Watkins, **Bullpen Coach**—Colby Suggs, **Assistant Pitching**—Luis Ramirez, **Quality Control**—Nate Dammann, **Bullpen Catchers**—Anderson De La Rosa, Connor Olson. **Equipment Manager:** Rod McCormick.

MEDICAL/TRAINING
Director, Medical High Performance: Dr. Christopher Camp. **Medical Director Emeritus:** Dr. John Steubs. **Club Physicians:** Dr. Rahul Kapur, Dr. Dave Olson, Dr. Corey Wulf, Dr. Amy Beacom. **Head Athletic Trainer:** Nick Paparesta. **Assistant Trainers:** Masamichi Abe, Jason Kirkman. **Physical Therapist:** Adam Diamond. **Director, Strength & Conditioning:** Ian Kadish. **Strength & Conditioning Coaches:** Chuck Bradway, Aaron Rhodes. **Massage Therapist:** Kelli Bergheim.

Derek Falvey

PLAYER DEVELOPMENT
Telephone: (612) 659-3480. **Fax:** (612) 659-4026.
Vice President, Hitting Development & Procurement: Alex Hassan. **Director, Player Development:** Drew MacPhail. **Director, Minor League and High Performance Operations:** Brian Maloney. **Director, Performance Nutrition:** Kara Lynch. **Director, Player Education:** Amanda Daley. **Assistant Directors, Player Development:** Tommy Bergjans, Frankie Padulo. **Assistant Director, Florida & Dominican Republic Operations:** Victor Gonzalez. **Assistant Director, Player Development Research:** Josh Ruffin. **Assistant Director, Sports Science:** Martijn Verhoeven. **Minor League Coordinators:** Kevin Morgan (field), Edgar Varela (Instruction), Justin Willard (pitching), Nat Ballenberg (assistant pitching), Bryce Berg (hitting), Ryan Smith (assistant hitting), Tucker Frawley (Infield and catching), Mike Quade (outfield). **Pitching Development & Acquisitions Specialist:** Matt Daniels.

FARM SYSTEM

Class	Club (League)	Manager	Hitting Coach	Pitching Coach
Triple-A	St. Paul (IL)	Toby Gardenhire	Nate Spears	C. Bello/P. Larson
Double-A	Wichita (SL)	Ramon Borrego	Shawn Schlechter	DJ Engle/Dan Urbina
High-A	Cedar Rapids (MWL)	Brian Dinkelman	C. Day/Y. Perez	C. Hernandez/J. Lovin
Low-A	Fort Myers (FSL)	Brian Meyer	Rayden Sierra	J. Gaynor/R.Salazar
Rookie	Twins (FCL)	Seth Feldman	Guerrero/Miranda/McBride	Angulo/Dzurak/Maduro
Rookie	Twins (DSL)	Rafael Martinez	J. Rodriguez/R. Santana	E. Julio/J. Sanchez

SCOUTING
Vice President, Amateur Scouting: Sean Johnson. **Senior Advisor, Scouting:** Deron Johnson. **Director, Latin American Scouting & US Integration:** Fred Guerrero. **Director, Professional Player Procurement:** Brad Steil. **Assistant Director, Amateur Scouting:** Tim O'Neil. **Assistant Director, Professional Player Procurement:** Navery Moore. **Senior International Scouting Advisor:** José León. **National Crosschecker:** Billy Corrigan. **Amateur Crosschecker:** Freddie Thon. **Scouting Supervisors: East**—Mark Quimuyog, **Mideast**—Derrick Dunbar, **Midwest**—Mike Ruth, **West**—Elliott Strankman. **Area Scouts:** Andrew Ayers, Joe Bisenius, Kyle Blackwell, Trevor Brown, Walt Burrows, Ty Dawson, J.R. DiMercurio, Brett Dowdy, John Leavitt, Mitch Morales, Jeff Pohl, Jack Powell, Dylan Tashjian, Brian Tripp, Kyle Van Hook, Nick Venuto, Chandler Wagoner, Matt Williams, John Wilson. **Dominican Republic:** Eduardo Soriano (DR Supervisor), Daniel Sánchez, Manuel Luciano, Luis Lajara, Samuel Pimentel. **Venezuela:** Andrés García (VZ Supervisor), Oswaldo Troconis, Edgar Guerra, Marlon Nava, John González. **Pro Scouts:** Ken Compton, Earl Frishman, Jason Hahn, John Manuel, Jose Marzan, Bill Milos, Keith Stohr, Gianfraco Wawoe, Wesley Wright, Rafael Yanez.

MAJOR LEAGUES

NEW YORK METS

Office Address: Citi Field, 41 Seaver Way, Flushing, NY 11368.
Telephone: (718) 507-6387. **Fax:** (718) 507-6395.
Website: www.mets.com. **Twitter:** @mets.

OWNERSHIP
Owner, Chairman and CEO: Steven A. Cohen. **Owner & President, Amazin' Mets Foundation:** Alexandra M. Cohen. **Vice Chairman:** Andrew B. Cohen. **Chairman Emeritus:** Fred Wilpon. **Board of Directors:** Jeanne Melino, Chris Christie.

BUSINESS OPERATIONS
President, Foundation: Alex Cohen. **Chief Technology Officer:** Mark Brubaker. **Chief Financial Officer & Treasurer:** Steve Canna. **Chief Communications Officer:** Nancy Elder. **Executive Vice President, General Manager:** Billy Eppler. **Executive Vice President & Chief Marketing Officer:** Andy Goldberg. **Executive Vice President & Chief Legal Officer:** Katie Pothier. **Head of Human Resources:** Ariel Speicher. **Executive Vice President, Operations:** Jeff White. **Executive Vice President & Chief Revenue Officer:** Jeff Deline. **Senior Vice President, Ticketing & Premium:** Jake Bye. **Senior Vice President, Ballpark Operations:** Sue Lucchi. **Senior Vice President, Partnerships:** Brenden Mallette. **Senior Vice President, Foundation & Community Engagement:** Jeanne Melino. **Senior Vice President & Chief of Staff:** John Ricco. **Senior Vice President, Finance:** Peter Woll. **Vice President, Guest Experience & Venue Operations:** Chris Brown. **Vice President, Facility Operations:** Peter Cassano. **Vice President, Brooklyn Administration:** Steven Cohen. **Vice President & Co-General Counsel:** James Denniston. **Vice President, Hospitality:** Taryn Donovan. **Vice President, Technology Solutions:** Oscar Fernandez. **Vice President, Alumni Public Relations & Team Historian:** Jay Horwitz.

Steve Cohen

MEDIA RELATIONS
Telephone: (718) 565-4330. **Fax:** (718) 639-3619.
Chief Communications Officer: Nancy Elder. **Senior Director, Communications and Publications:** Zach Weber. **Senior Director, Communications:** Ethan Wilson. **Manager, Communications/Translator:** Álan Suriel. **Manager, Communications:** Zack Becker. **Manager, Communications:** Katie Agostin. **Assistant, Communications:** Josh Lederman.

TRAVEL/CLUBHOUSE
Director, Team Travel: Brian Small. **Equipment Manager:** Kevin Kierst. **Visiting Clubhouse Manager:** Dave Berni. **Coordinator, Clubhouse Operations:** Scott Keltner.

BASEBALL OPERATIONS
Telephone: (718) 803-4013, (718) 565-4339. **Fax:** (718) 507-6391.
Executive Vice President, General Manager: Billy Eppler. **Assistant General Manager, Baseball Operations:** Ian Levin. **Assistant General Manager, Baseball Analytics:** Ben Zauzmer. **Vice President, Baseball Operations:** Jonathan Strangio. **Vice President, Amateur & International Scouting:** Thomas Tanous. **Director, Baseball Development:** Bryan Hayes. **Coordinator, Baseball Operations:** John Madsen. **Director, Major League Operations:** Elizabeth Benn. **Director, Baseball Operations:** Nick Spar.

MAJOR LEAGUE STAFF
Manager: Buck Showalter. **Bench Coach:** Eric Chavez. **Catching Coach:** Glenn Sherlock. **Pitching Coach:** Jeremy Hefner. **Hitting Coach:** Jeremy Barnes. **Assistant Hitting Coach:** Eric Hinske. **First Base Coach:** Wayne Kirby. **Third Base Coach:** Joey Cora. **Bullpen Coach:** Dom Chiti. **Assistant Coach:** Danny Barnes. **Bullpen Catcher:** Dave Racaniello. **Bullpen Catcher:** Eric Langill. **Major League Coaching Assistant:** Aaron Myers. **Major League Coaching Assistant:** Rafael Fernandez.

PLAYER DEVELOPMENT
Telephone: (718) 565-4302. **Fax:** (718) 205-7920.
Player Development Director: Kevin Howard. **Assistant Director, Player Development:** Andrew Christie. **Director, Minor League Operations:** Ronny Reyes. **Director, Latin America Operations:** Juan Henderson. **Manager of Minor League Education and Life Skills:** Neskys Liriano. **Coordinator, Minor League Operations:** Amy Ross. **Assistant, Minor League Travel:** Ches Goodman. **Manager, Minor League Equipment & Operations:** John Mullin. **Assistant Manager Minor League Clubhouse & Equipment:** Drew Dunton. **Director, Hitting Development:** Jeff Albert. **Director, Pitching Development:** Eric Jagers. **Field Coordinator:** Eddy Rodriguez. **Assistant Field Coordinator:** Ken Knutson. **Pitching Coordinator:** Jono Armold. **Assistant Pitching Coordinator/Pitching Coach:** Kyle Driscoll. **Coordinator, Player Development Programming:** Max Vogel-Freedman. **Infield Coordinator:** Miguel Cairo. **Catching Coordinator:** Robert Natal. **Pitching & Performance Integration Coordinator:** Kyle Rogers. **Outfield/Baserunning

GENERAL INFORMATION
Stadium (year opened): Citi Field (2009).
Team Colors: Blue and orange.
Home Dugout: First Base.
Playing Surface: Grass.

MAJOR LEAGUES

Coordinator: Shane Robinson. **Roving INF Instructor:** Luis Rivera. **Roving INF/Base Running Instructor:** Jemile Weeks

RESEARCH AND DEVELOPMENT

Assistant General Manager, Baseball Analytics: Ben Zauzmer. **Director, Baseball Analytics:** Joseph Lefkowitz. **Manager, Baseball Research & Development:** Jared Faust. **Coordinator, Pitching Analytics:** David Lang. **Coordinator, Minor League Analytics:** Daniel Schoenfeld. **Manager, Video Operations:** Joseph Scarola. **Senior Coordinator, Video Operations:** Sean Haggans. **Coordinator, Pitching Analysis & Evaluations:** Jack Bredeson. **Analyst, Major League Strategy:** Joey Keating. **Analyst, Major League Strategy:** Natalie Maurice. **Replay Analyst:** Harrison Friedland. **Senior Analyst, Baseball Analytics:** Michael Jerman. **Biomechanical Analyst, Baseball Analytics:** Siddhartha Thakur. **Analyst, Baseball Analytics:** Desmond McGowan. **Analyst, Baseball Analytics:** Tatiana DeRouen. **Analyst, Baseball Analytics:** Kuan-Cheng Fu. **Analyst, Baseball R&D:** Tim Wise. **Director, Baseball Systems:** Kevin Meehan.

Billy Eppler

MINOR LEAGUE PERFORMANCE

Director, Minor League Athletic Training and Reconditioning: JT Podell. **Minor League Medical Coordinator:** Bob Tarpey. **Medical Coordinator, Latin America:** Jhomelger Garcia. **Minor League Reconditioning Coordinator:** Luke Novosel. **Reconditioning Performance Coach:** Kory Wan. **Minor League Reconditioning Therapist:** Matt Witt. **Minor League Reconditioning Athletic Trainer:** Adam Devery. **Minor League Performance Coaching Coordinator:** Luke Passman. **Minor League Performance Nutrition Coordinator:** Geordan Stapleton. **Minor League Performance Nutritionist:** Bella Simpson. **Mental Performance Coach:** Maria Bogaert. **Mental Performance Coach:** Emmanuel Goico-Montes de Oca

FARM SYSTEM

Class	Club	Manager	Hitting Coach	Pitching Coach
Triple-A	Syracuse (IL)	Dick Scott	Collin Hetzler	Kyle Driscoll
Double-A	Binghamton (EL)	Reid Brignac	Darin Everson	AJ Sager
High-A	Brooklyn (SAL)	Chris Newell	Richie Benes	Victor Ramos
Low-A	St. Lucie (FSL)	Gilbert Gomez	Eduardo Nunez	Dan Mckinney
Rookie	Mets (FCL)	Jay Pecci	N. Ascue/A. Diaz	Luis Alvarado
Rookie	Mets 1 (DSL)	Danny Ortega	Leo Hernandez	Cristhian Martinez
Rookie	Mets 2 (DSL)	Mac Seibert IV	Bryce Wheary	Wander Cabrera

SCOUTING

Telephone: (718) 565-4311. **Fax:** (718) 205-7920.

Vice President, Amateur and International Scouting: Thomas Tanous. **Senior Advisor, Domestic and International Scouting:** Marc Tramuta. **Director, Amateur Scouting:** Drew Toussaint. **Manager, Amateur Scouting/Pacific Rim:** Tom Fleischman. **Coordinator, Amateur Scouting:** Cole Jaskoviak. **Senior Director, Pro Player Personnel:** Nate Horowitz. **Senior Manager, Pro Player Personnel:** Jason Stein. **Manager, Pro Player Personnel:** Ronnie Socash. **Assistant, Pro Player Personnel:** Bryan Ray Woolley. **Senior Advisor, Pro Player Personnel:** Joseph Kowal. **Special Advisor, Pro Player Personnel | International/Amateur Special Assignments:** David Keller. **Pacific Rim Evaluator, Japan:** Jeffrey Kusumoto. **Pacific Rim Evaluator, Korea:** Bon Kim. **Director, Pro Player Evaluation:** Jeff Lebow. **Coordinator, Pro Player Evaluation:** Jason Davis. **Pro Player Evaluators:** Jaymie Bane, Tony DeFrancesco, Pat Jones, Jim Kelly, Ash Lawson, Chad MacDonald, Shaun McNamara, Andy Pratt, Roy Smith, Rudy Terrasas, Ernie Young. **Regional Supervisor, Southeast:** Cesar Aranguren. **Senior Advisor, Amateur Scouting:** Eddie Bane. **Regional Supervisor, Midwest:** Nathan Beuster. **Underclass Supervisor:** Tom Clark. **National Pitching Crosschecker:** Chris Hervey. **Regional Supervisor, West:** Tyler Holmes. **Senior Advisor, Amateur Scouting:** Ron Hopkins. **Regional Supervisor, Northeast:** Mike Ledna. **Catching Evaluation Scout:** Joe Oliver. **National Crosschecker:** Doug Thurman. **Area Supervisors:** Gary Brown, Jet Butler, Brett Campbell, Daniel Coles, Chris Heidt, John Kocsiak, Rusty McNamara, Marlin McPhail, Nelson Mompierre, Rich Morales, Joe Raccuia, Brian Reid, Harry Shelton, Scott Thomas, Glenn Walker, Kevin Whiteside. **Data Tech Scout:** Jacob Dorris. **Scouts:** Johnny Magliozzi, Jason McLaughlin, Nathan Rode. **Director, International Scouting:** Steve Barningham. **Coordinator, International Scouting:** Rosario Chiovaro. **National Scout, Dominican Republic:** Moises de la Mota. **Supervisor, Pitching Evaluation & Development:** John Hendricks. **National Scout, Colombia, Panama, Mexico:** Harold Herrera. **National Scout, Venezuela:** Ismael Perez. **Supervisor, Dominican Republic & Cuba:** Oliver Dominguez. **Coordinator, Dominican Republic:** Felix Romero. **Coordinator, Mexico:** Martin Arvizu. **Caribbean Crosschecker:** Luis Scheker. **Scout, Dominican Republic:** Kelvin Dominguez. **Scout, Dominican Republic:** Wilson Peralta. **Scout, Venezuela:** Robert Espejo. **Scouts, Venezuela:** Manuel López, Andres Nunez, Carlos Perez. **Scout, Panama & Brazil:** Elvis Rios. **Video Coordinator, Dominican Republic:** Jose Luis de Leon. **Scout, Dominican Republic:** Carlos Pellerano. **Video Coordinator, Venezuela:** Miguel Chang. **Video Assistant, Dominican Republic:** Oliver Mieses.

MAJOR LEAGUES

NEW YORK YANKEES

Office Address: Yankee Stadium, One East 161st St., Bronx, NY 10451.
Telephone: (718) 293-4300.
Website: www.yankees.com, www.yankeesbeisbol.com.
Twitter: @Yankees, @YankeesPR, @LosYankees, @LosYankeesPR.

OWNERSHIP
Managing General Partner/Co-Chairperson: Harold Z. (Hal) Steinbrenner. **General Partner/Vice Chairperson:** Jennifer Steinbrenner Swindal. **General Partner/Vice Chairperson:** Jessica Steinbrenner.

BUSINESS OPERATIONS

President: Randy Levine, Esq. **Chief Operating Officer:** Lonn A. Trost, Esq. **Senior Vice President, General Manager:** Brian Cashman. **Senior Vice President, Asst. General Manager:** Jean Afterman, Esq.
Senior Vice President, Stadium Operations: Doug Behar. **Senior Vice President, Yankee Global Enterprises CFO:** Tony Bruno. **Senior Vice President & General Counsel:** Alan Chang, Esq. **Senior Vice President, Strategic Ventures:** Marty Greenspun. **Senior Vice President, Chief Security Officer:** Sonny Hight. **Senior Vice President, Assistant General Counsel:** Mike Lane. **Senior Vice President & CFO:** Scott M. Krug. **Senior Vice President, Chief Information Officer:** Mike Lane. **Senior Vice President & Chief Legal Officer:** Mike Mellis, Esq. **Senior Vice President, Corporate/Community Relations:** Brian E. Smith. **Senior Vice President, Partnerships:** Michael J. Tusiani.
Senior Vice President, Marketing: Deborah A. Tymon. **Vice President, Ticket Sales, Service & Operations:** Kevin Dart. **Vice President, Assistant General Manager:** Michael Fishman. **Vice President, Partnership Sales:** Daniel Gallivan. **Vice President, Non-Baseball Sports Events:** Mark Holtzman. **Vice President, Baseball Operations:** Tim Naehring. **Vice President, Domestic Amateur Scouting:** Damon Oppenheimer. **Vice President, Player Development:** Kevin Reese. **Vice President, Human Resources, Employment & Labor Law:** Aryn Sobo, Esq. **Vice President, Communications & Media Relations:** Jason Zillo.

Harold Z. Steinbrenner

COMMUNICATIONS/MEDIA RELATIONS
Telephone: (718) 579-4460. **Email:** media@yankees.com.
Senior Director: Michael Margolis. **Manager:** Kaitlyn Brennan. **Bilingual Media Relations Coordinator:** Marlon Abreu. **Assistants:** Jon Butensky, Parker Lougée, Jon Simon. **Administrative Assistant:** Germania Dolores Hernández-Simonetti. **Associate:** Tristan Vitale.

BASEBALL OPERATIONS

Special Assignment Scout: Jim Hendry. **Senior Advisor, Baseball Operations:** Omar Minaya. **Executive Advisor to the General Manager:** Brian Sabean. **Director, Pro Scouting:** Matt Daley. **Director, Quantitative Analysis:** David Grabiner. **Director, Baseball Operations:** Matthew Ferry. **Director, Baseball Systems:** Brian Nicosia. **Assistant Director, Baseball Operations:** Michael Pinsky. **Assistant Director, Pro Scouting:** Adam Charnin-Aker. **Assistant Directors, Quantitative Analysis:** John Morris, Sam Waters. **Lead Software Engineer:** Nick Eby. **Lead Mobile Engineer:** Michael Traverso. **Product Manager:** Matt Jones. **Senior Analysts, Quantitative Analysis:** Theodore Feder, Justin Sims. **Analysts, Quantitative Analysis:** Diana Faust, Walker Harrison, Antonio Ortiz. **Coordinators, Advance Scouting:** Amanda Brady, Shea Wingate. **Coordinator, Baseball Operations:** Jesse Lippin-Foster. **Coordinator, Professional Scouting:** Jimmy Stokes. **Assistant, Baseball Operations:** Lukas Koepke. **Assistant, Advance Scouting:** Rohan Gupta. **Senior Database Engineer:** Jesse Bradford. **Data Engineers:** Samuel Grigo, Kaden Han. **Mobile Engineer:** Rakibul Islam. **Senior Software Engineer:** James Dunn. **Database Engineers:** Eric Fitton, Patrick Gilligan. **Research Analyst, Quantitative Analysis:** John Benedetto. **Full-Stack Software Engineers:** Alex Herreid, Brian Minter, Andrew Mogg. **Quality Assurance Engineer:** Matt Zielonko. **Data Quality Engineer:** Henry Ryan. **Administrative Assistant:** Mary Pellino.

MAJOR LEAGUE STAFF
Manager: Aaron Boone.
Coaches: Bench—Carlos Mendoza; **Hitting**—Dillon Lawson; **Asst. Hitting**—Casey Dykes, Brad Wilkerson. **Pitching**—Matt Blake; **Asst. Pitching**—Desi Druschel. **First Base**—Travis Chapman; **Third Base**—Luis Rojas; **Bullpen**—Mike Harkey; **Quality Control/Catching**—Tanner Swanson.

MEDICAL/TRAINING
Head Team Physician: Christopher Ahmad, M.D. **Head Team Internist:** Paul Lee, M.D., M.P.H. **Team Internist:** William Turner, M.D. **Senior Advisor, Orthopedics:** Stuart Hershon, M.D. **Director, Player Health and Performance:** Eric Cressey. **Assistant Director, Player Health and Performance:** Donovan Santas. **Director of Sports Medicine**

GENERAL INFORMATION
Stadium (year opened): Yankee Stadium (2009).
Team Colors: Navy blue and white.
Home Dugout: First Base.
Playing Surface: Grass.

50 • Baseball America 2023 Directory BaseballAmerica.com

MAJOR LEAGUES

Brian Cashman

& Rehabilitation (ATC/PT): Michael Schuk. **Head Athletic Trainer:** Tim Lentych. **Assistant Athletic Trainer:** Alfonso Malaguti. **Major League Physical Therapist:** Joe Bello. **Major League Strength & Conditioning Coach:** Brett McCabe. **Assistant Major League Strength & Conditioning Coach:** Larry Adegoke. **Director of Medical Services:** Steve Donohue. **Major League Dietitian:** Drew Weisberg. **Massage Therapist:** Doug Cecil.

PLAYER DEVELOPMENT

Vice President, Player Development: Kevin Reese.

Director, Player Development: Eric Schmitt. **Assistant Director, Player Development:** Stephen Swindal Jr. **Director, Minor League Operations:** Nick Avanzato. **Director, International Operations:** Victor Roldan. **Manager, Player Development Analytics:** Dan Walco. **Baseball Solutions Engineer:** Rob Owens. **P.D., Equipment & Clubhouse Operations Manager:** Ryan Ornstein. **Clubhouse Manager, Player Development:** Jamie Ventura. **Analyst, Player Development:** Matt Reiland. **Assistant, International Operations:** Giuliano Montañez. **Assistant, Minor League Operations:** Nick Leon. **Assistant, Player Development:** Austin Zieg. **Player Development Advisor:** Pat McMahon. **Senior Director of Pitching:** Sam Briend. **Director, Baseball Development:** Mario Garza. **Rehab Pitching Coordinator:** John Kremer. **Complex Pitching Coordinator:** Ben Buck. **Minor League Hitting Coordinator:** Joe Migliaccio. **Assistant Minor League Hitting Coordinator:** Aaron Leanhardt. **Director of Speed Development & Baserunning/Roving Hitting Coach:** Matt Talarico. **Defensive Coordinator:** Aaron Gershenfeld. **Roving Infield/Outfield Instructors:** Dan Fiorito, Ryan Hunt. **Assistant Director, Player Health & Performance:** Donovan Santas. **Medical Coordinator:** Mark Littlefield. **Assistant Medical Coordinator:** Greg Spratt. **Rehabilitation Coordinator:** David Colvin. **Assistant Rehabilitation Coordinator:** Charlie Domnisch. **Rehab Strength Coach:** Ty Hill. **Manual Therapy & Corrective Exercise Coordinator:** Mike Wickland. **Minor League Nutrition Coordinator:** Chandler Falcon. **Associate Director, Mental Conditioning:** Chris Passarella. **Coordinator, Cultural Development:** Héctor González. **Video Coordinator, Mental Conditioning Coach:** David Schnabel. **Mental Conditioning Coaches:** Aaron Barnett, Noel Garcia. **Director:** David Whiteside. **Senior Biomechanist:** Gillian Weir. **Senior Analyst:** Christina Williamson. **Engineers:** Kimber Ashman, Lydia Brough. **Lab Technician:** Kelsey Klug. **Coordinator:** Joe Siara. **Skill Acquisition Specialist:** Tim Buszard. **Sports Scientist:** Patrick Hipes. **Minor League Video Coordinator:** Zach Iannarelli. **Asst. Minor League Video Coordinators:** Paul Henshaw, Luke Morris. **Video Coordinator, International P.D.:** Eliezer Beard. **Video-Trackman Assistants, International P.D:** Nelson B. Alvarez, Javier Deyan, Eduardo Yanes. **Director, International Baseball Operations:** David Adams. **Director, Latin Baseball Academy:** Joel Lithgow. **Assistants, International Baseball Ops:** Manuel Castillo, J.T. Hernandez.

FARM SYSTEM

Class	Club (League)	Manager	Hitting Coach	Pitching Coach
Triple-A	Scranton/WB (IL)	Shelley Duncan	Trevor Amicone	Graham Johnson
Double-A	Somerset (EL)	Raul Dominguez	Jake Hirst	Grayson Crawford
High-A	Hudson Valley (SAL)	Sergio Santos	Kevin Martir	Preston Claiborne
Low-A	Tampa (FSL)	Rachel Balkovec	Rick Guarno	Gerardo Casadiego
Rookie	Yankees (FCL)	James Cooper	Chipka/DeAngelis	DeGagne/Medick
Rookie	Yankees 1 (DSL)	TBD	TBD	TBD
Rookie	Yankees 2 (DSL)	TBD	TBD	TBD

SCOUTING

Telephone: (813) 875-7569. **Fax:** (813) 873-2302.

Vice President, Domestic Amateur Scouting: Damon Oppenheimer. **Asst. Dir., Dom. Amateur Scouting, Operations:** Mitch Colahan. **Asst. Dir., Dom. Amateur Scouting, Analytics:** Scott Benecke. **Amateur Scouting & Affiliate Pitching Analyst:** Scott Lovekamp. **National Crosscheckers:** Sam Hughes, Tim Kelly, Steve Kmetko, Jeff Patterson, Mike Wagner. **Draft Medical Coordinator:** Joe Metz. **Amateur Scouting Video & Administration Coordinators:** AJ Oppenheimer, Joe Wielbruda. **Area Scouts:** Troy Afenir, Tim Alexander, Chuck Bartlett, Denis Boucher, Ricky Castle, Jeff Deardorff, Bobby DeJardin, Mike Gibbons, Matt Hyde, David Keith, Steve Lemke, Mike Leuzinger, Ronnie Merrill, Darryl Monroe, Bill Pintard, Matt Ranson, Brian Rhees, Tyler Robertson, Stewart Smothers, Mike Thurman.

Director, Pro Scouting: Matt Daley. **Assistant Director, Pro Scouting:** Adam Charnin-Aker.

Professional Scouts: Scott Atchison, Kendall Carter, Jay Darnell, Marc DelPiano, Jonathan Diaz, Brandon Duckworth, Tyler Greene, Shawn Hill, Cory Melvin, Pat Murtaugh, Jaylon Pimentel, Jose Ravelo, JT Stotts, Alex Sunderland, Dennis Twombley, Aron Weston, Tom Wilson.

Director, International Scouting: Donny Rowland. **Assistant Director, International Scouting:** Brady LaRuffa. **Assistant to Director, Latin America:** Edgar Mateo. **Assistant to Director, Quality Control:** Ethan Sander. **Supervisors, International Scouting:** Ricardo Finol, Steve Wilson, Dennis Woody. **Crosschecker, International Scouting:** Juan Rosario. **Crosscheckers, Latin America:** Victor Mata, Jose Gavidia, Caonabo Cosme, Carlos Levy. **Video Coordinator, International Scouting:** Kurt Bathelt. **Video Assistants, Dominican Rep:** Smerling Lantigua, Miguel Mojica. **Video Assistant, Venezuela:** Wilelvis Salazar. **Manager, Data/Technology, Int'l Scouting:** Vianco Martinez. **Technology/Data Analyst, D.R.:** Carlos Ravelo. **Technology/Data Analyst, Venezuela:** Victor Deyan. **International Scouts:** Rudy Gomez, John Wadsworth, Alvaro Noriega, Luis Sierra, Esdras Abreu, Luis Brito, R. Arturo Peña, Juan Piron, Luis Rodriguez, Jose Sabino, Troy Williams, Kevin Valera, Lee Sigman, Doug Skiles, Edgard Rodriguez, Chi Lee, Peng Pu Lee, Alan Atacho, Darwin Bracho, Roney Calderon, Cesar Suarez, Jesus Taico, Luis Tinoco.

MAJOR LEAGUES

OAKLAND ATHLETICS

OWNERSHIP
President: David Kaval. **Senior Advisor to the Managing Partner:** Billy Beane. **Chairman Emeritus:** Lew Wolff
Board Members: Bill Gurtin, Keith Wolff, Sandy Dean.

BUSINESS OPERATIONS

OFFICE OF THE PRESIDENT
Special Assistants to the President: Rickey Henderson, Rollie Fingers, Dennis Eckersley.
Chief of Staff: Miguel Duarte. **Director, Project Finance:** Ross Bowen. **Manager, Operations:** Colette Lucas-Conwell. **Special Assistant & Investor Relations, Manager:** Curtis Wiggington. **Director, Alumni and Family Relations:** Detra Paige. **Manager, Alumni and Family Relations:** Melissa Guzman.

COMMUNICATIONS, COMMUNITY AND MARKETING
Vice President, Marketing, Communications and Community: Catherine Aker. **Executive Assistant:** Lupita Rodriguez. **Director of Communications:**. Erica George. **Director, Baseball Communications:** Mark Ling. **Baseball Information Manager:** Mike Selleck. **Baseball Communications Manager:** Olivia Hummer. **Baseball Communications Coordinator:** Greg Korn.

David Kaval

COMMUNITY ENGAGEMENT
Senior Director, Community: Stephanie Gaywood. **Senior Manager, Community:** Whitney Campbell. **Manager, Youth Baseball and Softball:** Mychael Jamison. **Coordinator, Community Engagement:** Annalise Lyons.

MARKETING & ADVERTISING
Senior Director, Marketing & Advertising: Vittorio DeBartolo. **Creative Director:** John Lemein. **Marketing Manager:** Parker Preston. **Manager, Marketing & Advertising:** Vanessa Mendy. **Marketing Coordinator:** Kira Griffin. **Marketing Project Coordinator:** Cecily Mitchell. **Graphic Designers:** Casey Brochhagen, Kristin Shum. **Team Photographer:** Michael Zagaris.

BROADCASTING
Coordinating Producer, Broadcasting: D'Aulaire Louwerse. **Multimedia Producer:** Cody Elias. **Broadcasting and Media Content Coordinator:** Ray Jensen. **Senior Broadcast Producer and Host:** Chris Townsend. **Team Announcers:** Ken Korach, Glen Kuiper, Vince Cotroneo, Dallas Braden.

TICKET SALES, PARTNERSHIPS AND ANALYTICS
Vice President, Sales & Business Operations: Steve Fanelli. **Senior Director of Business Analytics:** Mark Bashuk. **Senior Manager, Ticket Solutions:** Austin Redman. **Senior Manager, Business Analytics:** Anne Marie Rowe. **CRM & Sales Analyst:** Beau Muster. **Business Operations Analyst:** Kelsey Moeller. **Senior Director, Ticket Sales:** Josh Feinberg. **Manager, Ticket Sales:** Gavin Lituchy. **Senior Account Executive, Business Development:** Parker Newton. **Senior Account Executive, Ticket Sales:** Anton Calvin. **Account Executives:** Sean Dobbyn, Alyssa Mensinger, Matt Musoni, Carly Wade. **Ticket Sales Representatives:** Ethan Eliason, Simon Siggins-Bell. **Membership Services Representative:** Nick Sakoda.

STADIUM OPERATIONS
Vice President, Stadium Operations: David Rinetti. **Senior Director of Stadium Operations:** Paul La Veau. **Director of Concessions & Merchandise:** Nicole Morgan. **Director, Stadium Operations Events:** Kristy Ledbetter. **Director, Guest Services:** Elisabeth Aydelotte. **Director, Security:** Jason Silva. **Senior Manager of Stadium Services:** Randy Duran. **Stadium Operations Systems Coordinator:** Gokulesh Killer. **Stadium Operations Coordinator:** Olivia Ortiz-Ortiz. **Stadium Operations Scheduler:** Dawn Silva. **Stadium Operations Events Coordinator:** Isiah Clement. **Stadium Services Assistant:** Isaias Del Toro. **Guest Services Coordinator:** Robert Towne. **Guest Services Assistant:** Giancarlo Bautista. **Manager of Authentication:** Erik Farrell. **Head Groundskeeper:** Clay Wood. **Assistant Head Groundskeeper:** Samuel Turner. **Groundskeeper:** Andrew Egan.

FINANCE
Vice President of Finance: Matthew Causey. **Controller:** Thomas Hicks. **Senior Director of Finance:** Kasey Jarcik. **Senior Manager, Payroll:** Rose Dancil. **Senior Payroll Specialist:** Desiree Powers. **Senior Accountant:** Danna Mouat. **Senior Revenue Accountant:** Naima Peterson. **Accounts Payable Coordinator:** Carlos Hidalgo. **Senior Financial Analyst:** Ameela Li. **Jr. Accountant:** Marvin Hernandez.

BASEBALL OPERATIONS

GENERAL INFORMATION
Stadium (year opened): RingCentral Coliseum (1968).
Team Colors: Kelly green and gold.
Home Dugout: Third Base.
Playing Surface: Grass.

MAJOR LEAGUES

General Manager: David Forst. **Assistant GM, Major League & International Operations:** Dan Feinstein. **Assistant GM/Director, Player Personnel:** Billy Owens. **Sr. Director, Baseball Development & Technology:** Rob Naberhaus. **Special Assistants to GM:** Grady Fuson, Chris Pittaro, Scott Hatteberg. **Director, Baseball Administration:** Pamela Pitts. **Video Coordinator:** Adam Rhoden. **Special Assistant to Baseball Operations:** Scott Hatteberg. **Senior Research Scientist:** David Jackson-Hanen. **Director, Baseball Development:** Pike Goldschmidt. **Director, Research and Analytics:** Ben Lowry. **Analyst, Baseball Operations:** Samantha Schultz.

David Forst

MAJOR LEAGUE STAFF
Manager: Mark Kotsay. **Coaches: Bench**—Darren Bush; **Hitting**—Tommy Everidge; **Asst. Hitting**—Chris Cron; **Pitching**—Scott Emerson; **First Base**—Mike Aldrete; **Third Base**—Eric Martins; **Bullpen**—Mike McCarthy.

MEDICAL STAFF
Director of Sports Medicine and Rehabilitation: Brian Schulman. **Head Athletic Trainer:** Jeff Collins. **Assistant Athletic Trainers:** Elliot Diehl, Brad LaRosa. **Head Sport Performance Coach:** Josh Cuffe. **Assistant Sport Performance:** Coach Steven Candelaria. **Major League Massage Therapist:** Ozzie Lyles. **Head Team Physician:** Dr. Allan Pont. **Team Physician:** Dr. Grant Wang. **Head Team Orthopedist:** Dr. Will Workman. **Team Orthopedist:** Dr. Michael T Freehill. **Arizona Team Physician:** Dr. Fred Dicke. **Arizona Team Orthopedist:** Dr. Douglas Freedberg.

PLAYER DEVELOPMENT
Director of Player Development: Ed Sprague. **Director of Latin American Operations:** Raymond Abreu. **Director of Minor League Operations:** Manny Colón. **Assistant Director, Minor League Operations:** Nancy Moriuchi. **Assistant Director, Minor League Operations:** Thomas Miller. **Minor League Operations Coordinator:** Luis Victoria. **Minor League Hitting Coordinator:** Jim Eppard. **Minor League Pitching Coordinator:** Gil Patterson. **Minor League Infield Coordinator:** Juan Navarrete. **Arizona Field Coordinator and Minor League Outfield/Baserunning Coordinator:** Steve Scarsone. **Minor League Catching Coordinator:** Gabe Ortiz. **Hitting Development Coach:** Lloyd Turner. **Pitching Development Coach:** Dan Hubbs. **Minor League Pitching Coordinator Assistant:** Craig Lefferts. **Minor League Pitching Rehab Coordinator:** Rick Rodriguez. **Minor League Assistant Pitching Rehab Coordinator:** Steve Connelly. **Coordinator of Player Development, Latin America:** Veronica Alvarez. **Senior Coordinator of Medical Services:** Larry Davis. **Minor League Medical Coordinator:** Nate Brooks. **Latin America Medical Coordinator:** Nick Voelker. **Minor League Rehab Coordinator:** Javier Alvidres. **Minor League Rehab Assistant:** Brittany Bilodeau. **Minor League Sport Performance Coordinator:** J.D. Howell. **Assistant Minor League Sport Performance Coordinator:** Scott Smith. **Minor League Sport Performance Rehab Coordinator:** Derek Clovis. **Minor League Technology and Development Manager:** Ed Gitlitz. **Coordinator, Minor League Technology and Development:** Taylor Schmid. **Data Engineer:** Andrew Gibson. **Senior Coordinator of Educational and Cultural Programs:** Kelvin Todd. **Coordinator of Educational and Cultural Programs:** Leo Bejarán-Specht. **Senior Facility Manager, Arizona:** James Gibson. **Coordinator, Arizona Clubhouse Operations:** Ty Ketterling. **Assistants, Arizona Clubhouse Operations:** Alex Haas, Dylan Ruth, Mark Gallo. **Interpreter:** Yen Po Wang. **Arizona Head Groundskeeper:** Chad Huss. **Arizona Assistant Groundskeeper:** Greg Hofer.

FARM SYSTEM

Class	Club (League)	Manager	Hitting Coach	Pitching Coach
Triple-A	Las Vegas (PCL)	Fran Riordan	Brian McArn	Bryan Corey
Double-A	Midland (TL)	Bobby Crosby	Javier Godard	Chris Smith
High-A	Lansing (MWL)	Craig Conklin	Ron Witmeyer	Don Schulze
Low-A	Stockton (CAL)	Gregorio Petit	Kevin Kouzmanoff	Gabriel Ozuna
Rookie	Athletics (ACL)	Adam Rosales	Perez/Jeske/Esmay	Bronswell Patrick
Rookie	Athletics (DSL)	Cooper Goldby	Buhner/Vicente	Gott/Brito

SCOUTING
Director, Scouting: Eric Kubota. **Assistant Director, Scouting:** Sean Rooney. **Assistant Director, Scouting and Baseball Operations:** Haley Alvarez. **Assistant Director, Scouting and Baseball Operations:** Greg Ledford (San Francisco, CA). **Master Pitching Scout:** John Hughes. **West Coast Supervisor:** Scott Kidd. **Midwest Supervisors:** Mark Adair, Armann Brown. **East Coast Supervisor:** Marc Sauer. **Pro Scouts:** Shooty Babitt, Jeff Bittiger, Grant Brittain, Dan Freed, Tim Huff, Will Schock, Steve Springer, Tom Thomas, Mike Ziegler. **Area Scouts:** Steve Abney, Anthony Aliotti, Neil Avent, Chris Botsoe, Jim Coffman, Ruben Escalera, Tripp Faulk, Julio Franco, Matt Higginson, Derek Lee, Kelcey Mucker, Trevor Schaffer, Rich Sparks, Jemel Spearman, Troy Stewart, Dillon Tung, Jeff Urlaub, Ron Vaughn. **Director, International Scouting:** Steve Sharpe. **Director, Latin American Operations:** Raymond Abreu (Santo Domingo, D.R.). **Scouting Supervisor, Latin America:** Juan Mosquera (Panama). **Scouting Supervisor, Dominican Republic:** Fernando Encarnacion. **Coordinator, Pacific Rim:** Adam Hislop. **International Scouts:** Javier Agelvis (Mexico), Yendri Bachelor (D.R.), Jose Barradas (VZ), Dan Betreen (Australia), Clemens Cichocki (Europe), Juan Carlos De La Cruz (D.R.), Jose De Jesus (D.R., Video), Andri Garcia (Venezuela), Kevin Garcia (Venezuela), Oswaldo Garcia (Colombia), Lewis Kim (South Korea), Wilfredo Magallanes (D.R.), Argenis Paez (Venezuela), Tito Quintero (Colombia), Amaurys Reyes (D.R.), Toshiyuki Tomizuka (Japan), Oswaldo Troconis (VZ).

MAJOR LEAGUES

PHILADELPHIA PHILLIES

Office Address: Citizens Bank Park, One Citizens Bank Way, Philadelphia, PA 19148.
Telephone: (215) 463-6000. **Website:** www.phillies.com.

OWNERSHIP
Operated By: The Phillies. **Managing Partner:** John Middleton. **Chairman Emeritus:** Bill Giles.

BUSINESS OPERATIONS

EXECUTIVE MANAGEMENT
Executive VP: David Buck. **VP/General Counsel:** Leslie Safran. **Director, Human Resources:** Jon Madden. **VP, Administration:** Kathy Killian. **VP, Chief Technology Officer:** Sean Walker. **Director, Technology Services:** Matt Bryan. **Director, Technology Systems Architect:** Kevin Donahue. **Director, Information Technology:** Bob Tonnon. **Director, Enterprise Applications:** Michael Cunningham.

BUSINESS AFFAIRS
VP, Business Affairs: Howard Smith. **Director, Concession Development:** Bruce Leith. **Director, Retail Marketing:** Kristin Zeller. **VP, Operations/Security:** Sal DeAngelis. **Director, Facility Operations:** Ed Speer. **Director, Special Events:** Leila Graham-Willis.

COMMUNICATIONS
Telephone: (215) 463-6000. **Fax:** (215) 389-3050
VP, Communications: Bonnie Clark. **VP, Baseball Communications:** Kevin Gregg. **Director, Publications:** Christine Negley. **Director, Player Relations and Phillies Charities:** Sophie Riegel. **Director, Baseball Communications:** Chris Ware. **Director, Photography/Team Photographer:** Miles Kennedy. **PA Announcer:** Dan Baker. **Official Scorers:** Mark Gola, Mike Maconi, Dick Shute.

FINANCE
Sr. VP/CFO: John Nickolas. **Director, Business Analytics:** Josh Barbieri. **Director, Business Analytics Strategy:** Blake Summerfield. **VP, Finance and Controller:** Shannon Snellman. **Director, Payroll:** Bryan Humphreys. **Director, Accounts Payable & Cost Management:** Joann Milorey.

BROADCAST/VIDEO SERVICES
Director, Broadcasting/Video Services: Mark DiNardo. **Director, Video Production:** Sean Rainey. **Director, Video Engineering:** Martin Otremsky.

MARKETING/PROMOTIONS
Sr. VP, Partnership Sales and Corporate Marketing: Jacqueline Cuddeback. **VP, Marketing Programs & Events:** Kurt Funk. **VP, Marketing & New Media:** Michael Harris. **Sr. Director, Marketing Events & Special Projects:** James Trout. **Director, Promotions:** Scott Brandreth. **Director, Relationship Marketing:** John Brazer. **Director, Community and Charity Events:** Michele DeVicaris. **Director, Youth Baseball & Softball Development:** Jon Joaquin. **Director, Community Initiatives:** Mary Ann Moyer. **Director, Partnership Sales & Corporate Marketing:** Rob MacPherson. **Director, Corporate Sales:** Scott Nickle. **Director, Entertainment:** Teresa Harris.

SALES/TICKETS
Telephone: (215) 463-1000. **Fax:** (215) 463-9878.
Sr. VP, Ticket Operations & Projects: John Weber. **Sr. Director, Business Development and Suite Sales:** Kevin Beale. **Sr. Director, Sales:** Derek Schuster. **Sr. Director, Group Sales:** Vanessa Mapson. **Director, Ticket Technology & Development:** Christopher Pohl. **Director, Season Ticket Services:** Mike Holdren. **Director, Premium Sales & Services:** Matt Kessler. **Director, Ticket Operations:** Ken Duffy.

TRAVEL/CLUBHOUSE
Director, Clubhouse Services: Phil Sheridan. **Manager, Team Travel:** Jameson Hall. **Manager, Equipment/Umpire Services:** Dan O'Rourke. **Manager, Visiting Clubhouse:** Kevin Steinhour.

BASEBALL OPERATIONS
President, Baseball Operations: David Dombrowski. **VP/General Manager:** Sam Fuld. **Assistant GM:** Ani Kilambi. **Assistant GM:** Ned Rice. **Assistant GM:** Jorge Velandia. **Sr. Advisor:** Pat Gillick. **Sr. Advisor, GM:** Larry Bowa. **Sr. Advisor, GM:** Charlie Manuel. **Special Advisor to the President of Baseball Operations:** Jimmy Rollins. **Special Assistant, GM:** Howie Kendrick. **Director, Player Development:** Preston Mattingly. **Director, International Scouting:** Sal Agostinelli. **Director, Amateur Scouting:** Brian Barber. **Director, Professional Scouting:** Mike Ondo. **Director, Research and Development:** Alex Nakahara. **Director, Integrative Baseball Performance:** Rob Segedin. **Director, Amateur Scouting Administration:** Rob Holiday. **Director, Baseball Operations:** Corinne Landrey. **Director, Baseball

GENERAL INFORMATION
Stadium (year opened): Citizens Bank Park (2004).
Team Colors: Red, white and blue.
Home Dugout: First Base.
Playing Surface: Natural Grass.

MAJOR LEAGUES

Development: Ben Werthan. **Director, Staff Recruitment and Talent Development:** Steve Moser. **Director, Minor League Operations:** Lee McDaniel. **Director, Mental Performance, Life Skills & Education:** Ceci Craft. **Assistant Director, Quantitative Analysis:** Patrick McFarlane. **Assistant Director, Foundational Research:** Ryan Plunkett.

MAJOR LEAGUE STAFF

Manager: Rob Thomson. **Coaches: Bench**—Mike Calitri, **Pitching**—Caleb Cotham, **Hitting**—Kevin Long, **First Base**—Paco Figueroa, **Third Base**—Dusty Wathan, **Infield**—Bobby Dickerson, **Bullpen**—Dave Lundquist, **Assistant Pitching Coach/Director of Pitching Development:** Brian Kaplan. **Assistant Hitting Coach:** Jason Camilli. **Bullpen Catchers:** Brad Flanders, Hector Rabago.

Dave Dombrowski

MEDICAL/TRAINING

Director, Medical Services: Dr. Michael Ciccotti. **Head Athletic Trainer:** Paul Buchheit. **Assistant Athletic Trainers:** Joe Rauch, Christian Bermudez. **Director, Strength and Conditioning and Nutrition:** Morgan Gregory. **Assistant Strength & Conditioning Coach:** Furey Leva. **Major League Physical Therapist:** Alex Plum. **Major League Medical Operations Liaison:** Raul Perez.

PLAYER DEVELOPMENT

Director, Player Development: Preston Mattingly. **Director, Minor League Operations:** Lee McDaniel. **Director, Minor League Training Facilities and Equipment:** Joe Cynar. **Director, International Operations:** Ray Robles. **Assistant Director, Player Development:** Dana Parks. **Special Assistant to the Director of Player Development:** Matt Martin. **Manager, Player Development:** Edwin Soto. **Field Coordinator:** Kevin Bradshaw. **D.R. Academy Field Coordinator:** Manny Amador. **Director, Hitting Development:** Luke Murton. **Upper Level Hitting Coordinator/Development Analyst:** Kevin Mahala. **Lower Level Hitting Coordinator:** Jake Elmore. **Latin America Hitting Coordinator/Special Advisor to International Scouting:** Edwar González. **Director, Pitching Development:** Brian Kaplan. **Pitching Coordinator:** Travis Hergert. **Upper Level Pitching Coordinator/Development Analyst:** Mark Lowy. **Lower Level Pitching Coordinator:** Vic Diaz. **Florida Complex Coordinator:** Keith Werman. **Defensive Coordinator (Outfield):** Andy Abad. **Defensive Coordinator (Infield):** Adam Everett. **Medical Coordinator:** Justin Ahrens. **Rehab Coordinator:** Justin Tallard. **Physical Therapist:** Brittany Gooch. **Rehab Pitching Coordinator:** Aaron Barrett. **Strength and Conditioning Coordinator:** Pat Trainor. **Assistant Strength and Conditioning Coordinator:** José Salas. **Mental Performance Scouting and Rehab Coordinator:** Traci Statler. **Nutrition Coordinator:** Stephanie MacNeill. **Manager, Language Education and Cultural Assimilation:** Kiah Villamán. **Manager, Minor League Video and Technology:** Connor Carroll.

FARM SYSTEM

Class	Club (League)	Manager	Hitting Coach	Pitching Coach
Triple-A	Lehigh Valley (IL)	Anthony Contreras	Joe Thurston	Cesar Ramos
Double-A	Reading (EL)	Al Pedrique	Tyler Henson	Brad Bergesen
High-A	Jersey Shore (SAL)	Greg Brodzinski	Brock Stassi	Phil Cundari
Low-A	Clearwater (FSL)	Marty Malloy	Chris Heintz	Matt Hockenberry
Rookie	Phillies (FCL)	Shawn Williams	Rafael DeLima	R. McCauley/G. Armas
Rookie	Phillies Red (DSL)	Nerluis Martinez	Manny Martinez	Alex Concepcion
Rookie	Phillies White (DSL)	Orlando Munoz	Samuel Hiciano	Les Straker

SCOUTING

Director, Amateur Scouting: Brian Barber. **Director, Amateur Scouting Administration:** Rob Holiday. **National Scouting Coordinators:** David Crowson, Darrell Conner. **Coordinator, Amateur Scouting:** Connor Betbeze. **Regional Supervisors:** Alex Agostino, Shane Bowers, Buddy Hernandez, Brad Holland, Brian Kohlscheen. **Special Assignment Scouts:** Dean Albany, David Chadd, Craig Colbert, Erick Dalton, Todd Donovan, Dave Holliday, Charley Kerfeld, Mike Koplove, Jon Mercurio, Brad Sloan, Dan Wright. **Director, Professional Scouting:** Mike Ondo. **Professional Scouts:** Erick Dalton, Todd Donovan, Jon Mercurio. **Area Scouts:** Dave Dangler, Casey Fahy, Tommy Field, Zach Friedman, Ralph Garr Jr., Victor Gomez, Aaron Jersild, Kellan McKeon, Timi Moni, Justin Munson, Demerius Pittman, Hilton Richardson, Derrick Ross, Mike Stauffer, Jason Waugh, Bo Way, Jeff Zona Jr. **Director, International Scouting:** Sal Agostinelli. **Assistant Directors, International Scouting:** Derrick Chung, Josh Lipman. **Latin America Coordinators:** Jesús Méndez, Carlos Salas. **International Crosscheckers:** Oneri Fleita, Alex Mesa. **Crosschecker, Dominican Republic:** Andres Hiraldo. **Crosschecker, Dominican Republic:** Luis Garcia. **International Scouts:** Alvaro Blanco (Colombia), Jesus Blanco (Venezuela), Alex Choi (South Korea), Elvis García (Venezuela), Charlie Gastelum (Mexico), Gene Grimaldi (Associate Scout), Jose Guzman (Dominican Republic), Jonatan Hernandez (Venezuela), Takahashi Koji (Japan), Quincy Martina (Curacao), Jean Montalvo (Dominican Republic), William Mota (Venezuela), Howard Norsetter (Australia), Bernardo Pérez (Dominican Republic), Abdiel Ramos (Panama), Franklin Rojas (Venezuela), Victor Santana (Dominican Republic), Claudio Scerrato (Europe), Eddy Toledo (Dominican Republic) Ebert Velásquez (Venezuela), Youngster Wang (Taiwan). **International Video Scouting Assistants:** Gustavo Mogollon (Venezuela), Kelvin Paulino (Dominican Republic). **International Development Scout:** Cristobal Colon. **Dominican Republic Data Tracker:** Rafioby Ureña. **International Tryout Assistant:** Miguel De Jesus. **Performance Specialist:** Bryce Harman.

MAJOR LEAGUES

PITTSBURGH PIRATES

Office Address: PNC Park at North Shore, 115 Federal St., Pittsburgh, PA, 15212.
Mailing Address: PO Box 7000, Pittsburgh, PA 15212.
Telephone: (412) 323-5000. **Fax:** (412) 325-4412.
Website: www.pirates.com. **Twitter:** @Pirates.

Travis Williams

BUSINESS OPERATIONS

OWNERSHIP
Chairman of the Board: Bob Nutting.
President: Travis Williams. **Associate General Counsel:** Drew Singer.

COMMUNICATIONS
Senior VP, Communications/Broadcasting: Brian Warecki. **Director, Player Relations & Team Historian:** Jim Trdinich. **Director, Broadcasting:** Marc Garda. **Director, Media Relations:** Dan Hart. **Director, Baseball Communications:** Patrick Kurish. **Director, Communications:** Melissa Strozza.

MARKETING/CORPORATE SPONSORSHIPS
Director, Alumni Affairs/Promotions/Licensing: Joe Billetdeaux. **Senior Director, Integrated Marketing:** Carey Cox. **Director, Premium Partnerships & PNC Park Events:** Erinn Sander. **Director, Game Presentation:** Conrad Bradburn. **Director, Ballpark Productions:** Jon Cofer. **Director, Corporate & Premium Partnership Sales:** Chris Stevens. **Director, Corporate Partnership Activation:** Katie Shockey. **Director, Corporate & Premium Partnership Sales:** Dave Shinsky.

STADIUM OPERATIONS
Executive VP/General Manager, PNC Park: Dennis DaPra. **Vice President, Ballpark Operations:** Chris Hunter. **Senior VP, Florida and Dominican Operations:** Jeff Podobnik. **Director, Field Operations:** Matt Brown. **Director, PNC Park Operations:** J.J. McGraw. **Director, Facility Operations and Strategy:** Jackie Riggleman.

TRAVEL/CLUBHOUSE
Home Clubhouse Manager: Scott Bonnett. **Visiting Clubhouse Manager:** Kevin Conrad. **Assistant Equipment Manager:** Kiere Bulls. **Manager, Team Travel:** Ryan Denlinger.

GENERAL INFORMATION
Stadium (year opened): PNC Park (2001).
Team Colors: Black and gold.
Home Dugout: Third Base.
Playing Surface: Grass.

MAJOR LEAGUES

BASEBALL OPERATIONS

Executive Vice President, Baseball Operations and General Manager: Ben Cherington. **Assistant General Manager:** Kevan Graves. **Assistant General Manager:** Steve Sanders. **Senior Vice President, Baseball Operations:** Bryan Stroh. **Director, Pro Scouting:** Will Lawton. **Assistant Director, Baseball Operations:** Trey Rose. **Manager, Team Travel:** Ryan Denlinger. **Assistant, Baseball Operations:** Anthony Argenziano. **Business Assistant, Baseball Operations:** Zoe Lamb.

Ben Cherington

MAJOR LEAGUE STAFF

Manager: Derek Shelton. **Bench Coach:** Don Kelly. **Hitting Coach:** Andy Haines. **Pitching Coach:** Oscar Marin. **Assistant Hitting Coach:** Christian Marrero. **Major League Field Coordinator and 3rd Base Coach:** Mike Rabelo. **Major League First Base Coach:** Tarrik Brock. **Bullpen Coach:** Justin Meccage. **Major League Run Prevention & Game Planning Coach:** Radley Haddad. **Major League Bullpen Catcher and Catching Assistant:** Jordan Comadena. **Coordinator, Major League Pitching Operations:** Jeremy Bleich. **Coordinator, Mental Performance:** Andy Bass. **ML Integrated Baseball Performance Coach:** Tim McKeithan. **Major League Coach:** Mendy Lopez.

MEDICAL/TRAINING

Director, Sports Medicine: Todd Tomczyk. **Director, Sports Performance:** A.J. Patrick. **Head Strength and Conditioning Coach:** Terence Brannic. **Assistant Major League Strength & Conditioning Coach:** Adam Vish. **Major League Dietitian:** Hillary Ake. **Sport Nutrition Assistant:** Steffani Holmes. **Executive Chef, Home Clubhouse:** Tony Palatucci. **Head Major League Athletic Trainer:** Rafael Freitas. **Major League Assistant Athletic Trainer:** Tony Leo. **Major League Physical Therapist:** Seth Steinhauer. **Medical Director:** Dr. Patrick DeMeo. **Team Physicians:** Dr. Darren Frank, Dr. Dennis Phillips, Dr. Michael Scarpone, Dr. Robert Schilken, Dr. Edward Snell.

RESEARCH & DEVELOPMENT

Senior Director, Strategy & Research: Dan Fox. **Director, R&D:** Sean Ahmed. **Assistant Director, R&D:** Christine Harris. **Lead Quantitative Analyst:** Justin Newman. **Senior Performance Analyst, R&D:** Justin Perline. **Senior Software Engineers:** Brian Hulick, Frank Wolverton. **Systems Tech Lead:** Rosie Yu. **Analyst, Research & Development:** James Bueghly. **Sr. Data Engineer:** Matthew Reiersgaard. **Associate Data Engineers:** David Shapero, Mike Walsh.

PLAYER DEVELOPMENT

Director, Coaching and Player Development: John Baker. **Director, International Development:** Hector Morales. **Director, Mental Performance and Learning:** Bernie Holliday. **Assistant Director, Coaching and Player Development:** Michael Chernow. **Assistant Director, Coaching and Player Development:** Shawn Johnston. **Coordinator, Coaching and Player Development:** Julio Sepulveda. **Assistant, Coaching and Player Development:** Jack Cecil. **Special Assistant, Coaching and Player Development:** Brad Fischer. **Senior Advisor, Pitching Development:** Dewey Robinson. **Coordinator, Coaching & Player Development, R&D:** Matthew Kane. **Analyst, Coaching and Player Development:** Clarence Rivers. **Minor League Video Coordinator:** Marc Roche. **FCL/LA Mental Performance Coordinator:** Michael Gonzalez. **Senior Coordinator, Education:** Mayu Fielding. **Coordinator, Player Advocacy and Learning:** Paige Moshier. **Administrator, D.R. Academy:** Juan Carlos Mendoza. **Senior Director, Player Personnel:** Steve Williams. **Director, Player Personnel:** Max Kwan. **Assistant Director, Pro Player Valuation:** Joe Douglas. **Coordinator, Pro Player Strategy:** Grant Jones. **Pro Evaluation Team Leaders:** Sean McNally, Larry Broadway, Hadi Raad. **Player Valuation Analyst:** Zach Aldrich. **Player Valuation Analyst:** Aaron Razum.

FARM SYSTEM

Class	Club (League)	Manager	Hitting Coach	Pitching Coach
Triple-A	Indianapolis (IL)	Miguel Perez	Eric Munson	Dan Meyer
Double-A	Altoona (EL)	Callix Crabbe	Jon Nunnally	Cale Johnson
High-A	Greensboro (SAL)	Robby Hammock	Ruben Gotay	Fernando Nieve
Low-A	Bradenton (FSL)	Jonathan Johnston	Quentin Brown	Matt Ford
Rookie	Pirates (FCL)	Jose Mosquera	Curt Wilson	Mick Fieldbinder
Rookie	Pirates (DSL)	J. Mendez/E. Goforth	Khelyn Smith	Jose Cueto

SCOUTING

Fax: (412) 325-4414. **Senior Director, Amateur Scouting:** Joe DelliCarri. **Director, International Scouting:** Junior Vizcaino. **Assistant Director, Amateur Scouting:** Mike Mangan. **Assistant Director, Amateur Scouting Operations:** Matt Skirving. **Coordinator, International Operations:** Matt Benedict, Jose Cruz. **Global Crosschecker:** Rodney Henderson. **International Crosschecker:** Jesus Lantigua. **National Supervisors:** Jimmy Lester, Jack Bowen. **Regional Supervisors:** Trevor Haley, Sean Heffernan, Jason Ellison. **Area Supervisors:** Eddie Charles, Dan Radcliff, Brett Evert, Mike Sansoe, Brian Tracy, Derrick Van Dusen, Matt Bimeal, John Lombardo, Anthony Wycklendt, Wayne Mathis, Adam Bourassa, Michael Bradford, Darren Mazeroski, Cam Murphy, John Koronka. **Special Assignment Scouts:** Doug Strange, Blake Crosby. **Pro Scouts:** Michael Landestoy, Everett Russell, Kinza Baad, Carlos Berroa, Andrew Lorraine, Brendan Gawlowski, Tim Smith. **International Supervisors:** Saul Torres; Emmanuel Gomez; Raul Lopez; Tony Harris; Fu-Chun Chiang; Tom Gillespie. **International Scouts:** Esteban Alvarez, Daurys Nin, Leudy Castro, Cristino Valdez, Omelbis Corporan; Victor Alvarez, Gregory Bolivar, Pedro Avila, Omar Gonzalez, Jesus Morelli, Jessie Nava, Jose Partidas, Dirimo Chavez; Roberto Saucedo; Marcos Guimaraes; Eugene Helder; Mark Van Zanten; Jose Pineda.

MAJOR LEAGUES

ST. LOUIS CARDINALS

Office Address: 700 Clark Street, St. Louis MO 63102.
Telephone: (314) 345-9600. **Fax:** (314) 345-9523. **Website:** www.cardinals.com.

OWNERSHIP
Operated By: St. Louis Cardinals, LLC. **Chairman/Chief Executive Officer:** William DeWitt, Jr. **President:** Bill DeWitt III. **Senior Administrative Assistant to Chairman:** Grace Pak. **Senior Administrative Assistant to President:** Julie Laningham. **Sr. VP & General Counsel:** Mike Whittle. **Associate General Counsel:** Nick Garzia.

BUSINESS OPERATIONS

FINANCE
Fax: (314) 345-9520.
Senior VP/Chief Financial Officer: Brad Wood. **Vice President, Accounting & Payroll:** John Lowry. **Director, Risk Management:** Rex Carter. **VP, Human Resources:** Jayme Riester. **VP, Event Services/Merchandising:** Vicki Bryant.

MARKETING/SALES/COMMUNITY RELATIONS
Fax: (314) 345-9529.
Senior VP, Sales & Marketing: Dan Farrell. **Administrative Assistant, VP, Sales & Marketing:** Gail Ruhling. **VP, Corporate Sales & Broadcasting:** Thane Van Breusegen. **Director, Marketing & Brand Execution:** Martin Coco. **VP Community Relations & Exec. Director Cardinals Care:** Michael Hall.

Bill DeWitt III

COMMUNICATIONS
Fax: (314) 345-9530.
Director, Communications: Brian Bartow. **Asst. Director, Communications:** Michael Whitty. **Manager, Baseball Communications & Media Services:** Chris Tunno. **Manager, Communications & Public Relations:** Carson Shipley. **PA Announcer:** John Ulett. **Official Scorers:** Gary Muller, Mike Smith, Jonathan Webb.

STADIUM OPERATIONS
Fax: (314) 345-9535.
VP, Stadium Operations: Matt Gifford. **Director, Security:** Phil Melcher. **Director, Facility Operations & Planning:** Hosei Maruyama.

TICKETING
Fax: (314) 345-9522.
VP, Ticket Sales/Service: Joe Strohm. **Director, Ticket Sales & Retention:** Rob Fasoldt. **Director, Ticket Operations:** Kerry Emerson.

TRAVEL/CLUBHOUSE
Fax: (314) 345-9523.
Team Travel Director: Ernie Moore. **Equipment Manager:** Mark Walsh. **Visiting Clubhouse Manager:** Rip Rowan. **Video Coordinator:** Chad Blair.

BASEBALL OPERATIONS
President of Baseball Operations: John Mozeliak. **Senior Executive Assistant to the President of Baseball Operations:** Linda Brauer. **Vice President & General Manager:** Michael Girsch. **Assistant GM:** Moises Rodriguez. **Assistant GM & Director of Scouting:** Randy Flores. **Assistant GM, Director of Player Development:** Gary LaRocque. **Special Assistant to GM, Player Procurement:** Matt Slater. **Director, Baseball Administration:** John Vuch. **Manager, Player Communications:** Melody Yount. **Manager, Technology & Innovation:** Javier Duren

BASEBALL ANALYTICS
Sr. Director of Baseball Development: Jeremy Cohen. **Project Director:** Matt Bayer. **Director, Analytics:** Kevin Seats. **Lead Data Scientist:** Alan Kessler. **Senior Data Scientist:** Garrett Greenwood. **Amateur Scouting Analyst:** Julia Prusaczyk. **Analyst:** John Kern.

BASEBALL SYSTEMS
Senior Lead Application Developer: Brian Seyfert. **Lead Analytics Engineer:** Todd Heitmann. **Lead Data Engineer:** Nathan Nutter **Lead Cloud Architect:** John Weeks. **Application Developer:** Austin Lukaschewski. **Analytics Engineer:** Jack Hanley. **Systems Engineer:** Mike Noel

GENERAL INFORMATION
Stadium (year opened): Busch Stadium (2006).
Team Colors: Red and white.
Home Dugout: First Base.
Playing Surface: Grass.

MAJOR LEAGUES

MAJOR LEAGUE STAFF
Manager: Oliver Marmol. **Coaches: Bench**—Joe McEwing. **Pitching**—Dusty Blake. **Hitting**—Turner Ward. **Assistant Hitting Coaches**—Brendon Allen & Daniel Nicholaisen. **First Base**—Richard "Stubby" Clapp. **Third Base**—Ron "Pop" Warner. **Asst. Pitching Coach/Bullpen**—Julio Rangel. **Assistant Coach:** Willie McGee. **Game Planning Coach:** Patrick Elkins. **Bullpen Catchers**—Jamie Pogue, Kleininger Teran.

MEDICAL/PERFORMANCE
Head Orthopedist Surgeon: Dr. George Paletta. **Major League Medical Services Coordinator:** Brian Mahaffey. **Director of Medical Operations/Head Athletic Trainer:** Adam Olsen. **Director of Performance:** Robert Butler. **Assistant Athletic Trainers:** Chris Conroy. **Assistant Director, Performance:** Thomas Knox. **Performance Specialist & Physical Therapist:** Jason Shutt. **Strength & Conditioning Coach:** Lance Thomason. **Assistant Strength & Conditioning Coach:** Frank Witkowski. **Medical Adm/Asst Ath Trainer:** Keith Joynt. **Physical Therapist:** Matt Leonard. **Soft Tissue Specialist:** Cyrus Poitier.

John Mozeliak

PLAYER DEVELOPMENT
Asst. GM & Director, Player Development: Gary LaRocque. **Manager, Player Dev & Performance:** Emily Wiebe. **Coordinator, Player Development:** Antonio Mujica. **Minor League Instructors—Coordinator of Instruction:** Jose Oquendo. **Sr. Pitching Coordinator:** Tim Leveque. **Hitting Coordinator:** Russ Steinhorn. **Asst. Pitching Coordinator:** Dean Kiekhefer. **Jupiter Complex Pitching Coordinator:** Rick Harig. **Special Advisors:** Ryan Ludwick, Jason Isringhausen & Bryan Eversgerd. **Medical Coordinator:** Chris Whitman. **S&C Coordinator:** Jackie Gover. **Rehab Coordinator:** Victor Kuri. **Technology Integration:** DC MacLea. **Video & Technology Specialist:** Brady Hall. **Performance Specialist:** Ross Hasegawa. **Performance Specialist Rehab:** Nick Arpino. **DR Medical Coordinator:** Pedro Betancourt. **Minor League Athletic Trainers:** Dan Martin (Memphis), Alex Wolfinger (Springfield), Paden Eveland (Peoria), Jeff Case (Palm Beach), Kiomy Martinez-Ortiz & Riku Shabata (FCL), Albert Navarro (DSL). **Minor League Strength & Conditioning Coaches:** Henry Torres (Memphis), Spencer Clevenger (Springfield), Ryan Duffy (Peoria), Cambell Quirk (Palm Beach), Grace Cullen & Harben Filho Branco (FCL), Elvis Hernandez & Gerardo De Leon (DSL).

FARM SYSTEM

Class	Club (League)	Manager	Hitting Coach	Pitching Coach
Triple-A	Memphis (IL)	Ben Johnson	Howie Clark	Darwin Marrero
Double-A	Springfield (TL)	Jose Leger	Brock Hammit	Eric Peterson
High-A	Peoria (MWL)	Patrick Anderson	Casey Chenoweth	Edwin Moreno
Low-A	Palm Beach (FSL)	Gary Kendall	Willi Martin	Giovanni Carrara
Rookie	Cardinals (FCL)	Roberto Espinoza	Erick Almonte	Dernier Orozco
Rookie	Cardinals (DSL)	Frey Peniche	TBD	Bill Villallanueva

SCOUTING
Fax: (314) 345-9519.
Assistant General Manager & Director of Scouting: Randy Flores. **Special Advisor to the Scouting Director:** Jamal Strong. **Amateur Manager of Domestic Scouting:** Ty Boyles. **National Crosscheckers:** Aaron Looper (Shawnee, OK), Zachary Mortimer (Pilesgrove, NJ), Jamal Strong (Surpirse, AZ), Jabari Barnett (Dallas, TX), Aaron Krawiec (Gilbert, AZ), Clint Brown (Braselton, GA), Sean Moran (Furlong, PA) **Area Scouts:,** Jason Bryans (Tecumseh, ON), TC Calhoun (Abingdon, VA), Scott Cousins (Scottsdale, AZ), Keanan Lamb (Birmingham, AL), Josh Lopez (West Palm Beach, FL), Mike Garciaparra (Manhattan Beach, CA), Dirk Kinney (Lenexa, KS), Donnie Marbut (Olympia, WA), Brian Moehler (Atlanta, GA), Jim Negrych (Phoenixville, PA), Pete Parise (Dallas, TX), Stacey Pettis (Brentwood, CA), Joe Quezada (Houston, TX), Chris Rodriguez (Los Angeles, CA), Mauricio Rubio (Chicago, IL). **Part-Time Scouts:** Juan C Ramos (Caguas, PR), Paul Ah Yat (Hon, HI). **Manager, Pro Scouting:** Jared Odom (St. Louis, MO). **Special Assistant to Scouting Director:** Jeff Ishii (Chino, CA). **Professional Scouts:** Brian Hopkins (Holly Springs, NC), Jeff Ishii (Chino, CA), Aaron Klinic (Baltimore, MD), Deric McKamey (Cincinnati, OH), Craig Richmond (Tampa, FL) Joe Rigoli (Parsippany, NJ), Kerry Robinson (Ballwin, MO). **Assistant General Manager (International Scouting):** Moises Rodriguez. **Senior International Crosschecker:** Joe Almaraz. **International Crosschecker:** Damaso Espino. **Senior Latin American Crosschecker/DR Scouting Supervisor:** Angel Ovalles. **Latin American Crosschecker/DR Crosschecker:** Alix Martinez. **Dominican Republic Scouts:** Braly Guzman, Raymi Dicent, Filiberto Fernandez, Darluimis Almonte. **Venezuela Scouting Supervisor:** Jose Gonzalez Maestre. **Venezuela Scouts:** Estuar Ruiz, Jesus Perez, Neriel Morillo, Wilmer Castillo. **Mexico:** Ramon Garcia. **Colombia/Latin America:** Carlos Balcazar

MAJOR LEAGUES

SAN DIEGO PADRES

Office and Mailing Address: Petco Park, 100 Park Blvd., San Diego, CA 92101.
Telephone: (619) 795-5000.
E-mail address: comments@padres.com. **Website:** www.padres.com. **Twitter:** @padres.
Facebook: www.facebook.com/padres. **Instagram:** www.instagram.com/padres

OWNERSHIP
Operated By: Padres LP. **Chairman:** Peter Seidler.

BUSINESS OPERATIONS
Chief Executive Officer: Erik Greupner. **Chief Operating Officer:** Caroline Perry. **Senior Vice President, People & Culture:** Sara Greenspan. **Senior Vice President, Special Events:** Jaclyn Lash. **Vice President, Information Technology:** Ray Chan. **Vice President, Finance:** Greg Massey. **Vice President, Public Affairs:** Diana Puetz. **Vice President, Business Strategy & Analytics:** Scott Robish

LEGAL
Vice President/General Counsel: Terezka Zabka

COMMUNITY RELATIONS/MILITARY AFFAIRS
Telephone: (619) 795-5265. **Fax:** (619) 795-5266. **Senior Vice President, Community Relations & Military Affairs:** Tom Seidler. **Vice President, Community Relations:** Bill Johnston. **Director, Community Relations:** Connor Feeney.

Peter Seidler

ENTERTAINMENT/MARKETING/COMMUNICATIONS/CREATIVE SERVICES
Senior Vice President/Chief Marketing Officer: Chris Connolly. **Vice President, Communications:** Craig Hughner. **Vice President, Broadcasting and Entertainment:** Erik Meyer. **Senior Director, Content:** Nicky Patriarca. **Senior Director, Marketing:** Emily Wittig. **Senior Director, Game Day Presentation:** Shannon Landers. **Senior Director, Creative Digital Design:** Daniel Kim. **Senior Director, Fan Engagement:** Darryl Mendoza. **Director, Media Relations & Baseball Information:** Darren Feeney. **Director, Business Communications & Spanish Media Relations:** Danny Sanchez. **Director, Video Production:** Tom Higdon. **Director, Scoreboard Operations:** Jeff Praught

BALLPARK OPERATIONS/HOSPITALITY
Senior Vice President, Ballpark Operations: Ken Kawachi. **Vice President, Facilities and Special Projects:** Randy McWilliams. **Vice President, Hospitality:** Josh Momberg. **Senior Director, Security/Transportation:** Kevin Dooley. **Director, Ballpark Operations:** Christian Mua. **Senior Manager, Event Operations:** Kim Seaberg. **Official Scorers:** Jack Murray, Bill Zavestoski, Dave Matheson and Nick Canepa

TICKETING
Telephone: (619) 795-5500. **Fax:** (619) 795-5034. **Senior Vice President, Corporate Partnerships:** Sergio Del Prado. **Vice President, Ticket Sales and Service:** Curt Waugh. **Vice President, Partnership Services:** Eddie Quinn. **Senior Director, Membership Services:** Ashley Hoffman. **Senior Director, Premium, Membership & Suite Sales:** Jeffrey Gould. **Senior Director, Ticket Operations:** Jim Kiersnowski. **Senior Director, Toursism Development & Corporate Events:** Chelsea Dill.

TRAVEL/CLUBHOUSE
Director, Player & Staff Services: T.J. Lasita. **Manager, Clubhouse & Equipment:** TJ Laidlaw. **Assistant Equipment Manager & Umpire Room Attendant:** Tony Petricca. **Visiting Clubhouse Manager:** Spencer Dallin

BASEBALL OPERATIONS
Telephone: (619) 795-5077. **Fax:** (619) 795-5361.
President of Baseball Operations & General Manager: A.J. Preller. **VP, Assistant GM:** Fred Uhlman Jr. **VP, Assistant GM:** Josh Stein. **VP, Baseball Operations:** Nick Ennis. **Senior Advisor to GM, Player Personnel:** Logan White. **Special Assistants to the GM:** James Keller, David Post, Moises Alou. **Senior Advisor to Baseball Operations:** Trevor Hoffman, Glenn Hoffman. **Senior Advisor, Baseball Operations & Scouting:** Ron Rizzi. **Special Assistant, Baseball Operations:** A.J. Ellis. **Advisor, Baseball Operations:** Allen Craig. **Director, Baseball Research & Development:** Adam Esquer. **Assistant Director, Baseball Research & Development:** Cody Zupnick. **Senior Analysts, Baseball Research & Development:** Mario Paciuc, Joseph Sutcliffe. **Director, Baseball Systems:** Wells Oliver. **Developers & Data Engineer, Baseball Systems:** Garret Doe, Michael Vanger, Gustavo Montalvo, Mike Peterson. **Manager, Pro Scouting and Baseball Operations:** Brett Becker. **Coordinator, Advance Scouting and Baseball Operations:** Jim McKew

GENERAL INFORMATION
Stadium (year opened):
Petco Park (2004).
Team Colors: Padres Blue and White

Home Dugout: First Base.
Playing Surface: Grass.

MAJOR LEAGUES

MAJOR LEAGUE STAFF
Manager: Bob Melvin. **Associate Manager:** Ryan Christenson. **Bench Coach/Offensive Coordinator:** Ryan Flaherty. **Pitching Coach:** Ruben Niebla. **Bullpen Coach:** Ben Fritz. **Third Base Coach & Infield Instructor:** Matt Williams. **First Base Coach & Outfield Instructor:** David Macias. **Assistant Hitting Coach:** Oscar Bernard. **Assistant Hitting Coach:** Scott Coolbaugh. **Catching Coach:** Brian Esposito. **Game Planning & Coaching Assistant:** Peter Summerville. **Bullpen Catcher & Coaching Assistant:** Heberto Andrade. **Senior Advisor to Major League Coaching Staff:** Bryan Price. **Senior Advisor to Player Development & Major Leagues:** Mike Shildt

MEDICAL/TRAINING
Club Physicians: UC San Diego Health—Dr. Catherine Robertson, Dr. Kenneth Taylor, Dr. Daniel Slater, Dr. Amy Leu, Dr. Bryan Leek. **Director, Player Health and Performance:** Don Tricker. **Head Athletic Trainer:** Mark Rogow. **Physical Therapist:** Scott Hacker. **Assistant Athletic Trainers:** Ben Fraser, Ricky Huerta. **Strength & Conditioning Coaches:** Jay Young, Kenny Esquivel. **Massage Therapists:** Atsushi Nakasone, Yuji Nagahama. **Coordinator, Performance Nutrition and Dietician:** Whitney Milano. **Minor League Athletic Training Coordinator:** Paul Porter. **Minor League Physical Therapists:** Taylor McWilliams, Aaron Wengertsman. **Minor League Strength & Conditioning Coordinators:** Jon Hill, Ryo Naito. **Minor League Performance Dietitian:** Jaime Gottlieb. **Quality Assurance, Player Health and Performance:** Hillary Plummer

A.J. Preller

PLAYER DEVELOPMENT
Telephone: (619) 795-5392. **Fax:** (619) 795-5036.
Director, Player Development: Ryley Westman. **Assistant Director, Player Development:** Mike Daly. **Coordinator, Minor League Admin & Baseball Operations:** Allison Luneborg. **Coordinator, International Player Development:** Vicente Cafaro. **Coordinator, Player Development:** Clinton Sewell. **Director, Sports Science:** Nathan Landau. **Senior Performance Scientist, Sports Science:** Patrick Cherveny. **Performance Coach, Sports Science:** Christian Wonders. **Sports Scientist:** Jesus Ramos. **Coordinator, Sports Science:** Rebekah Lajoie. **Manager, Minor Leagues/Peoria:** Todd Stephenson. **Manager, Learning, Education & Life Skills:** Kaitlyn Simmons. **Manager, Video Operations and Pro Scout:** Ethan Dixon. **Manager, Minor League Equipment:** Zach Nelson. **Clubhouse Assistant:** Kyle Ross. **Lead ESL Instructor:** Sherly German. **Field Coordinator & Player Performance:** Vinny Lopez. **Assistant Field Coordinator/Infield Coordinator:** Ryan Barba. **Director, Pitching Development:** Rob Marcello. **Minor League Pitching Coordinator:** Jose Rada. **Minor League Hitting Coordinator:** Mike McCoy. **Minor League Catching Coordinator:** Brian Whatley. **Rehab Pitching Coordinator:** Matt Hancock. **Director, International Operations:** Cesar Rizik. **Administrator, D.R. Baseball Operations:** Franklyn Peguero. **Assistant Administrator, D.R. Baseball Operations:** Martina Pereyra. **Latin American Operations Assistant:** Joel Caro. **Mental Skills Coordinator:** Rosa Pou. **Mental Skills Coach:** Fabian Di Lorenzo. **Latin American Education Coordinator:** Belgica Reyes.

FARM SYSTEM

Class	Farm Club (League)	Manager	Hitting Coach	Pitching Coach
Triple-A	El Paso (PCL)	Philip Wellman	Raul Padron	Scott Mitchell
Double-A	San Antonio (TL)	Luke Montz	Pat O'Sullivan	Jeff Andrews
High-A	Fort Wayne (MWL)	Jonathan Mathews	Aaron Bray	Carlos Chavez
Low-A	Lake Elsinore (CAL)	Pete Zamora	Jed Morris	Thomas Eshelman
Rookie	Padres (ACL)	Lukas Ray	M. Del Castillo/E. Del Prado	R. Price/Y. Monzon/L. Rosales
Rookie	Padres (DSL)	Luis Mendez	Y. Garcia/D. Cedeno/R. Giron	N. Cruz/J. Quezada

SCOUTING
VP, Amateur & International Scouting: Chris Kemp. **Coordinator, Amateur Scouting:** Max Kraust. **Manager of Amateur Analysis, Baseball R&D:** Layne Gross. **Amateur Scout:** Doug Banks. **Assistant, Amateur Scouting:** Dylan Schoknecht. **Crosschecker, West Region:** Josh Emmerick. **Area Scout, Northwest:** Justin Baughman. **Area Scout, Northern California:** Tim Reynolds. **Area Scout, Southern California:** Spencer Babcock. **Area Scout, Southern California:** Jack Shannon. **Area Scout, Four Corners:** Will Scott. **Area Scout, Canada:** Chris Kemlo. **Area Scout, Upper Midwest:** Troy Hoerner. **Area Scout, Midwest:** Stephen Moritz. **Crosschecker, South Central Region:** Andrew Salvo. **Area Scout, North Texas:** Matthew Schaffner. **Area Scout, South Texas & Louisiana:** Tyler Watson. **Area Scout, Gulf States:** Clint Harrison. **Crosschecker, Southeast Region:** Nick Brannon. **Area Scout, Carolinas / Intl Crosschecker:** Jake Koenig. **Area Scout, Georgia & East Tennessee:** Tyler Stubblefield. **Area Scout, North Florida:** John Martin. **Area Scout, South Florida & Puerto Rico/Intl Scout:** Cliff Terracuso. **Scout, Puerto Rico (Part-time):** Willie Ronda. **Crosschecker, Northeast Region:** Mike Kanen. **Area Scout, Northeast:** John McNamara. **Area Scout, Mid-Atlantic:** Danny Sader. **Area Scout, Ohio Valley:** Matt Maloney. **Coordinator, Sports Science:** Rebekah Lajoie. **Senior Performance Scientist, Sports Science:** Patrick Cherveny.

MAJOR LEAGUES

SAN FRANCISCO GIANTS

Office Address: Oracle Park, 24 Willie Mays Plaza, San Francisco, CA 94107.
Telephone: (415) 972-2000. **Fax:** (415) 947-2800. **Website:** sfgiants.com, sfgigantes.com.

OWNERSHIP
Operated By: San Francisco Baseball Associates L.P.

BUSINESS OPERATIONS
President/Chief Executive Officer: Laurence M. Baer. **Senior Executive Advisor:** Staci Slaughter. **Special Assistants:** Will Clark, Willie Mays. **Special Advisor:** Barry Bonds.

FINANCE/LEGAL/INFORMATION TECHNOLOGY
Executive Vice President & Chief Legal Officer: Jack F. Bair. **Senior Vice President & General Counsel:** Amy Tovar. **Senior VP/Chief Financial Officer:** Lisa Pantages. **Senior VP/CIO:** Bill Schlough. **VP, Information Technology:** Ken Logan. **VP, Finance:** Chris Rossi.

ADMINISTRATION
Executive VP, Administration: Alfonso Felder. **Senior Vice President & Chief Venue Officer, Oracle Park:** Jorge Costa. **VP, Ballpark Operations:** Gene Telucci. **VP, Security:** Tinie Roberson. **Vice President, Guest Services:** Alexis Lustbader. **Senior Vice President & Chief People Officer:** Jose Martin. **Vice President, Human Resources:** Lan Huynh Lee. **President, Giants Enterprises:** Stephen Revetria. **VP, Giants Enterprises:** Joey Nevin. **Senior VP, Event Strategy & Services:** Sara Grauf.

Laurence M. Baer

COMMUNICATIONS
Telephone: (415) 972-2445. **Fax:** (415) 947-2800.
Telephone: (415) 972-2445. **Fax:** (415) 947-2800. **Senior Vice President, Communications & Community Relations:** Shana Daum. **Executive Assistant to the Senior VP, Communications & Community Relations:** Lyz Socha. **Senior Director, Business & Internal Communications:** Casey Baksa. **Executive Director, Giants Community Fund:** Sue Petersen. **Vice President, Media Relations:** Matt Chisholm. **Senior Director, Broadcast Communications & Media Operations:** Maria Jacinto. **Director, Hispanic Communications & Marketing:** Erwin Higueros. **Senior Manager, Media Relations:** Megan Brown. **Senior Manager, Baseball Information:** Mike Passanisi. **Coordinator, Media Relations:** Mariana de Paula. **Director, Player, Alumni & Community Relations:** Bobby Baksa.

BUSINESS OPERATIONS
Executive VP, Business Operations: Mario Alioto. **Senior Vice President & Chief Business Development Officer:** Jason Pearl. **Director, Marketing/Advertising:** Travis LoDolce. **Vice President, Content & Entertainment:** Paul Hodges. **Vice President, Brand Development & Digital Media:** Bryan Srabian. **PA Announcer:** Renel Brooks-Moon.

TICKETING
Telephone: (415) 972-2000. **Fax:** (415) 972-2500.
Senior VP, Ticket Sales/Services: Russ Stanley. **Vice President, Ticket & Premium Revenue:** Jeff Tucker. **VP, Business Analytics:** Rocky Koplik.

BASEBALL OPERATIONS
Telephone: (415) 972-1922. **Fax:** (415) 947-2929.
President of Baseball Ops.: Farhan Zaidi. **General Manager:** Pete Putila. **Senior Advisor to President of Baseball Ops:** JP Ricciardi, John Barr. **VP/Assistant GM:** Jeremy Shelley. **VP, Baseball Resources and Development:** Yeshayah Goldfarb. **VP, Player Performance and Wellness:** Colin Cahill. **VP, Pro Scouting:** Zack Minasian. **Special Assistant, Scouting:** Craig Weissmann. **Special Assistant to Baseball Ops:** Felipe Alou, Ron Wotus and Sam Geaney. **Executive Assistant to Baseball Ops/Administration:** Karen Sweeney. **VP, Baseball Analytics:** Paul Bien. **Director of Player Personnel Administration:** Clara Ho-Frawley. **Director, International Operations & Baseball Administration:** Jose Bonilla. **Director, Baseball Analytics:** Michael Schwartze. **Baseball Ops Analyst:** Rohanna Pacheco, Simon Ricci, Mark Ferraro, Jimmy Kerr. **Senior Data Scientist:** Greg Starek. **Data Scientist:** Brian Huey. **Staff Software Engineer, Baseball Systems:** Kevin Deggelman. **Senior Software Engineer, Baseball Systems:** Alex Case, Eddie Elliott. **Software Engineer:** Rob Bertucci, Krystine Xie, Matt Fong, Jack McGeary. **Assistant, Baseball Ops:** Josh Zimmerman.

MAJOR LEAGUE STAFF
Manager: Gabe Kapler. **Coaches: Bench**—Kai Correa. **Director of Pitching**—Brian Bannister. **Pitching Coach**—Andrew Bailey. **Asst Pitching Coach**—J.P. Martinez. **Hitting Coach**—Justin Viele. **Director of Hitting/ML Assistant Hitting Coach:** Dustin Lind. **Assistant Hitting Coach:** Pedro Guerrero. **Third Base Coach**—Mark Hallberg. **First Base Coach**—Antoan Richardson. **Bullpen**—Craig Albernaz. **Quality Assurance Coach:** Nick Ortiz. **Assistant Coaches:**

GENERAL INFORMATION
Stadium (year opened): Oracle Park (2000). **Playing Surface:** Grass.
Team Colors: Black, orange and cream.
Home Dugout: Third Base.

MAJOR LEAGUES

Alyssa Nakken, Taira Uematsu. **Director, Video Coaching:** Fernando Perez. **Bullpen Catchers:** Alex Burg, Brant Whiting. **Batting Practice Pitcher:** John Yandle.

MEDICAL/TRAINING
Head Team Physician: Dr. Anthony Saglimbeni. **Head Team Orthopedist:** Dr. Ken Akizuki. **Team Physicians:** Dr. Robert Murray, Dr. Chris Chung. **Team Orthopedist:** Dr. Ben Ma. **Senior Dir. of Athletic Training:** Dave Groeschner. **Head Athletic Trainer:** Anthony Reyes. **Asst. Athletic Trainer:** LJ Petra. **Physical Therapist:** Tony Reale. **Strength & Conditioning Coach:** Brad Lawson. **Asst. Strength & Conditioning Coach/Sports Science Specialist:** Saul Martinez. **Massage Therapist:** Hiroki Sato. **Coordinator, Medical Admin.:** Chrissy Yuen. **Dir. of Performance Nutrition:** Adam Rodrigues. **Medical Review Analyst:** Eric Ortega.

PLAYER DEVELOPMENT

Farhan Zaidi

Sr. Director, Player Development: Kyle Haines. **Assistant Director, Education & Cultural Development:** Laura Nuñez. **Minor League Medical Director:** Dustin Luepker. **Director, Arizona Field Operations:** Josh Warstler. **Manager, Minor League Operations:** Gabriel Alvarez. **Field Coordinator:** Tony Diggs. **Coordinator, Latin America Development:** Hector Borg. **Assistant Field/Infield Coordinator:** Jason Wood. **Pitching Coordinator:** Justin Lehr. **Hitting Coordinator:** Ed Lucas. **Assistant Pitching Coordinator:** Clay Rapada. **Assistant Hitting Coordinator:** Jacob Cruz. **Outfield/Baserunning Coordinator:** Tim Leiper. **Catching Coordinator:** Lance Burkhart. **Rehab Pitching Coordinator:** Matt Yourkin. **Hitting Instructor:** Pat Burrell. **Roving Pitching Instructor:** Ryan Vogelsong. **Baseball Operations Analyst:** Mark Ferraro. **Minor League Clubhouse and Equipment Coordinator:** Ryan Stiles. **Minor League Operations Coordinator:** Jacob Koch. **Minor League Video and Technology Coordinator:** Nick Horning. **Minor League Medical Coordinator:** Ryo Watanabe. **Minor League S&C Coordinator:** Andy King. **Mental Health Coordinator:** Emily Cheatum. **Latin America S&C Coordinators:** Sergio Rojas, Andrea Nuñez. **Mental Skills Coaches:** Kellen Lee, Francisco Rodriguez. **Performance Nutritionist:** Erika Gonzalez-Rebull. **Manager, Minor League Field Operations:** Jeff Winsor.

FARM SYSTEM

Class	Farm Club (League)	Manager	Hitting Coach	Pitching Coach
Triple-A	Sacramento (PCL)	Dave Brundage	Damon Minor	Garvin Alston
Double-A	Richmond (EL)	Dennis Pelfrey	Cory Elasik	Paul Oseguera
High-A	Eugene (NWL)	Carlos Valderrama	Tommy Joseph	Alain Quijano
Low-A	San Jose (CAL)	Jeremiah Knackstedt	Travis Ishikawa	Dan Runzler
Rookie	Giants 1 (ACL)	Jose Montilla	Jared Walker	Mario Rodriguez
Rookie	Giants 2 (ACL)	Jacob Heyward	TBD	Luis Pino
Rookie	Giants (DSL)	Drew Martinez	Juan Parra	TBD
Rookie	Giants 2 (DSL)	Juan Ciriaco	Rob Riggins	Osiris Matos

SCOUTING
Telephone: (415) 972-2360. **Fax:** (415) 947-2929.

VP, Pro Scouting: Zack Minasian. **Senior Director, Amateur Scouting:** Michael Holmes. **Senior Director, International Scouting:** Joe Salermo. **Director, International Scouting:** Felix Peguero. **Director of International Operations/Baseball Administration:** Jose Bonilla. **Coordinator of Amateur Scouting:** Mike Navolio. **Pro Scouts:** Ellis Burks, Keith Champion, Jim D'Aloia, Steve Decker, Jalal Leach, Ben McDonough, Ross Pruitt, Steve Riha, Ryan Thompson, Shane Turner, Brandon Anderson. **Senior Advisors to President:** JP Ricciardi, John Barr. **Special Assistant, Scouting:** Craig Weissmann. **National Crosscheckers:** Brian Bridges, John Castleberry. **National Pitching Coordinator:** Dan Murray. **Scouting Supervisors: Northeast**—Arnold Brathwaite, **Southeast**—Jim Buckley, **Midwest** —Andrew Jefferson, **West**—Matt Woodward. **Area Scouts:** Jose Alou, Ray Callari, Brad Cameron, Larry Casian, Todd Coryell, John DiCarlo, Paul Faulk, Jim Gabella, Chuck Hensley Jr., DJ Jauss, Michael Kendall, Nick Long, James Mouton, Jared Schlehuber, Tom Shafer, Keith Snider, Jeff Wood. **International Crosscheckers:** Jose Alou, Michael Silvestri, Charlie Sullivan. **Director, Venezuela Scouting:** Ciro Villalobos. **Venezuela Crosschecker:** Edgar Fernandez. **Asst. Director & Dominican Republic Crosschecker:** Jesus Stephens. **Supervisor, Dominican Republic:** Gabriel Elias. **Scouts, Dominican Republic:** Abner Abreu, Jonathan Bautista, Andrew Polonia, Michel De Jesus. **Scouting Video Coordinator:** Carlos Reyes. **Scouts, Venezuela:** Joanthan Arraiz, Jose Beyron, Carlos Leon, Juan Marquez, Oscar Montero, Robert Moron, Ciro Villalobos Jr. **Scout, Colombia:** Daniel Mavarez. **Scout, Nicaragua:** Sandy Moreno. **Scout, Panama:** Rogelio Castillo. **Scout, Pacific Rim:** Evan Hsueh.

MAJOR LEAGUES

SEATTLE MARINERS

Office Address: 1250 First Ave. South, Seattle, WA 98134.
Mailing Address: PO Box 4100, Seattle, WA 98194.
Telephone: (206) 346-4000. **Fax:** (206) 346-4400. **Website:** www.mariners.com.

OWNERSHIP
Board of Directors: John Stanton (Chairman), John Ellis, Howard Lincoln (Chairman Emeriti), Chris Larson, Jeff Raikes, Buck Ferguson, Betsy Pepper Larson. **President, Business Operations:** Catie Griggs.

BUSINESS OPERATIONS

FINANCE
Executive Vice President and CFO: Tim Kornegay. **Senior VP, Strategy and Analytics:** Chris Kennedy. **Senior Director, Finance:** Monica Marmolejo. **Director, Internal Audit Operations:** Connie McKay.

John Stanton

LEGAL & GOVERNMENTAL AFFAIRS/ COMMUNITY RELATIONS
Executive Vice President and General Counsel: Fred Rivera. **VP, Deputy General Counsel:** Melissa Robertson. **Senior VP, People and Culture:** Lisa Winsby. **VP, People and Culture:** Brooke Sullivan. **VP, People & Culture and Diversity:** Katherine Cheng.

SALES
Senior VP, Sales: Frances Traisman. **Senior VP, Corporate Partnerships:** Chris Voigt. **Senior Director, Partnerships & Strategy/Activation:** Ingrid Russell-Narcisse. **VP, Ticket Sales & Service:** Cory Carbary.

MARKETING/COMMUNICATIONS
Telephone: (206) 346-4000. **Fax:** (206) 346-4400.
Senior VP, Marketing/Communications: Kevin Martinez. **VP, Communications:** Tim Hevly. **VP, Marketing:** Gregg Greene. **Director, Band Communications:** Sarah Alamshaw. **Coordinators, Baseball Information:** Adam Gresch, Alex Mayer, Freddy Llanos. **Senior Director, Mariners Productions:** Ben Mertens. **Senior Director, Marketing:** Mandy Lincoln. **Director, Graphic Design:** Carl Morton. **Director, Strategic Marketing & Sales:** Haley Durmer. **Director, Digital Marketing:** Tim Walsh.

TICKETING
Telephone: (206) 346-4001. **Fax:** (206) 346-4100.
VP, Fan Experience: Malcolm Rogel. **Senior Director, Ticket Services:** Jennifer Sweigert.

STADIUM OPERATIONS
Senior VP, Ballpark Events & Operations: Trevor Gooby. **Senior Director, Event Sales:** Alisia Anderson. **Director, Ballpark Services:** Juan Rodriguez. **Director, Facilities:** Dave Wilke. **Senior VP, Information Technology:** Kari Escobedo. **VP, Product & Technology:** Letitia Selk. **Director, Information Systems:** Oliver Roy. **Director, Database/Applications:** Justin Stolmeier. **Director, Baseball Systems:** CJ Elger. **Senior Director, Procurement:** Norma Cantu. **Head Groundskeeper:** Tim Wilson. **PA Announcer:** Tom Hutyler.

MERCHANDISING
Sr. Director, Retail Operations: Julie McGillivray. **Director, Retail Merchandising:** Renee Steyh. **Director, Retail Stores:** Mary Beeman.

TRAVEL/CLUBHOUSE
Director, Major League Operations: Jack Mosimann. **Clubhouse Managers:** Chris DeWitt and Joe Van Vleck. **Visiting Clubhouse Manager:** Jeff Bopp. **Video Coordinator:** Patrick Hafner.

BASEBALL OPERATIONS
President, Baseball Operations: Jerry Dipoto.
Executive Vice President, General Manager: Justin Hollander. **Assistant GM:** Andy McKay. **Director, Major League Operations:** Jack Mosimann. **Director, Baseball Operations:** Tim Stanton. **Director, Baseball Projects:** David Hesslink. **Coordinator, Advance Scouting:** Sam Reinertsen. **Director, Data Strategy:** Skylar Shibayama. **Senior Director, Analytics:** Jesse Smith. **Director, Analytics:** Joel Firman. **Manager, Analytics:** John Choiniere.

MAJOR LEAGUE STAFF
Manager: Scott Servais. **Pitching**—Pete Woodworth. **Hitting**—Jarret DeHart. **Hitting**— Tony Arnerich. **First Base**—Kristopher Negrón. **Third Base**—Manny Acta. **Bullpen and Quality Control**—Stephen Vogt. **Infield Coach**—Perry Hill. **Field Coordinator**—Carson Vitale. **ML Coach**—Trent Blank. **Bullpen Catcher**—Fleming Báez, Justin Novak. **Batting**

GENERAL INFORMATION
Stadium (year opened): T-Mobile Park (1999). **Home Dugout:** First Base.
Team Colors: Northwest green, silver and navy blue. **Playing Surface:** Grass.

MAJOR LEAGUES

Practice Pitcher—Nasusel Cabrera. **Video Coordinator:** Patrick Hafner. **Video Assistant:** Dan Kaplan, Jake Kuruc.

MEDICAL/TRAINING
Head Orthopedist: Dr. Jason King. **Sr. Director, High Performance:** Rob Scheidegger. **Head Athletic Trainer:** Kyle Torgerson. **Asst. Athletic Trainer:** Taylor Bennett, Kevin Orloski. **Physical Therapist:** Ryan Bitzel. **Strength and Conditioning Coach:** Matt Rutledge. **Asst. Performance Specialist:** Derek Cantieni. **Director, Sports Science:** Kate Weiss.

PLAYER DEVELOPMENT
Telephone: (206) 346-4316. **Fax:** (206) 346-4300.
Director, Player Development: Justin Toole. **Coordinators, Player Development:** Mat Snider, Ryan McLaughlin. **Special Assistants, Player Development:** Alvin Davis, Dan Wilson, Mike Cameron, Franklin Gutiérrez, Hisashi Iwakuma. **Manager, Rehab and Return to Play:** John Walker. **Director, Hitting Strategy:** Jarret DeHart. **Director, Pitching Strategy:** Trent Blank. **Hitting Strategist:** Edward Paparella. **Pitching Strategist:** Ken Roberts. **Pitching Strategist and Rehab Coordinator:** Ari Ronick. **Field Coordinator:** Louis Boyd. **Hitting Coordinator:** CJ Gillman. **Asst. Hitting Coordinator:** Tyger Peterson. **Pitching Coordinator:** Max Weiner. **Asst. Pitching Coordinator:** Matt Pierpont. **Catching Coordinator:** Zac Livingston. **Performance Specialist Coordinator:** Jeff Mathers. **Mental Skills Coordinator:** Stephanie Hale.

Jerry Dipoto

FARM SYSTEM

Class	Club (League)	Manager	Hitting Coach	Pitching Coach
Triple-A	Tacoma (PCL)	John Russell	Brad Marcelino	Jairo Cuevas
Double-A	Arkansas (TL)	Mike Freeman	Shawn O'Malley	Michael Peoples
High-A	Everett (NWL)	Ryan Scott	Mike Fransoso	Cameron Ming
Low-A	Modesto (CAL)	Zach Vincej	Seth Mejias-Brean	Jake Witt
Rookie	Mariners (ACL)	Luis Caballero	Brett Schneider	Todd Carroll
Rookie	Mariners (DSL)	Jose Amanico	Devin Fujiyoka	Bryan Pall

SCOUTING
Director, Amateur Scouting: Scott Hunter. **Asst. Director, Amateur Scouting:** Frankie Piliere. **Director, Player Personnel:** Brendan Domaracki. **Global Crosschecker:** Carlos Gomez (Miami, FL). **Crosscheckers:** Ben Collman (German Valley, IL), Ryan Holmes (Thousand Oaks, CA), Jesse Kapellusch (Cooper City, FL), Mark Lummus (Godley, TX), Devitt Moore (Bryn Mawr, PA). **Regional Scouts:** Trevor Andresen (Solana Beach, CA), Ty Bowman (Phoenix, AZ), Randolph Gassaway (Sacramento, CA) Dan Holcomb (Nashville, TN), Tyler Holub (Durham, NC), Bobby Korecky (Estero, FL), Jackson Laumann (Florence, KY), Terry McClure (Atlanta, GA), Derek Miller (Sugar Land, TX), Rob Mummau (Palm Harbor, FL), Patrick O'Grady (Dallas, TX), David Pepe (Boonton, NJ), Joe Saunders (Chicago, IL). **Coordinator, Player Personnel:** Austin Yamada. **Scouting Analysts:** Matt Ault, Matt Doughty, Tyler Warmoth. **Director, International Amateur Scouting:** Frankie Thon (Doral, FL). **International Crosschecker:** Kevin Fox (Roseville, CA). **Supervisor, Dominican Republic:** Audo Vicente (Santo Domingo, DR). **Latin America Supervisor:** David Brito (Baranquilla, CO). **Venezuela Supervisor:** Federico Hernandez (Caracas, VZ). **International Admin:** Angel Contreras. **International Scouts:** Felipe Burin (Brazil), Alfredo Celestin (D.R.), Rodrigo Cortez (Venezuela) Franklin Diaz (D.R.) Luis Fuenmayor (Venezuela), Kenny Hart (Aruba & Curacao), Sam Kao (Taiwan), Luis Martinez (Venezuela), Rafael Mateo (D.R.), Manabu Noto (Japan), Rigoberto Rangel (Panama), Ismael Rosado (Dominican Republic), Illich Salazar (Venezuela), David Velazquez (Mexico).

MAJOR LEAGUES

TAMPA BAY RAYS

Office Address: Tropicana Field, One Tropicana Drive, St. Petersburg, FL 33705.
Telephone: (727) 825-3137. **Fax:** (727) 825-3111.

OWNERSHIP
Principal Owner: Stuart Sternberg

BUSINESS OPERATIONS
Presidents: Brian Auld, Matt Silverman. **Chief Planning & Development Officer:** Melanie Lenz. **Chief Public Affairs & Communications Officer:** Rafaela A. Amador. **Chief Financial Officer:** Rob Gagliardi. **Chief Technology Officer:** Juan Ramirez. **Chief People & Culture Officer:** Jennifer Lyn Tran. **Chief Business Officer:** William Walsh. **Chief People & Community Officer:** Bill Wiener Jr. **Senior VP, Administration/General Counsel:** John Higgins. **VP, Corporate Partnerships:** Anthony Rioles. **VP, Accounting:** Patrick Smith. **VP, Ticket Sales & Service:** Jeff Tanzer. **VP, Fan Experience:** Eric Weisberg. **VP, Development:** Robbie Artz. **VP, Communications & Public Affairs:** Devin O'Connell. **VP, Diversity, Equity & Inclusion:** Stephen Thomas. **VP, Communications & Baseball Information:** Jason Wallace. **VP, Communications & Broadcasting:** De Anna Sheffield Ward. **VP, Fan Experience:** Eric Weisberg. **VP, Accounting:** Patrick Smith. **VP, Creative & Brand:** Warren Hypes.

Stuart Sternberg

FINANCE
Director, Financial Planning & Analysis: Jason Gray.

MARKETING/COMMUNITY RELATIONS
Director, Marketing & Creative Services: Emily Miller. **Executive Director, Rays Baseball Foundation:** David Egles. **Director, Community Engagement:** Kimberly Couts.

GAME OPERATIONS
Director, Promotions: Stephon Thomas. **Director, Fan Experience:** Nicholas Armes. **Director, Game Presentation:** Stephen Boyer. **Director, Production & Broadcast Systems:** Michael Weinman.

COMMUNICATIONS/BROADCASTING
Director, Broadcasting: Christopher Mueller.

CORPORATE PARTNERSHIPS
Director, Corporate Partnerships Sales: John Pope. **Director, Corporate Partnerships Services:** Amanda Marquez.

STADIUM OPERATIONS
Senior Director, Building Operations: George Dowling. **Senior Director, Partner & VIP Relations:** Cass Halpin. **Senior Director, Security & Stadium Operations:** Jim Previtera. **Director, Building Operations:** Chris Raineri. **Director, Stadium Operations:** Mike Ferrario. **Head Groundskeeper & Director of Operations, Charlotte Sports Park:** Dan Moeller.

TICKET SALES & SERVICES
Director, Ticket Operations: Robert Bennett. **Director, Ticket Sales & Service:** Dan Newhart. **Director, Ticket Services & Technology:** Matt Fitzpatrick. **Director, Ticket Operations:** Ken Mallory. **Director, Ticketing & Digital:** Jimmy Reed.

STRATEGY & DEVELOPMENT
Director, Strategy & Development: Sanford Sternberg.

BASEBALL OPERATIONS
President: Erik Neander. **Senior VP, Baseball Operations/GM:** Peter Bendix. **VP, Baseball Operations/AGM:** Will Cousins, Chanda Lawdermilk, Carlos Rodriguez. **VP, Baseball Systems:** Brian Plexico. **VP, Player Personnel:** Kevin Ibach. **Special Assistant to the President and GM:** Bobby Heck. **Special Assistant, Baseball Operations:** Denard Span. **Senior Advisor, Player Development and Baseball Operations:** Mitch Lukevics. **Senior Advisor, Scouting/Baseball Operations:** R.J. Harrison. **Senior Director, Team Travel and Logistics:** Chris Westmoreland. **Director, Baseball Operations:** Cole Figueroa, Hamilton Marx. **Director, Baseball Performance Science:** Joe Myers. **Analyst, Performance Science:** Keegan Henderson. **Director, Predictive Modeling:** Taylor Smith. **Assistant Director, Baseball Operations:** Samantha Bireley. **Assistant Director, Major League Operations:** Jeremy Sowers. **Baseball Systems:** Rob Alonzi, Brandon Cordell, Todd Daniels, Luke Fair, Ted Lopez, Zack Strickland, Travis Trapp, Avery Wilkening. **Dev Ops Engineer:** Louis Palma. **Jr. Dev Ops Engineer:** Nick Zeak. **Jr. Data Engineer:** Rocco Matarazzo. **Lead Analysts,**

GENERAL INFORMATION
Stadium (year opened): Tropicana Field (1998). **Playing Surface:** AstroTurf Game Day Grass 3D-60 H.
Team Colors: Dark blue, light blue, yellow.
Home Dugout: First Base.

MAJOR LEAGUES

Erik Neander

R&D: Salem Marrero, David Marshall, Jason Pellettiere. **Senior Analysts R&D:** Emmie Dolfi, Michael McClellan. **Analysts:** Vibhor Agarwal, Josh Arthurs, Bryant Davis, Dylan Murphy, John Nicholson, Ben Smith, John Williams. **Junior Analysts, R&D:** Mason Kellett, Erik Larsen, Michael Model, Tim Morales, Dash Nusbaum, David Yamin, Kyle Young. **Analyst, Baseball Development:** Jeff Sullivan. **Coordinators:** Bobby Kinne, Brad Ballew, Dani Dockx, Grace Dowling, Mike Lambiaso, Vishnu Sarpeshkar, Erika Sperl, Elly Weller. **Assistants:** Mathew Bennett, Matt Bruno, Max Kassan, Randell Kanemaru, Isha Rahman. **Lead Sports Dietician:** Courtney Ellison. **Head of Mental Performance:** Justin Su'a. **Lead Biomechanist:** Mike McNally. **Applied Biomechanist:** Jillian Hawkins.

MAJOR LEAGUE STAFF

Manager: Kevin Cash. **Coaches: Bench**—Rodney Linares. **Pitching**—Kyle Snyder. **Assistant Pitching/Rehab**—Rick Knapp. **Hitting**—Chad Mottola. **Assistant Hitting**—Dan Dement, Brady North. **First Base**—Chris Prieto. **Third Base**—Brady Williams. **Bullpen**—Jorge Moncada. **Field Coordinator**—Tomas Francisco. **Process/Analytics Coach**—Jonathan Erlichman.

MEDICAL/TRAINING

Orthopedic Team Physician: Dr. Koco Eaton. **Internal Medicine Team Physician:** Dr. John Gross. **Massage Therapists:** Ray Allen, Homare Watanabe. **Head Athletic Trainer:** Joe Benge. **First Assistant ATC:** Michael Sandoval. **Assistant ATC:** Aaron Scott. **Assistant ATC/PT:** Wilson Diez. **Assistant ATC/Acupuncture:** Shin Fukuda. **Rehab Coordinator/PT:** Brad Epstein. **Rehab ATC:** Joel Smith. **Special Projects:** Mark Vinson. **S&C:** Trung Cao (Head), Joey Greany (Assistant), Bryan King (Rehab).

PLAYER DEVELOPMENT

Director, Minor League Operations: Jeff McLerran. **Assistant Director, Minor League Operations:** George Pappas. **Assistant Director, Minor League Operations/Baseball Development:** Simon Rosenbaum. **AD, Performance Science/Player Development:** Ryan Pennell. **Sr. Administrator, Minor League/International Operations:** Giovanna Rodriguez. **Coordinator, Player Development:** Jairo De La Rosa. **Pitching Strategist:** Winston Doom. **Manager, Team Travel and Logistics:** Karly Fisher. **Coordinator, Baseball Development:** Dani Dockz. **Coordinator, Mental Performance:** Josh Kozuch. **Coordinator, Training Methods:** Brett Ebers. **Coordinator, Minor League Operations:** Wilson Made. **Coordinator, Minor League and International Operations:** Jeremy Sanders. **Assistant, Minor League Operations:** Ryan Burnett. **Video Coordinator:** Michael O'Toole. **Minor League Equipment Manager:** Tim McKechney. **Assistant Minor League Equipment Manager:** Shane Rossetti. **Language Education Coordinator:** Lenore Sanchez. **Advisor, Player Education:** Milton Jamail. **EAP:** Vince Lodato. **Field Coordinator:** Alejandro Freire. **Assistant Field Coordinator:** Blake Butera. **Minor League Coordinators: Pitching:** Alberto Bastardo, Rolando Garza, Jim Paduch. **Hitting:** Will Bradley, Steve Livesey, Kyle Wilson. **Catching:** Jeff Smith. **Infield:** Ivan Ochoa. **OF/Baserunning:** Jared Sandberg. **Affiliate Medical:** Marty Brinker. **Complex Medical/Rehab:** Scott Thurston. **Latin America S&C:** Cesar Gutierrez. **S&C Coordinator:** Chris Osmond. **Asst S&C:** Paul Jones. **Nutrition:** Drew Jarmuz, Al Roth. **Latin America Medical Admin:** Oscar Orengo. **Mental Performance Coaches:** Kris Goodman, Jenny Ferriter, Carla Diaz. **Clubhouse/MnL Nutrition Asst:** Sean Jones.

FARM SYSTEM

Class	Club (League)	Manager	Hitting Coach	Pitching Coach
Triple-A	Durham (IL)	Michael Johns	Kenny Hook	Brian Reith
Double-A	Montgomery (SL)	Morgan Ensberg	Wuarnner Rincones	Steve Merriman
High-A	Bowling Green (SAL)	Rafael Valenzuela	Paul Rozzelle	R.C. Lichtenstein
Low-A	Charleston (CAR)	Sean Smedley	Perry Roth	Levi Romero
Rookie	Rays (FCL)	Frank Maldonado	J.Nelson/M. Castillo	J.Gonzalez/H. Bonilla
Rookie	Rays (DSL)	J. Zorrilla/H. Gimenez	O. Luna/J. Natera	L. Urena/J. Sanchez

SCOUTING

Director, Amateur Scouting: Chuck Ricci. **Assistant Director, Amateur Scouting:** David Hamlett. **Assistant Director, Pro Personnel & Pro Scouting:** Ryan Bristow. **Analyst, Pro Personnel & Pro Scouting:** Tyler Chamberlain-Simon. **Coordinator, Amateur Scouting:** Sydney Malone. **Assistant, Amateur Scouting:** Jake Girard. **Special Assignment Scout:** Jeff Cornell. **Pro Personnel Specialists:** Mike Brown, Max Cohen, Jason Cole, Jason Grey, Nate Howard, Mike Langill, Tyler Stohr. **Pro Scouts:** Ken Califano, JD Elliby, Ruddy Giron, Jose Gomez, Carlos Herazo, Ken Kravec, Jose Leroux, Dave Myers, Wood Myers, Cesar Ramirez, Eduardo Sanchez. **Regional Crosscheckers:** Rickey Drexler (South), Kevin Elfering (Southeast), Joe Hastings (Northeast), Brian Hickman (Midwest), Jake Wilson (West). **Pitching Crosschecker:** Ryan Henderson. **Scout Supervisors:** Matt Alison, Steve Ames, James Bonnici, Zach Clark, Austin Cousino, Tom Couston, Brett Foley, Tim Fortugno, Luke Harrigan, Milt Hill, Chris Hom, Jaime Jones, Reggie Lawson, ML Morgan, Brian Oliver. **Part-Time Area Scouts:** Jose Hernandez, Josh Jackson, Dave Jorn, Gil Martinez, Casey Onaga, Jack Sharp, Marcos Tovar, Lou Wieben. **Development Scouts:** Jeff Lavin, Jhonneris Mendez. **International Crosschecker/South Florida Supervisor:** Victor Rodriguez. **Director, International Scouting:** Steve Miller. **Director, International Operations:** Patrick Walters. **Assistant Director, International Operations:** Ronnie Blanco. **Coordinator, International Scouting:** Jeff Johnson. **International Crosschecker:** Brad Budzinski. **Consultant, International Operations:** John Gilmore. **Scouting Supervisor, Colombia:** Angel Contreras. **Scouting Supervisor, Dominican Republic:** Danny Santana. **Venezuela Crosschecker:** William Bergolla. **Regional Crosschecker, Dominican Republic:** Rigo De Los Santos. **International Scouts:** Miguel De La Cruz, Felix Fermin, Remmy Hernandez, Jorge Perez (Dominican Republic), Marlon Roche, Juan Francisco Castillo, Carlos Leon, Sergio Leon (Venezuela), Frank Tineo (Venezuela), Tiago Campos (Brazil), Karla Espinoza, Keith Hsu (Taiwan), Chairon Isenia (Curacao), Joe Park (Korea), Tateki Uchibori (Japan), Gustavo Zapata (Panama), Alex Zuniga (Colombia).

MAJOR LEAGUES

TEXAS RANGERS

Office Address: 734 Stadium Drive, Arlington, TX 76011.
Telephone: (817) 273-5222. **Website:** www.texasrangers.com. **Twitter:** @Rangers.

OWNERSHIP
Managing Partner & Majority Owner: Ray C. Davis. **Executive Committee:** Bob R. Simpson. **President, Business Operations & Chief Operating Officer:** Neil Leibman.

BUSINESS OPERATIONS
President, REV Entertainment: Sean Decker. **Executive VP/CFO:** Kellie Fischer. **Executive VP, Public Affairs:** John Blake. **Executive VP, Partnerships & Client Services:** Jim Cochrane. **Executive VP, Venue Operations & Guest Services:** Mike Healy. **Executive VP, Business Operations:** Rob Matwick. **Executive VP, Ballpark Entertainment/Productions:** Chuck Morgan. **Special Assistant:** Ivan Rodriguez.

HUMAN RESOURCES/LEGAL/INFORMATION TECHNOLOGY
Sr. VP, Info Technology: Mike Bullock. **Sr. VP, General Counsel:** Erin Kearney. **VP, Human Resources:** Jeff Miller. **Director, Human Resources:** Mercedes Riley. **Corporate Counsel:** Robert Fountain. **Sr. Director, IT Infrastructure & Security:** Chris Hedrick. **Director, IT Applications & Operations:** Graf Reiner. **Manager, IT Help Desk & Customer Service:** Greg Garrison. **Senior Engineers, Infrastructure & Security:** Justin Stockdale, Robert Wiggs.

Ray Davis

FINANCE
Sr. VP/Finance: Starr Gulledge. **Senior Accountant:** Kellie Alford. **Senior Treasury Accountant:** Michael Trybul.

COMMUNICATIONS/COMMUNITY IMPACT/FOUNDATION
Telephone: (817) 273-5203
VP, Broadcasting/Communications: Angie Swint. **VP, Baseball Communications:** Rich Rice. **Director, Baseball Communications:** Will Nadal. **Director, Business Communications:** Chad Seely. **Assistant Director, Baseball Communications:** Tyler Strachan. **Manager, Business Communications:** Lauren Wyatt. **Manager, Photography:** Ben Ludeman. **Manager, Alumni & Player Outreach:** Ashley Quintilone. **Sr. Vice President, Community Impact & Executive Director, Texas Rangers Foundation:** Karin Morris. **Sr. Director, Youth Baseball and Baseball Development:** Juan Leonel Garciga. **Director, Development:** Justin Henry. **Director, Community Impact:** Reynaldo Casas.

FACILITIES/GUEST SERVICES/SECURITY
Sr. Director, Security: Michael Smith. **Director, Event Security & Special Projects:** Donald Paisant. **Director, Major League Grounds:** Dennis Klein. **Director, Complex Grounds:** Steve Ballard. **Director, Facility Operations:** Gabriel Saenz. **Director, Guest Services:** Craig Hodnik. **Director, Engineering & Maintenance:** Grant Phifer. **Director, Venue Operations:** Josh King.

TICKET AND SPONSORSHIP SALES
Vice President, Business Analytics & Ticket Strategy: Katie Morgan. **Vice President, Ticket Sales:** Dan Hessling. **Vice President, Ticket Retention & New Business Development:** Nick Richardson. **Vice President, Corporate Partnerships:** Chad Wynn. **Sr. Director Ticket Operations & Strategy:** Mike Lentz. **Director, Group Sales:** Jamie Roberts. **Director, Suites & Premium Services:** Delia Willms. **Director, Business Partnerships:** Brian Nephew. **Director, Business Intelligence:** Machelle Noel.

MARKETING/GAME PRESENTATION
Sr. VP, Marketing: Travis Dillon. **Sr. Director, Game Entertainment/Productions:** Chris DeRuyscher. **Director, Marketing & Advertising:** Kyle Bartlett. **Creative Director:** Scott Biggers. **Director, Media:** Allison Archer. **Art Director:** Cole Smith. **Sr. Creative Producer, Ballpark Entertainment:** Hugo Carbajal. **Director, Promotions:** Zachary Geist.

EVENTS/REV ENTERTAINMENT
VP, Events: Jared Schrom. **VP, Communications & Marketing:** Madison SanFilippo. **Sr. Director, Marketing:** Lindsey Hopper. **Sr. Director, Event Operations:** Pedro Soto, Jr.

GENERAL INFORMATION
Stadium (year opened): Globe Life Field (2020).
Team Colors: Royal blue and red.
Home Dugout: First Base.
Playing Surface: Turf.

MAJOR LEAGUES

BASEBALL OPERATIONS
Telephone: (817) 273-5222.
Executive VP/General Manager: Chris Young. **VP/Assistant General Manager, Scouting:** Josh Boyd. **VP/Assistant General Manager, Player Development & International Scouting:** Ross Fenstermaker. **Sr. Advisor, Baseball Operations:** Dayton Moore. **Special Assistants to the GM:** Nick Hundley, Colby Lewis, Darren Oliver, Michael Young. **Sr. Director, Baseball Operations:** Michaelene Courtis. **Sr. Director, Baseball Research & Development:** Ryan Murray. **Sr. Director, Player & Family Services:** Taunee Paur Taylor. **Sr. Director, Research & Development, Applications:** Daren Willman. **Director, Leadership, Organizational Development & Mental Performance:** Ben Baroody. **Director, Pitching Analysis:** Todd Walther. **Director, Travel:** Josh Shelton. **Director, Team Security:** Blake Miller. **Assistant Director, Baseball Operations:** Vinesh Kanthan. **Assistant Director, Baseball Research & Development:** Alexander Booth. **Assistant Director, Research & Development, Baseball Systems:** Stephen Coward. **Assistant, Pitching Analysis:** Rich Birfer-Karlin. **Assistant, Baseball Operations:** Olivia Lord. **Analytics Coordinator, Player Development:** R.J. Walsh. **Senior Analysts:** Justin Brantley, Michael Topol. **Senior Data Engineer:** Jessica Zhang. **Analyst, Major League Operations:** Bobby Bandelow. **Analyst, Player Personnel:** Justin Bedard. **Analyst Sports Science:** Will Melville. **Analytics Engineer:** Eduardo Vasquez. **Junior Analysts:** Sam Linker, Taylor Rogers. **Applied Biochemist:** Caleb Watkins. **Major League Video Coordinator:** Adam Brenner. **Associate Data Engineer:** Oliver Dykstra. **Major League Video Assistant:** Bryson Asmus. **Equipment & Home Clubhouse Manager:** Brandon Boyd. **Assistant Clubhouse Managers:** Dave Bales, Parker Zavala. **Visiting Clubhouse Manager:** Mason McKenna.

Chris Young

MAJOR LEAGUE STAFF
Manager: Bruce Bochy. **Associate Manager:** Will Venable.
Coaches: Bench/Offensive Coordinator—Donnie Ecker. **Pitching**—Mike Maddux. **Hitting**—Tim Hyers. **First Base**—Corey Ragsdale. **Third Base**—Tony Beasley. **Bullpen**—Brett Hayes. **Catching**—Bobby Wilson. **Assistant Hitting Coach**—Seth Conner. **Assistant, Major League Staff**—Theo Hooper.

MEDICAL/TRAINING
Sr. Director, Medical Operations/Sports Science: Jamie Reed. **Team Physician:** Dr. Keith Meister. **Team Physician, Internal Medicine:** Dr. David Hunter. **Assistant Team Physicians:** Dr. Jesse Even, Dr. Tariq Hendawi, Dr. Shane Seroyer. **Head Trainer:** Matt Lucero. **Athletic Trainers:** Sean Fields, Jacob Newburn. **Physical Therapist:** Regan Wong. **Strength/Conditioning Coach:** José Vázquez. **Assistant Strength/Conditioning Coach:** Al Sandoval. **Major League Performance Dietician:** Katie McInnis. **Massage Therapist:** Raul Cardenas.

PLAYER DEVELOPMENT
Director, Player Development: Josh Bonifay. **Director, Minor League Operations:** Stosh Hoover. **Assistant Directors, Player Development:** Conner Gunn, Sam Niedorf. **Coordinators:** Kenny Holmberg (Field/Infield), Jordan Tiegs (pitching), Brendan Sagara (pitch design specialist), Cody Atkinson (director, hitting), Eric Dorton (full season hitting), Sharnol Adriana (flex hitting), Garrett Kennedy (catching), Keith Comstock (rehab). **Sr. Director, Performance:** Napoleon Pichardo. **Assistant Director, Performance:** Logan Frandsen. **Medical Coordinator:** Alex Rodriguez. **Mental Performance:** David Franco, Hannah Huesman. **Video Coordinator:** Hunter Schneider.

FARM SYSTEM

Class	Club (League)	Manager	Hitting Coach	Pitching Coach
Triple-A	Round Rock (PCL)	Doug Davis	Matt Lawson	Dave Borkowski
Double-A	Frisco (TL)	Carlos Cardoza	Ryan Tuntland	Josh Zeid
High-A	Hickory (SAL)	Chad Comer	Drew Sannes	Jon Goebel
Low-A	Down East (CAR)	Carlos Maldonado	Brian Pozos	Julio Valdez
Rookie	Rangers (ACL)	Gulider Rodriguez	E. Orona/T. Wolfe	J. Jaimes/ T. St. Clair
Rookie	Rangers (DSL)	Elevys Gonzalez	E. Kingsdale/D. Padilla/W. Veras	TBA

SCOUTING
Director, Pro Scouting: Mike Parnell. **Assistant Director, Pro Scouting:** Chandler Couch. **Senior Evaluators:** Scot Engler, Scott Littlefield, Rafic Saab. **Special Assignment Scout:** Jonathan George. **Pro Scouts:** Mike Anderson, Elliott Blair, Taylor Cameron, Kendall Coleman, Mike Grouse, Touré Harris, Curtis Jung, Donzell McDonald, Michael Quesada. **Senior Director, Amateur Scouting:** Kip Fagg. **Director, Amateur Scouting:** Adam Lewkowicz. **Special Assignment Crosschecker:** Bobby Crook. **West Coast Crosschecker:** Casey Harvie. **National Crosschecker:** Jake Krug. **Southeast Crosschecker:** Arthur McConnehead. **Midwest Crosschecker:** Demond Smith. **Northern Crosschecker:** Brian Williams. **Area Scouts:** Tyler Carroll, Chris Collias, Tommy Duenas, Steve Flores, Jay Heafner, Levi Lacey, Brian Matthews, Gray McGraw, Michael Medici, Brian Morrison, Patrick Perry, Takeshi Sakurayama, Gabe Sandy, Dustin Smith, Darin Vaughan, John Wiedenbauer. **Director, International Scouting & Development:** Hamilton Wise. **Assistant Director, International Scouting & Development:** Jonny Clum. **Assistant, International Scouting & Development:** Jack Marino. **Supervisor, Dominican Republic:** Willy Espinal. **International Crosscheckers:** Jhonny Gomez, Mark Muzzi. **International Scouts:** Arturo Barnetche, Mafel Brito, Rafael Cedeno, Anthony Dominguez, Jose Fernandez, Jesus "Chu" Halabi, Julio Justo, Daniel Liscano, Nelson Muniz, Kwangmin "Andre" Park, Carlos Plaza, Carlos Plaza Jr., Jose Gabriel Rodriguez, Juan Salazar, Hamilton Sarabia, Cesar Sarmiento, Pablo Savinon. **Senior Advisor, Major League Scouting (Hokkaido):** Randy Smith. **Coordinator, Pacific Rim Operations:** Joe Furukawa. **International Scouts:** Hajime Watabe (Japan), Daniel Chang (Taiwan). Furukawa (Japan).

MAJOR LEAGUES

TORONTO BLUE JAYS

Office/Mailing Address: 1 Blue Jays Way, Suite 3200, Toronto, Ontario M5V 1J1.
Telephone: (416) 341-1000. **Fax:** (416) 341-1245. **Website:** www.bluejays.com.

OWNERSHIP
Operated by: Toronto Blue Jays Baseball Club. **Principal Owner:** Rogers Communications Inc. **Chairman, Toronto Blue Jays:** Edward Rogers. **Vice Chairman, Rogers Communications Inc.:** Phil Lind. **President and CEO, Rogers Communication:** Anthony Staffieri. **President, Rogers Sports & Media, Rogers Communication:** Colette Watson.

BUSINESS OPERATIONS
President and CEO: Mark A. Shapiro. **President Emeritus:** Paul Beeston. **Executive Vice President, Baseball Operations/General Manager:** Ross Atkins. **Executive Vice President, Finance:** Ben Colabrese. **Executive Vice Presidents, Business Operations:** Anuk Karunaratne. **Executive Vice President, Marketing and Business Operations:** Marnie Starkman. **Executive Assistant to the President/CEO:** Gail Ricci.

Mark Shapiro

FINANCE/ADMINISTRATION
Director, Finance: Josh Hoffman. **Senior Manager, Blue Jays US Payroll & Benefits:** Sharon Dykstra. **Senior Manager, Finance:** Mark Murray. **Senior Manager, Finance:** Alex Haeussler. **Manager, Finance:** Leslie Galant-Gardiner. **Manager, Finance:** Troy Mercuri. **Manager, Treasury & Vault Operations:** Garrett Mercer. **Senior Financial Analysts:** Melissa Patterson, Bryanna Buckborough. **Senior Payroll Administrator:** Joyce Chan. **Senior Payroll Analyst:** Joy Baybayan. **Finance Associate:** Marisa Paine. **Coordinator, Vendor Administration:** Taylor Thompson.

MARKETING/COMMUNITY RELATIONS
Vice President, Brand & Digital Marketing: Christine DesJardine. **Director, Brand & Digital Marketing:** Sheldon Kiernan. **Director, Creative Services & Marketing Management:** Sherry Oosterhuis. **Director, Game Entertainment & Production:** Stefanie Wright. **Content Director:** George Skoutakis. **Content Producer:** John Woo. **Senior Marketing Manager:** Maureen Kinghorn. **Program Manager, Amateur Baseball:** T.J. Burton. **Marketing Department Manager & Alumni Relations:** Maria Cresswell. **Manager, Game Entertainment:** Sadie Perfetto. **Manager, Community Marketing & Family Programs:** Erinn White. **Senior Motion Graphics Designer:** Michael Campbell. **Motion Graphics Designer:** Ben Simpson. **Social Media Manager:** Alykhan Ravjiani. **Social Content Specialist:** Nico Canavo. **Social Media Specialist:** Richard Lee-Sam. **Photographer & Graphic Design:** Steven Crawford. **Specialist, Digital Marketing & Web/App:** Thomas Small. **Program Specialist, Amateur Baseball:** Jeff Holloway. **Authentics Specialist:** Mike Ferguson. **Program Assistant, Amateur Baseball:** Lucas McKernan. **Coordinator, In-Game Entertainment & Production:** Shaina Gibson.

COMMUNICATIONS
Vice President, Communications & Baseball Media: Andrea Goldstein. **Director, Business Communications:** Jessica Beard. **Manager, Business Communications:** Madeleine Davidson. **Manager, Baseball Communications:** Adam Felton. **Manager, Baseball Information:** Rodney Hiemstra. **Specialist, Baseball Communications:** Simon Wells.

TRAVEL/CLUBHOUSE
Director, Team Travel/Clubhouse Operations: Mike Shaw. **Senior Manager, Visiting Clubhouse:** Kevin Malloy. **Senior Manager, Clubhouse Operations:** Scott Blinn. **Manager, Home Clubhouse Operations:** Mustafa Hassan.

HIGH PERFORMANCE/MEDICAL STAFF
Assistant Director, High Performance Operations: Steve Rassel. **Assistant Director, High Performance Applied Performance Research:** Dehra Harris. **MiLB S&C Coordinator:** Aaron Spano. **S&C Latin American Coordinator:** Omar Aguilar. **ML Head S&C:** Scott Weberg. **ML Assistant S&C:** Jeremy Trach. **Rehab S&C:** Taylor Haslinger. **Dietitian Coordinator:** Kat Mangieri. **Mental Performance Coordinator:** Rob DiBernardo. **ML Mental Performance Coach:** Jimmy VanOstrand. **Senior Mental Performance Coach:** John Lannan. **Mental Performance Coach:** Raul Pimentel. **Assistant Mental Performance Coach:** Erika Monsalve. **Sports Science Coordinator:** Brandon Stone. **Biomechanist:** Clare Padmore. **Medical Director:** Andrew Pipkin. **Assistant Medical Director:** Adam Ingle. **MiLB ATC Coordinator:** Michael Rendon. **PDC ATC & Latin American Coordinator:** Jon Woodworth. **Rehab Coordinator:** Phillip Dimino. **Medical Research Coordinator:** Scott Peters. **ML Head ATC:** Jose Ministral. **ML Assistant ATCs:** Voon Chong, Drew MacDonald. **ML Physical Therapist:** John Biggar. **Physical Therapist:** Alex Suerte. **EAP Director:** Sam Lima.

GENERAL INFORMATION
Stadium (year opened): Rogers Centre (1989).
Team Colors: Blue and white.
Home Dugout: Third Base.
Playing Surface: AstroTurf 3D Xtreme.

MAJOR LEAGUES

BASEBALL OPERATIONS

Ross Atkins

Senior Vice President, Player Personnel: Tony LaCava. **Vice President, International Scouting & Baseball Operations:** Andrew Tinnish. **Assistant General Manager:** Joe Sheehan. **Assistant General Manager:** Michael Murov. **Director, Baseball Research:** Sanjay Choudhury. **Director, Baseball Operations:** Jeremy Reesor. **Director, Baseball Systems:** Peter Saunders. **Manager, Baseball Research:** Graydon Carruthers. **Coordinator, Baseball Research & Development:** Spencer Estey. **Coordinator, Game Planning:** Theron Simpson. **Coordinator, Baseball Research:** Liam Stevenson. **Coordinator, Baseball Operations:** Bryan Lee. **Player Personnel Analyst:** John Babocsi. **Assistant, Pro Scouting & Baseball Operations:** Megan Evans. **Major League Video Coordinator:** Eric Slotter. **Assistant, Advance Scouting:** Anthony Lucchese. **Executive Assistant to the General Manager:** Anna Coppola. **Analytics Developer:** John Meloche. **Research Analyst:** Dan Goldberg. **Baseball Systems Engineer:** Alex Robson. **Assistant, Baseball Research & Development:** Gabrielle Campos. **Assistant, Baseball Research:** Same Greene. **Assistant, Baseball Research:** Maxine Wang. **Assistant, Baseball Research:** Catherine Wu. **Assistant, Scouting:** Matt McCue. **Baseball Systems Cloud Engineer:** Antione Laplante. **Bilingual Player Interpreter:** Hector Lebron. **Bilingual Player Interpreter:** Jun Sung Park.

MAJOR LEAGUE STAFF

Manager: John Schneider. **Coaches: Bench**— Don Mattingly, **Pitching**—Pete Walker, **Hitting**—Guillermo Martinez, **First Base**—Mark Budzinski, **Third Base**—Luis Rivera. **Major League Field Coordinator** — Gil Kim. **Major League Hitting Strategist**—Dave Hudgens. **Assistant Hitting Coach**—Hunter Mense. **Major League Pitching Strategist**—David Howell. **Major League Coach** — Adam Yudelman. **Performance Coach:** Se Hong Jang. **Bullpen Catchers:** Alex Andreopoulos, Luis Hurtado.

PLAYER DEVELOPMENT

Telephone: (727) 734-8007. **Fax:** (727) 734-8162.

Director, Player Development: Joe Sclafani. **Director, Minor League Operations:** Charlie Wilson. **Director, Latin America Operations:** Sandy Rosario. **Field Coordinator:** Casey Candaele. **Short-Season Field Coordinator:** John Tamargo Jr. **Defense Coordinator:** Dallas McPherson. **Hitting Coordinator:** Hunter Mense. **Infield Coordinator:** Danny Solano. **Pitching Coordinator:** Cory Popham. **Pitching Coordinator:** Matt Tracy. **Coordinator, Player Development & HP Operations:** Will Habib. **Coordinator, Player Development & Amateur Scouting:** Reed Kienle. **Business Manager, Minor League Operations:** Michelle Rodgers. **Assistant, Player Development:** Michael Rivera. **MiLB Pitching Analyst:** Evan Short. **Coordinator, Technology Operations:** Matt von Roemer. **Assistant, Short-Season Player Development & Transitions:** Robelin Bautista. **Assistant, Player Development Technology:** Jordan Eaddy. **Special Assistant to Player Development:** Tim Raines. **Swing Consultant & Affiliate Hitting Coach:** Matt Hague. **Rehab Pitching Coach:** Greg Vogt. **Rehab Position Player Coach:** Luis Silva. **Hitting Lab Technician:** Ryan Beckman. **Equipment Coordinator:** Billy Wardlow. **Clubhouse Manager, Florida Operations:** Bobby Walker. **Education Coordinator:** Sonia De La Cruz.

FARM SYSTEM

Class	Club (League)	Manager	Hitting Coach	Pitching Coach
Triple-A	Buffalo (IL)	Casey Candaele	Matt Hague	Tim Norton
Double-A	New Hampshire (EL)	Cesar Martin	Mitch Huckabay	Drew Hayes
High-A	Vancouver (NWL)	Brent Lavallee	Danny Cannellas	Joel Bonnett
Low-A	Dunedin (FSL)	Donnie Murphy	Matt Young	Cory Riordan
Rookie	Blue Jays (FCL)	TBA	TBA	TBA
Rookie	Blue Jays (DSL)	TBA	TBA	TBA

SCOUTING

Director, Pro Scouting: Ryan Mittleman. **Special Assignment Scout:** Russ Bove. **Special Assignment Scout:** Dean Decillis. **Major League Scouts:** Sal Buter. **Professional Scouts:**, Kevin Briand, Justin Coleman, David May Jr., Stephen Yoo. **Pacific Rim Scout:** Hideaki Sato. **Player Personnel Coordinators:** Matt Anderson, Blake Bentley, Marc Lippman, Tim Rooney. **Player Personnel Managers:** Carson Cistulli, Jon Lalonde, Nick Manno, Brent Urcheck. **Pro Scouting Analyst:** Tommy Farah. **Pro Scouting Fellow:** Frank Herrmann, Dean Steinmann. **Director, Amateur Scouting:** Shane Farrell. **Manager, Amateur & International Scouting:** Harry Einbinder. **Manager, Amateur Scouting:** Kory Lafreniere. **Amateur Scouting Analyst:** Chris Weikel. **Assistant, Scouting:** Matt McCue. **National Supervisor:** Blake Crosby. **Regional Crosscheckers:** CJ Ebarb, Jamie Lehman, Greg Runser, Noah St. Urbain, Michael Youngberg. **Crosscheckers:** Brian Johnston, Paul Tinnell. **Area Scouts:** Adam Arnold, Joey Aversa, Coulson Barbiche, Brandon Bishoff, Tom Burns, Adrian Casanova, Chris Curtis, Ryan Fox, Pete Holmes, Matt Huck, Randy Kramer, Jim Lentine, Nate Murrie, Don Norris, Matt O'Brien, Wes Penick, Max Semler, Bud Smith, Mike Tidick. **Scouts:** Chris Lionetti, Roberto Santana. **Amateur & International Video Associate:** Tony Cho. **Canadian Scouting:** Patrick Griffin, Jay Lapp, Jasmin Roy, Rene Tosoni. **Director, Latin American Operations:** Sandy Rosario. **Scouting Supervisors:** Aaron Acosta (MX), Jose Contreras (VZ) Lorenzo Perez (DR). **Scouting Coordinator, South America:** Francisco Plasencia. **Assistant, International Scouting:** Julio Ramirez. **Assistant, International Operations:** Tyler Baldwin. **International Scouting:** Franklin Briceno (VZ), Alexis de la Cruz (DR), Luciano del Rosario (DR), Oscar Delgado (VZ), Enrique Falcon (COL), Jhoan Gomez (DR), Miguel Leal (VZ), Alirio Ledezma (VZ), Jose Natera (DR), Luis Natera (DR), Enmanuel Rojo (DR), Daniel Sotelo (NIC), Alex Zapata (PAN).

MAJOR LEAGUES

WASHINGTON NATIONALS

Office Address: 1500 South Capitol Street SE, Washington, DC 20003.
Telephone: (202) 640-7000. **Fax:** (202) 547-0025.
Website: www.nationals.com.

OWNERSHIP
Managing Principal Owner: Mark D. Lerner.
Principal Owners: Annette M. Lerner, Marla Lerner Tanenbaum, Debra Lerner Cohen, Robert K. Tanenbaum, Edward L. Cohen, Judy Lenkin Lerner.

BUSINESS OPERATIONS
Chief Operating Officer, Lerner Sports: Alan H. Gottlieb. **Chief Financial Officer:** Ted Towne. **Senior Vice President:** Elise Holman.

BALLPARK ENTERPRISES
Executive Director, Ballpark Enterprises: Keely O'Brien

LEGAL
Senior Vice President & General Counsel: Betsy Philpott. **Deputy General Counsel:** John Bramlette.

HUMAN RESOURCES
Vice President, Human Resources: Jason Beckwith. **Senior Director, Human Resources:** Tatiana Diener. **Director, Benefits:** Stephanie Giroux.

Mark D. Lerner

COMMUNICATIONS
Senior Vice President, Chief Communications Officer: Jennifer Giglio; **Executive Director, Communications:** Valerie Krebs. **Director, Communications:** Kyle Brostowitz. **Manager, Communications:** Daniel Kurish. **Manager, Communications:** Gabrielle Scheder-Bieschin. **Coordinator, Communications:** Devon Bridges.

COMMUNITY RELATIONS
Senior Vice President, Community Engagement: Gregory McCarthy. **Executive Director, Player & Community Relations:** Shawn Bertani. **Director, Community Relations:** Nicole Murray. **Director, Community Relations:** Alex Robbins.

BROADCASTING/GAME PRESENTATION
Director, Promotions & Events: Lindsey Norris. **Director, Game Production & Operations:** Emilee Harris. **Director, Video & Broadcast Engineering:** Benjamin Smith.

TICKETING
Vice President, Ticket Sales & Service: Ryan Bringger.

BALLPARK OPERATIONS
Senior Vice President & General Manager of Nationals Park: Frank Gambino. **Senior Vice President, Ballpark Operations:** Lisa Marie Czop.

BASEBALL OPERATIONS
President of Baseball Operations and General Manager: Mike Rizzo. **Assistant General Manager & Vice President, Scouting Operations:** Kris Kline. **Assistant General Manager & Vice President, International Operations:** Johnny DiPuglia. **Vice President & Assistant General Manager, Baseball Operations:** Michael DeBartolo. **Assistant General Manager, Player Personnel:** Mark Scialabba. **Senior Advisor to the General Manager:** Jack McKeon. **Assistant, Major League Administration:** Jordan Missal. **Director, Baseball Operations:** James Badas.

BASEBALL RESEARCH AND DEVELOPMENT
Senior Director, Baseball Research & Development: Lee Mendelowitz. **Director, Baseball Research & Strategy:** Max Ehrman. **Manager, Major League Strategy:** David Higgins. **Lead Analyst, Baseball Research & Development:** Michael Schatz. **Analyst, Baseball Research & Development:** David Gagnon. **Analyst, Baseball Research & Development:** Lee Przybylski. **Analyst, Baseball Research & Development:** Omar Taveras. **Coordinator, Player Development Analytics:** Jordan Rassmann. **Senior Developer, Baseball Research & Development:** Jason Holt. **Senior Developer, Baseball Research & Development:** Jay Liu. **Data Engineer:** Chris Jordan

MAJOR LEAGUE OPERATIONS
Vice President, Clubhouse Operations & Team Travel: Rob McDonald. **Clubhouse & Equipment Manager:** Mike Wallace. **Visiting Clubhouse Manager:** Matt Rosenthal. **Equipment Manager:** Dan Wallin. **Clubhouse Assistants:** Mike

GENERAL INFORMATION
Stadium (year opened):
Nationals Park (2008).
Team Colors: Red, white and blue.
Home Dugout: First Base.
Playing Surface: Grass.

MAJOR LEAGUES

Gordon, Andrew Melnick, Gregory Melnick.

MAJOR LEAGUE STAFF
Manager: Dave Martinez. **Coaches: Bench—** Tim Bogar. **Pitching—** Jim Hickey. **Hitting—** Darnell Coles. **First Base—** Eric Young Jr.. **Third Base—** Gary DiSarcina. **Bullpen—** Ricky Bones. **Catching & Strategy Coach—** Henry Blanco **Assistant Hitting Coach:** Pat Roessler.

MEDICAL/TRAINING
Executive Director, Medical Services: Harvey Sharman. **Lead Team Physician:** Dr. Robin West. **Director, Athletic Training:** Paul Lessard. **Head Athletic Trainer:** Dale Gilbert.

PLAYER DEVELOPMENT
Director, Player Development: De Jon Watson. **Director, Minor League and Florida Operations:** Ryan Thomas. **Director, Player Development Tech & Strategy:** David Longley. **Assistant Director, Player Development:** John Wulf. **Assistant Director, Minor League Operations:** JJ Estevez. **Assistant Director, Player Dev. Tech & Strategy:** Patrick Coghlan. **Manager, Florida Operations:** Diane Wiebe. **Coordinator, Minor League Operations & Player Education:** Andrew Scarlata. **Coordinator, Player Development Analytics:** Jordan Rassman. **Coordinator, Minor League Video:** Allan Bekerman. **Player Development Analyst:** Allen Ho. **Senior Biomechanist:** Bill Johnson. **Biomechanist:** Brittany Mills. **Minor League Clubhouse & Equipment Coordinator:** Carlos Felix. **Minor League Clubhouse Operations:** Scott Paquin. **Clubhouse Assistant:** Brandon Darnell. **DSL Academy Administrator:** Eduardo Castro. **DSL Clubhouse Assistant:** Edniel Rouancourt. **DSL Academy Administrative Assistant:** Lorena Rosario. **Field Coordinator:** Bob Henley. **Senior Advisor, Player Development:** Dave Jauss. **Quality Control Coordinator:** Bill Mueller. **Hitting Coordinator:** Joe Dillon. **Lower Level Hitting Coordinator:** Troy Gingrich. **Pitching Coordinator:** Sam Narron. **Lower Level Pitching Coordinator:** Michael Tejera. **Rehabilitation Pitching Coordinator:** Mark Grater. **Infield Coordinator:** Cody Ransom. **Outfield/Baserunning Coordinator:** Coco Crisp. **Catching Coordinator:** Randy Knorr. **Strength and Conditioning Coordinator:** Gabe Torres. **Assistant Strength and Conditioning Coordinator:** Shane Hill. **Medical Rehab Coordinator:** Gene Basham. **Assistant Medical Rehab Coordinator:** Jeff Allred. **Rehab Coordinator:** JR Wood. **Mental Skills Coordinator:** Dana Sinclair. **Minor League Dietitian:** Emily Kaley.

Mike Rizzo

FARM SYSTEM

Class	Club	Manager	Hitting Coach	Pitching Coach
Triple-A	Rochester (IL)	Matt LeCroy	Brian Daubach	Rafael Chaves
Double-A	Harrisburg (EL)	Delino Deshields	Tim Doherty	Joel Hanrahan
High-A	Wilmington (SAL)	Mario Lisson	Micah Franklin	Mark DiFelice
Low-A	Fredericksburg (CAR)	Jake Lowery	Delwyn Young	Justin Lord
Rookie	Nationals (FCL)	Luis Ordaz	Ender Chávez	Franklin Bravo
Rookie	Nationals (DSL)	Rafael Ozuna	Alex Valdez	Edwin Hurtado

SCOUTING
Director, Scouting Operations: Eddie Longosz. **Director, Player Procurement:** Kasey McKeon. **Director, Pitching Evaluation & Special Asst. to the President of Baseball Ops & GM:** Jeff Zona. **Assistant Director, Amateur Scouting:** Mark Baca. **Special Assistants to the President of Baseball Operations & GM:** Steve Arnieri, Mike Daughtry, Willie Fraser, Jeff Harris, Greg Hunter, Dan Jennings, John Mirabelli, Mike Pagliarulo, Jay Robertson, Bob Schaefer, Matt Ruebel, Jon Weil. **East Crosschecker:** Alan Marr. **Midwest Crosschecker:** Jimmy Gonzales. **West Crosschecker:** Fred Costello. **Southeast Crosschecker and Area Supervisor:** Alex Morales. **Area Supervisors:** Bryan Byrne, Brian Cleary, Ben Diggins, James Goodwin, Kevin Ham, Bob Hamelin, Tommy Jackson, Steve Leavitt, John Malzone, Bobby Myrick, Scott Ramsay, Mitch Sokol, Cody Staab. **Director, International Operations:** Mike Cadahia. **Director, Latin American Scouting:** Fausto Severino. **Assistant, International Scouting:** Taisuke Sato. **Crosscheckers:** Alex Rodriguez, Modesto Ulloa, Riki Vasquez. **Coordinator, Venezuela:** German Robles. **Colombia:** Eduardo Cabrera. **Curacao and Aruba:** David Leer. **Dominican Republic:** Abraham Despradel, Oscar Disla, Virgilio De Leon, Bolivar Pelletier. **Panama:** Miguel Ruiz. **Venezuela:** Salvador Donadelli, Juan Indriago, Ronald Morillo, Juan Munoz.

MEDIA INFORMATION

MAJOR LEAGUES

LOCAL MEDIA INFORMATION

AMERICAN LEAGUE

BALTIMORE ORIOLES
Radio/TV Announcers: Geoff Arnold, Kevin Brown, Scott Garceau, Brett Hollander, Dave Johnson, Rob Long, Ben McDonald, Melanie Newman, Jim Palmer. **Flagship Radio Stations:** 105.1-FM WBAL The Fan, 97.9-FM WIYY. **Flagship TV Station:** Mid-Atlantic Sports Network.

BOSTON RED SOX
Radio Announcers: Joe Castiglione, Will Flemming, Sean McDonough, Lou Merloni. **Flagship Station:** WEEI (93.7 FM). **TV Announcers:** Dave O'Brien. **Flagship Station:** New England Sports Network (regional cable).

CHICAGO WHITE SOX
Radio Announcers: Darrin Jackson, Len Kasper. **Flagship Station:** ESPN Radio Chicago AM 1000
TV Announcers: Steve Stone, Jason Benetti. **Flagship Stations:** WGN TV-9, WPWR-TV, NBC Sports Chicago (regional cable).

CLEVELAND GUARDIANS
Radio Announcers: Tom Hamilton, Jim Rosenhaus. **Flagship Station:** WTAM 1000-AM.
TV Announcers: Rick Manning, Matt Underwood, Andre Knott. **Flagship Station:** FOX Sports Ohio.

DETROIT TIGERS
Radio Announcers: Dan Dickerson, Jim Price. **Flagship Station:** WXYT 97.1 FM and AM 1270.
TV Announcers: Jack Morris, Kirk Gibson, Matt Shepherd, Craig Monroe, John Keating, Dan Petry. **Flagship Station:** Bally Sports Detroit (regional cable).

HOUSTON ASTROS
Radio Announcers: Steve Sparks, Robert Ford. **Spanish:** Francisco Romero, Alex Treviño.
Flagship Stations: KBME 790-AM, KLAT 1010-AM (Spanish).
TV Announcers: Todd Kalas, Geoff Blum, Julia Morales. **Flagship Station:** AT&T Sports Net Southwest.

KANSAS CITY ROYALS
Radio Announcers: Denny Matthews, Jake Eisenberg, Steve Stewart. **Kansas City Affiliate:** KCSP 610-AM.
TV Announcers: Ryan Lefebvre, Rex Hudler, Joel Goldberg, Jeff Montgomery (pre-game).
Flagship Station: Bally Sports Kansas City.

LOS ANGELES ANGELS
Radio Announcers: Terry Smith, Mark Langston. **Flagship Station:** AM 830, 1330 KWKW (Spanish).
TV Announcers: Wayne Randazzo, Matt Vasgersian, Patrick O'Neal, Mark Gubicza. **Flagship TV Station:** Bally Sports West.

MINNESOTA TWINS
Radio Announcers: Cory Provus, Dan Gladden. **Radio Network Studio Host:** Kris Atteberry. **Spanish Radio:** Alfonso Fernandez, Tony Oliva. **Flagship Station:** WCCO-AM 830. **TV Announcers:** Dick Bremer, Roy Smalley, LaTroy Hawkins, Justin Morneau, Glen Perkins, Jim Kaat. **Flagship Station:** Bally Sports North.

NEW YORK YANKEES
Radio Announcers: John Sterling, Suzyn Waldman. **Flagship Station:** WFAN 660-AM, WADO 1280-AM. **Spanish Radio Announcers:** Francisco Rivera, Rickie Ricardo. **TV Announcers:** David Cone, Jack Curry, John Flaherty, Michael Kay, Ryan Ruocco, Bob Lorenz, Meredith Marakovits, Nancy Newman, Paul O'Neill, Ryan Ruocco, Chris Shearn. **Flagship Station:** YES Network.

OAKLAND ATHLETICS
Radio Announcers: Vince Cotroneo, Ken Korach. **Flagship Station:** KTRB 860 AM.
TV Announcers: Glen Kuiper, Dallas Braden, Chris Townsend. **Flagship Stations:** NBC Sports California.

SEATTLE MARINERS
Radio Announcers: Rick Rizzs, Aaron Goldsmith. **Flagship Station:** 710 ESPN Seattle (KIRO-AM 710).
TV Announcers: Mike Blowers, Dave Sims, Dan Wilson, Alex Rivera. **Flagship Station:** ROOT Sports Northwest.

TAMPA BAY RAYS
Radio Announcers: Andy Freed, Dave Wills, Neil Solondz. **Flagship Station:** WDAE 620 AM/95.3 FM Tampa/St. Petersburg. **TV Announcers:** Brian Anderson, Dewayne Staats, Tricia Whitaker, Orestes Destrade, Rich Hollenberg, Doug Waechter. **Flagship Station:** Bally Sports Sun. **Spanish:** Enrique Oliu, Ricardo Taveras.

TEXAS RANGERS
Radio Announcers: Eric Nadel, Matt Hicks. **Spanish:** Eleno Ornelas, Jose Guzman. **Flagship Station:** 105.3 The FAN FM, KFLC 1270 AM (Spanish). **TV Announcers:** Dave Raymond, Tom Grieve, C.J. Nitkowski, David Murphy, Emily Jones, Jared Sandler. **Flagship Station:** Bally Sports Southwest (regional cable).

TORONTO BLUE JAYS
Radio Announcers: Ben Wagner. **Flagship Station:** SportsNet Radio Fan 590-AM.
TV Announcers: Buck Martinez, Dan Shulman, Jamie Campbell, Joe Siddall, Dan Shulman, Hazel Mae, Arash Madani. **Flagship Station:** Rogers Sportsnet.

BaseballAmerica.com

Baseball America 2023 Directory • **75**

MAJOR LEAGUES

NATIONAL LEAGUE

ARIZONA DIAMONDBACKS
Radio Announcers: Greg Schulte, Tom Candiotti, Rodrigo Lopez (Spanish), Oscar Soria (Spanish), Richard Saenz (Spanish). **Flagship Stations:** Arizona Sports 98.7 FM, TUDN 105.1 (Spanish).
TV Announcers: Steve Berthiaume, Bob Brenly. **Flagship Stations:** FOX Sports Arizona (regional cable).

ATLANTA BRAVES
Radio Announcers: Jim Powell, Joe Simpson, Ben Ingram. **Flagship Stations:** WCNN-AM 680 The Fan.
TV Announcers: Paul Byrd, Brian Jordan, Peter Moylan, Nick Green, Jeff Francoeur. **Flagship Stations:** Bally Sports South.

CHICAGO CUBS
Radio Announcers: Pat Hughes, Ron Coomer. **Flagship Station:** WSCR-670 The Score.
TV Announcers: Jon Sciambi, Jim Deshaies. **Flagship Stations:** Marquee Sports Network.

CINCINNATI REDS
Radio Announcers: Tommy Thrall, Jeff Brantley. **Flagship Station:** WLW 700-AM.
TV Announcers: John Sadak, Chris Welsh, Jeff Brantley, Barry Larkin. **Flagship Station:** Bally Sports Ohio.

COLORADO ROCKIES
Radio Announcers: Jack Corrigan, Jerry Schemmel, Salvador Hernandez (Spanish), Carlos Valdaz (Spanish), Hector Salazar (Spanish). **Flagship Station:** KOA 850-AM & 94.1 FM, Rockies Spanish Radio 1150 AM.
TV Announcers: Drew Goodman, Jeff Huson, Ryan Spilborghs. **Flagship Station:** AT&T SportsNet.

LOS ANGELES DODGERS
Radio Announcers: Rick Monday, Charley Steiner, Tim Neverett. **Spanish:** Jaime Jarrín, Jose Mota. **Flagship Stations:** AM570 Fox Sports LA, KTNQ 1020-AM (Spanish).
TV Announcers: Joe Davis, Orel Hershiser, Nomar Garciaparra, Dontrelle Willis, Tim Neverett. **Spanish:** Pepe Yniguez, Fernando Valenzuela. **Flagship Stations:** SportsNet LA (regional cable).

MIAMI MARLINS
Radio Announcers: TBA. **Flagship Stations:** WINZ 940-AM.
TV Announcers: Paul Severino, Tommy Hutton. **Flagship Stations:** Bally Sports Florida (regional cable).

MILWAUKEE BREWERS
Radio Announcers: Bob Uecker, Jeff Levering, Lane Grindle. **Flagship Station:** WTMJ 620-AM.
TV Announcers: Brian Anderson, Bill Schroeder, Sophia Minnaert. **Flagship Station:** Bally Sports Wisconsin.

NEW YORK METS
Radio Announcers: Howie Rose, Wayne Randazzo, Pat McCarthy, Keith Raad. **Flagship Station:** WCBS 880-AM.
TV Announcers: Gary Cohen, Keith Hernandez, Ron Darling, Steve Gelbs, Todd Zeile. **Flagship Stations:** Sports Net New York (regional cable), PIX11-TV.

PHILADELPHIA PHILLIES
Radio Announcers: Scott Franzke, Larry Andersen. **Flagship Station:** SportsRadio 94WIP (94.1 FM).
TV Announcers: Tom McCarthy, Ben Davis, Ruben Amaro Jr., John Kruk, Mike Schmidt. **Flagship Stations:** NBC 10 (regional cable).

PITTSBURGH PIRATES
Radio Announcers: Joe Block, Matt Capps, Kevin Young, Greg Brown, Bob Walk, John Wehner. **Flagship Station:** Sports Radio 93.7 FM The Fan.
TV Announcers: Joe Block, Matt Capps, Kevin Young, Greg Brown, Bob Walk, John Wehner. **Flagship Station:** AT&T SportsNet Pittsburgh (regional cable).

ST. LOUIS CARDINALS
Radio Announcers: John Rooney, Ricky Horton, Mike Claiborne. **Flagship Station:** KMOX 1120 AM. **Spanish Radio Announcers:** Polo Ascencio, Bengie Molina. **Flagship Station:** WJIR 880
TV Announcers: Chip Caray, Al Hrabosky, Brad Thompson, Jim Edmonds, Jim Hayes, Alexa Datt, Scott Warmann. **Flagship Station:** Bally Sports Midwest.

SAN DIEGO PADRES
Radio Announcers: Jesse Agler, Tony Gwynn Jr. **Flagship Stations:** 97.3 The Fan.
TV Announcers: Don Orsillo, Mark Grant. **Flagship Station:** Bally Sports San Diego. **Spanish Announcers:** Eduardo Ortega, Carlos Hernandez on XEMO-860-AM.

SAN FRANCISCO GIANTS
Radio Announcers: Mike Krukow, Duane Kuiper, Jon Miller, Dave Flemming.
Spanish: Tito Fuentes, Edwin Higueros. **Flagship Station:** KNBR 680-AM (English); ESPN Deportes-860AM (Spanish).
TV Announcers: Mike Krukow, Duane Kuiper, Jon Miller, Mike Krukow. **Flagship Stations:** KNTV-NBC 11, CSN Bay Area (regional cable).

WASHINGTON NATIONALS
Radio Announcers: Charlie Slowes, Dave Jageler. **Flagship Station:** WJFK 106.7 FM.
TV Announcers: Bob Carpenter, Kevin Frandsen. **Flagship Station:** Mid-Atlantic Sports Network.

76 · Baseball America 2023 Directory

BaseballAmerica.com

MAJOR LEAGUES

NATIONAL MEDIA INFORMATION

BASEBALL STATISTICS

ELIAS SPORTS BUREAU INC. NATIONAL MEDIA BASEBALL STATISTICS
Official Major League Statistician Mailing Address: 500 Fifth Ave., Suite 2140, New York, NY 10110.
Telephone: (212) 869-1530. **Fax:** (212) 354-0980. **Website:** esb.com.
President: Joe Gilston.
Vice President: Chris Thorn. **Email Address:** Chris.Thorn@ESB.com
Manager, Baseball Operations: John Labombarda. **Email Address:** John.Labombarda@ESB.com

MLB ADVANCED MEDIA
Official Minor League Statistician Mailing Address: 1271 Avenue of the Americas, New York, NY 10020.
Telephone: (212) 485-3444. **Fax:** (212) 485-3456. **Website:** MiLB.com.
Director, Stats: Chris Lentine. **Senior Manager, Stats:** Shawn Geraghty.
Senior Stats Supervisors: Jason Rigatti, Ian Schwartz. **Stats Supervisors:** Lawrence Fischer, Jake Fox, Dominic French, Kelvin Lee.

MILB.COM OFFICIAL WEBSITE OF MINOR LEAGUE BASEBALL
Mailing Address: 1271 Avenue of the Americas, New York, NY 10020.
Telephone: (212) 485-3444. **Fax:** (212) 485-3456. **Website:** MiLB.com.
Director, Minor League Club Initiatives: Nathan Blackmon. **Sr. Producer, MiLB.com:** Dan Marinis.

STATS PERFORM
Mailing Address: 203 N. LaSalle St. Chicago, IL, 60601.
Telephone: (847) 583-2100. **Fax:** (847) 470-9140. **Website:** statsperform.com.
Email: sales@stats.com. **Twitter:** @STATSBiznews; @STATS_MLB. **CEO:** Carl Mergale. **Chief Operating Officer:** Mike Perez. **Chief Revenue Officer:** Steve Xeller. **Chief Revenue Officer:** Steve Xeller.

GENERAL INFORMATION

MUSEUMS

NATIONAL BASEBALL HALL OF FAME AND MUSEUM
Address: 25 Main St., Cooperstown, NY 13326.
Telephone: (888) 425-5633, (607) 547-7200. **Fax:** (607) 547-2044. **E-mail Address:** info@baseballhall.org. **Website:** www.baseballhall.org.
Year Founded: 1939.
Chairman: Jane Forbes Clark. **President:** Josh Rawitch.
Museum Hours: Open daily, year-round, closed only Thanksgiving, Christmas and New Year's Day. 9 a.m.-5 p.m. Summer hours, 9 a.m.-9 p.m. (Memorial Day weekend through the day before Labor Day.)
2023 Hall of Fame Induction Ceremony: July 23, Cooperstown, N.Y.

NEGRO LEAGUES BASEBALL MUSEUM
Mailing Address: 1616 E. 18th St., Kansas City, MO 64108.
Telephone: (816) 221-1920. **Fax:** (816) 221-8424.
E-mail Address: bkendrick@nlbm.com. **Website:** www.nlbm.com.
Year Founded: 1990.
President: Bob Kendrick.
Museum Hours: Tues.-Sat. 10 a.m.-5 p.m.; Sun. noon-5 p.m.

RESEARCH

SOCIETY FOR AMERICAN BASEBALL RESEARCH
Mailing Address: Cronkite School at ASU, 555 N Central Ave., #416 , Phoenix, AZ 85004.
Website: www.sabr.org.
Year Founded: 1971.
President: Mark Armour. **Vice President:** Leslie Heaphy. **Secretary:** Todd Lebowitz. **Treasurer:** Daniel Levitt.
Directors: Dan Evans, Tara Krieger, Bill Nowlin, Allison Levin. **CEO:** Scott Bush. **Director of Editorial Content:** Jacob Pomrenke.

ALUMNI ASSOCIATIONS

MAJOR LEAGUE BASEBALL PLAYERS ALUMNI ASSOCIATION
Mailing Address: 1631 Mesa Ave., Copper Building, Suite D, Colorado Springs, CO 80906.
Telephone: (719) 477-1870. **Fax:** (719) 477-1875.
E-mail Address: postoffice@mlbpaa.com. **Website:** www.baseballalumni.com.

MAJOR LEAGUES

Facebook: facebook.com/majorleaguebaseballplayersalumniassociation. **Twitter:** @MLBPAA.
Chief Executive Officer: Dan Foster (dan@mlbpaa.com). **Chief Operating Officer:** Geoffrey Hixson (geoff@mlbpaa.com). **Vice President, Operations:** Mike Groll (mikeg@mlbpaa.com). **Director, Communications:** Kendall Meisner (kendall@mlbpaa.com). **VP, Membership & Development:** Kate Tyo (Kate@mlbpaa.com). **Director, Memorabilia Operations:** Greg Thomas (greg@shoplegends.com). **Director, IT:** Chris Burkeen (cburkeen@mlbpaa.com).

BASEBALL ASSISTANCE TEAM (B.A.T.)
Mailing Address: 245 Park Ave., 31st Floor, New York, NY 10167.
Telephone: (212) 931-7822, **Fax:** (212) 949-5433.
Website: www.baseballassistanceteam.com.

MINISTRY

BASEBALL CHAPEL
Mailing Address: P.O. Box 10102, Largo FL 33773.
Telephone: (610) 999-3600.
E-mail Address: office@baseballchapel.org. **Website:** www.baseballchapel.org.
Year Founded: 1973.
President: Vince Nauss. **Hispanic Ministry:** Luke Sawyer. **Women's Ministry:** Gio Llerena. **Ministry Operations:** Rob Crose, Steve Sisco.

CATHOLIC ATHLETES FOR CHRIST
Mailing Address: 3703 Cameron Mills Road, Alexandria, VA 22305.
Telephone: (703) 239-3070.
E-mail Address: info@catholicathletesforchrist.org. **Website:** www.catholicathletesforchrist.org.
Year Founded: 2006.
President: Ray McKenna. **MLB Ministry Coordinator:** Kevin O'Malley. **MLB Athlete Advisory Board Members:** Mike Sweeney (Chairman), Jeff Suppan (Vice Chairman), Lauren Bauer, David Eckstein, Terry Kennedy, Jack McKeon, Darrell Miller, Mike Piazza, Vinny Rottino, Craig Stammen.

TRADE/EMPLOYMENT

BASEBALL WINTER MEETINGS
2023 Convention: Dec. 4-7, Nashville

REVIVING BASEBALL IN INNER CITIES

Mailing Address: 1271 Avenue of the Americas, New York, NY 10020.
Telephone: (212) 931-7800. **Fax:** (212) 949-5695
Year Founded: 1989
Chief Baseball Development Officer: Tony Reagins. **VP, Baseball & Softball Development:** David James. **VP, Youth & Facility Development:** Darrell Miller. **VP, Baseball Development:** Del Matthews. **Sr. Directors, Baseball & Softball Development:** Chris Haydock, Chuck Fox. **Youth Protection Compliance Officer:** Katherine Anderson. **Director, New Orleans Youth Academy:** Eddie Davis. **Sr. Manager, Play Ball & RBI:** Bennett Shields. **General Manager Baseball Development, Asia:** Rick Dell. **Manager, Baseball and Softball Development and Legal:** Sarah Padove. **Sr. Coordinator, Baseball Development, RBI:** Steven Smiegocki. **Sr. Coordinator, International Baseball Development, RBI:** Chris Madden. **Sr. Coordinator, Baseball Development:** Kindu Jones. **Coordinators, Softball Development:** Rachel Hubertus, Natalia Reynoso. **Coordinator, Baseball & Softball Development:** Cameron Scott. **Managing Director, Jackie Robinson Training Complex:** Rachelle Madrigal. **Coordinator, MLB Compton Youth Academy:** Kenneth Landreaux. **Coordinator, MLB Compton Youth Academy Softball:** Eliza Crawford. **Sr. Administrative Assistant:** Grace Carrasco. **E-mail:** rbi@mlb.com. **Website:** www.mlb.com/rbi

MLB YOUTH ACADEMIES

CINCINNATI REDS YOUTH ACADEMY
Director: Jerome Wright
Asst. Director: Jeremy Hamilton
Mailing Address: 2026 E. Seymour Avenue. Cincinnati , OH 45327
Phone Number: 513-765-5000

COMPTON YOUTH ACADEMY
Vice President: Darrell Miller
Mailing Address: 901 East Artesia Blvd. Compton, CA
Phone: 310-763-3479

78 · Baseball America 2023 Directory

BaseballAmerica.com

MAJOR LEAGUES

HOUSTON ASTROS YOUTH ACADEMY
Director: Daryl Wade
Mailing Address: 2801 South Victory Drive. Houston, TX 77088.
Email: uya@astros.com

KANSAS CITY ROYALS URBAN YOUTH ACADEMY
Address: 1622 E. 17th Terrace, Kansas City, MO 64108
Phone: 816-242-5728
Email: kcuya@royals.com

NEW ORLEANS YOUTH ACADEMY
Director: Eddie Anthony Davis III
Mailing Address: 6403 Press Drive. New Orleans, LA 70126
Phone Number: 504-282-0443

PHILADELPHIA PHILLIES YOUTH ACADEMY
Director: Jon Joaquin
Phone Number: 215-218-5634
Director: Rob Holiday
Phone Number: 215-218-5204

TEXAS RANGERS YOUTH ACADEMY
Director: Juan Leonel Garciga
Mailing Address: 1000 Ballpark Way, Arlington, TX 76011
Phone Number: 817-273-5297

WASHINGTON NATIONALS YOUTH ACADEMY
Executive Director: Tal Alter
Mailing Address: 3675 Ely Place SE. Washington, DC 20019
Phone Number: 202-827-8960

MAJOR LEAGUES

SPRING TRAINING

CACTUS LEAGUE

ARIZONA DIAMONDBACKS

MAJOR LEAGUE

Complex Address: Salt River Fields at Talking Stick, 7555 North Pima Road, Scottsdale, AZ 85256. **Telephone:** (480) 270-5000. **Seating Capacity:** 11,000 (7,000 fixed seats, 4,000 lawn seats). **Location:** From Loop-101, use exit 44 (Indian Bend Road) and proceed west for approximately one-half mile; turn right at Pima Road to travel north and proceed one-quarter mile; three entrances to Salt River Fields will be available on the right-hand side.

MINOR LEAGUE

Complex Address: Same as major league club.

CHICAGO CUBS

MAJOR LEAGUE

Complex Address: Sloan Park, 2330 West Rio Salado Parkway, Mesa, AZ 85201. **Telephone:** (480) 668-0500. **Seating Capacity:** 15,000. **Location:** on the land of the former Riverview Golf Course, bordered by the 101 and 202 interchange in Mesa.

MINOR LEAGUE

Complex Address: 2510 W. Rio Salado Parkway, Mesa, AZ 85201. **Telephone:** (480) 668-0500

CHICAGO WHITE SOX

MAJOR LEAGUE

Complex Address: Camelback Ranch-Glendale, 10710 West Camelback Road, Phoenix, AZ 85037. **Telephone:** (623) 302-5000. **Seating Capacity:** 13,000. **Hotel Address:** Residence Inn Phoenix Glendale Sports and Entertainment District, 7350 N Zanjero Blvd, Glendale, AZ 85305, **Telephone:** (623) 772-8900. **Hotel Address:** Renaissance Glendale Hotel & Spa, 9495 W Coyotes Blvd, Glendale, AZ 85305. **Telephone:** 629-937-3700.

MINOR LEAGUE

Complex/Hotel Address: Same as major league club.

CINCINNATI REDS

MAJOR LEAGUE

Complex Address: Cincinnati Reds Player Development Complex, 3125 S Wood Blvd, Goodyear, AZ 85338. **Telephone:** (623) 932-6590. **Ballpark Address:** Goodyear Ballpark, 1933 S Ballpark Way, Goodyear, AZ 85338. **Telephone:** (623) 882-3120. **Hotel Address:** Marriott Residence Inn, 7350 N Zanjero Blvd, Glendale, AZ 85305. **Telephone:** (623) 772-8900. **Fax:** (623) 772-8905.

MINOR LEAGUE

Complex/Hotel Address: Same as major league club.

CLEVELAND GUARDIANS

MAJOR LEAGUE

Complex Address: Cleveland Guardians Player Development Complex 2601 S Wood Blvd, Goodyear, AZ 85338; Goodyear Ballpark 1933 S Ballpark Way, Goodyear, AZ 85338. **Telephone:** (623) 882-3120. **Location: From Downtown Phoenix/East Valley:** West on I-10 to Exit 127, Bullard Avenue and proceed south (left off exit), Bullard Avenue turns into West Lower Buckeye Road. Turn left onto Wood Blvd. **Hotel Address:** (Media) Hampton Inn and Suites, 2000 N Litchfield Rd, Goodyear, AZ 85395. **Telephone:** (623) 536-1313. **Hotel Address:** Holiday Inn Express, 1313 N Litchfield Rd, Goodyear, AZ 85395. **Telephone:** (623) 535-1313. **Hotel Address:** TownePlace Suites, 13971 West Celebrate Life Way, Goodyear, AZ 85338. **Telephone:** (623) 535-5009. **Hotel Address:** Residence Inn by Marriott, 2020 N Litchfield Rd, Goodyear, AZ 85395. **Telephone:** (623) 866-1313.

MINOR LEAGUE

Complex Address: Same as major league club.

COLORADO ROCKIES

MAJOR LEAGUE

Complex Address: Salt River Fields at Talking Stick, 7555 North Pima Rd, Scottsdale, AZ 85258. **Telephone:** (480) 270-5800. **Seating Capacity:** 11,000 (7,000 fixed seats, 4,000 lawn seats). **Location:** From Loop-101, use exit 44 (Indian Bend Road Talking Stick Way) and proceed west for approximately one-half mile; turn right at Pima Road to travel north and proceed one-quarter mile; three entrances to Salt River Fields will be available on the right-hand side. **Visiting Team Hotel:** The Scottsdale Plaza Resort, 7200 North Scottsdale Road, Scottsdale, AZ 85253. **Telephone:** (480) 948-5000. **Fax:** (480) 951-5100.

MINOR LEAGUE

Complex/Hotel Address: Same as major league club.

KANSAS CITY ROYALS

MAJOR LEAGUE

Complex Address: Surprise Stadium, 15850 North Bullard Ave, Surprise, AZ 85374. **Telephone:** (623) 222-2000. **Seating Capacity:** 10,700. **Location:** I-10 West to Route 101 North, 101 North to Bell Road, left on Bell for five miles, stadium on left. **Hotel Address:** Wigwam Resort, 300 East Wigwam Blvd, Litchfield Park, Arizona 85340. **Telephone:** (623) 935-3811.

MINOR LEAGUE

Complex Address: Same as major league club. **Hotel Address:** Comfort Hotel and Suites, 13337 W Grand Ave, Surprise, AZ 85374. **Telephone:** (623) 583-3500.

LOS ANGELES ANGELS

MAJOR LEAGUE

Complex Address: Tempe Diablo Stadium, 2200 West Alameda Drive, Tempe, AZ 85282. **Telephone:** (480) 858-7500. **Fax:** (480) 438-7583. **Seating Capacity:** 9,558. **Location:** I-10 to exit 153B (48th Street), south one mile on 48th Street to Alameda Drive, left on Alameda.

MINOR LEAGUE

Complex Address: Tempe Diablo Minor League Complex, 2225 W Westcourt Way, Tempe, AZ 85282. **Telephone:** (480) 858-7558.

80 · Baseball America 2023 Directory

BaseballAmerica.com

MAJOR LEAGUES

LOS ANGELES DODGERS

MAJOR LEAGUE

Complex Address: Camelback Ranch, 10710 West Camelback Rd, Phoenix, AZ 85037. **Seating Capacity:** 13,000, plus standing room. **Location:** I-10 or I-17 to Loop 101 West or North, Take Exit 5, Camelback Road West to ballpark. **Telephone:** (623) 302-5000. **Hotel:** Unavailable.

MINOR LEAGUE

Complex/Hotel Address: Same as major league club.

MILWAUKEE BREWERS

MAJOR LEAGUE

Complex Address: Maryvale Baseball Park, 3600 N 51st Ave, Phoenix, AZ 85031. **Telephone:** (623) 245-5555. **Seating Capacity:** 9,000. **Location:** I-10 to 51st Ave, north on 51st Ave. **Hotel Address:** Unavailable.

MINOR LEAGUE

Complex Address: Maryvale Baseball Complex, 3805 N 53rd Ave, Phoenix, AZ 85031. **Telephone:** (623) 245-5600. **Hotel Address:** Unavailable.

OAKLAND ATHLETICS

MAJOR LEAGUE

Complex Address: Hohokam Stadium, 1235 North Center Street, Mesa, AZ 85201. **Telephone:** 480-907-5489. **Seating Capacity:** 10,000.

MINOR LEAGUE

Complex Address: Fitch Park, 160 East 6th Place, Mesa, AZ 85201. **Telephone:** 480-387-5800.

SAN DIEGO PADRES

MAJOR LEAGUE

Complex Address: Peoria Sports Complex, 8131 West Paradise Lane, Peoria, AZ 85382. **Telephone:** (619) 795-5720. **Fax:** (623) 486-7154. **Seating Capacity:** 12,000. **Location:** I-17 to Bell Road exit, west on Bell to 83rd Ave. **Hotel Address:** La Quinta Inn & Suites (623) 487-1900, 16321 N 83rd Avenue, Peoria, AZ 85382.

MINOR LEAGUE

Complex/Hotel: Country Inn and Suites (623) 879-9000, 20221 N 29th Avenue, Phoenix, AZ 85027.

SAN FRANCISCO GIANTS

MAJOR LEAGUE

Complex Address: Scottsdale Stadium, 7408 East Osborn Rd, Scottsdale, AZ 85251. **Telephone:** (480) 990-7972. **Fax:** (480) 990-2643. **Seating Capacity:** 11,500. **Location:** Scottsdale Road to Osborne Road, east on Osborne for a 1/2 mile. **Hotel Address:** Hilton Garden Inn Scottsdale Old Town, 7324 East Indian School Rd, Scottsdale, AZ 85251. **Telephone:** (480) 481-0400.

MINOR LEAGUE

Complex Address: Giants Minor League Complex 8045 E Camelback Road, Scottsdale, AZ 85251. **Telephone:** (480) 990-0052. **Fax:** (480) 990-2349.

SEATTLE MARINERS

MAJOR LEAGUE

Complex Address: Seattle Mariners, 15707 North 83rd Street, Peoria, AZ 85382. **Telephone:** (623) 776-4800. **Fax:** (623) 776-4829. **Seating Capacity:** 12,339. **Location:** Hwy 101 to Bell Road exit, east on Bell to 83rd Ave, south on 83rd Ave. **Hotel Address:** La Quinta Inn & Suites, 16321 N 83rd Ave, Peoria, AZ 85382. **Telephone:** (623) 487-1900.

MINOR LEAGUE

Complex Address: Peoria Sports Complex (1993), 15707 N 83rd Ave, Peoria, AZ 85382. **Telephone:** (623) 776-4800. **Fax:** (623) 776-4828. **Hotel Address:** Hampton Inn, 8408 W Paradise Lane, Peoria, AZ 85382. **Telephone:** (623) 486-9918.

TEXAS RANGERS

MAJOR LEAGUE

Complex Address: Surprise Stadium, 15754 North Bullard Ave, Surprise, AZ 85374. **Telephone:** (623) 266-8100. **Seating Capacity:** 10,714. **Location:** I-10 West to Route 101 North, 101 North to Bell Road, left at Bell for seven miles, stadium on left. **Hotel Address:** Residence Inn Surprise, 16418 N Bullard Ave, Surprise, AZ 85374. **Telephone:** (623) 249-6333.

MINOR LEAGUE

Complex Address: Same as major league club. **Hotel Address:** Holiday Inn Express and Suites Surprise, 16549 North Bullard Ave, Surprise AZ 85374.

MAJOR LEAGUES

GRAPEFRUIT LEAGUE

ATLANTA BRAVES

MAJOR LEAGUE

Complex Address: Cool Today Park, 18800 South West Villages Pkwy Venice, FL 34293. **Telephone:** (941) 413-5000. **Seating Capacity:** 8,000. **Location:** From I-75S: Take Exit 191 (River Rd Englewood/North Port). Keep Right onto River Road for 3.9 miles. Turn Right onto US 41/Tamiami Trail. In 1.5 miles take a left onto W. Villages Pkwy. Continue on W. Villages Pkwy for .75 miles.

From I-75N: Take Exit 191 (River Rd Englewood/North Port). Turn left onto River Road. Continue for 3.9 miles. Turn Right onto US 41/Tamiami Trail. In 1.5 miles take a left onto W. Villages Pkwy. Continue on W. Villages Pkwy for .75 miles.

Hotel Address: Unavailable.

MINOR LEAGUE

Complex Address: Same as major league club. **Telephone:** (407) 939-2232. **Fax:** (407) 939-2225. **Hotel Address:** Marriot Village at Lake Buena Vista, 8623 Vineland Ave, Orlando, FL 32821. **Telephone:** (407) 938-9001.

BALTIMORE ORIOLES

MAJOR LEAGUE

Complex Address: Ed Smith Stadium, 2700 12th Street, Sarasota, FL 34237. **Telephone:** (941) 893-6300. **Fax:** (941) 893-6377. **Seating Capacity:** 7,500. **Location:** I-75 to exit 210, West on Fruitville Road, right on Tuttle Avenue.

MINOR LEAGUE

Complex Address: Buck O'Neil Baseball Complex at Twin Lakes Park, 6700 Clark Rd, Sarasota, FL 34241. **Telephone:** (941) 923-1996.

BOSTON RED SOX

MAJOR LEAGUE

Complex Address: JetBlue Park at Fenway South, 11500 Fenway South Drive, Fort Myers, FL 33913. **Telephone:** (239) 334-4700. **Directions: From the North:** Take I-75 South to Exit 131 (Daniels Parkway); Make a left off the exit and go east for approximately two miles; JetBlue Park will be on your left. **From the South:** Take I-75 North to Exit 131 (Daniels Parkway); Make a right off exit and go east for approximately two miles; JetBlue Park will be on your left.

MINOR LEAGUE

Complex/Hotel Address: Fenway South, 11500 Fenway South Drive, Fort Myers, FL 33913.

DETROIT TIGERS

MAJOR LEAGUE

Complex Address: Joker Marchant Stadium, 2301 Lakeland Hills Blvd, Lakeland, FL 33805. **Telephone:** (863) 686-8075. **Seating Capacity:** 9,568. **Location:** I-4 to exit 33 (Lakeland Hills Boulevard).

MINOR LEAGUE

Complex Address: Tigertown, 2125 N Lake Ave, Lakeland, FL 33805. **Telephone:** (863) 686-8075.

HOUSTON ASTROS

MAJOR LEAGUE

Complex Address: The Ballpark of the Palm Beaches, 5444 Haverhill Road, West Palm Beach, FL 33407. **Telephone:** (844) 676-2017. **Seating Capacity:** 7,838. **Location:** Exit Florida's Turnpike onto Okeechobee Blvd. Proceed east to Haverhill Road turning left onto Haverhill Road. On game days, all vehicles may park in one of two grass parking areas. Proceed toward the stadium for disabled parking or drop-off. The North entrance on Haverhill Road will be right-out only.

MINOR LEAGUE

Complex Information: Same as major league club. **Hotel Address:** Unavailable.

MIAMI MARLINS

MAJOR LEAGUE

Complex Address: Roger Dean Stadium, 4751 Main Street, Jupiter, FL 33458. **Telephone:** (561) 775-1818. **Telephone:** (561) 799-1346. **Seating Capacity:** 7,000. **Location:** I-95 to exit 83, east on Donald Ross Road for one mile to Central Blvd, left at light, follow Central Boulevard to circle and take Main Street to Roger Dean Stadium. **Hotel Address:** Palm Beach Gardens Marriott, 4000 RCA Boulevard, Palm Beach Gardens, FL 33410. **Telephone:** (561) 622-8888. **Fax:** (561) 622-0052.

MINOR LEAGUE

Complex/Hotel Address: Same as major league club.

MINNESOTA TWINS

MAJOR LEAGUE

Complex Address: Centurylink Sports Complex/Hammond Stadium, 14100 Six Mile Cypress Parkway, Fort Myers, FL 33912. **Telephone:** (239) 533-7610. **Seating Capacity:** 8,100. **Location:** Exit 21 off I-75, west on Daniels Parkway, left on Six Mile Cypress Parkway. **Hotel Address:** Four Points by Sheraton, 13600 Treeline Avenue South, Ft. Myers, FL 33913. **Telephone:** (800) 338-9467.

MINOR LEAGUE

Complex/Hotel Address: Same as major league club.

NEW YORK METS

MAJOR LEAGUE

Complex Address: Tradition Field, 525 NW Peacock Blvd, Port St. Lucie, FL 34986. **Telephone:** (772) 871-2100. **Seating Capacity:** 7,000. **Location:** Exit 121C (St Lucie West Blvd) off I-95, east 1/4 mile, left onto NW Peacock. **Hotel Address:** Hilton Hotel, 8542 Commerce Centre Drive, Port St. Lucie, FL 34986. **Telephone:** (772) 871-6850.

MINOR LEAGUE

Complex Address: Same as major league club. **Hotel Address:** Main Stay Suites, 8501 Champions Way, Port St. Lucie, FL 34986. **Telephone:** (772) 460-8882.

NEW YORK YANKEES

MAJOR LEAGUE

Complex Address: George M. Steinbrenner Field, One Steinbrenner Drive, Tampa, FL 33614. **Telephone:** (813) 875-7753. **Hotel:** Unavailable.

82 · Baseball America 2023 Directory

BaseballAmerica.com

MAJOR LEAGUES

MINOR LEAGUE
Complex Address: Yankees Player Development/Scouting Complex, 3102 N Himes Ave, Tampa, FL 33607. **Telephone:** (813) 875-7569. **Hotel:** Unavailable.

PHILADELPHIA PHILLIES

MAJOR LEAGUE
Complex Address: BayCare Ballpark, 601 N Old Coachman Road, Clearwater, FL 33765. **Telephone:** (727) 467-4457. **Fax:** (727) 712-4498. **Seating Capacity:** 8,500. **Location:** Route 60 West, right on Old Coachman Road, ballpark on right after Drew Street. **Hotel Address:** Holiday Inn Express, 2580 Gulf to Bay Blvd, Clearwater, FL 33765. **Telephone:** (727) 797-6300. **Hotel Address:** La Quinta Inn, 21338 US 19 North, Clearwater, FL 33765. **Telephone:** (727) 799-1565.

MINOR LEAGUE
Complex Address: Carpenter Complex, 651 N Old Coachman Rd, Clearwater, FL 33765. **Telephone:** (727) 799-0503. **Fax:** (727) 726-1793. **Hotel Addresses:** Hampton Inn, 21030 US Highway 19 North, Clearwater, FL 34625. **Telephone:** (727) 797-8173. **Hotel Address:** Econolodge, 21252 US Hwy 19, Clearwater, FL 34625. **Telephone:** (727) 799-1569.

PITTSBURGH PIRATES

MAJOR LEAGUE
Stadium Address: 17th Ave West and Ninth Street West, Bradenton, FL 34205. **Seating Capacity:** 8,500. **Location:** US 41 to 17th Ave, west to 9th Street. **Telephone:** (941) 747-3031. **Fax:** (941) 747-9549.

MINOR LEAGUE
Complex: Pirate City, 1701 27th St E, Bradenton, FL 34208.

ST. LOUIS CARDINALS

MAJOR LEAGUE
Complex Address: Roger Dean Stadium, 4751 Main Street, Jupiter, FL 33458. **Telephone:** (561) 775-1818. **Fax:** (561) 799-1380. **Seating Capacity:** 7,000. **Location:** I-95 to exit 58, east on Donald Ross Road for 1⁄4 mile. **Hotel**

Address: Embassy Suites, 4350 PGA Blvd, Palm Beach Gardens, FL 33410. **Telephone:** (561) 622-1000.

MINOR LEAGUE
Complex: Same as major league club. **Hotel:** Double Tree Palm Beach Gardens. **Telephone:** (561) 622-2260.

TAMPA BAY RAYS

MAJOR LEAGUE
Stadium Address: Charlotte Sports Park, 2300 El Jobean Road, Port Charlotte, FL 33948. **Telephone:** (941) 206-4487. **Seating Capacity:** 6,823 (5,028 fixed seats). **Location:** I-75 to US-17 to US-41, turn left onto El Jobean Rd. **Hotel Address:** None.

MINOR LEAGUE
Complex: Same as major league club.

TORONTO BLUE JAYS

MAJOR LEAGUE
Stadium Address: Florida Auto Exchange Stadium, 373 Douglas Ave, Dunedin, FL 34698. **Telephone:** (727) 733-9302. **Seating Capacity:** 5,509. **Location:** US 19 North to Sunset Point; west on Sunset Point to Douglas Avenue; north on Douglas to Stadium; ballpark is on the southeast corner of Douglas and Beltrees.

MINOR LEAGUE
Complex Address: Bobby Mattick Training Center at Englebert Complex, 1700 Solon Ave, Dunedin, FL 34698. **Telephone:** (727) 734-8007. **Hotel Address:** Clarion Inn & Suites, 20967 US Highway 19 North Clearwater, FL 33765. **Telephone:** (727) 799-1181.

WASHINGTON NATIONALS

MAJOR LEAGUE
Stadium Address: The Ballpark of the Palm Beaches, 5444 N. Haverhill Road, West Palm Beach, FL 33407. **Telephone:** (844) 676-2017.

MINOR LEAGUE
Complex: Same as major league club.

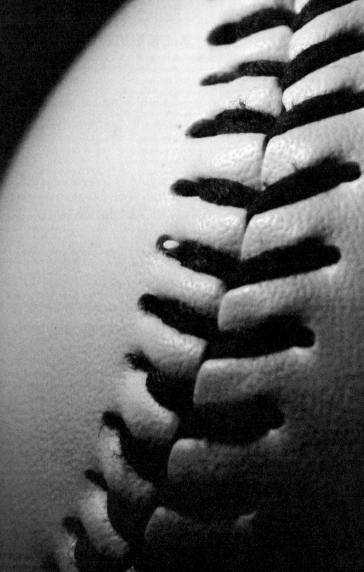

MINOR LEAGUES

MINOR LEAGUES

INTERNATIONAL LEAGUE

STADIUM INFORMATION

Club	Stadium	Opened	LF	CF	RF	Capacity	2022 Att.
Buffalo	Sahlen Field	1988	325	404	325	18,025	451,859
Charlotte	Truist Field	2015	325	400	315	10,002	531,465
Columbus	Huntington Park	2009	325	400	318	10,100	534,393
Durham	Durham Bulls Athletic Park	1995	305	400	327	10,000	472,090
Gwinnett	Coolray Field	2009	335	400	335	10,427	216,177
Indianapolis	Victory Field	1996	320	402	320	14,500	534,610
Iowa	Principal Park	1992	335	400	335	11,000	437,543
Jacksonville	121 Financial Ballpark	2003	321	420	317	11,000	358,094
Lehigh Valley	Coca-Cola Park	2008	336	400	325	10,000	544,220
Louisville	Louisville Slugger Field	2000	325	400	340	13,131	424,035
Memphis	AutoZone Park	2000	319	400	322	10,000	239,605
Nashville	First Horizon Park	2015	330	405	310	10,000	555,576
Norfolk	Harbor Park	1993	333	400	318	12,067	365,292
Omaha	Werner Park	2011	310	402	315	9,023	294,511
Rochester	Frontier Field	1997	335	402	325	10,840	432,580
St. Paul	CHS Field	2015	330	396	320	7,140	473,911
Scranton/WB	PNC Field	2013	330	408	330	10,000	331,286
Syracuse	NBT Bank Stadium	1997	330	400	330	11,671	335,490
Toledo	Fifth Third Field	2002	320	408	315	10,300	426,499
Worcester	Polar Park	2021	330	403	320	9,508	532,152

BUFFALO BISONS

Address: Sahlen Field, One James D. Griffin Plaza, Buffalo, NY 14203.
Telephone: (716) 846-2000. **Fax:** (716) 852-6530.
E-Mail Address: info@bisons.com. **Website:** www.bisons.com.
Affiliation (first year): Toronto Blue Jays (2013). **Years in League:** 1998-

OWNERSHIP/MANAGEMENT
Operated By: Rich Products Corp. **Principal Owner/President:** Robert Rich Jr. **Executive President, Rich Entertainment Group:** Melinda Rich. **President, Rich Entertainment Group, Senior Vice President, Finance & Family Office:** Joseph Segarra. **President, Rich Baseball Operations:** Mike Buczkowski. **VP/Secretary:** William Gisel. **Corporate Counsel:** Jill Bond, William Grieshober. **VP/Operations & Finance:** Kevin Parkinson. **VP/Food Service Operations:** Robert Free. **General Manager:** Anthony Sprague. **Assistant General Manager/Marketing & PR:** Brad Bisbing. **Director, Stadium Operations:** Brian Phillips. **Senior Accountant:** Chas Fiscella. **Accountants:** Amy Delaney, Tori Dwyer. **Director, Ticket Operations:** Mike Poreda. **Director, Corporate Sales:** Jim Harrington. **Director, Sales:** Geoff Lundquist. **Account Executives:** Sara Acker, Mark Gordon, Shaun O'Lay. **Ticket Office & Sales Coordinator:** Kimberly Milleville. **Retail, Licensing & Entertainment Manager:** Theresa Cerabone. **Manager, Baseball Communications & "Voice of the Bisons,":** Pat Malacaro. **Executive Assistant:** Tina Lesher. **Community Relations:** Gail Hodges. **Director, Food & Beverage Operations:** Sean Regan. **Food Service Operations Supervisor:** Curt Anderson. **Manager, Pub at the Park:** Kailey Gyorffy. **Kitchen Manager:** Dean Williams. **Commissary Manager:** Eugene Steele. **Chief Engineer:** Gerald Hamilton. **Head Groundskeeper:** Kelly Rensel. **Home Clubhouse/Baseball Operations Coordinator:** Scott Lesher. **Visiting Clubhouse Manager:** Steve Morris. **Graphic Designer:** Allison Marcano. **Digital & Social Content Coordinator:** Marissa Packard. **Entertainment & Promotions Coordinator:** Amanda Ballestero.

FIELD STAFF
Manager: TBA. **Hitting Coach:** TBA. **Pitching Coach:** TBA. **Fundamentals Coach:** TBA. **Athletic Trainer:** TBA. **Strength Coach:** TBA.

GAME INFORMATION
Radio Announcers: Pat Malacaro, Duke McGuire. **No. of Games Broadcast:** 150. **Flagship Station:** ESPN 1520. **PA Announcer:** Tom Burns, Jim McGee, Jerry Reo. **Official Scorers:** Kevin Lester, Jon Dare. **Stadium Name:** Sahlen Field. **Location:** From north, take I-190 to Elm Street exit, left onto Swan Street; From east, take I-190 West to exit 51 (Route 33) to end, exit at Oak Street, right onto Swan Street; From west, take I-190 East, exit 53 to I-90 North, exit at Elm Street, left onto Swan Street. **Standard Game Times:** 7:05 pm, Sun. 1:05. **Ticket Price Range:** TBA.

CHARLOTTE KNIGHTS

Address: Truist Field, 324 S. Mint St., Charlotte, NC 28202.
Telephone: (704) 274-8300. **Fax:** 704-274-8330.
E-Mail Address: knights@charlotteknights.com. **Website:** charlotteknights.com.

MINOR LEAGUES

Affiliation (first year): Chicago White Sox (1999). **Years in League:** 2021-

OWNERSHIP/MANAGEMENT
Operated by: Knights Baseball, LLC. **Principal Owners:** Don Beaver, Bill Allen. **Chief Operating Officer:** Dan Rajkowski. **General Manager:** Rob Egan. **Director, Special Projects:** Julie Clark. **Finance/HR Manager:** Sara Maple. **VP, Communications:** Tommy Viola. **VP, Sponsorship Sales:** Marty Steele. **VP, Marketing:** Matt DuBois. **VP, Stadium Operations:** Tom Gorter. **VP, Ticket Sales:** Matt Harper. **VP, Special Events:** Grace Eng. **Senior Director of Game Entertainment & Creative Services:** Tommy Bean. **Creative/IT Director:** Bill Walker. **Director, Field Operations:** Matt Parrott. **Director, Broadcasting/Team Travel:** Matt Swierad. **Director, Community Relations:** Megan Smithers. **Director, Video Production:** Cameron Moist. **Director, Special Events:** Troy Rodrigues. **Director, Ticket Sales:** Alex Michel. **Director, Merchandise/Retail Operations:** Ryan Echerd. **Business Development Executives:** Ryan Meagher, Ryan Sorrow. **Partnership Services Manager:** Taylor Fike. **Group Sales Manager:** T.J. King. **Ticket Operations Manager:** Leighton Foster. **Hospitality Sales Manager:** Cooper Kinsey. **Ticket Sales and Service Representative:** Jack Doran. **Ticket Sales Account Executives:** Bradley Fabian, Kelsey Kandil, Victoria Liefert. **Promotions Manager:** Chris Dillon. **Community & Promotions Coordinator:** Jules D'Aiello. **Digital Media and Graphic Design Manager:** Jason Furst. **Manager of Ticket Services:** Emily Mitchell. **Partnership Services Coordinator:** Jacelyn Shepherd. **Mascot Coordinator:** Phillip Potter. **Operations Manager:** Matt Fisher. **Field Operations Manager:** Nick Verzal. **Assistant Manager, Clubhouse/Ballpark Operations:** Corbin Balzer. **Assistant, Groundskeeper:** Julian Brown. **Graphics and Social Media Assistant:** Kelly Teseny. **Front Desk Receptionist/Administrative Assistant:** Shelby Reasor.

FIELD STAFF
Manager: Justin Jirschele. **Hitting Coach:** Cameron Seitzer. **Pitching Coach:** Matt Zaleski. **Fundamentals Coach:** TBA. **Athletic Trainer:** TBA. **Strength Coach:** TBA.

GAME INFORMATION
Radio Announcers: Matt Swierad, Mike Pacheco. **No. of Games Broadcast:** 150. **Flagship Station:** 730 The Game ESPN Charlotte. **PA Announcer:** Ken Conrad. **Official Scorers:** Jerry Bowers, Jim Morrison, Richard Walker. **Stadium Name:** Truist Field. **Location:** Exit 10 off Interstate 77. **Ticket Price Range:** $12-$24. **Visiting Club Hotel:** DoubleTree by Hilton Charlotte, 895 W. Trade St., Charlotte, NC 28202.

COLUMBUS CLIPPERS

Address: 330 Huntington Park Lane, Columbus, OH 43215.
Telephone: (614) 462-5250. **Fax:** (614) 462-3271. **Tickets:** (614) 462-2757.
E-Mail Address: info@clippersbaseball.com. **Website:** www.clippersbaseball.com.
Affiliation (first year): Cleveland Guardians (2009). **Years in League:** 2021-

OWNERSHIP/MANAGEMENT
President & General Manager: Ken Schnacke. **Vice President, Assistant GM:** Mark Galuska. **Vice President, Business:** Mark Warren. **Vice President, Tickets:** Scott Ziegler. **Executive Assistant:** Ashly Held. **Team Historian:** Joe Santry. **Director, Merchandising:** Krista Oberlander. **Director, Ticket Operations:** Eddie Langhenry. **Director, Media & Ticket Services:** Chris Sprague. **Director, Ticket Sales:** Kevin Daniels. **Assistant Director, Ticket Sales:** Max Dreisbach. **Director, Group Sales:** Matt Harrison. **Assistant Director, Group Sales:** Jordan Aronowitz. **Director, Finance & Administration:** Ashley Ramirez. **Director, Administration & Travel:** Shelby White. **Director, Multimedia:** Larry Mitchell. **Assistant Director, Multimedia:** Pat Welch. **Director, Marketing/In-Game Entertainment:** Steve Kuilder. **Director, Social Media:** Aaliyah Phounsavath. **Marketing Coordinator:** Ian Gillen. **Director, Game Operations/Creative Services:** Yoshi Ando. **Director, Pressbox Operations/Statistics:** Anthony Slosser. **Director, Sales:** Austin Smith. **Director, Corporate Sales:** TBA. **Director, Ballpark Operations:** Tom Rinto. **Director, Group Sales:** Spencer Harrison. **Director, Community Relations:** Emily Poynter. **Director, Website/Media Relations:** Matt Leininger. **Ballpark Superintendent:** Gary Delozier. **Maintenance Supervisor:** Curt Marcum. **Director, Event Planning:** Micki Shier. **Director, Broadcasting:** Ryan Mitchell. **Director, Field Operations:** Wes Ganobcik. **Manager, Field Operations:** L.J. Black. **Supervisor of Grounds:** TBA. **GM, Levy Food & Beverage:** Jeff Roberts. **Support Services:** Marvin Dill, Beth Morris. **Home Clubhouse:** John McCausland. **Visiting Clubhouse:** Adam Meader.

FIELD STAFF
Manager: Andy Tracy. **Pitching Coach:** Owen Dew. **Pitching Strategist:** TBA. **Hitting Coach:** Junior Betances. **Bench Coach:** TBA. **Trainer:** Jeremy Heller. **Strength Coach:** TBA. **Video Coordinator:** TBA.

GAME INFORMATION
Stadium Name: Huntington Park. **No. of Games Broadcast:** 150. **Location: From North:** South on I-71 to I-670 west, exit at Neil Avenue, turn left at intersection onto Neil Avenue. **From South:** North on I-71, exit at Front Street (#100A); turn left at intersection onto Front Street, turn left onto Nationwide Blvd. **From East:** West on I-70, exit at Fourth Street, continue on Fulton Street to Front Street, turn right onto Front Street, turn left onto Nationwide Blvd. **From West:** East on I-70, exit at Fourth Street, continue on Fulton Street to Front Street, turn right onto Front Street, turn left onto Nationwide Blvd. **Ticket Price Range:** $6-21. **Visiting Club Hotel:** Sonesta Columbus Downtown (formerly Crowne Plaza), 33 East Nationwide Blvd, Columbus, OH 43215. **Telephone:** (614) 461-4100. **Visiting Club Hotel:** Drury Hotels Columbus Convention Center, 88 East Nationwide Blvd, Columbus, OH 43215. **Telephone:** (614) 221-7008. **Visiting Club Hotel:** Hyatt Regency Downtown, 350 North High Street, Columbus, OH 43215. **Telephone:** (614) 463-1234. **Visiting Club Hotel:** Red Roof Inn, 111 East Nationwide Blvd., Columbus Ohio 43215. **Telephone:** 614-224-6539.

MINOR LEAGUES

DURHAM BULLS

Office Address: 409 Blackwell St., Durham, NC 27701.
Mailing Address: PO Box 507, Durham, NC 27702
Telephone: (919) 687-6500. **Fax:** (919) 687-6560
Website: durhambulls.com. **Twitter:** @DurhamBulls
Affiliation (first year): Tampa Bay Rays (1998). **Years in League:** 2021-

OWNERSHIP/MANAGEMENT
Operated by: Capitol Broadcasting Company, Inc. **President/COO:** Jimmy Goodmon. **Vice President of Baseball Operations:** Mike Birling. **Assistant General Manager, Operations:** Scott Strickland. **Business Manager:** Theresa Stocking. **Senior Accountant:** Jordan Tucker. **Senior & Special Projects Accountant:** Nick Bornhoft. **Sponsorship Account Executives:** Jackson Faerber, Sara Killeen. **Head Groundskeeper:** Cameron Brendle. **Head Groundskeeper, Durham Athletic Park:** Luke Lewallen. **Stadium Operations Manager:** Will Bender. **Director, Promotions:** Leslie Martin. **Video & Digital Production Manager:** Patrick Norwood. **Digital & Social Content Manager:** Andrew Green. **Production Designer:** Paxton Rembis. **Mascot & Community Relations Coordinator:** Eric Topolewski. **Manager of Membership Services:** Timothy Troy. **Account Executive, Corporate Sales:** Austin DeFilippo. **Account Executives, Corporate Sales:** Tiler Dixon, Kyle Nekoloff. **Account Executive, Group Sales:** Andre Jackson. **Box Office Manager:** Erin Thompson. **Director of Merchandising and Team Travel:** Bryan Wilson. **Assistant Director of Merchandise, E-Commerce:** Emily Goddard. **Director of Food and Beverage:** Dave Levey. **Assistant Director of Food and Beverage:** Todd Feneley. **Concessions Manager:** Andrew Houston. **Hospitality Executive Chef:** Derek Crayton.

FIELD STAFF
Manager: Michael Johns. **Pitching Coach:** Brian Reith. **Hitting Coach:** Kenny Hook. **Bench Coach:** TBA. **Athletic Trainers:** TBA. **Strength Coach:** TBA.

GAME INFORMATION
Broadcasters: Patrick Kinas. **No. of Games Broadcast:** 150. **Flagship Station:** 96.5 FM and 99.3 FM. **PA Announcer:** Tony Riggsbee. **Official Scorer:** Brent Belvin. **Stadium Name:** Durham Bulls Athletic Park. **Location:** From Raleigh, I-40 West to Highway 147 North, exit 12B to Willard, two blocks on Willard to stadium; From I-85, Gregson Street exit to downtown, left on Chapel Hill Street, right on Mangum Street. **Standard Game Times:** 7:05 pm, Sat. 6:35 pm, Sun. 5:05 pm. **Ticket Price Range:** $7-14. **Visiting Club Hotel:** TBA. **Telephone:** TBA.

GWINNETT STRIPERS

Office Address: 2500 Buford Drive, Lawrenceville, GA 30043.
Mailing Address: P.O. Box 490310, Lawrenceville, GA 30049.
Telephone: (678) 277-0300. **Fax:** (678) 277-0338.
E-Mail Address: stripersinfo@braves.com. **Website:** www.gostripers.com.
Affiliation (first year): Atlanta Braves (1966). **Years in League:** 2021-

OWNERSHIP/MANAGEMENT
Ownership: Diamond Baseball Holdings, LLC. **Vice President & General Manager:** Erin McCormick. **Senior Director of Ticket Sales:** Peter Billups. **Office Manager:** Tyra Williams. **Ticket Sales Manager:** Zack Mandelblatt. **Account Executives, Ticket Sales:** Will Johnson, Taylor Poff, Virginia Nelle Reid, Christian Wilkes. **Ticket Operations Coordinator:** Richard Moseley. **Media Relations Manager & Broadcaster:** Dave Lezotte. **Creative Services Manager:** Nick Gosen. **Marketing Manager:** Kyle Kamerbeek. **Stadium Operations Manager:** Avery Kesler. **Facilities Engineer:** Gary Hoopaugh. **Director of Sports Turf Management:** McClain Murphy. **Sports Turf Coordinator:** Kiley Coursey. **Home Clubhouse Manager:** Nick Dixon. **Merchandise Coordinator:** Malik Perkins. **Director of Operations, Professional Sports Catering:** Chiara Perkins.

FIELD STAFF
Manager: Matt Tuiasosopo. **Hitting Coach:** Carlos Mendez. **Pitching Coach:** Craig Bjornson. **Coach:** TBD. **Athletic Trainer:** TBD

GAME INFORMATION
Radio Announcer: Dave Lezotte. **No. of Games Broadcast:** 150. **Flagship Station:** My Country 99.3 WCON (streaming online only at MyCountry993.com). **PA Announcer:** Kevin Kraus. **Official Scorers:** Jack Woodard, Guy Curtright, Stan Awtrey, Phil Engel. **Stadium Name:** Coolray Field. **Location:** I-85 (at Exit 115, State Road 20 West) and I-985 (at Exit 4); follow signs to park. **Ticket Price Range:** $8-30 (advance) or $11-33 (day-of-game). **Visiting Club Hotels:** Courtyard by Marriott Buford/Mall of Georgia, 1405 Mall of Georgia Boulevard, Buford, GA 30519. **Telephone:** (678) 745-3380. Fairfield Inn & Suites Atlanta Buford/Mall of Georgia, 1355 Mall of Georgia Boulevard, Buford, GA 30519. **Telephone:** (678) 714-0248.

INDIANAPOLIS INDIANS

Address: 501 W. Maryland Street, Indianapolis, IN 46225.
Telephone: (317) 269-3542. **Fax:** (317) 269-3541.
E-Mail Address: Indians@IndyIndians.com. **Website:** www.indyindians.com.

MINOR LEAGUES

Affiliation (first year): Pittsburgh Pirates (2005). **Years in League:** 2021-

OWNERSHIP/MANAGEMENT

Chairman of the Board & Chief Executive Officer: Bruce Schumacher. **President & General Manager:** Randy Lewandowski. **Chairman Emeritus:** Max Schumacher. **Assistant General Manager, Corporate Sales & Marketing:** Joel Zawacki. **Assistant General Manager, Tickets & Operations:** Matt Guay. **Director, Business Systems & Talent:** Bryan Spisak. **Business Intelligence Analyst:** Bill Fulton. **Business Operations Manager:** Sarah Haynes. **Business Operations Coordinator:** Sana Beotra. **Guest Relations Coordinator:** Michelle Treviño. **Director, Communications:** Cheyne Reiter. **Communications Manager:** Anna Kayser. **Social Media Coordinator:** Katie Bostic. **Voice of the Indians:** Howard Kellman. **Director, Creative:** Adam Pintar. **Videographer:** Alex Leachman. **Graphic Designer:** Ryan Lane. **Director, Marketing:** Kim Stoebick. **Senior Marketing Manager:** Heidi Gahm. **Digital Marketing Manager:** Max Freeman. **Marketing Coordinator:** Hannah O'Brien. **Game Operations Coordinator:** Eric Barnes. **Mascot Program Coordinator:** Jake Martinez. **Director, Corporate Sales:** Christina Toler. **Corporate Sales Account Executive:** Chandler McKinney. **Director, Community & Partnership Activation:** Kylie Kinder. **Community Outreach Coordinator:** Mary Mueller. **Partnership Activation Coordinator:** Ben Kayser. **Senior Director, Facilities:** Tim Hughes. **Senior Facilities Manager:** Allan Danehy. **Facilities Maintenance Tech:** Kyle Winters. **Director, Field Operations:** Joey Stevenson. **Field Operations Manager:** Nick Farfan. **Field Operations Coordinator:** Bryce Huebner. **Director, Merchandise:** Mark Schumacher. **Merchandise Manager:** Patrick Westrick. **Director, Stadium Operations:** Tyler Jacobs. **Stadium Operations Manager:** Kim Duplak. **Operations Support:** Ki Hubbard, Sandra Reaves. **Home Clubhouse Manager:** Bobby Martin. **Visiting Clubhouse Manager:** Jeremy Martin. **Director, Ticket Sales:** Chad Bohm. **Director of Tickets, Premium Services & Events:** Kerry Vick. **Stadium Events Manager:** Paige McClung. **Premium & Ticket Services Manager:** Kathryn Bobel.

FIELD STAFF

Manager: Miguel Perez. **Pitching Coach:** Dan Meyer. **Hitting Coach:** Eric Munson. **Bench Coach:** Dallas McPherson. **Bullpen Coach:** Drew Benes. **Integrated Performance Coach:** Brady Conlan. **Athletic Trainer:** Tyler Brooks. **Strength & Conditioning Coach:** Alan Burr.

GAME INFORMATION

Radio Announcers: Howard Kellman, Andrew Kappes, Jack McMullen. **Flagship Station:** Fox Sports 1260.
PA Announcer: David Pygman. **Official Scorers:** Ed Holdaway, Kim Rogers, Will Roleson, Geoff Sherman, Jeff Williams. **Stadium Name:** Victory Field. **Location:** I-70 to West Street exit, north on West Street to ballpark; I-65 to Martin Luther King and West Street exit, south on West Street to ballpark. **Standard Game Times:** 7:05 pm; 6:35 (select weekdays and Sat. in April/May/Sept.); 1:35 (Wed./Sun.). **Ticket Price Range:** $12-18. **Visiting Club Hotel:** Fairfield Indianapolis Downtown, 501 W. Washington Street, Indianapolis, IN 46204. **Telephone:** (317) 636-7678.

IOWA CUBS

Address: One Line Drive, Des Moines IA 50309.
Telephone: (515) 243-6111. **Fax:** (515) 243-5152.
Website: www.iowacubs.com.
Affiliation (first year): Chicago Cubs (1981). **Years in League:** 2021-

OWNERSHIP/MANAGEMENT

Owner: Diamond Baseball Holdings. **Executive Chairman:** Pat Battle. **Chief Executive Officer:** Peter B. Freund. **President/General Manager:** Sam Bernabe. **Assistant GM:** Randy Wehofer. **Manager, Media/Public Relations:** Colin Connolly. **Broadcaster/Account Executive, Partnerships:** Alex Cohen. **Manager, Video Operations & Production:** Justin Walters. **Manager, Creative Services:** Matt Evers. **Manager, Marketing:** Deonne Witherspoon. **VP, Premium Ticket Sales & Partnerships:** Brent Conkel. **Manager, Ticket Operations:** Clayton Grandquist. **Manager, Group Ticket Sales/Account Executive, Partnerships:** Jason Gellis. **Account Executive, Partnerships:** John Rodgers. **Account Executives, Ticket Sales:** Amanda Dale, Sam Jochimsen, & Neysa Halverson. **Director, Retail Merchandise:** Lisa Hufford. **Manager, Retail Merchandise:** Katie Kral. **VP, Stadium Operations:** Jeff Tilley. **Managers, Stadium Operations:** Andrew Quillin, Dustin Halderson, & Josh Stephens. **VP, Field Operations:** Chris Schlosser. **Assistant Managers, Field Operations:** Brooks Montange & Bridger Claassen. **Outside Grounds:** Shari Kramer. **Chief Technology Officer:** Ryan Clutter. **Manager, Special Projects:** Scott Sailor. **VP, Finance:** Sue Tollefson. **Manager, Accounting:** Lori Heaberlin.

FIELD STAFF

Manager: Marty Pevey. **Hitting Coach:** John Mallee. **Pitching Coach:** Ron Villone. **Bench Coach:** Eric Patterson. **Athletic Trainers:** Logan Severson and Ed Halbur. **Strength/Conditioning:** Nathan Garza.

GAME INFORMATION

Radio Announcer: Alex Cohen. **No. of Games Broadcast:** 150. **Flagship Station:** AM 940 KPSZ. **PA Announcers:** Mark Pierce, Corey Coon, Rick Stageman, Joe Hammen. **Official Scorers:** Michael Pecina, James Hilchen, Steve Mohr. **Stadium Name:** Principal Park. **Location:** I-80 or I-35 to I-235, to Third Street exit, south on Third Street, left on Line Drive. **Standard Game Times:** Tues./Thurs. 6:38, Wed. 12:08, Fri. 7:08, Sat. 6:08, Sun. 1:08. **Ticket Price Range:** $6-40. **Visiting Hotel:** Hampton Inn and Suites Downtown, 120 SW Water Street, Des Moines IA 50309. **Telephone:** (515) 244-1650.

MINOR LEAGUES

JACKSONVILLE JUMBO SHRIMP

Office Address: 301 A. Philip Randolph Blvd, Jacksonville, FL 32202.
Telephone: (904) 358-2846. **Fax:** (904) 358-2845.
E-Mail Address: info@jaxshrimp.com. **Website:** www.jaxshrimp.com.
Affiliation (first year): Miami Marlins (2009). **Years In League:** 2021–.

OWNERSHIP/MANAGEMENT
Operated by: Jacksonville Baseball LLC.
Owner & Chief Executive Officer: Ken Babby. **Executive Assistant to Ken Babby:** Jill Popov. **President, Fast Forward Sports Group:** Jim Pfander. **Chief Human Resources Office:** Leatrice Buck. **Chief Financial Officer:** Shawn Carlson. **Executive Vice President/General Manager:** Harold Craw. **Vice President, Marketing and Media:** Noel Blaha. **Senior Vice President, Sales:** Linda McNabb. **Assistant General Manager:** Matt Goudreau. **Director, Field Operations:** Christian Galen. **Director, Promotions & Special Events:** David Ratz. **Director of Corporate Partnerships:** Terry O'Grady. **Director of Ticket Operations:** Peter Ercey. **Director of Broadcasting and Media Relations:** Scott Kornberg. **Assistant Director, Food & Beverage:** Nevious Love. **Stadium Operations Manager:** Tom Snyder. **Creative Services Manager:** Brian DeLettre. **Director of Merchandise:** Brennan Earley. **Community Relations Manager:** Carolyn Bosworth. **Accounting Manager:** Bryson Lenderman. **Box Office Manager:** Cody Davis. **Partner Services Manager:** Holden Hitchcock. **Chef, Food & Beverage:** Travis Bosche. **Account Executives:** Marc Spera, Zachary Quillian, Devin Walker. **Stadium Operations Assistant:** Matthew Maynard. **Field Operations Assistant:** Chris Campbell. **Finance Assistant:** Patrick Jordan. **Travel Coordinator/Office Administrator:** Christine Collins. **Broadcast & Media Relations Assistant:** Matt Davis. **Payroll Coordinator:** Teresa Lively-Hall. **Video Manager:** Victor Di Diego

FIELD STAFF
Manager: Daren Brown. **Pitching Coach:** Jeremy Powell. **Hitting Coach:** Greg Colbrunn. **Defensive Coach:** Jose Ceballos. **Athletic Trainer:** Eric Reigelsberger. **Strength & Conditioning Coach:** Tim Rodmaker.

GAME INFORMATION
Radio Announcer: Scott Kornberg. **No. of Games Broadcast:** 150. **Flagship Station:** ESPN 690.
PA Announcer: John Leard. **Official Scorer:** Jason Eliopulos. **Stadium Name:** 121 Financial Ballpark. **Location:** I-95 South to Martin Luther King Parkway exit, follow Gator Bowl Blvd around TIAA Bank Field; I-95 North to Exit 347 (Emerson Street), go right to Hart Bridge Expressway, take Sports Complex exit, left at light to stop sign, take left and follow around TIAA Bank Field; From Mathews Bridge, take A Philip Randolph exit, right on A Philip Randolph, straight to ballpark. **Standard Game Times:** 7:05 pm, Sat. 6:35 pm, Sun. 3:05 pm. **Ticket Price Range:** $5-$28. **Visiting Club Hotel:** Doubletree by Hilton Hotel Jacksonville Riverfront, 1201 Riverplace Blvd., Jacksonville, FL 32207. **Telephone:** (904) 398-8800.

LEHIGH VALLEY IRONPIGS

Address: 1050 IronPigs Way, Allentown, PA 18109
Telephone: (610) 841-7447. **Fax:** (610) 841-1509
E-Mail Address: info@ironpigsbaseball.com. **Website:** www.ironpigsbaseball.com.
Affiliation (first year): Philadelphia Phillies (2008). **Years in League:** 2021–.

OWNERSHIP/MANAGEMENT
Ownership: LV Baseball LP. **President & General Manager:** Kurt Landes. **Administrative Assistant:** Pat Golden. **Senior Vice President, Administration:** Michelle Perl. **Director, Finance:** Eric Hinkle. **Manager, Finance:** Alexis Junge. **Vice President, Marketing & Entertainment:** Matthew Bari. **Director, Promotions & Entertainment:** TBA. **Director, Multimedia Design & Entertainment:** Kevin Whitehead. **Director, Digital Media & Communications:** TBA. **Manager, Multimedia & Design:** Alex Schempp. **Manager, IronPigs Charities:** Matt Sommers. **Manager, Media Relations & Communications:** TBA. **Manager, Community Relations:** Aaron Weisberg. **Vice President, Ticket Sales:** Andy Beuster. **Director, Ticket Operations:** Brittany Balonis. **Director, Group Sales:** Ryan Hines. **Director, Memberships:** Nick DiPaola. **Senior Manager, Ticket Operations & Analytics:** Collin DeJong. **Senior Manager, Group Sales:** Chad Mazepa, Daniel Sterenberg. **Senior Manager, Corporate Ticket Sales:** Dante Strella. **Manager, Ticket Coordinator:** Chris DeSpirito. **Manager, Group Sales:** Zach Groover, Nikki Homanick. **Manager, Corporate Tickets:** Chase Adams, Reagan McKeon. **Manager, Memberships:** Braeden Keith, Stephanie Kinsella. **Senior Director, Corporate Partnerships:** TBA. **Senior Manager, Sponsorship Services:** Emily Frajdofer. **Senior Manager, Corporate Partnerships:** Jordan Perrine. **Manager, Corporate Partnerships:** Molly Payne, Ryan Davey.

FIELD STAFF
Manager: Anthony Contreras. **Pitching Coach:** Cesar Ramos. **Hitting Coach:** Joe Thurston. **Bench Coach:** Pat Listach. **Athletic Trainer:** Andrew Dodgson. **Strength/Conditioning Coach:** Mike Lidge

GAME INFORMATION
Radio Announcers: Pat McCarthy. **No. of Games Broadcast:** 150. **Flagship Radio Station:** FOX Sports Radio 1230 AM & 94.7 FM. **Television Station:** Service Electric Network. **Television Announcers:** Mike Zambelli, Steve Degler, Doug Heater. **No. of Games Televised:** 75 (all home games). **PA Announcer:** Justin Choate. **Official Scorers:** Mike Falk, Jack Logic, David Sheriff, Dick Shute. **Stadium Name:** Coca-Cola Park. **Location:** Take US 22 to exit for Airport Road South, head south, make right on. American Parkway, left into stadium. **Standard Game Times:** 7:05 pm, Sat. 6:35 pm, Sun. 1:35.

MINOR LEAGUES

LOUISVILLE BATS

Address: 401 E Main St, Louisville, KY 40202.
Telephone: (502) 212-2287. **Fax:** (502) 515-2255.
E-Mail Address: info@batsbaseball.com. **Website:** www.batsbaseball.com.
Affiliation (first year): Cincinnati Reds (2000). **Years in League:** 1998 - Present

OWNERSHIP/MANAGEMENT
Chairman: Stuart and Jerry Katzoff (MC Sports). **President:** Greg Galliete. **Executive Vice President, Controller:** Michele Anderson. **Vice President of Stadium Operations:** Brett Myers. **Vice President of Ticket Sales:** David Barry. **Public Relations Manager:** Conor Mullaney. **Marketing and Community Outreach Manager:** Sam Delph. **Head Clubhouse Manager:** TJ Leonard. **Club Physicians:** Walter Badenhausen, M.D.; John A. Lach, Jr., M.D. **Club Dentist:** Pat Carroll, D.M.D. **Chaplains:** Jose Castillo.

FIELD STAFF
Manager: Pat Kelly. **Pitching Coach:** Virgil Vasquez. **Hitting Coach:** Alex Pelaez. **Coach:** Mike Jacobs. **Coach:** Vince Harrison. **Athletic Trainer:** Steve Gober. **Strength/Conditioning Coach:** Dan Donohue.

GAME INFORMATION
Radio Announcers: Nick Curran, Jim Kelch. **No. of Games Broadcast:** 150. **Flagship Station:** WXVW 1450 AM and 96.1 FM. **PA Announcer:** Charles Gazaway. **Official Scorers:** Nick Evans, Neil Rohrer, Ryan Ritchey, Jeff Hollis, Ed Peak. **Stadium Name:** Louisville Slugger Field. **Location:** I-64 and I-71 to I-65 South/North to Brook Street exit, right on Market Street, left on Jackson Street; stadium on Main Street between Jackson and Preston. **Ticket Price Range:** $9-55. **Visiting Club Hotel:** Omni Hotel, 400 South 2nd Street, Louisville, KY 40202. **Telephone:** (502) 313-6664.

MEMPHIS REDBIRDS

Office Address: 198 Union, Memphis, TN 38103.
Stadium Address: 198 Union Ave, Memphis, TN 38103.
Telephone: (901) 721-6000. **Fax:** (901) 328-1102.
Website: www.memphisredbirds.com.
Affiliation (first year): St. Louis Cardinals (1998). **Years in League:** 2021-

OWNERSHIP/MANAGEMENT
Ownership: Peter B. Freund. **President/General Manager:** Craig Unger. **Vice President, Stadium and Baseball Operations:** Mike Voutsinas. **Manager, Group Sales:** Dylan Powers. **Manager, Field Operations:** Tylor Meppelink. **Manager, Ticket Operations:** Michael Magwood. **Director, Corporate Sales:** Tyler Gilles. **Coordinator, Integrated Marketing:** Sarah Jent. **Graphic Designer:** John Privitera. **Manager, Retail Operations:** Kirsten Porch. **Accounting Manager:** Cindy Neal.

FIELD STAFF
Manager: Ben Johnson. **Hitting Coach:** Howie Clark. **Pitching Coach:** Darwin Marrero. **Coach:** Will Peterson. **Trainer:** Dan Martin. **Strength & Conditioning:** Jacqueline Grover.

GAME INFORMATION
Radio Announcer: TBA **No. of Games Broadcast:** 150. **Flagship Station:** online. **PA Announcer:** Greg Ratliff. **Official Scorers:** TBA. **Stadium Name:** AutoZone Park. **Location:** North on I-240, exit at Union Avenue West, one and half miles to park. **Standard Game Times:** Mon-Wed. 6:45, Thu-Fri. 7:10, Sat. 6:35, Sun 2:05. **Ticket Price Range:** $9-24. **Visiting Club Hotel:** TBA.

NASHVILLE SOUNDS

Address: 19 Junior Gilliam Way, Nashville, TN 37219.
Telephone: (615) 690-HITS. **Fax:** (615) 256-5684.
E-Mail address: info@nashvillesounds.com. **Website:** www.nashvillesounds.com.
Affiliation (first year): Milwaukee Brewers (2021). **Years in League:** 2021-

OWNERSHIP/MANAGEMENT
Operated By: MFP Baseball. **Owners:** Frank Ward, Masahiro Honzawa. **GM/Chief Operating Officer:** Adam English. **Asst. GM/VP, Operations:** Doug Scopel. **VP, Corporate Partnerships:** Danielle Gaw. **VP, Ticket Sales and Service:** Taylor Fisher. **Director, Accounting:** Katie Sigman. **Director, Marketing:** Abby Holman. **Director, Broadcasting:** Jeff Hem. **Director, Creative Services:** Neil Rosan. **Director, Stadium Operations:** Hannah Onken. **Director, Ticket Sales:** Kevin Kurowski. **Director, Ticket Operations:** Kyle Hargrove. **Director, Retail:** Wade Becker. **Director, Special Events:** Sierra Siegel. **Manager, Fan Experience and Community Relations:** Travis Williams. **Manager, Business Development:** Jon Brownfield. **Managaers, Partnership Activation:** Nicole Cholski and Benjamin Whalen. **Manager, Entertainment and Promotions:** Karly Deland. **Coordinator, Group Theme:** Rae Nead. **Manager, Merchandise:** Frank Paruzynski. **Manager, Communications:** Collin Perry. **Manager, Senior Stadium Operations:** Caleb Yorks. **Managers,**

MINOR LEAGUES

Stadium Operations: Colin Brennan and Diana Graber Dovenspike. **Manager, Inside Sales:** Kelsen Adeni. **Account Executive:** Reghan Brands, Jay Evans, Jacob Friehauf, Ben Whalin, Kelsey Wisner, Luke Povolny. **Manager, Ticket Operations:** Lyndsey Tarver. **Coordinator, Ticket Operations:** Nicholas Carr. **Coordinator, Mascot:** Buddy Yelton. **Coordinator, Event Prouduction:** Hunter Gipson. **Coordinator, Digital Marketing:** Shannon Gadomski. **Lead Graphic Designer:** Drew Gibby. **Ticket Sales Representatives:** Sarah Norton and John Siebert.

FIELD STAFF
Manager: Rick Sweet. **Hitting Coach:** Al LeBoeuf. **Pitching Coach:** Jeremy Accardo. **Coach:** Ned Yost IV. **Coach:** Liu Rodriguez. **Bullpen Coach:** Patrick McGuff. **Athletic Trainer:** Jeff Paxson. **Assistant Athletic Trainer:** Jon Harris. **Strength & Conditioning Specialist:** Andrew Emmick. **Assistant Strength & Conditioning Specialist:** Jonathan Christensen.

GAME INFORMATION
Radio Announcer: Jeff Hem. **No. of Games Broadcast:** 150. **Flagship Station:** 94.9 ESPN. **Official Scorers:** Eric Jones, Cody Bush, Eric Moyer. **Stadium Name:** First Horizon Park. **Location:** I-65 to exit 85 (Rosa L Parks Blvd) and head south; Turn left on Jefferson St, then turn right onto Rep. John Lewis Way, then turn left on Jackson St. **Standard Game Times:** 7:05, 6:35, 6:05, 2:05. **Ticket Price Range:** $10-42. **Visiting Club Hotel:** Sonesta Nashville. 600 Marriott Drive, Nashville, TN 37214.

NORFOLK TIDES

Address: 150 Park Ave, Norfolk, VA 23510.
Telephone: (757) 622-2222. **Fax:** (757) 624-9090.
E-Mail Address: receptionist@norfolktides.com. **Website:** www.norfolktides.com.
Affiliation (first year): Baltimore Orioles (2007). **Years in League:** 2021-

OWNERSHIP/MANAGEMENT
Operated By: Tides Baseball Club Inc. **President:** Ken Young. **General Manager:** Joe Gregory. **Assistant General Managers:** Mike Watkins, Mike Zeman. **Director, Ticket Operations:** Sze Fong. **Director, Ticket Sales:** John Muszkewycz. **Director of Finance and Human Resources:** Dawn Coutts. **Head Groundskeeper:** Kenny Magner. **Home Clubhouse Manager:** Adam Sehlmeyer. **Visiting Clubhouse Manager:** Jack Brenner.

FIELD STAFF
Manager: Buck Britton. **Hitting Coach:** Brink Ambler. **Pitching Coach:** Justin Ramsey. **Fundamentals Coach:** TBA. **Athletic Trainer:** TBA. **Strength Coach:** TBA.

GAME INFORMATION
Radio Announcers: Pete Michaud. **No. of Games Broadcast:** 150. **Flagship Station:** ESPN 94.1 FM. **PA Announcer:** Jack Ankerson. **Official Scorers:** Mike Holtzclaw, Jim Hodges. **Stadium Name:** Harbor Park. **Location:** Exit 9, 11A or 11B off I-264, adjacent to the Elizabeth River in downtown Norfolk. **Standard Game Times:** 6:35 pm Monday-Thursday and Saturday, Friday 7:05 pm, Sun 1:05 pm (first half of season); 4:05 pm (second half of season). **Ticket Price Range:** $12-15. **Visiting Club Hotel:** Sheraton Waterside, 777 Waterside Dr, Norfolk, VA 23510. **Telephone:** (757) 622-6664.

OMAHA STORM CHASERS

Address: Werner Park, 12356 Ballpark Way, Papillion, NE 68046.
Administrative Office Phone: (402) 734-2550.
Ticket Office Phone: (402) 738-5100. **Fax:** (402) 734-7166.
E-mail Address: info@omahastormchasers.com. **Website:** www.omahastormchasers.com.
Affiliation (first year): Kansas City Royals (1969). **Years in League:** 2021-

OWNERSHIP/MANAGEMENT
Operated By: Alliance Baseball Managing Partners. **Owners:** Gary Green, Larry Botel, Brian Callaghan, Eric Foss, Stephen Alepa, Peter Huff, Evan Friend. **CEO:** Gary Green. **President:** Martie Cordaro. **Vice President/General Manager:** Laurie Schlender. **Assistant General Manager, Sales:** Marcus Sabata. **Assistant General Manager, Tickets & Operations:** Zach Ziler. **Broadcast & Media Relations Manager:** Nicholas Badders. **Creator of Fun—Promotions & Products:** Emily Hintz. **Mascot Coordinator:** Jack Livers. **Game Operations Manager:** Andrew Rosenau. **Creative Content Manager:** Alex Seder. **Social Media Manager:** Nina Sobotka. **Video & Multimedia Coordinator:** Clayton Van Horn. **Manager of Human Resources & Community Affairs:** Aniya Tate. **Retail Operations Manager:** Mitch Cunningham. **Client Services Manager:** Skyler Clough. **Senior Corporate Sales Executive:** Bob Flannery. **Ticket Operations Manager:** Reilly Raube. **Manager of Lead Development:** Blake Paris. **Director of Business Development:** Dustin True. **Group Sales Manager:** Dru Sauer. **Group Ticket Sales Executive:** Landon Caldwell. **Group Ticket Sales Executive:** Josh Kalin. **Ticket Operations & Retail Assistant:** Stevie Buck. **Events Coordinator:** Anthony Goetz. **Ballpark Operations Manager:** Tyler Shaw. **Director of Operations:** Matt Sutter. **Grounds Manager:** Tom Walter.

FIELD STAFF
Manager: Mike Jirschele. **Hitting Coach:** Bijan Rademacher. **Pitching Coach:** Dane Johnson. **Assistant Coach:** Chris Nelson. **Athletic Trainer:** James Stone. **Strength Coach:** Yannick Plante. **Coordinator of Clubhouse Operations:** Mike Brown.

MINOR LEAGUES

GAME INFORMATION
Radio Announcers: Nicholas Badders. **No. of Games Broadcast:** 150. **Broadcasts:** omahastormchasers.com **PA Announcer:** Craig Evans. **Official Scorers:** Gary Sharp & Ryan White. **Stadium Name:** Werner Park. **Location:** Highway 370, just east of I-80 (exit 439). **Standard Game Times:** 6:35 pm (April-May, August-September), 7:05 (June-July), Sun. 2:05. **Visiting Club Hotel:** Courtyard Omaha La Vista, 12560 Westport Parkway, La Vista, NE 68128. **Telephone:** (402) 339-4900. **Fax:** (402) 339-4901.

ROCHESTER RED WINGS

Address: One Morrie Silver Way, Rochester, NY 14608.
Telephone: (585) 454-1001. **Fax:** (585) 454-1056.
E-Mail: info@redwingsbaseball.com. **Website:** RedWingsBaseball.com.
Affiliation (first year): Washington Nationals (2021). **Years in League:** 2021-

OWNERSHIP/MANAGEMENT
Operated by: Rochester Community Baseball, Inc.
President/CEO/COO: Naomi Silver.
Chairman: Gary Larder. **General Manager:** Dan Mason. **Assistant GM:** Will Rumbold. **Assistant GM, Sales:** Bob Craig. **Senior Director, Tickets & Group Sales:** Eric Friedman. **Director, Communications:** Morrie Silver. **Director, Corporate Development:** Nick Sciarratta. **Director, Video Production:** John Blotzer. **Director, Ticket Operations:** Mike Ewing. **Director, Promotions and Merchandising:** Nicole Boyle. **Director, Ballpark Operations:** Cam Mason. **Coordinator, Digital Media:** Stephen Lasnick. **Head Groundskepper:** Gene Buonomo. **Assistant Groundskeeper:** Geno Buonomo. **Office Manager:** Annamarie Marsha. **Controller:** Michelle Schiefer. **Director, Human Resources:** Paula LoVerde. **Ticket Office Mgr. & Business Coordinator:** Dave Welker. **GM, Food & Beverage:** Jeff DeSantis. **Business Manager, F&B:** Dave Bills. **Director, Catering & Hospitality:** Megan Ridings. **Manager, Catering Sales:** Emily Chard.

FIELD STAFF
Manager: Matthew LeCroy. **Hitting Coach:** Brian Daubach. **Pitching Coach:** Rafael Chaves. **Development Coach:** Billy McMillon. **Athletic Trainer:** Eric Montague. **Strength & Conditioning Coach:** Mike Warren.

GAME INFORMATION
Radio Announcer: Josh Whetzel. **No. of Games Broadcast:** 150. **Flagship Stations:** WHTK 1280-AM.
PA Announcers: Kevin Spears, Rocky Perrotta. **Official Scorers:** Warren Kozireski, Brendan Harrington, Craig Bodensteiner, Bob Simms. **Stadium Name:** Frontier Field. **Location:** I-490 East to exit 12 (Brown/Broad Street) and follow signs; I-490 West to exit 14 (Plymouth Ave) and follow signs. **Standard Game Times:** 7:05 pm, Sun 1:05. **Ticket Price Range:** $13-19. **Visiting Club Hotel:** Hyatt Regency Rochester, 125 E Main St, Rochester, NY 14604. **Telephone:** (585) 546-1234.

ST. PAUL SAINTS

Office Address: 360 Broadway Street, St. Paul, MN 55101.
Telephone: (651) 644-3517. **Fax:** (651) 644-1627.
Email Address: funisgood@saintsbaseball.com.
Website: saintsbaseball.com.
Affiliation: Minnesota Twins (2021). **Years in League:** 2021-

OWNERSHIP/MANAGEMENT
Chairman of the Board: Marvin Goldklang. **President:** Mike Veeck. **Executive VP/General Manager:** Derek Sharrer. **Executive VP/Business Development:** Tom Whaley. **Executive Vice President, Sales and Operations:** Chris Schwab. **Vice President, Director of Media Relations/Broadcasting:** Sean Aronson. **Vice President/Assistant General Manager, Brand Marketing and Experience:** Sierra Bailey. **Director, Community Partnerships and Fan Services:** Eddie Coblentz. **Director, Creative Services:** Rob Thompson. **Creative Services Coordinator:** Jordan Dawkins. **Director, Box Office Manager:** Shana McGlynn. **Digital Media & Video Production Coordinator:** Cameron Surdyk. **Content Producer:** Jason Wondhorn. **Digital Media Specialist:** Aly May. **Director of Sales & Corporate Partnerships:** Austyn Ruback. **Corporate Sales & Ticket Sales Executive:** Kailyn Johnson. **Senior Ticket Sales Executive:** Eric Simon. **Ticket Sales Executive:** Adam Lillestol, Jake McGeorge, Morgan Stienessen. **CHS Field Events Coordinators:** Julia Jaffee, Sarah Olsen. **Youth Sports Coordinator:** Sarah Gottfredsen. **Business Manager/Community Relations:** Krista Schnelle. **Office Manager:** Gina Kray. **Director, Ballpark Operations:** Curtis Nachtsheim. **Director of Field Operations:** Marcus Campbell.

FIELD STAFF
Manager: Toby Gardenhire. **Pitching Coaches:** Cibney Bello, Peter Larson. **Hitting Coach:** Nate Spears. **Defensive Coach:** Tyler Smarslok. **Athletic Trainer:** Ben Myers. **Assistant Athletic Trainer:** Taylor Carpenter. **Strength & Conditioning Coach:** Cody Drouin. **Clubhouse Manager/Assistant, Baseball Operations:** Matt Tramp. **Coordinators, Baseball Technology:** Lincoln Ficek, Alek Hughes.

GAME INFORMATION
Radio Announcer: Sean Aronson. **Games Broadcast:** 150. **Flagship Station:** KFAN+ 96.7 FM. **Webcast Address:** www.saintsbaseball.com. **Stadium Name:** CHS Field. **Location:** From the west take I-94 to the 7th St. Exit and head south to 5th & Broadway. From the east take I-94 to the Mounds Blvd/US-61N exit. Turn left on Kellogg and a right on

MINOR LEAGUES

Broadway until you reach 5th St. **Standard Game Times:** (Games through May 14) **Tue.- Fri.:** 6:37 pm, **Sat:** 2:07 p.m., **Sun.:** 2:07 pm. (Games from May 23-September 23): **Tue-Sat:** 7:07 p.m., **Sun:** 2:07 p.m. (Games from September 19-24) **Tuesday-Saturday:** 6:37 p.m., **Sun:** 12:07 p.m.

SCRANTON/WILKES-BARRE RAILRIDERS

Address: 235 Montage Mountain Rd., Moosic, PA 18507.
Telephone: (570) 969-2255. **Fax:** (570) 963-6564.
E-Mail Address: info@swbrailriders.com.
Website: www.swbrailriders.com.
Affiliation (first year): New York Yankees (2007). **Years in League:** 2021-

OWNERSHIP/MANAGEMENT
Ownership: Diamond Baseball Holdings. **Executive Chairman:** Pat Battle. **CEO:** Peter Freund. **General Manager:** Katie Beekman. **Assistant General Manager:** Matt Hamilton. **Director, Communications/Broadcaster:** Adam Marco. **Manager, Community Relations:** Krista Lutzick. **Corporate Services Manager:** Kate Mummert. **Director, Finance:** Patrick Cawley. **Senior Accountant:** Holly Gumble. **Director, Marketing:** Jordan Calvey. **Marketing Manager:** Katherine Arata. **Social Media/ Special Events Manager:** Kirsten Peters. **Sr. Director, Partnership Management & Marketing:** Kristina Knight. **Director, Season Ticket Sales & Service:** Kelly Cusick. **Account Executives, Season Tickets:** Mark Ambrose, Anthony Daniel & Kyle Davis. **Director, Group Sales:** Mike Harvey. **Group Sales Executives:** Anthony D'Andrea & Colby Emma. **Director, Youth Baseball & Sports Sales:** Robby Judge. **Premium Sales Manager:** Mike Phipps. **Premium Sales Executives:** Spencer Barbarree & Cody Purks. **Manager, Ticket Operations:** Dan Ross. **Director, Field Operations:** Steve Horne. **Manager, Field Operations:** Dustin Spiegel. **Sr. Director, Stadium Operations:** Ryan Long. **Manager, Stadium Operations:** Brandon Brzenski.

FIELD STAFF
Manager: Shelley Duncan. **Pitching Coach:** Graham Johnson. **Hitting Coach:** Trevor Amicone. **Defensive Coach:** Jose Javier. **Athletic Trainer:** Jimmy Downam. **Strength/Conditioning Coach:** Ryan Williams. **Advance Scouting Analyst:** Nick Loeffelholz.

GAME INFORMATION
Radio Announcer: Adam Marco. **No. of Games Broadcast:** 150. **Flagship Stations:** 1340 WYCK-AM, 1400 WICK-AM, 1440 WCDL-AM. **Television Announcer:** Adam Marco. **No. of Games Broadcast:** TBA. **Flagship Station:** TBA. **PA Announcers:** Unavailable. **Official Scorers:** Dean Corwin, Dick Devans, Mark Ligi & Armand Rosamilia. **Stadium Name:** PNC Field. **Location:** Exit 182 off Interstate 81; stadium is on Montage Mountain Road. **Standard Game Times:** Mon.-Fri. 6:35 pm, Sat- 4:05 pm (April, May & Sept) & 6:05 pm (June-August); Sun. 1:05 pm. **Ticket Price Range:** $10-$16. **Visiting Club Hotel:** Hilton Scranton & Conference Center. **Telephone:** (570) 343-3000.

SYRACUSE METS

Address: One Tex Simone Drive, Syracuse NY, 13208
Telephone: 315-474-7833. **Fax:** 315-474-2658.
E-Mail Address: baseball@syracusemets.com. **website:** syracusemets.com
Affiliation (First year): New York Mets (2019). **Years in league:** 1961-Present

OWNERSHIP/MANAGEMENT
Operated by: NY Mets. **General Manager:** Jason Smorol. **Assistant GM, Business Development:** Katie Stewart. **Assistant GM, Stadium/Business Ops:** Brian Paupeck. **Director, Sales/Marketing:** Kathleen McCormick. **Manager, Corporate Sales:** Julie Cardinali. **Senior Accountant:** Patrick Taylor. **Director, Finance:** Frank Santoro. **Director, Broadcasting/Media Relations:** Michael Tricarico. **Director, Ticket Operations:** Will Commisso. **Director, Multimedia Production:** Anthony Cianchetta. **Manager, Suites/Hospitality:** Bill Ryan. **Manager, Social Media/Graphics:** Jed Davis. **Manager, Equipment/Clubhouse Operations:** Craig Nielsen. **Head Groundskeeper/Director, Turf Management:** John Stewart.

FIELD STAFF
Manager: Dick Scott. **Pitching Coach:** Kyle Driscoll. **Hitting Coach:** Collin Hetzler. **Bench Coach:** J.P. Arencibia.

GAME INFORMATION
Radio Announcers: Michael Tricarico and Evan Stockton. **No. of Games Broadcast:** 150. **Flagship Station:** The Score 1260 AM. **PA Announcer:** Nick Aversa. **Official Scorer:** Dom Leo. **Stadium Name:** NBT Bank Stadium. **Location:** New York State Thruway to exit 36 (I-81 South); to 7th North Street exit, left on 7th North, right on Hiawatha Boulevard. **Standard Game Times:** 6:35 pm, Sun. 1:05 pm. **Ticket Price Range:** $12-$20. **Visiting Club Hotel:** Embassy Suites @ Destiny USA.

MINOR LEAGUES

TOLEDO MUD HENS

Address: 406 Washington St., Toledo, OH 43604.
Telephone: (419) 725-4367. **Fax:** (419) 725-4368.
E-Mail Address: mudhens@mudhens.com. **Website:** www.mudhens.com.
Affiliation (first year): Detroit Tigers (1987). **Years in League:** 2021-

OWNERSHIP/MANAGEMENT
Operated By: Toledo Mud Hens Baseball Club, Inc. **Chairman of the Board:** Michael Miller. **Vice President:** David Huey. **Secretary/Treasurer:** Charles Bracken. **President/CEO:** Joseph Napoli. **GM/Executive Vice President:** Erik Ibsen. **President, CFO:** Brian Leverenz. **Assistant Controller:** Tom Mitchell. **Social Media Coordinator:** Amanda Jerzykowski. **Director Corporate Partnerships:** Ed Sintic. **Director Ticket Sales:** Rita Natter and Adam Haman. **Manager, Box Office Sales:** Jessica MacFarlane. **Game Day Coordinators:** Taylor Vandenbroek and Nathan Permar. **Director, Merchandise & Licensing:** Craig Katz. **Turf Manager:** Kyle Leppelmeier. **Clubhouse Manager:** Joe Sarkisian.

FIELD STAFF
Manager: Anthony Iapoce. **Hitting Coach:** Mike Hessman. **Pitching Coach:** Doug Bochtler. **Bench Coach:** Tony Cappucilli. **Athletic Trainer:** Jason Schwartzman. **Strength Coach:** Phill Hartt.

GAME INFORMATION
Radio Announcer: Jim Weber. **No. of Games Broadcast:** 150. **Flagship Station:** WCWA 1230-AM. **TV Announcers:** Jim Weber, Matt Melzak. **No. of Games Broadcast:** 72 (all home games). **TV Flagship:** Buckeye Cable Sports Network (BCSN). **PA Announcer:** Mason. **Official Scorers:** Jeff Businger, Ron Kleinfelter, John Malkoski Jr., Jack Malkoski, Lee Schuh. **Stadium Name:** Fifth Third Field. **Location:** From Ohio Turnpike 80/90, exit 54 (4A) to I-75 North, follow I-75 North to exit 201-B, left onto Erie Street, right onto Washington Street; From Detroit, I-75 South to exit 202-A, right onto Washington Street; From Dayton, I-75 North to exit 201-B, left onto Erie Street, right onto Washington Street; From Ann Arbor, Route 23 South to I-475 East, I-475 east to I-75 South, I-75 South to exit 202-A, right onto Washington Street. **Ticket Price Range:** $12. **Visiting Club Hotel:** Park Inn, 101 North Summit, Toledo, OH 43604. **Telephone:** (419) 241-3000.

WORCESTER RED SOX

Office Address: Polar Park, 100 Madison St., Worcester, MA 01608.
Mailing Address: PO Box 3180, Worcester, MA 01613.
Telephone: (508) 500-8888 and (508) 500-1000
E-Mail Address: info@woosox.com. **Website:** www.woosox.com.
Affiliation (first year): Boston Red Sox (2021). **Years in League:** 2021-

OWNERSHIP/MANAGEMENT
Principal Owner & Chairman: Larry Lucchino. **Vice Chairman:** Mike Tamburro. **President:** Dr. Charles Steinberg. **Executive Vice President-General Manager/Business and Real Estate:** Dan Rea III. **Executive Vice President/General Counsel:** Kim Miner, Esq. **Senior Vice President/Communications:** Bill Wanless. **Senior Vice President/Corporate Partnerships:** Michael Gwynn. **Senior Vice President/Corporate Partnerships:** Jack Verducci. **Vice President/Marketing:** Steve Oliveira. **Vice President/Baseball Operations & Community Relations:** Joe Bradlee. **Executive Assistant to the Chairman:** Fay Scheer. **Special Assistant to the President & Intern Coordinator:** Jackie Wilkes. **Executive Vice President, Treasurer:** Jason Emmett. **Chief Ambassador:** Rick Medeiros. **Vice President, Ticket Operations:** Samantha Saccoia-Beggs. **Vice President, Marketing Programs:** Steve Oliveira. **Vice President, Ballpark Facilities:** Robert Malone. **Director of Graphic Design:** Courtney Cowsill. **Senior Director of Polar Park Events:** Hannah Butler. **Office Manager:** Carol Krushnowski. **Corporate & Community Partnerships:** Mike Lyons. **Senior Director of Facilities:** Jeff Caster. **Merchandising Manager:** Kyla Frates. **Broadcaster & Corporate Event Manager:** Jim Cain. **Group Event Managers:** Joe Foley, Tom Steiger. **Manager of Accounting:** Dan Fontaine. **Director of Baseball & Gameday Operations:** Alex Richardson. **Radio/TV Broadcasters:** Jim Cain, Tyler Murray, Mike Antonellis, Jay Burnham, Cooper Boardman.

FIELD STAFF
Field Manager: Chad Tracy. **Hitting Coach:** Rich Gedman. **Pitching Coach:** Paul Abbott. **Coaches:** Jose Flores & Mike Montville. **Trainers:** Nick Kuchwara & Scott Gallon. **Strength & Conditioning Coach:** Ben Chadwick.

GAME INFORMATION
Radio Announcers: Jim Cain. **No. of Games Broadcast:** 150. **Flagship Station:** NASH Icon 98.9-FM. **PA Announcer:** Ben DeCastro. **Official Scorer:** Bruce Guindon. **Stadium Name:** Polar Park. **Location:** Canal District, **Worcester, MA Standard Game Times:** 6:45 pm, Sat. 4:**05**, Sun 1:**05**. **Ticket Price Range:** $8-21. **Visiting Club Hotel:** Hilton Garden Inn, Worcester, MA.

MINOR LEAGUES

PACIFIC COAST LEAGUE

STADIUM INFORMATION

Club	Stadium	Opened	LF	CF	RF	Capacity	2022 Att.
Albuquerque	Isotopes Park	2003	340	400	340	13,500	515,498
El Paso	Southwest University Park	2014	322	406	322	8,018	496,805
Las Vegas	Las Vegas Ballpark	2019	340	415	340	8,196	518,221
Oklahoma City	Chickasaw Bricktown Ballpark	1998	325	400	325	9,000	410,730
Reno	Greater Nevada Field	2009	339	410	340	9,100	336,079
Round Rock	Dell Diamond	2000	330	405	325	8,722	412,988
Sacramento	Sutter Health Park	2000	330	403	325	14,014	372,769
Salt Lake	Smith's Ballpark	1994	345	420	315	14,511	434,616
Sugar Land	Constellation Field	2012	348	405	325	7,500	285,827
Tacoma	Cheney Stadium	1960	325	425	325	6,500	366,469

ALBUQUERQUE ISOTOPES

Address: 1601 Avenida Cesar Chavez SE, Albuquerque, NM 87106
Telephone: (505) 924-2255. **Fax:** (505) 242-8899.
E-Mail Address: info@abqisotopes.com. **Website:** www.abqisotopes.com.
Affiliation (first year): Colorado Rockies (2015). **Years in League:** 2021-

OWNERSHIP/MANAGEMENT

President: Ken Young. **Vice President/Secretary/Treasurer:** Emmett Hammond. **VP/GM:** John Traub. **Assistant GM, Business Operations:** Chrissy Baines. **Assistant GM, Sales/Marketing:** Adam Beggs. **Media Relations Manager:** Forest Stulting. **Director, Retail Operations:** Michael Malgieri. **Director, Stadium Operations:** Bobby Atencio. **Director, Accounting/Human Resources:** Cynthia DiFrancesco. **Box Office/Administration Director:** Mark Otero. **Director, Community Relations:** Michelle Montoya. **Marketing/Promotions Manager:** Dylan Storm. **Director of Game Production:** Kris Shepard. **Front Office Assistant:** Alexia Gutierrez. **Suite Relations Manager:** TBD. **Director of Baseball Operations:** Ryan Maxwell. **Season Ticket, Group Sales Manager:** CJ Scroger. **Ticket Sales Executives:** Aaron Robinson, Josh Woisin, Terry Clark, Piper Le Jeune. **Creative Services Manager:** Rebecca Zook. **Head Groundskeeper:** Ed Attalla. **Assistant Groundskeeper:** Thomas Gallegos. **GM:** Brad Six. **Executive Chef:** Jim Griego.

FIELD STAFF

Manager: Warren Schaeffer. **Hitting Coach:** Jordan Pacheco. **Pitching Coach:** Frank Gonzales. **Bench Coach:** Bobby Meacham. **Athletic Trainer:** Hoshi Mizutani. **Physical Performance Coach:** TBA.

GAME INFORMATION

Radio Announcer: Josh Suchon. **No. of Games Broadcast:** 150. **Flagship Station:** KNML 95.9-FM & 610-AM. **PA Announcer:** Francina Walker. **Official Scorers:** Gary Herron, Brent Carey, John Miller, Frank Mercogliano. **Stadium Name:** Isotopes Park. **Location:** From 1-25, exit east on Avenida Cesar Chavez SE to University Boulevard; From I-40, exit south on UniversityBoulevard SE to Avenida Cesar Chavez. **Standard Game Times:** 6:35 pm/7:05 pm. Sun 1:35/6:05 pm. **Ticket Price Range:** $8-$27. **Visiting Club Hotel:** Sheraton Albuquerque Airport Hotel, 2910 Yale Blvd SE, Albuquerque, NM 87106. **Telephone:** (505) 843-7000.

EL PASO CHIHUAHUAS

Address: 1 Ballpark Plaza, El Paso, TX 79901.
Telephone: (915) 533-2273. **Fax:** (915) 242-2031.
E-Mail Address: info@epchihuahuas.com. **Website:** www.epchihuahuas.com
Affiliation (first year): San Diego Padres (2014). **Years in League:** 2021-

OWNERSHIP/MANAGEMENT

Owners: Alejandra de la Vega Foster, Woody Hunt, Josh Hunt, Paul Foster. **President:** Alan Ledford. **Senior Vice President/General Manager:** Brad Taylor. **Vice President, Operations & Special Events:** Matt LaRose. **Senior Director, Finance & Administration:** Pamela De La O. **Accounts Payable/Accounts Receivable Supervisor and Payroll Coordinator:** Pamela Nieto. **Staff Accountant:** Jasmine Alcantara. **Senior Director, Corporate Partnerships & Suites:** Judge Scott. **Senior Account Executive, Corporate Partnerships:** Cole Buck. **Corporate Partnerships Activations Specialist:** Kate Starr. **Senior Director, Ticket Sales & Service:** Nick Seckerson. **Director, Season Seat Sales:** Primo Martinez. **Senior Director, Strategy & Analytics:** Ross Rotwein. **Director, Group Sales:** Brittany Morgan. **Senior Account Executive, Ticket Sales:** Ethan Andersen. **Account Executives, Ticket Sales:** Daniel Press, Jake Spitz. **Senior Account Executive, Group Sales & Inside Sales Manager:** Janine Quiroz. **Senior Account Executive, Group Sales:** Austin Weber. **Account Executive, Group Sales:** Joshalyn Estrada. **Senior Manager, Ticket Operations:** Ruben Armendariz. **Ticket Operations Coordinator:** Hector Marquez. **Senior Director, Marketing & Communications:** Angela Olivas. **Senior Manager, Video & Digital Production:** Juan Gutierrez. **Senior Manager, Broadcast & Media

MINOR LEAGUES

Relations: Tim Hagerty. **Director, Promotions & Community Relations:** Andy Imfeld. **Manager, Digital Strategies & Production:** Gage Freeman. **Community Relations & Promotions Senior Coordinator:** Matt Clarkson. **Lead Graphic Designer & Creative Services:** Ilene Serna. **Lead, Baseball Operations:** Anthony Rifenburg. **Director, Grounds & Building Operations:** Travis Howard. **Assistant Groundskeepers:** Alex Orona, Bryan Shira, Tony Tafoya, Gordon Von Weyhe. **Manager, Facilities:** Michael Raymundo. **Facilities Supervisors:** Victor Estrada, Manny Garcia. **Manager, Guest Services & Operations:** Chris Flores. **Coordinator, Guest Services:** Warren Hartley. **Manager, Retail & Merchandise Operations:** David Apodaca. **Director, Special Events:** Gina Roe-Davis.

FIELD STAFF
Manager: Philip Wellman. **Hitting Coach:** Raul Padron. **Pitching Coach:** Scott Mitchell. **Assistant Pitching Coach:** Jimmy Jones. **Strength Coach:** A.J. Russell. **Athletic Trainers:** Josh DiLoreto, Maritza Castro.

GAME INFORMATION
Broadcaster: Tim Hagerty. **No. of Games Broadcast:** 150. **Flagship Station:** ESPN 600 AM El Paso. **PA Announcer:** TBA. **Official Scorer:** TBD. **Stadium Name:** Southwest University Park. **Standard Game Times:** TBD. **Ticket Price Range:** $5-10.50. **Visiting Club Hotel:** TBD

LAS VEGAS AVIATORS

Address: 1650 S. Pavilion Center Drive, Las Vegas, NV 89135.
Telephone: (702) 943-7200. **Fax:** (702) 943-7214.
E-Mail Address: info@aviatorslv.com. **Website:** www.aviatorslv.com.
Affiliation (first year): Oakland Athletics (2019). **Years in League:** 1983 -

OWNERSHIP/MANAGEMENT
Operated By: Summerlin Las Vegas Baseball Club LLC
President/COO: Don Logan. **General Manager/Vice President, Sales/Marketing:** Chuck Johnson. **Vice President, Ticket Sales:** Erik Eisenberg. **Vice President/Ballpark Operations:** Jason Weber. **Vice President/Ticket Operations:** Siobhan Steiermann. **Vice President/Public Safety:** Bill Corder. **Vice President/Retail Operations:** Edward Dorville. **Director, Sponsorships:** James Jensen. **Director/Team Operations:** Steve Dwyer. **Director, Ticket Sales:** Bryan Frey. **Director, Broadcasting:** Russ Langer. **Director, Business Development:** Larry Brown. **Media Relations Director:** Jim Gemma. **Director/Game Entertainment:** Gary Arlitz. **Senior Account Executive:** Nathan Erbach. **Account Executives, Ticket Sales:** Daniel Crawford, Michael Kuchinski, Rickie Ritchie, Brock Shively. **Controller:** Brian Winslow. **Senior Accountant:** Melissa Murray. **Staff Accountant:** Jessica Cullen. **Ballpark Support Manager:** Chip Vespe. **Marketing & Social Media Manager:** Elsye Jones. **Box Office Manager:** Annette Evans. **Ticket Operations Supervisor:** Michelle Taggart. **Ticket Services Specialist:** Jessica Becerra. **Director, Special Events:** Jenna Potter. **Special Events Manager:** Olivia Perry. **Premium Ticket Services Coordinator:** Katie Greener. **Executive Administrative Assistant:** Jan Dillard. **Administrative Support Specialist:** Kirsten Sheff. **Manager/Retail Operations:** Tom Brazile. **Coordinator/Retail Operations:** Andrew Lockhart. **Retail Sales Associate:** Daymian Yohner. **Radio Broadcaster/Game Entertainment Specialist:** Matt Neverett. **Engineering Manager:** Ronnie Cabrera. **Facility Maintenance Engineers:** Mason Piccinetti, Gus Wagasky. **IT Las Vegas Ballpark Support:** Reko Pinson. **Dockmaster:** Robert Whittaker. **Head Groundskeeper:** Isaiah Lienau.

FIELD STAFF
Manager: Fran Riordan. **Hitting Coach:** Brian McArn. **Pitching Coach:** Bryan Corey. **Assistant Hitting Coach:** Todd Takayoshi. **Head Athletic Trainer:** Shane Zdebiak. **Assistant Athletic Trainer:** Dave Comeau. **Sport Performance Coach:** Matt Mosiman.

GAME INFORMATION
Radio Announcer: Russ Langer. **No. of Games Broadcast:** 150. **Flagship Station:** Raider Nation Radio 920 AM
PA Announcer: Dan Bickmore. **Official Scorer:** Peter Legner. **Stadium Name:** Las Vegas Ballpark. **Location:** I 215 North Beltway to Sahara Avenue (exit east), left on Pavilion Center Drive; 1 215 South Beltway to Charleston Blvd. (exit east), right on Pavilion Center Drive. **Standard Game Time:** 7:05 pm. **Ticket Price Range:** $13-50. **Visiting Club Hotel:** Red Rock Casino Resort & Spa, 11011 W. Charleston Blvd. Las Vegas, NV 89135. **Telephone:** (702) 797-7777.

OKLAHOMA CITY DODGERS

Address: 2 S Mickey Mantle Dr., Oklahoma City, OK 73104.
Telephone: (405) 218-1000. **Fax:** (405) 218-1011.
E-Mail Address: info@okcdodgers.com. **Website:** www.okcdodgers.com.
Affiliation (first year): Los Angeles Dodgers (2015). **Years in League:** 1998–

OWNERSHIP/MANAGEMENT
Operated By: Diamond Baseball Holdings, LLC. **Principal Owner:** Diamond Baseball Holdings, LLC.
President/General Manager: Michael Byrnes. **Senior Vice President:** Jenna Byrnes. **Vice President, Ticket Sales:** Kyle Daugherty. **Vice President, Finance/Accounting:** John MacDonald. **Vice President, Operations:** Mitch Stubenhofer. **Vice President, Marketing/Communications:** Ben Beecken. **Vice President, Corporate Partnerships:** Jim Flavin. **Director, Partnership Sales:** Ryan Vanlow. **Director, Communications/Broadcasting:** Alex Freedman. **Director, Food Service Operations:** Will Fenwick. **Director, Game Presentation & Video:** A.J. Navarro. **Executive**

MINOR LEAGUES

Director, OKC Dodgers Baseball Foundation: Carol Herrick. **Director, Special Events:** Shelby Kirkes. **Director, Merchandise:** Jasmine Buchanan. **Director, Customer Experience:** Caleb Beverly. **Communications Manager:** Lisa Johnson. **Baseball Operations Coordinator:** Billy Maloney. **Operations Coordinator:** Jarett Wolfe. **Office Administrator:** Travis Hunter. **Head Groundskeeper:** Jeff Jackson. **Assistant Groundskeeper:** Joseph Golding. **Clubhouse Manager:** Clyde Howard.

FIELD STAFF
Manager: Travis Barbary. **Hitting Coach:** Emmanuel Burriss. **Pitching Coach:** Doug Mathis. **Coach:** Chris Gutierrez. **Bullpen Coach:** Justin DeFratus. **Athletic Trainers:** Chelsea Willette & Griffin Boyte. **Performance Coach:** Paul Fournier.

GAME INFORMATION
Radio Announcer: Alex Freedman. **No. of Games Broadcast:** 150. **Station:** KGHM-AM 1340 (www.1340thegame.com). **PA Announcer:** Kennan Garrett. **Official Scorers:** Jim Byers, Mark Heusman, Rich Tortorelli. **Stadium Name:** Chickasaw Bricktown Ballpark. **Location:** Bricktown area in downtown Oklahoma City, near interchange of I-235 and I-40, off I-235 take Sheridan exit to Bricktown; off I-40 take Shields exit, north to Bricktown. **Standard Game Times: Tue-Sat:** 7:05 pm, **Sun:** 2:05 (April-June; Sept.), 6:05 (July-Aug). **Ticket Price Range:** $12-33. **Visiting Club Hotel:** Courtyard Oklahoma City Downtown, 2 West Reno Ave., Oklahoma City, OK 73102. **Telephone:** (405) 232-2290.

RENO ACES

Address: 250 Evans Ave, Reno, NV 89501.
Telephone: (775) 334-4700. **Fax:** (775) 334-4701.
Website: www.renoaces.com.
Affiliation (first year): Arizona Diamondbacks (2009). **Years in League:** 2021-

OWNERSHIP/MANAGEMENT
General Manager/Chief Operations Officer: Chris Phillips. **Chief Commercial Officer:** Mike Murray. **Chief Financial Officer:** Stacey Bowman. **VP of Business Development:** Brian Moss. **VP of Corporate Partnerships:** Max Margulies. **VP of Event Experience:** Sarah Bliss. **VP of Marketing and Communications:** Vince Ruffino. **VP of Operations:** Anthony Altamura. **VP of Ticket Sales:** Alex Strathearn. **Senior Director of Ticket Services & Operations:** Laura Raymond. **Accounting Director:** Adam Hyde. **Creative Director:** Blake O'Brien. **Marketing Director:** AJ Grimm. **Ticket Operations Director:** Kristina Solis. **Ballpark Operations Manager:** Brandon Wildman. **Communications Manager:** Adam Nichols. **Corporate Partnerships Services Manager:** Hannah Jurgens. **Facilities Manager:** Maurice Lewis. **Facility Maintenance Manager:** Myles Fresquez. **Fan Experience Manager:** Marisa Ochoa. **Production & Game Entertainment Manager:** Dora Cantu. **Team Store & Merchandise Manager:** Jennifer Lieber. **Ballpark Operations Coordinator:** Joe Creason. **Corporate Partnerships Services Coordinator:** Gracie Gribble. **Corporate Partnerships Services Coordinator:** Olivia Reese. **Human Resources & Payroll Coordinator:** Joanna Torres. **Marketing Coordinator:** Chase Grodin. **Senior Membership Service Coordinator:** Kyle McAndrew. **Senior Account Executive:** Henry Travland. **Senior Account Executive:** Max Middendorf. **Account Executive-Business Development:** Adam Plyler. **Account Executive:** Benji Meshek. **Account Executive:** Spencer Jackson. **Account Executive:** Valerie Garcia. **Inside Sales Executive:** Nick Marimberga. **Inside Sales Executive:** Russell Hicks. **Inside Sales Executive:** Brandon Lozano. **Staff Accountant:** Chase Jackson. **Head Groundskeeper:** Leah Withrow. **Assistant Groundskeeper:** Max Casper. **Home Clubhouse Manager:** Paul Whatley. **Visiting Clubhouse Manager:** Samuel Midgette.

FIELD STAFF
Manager: Blake Lalli. **Hitting Coaches:** Mark Reed and Travis Denker. **Pitching Coach:** Doug Drabek and Jeff Bajenaru. **Athletic Trainer:** Damon Reel. **Strength & Conditioning Coach:** Nate Friedman.

GAME INFORMATION
Radio Announcer: Kevin DiDomenico. **No. of Games Broadcast:** 150. **PA Announcers:** Taylor Morgan, Phillip Goodman, Chris Payne. **Official Scorers:** Alan Means, Greg Erny, Gregg Zive. **Stadium Name:** Greater Nevada Field. **Location:** From north, south and east: I-80 West, Exit 14 (Wells Ave.), left on Wells, right at Kuenzil St., field on right; From West, I-80 East to Exit 13 (Virginia St.), right on Virginia, left on Second, field on left. **Standard Game Times:** 7:05 p.m., 6:35 p.m., 1:05 p.m. **Ticket Price Range:** $8-35.

ROUND ROCK EXPRESS

Address: 3400 East Palm Valley Blvd, Round Rock, TX 78565.
Telephone: (512) 255-2255. **Fax:** (512) 255-1558.
E-Mail Address: info@rrexpress.com. **Website:** www.RRExpress.com.
Affiliation (first year): Texas Rangers (2011). **Year in League:** 2021-

OWNERSHIP/MANAGEMENT
Operated By: Ryan Sanders Sports & Entertainment. **Principal Owners:** Nolan Ryan, Don Sanders. **Owners:** Reid Ryan, Reese Ryan, Bret Sanders, Brad Sanders. **Chief Executive Officer, Ryan Sanders Sports & Entertainment:** Reid Ryan. **Chief Financial Officer, Ryan Sanders Sports & Entertainment:** Jonathan Germer. **President:** Chris Almendarez. **General Manager:** Tim Jackson. **Executive Advisor to President & General Manager:** Dave Fendrick. **Senior Vice President, Marketing:** Laura Fragoso. **Vice President, Administration & Accounting:** Debbie Coughlin. **Assistant General Manager, Sales:** Stuart Scally. **Senior Director, Stadium Operations & Security:** Gene Kropff.

MINOR LEAGUES

Senior Director, United Heritage Conference Center: Scott Allen. **Director, Broadcasting:** Mike Capps. **Director, Nolan Ryan Foundation:** Mary Conley Thompson. **Director, Information Technology:** Mark Ramos. **Director, Retail:** Joe Belger. **Director, Sales:** Oscar Rodriguez. **Director, Stadium Maintenance:** Aurelio Martinez. **Director, Ticket Operations:** Aschley Carvalho. **Manager, Clubhouse Operations:** Kenny Bufton. **Manager, Office:** Wendy Abrahamsen. **Manager, PR & Communications:** Rylan Kobre. **Manager, Communications & Travel:** Aubrey Losack. **Manager, Client Services & Promotions:** Emily Rutherford. **Manager, Home Run Dugout:** Paul Ponzio. **Coordinator, Digital Marketing & Community Relations:** Reilly Low. **Coordinator, Game Entertainment & Promotions:** Annalicia Lugo. **Coordinator, Nolan Ryan Foundation:** Jules McCormack. **Coordinator, Multimedia Marketing:** Colin Perry. **Coordinator, Baseball Operations:** Jackson Ryan. **Coordinator, Operations & Event Fulfillment:** Robbie Price. **Senior Account Executives:** Connor Truitt, John Watts. **Specialist, Ticket Operations:** Garrett Smith. **Account Executives:** Anthony Pollo, Casey Schneider, Heaven Walker. **Head Groundskeeper:** Nick Rozdilski. **Assistant Head, Groundskeeper:** Brett Maida. **Assistant, Facilities:** Austin Rotramel. **Housekeeping Staff:** Ofelia Gonzalez. **Electrician/HVAC Maintenance Staff:** Leslie Hitt. **Painter:** Roger Calkins.

FIELD STAFF
Manager: Doug Davis. **Hitting Coach:** Matt Lawson. **Pitching Coach:** Dave Borkowski. **Bench Coach:** Chase Lambin. **Development Coach:** Josh Johnson. **Bullpen Coach:** Demetre Kokoris. **Athletic Trainer:** Will Whitehead. **Strength and Conditioning Coach:** Wade Lamont.

GAME INFORMATION
Radio Announcer: Mike Capps. **No. of Games Broadcast:** 150. **Flagship Station:** AM 1300 The Zone. **PA Announcer:** Glen Norman. **Official Scorer:** Larry Little, Andrew Haynes. **Stadium Name:** Dell Diamond. **Location:** US Highway 79, 3.5 miles east of Interstate 35 (exit 253) or 1.5 miles west of Texas Tollway 130. **Standard Game Times:** 7:05 pm, 6:35, 6:05, 1:05, 12:05. **Ticket Price Range:** $7-$30. **Visiting Club Hotel:** LaQuinta Inn & Suites by Wyndham Round Rock East, 3900 East Palm Valley Blvd., Round Rock, TX 78665. **Telephone:** (737) 346-6652.

SACRAMENTO RIVER CATS

Address: Sutter Health Park - 400 Ballpark Drive, West Sacramento, CA 95691
Telephone: (916) 376-4700. **Fax:** (916) 376-4710.
E-Mail Address: reception@rivercats.com. **Website:** www.rivercats.com
Affiliation (first year): San Francisco Giants (2015). **Years in League:** 2021-

OWNERSHIP/MANAGEMENT
President/COO: Chip Maxson. **Executive Vice President, Finance:** Maddie Strika. **Vice President, Partner Services:** Greg Coletti. **Vice President, Ticket Sales & Marketing:** Troy Loparco. **Vice President, Facilities & Events:** Brittney Nizuk. **Manager, Human Resources:** JP Mora. **Assistant, Executive:** Katie Howard. **Coordinator, Accounting:** Lisa Foster. **Assistant, Administrative:** Abigail Delao. **Sr. Director, Ticket Operations:** Joe Carlucci. **Director, Ticket Sales:** Justice Hoyt. **Sr. Coordinator, Membership & Suite Services:** Gabriela Salazar. **Membership Experience Specialist:** Rachel Rus. **Membership Experience Specialist:** Bailey Metcalf. **Account Executive, Group Sales:** Cory Takiguchi. **Account Executive, Group Sales:** Henry Weiss. **Account Executive, Group Sales:** Bryson Martin. **Account Executive, Group Sales:** Dylan Rozema. **Account Executive, Inside Sales:** Amaya Barnes. **Account Executive, Inside Sales:** Kai Martin. **Account Executive, Inside Sales:** Axel Gomez Padilla. **Account Executive, Inside Sales:** Niko Dugay. **Account Executive, Corporate Sales:** Tim Williams. **Account Executive, Corporate Sales:** Austin Staab. **Account Executive, Corporate Sales:** Jason Green. **Account Executive, Corporate Sales:** Zac Alfers. **Account Executive, Corporate Sales:** Michael Mitchell. **Account Executive, Corporate Sales:** Jason Visesratana. **Director, Business Development:** Kelly Bott. **Coordinator, Partnership Activation:** Natalie Torres. **Assistant, Corporate Partnerships:** Judy Nguyen. **Director, Marketing:** Sarah Hebel. **Coordinator, Social Media & Marketing:** Kevin Peters. **Coordinator, Marketing & Community Engagement:** Ashley Magdaleno. **Assistant, Social Media & Marketing:** Caleb Hanna. **Coordinator, Mascot:** Matthew Francis. **Coordinator, Graphic Design:** Jay Rivett. **Coordinator: Baseball Operations:** Matthew Grone. **Coordinator, Communications:** Maverick Pallack. **Manager, Security:** Darrell Graham. **Manager, Guest Services:** Jessa Carlson. **Manager, Events & Entertainment:** Micaela Brewer. **Coordinator, Events & Entertainment:** Evelyn Chavez. **Manager, Stadium Operations:** Mike Correa. **Coordinator, Stadium Operations:** Hank Forrest. **Sr. Director, Field Operations:** Chris Shastid. **Coordinator, Field Operations:** Marcello Clamar. **Director, Merchandise:** Erin Kilby. **Director, Food & Beverage:** Gabe Erhartic. **Executive Chef:** Johnny Frink. **Manager, Concessions:** James Thompson. **Office Coordinator, Food & Beverage:** Leticia Perez.

FIELD STAFF
Manager: Dave Brundage. **Hitting Coach:** Damon Minor. **Pitching Coach:** Garvin Alston. **Fundamentals Coach:** Jolbert Cabrera. **Coach:** TBD. **Athletic Trainers:** David Getsoff, Brian Reinker. **Strength & Conditioning Coach:** TBD.

GAME INFORMATION
Radio Broadcaster: TBD. **No. of Games Broadcast:** 150. **PA Announcer:** Carolyn McCardle. **Official Scorers:** Mark Honbo, Matthew Benham, Doug Kelly, Chris Holtz, Kassandra Lopez, Corey Neal. **Stadium Name:** Sutter Health Park. **Location:** I-5 to Business-80 West, exit at Jefferson Boulevard. **Standard Game Time:** 6:45 p.m. **Ticket Price Range:** $10-$80.

MINOR LEAGUES

SALT LAKE BEES

Address: 77 W 1300 South, Salt Lake City, UT 84115.
Telephone: (801) 325-2337. **Fax:** (801) 485-6818.
E-Mail Address: info@slbees.com. **Website:** www.slbees.com.
Affiliation (first year): Los Angeles Angels (2001). **Years in League:** 2021-.

OWNERSHIP/MANAGEMENT
Principal Owner: Gail Miller. **President/General Manager:** Marc Amicone. **Assistant GM:** Bryan Kinneberg. **Director of Broadcasting:** Steve Klauke. **Director of Communications:** Kraig Williams. **Social and Digital Media Manager:** Kylee Rasmussen. **Director of Marketing and Game Presentation:** Brady Brown. **Director of Fan Engagement:** Tony Parks. **Graphic Designer:** Brayden Erickson. **Director of Ticket Operations:** Derrek Degraaff. **Box Office Supervisor:** Duane Sartori. **Receptionist:** Caytee Black. **Senior Director of Sales and Service:** Brad Jacoway. **Senior Director of Sales and Service:** Koy Pruitt. **Group Sales Manager:** Tanner Lund. **Ticket Sales Account Executive:** Abigail Scott. **Ticket Sales Account Executive:** Tim Morrissey. **Ticket Sales Account Executive:** Ian Schafer. **Ticket Sales Account Executive:** Bryce Justrom. **Ticket Sales Account Executive:** Madison Sherwood. **Membership Service Manager:** Sam Cook. **Membership Service Manager:** Ryan Corbett. **VP of Corporate Sponsorship:** Brian Devir. **Corporate Sponsorship Manager:** Dustin Dehlin. **Sponsorship Activation Manager:** Ariell Maesta. **Home Clubhouse Manager:** Cole Filosa. **Visiting Clubhouse Manager:** Chris Simonsen. **Director of Field Operations:** Brian Soukup. **Manager of Field Operations:** Jacob Fender. **Assistant Manager of Field Operations:** Bryce Bannock.

FIELD STAFF
Manager: Keith Johnson. **Pitching Coach:** Darrin Ebert. **Hitting Coach:** Joel Chimelis. **Coach:** Jack Santora. **Trainer:** Jonathan Fierro. **Strength & Conditioning Coach:** Henry Aleck

GAME INFORMATION
Radio Announcer: Steve Klauke. **No. of Games Broadcast:** 150. **Flagship Station:** 1280 AM. **PA Announcer:** Jeff Reeves. **Official Scorers:** Jeff Cluff, Brooke Frederickson, Randy Upton. **Stadium Name:** Smith's Ballpark. **Location:** I-15 North/South to 1300 South exit, east to ballpark at West Temple. **Standard Game Times:** 6:35 (Night games), 1:05 Sunday day games. **Ticket Price Range:** $10-24.

SUGAR LAND SPACE COWBOYS

Office Address: 1 Stadium Drive, Sugar Land, Texas, 77498.
Telephone: (281) 240-4487.
Affiliation (first year): Houston Astros (2021). **Years in League:** 2021-

OWNERSHIP/MANAGEMENT
Owner: Jim Crane. **Senior Vice President, Affiliate Business Operations:** Creighton Kahoalii. **Vice President Affiliate Operations:** Thomas Bell. **General Manager:** Tyler Stamm. **Assistant General Manager:** Chris Parsons. **Special Assistant:** Deacon Jones. **Senior Accountant:** Jen Schwarz. **Retail Manager:** Shamaine St. Julien. **Affiliate Business Operations Coordinator:** Philip Raven. **Director of Corporate Partnerships:** John Gray. **Senior Manager of Corporate Partnerships:** Teneisha Richardson. **Account Executive:** Alex Rodriguez. **Account Executive:** Samuel Stubbs. **Account Executive:** Tyler Tumbleson. **Community Relations Coordinator:** Megan Brown. **Community Relations Manager:** Sallie Ferris. **Graphic Design Coordinator:** Michael Kloska. **Marketing and Digital Media Coordinator:** Megan Murnane. **Media Relations Manager:** Ryan Posner. **Manager of Partnership Activation:** Erin Williams. **Director of Special Events:** Eddy Juarez. **Event Operations Manager:** Russell Wohldman. **Manager of Special Events Sales:** Kiersten Stiers. **Director of Stadium Operations:** Chris Cominse. **Manager of Stadium Operations:** Tim Hunter. **Director of Field Operations:** Brad Detmore. **Manager of Field Operations:** Corbin Zamora. **Clubhouse Manager:** DJ Pirson. **Visiting Clubhouse Manager:** Don Pirson.

FIELD STAFF
Manager: Mickey Storey. **Pitching Coach:** Erick Abreu. **Hitting Coach:** TBA. **Athletic Trainer:** Brandon Zumbach. **Strength and Conditioning Coach:** Zach Reding.

GAME INFORMATION
Radio Announcer: Gerald Sanchez. **No. of Games Broadcast:** 150. **Flagship Streaming Station:** MiLBTV. **Flagship Radio Station:** ESPN 92.5 FM (Gow Media). **Standard Game Times:** Mon.-Fri., 7:05 pm, Sat-Sun.: 6:05 pm. **Visiting Club Hotel:** Sugar Land Marriott Town Square. **Telephone:** (281) 275-8400.

TACOMA RAINIERS

Address: 2502 South Tyler St, Tacoma, WA 98405.
Telephone: (253) 752-7707. **Fax:** (253) 752-7135.
Website: www.tacomarainiers.com
Affiliation (first year): Seattle Mariners (1995). **Years in League:** 1960-

MINOR LEAGUES

OWNERSHIP/MANAGEMENT

Owners: The Baseball Club of Tacoma. **President:** Aaron Artman. **CFO:** Brian Coombe. **Vice President, Sales:** Shane Santman. **Director of Administration and Assistant to the President:** Patti Stacy. **Senior Director, Sales:** Tim O'Hollaren. **Director, Business Development:** Ben Nelson. **Senior Manager, Corporate Sales:** Kevin Drugge. **Manager, Corporate Sales:** Devon Barker. **Director, Group Sales and Event Marketing:** Caitlin Calnan. **Senior Manager, Group Sales:** Chris Aubertin. **Director of Fan Experience:** Cassidy Larson. **Director, Ticket Operations:** Alexa Covarrubias. **Manager, Ticket Operations:** Arturo Nava. **Manager, Box Office:** Necia Borba. **Senior Coordinator, Group Events:** Hayley Hacker. **Vice President, Marketing:** Megan Mead. **Director, Game Entertainment:** Madison Bukata. **Director, Media Relations and Baseball Information:** Paul Braverman. **Illustrator:** Delaney Saul. **Graphic Designer:** Erin Fogerty. **Director, Technical:** Anthony Phinney. **Specialist, Multimedia:** Branson Gustafson. **Marketing Manager:** Elliet Bradshaw. **Broadcaster:** Mike Curto. **Manager, Partner Services:** Hannah McArthur. **Manager, Partner Services:** Will Hamilton. **Director, Baseball Ops and Merchandise:** Ashley Schutt. **Manager, Retail Operations and Merchandise:** Kyle McGilvray. **Director of Finance and Operations:** Amy Tucci. **Head Groundskeeper:** Michael Huie. **Director, Stadium Operations:** Phillip Haywood.

FIELD STAFF

Manager: John Russell. **Hitting Coach:** Brad Marcelino. **Pitching Coach:** Jairo Cuevas. **Infield/Baserunning Coach:** Eric Farris. **Trainer:** Aric Quinney. **Strength and Conditioning:** Michael Sadler

GAME INFORMATION

Radio Broadcaster: Mike Curto. **No. of Games Broadcast:** 150. **Flagship Station:** TBA. **PA Announcer:** Randy McNair. **Official Scorers:** Kevin Kalal, Gary Brooks, Jon Gilbert, Scott Hauter. **Stadium Name:** Cheney Stadium. **Location:** From I-5, take exit 132 (Highway 16 West) for 1.2 miles to 19th Street East exit, merge right onto 19th Street, right onto Clay Huntington Way and follow into parking lot of ballpark. **Standard Game Times:** 7:05, Sun. 1:05. (Monday–Wednesday games start at 6:05pm in April–June, Saturday at 5:05pm in April, May, June & September.) **Ticket Price Range:** $7.50-$25.50. **Visiting Club Hotel:** Hotel Murano, 1320 Broadway Plaza, Tacoma, WA 98402. **Telephone:** (253) 238-8000.

MINOR LEAGUES

EASTERN LEAGUE

STADIUM INFORMATION

Club	Stadium	Opened	LF	CF	RF	Capacity	2022 Att.
Akron	Canal Park	1997	331	400	337	7,630	253,735
Altoona	Peoples Natural Gas Field	1999	325	405	325	7,210	285,777
Binghamton	Mirabito Stadium	1992	330	400	330	6,012	146,679
Bowie	Prince George's Stadium	1994	309	405	309	10,000	174,537
Erie	UPMC Park	1995	317	400	328	6,000	175,810
Harrisburg	Metro Bank Park	1987	325	400	325	6,300	244,433
Hartford	Dunkin' Donuts Park	2018	325	400	325	6,146	402,123
New Hampshire	Northeast Delta Dental Stadium	2005	326	400	306	6,500	282,514
Portland	Hadlock Field	1994	315	400	330	7,368	379,100
Reading	FirstEnergy Stadium	1951	330	400	330	9,000	368,068
Richmond	The Diamond	1985	330	402	330	9,560	406,560
Somerset	TD Bank Ballpark	1999	317	402	315	6,100	351,142

AKRON RUBBERDUCKS

Address: 300 S Main St, Akron, OH 44308.
Telephone: (330) 253-5151. (855) 97-QUACK. **Fax:** (330) 253-3300.
E-Mail Address: information@akronrubberducks.com.
Website: www.akronrubberducks.com.
Affiliation (first year): Cleveland Guardians (1989). **Years in League:** 2021-

OWNERSHIP/MANAGEMENT

Operated by: Fast Forward Sports Group/Akron Baseball, LLC. **Principal Owner/CEO:** Ken Babby. **President:** Jim Pfander. **CFO:** Shawn Carlson. **Chief Human Resource Officer:** Leatrice Buck. **Executive Assistant to Ken Babby:** Jill Popov. **Financial Reporting Analyst:** Mark Gupko. **President and General Manager:** Jim Pfander. **Vice President, Sales:** Dave Burke. **Vice President, Premium Experience:** Sam Dankoff. **Vice President, Ballpark Operations:** Adam Horner. **Office Manager:** Missy Dies. **Vice President, Ballpark Operations:** Adam Horner. **Director, Ballpark Operations:** James Parsons. **Head Groundskeeper:** Chris Walsh. **Assistant Groundskeeper:** Colt Boxler. **Director, Player Facilities:** Shad Gross. **Manger, Promotions and Community Relations:** Austin Stephens. **Coordinator, Promotions and Community Relations:** Zak Gordon. **Art Director:** Scott Watkins. **Manager, Creative Services:** Jack Haines. **Coordinator, Media Relations:** Jimmy Farmer. **Lead Broadcaster:** Marco LaNave. **Manager, Corporate Partnerships and Special Events:** Brian Lobban. **Coordinator, Corporate Partnerships:** Nick Bello. **Manager, Accounting:** Trevor Burk. **Coordinator, Accounting:** Breana Burkhart. **Supervisor, Food and Beverage:** Maddie Smith. **Coordinator, Food & Beverage:** Joe Kline. **Manager, Culinary Operations:** Louis Willmon-Holland. **Coordinator, Merchandise:** Luke Trese. **Director, Amateur Baseball Development/RubberDucks Baseball Academy:** Roy Jacobs. **Manager, Season Ticket Service and Sales:** Trevor McGuire. **Coordinator, Ticket Operations:** Luke Farmer. **Ticket Sales Executives:** Ethan Graham, Kyle Magovac, Noah Finley, Austin Havekost.

FIELD STAFF

Manager: Rouglas Odor. **Hitting Coach:** Mike Mergenthaler. **Pitching Coach:** Brad Goldberg. **Asst. Hitting Coach:** Ian Forster. **Bench Coach:** Daniel Robertson. **Athletic Trainer:** Jake Legan. **Strength Coach:** Mo Cuevas.

GAME INFORMATION

Radio Announcers: Marco LaNave, Jim Clark. **No. of Games Broadcast:** 138. **Flagship Station:** WHLO 640-AM. **PA Announcer:** Ethan Graham. **Official Scorer:** Chuck Murr. **Stadium Name:** Canal Park. **Location:** From I-76 East or I-77 South, exit onto Route 59 East, exit at Exchange/Cedar, right onto Cedar, left at Main Street; From I-76 West or I-77 North, exit at Main Street/Downtown, follow exit onto Broadway Street, left onto Exchange Street, right at Main Street. **Standard Game Time:** 6:35 (non-fireworks game); 7:05 pm (fireworks games), Sun 2:05. **Ticket Price Range:** $5-25. **Visiting Club Hotel:** Fairfield Inn & Suites by Marriott Akron Fairlawn. **Telephone:** (330) 665-0641.

ALTOONA CURVE

Address: Peoples Natural Gas Field, 1000 Park Avenue, Altoona, PA 16602
Telephone: (814) 943-5400. **Fax:** (814) 942-9132
E-Mail Address: frontoffice@altoonacurve.com. **Website:** www.altoonacurve.com
Affiliation (first year): Pittsburgh Pirates (1999). **Years in League:** 2021-

OWNERSHIP/MANAGEMENT

Operated By: Lozinak Professional Baseball. **Managing Members:** Bob and Joan Lozinak. **COO:** David Lozinak. **CFO:** Mike Lozinak. **General Manager:** Nate Bowen. **Assistant General Manager/Director of Merchandise:** Michelle Gravert. **Senior Advisor:** Sal Baglieri, Derek Martin. **Director of Finance:** Mary Lamb. **Assistant Finance Manager:**

BaseballAmerica.com

Baseball America 2023 Directory • **101**

MINOR LEAGUES

Hannah Reading. **Administrative Assistant:** Michelle Anna. **Director of Communications & Broadcasting:** Jon Mozes. **Assistant Director of Communications & Broadcasting:** Preston Shoemaker. **Director of Ticketing:** Ed Moffett. **Box Office Manager:** Austin Finochio. **Ticket Account Managers:** Rebekah Grainer, Tony Talarigo, Logan Ulmer. **Director of Community Relations & Social Media:** Annie Choiniere. **Director of Ballpark Operations:** Doug Mattern. **Operations Assistant:** Louis Miller. **Operations Ninja:** Will Lozinak. **Head Groundskeeper:** Mac Watson. **Assistant Groundskeeper:** Matt Clark. **Director of Concessions:** Jaime Skipper. **Assistant Director of Concessions:** Glenn McComas. **Assistant Concessions Manager:** Ryan Long. **Mascot Coordinator:** Ryan Neely. **Director of Creative Services:** Jon Weaver. **Creative Services Assistant:** Reid Pohland. **Director of Marketing, Promotions & Special Events:** Mike Kessling.

FIELD STAFF
Manager: Callix Crabbe. **Hitting Coach:** Jon Nunnally. **Pitching Coach:** Cale Johnson. **Integrated Baseball Performance Coach:** Blake Butler. **Bench Coach:** Gary Green. **Athletic Trainer:** Victor Silva. **Strength & Conditioning Coach:** Glenn Nutting.

GAME INFORMATION
Radio Announcers: Jon Mozes, Preston Shoemaker. **No. of Games Broadcast:** 138. **Flagship Station:** WRTA 98.5 FM and 1240 AM. **PA Announcer:** Rich DeLeo. **Official Scorers:** Ted Beam, David Musil, Chris Strawmier. **Stadium Name:** Peoples Natural Gas Field. **Location:** Located just off the Frankstown Road Exit off I-99. **Standard Game Times:** 6:00 p.m., 4:00 p.m. (Saturday's April – May), 1:00 p.m. (Sunday's)

BINGHAMTON RUMBLE PONIES

Office Address: 211 Henry St., Binghamton, NY 13901.
Mailing Address: PO Box 598, Binghamton, NY 13902.
Telephone: (607) 722-3866. **Fax:** (607) 723-7779.
E-Mail Address: info@bingrp.com. **Website:** www.bingrp.com.
Affiliation (first year): New York Mets (1992). **Years in League:** 2021-

OWNERSHIP/MANAGEMENT
President: David Sobotka. **General Manager:** John Bayne. **Creative Director:** Karen Sobotka. **Director of Business Operations:** Kelly Hust. **Director of Stadium Operations:** Craig Baker. **Director of Community Engagement:** Eddie Saunders. **Director of Marketing and Creative Services:** Henry Feigen. **Director of Operations and Sales:** Richard Tylicki. **Box Office Manager:** Molly Hawley.

FIELD STAFF
Manager: TBA. **Hitting Coach:** TBA. **Pitching Coach:** TBA. **Fundamentals Coach:** TBA. **Athletic Trainer:** TBA. **Strength Coach:** TBA.

GAME INFORMATION
Radio Announcer: TBA. **No. of Games Broadcast:** 138. **PA Announcer:** Frank Perney. **Official Scorer:** TBD. **Stadium Name:** Mirabito Stadium. **Stadium Location:** I-81 to exit 4S (Binghamton), Route 11 exit to Henry Street. **Standard Game Times:** 6:35, 7:05 (Fri), 1:05 (Day Games). **Ticket Price Range:** $8-$14. **Visiting Club Hotel:** Holiday Inn Downtown.

BOWIE BAYSOX

Address: Prince George's Stadium, 4101 Crain Hwy, Bowie, MD 20716.
Telephone: (301) 805-6000. **Fax:** (301) 464-4911.
E-Mail Address: info@baysox.com. **Website:** www.baysox.com.
Affiliation (first year): Baltimore Orioles (1993). **Years in League:** 2021-

OWNERSHIP/MANAGEMENT
Owned By: Attain Sports and Entertainment. **General Manager:** Brian Shallcross. **Business Manager:** Landon Ferrell. **Director, Ticket Operations:** Charlene Fewer. **Director, Sponsorships:** Matt McLaughlin. **Head Groundskeeper:** Ben Baker. **Stadium Operations Manager:** Justin Corsa. **Director, Gameday Personnel:** Darlene Mingioli. **Clubhouse Manager:** Jon Weinberg.

FIELD STAFF
Manager: Kyle Moore. **Hitting Coach:** Sherman Johnson. **Pitching Coach:** Forrest Herrmann. **Fundamentals Coach:** TBA. **Athletic Trainer:** TBA. **Strength Coach:** TBA.

GAME INFORMATION
Radio Broadcaster: Matt Sabados. **No. of Games Broadcast:** 138. **PA Announcer:** Tom DeGroff.
Official Scorers: Dan Gretz, Ted Black, Peter O'Reilly.
Stadium Name: Prince George's Stadium. **Location:** 1/4 mile south of US 50/Route 301 Interchange in Bowie. **Standard Game Times:** Mon-Thu, Sat. 6:**35 pm**, Fri 7:**05 pm**, Sun 1:**35 pm**. **Ticket Price Range:** $8-$18. **Visiting Club Hotel:** Crowne Plaza Annapolis, 173 Jennifer Rd, Annapolis, MD 21401; **Telephone:** (410) 266-3131.

MINOR LEAGUES

ERIE SEAWOLVES

Address: 831 French St, Erie, PA 16501.
Telephone: (814) 456-1300.
E-Mail Address: seawolves@seawolves.com. **Website:** www.seawolves.com.
Affiliation (first year): Detroit Tigers (2001). **Years in League:** 2021-

OWNERSHIP/MANAGEMENT
Principal Owners: At Bat Group, LLC.
CEO: Fernando Aguirre. **President:** Greg Coleman. **Assistant GM, Communications:** Greg Gania. **Assistant GM, Sales:** Mark Pirrello. **Director, Accounting/Finance:** Amy McArdle. **Director, Operations:** Drew Barajas. **Director, Entertainment:** Jason Dougherty. **Director, Fan Engagement:** Laina Banic. **Director, Merchandise:** Christy Buchar. **Director, Food/Beverage:** Jeff Burgess. **Assistant Director, Food & Beverage:** Mat Turner. **Director of Ticket Operations:** Tom Barnes. **Account Executive:** Sean Taylor. **Account Executive:** Trap Wentling

FIELD STAFF
Manager: Gabe Alvarez. **Hitting Coach:** John Murrian. **Pitching Coach:** Juan Pimentel. **Bench Coach:** Matt Malott. **Athletic Trainer:** Chris Vick. **Strength/Conditioning Coach:** Donny Trapp.

GAME INFORMATION
Radio Announcer: Greg Gania. **No. of Games Broadcast:** 138. **Flagship Station:** Fox Sports Radio WFNN 1330-AM. **PA Announcer:** TBA. **Official Scorer:** TBA. **Stadium Name:** UPMC Park. **Location:** US 79 North to East 12th Street exit, left on State Street, right on 9th Street. **Standard Game Times:** 6:05 p.m., **Sun** 1:35 p.m. **Ticket Price Range:** $12/$15 in advance| $15/$18 on game day. **Visiting Club Hotel:** Baymont by Wyndham Erie, 8170 Perry Hwy., Erie, PA 16509. **Telephone:** (814) 866-8808.

HARRISBURG SENATORS

Office Address: FNB Field, City Island, Harrisburg, PA 17101.
Mailing Address: PO Box 15757, Harrisburg, PA 17105.
Telephone: (717) 231-4444. **Fax:** (717) 231-4445.
E-Mail address: information@senatorsbaseball.com. **Website:** www.senatorsbaseball.com.
Affiliation (first year): Washington Nationals (2005). **Years in League:** 2021-

OWNERSHIP/MANAGEMENT
President: Kevin Kulp. **Vice President/General Manager:** Randy Whitaker. **Assistant General Manager, Marketing:** Ashley Grotte. **Vice President of Stadium Operations:** Tim Foreman. **Accounting Manager:** Donna Demczak. **Accounting Assistant:** Courtney Keller. **Sr. Corporate Corporate Sales Executive:** Nathan Rovenolt. **Director of Ticket Operations:** Matt McGrady. **Sales Service Coordinator:** Corey Pierce. **Group Event Coordinator:** Cole Single. **Ticket Account Executives:** Josh Troutman, Cody Nelson, and Zach Taylor. **Radio Broadcaster:** Terry Byrom. **Director of Community Relations:** JK McKay. **Director of Game Entertainment:** Jess Knaster. **Video Production Manager:** Troy Matthews. **Digital Marketing Coordinator:** Casey Saussaman. **Creative Services Coordinator:** Delaney Mitchell. **Head Groundskeeper:** Brandon Forsburg. **Stadium Operations Manager:** Tyler Rivera.
2023 Intern Class: Ashley Ward, Brennen Eshleman, Colin Snyder, Devon Grunderson, Ethan Shellenberger, and Jackson Fowler.

FIELD STAFF
Manager: Delino DeShields. **Hitting Coach:** Tim Doherty. **Pitching Coach:** Joel Hanrahan. **Developmental Coach:** Oscar Salazar. **Trainer:** Don Neidig. **Strength Coach:** Ryan Grose.

GAME INFORMATION
Radio Announcers: Terry Byrom & Frankie Vernouski. **No. of Games Broadcast:** 138. **Flagship Station:** CBS Sports Radio Harrisburg. **PA Announcer:** TBA. **Official Scorers:** Andy Linker and Mick Reinhard. **Stadium Name:** FNB Field. **Location:** I-83, exit 23 (Second Street) to Market Street, bridge to City Island. **Ticket Price Range:** $9-35. **Visiting Club Hotel:** Hotel Indigo Harrisburg-Hershey, 765 Eisenhower Blvd, Harrisburg, Pa, **17111, Phone:** 717-558-7676 . **Telephone:** (717) 857-8776. **Visiting Team Workout Facility:** TBD.

HARTFORD YARD GOATS

Address: Dunkin' Park, 1214 Main Street, Hartford CT 06103
Telephone: (860) 246-4628. **Fax:** (860) 247-4628
E-Mail Address: info@yardgoatsbaseball.com. **Website:** www.YardGoatsBaseball.com
Affiliation (first year): Colorado Rockies (2015). **Years in League:** 2021-

OWNERSHIP/MANAGEMENT
President: Tim Restall. **General Manager:** Mike Abramson.
Assistant General Manager, Sales: Josh Montinieri. **Assistant General Manager, Operations:** Dean Zappalorti.

MINOR LEAGUES

Controller: Jim Bonfiglio. **Director, Broadcasting & Media Relations:** Jeff Dooley. **Executive Director of Business Development:** Steve Given. **Executive Director of Ballpark Operations:** Kyle Calhoon. **Executive Director, Community Partnerships:** Aisha Petteway. **Director of Ticket Sales:** Steve Mekkelsen. **Director of Stadium Events:** Jessica Skelly. **Director of Production and Creative Services:** Mike Delgado. **Director of Stadium Operations:** Joe Bossi. **Hospitality Manager:** Matt DiBona. **Human Resources Manager:** Monique Skyers. **Field Operations Manager:** Matt Piersanti. **Promotions & Client Services Manager:** Isabelle Meckfessel. **Creative Services & Digital Marketing Coordinator:** Monica Porth. **Event Coordinator:** Courtney Angers. **Senior Account Executive:** Shawn Perry. **Group Sales Manager:** Jacob Michney. **Ticket Sales Account Executive:** Matt Johnson. **Ticket Sales Account Executive:** Odane Artwell. **Ticket Sales Account Executive:** Olivia Besthoff. **Ticket Operations Manager:** Maddie Clark. **Box Office Coordinator:** Eric Morin. **Merchandise Coordinator:** Ryan Sandler. **Community Programs Coordinator:** Dazmarie Maldonado. **Promotions Coordinator:** Andrew Meagher. **Operations Assistant:** Anthony Marcel. **Front Office Receptionist:** Shirelle Buie. **Professional Sports Catering Concessions Manager:** Andrew Labov. **Business Manager:** Kevin Molde. **Executive Chef:** Joe Bartlett.

FIELD STAFF
Manager: Chris Denorfia. **Bench Coach:** Luis Lopez. **Pitching Coach:** Blaine Beatty. **Hitting Coach:** Tom Sutaris.

GAME INFORMATION
Radio Announcers: Jeff Dooley, Dan Lovallo. **No. of Games Broadcast:** 138. **Flagship Station:** News Radio 1410 AM/100.9 FM Spanish AM 1120 Danny Rodriguez, Derik Rodriguez. **PA Announcer:** Jared Doyon. **Official Scorer:** Jim Keener. **Stadium Name:** Dunkin' Park. **Directions: From the West:** Take 84 East to Exit 50 (Main Street). Take Exit 50 toward Main St. Use the left lane to merge onto Chapel St S. Turn left onto Trumbull St. Use the middle lane to turn left onto Main St. **From the East:** Take 84 West to Exit 50 (US-44 W/Morgan Street). Follow I-91 S/Main St. Take a slight right onto Main St. **From the North:** Take 91 South to Exit 32A - 32B (Trumbull St). Turn left onto Market St. Turn right onto Morgan St. Take a slight right onto Main St. **From the South:** Take 91 North to Exit 32A - 32B (Market St). Use the left lane to take Exit 32A-32B for Trumbull St. Use the middle lane to turn left onto Market St. Turn right onto Morgan St. Take a slight right onto Main St. **Ticket Price Range:** $6-22. **Visiting Club Hotel:** Hilton Garden Inn Hartford South/Glastonbury. **Address:** 85 Glastonbury Boulevard, Glastonbury, CT. **Phone:** 860-659-1025

NEW HAMPSHIRE
FISHER CATS

Address: 1 Line Dr, Manchester, NH 03101.
Telephone: (603) 641-2005. **Fax:** (603) 641-2055.
E-Mail Address: info@nhfishercats.com. **Website:** www.nhfishercats.com.
Affiliation (first year): Toronto Blue Jays (2004). **Years in League:** 2021-

OWNERSHIP/MANAGEMENT
Operated By: DSF Sports Group & NHSC LLC. **Partner:** Art Solomon. **Partner:** Rick Brenner. **Partner:** Tom Silvia. **President:** Mike Ramshaw. **General Manager:** Mike Neis. **Executive Director of Finance:** Rich Engler. **Senior Vice President, Sales:** Jeff Tagliaferro. **Executive Director of Special Events and the Fisher Cats Foundation:** Stephanie Fournier. **Executive Director of Facilities:** Shawn Greenough. **Corporate Sales and Promotions Coordinator:** Andrew Marais. **Box Office Manager:** Tara Leeth. **Broadcasting and Media Relations Manager:** Steve Goldberg. **Graphic Design and Production Manager:** Amy Cecil. **Merchandise Manager:** Jacob Madsen. **Ticket Service Manager:** Nate Newcombe. **Facilities Manager:** Kevin Sweeney. **Head Groundskeeper:** Mike Georgiadis. **Ticket Sales Account Executive:** Caleb Baum. **Ticket Sales Account Executive:** Darrin Messier. **Account Executive:** Jared Brescia. **Account Executive:** Nathan Ward. **Special Assistant to the Team President and Front Office Manager:** Aubrey Smith.

FIELD STAFF
Manager: TBA. **Hitting Coach:** TBA. **Pitching Coach:** TBA. **Fundamentals Coach:** TBA. **Athletic Trainer:** TBA. **Strength Coach:** TBA.

GAME INFORMATION
Radio Announcers: Steve Goldberg, Bob Lipman. **No. of Games Broadcast:** 138. **Flagship Station:** WGIR 610-AM. **PA Announcers:** Adam LaFleur, Ben Altsher. **Official Scorers:** Chick Smith, Lenny Parker, Mitch Mastromatteo, Wally Hauser. **Stadium Name:** Delta Dental Stadium. **Location:** From I-93 North, take I-293 North to exit 5 (Granite Street), right on Granite Street, right on South Commercial Street, right on Line Drive. **Ticket Price Range:** $10-$14. **Visiting Club Hotel:** Tru by Hilton Manchester Downtown 135 Spring St, Manchester, NH 03101. **Telephone:** (603) 669-3000.

PORTLAND SEA DOGS

Office Address: 271 Park Ave, Portland, ME 04102.
Mailing Address: PO Box 636, Portland, ME 04104.
Telephone: (207) 874-9300. **Fax:** (207) 780-0317.
E-Mail address: seadogs@seadogs.com. **Website:** www.seadogs.com.
Affiliation (first year): Boston Red Sox (2003). **Years in League:** 1994-

MINOR LEAGUES

OWNERSHIP/MANAGEMENT
Operated By: Diamond Baseball Holdings
President/General Manager: Geoff Iacuessa. **VP/Financial Affairs & Game Operations:** Jim Heffley. **VP/Communications & Fan Experience:** Chris Cameron. **Assistant General Manager/Sales:** Dennis Meehan. **Director of Ticket Operations:** Jesse Scaglion. **Director of Promotions:** Allison Casiles. **Director, Media Relations & Broadcasting:** Emma Tiedemann. **Director, Business Development:** Alan Barker. **Director, Creative Services:** Chelsea Roemer. **Mascot Coordinator:** Tim Jorn. **Account Executive- Corporate Sales:** Justin Kelleher. **Account Executive- Ticket Sales:** Lauren Gasaway. **Account Executive- Ticket Sales:** Madison Spencer. **Director, Food Services:** Mike Scorza. **Assistant Director, Food Services:** Greg Moyes. **Clubhouse Manager:** Mike Coziahr. **Head Groundskeeper:** Jason Cooke. **Assistant Groundskeeper:** Cam Eggeman. **Assistant Groundskeeper:** Brandon Rolfe.

FIELD STAFF
Manager: Chad Epperson. **Hitting Coach:** Doug Clark. **Pitching Coach:** Sean Isaac. **Development Coach:** Joe Cronin. **Athletic Trainer:** Bobby Stachura. **Strength & Conditioning Coach:** Joe Hudson.

GAME INFORMATION
Radio Announcer: Emma Tiedemann. **No. of Games Broadcast:** 138. **Flagship Station:** WPEI 95.9 FM. **PA Announcer:** Paul Coughlin. **Official Scorer:** Thom Hinton. **Stadium Name:** Hadlock Field. **Location:** From South, I-295 to exit 5, merge onto Congress Street, left at St John Street, merge right onto Park Ave; From North, I-295 to exit 6A, right onto Park Ave. **Ticket Price Range:** $8-13. **Visiting Club Hotel:** Holiday Inn Express, 303 Sable Oaks Dr., South Portland, ME 04106. **Telephone:** (207) 775-3900.

READING FIGHTIN PHILS

Office Address: Route 61 South/1900 Centre Ave, Reading, PA 19605. **Mailing Address:** PO Box 15050, Reading, PA 19612.
Telephone: (610) 370-2255. **Fax:** (610) 373-5868.
E-Mail Address: info@fightins.com. **Website:** www.fightins.com.
Affiliation: Philadelphia Phillies (1967). **Years in League:** 2021-

OWNERSHIP/MANAGEMENT
Operated By: E&J Baseball Club, Inc. **Principal Owner:** Reading Baseball LP. **Managing Partner:** Craig Stein.
General Manager: Scott Hunsicker. **Assistant General Manager:** Matt Hoffmaster. **Exec. Director, Sales:** Joe Bialek. **Exec. Director, Baseball Operations:** Kevin Sklenarik. **Exec. Director, Tickets & Groups:** Mike Becker. **Exec. Director, Community & Fan Development:** Mike Robinson. **Exec. Director, Business Development:** Anthony Pignetti. **Exec. Director, Promotions, Entertainment & Education:** Todd Hunsicker. **Controller:** Kris Haver. **Head Groundskeeper:** Dan Douglas. **Director, Marketing & Exec. Director, Baseballtown Charities:** Tonya Petrunak. **Video Director:** Andy Kauffman. **Director, Food & Beverage:** Travis Hart. **Office Manager:** Deneen Giesen. **Director, Groups:** Jon Nally. **Director, Client Fulfillment/Clubhouse Operations:** Andrew Nelson. **Director, Graphic Arts/Merchandise:** Ryan Springborn. **Account Executive:** Nick Helber. **Account Executive:** Mara Fulmer. **Media Relations/Broadcasting Manager:** TBA. **Account Executive:** Matt Koch. **Stadium Operations Manager:** Ricky Bruno.

FIELD STAFF
Manager: Al Pedrique. **Hitting Coach:** Tyler Henson. **Pitching Coach:** Brad Bergesen. **Position Coach:** Ray Ricker. **Athletic Trainer:** Steve Torregrosa. **Strength and Conditioning Coach:** Bruce Peditto.

GAME INFORMATION
Radio Announcer: TBA. **No. of Games Broadcast:** 138. Internet Stream. **Official Scorers:** Kyle Matschke, Brian Kopetsky, Josh Leiboff, Dick Shute. **Stadium Name:** FirstEnergy Stadium. **Location:** From east, take Pennsylvania Turnpike West to Morgantown exit, to 176 North, to 422 West, to Route 12 East, to Route 61 South exit; From west, take 422 East to Route 12 East, to Route 61 South exit; From north, take 222 South to Route 12 exit, to Route 61 South exit; From south, take 222 North to 422 West, to Route 12 East exit at Route 61 South. **Standard Game Times:** 6:45 or 7:00pm, **Sundays** 3:15 or 5:15. **Ticket Price Range:** $7-13. **Visiting Club Hotel:** DoubleTree by Hilton Hotel Reading, 701 Penn St., Reading, PA 19601. **Telephone:** (610) 375-8000.

RICHMOND FLYING SQUIRRELS

Address: 3001 N Arthur Ashe Boulevard, Richmond, VA 23230.
Telephone: (804) 359-3866. **Fax:** (804) 359-1373.
E-Mail Address: info@squirrelsbaseball.com. **Website:** www.squirrelsbaseball.com.
Affiliation: San Francisco Giants (2010). **Years in League:** 2021-

OWNERSHIP/MANAGEMENT
Operated By: Navigators Baseball LP. **President/Managing Partner:** Lou DiBella.
CEO: Todd "Parney" Parnell. **Vice President/General Manager:** Ben Rothrock. **Assistant General Manager:** Ben Terry. **Assistant General Manager:** Anthony Oppermann. **Controller:** Faith Casey-Harriss. **Assistant Controller:** Lisa Bennette. **Director of Corporate Partnerships:** Jamie Gordon. **Director of Group Sales:** Garrett Erwin. **Assistant Director of Group Sales:** Wesley Donald. **Box Office Manager:** Derrick McCabe. **Group Sales & Box Office Assistant:** James Dillard. **Group & Ticket Sales Executive:** Clayton Cotner. **Group & Ticket Sales Executive:** Jackson Strickler.

MINOR LEAGUES

Group Hospitality Manager: Carnie Bragg. **Hospitality & Merchandising Assistant:** Kayce Battle. **Director of Communications & Broadcasting:** Trey Wilson. **Media Assistant & Corporate Sales Executive:** Blaine McCormick. **Director of Entertainment:** Caroline Phipps. **Director of Business Operations:** Hannah DeFrank. **Creative Services & Production Director:** Nick Elder. **Graphic Design & Creative Services Manager:** Hunter Glotz. **Community Relations Manager:** Bailey Johnson. **Marketing & Social Media Manager:** Samantha McCloskey. **Mascot & Performance Manager:** Jack Caldwell. **Promotions Assistant & Office Manager:** Janell Armstead. **Director of Field Operations:** James Petrella. **Director of Stadium Operations:** Austin Doherty. **Operations Manager:** Drew Fagaly. **Director of Food & Beverage:** Steve Bales. **Assistant Director of Food & Beverage:** Justin Stone. **Food & Beverage Manager:** Michael Evans. **Director of Merchandising:** Jackson Hairfield.

FIELD STAFF
Manager: Dennis Pelfrey. **Hitting Coach:** Cory Elasik. **Pitching Coach:** Paul Oseguera. **Fundamentals Coach:** Lipso Nava. **Athletic Trainer:** Chris Walsh. **Strength Coach:** Matt Jordan.

GAME INFORMATION
Radio Announcers: Trey Wilson & Blaine McCormick. **No. of Games Broadcast:** 138. **Flagship Station:** Sports Radio 910 The Fan WRNL. **PA Announcer:** Bianca Bryan. **Official Scorer:** Bob Flynn. **Stadium Name:** The Diamond. **Location:** Right off I-64 at the Boulevard exit. **Standard Game Times:** 6:35 pm, Fri., 7:05, Sat. 6:05, Sun. 1:35. **Ticket Price Range:** $10-17. **Visiting Club Hotel:** Fairfield Inn & Suites by Marriott Richmond Short Pump/1-64. **Telephone:** (804) 545-4200.

SOMERSET PATRIOTS

Office Address: One Patriots Park, Bridgewater, NJ 08807.
Telephone: (908) 252-0700. **Fax:** (908) 252-0776.
Website: somersetpatriots.com.
Affiliation: New York Yankees (2021). **Years in League:** 2021-

OWNERSHIP/MANAGEMENT
Operated by: Somerset Baseball Partners, LLC. **Ownership:** Jonathan Kalafer and Josh Kalafer. **Co-Chairmen:** Jonathan Kalafer and Josh Kalafer. **President/GM:** Patrick McVerry. **Senior VP, Marketing:** Dave Marek. **VP, Communications & Media Relations:** Marc Russinoff. **VP, Operations:** Bryan Iwicki. **VP, Ticket Operations:** Matt Kupas. **Senior Director, Merchandise:** Rob Crossman. **Director, Tickets:** Nick Cherrillo. **Director, Marketing:** Hal Hansen. **Director, Business Development:** Ken Smith. **Director, Administration:** Michele DaCosta. **Manager, Media Relations & Broadcasting:** Steven Cusumano. **Account Executives:** Stephen Goldsmith, Molly Swayne, Jacob Unger, Matt Godlewski, James Killeen. **Controller:** Suzanne Colon. **Accountant:** Stephanie DePass. **Head Groundskeeper:** Dan Purner. **Homeplate Catering and Hospitality VP/General Manager:** Mike McDermott. **Assistant General Manager of Homeplate Catering and Hospitality:** Jimmy Search. **Director, Operations of HomePlate Catering:** Aly McGrath. **Accounting/Office Manager:** Kelly Bradshaw.

FIELD STAFF
Manager: Raul Dominguez. **Hitting Coach:** Jake Hirst. **Pitching Coach:** Grayson Crawford. **Defensive Coach:** Aaron Bossi. **Athletic Trainer:** Mike Becker. **Strength Coach:** Danny Smith. **Advance Scouting Analyst:** Steven DiMaria.

GAME INFORMATION
Lead Play-By-Play: Steven Cusumano. **No. of Games Broadcast:** 138. **Flagship Station:** FOX Sports New Jersey 93.5 FM/ 1450 AM. **Video Streams:** MiLB.tv. **Ballpark Name:** TD Bank Ballpark. **Standard Game Times:** Mon.- Thurs. 6:05 pm/ 6:35 pm/ 7:05 pm, Fri & Sat., 6:35 pm / 7:05 pm, Sun., 1:05 pm/ 5:05 pm.

MINOR LEAGUES

SOUTHERN LEAGUE

STADIUM INFORMATION

Club	Stadium	Opened	LF	CF	RF	Capacity	2022 Att.
Biloxi	MGM Park	2015	335	400	335	6,000	148,865
Birmingham	Regions Field	2013	320	400	325	8,500	266,921
Chattanooga	AT&T Field	2000	325	400	330	6,362	213,685
Mississippi	Trustmark Park	2005	335	402	332	7,416	150,491
Montgomery	Riverwalk Stadium	2004	314	380	332	7,000	156,356
Pensacola	Blue Wahoos Stadium	2012	325	400	335	6,000	281,972
Rocket City	Toyota Field	2021	326	400	326	7,500	327,007
Tennessee	Smokies Stadium	2000	330	400	330	6,000	294,334

BILOXI SHUCKERS

Address: 105 Caillavet Street, Biloxi, MS 39530
Telephone: (228) 233-3465
E-Mail Address: info@biloxishuckers.com. **Website:** www.biloxishuckers.com.
Affiliation (first year): Milwaukee Brewers (2015). **Years in League:** 2015-

OWNERSHIP/MANAGEMENT
Operated By: Biloxi Baseball LLC.
President: Ken Young. **General Manager:** Hunter Reed. **Assistant General Manager:** Trevor Matifes. **Ticket Operations Coordinator:** Johnny Tribbett. **Ballpark Entertainment Manager:** Daniel Clapper. **Media Relations Manager and Broadcaster:** Garrett Greene. **Community Relations Manager:** David Blackwell. **Stadium Operations Manager:** Vandy Mitchell. **Marketing & Social Media Coordinator:** Makenzie Crampton. **Retail Manager:** Veronica Wright. **Head Groundskeeper:** Trey Bowman. **Accounting Manager:** Pam Hendrickson.

FIELD STAFF
Manager: Mike Guerrero. **Pitching Coach:** Will Schierholz. **Hitting Coach:** Chuckie Caufield. **Bench Coach:** Nick Stanley. **Coach:** Josh Spence. **Athletic Trainer:** Andrew Staehling. **Associate Athletic Trainer:** Tanner Bos. **Strength and Conditioning Specialist:** Grant Kastelan

GAME INFORMATION
PA Announcer: Kyle Curley. **Official Scorer:** Scotty Berkowitz. **No. of Games Broadcast:** 138. **Stadium Name:** MGM Park. **Directions:** I-10 to I-110 South toward beach, take Ocean Springs exit onto US 90 (Beach Blvd), travel east one block, turn left on Caillavet Street, stadium is on the left. **Ticket Price Range:** $8-$26. **Visiting Club Hotel:** DoubleTree by Hilton Biloxi on Beach Blvd.

BIRMINGHAM BARONS

Office Address: 1401 1st Ave South, Birmingham, AL, 35233.
Mailing Address: PO Box 877, Birmingham, AL, 35201.
Telephone: (205) 988-3200. **Fax:** (205) 988-9698.
E-Mail Address: barons@barons.com. **Website:** www.barons.com.
Affiliation (first year): Chicago White Sox (1986). **Years in League:** 2021-

OWNERSHIP/MANAGEMENT
Principal Owners: Don Logan, Jeff Logan, Stan Logan. **President/General Manager:** Jonathan Nelson. **Vice President of Business Development & Entertainment:** John Cook. **CFO:** Blake Boozer. **Assistant Controller:** Cary Southerland. **Inventory Control Accountant:** Jonathan Judge. **Director of Group Sales:** Kevin Piotrzkowski. **Group Sales Manager:** Allie Darden. **Group Sales Manager:** Coty Holloway. **Group Sales Manager:** Will Larsen. **Group Sales Manager:** Tyler Baker. **Ticket Sales & Operations Director:** Josh Freund. **Director of Broadcasting:** Curt Bloom. **Head Groundskeeper:** Caleb Paullus. **Director of Stadium Operations:** Corey Johnson. **Director of Customer Service:** George Chavous. **Receptionist & Data Clerk:** Ashlee Bryan. **Director of Food & Beverage:** Gus Stoudemire. **Concessions Manager:** Tametrius Motley. **Catering Managers:** Sydney Boatner, Jordan Carmichael. **Premium Services Manager:** Maddie Doran. **Executive Chef:** Nick Tittle. **Sous Chef:** Vic Arnold.

FIELD STAFF
Manager: Lorenzo Bundy. **Hitting Coach:** Nicky Delmonico. **Pitching Coach:** Danny Farquhar. **Fundamentals Coach:** TBA. **Athletic Trainer:** TBA. **Strength Coach:** TBA.

GAME INFORMATION
Radio Announcer: Curt Bloom. **No of Games Broadcast:** 69. **Flagship Station:** JOX 94.5-WJOX-FM. **PA**

MINOR LEAGUES

Announcers: Derek Scudder, Andy Parish. **Official Scorers:** Jeff Allison, David Tompkins. **Stadium Name:** Regions Field. **Location:** I-65 (exit 259B) in Birmingham. **Standard Game Times:** 7:05 pm, Sat. 6:30, Sun 4:00. **Ticket Price Range:** $10-23. **Visiting Club Hotel:** Hyatt Regency Birmingham - The Wynfrey Hotel, 1000 Riverchase Galleria, Birmingham, AL 35244. **Telephone:** (205) 988-3200

CHATTANOOGA LOOKOUTS

Office Address: 201 Power Alley, Chattanooga, TN 37402.
Mailing Address: PO Box 11002, Chattanooga, TN 37401.
Telephone: (423) 267-2208. **Fax:** (423) 267-4258.
E-Mail Address: lookouts@lookouts.com. **Website:** www.lookouts.com.
Affiliation (first year): Cincinnati Reds (2019). **Years in League:** 2021-

OWNERSHIP/MANAGEMENT
Operated By: Chattanooga Lookouts, LLC. **Principal Owner:** Hardball Capital. **Managing Partner:** Jason Freier. **President:** Rich Mozingo. **Vice President:** Andrew Zito. **Vice President, Finance & Business Operations:** Jennifer Crum. **Vice President, Food and Beverage:** Scott Burton. **Director, Public Relations:** Dan Kopf. **Director, Marketing & Entertainment:** Alex Tanish. **Director, Food & Beverage:** William Marr. **Senior Ticket Partnership Manager:** Jarrah Vella-Wright. **Ticket Partnership Manager:** Mark Curtis. **Ticket Partnership & Retail Manager:** Kansas Carpenter. **Ticket Operations Manager:** Sidney Hooper. **Operations Manager:** Michael Matheson. **Broadcaster:** Larry "The Voice" Ward.

FIELD STAFF
Manager: Jose Moreno. **Hitting Coach:** Daryle Ward. **Pitching Coach:** Brian Garman. **Coach:** Jefry Sierra

GAME INFORMATION
Radio Announcers: Larry Ward. **No. of Games Broadcast:** 138. **Flagship Station:** 98.1 The LAKE. **PA Announcer:** Gracen Shook, Tom McElligot. **Official Scorers:** Adam Belford, Howard Runyan. **Stadium Name:** AT&T Field. **Location:** From I-24, take US 27 North to exit 1C (4th Street), first left onto Chestnut Street, left onto Third Street. **Ticket Price Range:** TBD. **Visiting Club Hotel:** DoubleTree, 2232 Center Street, Chattanooga, TN 37421. **Telephone:** (423) 485-1185.

MISSISSIPPI BRAVES

Office Address: Trustmark Park, 1 Braves Way, Pearl, MS 39208.
Mailing Address: PO Box 97389, Pearl, MS 39288.
Telephone: (601) 932-8788. **Fax:** (601) 936-3567.
E-Mail Address: mississippibraves@braves.com. **Web site:** www.mississippibraves.com.
Affiliation (first year): Atlanta Braves (2005). **Years in League:** 2021-

OWNERSHIP/MANAGEMENT
Ownership: Diamond Baseball Holdings, LLC.
Vice President & General Manager: Pete Laven. **Assistant General Manager/Director of Sales:** Tim Mueller. **Office Manager:** Christy Shaw. **Ticket Manager:** Matthew Dispenza. **Account Executives:** Sean Bowden, Garrett Butler. **Head Groundskeeper:** Evan Berry. **Director of Group Sales:** David Kerr. **Director of Stadium Operations:** Zach Evans. **Director of Communications, Media & Broadcasting:** Chris Harris. **Food & Beverage Director:** Thomas Gazda.

FIELD STAFF
Manager: Kaneoka Texeira. **Hitting Coach:** Danny Santiesteban. **Pitching Coach:** Bo Henning. **Trainer:** TBD. **Coach:** TBD.

GAME INFORMATION
Radio Announcer: Chris Harris. **No. of Games Broadcast:** 138. **Flagship Station:** TBA
PA Announcer: Greg Flynn. **Official Scorer:** Mark Beason.
Stadium Name: Trustmark Park. **Location:** I-20 to exit 48/Pearl (Pearson Road). **Ticket Price Range:** $6-$25.
Visiting Club Hotel: Hilton Garden Inn Jackson Flowood, 118 Laurel Park Cove, Flowood, MS 39232. **Telephone:** (601) 487-0800.

MONTGOMERY BISCUITS

Address: 200 Coosa St., Montgomery, AL 36104.
Telephone: (334) 323-2255. **Fax:** (334) 323-2225.
E-Mail address: info@biscuitsbaseball.com. **Website:** www.biscuitsbaseball.com.
Affiliation (first year): Tampa Bay Rays (2004). **Years in League:** 2021-

OWNERSHIP/MANAGEMENT
Operated By: Biscuits Baseball LLC. **Chief Executive Officer:** Lou DiBella.
President: Todd "Parney" Parnell. **Chief Operating Officer:** Brendon Porter. **General Manager:** Michael Murphy.

MINOR LEAGUES

Corporate & Military Partnerships: Jay Jones. **Director of Group Sales:** Chris Walker. **Director of Entertainment & Uniforms:** I.J. Balaban. **Box Office Manager, Season Ticket Coordinator:** Justin Ross. **Marketing & Creative Services:** Jared McCarthy. **Broadcaster, Media Relations:** Chris Adams-Wall. **Retail Manager:** Ashley Williams. **Director, Food & Beverage:** Risa Juliano. **Assistant Director of Food & Beverage:** Nathan Edwards. **Director, Stadium Operations:** Steve Blackwell. **Assistant Director of Stadium Operations/Head Groundskeeper:** Alex English. **Business Manager:** Tracy Mims. **Executive Administrator:** Jeannie Burke. **Group Sales Executive:** Zach Proctor, Luke Wheeldon. **Ticket Sales Executive:** Jason Wieczorek.

FIELD STAFF
Manager: Morgan Ensberg. **Pitching Coach:** Steve Merriman. **Hitting Coach:** Wuarnner Rincones. **Bench Coach:** Frank Jagoda. **Athletic Trainer:** James Ramsdell. **Conditioning Coach:** Austin Teets

GAME INFORMATION
Radio Announcer: Chris Adams-Wall. **No of Games Broadcast:** 138. **Flagship Station:** WMSP 740-AM. **PA Announcer:** Rick Hendrick. **Official Scorer:** Brian Wilson. **Stadium Name:** Montgomery Riverwalk Stadium. **Location:** I-65 to exit 172, east on Herron Street, left on Coosa Street. **Ticket Price Range:** $8-16. **Visiting Club Hotel:** TBA.

PENSACOLA BLUE WAHOOS

Telephone: (850) 934-8444. **Fax:** (850) 791-6256.
E-Mail Address: info@bluewahoos.com. **Website:** www.bluewahoos.com
Affiliation (first year): Miami Marlins (2021). **Years in League:** 2012-

OWNERSHIP/MANAGEMENT
Operated by: Northwest Florida Professional Baseball LLC. **Principal Owners:** Quint Studer, Rishy Studer. **Minority Owners:** Bubba Watson, Derrick Brooks, Randall Wells, John List, Dana Suskind. **President:** Jonathan Griffith. **Executive Vice President & General Manager:** Steve Brice. **Vice President, Experience:** Donna Kirby. **Facilities Manager:** Mike Crenshaw, Mike Fitzgerald. **Head Groundskeeper:** Scotty Atkins. **Senior Writer:** Bill Vilona. **Broadcaster:** Erik Bremer. **Merchandise and Community Relations Manager:** Lauren Scott. **Ticket Operations Manager:** Brandon Miller. **Group Sales Executives:** Emily Mann, Tori Perkins, Steven Unser. **Corporate Sales Executive:** TJ Johnson. **Season Ticket Concierge:** Ryan O'Callaghan. **CFO:** Kathy Cadwell. **Accounts Payable:** Lea Howard. **Receptionist:** Pamela Ward.

FIELD STAFF
Manager: Kevin Randel. **Pitching Coach:** Dave Eiland. **Hitting Coach:** Matt Snyder. **Defensive Coach:** Danny Black. **Athletic Trainer:** Melissa Hampton. **Strength Coach:** Seth Gregorich.

GAME INFORMATION
Radio Announcer: Erik Bremer. **No. of Games Broadcast:** 138. **Flagship Station:** ESPN Pensacola. **PA Announcer:** Josh Gay, Kevin Peterson, Shane Tucker. **Official Standard Game Times:** 6:35 pm, Sat. 6:05, Sun. 4:05. **Ticket Price Range:** $6-$22

ROCKET CITY TRASH PANDAS

Address: 500 Trash Panda Way. Madison, AL 35758.
Telephone: (256) 325-1403.
E-Mail Address: Info@trashpandasbaseball.com. **Website:** trashpandasbaseball.com.
Affiliation (first year): Los Angeles Angels (2020). **Years in League:** 2020-

OWNERSHIP/MANAGEMENT
Owned and Operated by: BallCorps, LLC. **Managing Partner:** Mark Holland. **Executive Vice President and General Manager:** Garrett Fahrmann. **Executive Vice President:** Lindsey Knupp. **Vice President, Production and Entertainment:** Rob Sternberg. **Director, Finance:** Angy Blailock. **Senior Director, Operations:** Ken Clary. **Director, Food and Beverage:** Garien Shelby. **Director, Community Relations:** Maddison Kendrick. **Director, Ticket Operations:** Nate Leaser. **Director, Sales:** Cory Ausderau. **Director, Client Relations and Fan Experience:** Mareca Watson. **Director, Corporate Partnerships:** Trevor Kelly. **Director, Facility Maintenance:** Jason Marriott. **Head Groundskeeper:** Charlie Weaver.

FIELD STAFF
Manager: Andy Schatzley. **Hitting Coach:** Sean Kazmar Jr. **Pitching Coach:** Michael Wuertz. **Coach:** Dann Bilardello. **Strength & Conditioning Coach:** David Robertson. **Athletic Trainer:** T.D. Swinford

GAME INFORMATION
Director, Broadcasting and Baseball Information: Josh Caray. **No. of Games Broadcast:** 138. **Radio:** WUMP-FM 103.9 & 730 AM SportsRadio. **Website:** www.umpsports.com. **PA Announcer:** Antonio MacBeath. **Stadium Name:** Toyota Field. **Location:** I-565 to Toyota Field Exit. **Standard Game Times:** 6:35 pm (Tuesday-Saturday) 2:35 pm (Sundays, April-May, Sept.), 4:05 pm (Sundays, June-Aug). **Ticket Price Range:** $8-55. **Visiting Club Hotel:** AVID Hotel 125 Graphics Dr, Madison, AL 35758 (256) 325-1800

MINOR LEAGUES

TENNESSEE SMOKIES

Address: 3540 Line Drive, Kodak, TN 37764.
Telephone: (865) 286-2300. **Fax:** (865) 523-9913.
E-Mail Address: info@smokiesbaseball.com. **Website:** www.smokiesbaseball.com.
Affiliation (first year): Chicago Cubs (2007-). **Years in League:** 2021-

OWNERSHIP/MANAGEMENT

Owners: Randy and Jenny Boyd. **CEO:** Doug Kirchhofer. **President/COO:** Chris Allen. **Vice President:** Jeremy Boler. **General Manager:** Tim Volk. **Assistant General Manager, Stadium Operations:** Bryan Webster. **Assistant General Manager, Hospitality:** Chris Franklin. **Assistant General Manager, Marketing & Entertainment:** Aris M Theofanopoulos. **Director of Broadcasting:** Mick Gillispie. **Director of Outside Events:** Morgan Messick. **Assistant Director of Corporate Partnerships:** Baylor Love. **Corporate Sales Executive:** Trey Hinton. **Administrative Assistant:** Tolena Trout. **Director of Finance:** Paul Makres. **Admin/Finance Assistant:** Michelle Conway. **Accounting/HR Specialist:** Cheryl Brown. **Creative Services Manager:** Lindsay Coward. **Merchandise Manager:** Kenny Clawson. **Hospitality Manager:** David Branam. **Concessions Manager:** Tyler Kennedy. **Concessions Manager:** Caleb Mills. **Food & Beverage Assistant Manager:** Drew Miller. **Director of Ticket & Group Sales:** Emily Butler. **Box Office Manager:** Brett Adams. **Account Executive:** Stephen Haselton. **Account Executive:** Breanna Foy. **Account Executive:** Jake Blevins. **Stadium Operations Manager:** Bill Oaf. **Head Groundskeeper:** Duncan Long.

FIELD STAFF

Manager: Michael Ryan. **Hitting Coach:** Rick Strickland. **Pitching Coach:** Jamie Vermilyea. **Bench Coach:** Nick Lovullo. **Strength Coach:** TBD. **Athletic Trainer:** TBD.

GAME INFORMATION

Radio Announcer: Mick Gillispie. **No. of Games Broadcast:** 138. **Flagship Station:** WNML 99.1-FM/990-AM.

PA Announcer: George Yardley. **Official Scorer:** Wade Mitchell. **Stadium Name:** Smokies Stadium. **Location:** I-40 to exit 407, Highway 66 North. **Standard Game Times:** 7:00 pm, Sat. 7:00 pm, Sun. 2:00 pm. **Ticket Price Range:** $10-$16.

Visiting Club Hotel: Hampton Inn & Suites Sevierville, 105 Stadium Drive, Kodak, TN 37764. **Telephone:** (865) 465-0590.

MINOR LEAGUES

TEXAS LEAGUE

STADIUM INFORMATION

Club	Stadium	Opened	LF	CF	RF	Capacity	2022 Att.
Amarillo	Hodgetown	2019	325	405	325	7,300	379,029
Arkansas	Dickey-Stephens Park	2007	332	413	330	5,842	300,042
Corpus Christi	Whataburger Field	2005	325	400	315	5,362	257,991
Frisco	Dr Pepper Ballpark	2003	335	409	335	10,216	341,243
Midland	Security Bank Ballpark	2002	330	410	322	4,669	226,249
NW Arkansas	Arvest Ballpark	2008	325	400	325	6,500	240,615
San Antonio	Wolff Stadium	1994	310	402	340	9,200	272,144
Springfield	John Q. Hammons Field	2003	315	400	330	6,750	259,044
Tulsa	ONEOK Field	2010	330	400	307	7,833	357,200
Wichita	Riverfront Stadium	2021	340	400	325	10,000	220,528

AMARILLO SOD POODLES

Ballpark Address: 715. S Buchanan Street, Amarillo, TX 79101
Mailing Address: P.O. Box 9880, Amarillo, TX 79105
Main Phone: (806) 803-7762
Stadium Name: HODGETOWN. **Estimated Capacity:** 7,421
Affiliation (first year): Arizona Diamondbacks (2021). **Years In League:** 2019-

OWNERSHIP/MANAGEMENT

Owners: Elmore Sports Group. **President & General Manager:** Tony Ensor. **Assistant General Manager, Director of Ticket Sales:** Jeff Turner. **Director of Finance:** Ben Knowles. **Director of Media Relations & Baseball Operations:** Cory Hilborne. **Director of Food & Beverage:** Mike Lindal. **Director of Catering:** Nicole Lamontagne. **Executive Chef:** Mary Maddox. **Director of Marketing:** Anna Spinks. **Director of Corporate Partnerships:** Grant Norman. **Senior Group Sales Manager:** Noah St. Cyr. **Director of Merchandise:** Lynn Ensor. **Promotions & Corporate Partnerships Manager:** Sierra Todd. **Director of Stadium Operations:** Cody Grube. **Co-Head Groundskeeper:** Jason Floyd. **Co-Head Groundskeeper:** Jeff Schwartzenberg. **Community Relations & Mascot Coordinator:** Austin Jackson. **Box Office Manager:** Samantha Cook. **Senior Group Sales & Events Manager:** Zak McGrath. **Senior Tickets & Inside Sales Manager:** Matt Sutherland. **Ticket/Group Sales Account Executive:** Adam Padgett. **Video & Digital Production Manager:** Adrian Garcia. **Creative Services Manager:** Jordan Lank. **Corporate Partnerships Manager:** Adam Vrzal. **Corporate Partnership Activation & Fulfillment Specialist:** Isaac Galan. **Assistant Director of Stadium Operations:** Justin Garcia. **Team Store Assistant Manager:** Kendall Brown.

FIELD STAFF
Manager: Shawn Roof. **Hitting Coach:** Terrmel Sledge. **Pitching Coach:** Tom Gorzelanny. **Coach:** Javier Colina. **Strength & Conditioning Coach:** Mitchell Ho. **Athletic Trainer:** Chris Mudd.

GAME INFORMATION
Radio Announcers: Chris Cary & Stefan Caray. **No. of Games Broadcast:** 138. **Flagship Station:** Panhandle Sports Star 102.9 FM (Alpha Media USA-Amarillo). **PA Announcer:** N/A. **Official Scorer:** N/A. **Stadium Name:** HODGETOWN. **Game Times:** 7:05 p.m., 6:35 p.m., 1:05 p.m. CT. **Ticket Price Range:** $7-20. **Visiting Club Hotel:** Four Points by Sheraton.

ARKANSAS TRAVELERS

Office Address: Dickey-Stephens Park, 400 West Broadway, North Little Rock, AR 72114.
Mailing Address: PO Box 3177, Little Rock, AR 72203.
Telephone: (501) 664-1555. **Ticket Office:** (501) 664-7559
E-Mail address: travs@travs.com. **Website:** www.travs.com.
Affiliation (first year): Seattle Mariners (2017). **Years in League:** 1966-

OWNERSHIP/MANAGEMENT
Ownership: Arkansas Travelers Baseball Club, Inc.
President: Russ Meeks.
Executive Vice President/Chief Executive Officer: Rusty Meeks. **Chief Financial Officer:** Brad Eagle. **General Manager:** Sophie Ozier. **Assistant General Manager:** Ben Hornbrook. **Assistant General Manager:** John Sjobek. **Director of Finance/Corporate Assistant Secretary:** Patti Clark. **Director of Group Sales:** Montag Genser. **Director of Charities and Community Support:** Lance Restum. **Broadcaster/Baseball Operations Director:** Steven Davis. **Director of Food and Beverage:** Hunter Johnston. **Park Superintendent:** Greg Johnston. **Assistant Park Superintendent:** Reggie Temple. **Assistant Groundskeeper:** Grant Cross. **Creative Services Manager:** Bradley

MINOR LEAGUES

Field. **Suite and Ticket Sales Manager:** Megan Girton. **Creative Services and Merchandise Coordinator:** Tori Heck. **Corporate Event Planners:** Shelby Chenault, Jacob Titsworth.

FIELD STAFF
Manager: Mike Freeman. **Hitting Coach:** Shawn O'Malley. **Pitching Coach:** Michael Peoples. **Asst. Hitting/Catching Coach:** Jose Umbria.

GAME INFORMATION
Radio Announcer: Steven Davis. **No. of Games Broadcast:** All. **Flagship Station:** 106.7 FM Buz2
PA Announcer: Various. **Official Scorer:** Various. **Stadium Name:** Dickey-Stephens Park. **Location:** I-30 to Broadway exit, proceed west to ballpark, located at Broadway Avenue and the Broadway Bridge. **Standard Game Time:** Tue-Thur: 6:35 p.m.; Fri-Sat: 7:05 p.m.; Sun: 1:35 p.m. **Ticket Price Range:** $7-15. **Visiting Club Hotel:** Delta Hotel by Marriott Little Rock West

CORPUS CHRISTI HOOKS

Address: 734 East Port Ave, Corpus Christi, TX 78401.
Telephone: (361) 561-4665. **Fax:** (361) 561-4666.
E-Mail Address: info@cchooks.com. **Website:** www.cchooks.com.
Affiliation (first year): Houston Astros (2005). **Years in League:** 2021-

OWNERSHIP/MANAGEMENT
Owned/Operated By: Houston Astros. **General Manager:** Brady Ballard. **Director, Business Development:** Maggie Freeborn. **Account Executive, Corporate Partnerships:** Kaleb Womack. **Community Outreach Coordinator:** Emily Carney. **Director, Sales:** Pat McCarthy. **Manager, Tickets:** Liz Adams. **Account Executive:** Agustin Brizuela. **Account Executive:** Cassie Reyna. **Account Executive:** Veronica Hartman. **Director, Media Relations/Broadcasting:** Michael Coffin. **Director, Marketing & Entertainment:** Dustin Fishman. **Manager, Creative Services:** Courtney Merritt. **Manager, Marketing:** Emma Spotts. **Manager, Ballpark Entertainment:** Val Chapa. **Video Editor:** J.T. Garza. **Director, Operations:** Brett Howsley. **Manager, Home Clubhouse:** Marcus Tramp. **Coordinator, Special Events/Operations:** Shelby Forward. **Stadium Operations:** Mike Shedd. **Stadium Operations:** Mike Hoffman. **Head Groundskeeper:** Taylor Balhoff. **Assistant Groundskeeper:** Anthony Hernandez. **Director, Accounting:** Jessica Fearn. **Operations Manager/Store Supervisor:** Eric Suniga. **Accounting Associate:** Jordan Arizpe. **Administrative Assistant:** Barbara Funke. **Administrative Assistant:** Dalilah Maldonado.

FIELD STAFF
Manager: Joe Thon. **Hitting Coach:** TBA. **Pitching Coach:** Erick Abreu. **Fundamentals Coach:** TBA. **Athletic Trainer:** TBA. **Strength Coach:** TBA.

GAME INFORMATION
Radio Announcers: Michael Coffin, Gene Kasprzyk. **No. of Games Broadcast:** 138. **Flagship Station:** KKTX-AM 1360. **PA Announcer:** Amy Montez Frye. **Stadium Name:** Whataburger Field. **Location:** 734 E. Port Ave: I-37 to end of interstate, left at Chaparral, left at Hirsh Ave. **Ticket Price Range:** $6-20. **Visiting Club Hotel:** Best Western Corpus Christi; 300 N Shoreline Blvd, Corpus Christi, TX 78401; (361) 883-5111.

FRISCO ROUGHRIDERS

Address: 7300 RoughRiders Trail, Frisco, TX 75034.
Telephone: (972) 731-9200. **Fax:** (972) 731-5355.
E-Mail Address: info@ridersbaseball.com. **Website:** www.ridersbaseball.com.
Affiliation (first year): Texas Rangers (2003). **Years in League:** 2003-

OWNERSHIP/MANAGEMENT
Operated by: Frisco RoughRiders LP. **Chairman/CEO/General Partner:** Chuck Greenberg. **General Manager:** Scott Burchett. **Director of Business Partnerships:** Jeff Brown. **Director of Partner Services:** Eric Moore. **Customer Service Agents:** Claudia Kipp, Vicki Sohn. **Vice President of Sales:** Ross Lanford. **Director, Ticket Sales:** Alex Sandborn. **Director, Analytics & Ticket Strategy:** Jesse Evans. **Senior Corporate Sales Executive:** Tom Baker, Sydney Peterson. **Corporate Sales Executive:** Toufie J. Mazzawy, Jacob Gibson. **Group Sales Executives:** Natalie Brown, Jackson Burgess, Ryan Wooten, Adam Graham. **Inside Sales and Service:** Nestor Diaz, Darby Angle, Ty Young, Carlos Aguilar-Mendez. **Box Office Coordinator:** Chris Donawho. **Director of Finance:** Rick Maddox. **Merchandise Manager:** Lorraine Spencer. **VP, Community Development:** Breon Dennis, Jr. **Director of Marketing:** Krystin King. **Manager of Media Development/Broadcaster:** Zach Bigley. **Broadcast and Media Relations Assistant:** Josh Worden. **Senior Director, Sports Turf & Grounds Manager:** David Bicknell. **Maintenance Director:** Alfonzo Bailon. **Operations Coordinator:** Ryan Wojdula. **Team Dog:** Brooks.

FIELD STAFF
Manager: Carlos Cardoza. **Hitting Coach:** Ryan Tuntland. **Pitching Coach:** Josh Zeid. **Bench Coach:** Tripp Keister. **Development Coach:** Kawika-Emsley-Pai. **Athletic Trainer:** Ichi Takizawa. **Strength Coach:** Andru Cardenas.

GAME INFORMATION
Broadcaster: Zach Bigley. **No. of Games Broadcast:** 138. **Flagship Station:** www.RidersBaseball.com. **Stadium**

MINOR LEAGUES

Name: Riders Field. **Location:** Intersection of Dallas North Tollway & State Highway 121. **Standard Game Times:** 6:35 PM (April-May, September), 7:05 PM (June-August), **Sunday 4:**05 PM (April-May, September), 6:05 PM (June-August). **Visiting Club Hotel:** TBD. **Visiting Club Hotel Phone:** (972) 668-9700. **Visiting Club Hotel Fax:** (972) 668-9701.

MIDLAND ROCKHOUNDS

Address: Momentum Bank Ballpark, 5514 Champions Drive, Midland, TX 79706.
Telephone: (432) 520-2255. **Fax:** (432) 520-8326.
Website: www.midlandrockhounds.org.
Affiliation (first year): Oakland Athletics (1999). **Years in League:** 2021-

OWNERSHIP/MANAGEMENT
Operated By: Midland Sports, Inc. **Principal Owners:** Miles Prentice, Bob Richmond. **President:** Miles Prentice. **Executive Vice President:** Bob Richmond. **General Manager:** Monty Hoppel. **Assistant GM:** Jeff VonHolle. **Assistant GM, Operations:** Ray Fieldhouse. **Director, Broadcasting/Publications:** Bob Hards. **Director, Business Operations:** Denessa Leary. **Director, Ticketing:** Ryan Artzer. **Director, Client Services/ Marketing:** Shelly Haenggi. **Sales and Media Relations Executive:** Zelyn Zapata. **Director, Operations:** Dan Knapinski. **Sales and Community Relations Executive:** Jonathan Simmons. **Sales Executive:** Joey Gennusa. **Head Groundskeeper:** Brian Mitchell. **Director, Game Entertainment/Video Board:** Peyton Wilkins. **Grounds Assistant:** Mitch Riddle. **Concessions Operations Manager:** Al Melville. **Office Manager:** Vanessa Redman-Bynum. **Home Clubhouse Manager:** Austen Burgdorf. **Visiting Clubhouse Manager:** Blake Glass.

FIELD STAFF
Manager: Bobby Crosby. **Pitching Coach:** Chris Smith. **Hitting Coach:** Todd Takayoshi. **Assistant Hitting Coach:** Juan Dilone. **Athletic Trainer:** Jake Routhier. **Sport Performance Coach:** Connor Hughes

GAME INFORMATION
Radio Announcer: Bob Hards. **No. of Games Broadcast:** 138. **Flagship Station:** Streamed on Website. **PA Announcer:** Wes Coles. **Official Scorer:** TBA. **Stadium Name:** Momentum Bank Ballpark. **Location:** From I-20, exit Loop 250 North to Highway 191 intersection. **Standard Game Times: Sunday:** 2:00 pm, **Monday-Wednesday:** 6:30 pm, **Thursday-Saturday:** 7:00 pm. **Ticket Price Range:** $8-16. **Visiting Club Hotel:** Sleep Inn& Suites, 5612 Deauville Blvd, Midland, TX 79706. **Telephone:** (432) 694-4200.

NORTHWEST ARKANSAS NATURALS

Address: 3000 Gene George Blvd, Springdale, AR 72762.
Telephone: (479) 927-4900. **Fax:** (479) 756-8088.
E-Mail Address: tickets@nwanaturals.com. **Website:** www.nwanaturals.com.
Affiliation (first year): Kansas City Royals (1995). **Years in League:** 2021-

OWNERSHIP/MANAGEMENT
Principal Owner: Rich Products Corp. **Senior Chairman, Rich Products Corporation:** Robert Rich Jr. **Chairman, Rich Products Corporation/Executive Vice Chair, Rich Entertainment Group:** Melinda Rich. **President, Rich Entertainment Group:** Joseph Segarra. **President, Rich Baseball Operations:** Mike Buczkowski. **Vice President/ General Manager:** Justin Cole. **Assistant General Manager:** Mark Zaiger. **Senior Director of Retail Licensing, & Event Experience:** Morgan Helmer. **Senior Director of Marketing:** Dustin Dethlefs. **Director, Ballpark Operations:** Brock White. **Ballpark Operations Manager:** Brad Ziegler. **Head Groundskeeper:** Stephen Crockett. **Assistant Groundskeeper:** Lee Anderson. **Creative Services Coordinator:** Adam Annaratone. **Marketing Coordinator:** Jake Bay. **Ticket Office Manager:** Matt Fanning. **Account Executive/Event Coordinator:** Amber McCarthy. **Account Executive/ Gameday Coordinator:** Joy Clingan. **Account Executive:** Stevin Blackiston.

FIELD STAFF
Manager: Tommy Shields. **Pitching Coach:** Larry Carter. **Hitting Coach:** Andy LaRoche. **Bench Coach:** Christian Colón. **Assistant Coach:** Kevin Kuntz. **Strength & Conditioning Coach:** CJ Mikkelsen. **Athletic Trainer:** Danny Accola. **Coordinator of Clubhouse Operations:** Danny Helmer.

GAME INFORMATION
Radio Announcer: Shawn Murnin. **No. of Games Broadcast:** 138. **Flagship Station:** Streamed Online. **PA Announcer:** TBA. **Official Scorers:** Kyle Stiles, Walter Woodie, & Ken Foxx. **Stadium Name:** Arvest Ballpark. **Location:** I-49 to US 412 West (Sunset Ave), Left on Gene George Blvd. **Standard Game Times:** 705 pm, 605 pm (Saturday), 2:05 pm (Sunday). **Visiting Club Hotel:** Holiday Inn Springdale, 1500 S 48th St, Springdale, AR 72762. **Telephone:** (479) 751-8300.

MINOR LEAGUES

SAN ANTONIO MISSIONS

Address: 5757 Highway 90 W, San Antonio, TX 78227
Telephone: 210-675-7275 | **Fax:** 210-670-0001
Email Address: sainfo@samissions.com. **Website:** www.samissions.com
Affiliation (First Year): San Diego Padres (2021). **Years in League:** 2021-

OWNERSHIP/MANAGEMENT
Ownership: Designated Bidders, LLC. **President:** Burl Yarbrough. **General Manager:** Dave Gasaway. **Assistant GM:** Mickey Holt. **Assistant GM:** Jeff Long. **Assistant GM:** Bill Gerlt. **Director of Finance:** TBD. **Office Manager:** Delia Rodriguez. **Director of Ticketing:** JJ Jimenez. **Account Executives:** Alexandra Curtin, Gabriel Trejo, Tyler King, Alex Flynn, Elizabeth Woeste, Cruz Raymond, Daniel Oliva. **Director of Public Relations:** Jeremy Sneed. **Creative Director:** TBD. **Social Media/Marketing Manager:** Analee Reyes. **Maintenance Director:** Danny Pena. **Assistant Maintenance Director:** Chris Castillo. **Clubhouse Manager:** TBD. **Head Groundskeeper:** TBD. **Assistant Groundskeeper:** Nash Opperman.

FIELD STAFF
Manager: Luke Montz. **Pitching Coach:** Jeff Andrews. **Hitting Coach:** Pat O'Sullivan. **Bench Coach:** Felipe Blanco. **Athletic Trainer:** David Bryan. **Strength Coach:** TBD

GAME INFORMATION
No. of Games: 138. **Flagship Station:** 93.3 FM. **PA Announcer:** Roland Ruiz. **Official Scorer:** David Humphrey. **Stadium Name:** Nelson Wolff Stadium. **Location:** From I-10, I-35 or I-37, take US Hwy 90 West to Callaghan Road exit. **Standard Game Times:** 7:05 p.m., **Sunday** 2:05 p.m./6:05 p.m. **Visiting Club Hotel:** TBA.

SPRINGFIELD CARDINALS

Address: 955 East Trafficway, Springfield, MO 65802.
Telephone: (417) 863-0395. **Fax:** (417) 832-3004.
E-Mail Address: springfield@cardinals.com. **Website:** springfieldcardinals.com.
Affiliation (first year): St. Louis Cardinals (2005). **Years in League:** 2021-

OWNERSHIP/MANAGEMENT
Operated By: St. Louis Cardinals.
Vice President/General Manager: Dan Reiter. **VP, Baseball/Business Operations:** Scott Smulczenski. **Director, Market Development:** Brad Beattie. **Senior Director, Ticket Technology & Operations:** Angela Deke. **Director, Branding & Communications/Broadcaster:** Andrew Buchbinder. **Public Relations/Digital Media Specialist:** Kimberly Bates. **Manager, Fan Engagement & Special Events:** Regina Hess. **Manager, Production:** Tysen Hathcock. **Graphic Designer:** T.J. Patton. **Director, Ticket Sales & Marketing Operations:** Zack Pemberton. **Manager, Ticket Sales:** Eric Tomb. **VP, Stadium Operations:** Aaron Lowrey. **Director, Field & Stadium Operations:** Derek Edwards.

FIELD STAFF
Manager: Jose Leger. **Hitting Coach:** Brock Hammit. **Pitching Coach:** Eric Peterson. **Coach:** Will Hawks. **Athletic Trainer:** Alex Wolfinger. **Strength Coach:** Spencer Clevenger.

GAME INFORMATION
Radio Announcer: Andrew Buchbinder. **No. of Games Broadcast:** 138. **Flagship Station:** TBA. **PA Announcer:** Eric Tomb. **Official Scorers:** TBA. **Stadium Name:** Hammons Field. **Location:** Highway 65 to Chestnut Expressway exit, west to National, south on National, west on Trafficway. **Standard Game Time:** 7:10 pm. **Ticket Price Range:** $8-50. **Visiting Club Hotel:** University Plaza Hotel, 333 John Q Hammons Parkway, Springfield, MO 65806. **Telephone:** (417) 864-7333.

TULSA DRILLERS

Address: 201 N. Elgin Ave, Tulsa, OK 74120.
Telephone: (918) 744-5998. **Fax:** (918) 747-3267.
E-Mail Address: mail@tulsadrillers.com. **Website:** www.tulsadrillers.com.
Affiliation (first year): Los Angeles Dodgers (2015). **Years in League:** 1977-present.

OWNERSHIP/MANAGEMENT
Operated By: Tulsa Baseball Inc.
Co-Chairman: Dale Hubbard. **Co-Chairman:** Jeff Hubbard. **President & General Manager:** Mike Melega. **Assistant General Manager & Vice President of Public Relations & Baseball Operations:** Brian Carroll. **Assistant General Manager & Vice President of Marketing:** Justin Gorski. **Chief Financial Officer:** Jenna Savill. **Vice President, Ticket Sales:** Andrew Aldenderfer. **Director, Ticket Operations:** Justin Perkins. **Director of Stadium Operations:** Marshall Schellhardt. **Director of Community Relations:** Taylor Levacy. **Director of Food & Beverage:** Christopher Bullis. **Director of Food & Beverage:** Amanda Coe. **Director of Corporate Sales:** Jennifer Carthel. **Director of Promotions & Merchandise:** Alex Kossakoski. **Manager, Corporate Partnerships & Premium Services:** Cameron Gordon. **Creative**

MINOR LEAGUES

Services Manager: Mikki Downey. **Office & Special Events Manager/Assistant Director of Merchandise:** Kelsie Tulk. **Maintenance Manager:** Micah Wade. **Business Manager of F&B:** Belinda Shepherd. **Concessions Manager:** Mike Phipps. **Account Executive & Marketing Coordinator:** Brianna Root. **Mascot Coordinator:** Diego Davila. **Account Executive:** Nate Johnston. **Account Executive:** Ryan Christy. **Account Executive:** Seth Distler. **Video Production Assistant:** Blake Mathews. **Public Relations Assistant:** Brandon Hawkins. **Ticket Operations Assistant:** Bailey Conner. **Hospitality Assistant Manager:** Keith Carlton. **Community Relations Assistant:** Caitlin Perry. **Stadium Operations Assistant:** Collin Wilson. **Ticket Sales Associate:** Dylan Pham. **Ticket Sales Associate:** Michael Nickel. **Ticket Sales Associate:** Nick Copeland. **Accounting Assistant:** Terry Jenner. **Cleaning Supervisor:** Tre Springer. **Head Groundskeeper:** Gary Shepherd. **Radio Broadcaster:** Dennis Higgins. **Team Photographers:** Rich Crimi & Tim Campbell.

FIELD STAFF
Manager: Scott Hennessey. **Hitting Coach:** Lou Iannotti. **Pitching Coach:** Ryan Dennick. **Pitching Coach:** Durin O'Linger. **Bench Coach:** Juan Apodaca. **Performance Coach:** Noah Huff. **Athletic Trainer:** Jesse Guffey. **Video Associate:** Mikael Mogues.

GAME INFORMATION
Radio Announcer: Dennis Higgins. **No. of Games Broadcast:** 138. **Flagship Station:** KTBZ 1430-AM.
PA Announcer: Kirk McAnany. **Official Scorers:** Bruce Howard, Duane DaPron, Larry Lewis, Barry Lewis. **Stadium Name:** ONEOK Field. **Location:** I-244 to Cincinnati/Detroit Exit (6A), north on Detroit Ave, right onto John Hope Franklin Blvd, right on Elgin Ave. **Standard Game Times:** 7:05 pm (Tuesday-Saturday), Sun. 1:05. **Visiting Club Hotel:** Marriott Tulsa Southern Hills, 1902 E 71st Street, Tulsa, OK 74136. **Telephone:** (918) 493-7000.

WICHITA WIND SURGE

Address: 275 S. McLean Blvd, Wichita KS 67213
Telephone: (316) 221-8000. **Fax:** TBD
E-Mail Address: info@windsurge.com. **Website:** www.windsurge.com
Affiliation (first year): Minnesota Twins (2021). **Years in League:** 2021-

OWNERSHIP/MANAGEMENT
Ownership: Diamond Baseball Holdings, LLC. **President:** Jay Miller. **General Manager:** Bob Moullette. **Assistant General Manager:** Tara Tallman. **Senior Director, Corporate Sponsorships:** David Kirk. **Director of Corporate Partnerships & Public Relations:** Tim Grubbs. **Director, Marketing:** Kylee Sorrells. **Marketing Manager:** Jenn Schwechheimer. **Director, Ticket Sales:** Adam Mettler. **Manager, Special Events:** Maggie McLaughlin. **Promotions and Creative Services Manager:** Alvin Garcia. **Director of Business Operations:** April Houle. **Finance Manager:** Tanner Olmstead. **Video Operations & Production Coordinator:** Chance Fernandez. **Retail Merchandise Manager:** Jake Cassidy. **Community Relations Manager:** Hannah Jasinski. **Account Executive, Corporate Partnerships:** Christian Newell. **Account Executive, Ticket Sales:** Nick Nelson. **Account Executive, Ticket Sales:** Nick O'Brien. **Account Executive, Ticket Sales:** Adam Krichati. **Account Executive, Ticket Sales:** Tre Gray. **Sales Account Executive, Ticket Sales:** Colin Parks. **Manager, Ticket Operations:** Megan Overmann. **Coordinator Ticket Operations:** Dalton Colin. **Director Stadium Operations:** Ben Hartman. **Coordinator Stadium Operations:** Jacob Koch. **Assistant Field Operations:** Jake Cooley. **Director, Museum Operations:** Neleigh Higgins. **Director of Food & Beverage:** Jason Wilson. **Manager, Food & Beverage:** Justin Thomas. **Manager, Hospitality:** Madison White.

FIELD STAFF
Manager: Ramon Borrego. **Hitting Coach:** Shawn Schlechter. **Pitching Coach:** Dan Urbina and DJ Engle. **Bench Coach:** Takashi Miyoshi. **Strength Coach:** Jacob Needham. **Athletic Trainer:** Tyler Blair. **Asst. Athletic Trainer:** Katie Lortie. **Video Coach:** Chase Carder.

GAME INFORMATION
Radio Announcers: Tim Grubbs. **No. of Games Broadcast:** 138. **Flagship Station:** KKGQ 92.3 FM ESPN Radio.
PA Announcer: Derek Aalders. **Official Scorer:** Dave Glennemeier, Fred Martin, Wyatt Ebersole, Jeff Lutz. **Stadium Name:** Riverfront Stadium. **Location: From Airport:** US-400 E/US-54 E from Eisenhower Airport Pkwy, Take the Seneca/Sycamore exit from US-400 E/US-54 E, Continue on S Sycamore St to your destination. **Standard Game Times:** M-F 7:05; Sat. 6:05; Sun. 1:05. **Ticket Price Range:** $8-19. **Visiting Club Hotel:** Hyatt Regency Wichita, 400 W Waterman Street, Wichita, KS 67202. **Telephone:** (316) 293-1234.

MINOR LEAGUES

MIDWEST LEAGUE

STADIUM INFORMATION

Club	Stadium	Opened	LF	CF	RF	Capacity	2022 Att.
Beloit	ABC Supply Stadium	2021	345	400	325	3,850	102,794
Cedar Rapids	Veterans Memorial Stadium	2002	315	400	325	5,300	136,360
Dayton	Day Air Ballpark	2000	338	402	338	6,830	444,346
Fort Wayne	Parkview Field	2009	336	400	318	8,100	303,680
Great Lakes	Dow Diamond	2007	332	400	325	5,200	174,050
Lake County	Classic Park	2003	320	400	320	6,157	169,574
Lansing	Cooley Law School Stadium	1996	305	412	305	11,000	288,840
Peoria	Dozer Park	2002	310	400	310	7,000	135,784
Quad Cities	Modern Woodmen Park	1931	343	400	318	7,140	170,731
South Bend	Four Winds Fields	1987	336	405	336	5,000	285,977
West Michigan	Fifth Third Ballpark	1994	317	402	327	9,281	337,167
Wisconsin	Neuroscience Group Field	1995	325	400	325	5,170	206,805

BELOIT SKY CARP

Office Address: 217 Shirland Ave., Beloit, WI 53511 (ABC Supply Stadium)
Mailing Address: P.O. Box 855, Beloit, WI 53512. **Telephone:** (608) 362-2272.
E-Mail: info@skycarp.com. **Website:** www.skycarp.com.
Affiliation (first year): Miami Marlins (2021). **Years in League:** 2021-

OWNERSHIP/MANAGEMENT
President: Zach Brockman. **VP, Entertainment:** Maria Valentyn. **VP, Sales:** Drew Olstead. **Box Office Manager:** TBD. **Merchandise Manager:** Bob Villarreal. **Media & Public Relations Manager:** Josh Flickinger. **Head Groundskeeper:** Jaymeson Wilcox. **Events Manager:** Gracey McDonald. **Operations Manager:** Ben St. Peter. **Sales Executive:** Joe Valentyn. **GM of Food & Beverage:** Blair Schmitz. **Executive Chef:** Matthew A. Austin.

FIELD STAFF
Manager: Billy Gardner Jr. **Pitching Coach:** Jason Erickson. **Hitting Coach:** Dan Radison. **Trainer:** Melissa Hampton.

GAME INFORMATION
Radio Announcer: Larry Larson. **No. of Games Broadcast:** 132. **Flagship Station:** Big Radio App. **Stadium Name:** ABC Supply Stadium. **Standard Game Times:** Mon-Fri: 6:35, Sat-3:05/6:05, Sun 1:05pm. **Ticket Price Range:** $8-22. **Visiting Club Hotel:** Home2 Suites by Hilton. 2750 Cranston Road. Beloit, WI 53511. **Telephone:** (608) 467-5500.

CEDAR RAPIDS KERNELS

Office Address: 950 Rockford Road SW, Cedar Rapids, IA 52404.
Mailing Address: PO Box 2001, Cedar Rapids, IA 52406.
Telephone: (319) 363-3887. **Fax:** (319) 363-5631.
E-Mail: kernels@kernels.com. **Website:** www.kernels.com.
Affiliation (first year): Minnesota Twins (2013). **Years in League:** 2021-

OWNERSHIP/MANAGEMENT
President: Greg Churchill. **Chief Executive Officer:** Doug Nelson. **General Manager:** Scott Wilson. **Senior Director Business Development:** Jessica Fergesen. **Director of Food and Beverage:** Dan McAlpine. **Controller:** Shannon VanTine. **Assistant Director of Food and Beverage:** Tyler Benton. **Food & Beverage Staffing Manager:** Allie Mormann. **Social Media Manager & Graphic Designer:** McKenzie Short. **Baseball Operations Manager:** Logan Larson. **Stadium Operations Manager:** Dave Soper. **Box Office Manager:** Ben Steidler. **Sports Turf Manager:** Jesse Roeder. **Radio Broadcaster:** Calvin Christoforo. **Mascot Coordinator:** TBD. **Clubhouse Manager:** Chancelor Miller.

FIELD STAFF
Manager: Brian Dinkelman. **Hitting Coaches:** Corbin Day, Yeison Perez. **Pitching Coaches:** Carlos Hernandez, Jonas Lovin. **Trainers:** Matt Smith, Randy Yang. **Strength Coach:** Blake Kretovics.

GAME INFORMATION
Radio Announcer: Calvin Christoforo. **No. of Games Broadcast:** 120. Streaming Internet Only. **Stadium Name:** Perfect Game Field at Veterans Memorial Stadium. **Directions to Stadium:** From I-380 North, take the Wilson Ave exit, turn left on Wilson Ave, after the railroad tracks, turn right on Rockford Road, pro- ceed .8 miles, stadium is on left; from I-380 South, exit at First Avenue West (exit 19b), Go west to 15th Street, and turn left. Turn left onto 8th Ave, then right onto Kurt Warner Way. **Standard Game Times:** Mon.-Sat., 6:35 pm, Sun. 1:05 pm. **Ticket Price Range:** $10-16. **Visiting Club Hotel:** Double Tree 350 1st Ave NE Cedar Rapids, IA 52401. **Telephone:** (319) 731-4444.

MINOR LEAGUES

DAYTON DRAGONS

Office Address: Day Air Ballpark, 220 N. Patterson Blvd., Dayton, OH 45402.
Mailing Address: PO Box 2107, Dayton, OH 45401.
Telephone: (937) 228-2287. **Fax:** (937) 228-2284.
E-Mail Address: dragons@daytondragons.com. **Website:** www.daytondragons.com.
Affiliation (first year): Cincinnati Reds (2000). **Years in League:** 2000-

OWNERSHIP/MANAGEMENT
Operated By: Palisades Arcadia Baseball LLC.
President & General Manager: Robert Murphy. **Executive Vice President:** Eric Deutsch. **VP, Assistant General Manager:** Brandy Guinaugh. **VP, Accounting/Finance:** Mark Schlein. **VP, Corporate Partnerships:** Andrew Hayes. **Director, Media Relations & Broadcasting:** Tom Nichols. **Senior Director, Operations:** John Wallace. **Senior Director, Entertainment:** Kaitlin Rohrer. **Director, Entertainment:** Katrina Gibbs. **Director, Ticket Administration & Box Office:** Lindzey Watson. **Director, Group Sales:** Carl Hertzberg. **Entertainment Manager:** Jamie Penwell. **Business Development Managers:** Brice Odel, Andrew Zellers. **Senior Manager, Corporate Communications:** Megan Chamberlain. **Senior Manager, Corporate Partnerships:** Brittany Snyder. **Corporate Partnerships Managers:** Nicole Annucci, Jake Arthur, Tanner Buhrts, Alex Livingston, Kaylie Marshall, Jack Twomey. **Motion Graphics Designer & Production Manager:** David Luehring. **Graphic Designer:** Shawn Dewey. **Motion Graphics Designer & Production Manager:** Ian Kallmeyer. **Group Sales Managers:** Madison Berlinger, Andrew Majzan, Grant Noffsinger. **Inside Sales Manager:** Mandi Napier. **Merchandise & Ticket Manager:** Lamont Fox. **Assistant Box Office Manager:** Jacob Offenbacker. **Director of Field Operations:** Brent White. **Operations Managers:** Nick Hall, Sami Jones. **Corporate Partnerships Assistant:** Keegan Blosser. **Entertainment Assistant:** Fiona Holahan. **Media Relations Assistant:** Patrick Geshan. **Administrative Assistant to the President:** Mary Cleveland.

FIELD STAFF
Manager: Bryan LaHair. **Hitting Coach:** Eric Richardson. **Pitching Coach:** Todd Naskedov. **Coach:** Osmin Melendez. **Trainer:** Josh Hobson. **Strength/Conditioning:** Joel Canacoo. **Performance:** Peterson Plaz.

GAME INFORMATION
Radio Announcers: Tom Nichols and Patrick Geshan. **No. of Games Broadcast:** 132. **Flagship Station:** WONE 980 AM. **Television Announcer:** Tom Nichols and Jack Pohl. **No. of Games Broadcast:** Home-25. **Flagship Station:** WBDT Channel 26. **Official Scorers:** Matt Lindsay, Mike Lucas, Mark Miller. **Stadium Name:** Day Air Ballpark. **Location:** I-75 South to downtown Dayton, left at First Street; I-75 North, right at First Street exit. **Ticket Price Range:** $10-$20.
Visiting Club Hotel: Courtyard by Marriott, 100 Prestige Place, Miamisburg, OH 45342. **Telephone:** 937-433-3131. **Fax:** 937-433-0285.

FORT WAYNE TINCAPS

Address: 1301 Ewing St., Fort Wayne, IN 46802.
Telephone: (260) 482-6400. **Fax:** (260) 471-4678.
E-Mail Address: info@tincaps.com. **Website:** www.tincaps.com.
Affiliation (first year): San Diego Padres (1999). **Years in League:** 2021-

OWNERSHIP/MANAGEMENT
Operated By: Hardball Capital. **Owner:** Jason Freier. **President:** Mike Nutter. **Vice President, Corporate Partnerships:** David Lorenz. **VP, Finance:** Brian Schackow. **VP, Marketing & Promotions:** Michael Limmer. **Creative Director:** Tony DesPlaines. **Director of Video Production:** Melissa Darby. **Assistant Video Production Manager:** Jared Law. **Broadcasting/Media Relations Manager:** John Nolan. **Assistant Director of Marketing & Promotions:** Morgan Olson. **Community & Fan Engagement Manager:** Brenda Feasby. **Merchandise Manager:** Emma Reese. **Digital Marketing Manager:** Chris Darby. **Group Sales Manager:** Brent Harring. **Assistant Director of Group Sales:** Austin Allen. **Senior Ticket Account Manager:** Dalton McGill. **Ticket & Corporate Account Manager:** Jenn Sylvester. **Ticketing Director:** Kade Zvokel. **Reading Program Director/Assistant Director of Ticketing:** Blaine Jerome. **Special Events Coordinator:** Holly Raney. **Banquet Event Manager:** Alexis Strabala. **Food/Beverage Director:** Bill Lehn. **Executive Chef/Culinary Director:** Pisarn Amornarthakij. **Inventory & Reporting Manager:** Michael Shidler. **Food/Beverage Operations Manager:** Alec Bayman. **Commissary Manager:** Andrew Frank. **Assistant Concessions Operation Manager:** Jordyn Fitzgerald. **VIP Services Manager:** Maley Tinstman. **Head Groundskeeper:** Keith Winter. **Facilities Director:** Tim Burkhart. **Accounting Manager/Facilities Manager:** Erik Lose. **Groundskeeping/Ballpark Operations Assistant:** Jake Sperry. **Groundskeeping Assistant:** Dakota Steele. **Human Resources/Office Manager:** Cathy Tinney.

FIELD STAFF
Manager: Jonathan Mathews. **Pitching Coach:** Carlos Chavez. **Hitting Coach:** Aaron Bray. **Bench Coach:** Shane Robinson. **Athletic Trainer:** Lauren Gottschall. **Strength Coach:** Chandler Craig. **Performance Analyst:** Greg Bender.

GAME INFORMATION
Radio Announcers: John Nolan, Mike Maahs. **No. of Games Broadcast:** 132. **Flagship Station:** WKJG 1380-AM/100.9-FM. **TV Announcers:** John Nolan, Brett Rump, Tracy Coffman. **No. of TV Games Broadcast:** Home-66. **Flagship Station:** Comcast Network 81. **PA Announcer:** Jared Parcell. **Official Scorers:** Rich Tavierne, Bill Scott, Dan Watson. **Stadium Name:** Parkview Field. **Location:** 1301 Ewing St., Fort Wayne, IN, 46802. **Ticket Price Range:** $7-$14.

MINOR LEAGUES

GREAT LAKES LOONS

Address: 825 East Main St., Midland, MI 48640.
Telephone: (989) 837-2255. **Fax:** (989) 837-8780.
E-MailAddress: tickets@loons.com. **Website:** www.loons.com.
Affiliation (first year): Los Angeles Dodgers (2007). **Years in League:** 2021-

OWNERSHIP/MANAGEMENT

Stadium Ownership: Michigan Baseball Foundation. **Founder, CEO:** William Stavropoulos. **President, GM:** Chris Mundhenk. **Vice President, CFO:** Jana Chotivkova. **Vice President, COO:** Eric Ramseyer. **Director, Entertainment & Community Outreach:** Cameron Bloch. **Assistant General Manager, Ticket Sales:** Kevin Schunk. **Coordinator, Creative & Services and Content:** Elizabeth Getzinger. **Corporate Partnership and Entertainment Manager:** Eric Vandefifier. **Executive Assistant/HR Assistant:** Jessica Gillespie. **General Manager, Dow Diamond Events:** Dave Gomola. **Director, ESPN100.9-FM Sales:** Rich Juday. **Assistant GM, Corporate Partnerships:** Brandon Loker. **Box Office Manager:** Rickey Rissman. **Manager, Video Production:** Jimmy Metiva. **Director, Operations/Executive Chef:** Andrea Noonan. **Manager, Merchandise and Business:** Lauren Ouellette. **Director, ESPN 100.9-FM Production & Operations:** Jerry O'Donnell. **Ticket Account Executives:** Travis Webb, Scott Bejcek, Luke Gunsell, Austin Johnson. **Head Groundskeeper:** Jeff Ross. **Director, Accounting:** Jamie Start. **Assistant GM, Facility Operations:** Dan Straley. **Food and Beverage Business Coordinator:** Stephanie Tithof. **Manager, ESPN 100.9-FM Programming & Play-by-Play Broadcaster:** Brad Tunney. **Executive Chef:** Carlos Valles. **Director, Corporate Accounts:** Joe Volk. **Vice President, Baseball Operations & Gameday Experience:** Tiffany Wardynski. **Concessions Manager:** Cameron Koch. **Facilities Operation Managers:** Christopher Earl Eugene Backus, Basilio Gonzalez.

FIELD STAFF

Manager: Daniel Nava. **Hitting Coach:** O'Koyea Dickson. **Pitching Coach:** David Anderson. **Assistant Pitching Coach:** Richard De Los Santos. **Bench Coach:** Elian Herrera. **Athletic Trainer:** Ikuo Kato. **Performance Coach:** Ethan Quarles. **Video Associate:** Joe Manno.

GAME INFORMATION

Play-by-Play Broadcaster: Brad Tunney and Eric Bach. **No. of Games Broadcast:** 132. **Flagship Station:** WLUN, ESPN 100.9-FM (ESPN1009.com). **PA Announcer:** Jerry O'Donnell. **Official Scorers:** Steve Robb, Jason Wirtz. **Stadium Name:** Dow Diamond. **Location:** I-75 to US-10 W, Take the M-20/US-10 Business exit on the left toward downtown Midland, Merge onto US-10 W/MI-20 W (also known as Indian Street), Turn left onto State Street, the entrance to the stadium is at the intersection of Ellsworth and State Streets. **Standard Game Times:** M-F: 6:05 PM (April–May), **Sat & Sun:** 1:05 PM (April–May), **Mon-Sat:** 7:05 PM (June–Sept.), **Sun:** 1:05 PM (June–Sept.). **Ticket Price Range:** $10-18. **Visiting Club Hotel:** Fairfield Inn & Suites by Mariott; 506 Buttles Street, Midland, MI 48640. 989-631-7100.

LAKE COUNTY CAPTAINS

Address: 35300 Vine St., Eastlake, OH 44095-3142.
Telephone: (440) 975-8085. **Fax:** (440) 975-8958.
E-Mail Address: jyorko@captainsbaseball.com
Website: www.captainsbaseball.com.
Affiliation (first year): Cleveland Guardians (2003). **Years in League:** 2021-

OWNERSHIP/MANAGEMENT

Operated By: COLLiDE NEO. **Owners:** Alan Miller. **Chairman/Secretary/Treasurer:** Peter Carfagna. **Vice Chairman:** Rita Carfagna. **Vice President:** Ray Murphy. **General Manager:** Jen Yorko. **Assistant General Manager:** Drew LaFollette. **Director, Turf Management:** Drew Maskey. **Director, Ticket Sales & Partnerships:** Andrew Grover. **Director, Ticket Operations:** Kenny Cole. **Director, Stadium Operations:** Jason Schwab. **Manager, Merchandise & Special Events:** Jakob Hites. **Manager, Social Media:** Morgan Mattimore. **Ticket Sales Account Executive:** Dylan NiCastro.

FIELD STAFF

Manager: Omir Santos. **Hitting Coach:** Jordan Becker. **Pitching Coach:** Kevin Erminio. **Bench Coach:** Kyle Lindquist. **Athletic Trainer:** Matt Beauregard. **Strength & Conditioning Coach:** TBD.

GAME INFORMATION

Radio Announcer: TBD. **No. of Games Broadcast:** 132. **PA Announcer:** Jasen Sokol, Wayne Blankenship. **Official Scorers:** TBD. **Location:** From Ohio State Route 2 East, exit at Ohio 91, go left and the stadium is 1/4 mile north on your right; From Ohio State Route 90 East, exit at Ohio 91, go right and the stadium is approximately five miles north on your right. **Standard Game Times:** Mon.-Sat. 6:35 pm, Sun. at 1 pm, Mon-Sat. in June and July at 7 pm. **Visiting Club Hotel:** Four Points by Sheraton Cleveland-Eastlake, 35000 Curtis Blvd, Eastlake, OH 44095. **Telephone:** (440) 953-8000.

MINOR LEAGUES

LANSING LUGNUTS

Address: 505 E. Michigan Ave., Lansing, MI 48912.
Telephone: (517) 485-4500. **Fax:** (517) 485-4518.
E-Mail Address: info@lansinglugnuts.com. **Website:** lansinglugnuts.com.
Affiliation (first year): Oakland Athletics (2021). **Years in League:** 2021-

OWNERSHIP/MANAGEMENT
Operated By: Take Me Out to the Ballgame LLC. **Principal Owners:** Tom Dickson, Sherrie Myers. **General Manager:** Zac Clark. **Assistant General Manager:** Greg Kigar. **Head Groundskeeper:** Joe Trautner. **Director of Creative Services:** Terry Alapert. **Director of Finance:** Rebecca Pensyl. **Director of Food and Beverage:** Phil Wilder. **Director of Ticket Sales:** Nick Bertoia. **Director of Human Resource and Business Operations:** Angela Sees. **Director of Retail:** Matt Hicks. **Assistant Food and Beverage Director:** Tyler Quick. **Marketing and Fan Engagement Manager:** Amanda Rich. **Group Sales Manager:** Marcos Martinez. **Senior Account Executive:** Jacob Darnell. **Season Memberships Manager:** Nicholas Piechowiak. **Manager of Partnership Activation:** Meg Thompson. **Manager of Stadium Operations:** Jake Warren-Kraatz. **Box Office Manager:** Travis Drummond. **Special Events and Premium Manager:** Jamie Humphrey.

FIELD STAFF
Manager: Craig Conklin. **Hitting Coach:** Ron Witmeyer. **Pitching Coach:** Don Schulze. **Assistant Hitting Coach:** Luis Báez. **Athletic Trainer:** Eric Fasth. **Strength & Conditioning Coach:** Steven Thayer.

GAME INFORMATION
Broadcasters: Jesse Goldberg-Strassler, Adam Jaksa. **No. of Games Broadcast:** 132. **Flagship Station:** N/A. **PA Announcer:** Chris Snyder. **Official Scorer:** Timothy Zeko. **Stadium Name:** Jackson Field. **Location:** I-96 East/ West to US 496, exit at Larch Street, north of Larch, stadium on left. **Ticket Price Range:** $8-$36. **Visiting Club Hotel:** Radisson Hotel.

PEORIA CHIEFS

Address: 730 SW Jefferson, Peoria, IL 61605.
Telephone: (309) 680-4000. **Fax:** (309) 680-4080.
E-Mail Address: feedback@chiefsnet.com. **Website:** www.peoriachiefs.com.
Affiliation (first year): St. Louis Cardinals (2013). **Years in League:** 2021-

OWNERSHIP/MANAGEMENT
Operated By: Peoria Chiefs Community Baseball Club LLC.
General Manager: Jason Mott. **Assistant General Manager:** Gary Olson. **Social and Marketing Manager:** Audrey Wall. **Director of Ticket Operations:** Matthew Vetter. **Director of Operations:** Dan Busch. **Manger of Community Relations:** Payton Leverton. **Manager of Media Relations:** Cody Schindler. **Head Groundskeeper:** Mike Reno.

FIELD STAFF
Manager: Patrick Anderson. **Hitting Coach:** Willi Martin. **Pitching Coach:** Edwin Moreno. **Trainer:** TBD. **Strength Coach:** TBD.

GAME INFORMATION
Radio Announcer: Cody Schinder. **No. of Games Broadcast:** 132. **Flagship Station:** www.peoriachiefs.com, Tune-In Radio. **PA Announcer:** Dustin Fitzpatrick. **Official Scorers:** Cody Schindler & TBA. **Stadium Name:** Dozer Park. **Location:** From South/East, I-74 to exit 93 (Jefferson St), continue one mile, stadium is one block on left; From North/West, I-74 to Glen Oak Exit, turn right on Glendale, which turns into Kumpf Blvd, turn right on Jefferson, stadium on left. **Standard Game Times:** Mon.-Sat., 6:35 p.m. Sun., 1:35 pm. **Ticket Price Range:** $9-16. **Visiting Club Hotel:** Holiday Inn Express and Suites, 1100 Bass Pro Drive East Peoria, IL 61611. **Telephone:** (309) 694-9800.

QUAD CITIES RIVER BANDITS

Address: 209 South Gaines Street, Davenport, IA 52802
Telephone: (563) 324-3000. **Fax:** (563) 324- 3109
Email Address: bandit@riverbandits.com. **Website:** riverbandits.com
Affiliation (first year): Kansas City Royals (2021). **Years in League:** 2022

OWNERSHIP/MANAGEMENT
Operated by: Main Street Baseball LLC, Dave Heller, Roby Smith, Ken Croken. **Chief Operating Officer, Main Street Baseball:** Joe Kubly. **General Manager:** Paul Kleinhans-Schulz. **Vice President Sales:** Shawn Brown. **Executive Director, Special Events and Human Resources:** Taylor Kubly. **Assistant General Manager, Baseball Operations:** Julia McNeil. **Assistant General Manager, Marketing:** Josh Michalsen. **Director, Marketing:** Dan Straney. **Director, Production and Creative Services:** Justin Hodge. **Director, Finance:** Julie James. **Director Field Services/Head Groundskeeper:** Morgan Hunter. **Director, Food and Beverage:** Joey Kaye. **Director, Amusements:** Sam Carnes. **Broadcaster/Manager Media Relations and Season Tickets:** Kyle Kercheval. **Manager, Ballpark Operations and**

MINOR LEAGUES

Grounds: Vance Young. **Box Office Manager:** Tyler Phillips. **Event Manager:** Kara Fairfield. **Assistant Food and Beverage Director/Manager, Hospitality and Catering:** Bri Marxen. **Office and Merchandise Manager:** Haleigh Carnes.

FIELD STAFF
Manager: Brooks Conrad. **Hitting Coach:** Ryan Powers. **Pitching Coach:** Derrick Lewis. **Bench Coach:** David Noworyta. **Strength Coach:** Joe Pedulla. **Athletic Trainer:** Brad Groleau.

GAME INFORMATION
Broadcaster: Kyle Kercheval. **No. of Games Broadcast:** 132. **Flagship Station:** MiLB.TV and riverbandits.com (audio stream). **Stadium Name:** Modern Woodmen Park. **Location:** From I-74, take Grant Street exit left, west on River Drive, left on South Gaines Street; from I-80, take Brady Street exit south, right on River Drive, left on South Gaines Street. **Standard Game Times:** 6:30pm CT. **Single Game Ticket Price Range:** $8-$20

SOUTH BEND CUBS

Office Address: 501 W. South St., South Bend, IN 46601.
Mailing Address: PO Box 4218, South Bend, IN 46634.
Telephone: (574) 235-9988. **Fax:** (574) 235-9950.
E-Mail Address: cubs@southbendcubs.com. **Website:** www.southbendcubs.com
Affiliation (first year): Chicago Cubs (2015). **Years in League:** 2021-

OWNERSHIP/MANAGEMENT
Owner: Andrew Berlin. **President:** Joe Hart. **General Manager & V.P., Corporate Partnerships:** Nick Brown. **Assistant General Manager, Marketing/Media:** Chris Hagstrom-Jones. **Assistant General Manager, Operations:** Peter Argueta. **Assistant General Manager, Tickets:** Andy Francis. **Box Office Manager:** Anthony Burchette. **Merchandise Manager:** Mary Lou Pallo. **Account Executives:** Kyle Cavanaugh, Tessa Schrager, Kyle Vincent, Wyatt Helms, Jake Klimcak. **Director of Finance & Administration:** Melissa Christlieb. **Finance & Administrative Assistant:** Amber Hayes. **Head Groundskeeper:** Jairo Rubio. **Director of Food and Beverage:** Tyler Hopple. **Business and Catering Manager:** Chloe Greenboam. **Executive Chef:** Scott Craig. **Radio Broadcasters:** Brendan King, Max Thoma. **Production Manager:** Kayleigh Sedlace

FIELD STAFF
Manager: Lance Rymel. **Hitting Coach:** Dan Puente. **Pitching Coach:** Clayton Mortensen. **Coach:** D'Angelo Jimenez.

GAME INFORMATION
Radio Announcers: Brendan King & Max Thoma. **Flagship Station:** Sports Radio 960 AM WSBT. **PA Announcer:** Gregg Sims, Jon Thompson. **Official Scorer:** Peter Yarbro. **Stadium Name:** Four Winds Field. **Location:** I-80/90 toll road to exit 77, take US 31/33 south to South Bend to downtown (Main Street), to Western Ave., right on Western, left on Taylor. **Standard Game Times:** Mon.-Sat., 7:05 pm, Sun. 2:05 pm. **Ticket Price Range:** Advance $12-15, Day of Game $13-15. **Visiting Club Hotel:** Aloft South Bend. **Hotel Telephone:** (574) 288-8000.

WEST MICHIGAN WHITECAPS

Office Address: 4500 West River Dr., Comstock Park, MI 49321.
Mailing Address: PO Box 428, Comstock Park, MI 49321.
Telephone: (616) 784-4131. **Fax:** (616) 784-4911.
E-Mail Address: playball@whitecapsbaseball.com.
Website: www.whitecapsbaseball.com.
Affiliation (first year): Detroit Tigers (1997). **Years in League:** 2021-

OWNERSHIP/MANAGEMENT
Chairmen and Founders: Lew Chamberlin/Denny Baxter. **CEO:** Joe Chamberlin. **President:** Steve McCarthy. **Vice President/General Manager:** Jim Jarecki. **Vice President, Sales:** Dan Morrison. **Director of Marketing:** Lynn Tuori. **Multimedia Coordinator:** Kelly Gonzalez Diaz. **Director of Ticket Sales:** Shaun Pynnonen. **Director of Food and Beverage:** Matt Timon. **Senior Design & Brand Specialist:** Jack Powers. **Promotions and Fan Entertainment Manager:** Ben Love. **Ticket Sales Manager:** Mike Epstein. **Box Office Manager:** Kaitlyn Reed. **Ticket Operations Coordinator:** Emily Milne. **Ticket Sales Account Executives:** Riley Paulus, Nick Bradshaw, Brandon Olson, Tyler Glave. **Corporate Partner Sales Executives:** Brittney Behrens, JD Triemstra, Ernie McCallum. **Corporate Partnership Coordinator:** Leah Austin. **Community Relations Manager:** Jenny Garone. **Merchandise Manager:** Lori Ashcroft. **Hospitality Manager:** Amanda Stephan. **Food and Beverage Operations Manager:** Danielle O'Connor. **Event Chef:** Matt Schumaker. **Operations Manager:** Brett Frieze. **Facility Maintenance Manager:** Kipp Jelinski. **Facility Maintenance Assistant:** Matt Richardson. **Head Groundskeeper:** Mitch Hooten. **Special Events Manager:** April Butler. **Director of People:** Courtney Walsh. **Controller:** Dave Rozema. **IT Administrator:** Scott Lutz. **IT Assistant:** Kyle Willacker. **Administrative Assistants:** Martha Beals, Melanie Lonsway, Chris Parsons.

MINOR LEAGUES

FIELD STAFF
Manager: Brayan Peña. **Hitting Coach:** Francisco Contreras. **Pitching Coach:** Dan Ricabal. **Bench Coach:** Tim Garland. **Athletic Trainer:** Sean McFarland. **Strength Coach:** TBD.

GAME INFORMATION
Play-by-Play Broadcasters: Dan Hasty, Nate Wangler. **No. of Games Broadcast:** 132. **Flagship Station:** The TICKET 106.1FM Grand Rapids. **PA Announcers:** Mike Newell, Bob Wells. **Official Scorers:** Aaron Sagraves, Joey Sutherlin. **Stadium Name:** LMCU Ballpark. **Location:** US 131 North from Grand Rapids to exit 91 (West River Drive). **Ticket Price Range:** $9-18. **Visiting Club Hotel:** Hampton Inn, 500 Center Dr NW, Grand Rapids, MI 49544 . **Telephone:** (616) 647-1000.

WISCONSIN TIMBER RATTLERS

Office Address: 2400 N. Casaloma Dr., Appleton, WI 54913.
Mailing Address: PO Box 7464, Appleton, WI 54912.
Telephone: (920) 733-4152. **Fax:** (920) 733-8032.
E-Mail Address: info@timberrattlers.com. **Website:** www.timberrattlers.com.
Affiliation (first year): Milwaukee Brewers (2009). **Years in League:** 2021-

OWNERSHIP/MANAGEMENT
Owned by: Third Base Ventures, LLC
Principal Owner: Craig Dickman. **President/CEO:** Rob Zerjav. **Vice President of Baseball & Stadium Operations:** Aaron Hahn. **Vice President of Business Operations:** Ryan Moede. **Vice President of Marketing:** Hilary Bauer. **Director of Food & Beverage:** Ryan Grossman. **Director of Security:** Scott Hoelzel. **Director of Community Relations:** Dayna Baitinger. **Director of Business Development:** Seth Merrill. **Director of Corporate Partnerships:** Ryan Cunniff. **Director of Media Relations:** Chris Mehring. **Director of Ticket Sales:** Kyle Fargen. **Senior Ticket Account Manager:** TBA. **Director of Ticket Operations:** Tyler Van Rossum. **Box Office Manager:** Alex Patchak. **Controller:** Eric Dresang. **Banquet Sales & Event Managers:** Mackenzie Liedtky, Brandy O'Marro. **Executive Chef:** Charles Behrmann. **Executive Sous Chef:** Chris Prentice. **Assistant Director of Food & Beverage:** Megan Andrews. **Director of Stadium Operations:** Justin Peterson. **Stadium Operations Manager:** Jeromy Luebke. **Entertainment Coordinator:** Jacob Jirschele. **Senior Graphic Designer:** Nick Guenther. **Graphic Designer:** Jared Klein. **Accounting/Human Resources Manager:** Brooke Brefczynski. **Production Manager:** Noah Hintz. **Social Media & Merchandise Manager:** Jessica Amo. **Clubhouse Manager:** Mason Kubly. **Office Manager:** Mary Robinson.

FIELD STAFF
Manager: Joe Ayrault. **Hitting Coach:** Ken Joyce. **Pitching Coach:** Drew Thomas. **Bench Coach:** David Tufo. **Development Coach:** Bryan Delgado. **Trainer:** Benny Arroyo. **Strength Coach:** Jim Buckley.

GAME INFORMATION
Radio Announcer: Chris Mehring. **No. of Games Broadcast:** All. **Flagship Station:** WNAM 1280-AM. **Television Announcer:** Chris Mehring (Radio Simulcast). **Television Affiliates:** TBA. **No. of Games Broadcast:** TBA. **PA Announcer:** Joey D. **Official Scorer:** Kyle Lobner. **Stadium Name:** Neuroscience Group Field at Fox Cities Stadium. **Location:** Highway 41 to Highway 15 (00) exit, west to Casaloma Drive, left to stadium. **Standard Game Times:** Mon.-Fri.: 6:40 pm, Wed. (Day): 12:10, Sat.: (Apr-May), 1:10pm, Sat.: (June-Sept), 6:40 pm, Sun.: 1:10 pm. **Ticket Price Range:** $10-40. **Visiting Club Hotel:** AmericInn by Wyndham 132 N. Mall Drive, Appleton, WI 54913.

MINOR LEAGUES

STADIUM INFORMATION

Club	Stadium	Opened	LF	CF	RF	Capacity	2022 Att.
Aberdeen	Ripken Stadium	2002	310	400	310	6,000	121,916
Asheville	McCormick Field	1992	326	373	297	4,000	172,726
Bowling Green	Bowling Green Ballpark	2009	318	400	326	4,559	155,975
Brooklyn	MCU Park	2001	315	412	325	7,500	167,846
Greensboro	First National Bank Field	2005	322	400	320	7,599	265,943
Greenville	Fluor Field at the West End	2006	310	400	302	5,000	317,150
Hickory	L.P. Frans Stadium	1993	330	401	330	5,062	105,378
Hudson Valley	Dutchess Stadium	1994	325	400	325	4,494	184,055
Jersey Shore	ShoreTown Ballpark	2001	325	400	325	6,588	256,141
Rome	AdventHealth Stadium	2003	335	400	330	5,100	89,176
Wilmington	Frawley Stadium	1993	325	400	325	6,532	118,754
Winston-Salem	BB&T Ballpark	2010	315	399	323	5,500	287,529

ABERDEEN IRONBIRDS

Address: 873 Long Drive, Aberdeen, MD 21001
Telephone: (410) 297-9292. **Fax:** (210) 297-6653
E-Mail Address: Info@ironbirdsbaseball.com. **Website:** ironbirdsbaseball.com
Affiliation (first year): Baltimore Orioles (2002). **Years in league:** 2021-

OWNERSHIP/MANAGEMENT
Operated By: Ripken Professional Baseball LLC. **Principal Owner:** Cal Ripken Jr. **Co-Owner/Executive Vice President:** Bill Ripken. **General Manager:** Jack Graham. **Assistant General Manager, Baseball Operations:** Todd Bradley. **Director, Ticketing:** Justin Gentilcore. **Box Office Manager:** Daniel Carey. **Manager, Group Ticket Sales:** Andrew Spanos. **Account Executive:** Dan Edgren. **Account Executive:** Kyler Albert. **Director, Creative Services:** Kevin Jimenez. **Director, Partnerships & Marketing:** Brekke Autry. **Sr. Coordinator, Marketing & Communications:** Olivia Taddeo. **Manager, Facilities:** Larry Gluch. **Facilities Assistant:** David Dawson. **Manager, Merchandise and Operations:** Skye Truss. **Coordinator, Partnership Activation:** TBA. **Manager, Non-Gameday Events:** Becca Ashman.

FIELD STAFF
Manager: Roberto Mercado. **Hitting Coach:** Zach Cole. **Pitching Coach:** Austin Meine. **Fundamentals Coach:** Chase Sebby. **Development Coach:** Billy Facteau. **Athletic Trainer:** Tori Atencio. **Strength & Conditioning:** Sam Sauer.

GAME INFORMATION
No. of Games Broadcast on MiLB.tv: 66. **MiLB.tv Broadcaster:** Michael Marcantonini. **PA Announcer:** Ray Atkinson. **Official Scorer:** Jason King. **Stadium Name:** Leidos Field at Ripken Stadium. **Location:** I-95 to exit 85 (route 22), west on 22, right onto long drive. **Ticket Price Range:** $17-$42.

ASHEVILLE TOURISTS

Address: McCormick Field, 30 Buchanan Place, Asheville, NC 28801.
Telephone: (828) 258-0428. **E-Mail Address:** info@theashevilletourists.com.
Website: www.theashevilletourists.com.
Affiliation (first year): Houston Astros (2021). **Years in League:** 2021-

OWNERSHIP/MANAGEMENT
Operated By: DeWine Seeds-Silver Dollar Baseball, LLC. **President:** Brian DeWine. **General Manager:** Larry Hawkins. **Assistant General Manager:** Hannah Martin. **Director of Broadcasting/Media Relations:** Doug Maurer. **Stadium Operations Director:** Michael Mueller. **Director of Food & Beverage:** Tyler Holt. **Sports Turf Manager:** Joey Elmore. **Promotions Manager:** Alyssa Quirk. **Client Services Manager:** Jamie Unternaher. **Director of Ticket Operations:** Shannon Wladyka. **Account Executives:** Jess McGee and Hanna Rosenberger. **Merchandise Manager:** Kali DeWine.

FIELD STAFF
Manager: Nate Shaver. **Hitting Coach:** Rene Rojas. **Pitching Coach:** Jose Rada.

GAME INFORMATION
Radio Announcer: Doug Maurer. **No. of Games Broadcast:** 132. **Flagship Station:** Asheville Tourists Online Radio Network. **PA Announcer:** Tim Lolley. **Official Scorers:** Steven Grady, Adam Williams, Joseph Marvin. **Stadium Name:** McCormick Field. **Location:** I-240 to Charlotte Street South exit, south one mile on Charlotte, left on McCormick Place. **Ticket Price Range:** $10.50-$18.50.

MINOR LEAGUES

BOWLING GREEN HOT RODS

Address: Bowling Green Ballpark, 300 8th Avenue, Bowling Green, KY 42101.
Telephone: (270) 901-2121. **Fax:** (270) 901-2165.
E-Mail Address: fun@bghotrods.com. **Website:** www.bghotrods.com.
Affiliation (first year): Tampa Bay Rays (2009). **Years in League:** 2021-

OWNERSHIP/MANAGEMENT

Operated By: BG SKY, LLC. **Owner:** Jack Blackstock. **President/COO:** Eric C. Leach. **General Manager:** Kyle Wolz. **Assistant General Manager:** Ashlee Wilson. **Stadium Operations Manager:** Jeff Ciocco. **Stadium Operations Manager:** Garret Browning. **Head Groundskeeper:** Matt Hill. **Broadcasting/Media Relations Manager:** Riley Edwards. **Box Office Manager & Account Executive:** Alex Meyer. **Account Executive:** Marshall Stuart. **Account Executive:** Heath Monroe. **Video Production and Social Media Manager:** Chris Poindexter. **Graphic Design Manager:** Karley Livingston. **Promotions and Community Relations Manager:** Hunter Caldwell. **Seasonal Merchandise Manager:** Lyam French. **Bookkeeper:** Kim Myers.

FIELD STAFF

Manager: Rafael Valenzuela. **Pitching Coach:** R.C. Lichtenstein. **Hitting Coach:** Paul Rozzelle. **Bench Coach:** Skeeter Barnes. **Athletic Trainer:** Ruben Santiago. **Strength & Conditioning Coach:** Garrett Hudson.

GAME INFORMATION

Radio Announcer: Riley Edwards. **No. of Games Broadcast:** 132. **Flagship Station:** Talk 104.1 FM. **PA Announcer:** Unavailable. **Official Scorer:** Micky Strader. **Stadium Name:** Bowling Green Ballpark. **Location:** From I-65, take Exit 26 (KY-234/Cemetery Road) into Bowling Green for 3 miles, left onto College Street for .2 miles, right onto 8th Avenue. **Standard Game Times:** Mon.-Sat., 6:35 pm, Sun., 2:05/5:05 pm. **Ticket Price Range:** $8-25. **Visiting Club Hotel:** Tru by Hilton. **Telephone:** (270) 904-2260.

BROOKLYN CYCLONES

Address: 1904 Surf Ave, Brooklyn, NY 11224.
Telephone: (718) 372-5596. **Fax:** (718) 449-6368.
E-Mail Address: info@brooklyncyclones.com. **Website:** brooklyncyclones.com.
Affiliation (first year): New York Mets (2001). **Years in League:** 2021-

OWNERSHIP/MANAGEMENT

Owner, Chairman & CEO: Steven A. Cohen. **Owner & President, Amazin Mets Foundation:** Alexandra M. Cohen. **Vice Chariman & Owner:** Andrew B. Cohen. **Chairman Emeritus:** Fred Wilpon. **Vice President:** Steve Cohen. **General Manager:** Kevin Mahoney. **Assistant GM:** Billy Harner. **Operations Manager:** Vladimir Lipsman. **Director, Ticket Sales & Operations:** Michael Charyn. **Manager, Corporate Partnerships & Development:** Jennifer Reilly. **Director, Partnership Development:** Tommy Cardona. **Manager, Special Events:** Bryan Wynne. **Graphics & Social Media Manager:** Lily Clark. **Account Executives:** Ryan Dougherty, Mordechai Twersky, Ricky Viola. **Senior Accountant:** Tatiana Isdith. **Accounting:** Michael Cheung. **Administrative Assistant, Community Relations:** Sharon Lundy. **Clubhouse Manager:** Max Colten. **Operations:** Nariman Kyhydrov, Jesse Rivera, Angelo Cyriaque.

FIELD STAFF

Manager: Chris Newell. **Hitting Coach:** Richie Benes. **Pitching Coach:** Victor Ramos. **Bench Coach:** John Vaughn. **Athletic Trainer:** Paul Gonzales. **Performance Coach:** Drew Skrocki.

GAME INFORMATION

No. of Games Broadcast: 132. **Flagship Station:** Web Streaming Only. **PA Announcer:** Rick Rissetto. **Official Scorer:** Howard Kaplan & Charles O'Brien. **Stadium Name:** Maimonides Park. **Location:** Belt Parkway to Cropsey Ave South, continue on Cropsey until it becomes West 17th St, continue to Surf Ave, stadium on south side of Surf Ave; By subway, west/south to Stillwell Ave./Coney Island station. **Ticket Price Range:** $9-20. **Visiting Club Hotel:** Unavailable.

GREENSBORO GRASSHOPPERS

Address: 408 Bellemeade St, Greensboro, NC 27401.
Telephone: (336) 268-2255. **Fax:** (336) 273-7350.
E-Mail Address: info@gsohoppers.com. **Website:** www.gsohoppers.com.
Affiliation (first year): Pittsburgh Pirates (2019). **Years in League:** 2021-

OWNERSHIP/MANAGEMENT

Operated By: Temerity Baseball. **Principal Owner:** Andy Sandler.
President/General Manager: Donald Moore. **Assistant General Manager:** Tim Vangel. **Chief Financial Officer:** Brad Falkiewicz. **Director of Sales:** Todd Olson. **Director, Ticket Sales/Services:** Erich Dietz. **Ticket Sales Manager:** Dylan James. **Director, Creative Services:** Amanda Williams. **Director, Promotions/Community Relations:** Stephen Johnson. **Manager, Video Production:** Stephen Long. **Manager of Social Media and Media Services:** Callie Cline. **Office Administrator and Suite Coordinator:** Tony Roberts. **Director of Food and Beverage:** Drew Gill. **Concessions Manager:** Brandon Steele. **Director of Stadium Operations:** Davis Tomlinson. **Head Groundskeeper:** Anthony Alejo.

MINOR LEAGUES

FIELD STAFF
Manager: Robby Hammock. **Hitting Coach:** Ruben Gotay. **Pitching Coach:** Fernando Nieve. **Performance Coach:** Justin Orton. **Development Coach:** Collin Wilber. **Athletic Trainer:** Casey Lee. **Strength Coach:** Ryoji Ejima.

GAME INFORMATION
Announcer: Stuart Barefoot. **Official Scorer:** Jeff Mills. **Stadium Name:** First National Bank Field. **Location:** From I-85, take Highway 220 South (exit 36) to Coliseum Blvd, continue on Edgeworth Street, ballpark at corner of Edgeworth and Bellemeade Streets. **Standard Game Times:** 6:30 pm. **Ticket Price Range:** $9-14. **Visiting Club Hotel:** LaQuinta Inn at Greensboro Airport—7905 Triad Center Drive, Greensboro, NC 27409. **Telephone:** (336) 840.1550.

GREENVILLE DRIVE

Mailing Address: 935 South Main St, Suite 202, Greenville, SC 29601.
Stadium Address: 945 South Main St. Greenville, SC 29601.
Telephone: (864) 240-4500. **E-Mail Address:** info@greenvilledrive.com
Website: www.greenvilledrive.com
Affiliation (first year): Boston Red Sox (2005). **Years in League:** 2021-

OWNERSHIP/MANAGEMENT
Owner/Chairman: Craig Brown. **President:** Jeff Brown. **General Manager:** Eric Jarinko. **VP, Finance/Administration:** Jordan Smith. **VP, Ticketing:** Phil Bargardi. **VP, Grounds/Operations:** Greg Burgess. **VP, Sponsorships/Community Engagement:** Katie Batista. **VP, Business Development:** Suzanne Foody. **VP, Food & Beverage Operations:** Logan Taylor. **Director, Game Entertainment:** Alex Guest. **Director, Media/Creative Services:** Stephen Olschanski. **Director, Merchandise:** Jenny Burgdorfer. **Director, Video Production:** Lance Fowler. **Director, Facility Operations:** Timmy Hinds. **Director, Food & Beverage:** Preston Madill. **Director, Ticket Operations:** Elise Parish. **Director, Premium Hospitality & Catering:** Kimberly Black. **Director, West End Events at Fluor Field:** Dayna Mercer. **Executive Chef:** Wilbert Sauceda. **Accounting Manager:** Daniel Baker. **Office Manager:** Allison Roedell. **Retail Manager:** Emily Saunders. **Partner Activations Manager:** Emily Peeler. **Concessions Manager:** Mike Honeycutt. **Ticket Account Executives:** Brenden Campbell, Nathan Fenters, Caden Risen, Sydney Richardson. **Inside Sales Representatives:** Blakely Addis, Devin Foster. **Facilities Operations Assistant:** Nick Brafford. **Assistant Groundskeeper:** Jed Huth. **Clubhouse Manager:** Brady Andrews. **West End Events at Fluor Field Managers:** Katy Beverly, Ashley Hall. **Event Operations Assistant:** James Ervin.

FIELD STAFF
Manager: Iggy Suarez. **Pitching Coach:** Bob Kipper. **Hitting Coach:** Chris Hess. **Development Coach:** Alex Reynolds. **Coach:** Taylor Jackson. **ATC:** Charysse Berkowski. **S/C Coach:** Donny Gress.

GAME INFORMATION
Radio Announcer: Dan Scott & Tom Van Hoy. **Flagship Station:** GreenvilleDrive.com. **PA Announcer:** Chuck Hussion, William Qualkinbush. **Official Scorer:** Jordan Caskey. Scott Keeler. Chandler Simpson. **Stadium Name:** Fluor Field at the West End. **Location:** I-385 into Downtown Greenville; Left onto Church Street; Right onto University Ridge; Right onto Augusta Street; Left onto Field Street. **Standard Game Times:** Mon.-Sat., 7:05 p.m., Sun. 3:05 p.m. **Ticket Price Range:** Advance $8-$14, Day of Game $9-15. **Visiting Club Hotel:** Wingate by Wyndham. **Hotel Telephone:** (864) 281-1281.

HUDSON VALLEY RENEGADES

Office Address: Dutchess Stadium, 1500 Route 9D, Wappingers Falls, NY 12590.
Mailing Address: PO Box 661, Fishkill, NY 12524.
Telephone: (845) 838-0094. **Fax:** (845) 838-0014.
E-Mail Address: info@hvrenegades.com. **Website:** www.hvrenegades.com.
Affiliation (first year): New York Yankees (2021). **Years in League:** 2021-

OWNERSHIP/MANAGEMENT
Owner/Operator: Diamond Baseball Holdings, LLC. **General Manager:** Tyson Jeffers. **Assistant General Manager:** Zach Betkowski. **Vice President, Game Day Promotions & Programming:** Rick Zolzer. **Director, Marketing & Creative Services:** Zach Neubauer. **Director, Public Relations:** Joe Vasile. **Director, Stadium Operations & Special Events:** Tom Hubmaster. **Director, Stadium Operations:** Jack Dumoulin. **Director, Ticket Sales:** Will Young. **Manager, Community Relations:** Marcella Costello. **Manager, Corporate Partnerships & Activation:** Alex Gluckman. **Manager, Field Operations:** Tanner Puff. **Manager, Finance:** Peggie Hyatt. **Manager, Merchandise:** Luis Flores. **Account Executives, Ticket Sales:** Mariah Tlougan, Isaac Hennen, Erin Dietz.

FIELD STAFF
Manager: Sergio Santos. **Hitting Coach:** Kevin Martir. **Pitching Coach:** Preston Claiborne. **Defensive Coach:** Rob Benjamin, Derek Woodley. **Trainer:** Brandon Rodriguez. **Strength Coach:** Isiah McDonald. **Scouting Analyst:** Matt Wells.

GAME INFORMATION
Radio Announcer: Joe Vasile. **No. of Games Broadcast:** All 132 home and road games broadcast on Z93 (93.3 FM-Poughkeepsie) and the iHeartRadio App. **PA Announcer:** Rob Adams. **Official Scorer:** Dennis Sheehan. **Stadium Name:** Dutchess Stadium. **Location:** I-84 to exit 41 (NY-9D North), north one mile to stadium. **Standard Game Times: April & May:** Tues.-Fri., 6:05 p.m. | Sat. 4:05 p.m., Sun. 2:05 p.m. **June-Sept.:** Tues.-Fri., 7:05 p.m., Sat. 6:05 p.m., Sun., 2:05 p.m. **Visiting Club Hotel:** Courtyard by Marriott Fishkill, 17 Westage Drive, Fishkill, NY, 12524. **Telephone:** (845) 897-2400.

MINOR LEAGUES

HICKORY CRAWDADS

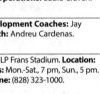

Office and Mailing Address: 2500 Clement Blvd. NW, Hickory, NC 28601.
Telephone: (828) 322-3000.
E-Mail Address: crawdad@hickorycrawdads.com.
Website: www.hickorycrawdads.com.
Affiliation (first year): Texas Rangers (2009). **Years in League:** 2021-

OWNERSHIP/MANAGEMENT
Operated by: Hickory Baseball Inc. **Principal Owners:** Texas Rangers. **President:** Neil Leibman. **General Manager:** Douglas Locascio. **Business Manager:** Donna White. **Assistant General Manager of Marketing:** Ashley Salinas. **Assistant General Manager of Sales:** Robby Willis. **Director of Operations & Special Events:** Daniel Barkley. **Head Groundskeeper:** Corey Church. **Director of Promotions and Community Relations:** Karly Vollgrebe. **Group Sales Executive:** Joey Norris. **Stadium Operations Manager:** Alex Cook. **General Manager, REV Food Service:** Ashley Pyatte. **Director, Food and Beverage Operations:** Sadie Craven.

FIELD STAFF
Manager: Chad Comer. **Hitting Coach:** Drew Sannes. **Pitching Coach:** Jon Goebel. **Development Coaches:** Jay Sullenger, Justin Jacobs. **Athletic Trainer:** Derrick Decker. **Strength and Conditioning Coach:** Andreu Cardenas.

GAME INFORMATION
PA Announcers: Rob Eastwood, Rodney Pyatt. **Official Scorers:** Mark Parker. **Stadium Name:** LP Frans Stadium. **Location:** I-40 to exit 123 (Lenoir North), 321 North to Clement Blvd, left for 1/2 mile. **Standard Game Times:** Mon.-Sat., 7 pm, Sun., 5 pm. **Visiting Club Hotel:** Crowne Plaza, 1385 Lenior-Rhyne Boulevard SE, Hickory, NC 28602. **Telephone:** (828) 323-1000.

JERSEY SHORE BLUECLAWS

Address: 2 Stadium Way Lakewood, NJ 08701
Telephone: 732-901-7000. **Fax:** 732-901-3967
Email Address: info@blueclaws.com
Website: www.blueclaws.com
Affiliation: Philadelphia Phillies (2001-) **Years In League:** 2021-

OWNERSHIP/MANAGEMENT
Managing Partner, Shore Town Baseball: Art Matin. **President/General Manager:** Joe Ricciutti. **Assistant General Manager:** Kevin Fenstermacher. **Senior VP, Ticket Sales & Service:** Bob McLane. **VP, Finance:** Don Rodgers. **VP, Community Relations & Sales / Executive Director, BlueClaws Charities:** Jim McNamara. **VP, Promotions & Entertainment:** Jamie Bertram. **VP, Corporate Partnerships:** Rob Vota. **Sr. Director, Partnership Services:** Zack Nicol. **Director, Communications:** Greg Giombarrese. **Director, Events & Operations:** Kayla Reilly. **Director, Regional Outreach:** Rob McGillick. **Director, Ticket Operations:** Garrett Herr. **Director, Grounds:** Mike Morvay. **Director, Merchandise & Ticket Sales:** Jamie Wagner. **Senior Sales Executive:** Craig Ebinger. **Ticket Membership Manager:** Joel Podos. **Ticket Membership Manager:** Kristen Larkin. **Group Ticket Manager:** Killian Vallieu. **Account Executive:** Jimmy Donnelly. **Manager, Accounting:** Phil Armstrong. **Manager, Food & Beverage:** Rachael Pabon. **Manager, Concourse:** Margaret De Rosa. **Manager, Hospitality:** Susan Wallace. **Manager, Promotions:** Gianna Fiocco. **Manager, Digital Marketing:** Raechel Kronyak. **Manager, Partnership Services:** Ben Wilson. **Manager, Events & Operations:** Ryan Mead. **Manager, Operations:** Shane Eldridge. **Ticket & Fan Services Coordinator:** Haley Kopf.

FIELD STAFF
Manager: Greg Brodzinski. **Pitching Coach:** Phil Cundari. **Pitching Development:** Brady Lail. **Hitting Coach:** Brock Stassi. **Bench Coach:** Chris Adamson. **Trainer:** Meaghan Flaherty. **Strength & Conditioning Coach:** Mark Jesse Jr.

GAME INFORMATION
Radio Announcers: Greg Giombarrese. **No. of Games Broadcast:** 66. **Flagship Station:** BlueClaws.com. **PA Announcers:** Jeff Fromm. **Official Scorers:** Joe Erickson. **Stadium Name:** ShoreTown Ballpark. **Location:** Route 70 to New Hampshire Avenue, North on New Hampshire for 2.5 miles to ballpark. **Standard Game Times:** 7:05 pm, 6:35 pm (April-May); Sun 1:05. **Ticket Price Range:** $9-18. **Visiting Team Hotel:** Clarion Hotel & Conference Center, 815 Rt. 37 West | Toms River, NJ 08755NJ 08755.

ROME BRAVES

Office Address: State Mutual Stadium, 755 Braves Blvd, Rome, GA 30161.
Mailing Address: PO Box 1915, Rome, GA 30162-1915.
Telephone: (706) 378-5100. **Fax:** (706) 368-6525.
E-Mail Address: romebraves@braves.com. **Website:** www.romebraves.com.
Affiliation (first year): Atlanta Braves (2003). **Years in League:** 2021-

OWNERSHIP MANAGEMENT
Operated By: Diamond Baseball Holdings, LLC. **General Manager:** David Lane. **Director, Stadium Operations:** Tyler Stinson. **Coordinator, Stadium Operations:** Brad Hobbs. **Director, Sales:** TBD. **Group Sales Manager:** Katie Aspin. **Box Office Manager:** Jackie O'Reilly. **Marketing Manager:** TBD. **Marketing & Media**

MINOR LEAGUES

Relations Coordinator: Justin Franklin. Account Representative: Patrick Gallagher. Account Representative: Hunter Coutts. Field Turf Manager: Joseph Brooks. Retail Manager: Starla Roden. Food and Beverage Director: Jonathan Jackson.

FIELD STAFF
Manager: Angel Flores. Hitting Coach: Garrett Wilkinson. Pitching Coach: Wes McGuire.

GAME INFORMATION
Radio Announcer: Logan Maddox. No. of Games Broadcast: 66 (Home only). Flagship Station: RomeBraves.com (home games). PA Announcer: TBD. Official Scorers: Jim O'Hara, Lyndon Huckaby. Stadium Name: AdventHealth Stadium. Location: I-75 North to exit 190 (Rome/Canton), left off exit and follow Highway 411/Highway 20 to Rome, right at inter- section on Highway 411 and Highway 1 (Veterans Memorial Highway), stadium is at intersection of Veterans Memorial Highway and Riverside Parkway. Ticket Price Range: $7-20. (purchased in advance). Visiting Club Hotel: Holiday Inn Express & Suites, 35 Hobson Way, Rome, GA 30161. Telephone: (706) 232-0021.

WILMINGTON BLUE ROCKS

Address: 801 Shipyard Drive, Wilmington, DE 19801.
Telephone: (302) 888-2015. Fax: (302) 888-2032.
E-Mail Address: info@bluerocks.com. Website: www.bluerocks.com.
Affiliation: Washington Nationals (2021). Years in League: 2021-

OWNERSHIP/MANAGEMENT
Operated by: Wilmington Blue Rocks LP. Honorary President: Matt Minker. Club President: Clark Minker. Owners: Main Street Baseball. Managing Partner/League Director & CEO, Main Street Baseball: Dave Heller. Assistant General Manager: Liz Welch, Gil Addeo. Director of Web and Creative Services: Mark Lavis. VP, Business Development: Robert Ford. Box Office Manager: Ian Porter. Director, Groups & Groups Experiences: Bill Levy. Director, Stadium Operations: Sean Mason. Director, Field Operations: Steve Gold. Controller: Steve Burdick. Director, Business Development: Kevin Linton.

FIELD STAFF
Manager: Mario Lisson. Hitting Coach: Micah Franklin. Pitching Coach: Mark DiFelice. Developmental Coach: Mark Harris.

GAME INFORMATION
No. of Games Broadcast: 66. Flagship Station: WGLS 89.7 Online Stream. PA Announcer: Kevin Linton. Official Scorer: Dick Shute. Stadium Name: Judy Johnson Field at Daniel S. Frawley Stadium. Location: I-95 North to Maryland Ave (exit 6), right on Maryland Ave, and through traffic light onto Martin Luther King Blvd, right at traffic light on Justison St, follow to Shipyard Dr; I-95 South to Maryland Ave (exit 6), left at fourth light on Martin Luther King Blvd, right at fourth light on Justison St, follow to Shipyard Drive. Standard Game Times: 6:35 pm, (Tue- Sat) Sun. 1:05 p.m. Ticket Price Range: $13-$17.

WINSTON-SALEM DASH

Office Address: 300 S. Liberty St., Suite 100, Winston-Salem, NC 27101.
Stadium Address: 951 Ballpark Way, Winston-Salem, NC 27101.
Telephone: (336) 714-2287. Fax: (336) 714-2288.
E-Mail Address: info@wsdash.com. Website: www.wsdash.com.
Affiliation (first year): Chicago White Sox (1997). Years in League: 2021-

OWNERSHIP/MANAGEMENT
Operated by: W-S Dash. Principal Owner: Billy Prim.
President & General Manager: Brian DeAngelis. VP, Chief Financial Officer: Kurt Gehsmann. Accounting Manager: Diane Pitts. Receptionist: Alisa May. VP, Baseball Operations: Ryan Manuel. Director, Stadium Operations: Mike Craven. Director of Facility Management: Jeff Kelly. Director of Grounds: Josh Leo. Director, Tickets: Cody Hallman. Managers, Tickets: Matt Beksinski, Josh Van Noy, Andrew Murphy, Kalen Thigpen, Joshua Eberhard, Junior Smart. Manager, Ticket Operations: Josh Soto. VP, Corporate Partnerships: Josh Strickland. Manager, Corporate Partnerships: Alex Barnes. VP, Marketing/Corporate Partnership Services: Morgan Clausel. Director, Entertainment: Caela McBride. Director, Merchandise: Sidney Laughlin. Manager, Marketing and Communications: Amanda Weaver. Manager, Partnership Services: Ryan Miller. Content Creator: Carson Lesser. Manager, Creative Services: Mark Lavis. Director, Food and Beverage: Kit Edwards. Manager, Catering: Beverly Becker. Manager, Concessions: Zachary Mounce. Manager, Hospitality Operations: Tanner Mounce.

FIELD STAFF
Manager: Guillermo Quiroz. Hitting Coach: Jason Krizan. Pitching Coach: John Ely.

GAME INFORMATION
Broadcaster/Media Relations: Andrew Murphy. No. of Games Broadcast: All Home (66) and Select Road. Flagship Station: Audio feed available on wsdash.com. PA Announcer: Jeffrey Griffin. Official Scorer: Kevin Williams Stadium Name: Truist Stadium. Location: Salem Parkway to Peters Creek Parkway exit. Standard Game Times: T-Sat 7 p.m., Sun. 2 p.m. Visiting Club Hotel: Fairfield Inn & Suites by Marriott - Winston-Salem Downtown.

MINOR LEAGUES

NORTHWEST LEAGUE

STADIUM INFORMATION

Club	Stadium	Opened	LF	CF	RF	Capacity	2022 Att.
Eugene	PK Park	2010	335	400	325	4,000	136,360
Everett	Everett Memorial Stadium	1984	324	380	330	3,682	128,836
Hillsboro	Hillsboro Ballpark	2013	325	400	325	4,500	150,792
Spokane	Avista Stadium	1958	335	398	335	7,162	231,081
Tri-City	Dust Devils Stadium	1995	335	400	335	3,700	108,136
Vancouver	Nat Bailey Stadium	1951	335	395	335	6,500	313,256

(Dimensions)

EUGENE EMERALDS

Office Address: 2760 Martin Luther King Jr. Blvd, Eugene, OR 97401.
Mailing Address: PO Box 10911, Eugene, OR 97440.
Telephone: (541) 342-5367. **Fax:** (541) 342-6089.
E-Mail Address: info@emeraldsbaseball.com. **Website:** www.emeraldsbaseball.com.
Affiliation (first year): San Francisco Giants (2021). **Years in League:** 2021-

OWNERSHIP/MANAGEMENT
Operated By: Elmore Sports Group Ltd. **Principal Owner:** David Elmore.
General Manager: Allan Benavides. **Assistant GM:** Matt Dompe. **Director, Food/Beverage:** Turner Elmore. **Director, Tickets:** Emilio Ziolkowski. **Event Managers:** Chris Bowers, Joe McIntyre, Trent Bennett, Garret Diegel and Andrew Brown. **Graphic Designer:** Kyrstin Ginter. **Director, Community Affairs:** Anne Culhane. **Sponsorship Sales:** Matt Dompe. **Home Radio:** Matt Dompe. **Away Radio:** Jacob Archer

FIELD STAFF
Manager: Carlos Valderrama. **Hitting Coach:** Tommy Joseph. **Pitching Coach:** Alain Quijano. **Fundamentals Coach:** Eliezer Zambrano. **Athletic Trainer:** Tim Vigue. **Strength Coach:** Chris Harms.

GAME INFORMATION
Radio Announcer: Matt Dompe. **No. of Games Broadcast:** 132. **Flagship Station:** 95.3-FM The Score. **PA Announcer:** Jill Cole. **Official Scorer:** George McPherson. **Stadium Name:** PK Park. **Standard Game Time:** Mon.- Sat., TBD, Sun., TBD. **Ticket Price Range:** $13-$22. **Visiting Club Hotel:** Even Hotel Eugene.

EVERETT AQUASOX

Mailing Address: 3802 Broadway, Everett, WA 98201.
Telephone: (425) 258-3673. **Fax:** (425) 258-3675.
E-Mail Address: info@aquasox.com. **Website:** www.aquasox.com.
Affiliation (first year): Seattle Mariners (1995). **Years in League:** 2021-

OWNERSHIP/MANAGEMENT
Operated by: 7th Inning Stretch, LLC.
Directors: Chad Volpe, Pat Filippone. **General Manager:** Danny Tetzlaff. **Director of Broadcasting:** Pat Dillon. **Director of Corporate Partnerships:** Mike MacCulloch. **Director of Tickets:** Jim Bergem. **Ticket Operations Manager:** Scott Brownlee. **Corporate Partnership Manager:** Bailey Walsh. **Director of Merchandise & Community Relations:** Nellie Kemp. **Account Executive:** Peyton Kelley. **Finance Manager:** Connor Doolin. **Ballpark Operations & Ticket Sales:** Chad Gates. **Director of Food & Beverage:** Liz Cox. **On-Field Emcee/Road Radio Broadcaster:** Steve Willits.

FIELD STAFF
Manager: Ryan Scott. **Hitting Coach:** Mike Fransoso. **Pitching Coach:** Cameron Ming. **Coach:** Sergio Plasencia. **Athletic Trainers:** Dan Laberry, Stephanie McLain. **Strength and Conditioning:** Drew Weidner.

GAME INFORMATION
Radio Announcers: Pat Dillon, Steve Willits. **No. of Games Broadcast:** 132. **Flagship Station:** KRKO 1380-AM, 95.3-FM. **PA Announcer:** Tom Lafferty. **Official Scorer:** Patrick Lafferty. **Stadium Name:** Funko Field at Everett Memorial Stadium. **Location:** I-5, exit 192. **Standard Game Times:** Mon.-Sat., 7:05 pm, Sun., 4:05 pm. **Ticket Price Range:** $10-22. **Visiting Club Hotel:** Courtyard by Marriott, 3003 Colby Ave, Everett, WA 98201. **Telephone:** (425) 259-2200.

HILLSBORO HOPS

Address: 4460 NE Century Blvd., Hillsboro, OR, 97124.
Telephone: (503) 640-0887.
E-Mail Address: info@hillsborohops.com. **Website:** www.hillsborohops.com.

MINOR LEAGUES

Affiliation (first year): Arizona Diamondbacks (2001). **Years in League:** 2021-

OWNERSHIP/MANAGEMENT
Operated by: Short Season LLC. **Managing Partners:** Mike McMurray, Josh Weinman, Myron Levin. **Chairman and CEO:** Mike McMurray. **President and General Manager:** K.L. Wombacher. **Chief Financial Officer:** Laura McMurray. **Vice President Corporate Partnerships:** Matt Kolasinski. **Vice President, Tickets:** Brett Breece. **Director, Merchandise:** Hannah August. **Director, Marketing and Communications:** Casey Sawyer. **Director, Broadcasting:** Rich Burk.

FIELD STAFF
Manager: Ronnie Gajownik. **Hitting Coach:** Ty Wright. **Pitching Coach:** Gabriel Hernandez. **Athletic Trainer:** Haruki Mukohchi. **Strength Coach:** Ryan Harrel.

GAME INFORMATION
PA Announcer: Jason Swygard. **Official Scorer:** Blair Cash. **Stadium Name:** Ron Tonkin Field. **Location:** 4460 NE Century Blvd., Hillsboro, OR. 97124. **Standard Game Times:** Mon.-Sat., 7:05 pm, Sun., 1:05 pm. **Ticket Price Range:** $7-$22. **Visiting Club Hotel:** Aloft by Marriott, Hillsboro, OR. **Telephone:** (503) 277-1900.

SPOKANE INDIANS

Office Address: Avista Stadium, 602 N Havana, Spokane, WA 99202.
Mailing Address: PO Box 4758, Spokane, WA 99220.
Telephone: (509) 535-2922. **Fax:** (509) 534-5368.
E-Mail Address: mail@spokaneindians.com. **Website:** www.spokaneindians.com.
Affiliation (first year): Colorado Rockies (2021). **Years in League:** 2021-

OWNERSHIP/MANAGEMENT
Operated By: Longball Inc. **Principal Owner:** Bobby Brett. **CEO:** Andrew Billig.
President: Chris Duff. **Senior Vice President:** Otto Klein. **VP, Concessions & Hospitality:** Josh Roys. **VP, Business Operations:** Lesley DeHart. **VP, General Manager:** Kyle Day. **VP, Ticket Services:** Nick Gaebe. **Director of Stadium Operations:** Chris Ackerman. **Director of Public Relations:** Bud Bareither. **Director of Corporate Partnerships:** Sean Dorsey. **Director of Grounds:** Tony Lee. **Director of Hospitality & Stadium Events:** Darby Moore. **Director of Employee Development & Culture:** MacKenzie White. **Director of Ticket Services:** Ryan Songey. **Partner Services Manager:** Gina Giesseman. **Concessions & Hospitality Manager:** Chayton Roberts. **Group Ticket Coordinator:** Sam Beeman. **Partner Services Coordinator:** Aaron Croom. **Group Ticket Coordinator:** Tyler Curtis. **Ticket Services Coordinator:** Daniel Homans. **Group Ticket Coordinator:** Andy Johnson. **Merchandise Coordinator:** Hanna Jones. **Employee Engagement Coordinator:** Jimmy Lasswell. **Ticket Services Coordinator:** Justus Reimer. **Partner Services Coordinator:** Emily Shields. **Ticket Services Coordinator:** Ben Wintringer.

FIELD STAFF
Manager: Robinson Cancel. **Pitching Coach:** Ryan Kibler. **Hitting Coach:** Zach Osborne. **Bench Coach:** Joe Mikulik.

GAME INFORMATION
Radio Announcer: Mike Boyle. **Flagship Station:** 1510 AM/103.5 FM. **PA Announcer:** Chadron Hazelbaker. **Official Scorer:** Todd Gilkey. **Stadium Name:** Avista Stadium. **Location:** From west, I-90 to exit 283B (Thor/Freya), east on Third Avenue, left onto Havana; From east, I-90 to Broadway exit, right onto Broadway, left onto Havana. **Standard Game Time:** Mon.-Sat., 6:30 pm, Sun., 5:09 pm. **Ticket Price Range:** $5-24. **Visiting Club Hotel:** Mirabeau Park Hotel & Convention Center, 1100 N. Sullivan Rd, Spokane, WA 99037. **Telephone:** (509) 343-6886.

TRI-CITY DUST DEVILS

Address: 6200 Burden Blvd, Pasco, WA 99301.
Telephone: (509) 544-8789. **Fax:** (509) 547-9570.
E-Mail Address: info@dustdevilsbaseball.com.
Website: dustdevilsbaseball.com.
Affiliation (first year): Los Angeles Angels (2021). **Years in League:** 2021-

OWNERSHIP/MANAGEMENT
Operated by: Northwest Baseball Ventures. **Principal Owners:** George Brett, Yoshi Okamoto, Brent Miles. **President:** Brent Miles. **Vice President/General Manager:** Derrel Ebert. **Assistant General Manager, Sponsorships:** Ann Shively. **Assistant General Manager, Tickets:** Trevor Shively. **Group Sales Manager:** Collin Ames. **Group Sales Coordinator:** Sam Villa. **Ticket Sales Account Executive:** Trevor Smith. **Sponsorship Operations Manager:** Brennan McIntire. **Promotions Coordinator:** Austen Serrata. **Head Groundskeeper:** Michael Angel.

FIELD STAFF
Manager: Jack Howell. **Hitting Coach:** Ryan Sebra. **Pitching Coach:** Doug Henry. **Defensive Coach:** Trevor Nyp. **Trainer:** Dylan Culwell. **Strength Coach:** Luis Cervantes.

GAME INFORMATION
Radio Announcer: Doug Taylor **No. of Games Broadcast:** 132. **Flagship Station:** Internet Broadcast. **PA**

Announcer: Patrick Harvey. **Official Scorers:** Tony Wise, Shane Kelley, Scott Tylinski. **Stadium Name:** Gesa Stadium. **Location:** I-182 to exit 9 (Road 68), north to Burden Blvd, right to stadium. **Standard Game Time:** Varies. **Ticket Price Range:** $9-17. **Visiting Club Hotel:** Hampton Inn & Suites Pasco/Tri-Cities, 6826 Burden Blvd., Pasco, WA 99301. **Telephone:** (509) 792-1660.

VANCOUVER CANADIANS

Address: Nat Bailey Stadium, 4601 Ontario St, Vancouver, B.C. V5V 3H4.
Telephone: (604) 872-5232. **Fax:** (604) 872-1714.
E-Mail Address: staff@canadiansbaseball.com.
Website: www.canadiansbaseball.com.
Affiliation (first year): Toronto Blue Jays (2011). **Years in League:** 2021-

OWNERSHIP/MANAGEMENT
Operated by: Vancouver Canadians Professional Baseball LLP.
Managing General Partner: Jake Kerr. **Co-Owner:** Jeff Mooney. **President:** Andy Dunn. **General Manager:** Allan Bailey. **Assistant General Manager:** Stephani Ellis. **Financial Controller:** Brenda Chmiliar. **Vice President Sales & Marketing:** Walter Cosman. **Manager, Ticket Operations:** Steven Maisey. **Manager, Stadium Operations:** Charles O'Neill. **Coordinator, Marketing Services:** Kendra Chin. **Assistant Financial Controller:** Charlene Shamku.

FIELD STAFF
Manager: Brent Lavallee. **Hitting Coach:** Ryan Wright. **Pitching Coach:** Joel Bonnett. **Coaching Assistant:** Ashley Ponce.

GAME INFORMATION
Radio/TV Announcer: Tyler Zickel. **No. of Games Broadcast:** 132. **Flagship Station:** Sportsnet 650 AM. **PA Announcer:** Niall O'Donohoe. **Official Scorer:** Mike Hanafin. **Stadium Name:** Nat Bailey Stadium. **Location:** From downtown, take Cambie Street Bridge, left on East 29th Ave., left on Ontario St. to stadium; From south, take Highway 99 to Oak Street, right on 41st Ave, left on Cambie St. right on East 29th Ave., left on Ontario St to stadium. **Standard Game Times:** Mon.-Sat., 7:05 pm, Sun., 1:05 pm. **Ticket Price Range:** $20-32. **Visiting Club Hotel:** Sandman Hotel Vancouver Airport, 3233 St. Edwards Dr., Richmond, B.C., V6X 1N4. **Telephone:** (604) 303-8888.

MINOR LEAGUES

CALIFORNIA LEAGUE

STADIUM INFORMATION

Club	Stadium	Opened	LF	CF	RF	Capacity	2022 Att.
Fresno	Chukchansi Park	2002	324	400	335	12,500	261,652
Inland Empire	San Manuel Stadium	1996	330	410	330	5,000	141,792
Lake Elsinore	The Diamond	1994	330	400	310	7,866	102,950
Modesto	John Thurman Field	1952	312	400	319	4,000	94,253
Rancho Cucamo.	LoanMart Field	1993	335	400	335	6,615	138,533
San Jose	Municipal Stadium	1942	320	390	320	5,208	115,074
Stockton	Banner Island Ballpark	2005	300	399	326	5,200	114,480
Visalia	Recreation Ballpark	1946	320	405	320	2,468	121,006

FRESNO GRIZZLIES

Address: 1800 Tulare St, Fresno, CA 93721.
Telephone: (559) 320-4487. **Fax:** (559) 264-0795.
E-Mail Address: info@fresnogrizzlies.com. **Website:** www.FresnoGrizzlies.com.
Affiliation (first year): Colorado Rockies (2021). **Years in League:** 2021-

OWNERSHIP/MANAGEMENT
Operated By: Fresno Sports & Events. **Managing Partner:** Michael Baker. **Chief Financial Officer:** Michael Moran. **President:** Derek Franks. **Assistant General Manager:** Andrew Milios. **VP of Finance:** James Thompson.

FIELD STAFF
Manager: Steve Soliz. **Hitting Coach:** Nic Wilson. **Pitching Coach:** Marc Brewer. **Bench Coach:** Cesar Galvez.

GAME INFORMATION
No. of Games Broadcast: 132. **Stadium Name:** Chukchansi Park. **Location:** 1800 Tulare St, Fresno, CA 93721. **Directions:** From 99 North, take Fresno Street exit, left on Fresno Street, left on Inyo or Tulare to stadium. From 99 South, take Fresno Street exit, left on Fresno Street, right on Broadway to H Street. From 41 North, take Van Ness exit toward Fresno, left on Van Ness, left on Inyo or Tulare, stadium is straight ahead. From 41 South, take Tulare exit, stadium is located at Tulare and H Streets, or take Van Ness exit, right on Van Ness, left on Inyo or Tulare, stadium is straight ahead. **Ticket Price Range:** TBD.

INLAND EMPIRE 66ERS

Address: 280 South E St., San Bernardino, CA 92401.
Telephone: (909) 888-9922. **Fax:** (909) 888-5251. **Website:** www.66ers.com.
Affiliation (first year): Los Angeles Angels (2011). **Years in League:** 2021-

OWNERSHIP/MANAGEMENT
Co-Owners: Dave Elmore, Donna Tuttle. **General Manager:** Joe Hudson. **Assistant General Manager:** Daniel Vasquez. **Director of Sales:** Hollee Haines. **Group Sales Account Executive:** Jarrett Stark. **Director of Promotions & Assistant to the General Manager:** Mary Grinnan. **Director of Food & Beverage:** Jacob DeJong. **Director of Broadcasting:** Steve Wendt. **Box Office Manager:** Ryan Williams. **Creative Services Manager:** Dusty Ferguson. **Social Media Coordinator:** Edza Gomez. **Account Executives:** Alec Aguilera, Shannon Axelson, Alejandro Cassal, Chris Holzknecht. **Operations Assistant:** Alfred Vargas.

FIELD STAFF
Manager: Dave Stapleton. **Hitting Coach:** Willie Romero. **Pitching Coach:** Elmer Dessens. **Coach:** Brian Rupp. **Athletic Trainer:** TBD. **Strength and Conditioning Coach:** TBD.

GAME INFORMATION
Radio Announcer: Steve Wendt. **Flagship Station:** 66ers.com. **PA Announcer:** TBA. **Official Scorer:** TBA. **Stadium Name:** San Manuel Stadium. **Location:** From south, I-215 to 2nd Street exit, east on 2nd, right on G Street; from north, I-215 to 3rd Street exit, left on Rialto, right on G Street. **Standard Game Times:** Mon.-Sat. 7:05 pm; Sun. 2:05 pm (1st Half) 5:35 pm (2nd Half). **Ticket Price Range:** $9-$28. **Visiting Club Hotel:** TBD. **Telephone:** TBD.

LAKE ELSINORE STORM

Address: 500 Diamond Drive, Lake Elsinore, CA 92530
Telephone: (951) 245-4487. **Fax:** (951) 245-0305.
E-Mail Address: info@stormbaseball.com. **Website:** www.stormbaseball.com.
Affiliation (first year): San Diego Padres (2001). **Years in League:** 2021-

MINOR LEAGUES

OWNERSHIP/MANAGEMENT
Owners: Gary Jacobs, Len Simon. **CEO/Co-General Manager:** Shaun Brock. **CFO/Co-General Manager:** Christine Kavic. **General Manager of Game Presentation and Events:** Mark Beskid. **Assistant General Manager of Baseball:** Terrance Tucker. **Assistant CFO:** Andres Pagan. **Box Office Manager:** Krista Williams. **Director of Hospitality:** Natalie Gates. **On-Field Emcee/Corporate Sales Executive/Promotions Director:** Kaz Egan. **Director of Entertainment:** Jon Gripe. **Multimedia Manager:** Justin Jett Pickard. **Head Groundskeeper:** Matt Siegel. **Operations and Facilities Manager:** Jason Natale. **Director of Food and Beverage:** Jason Wozniak. **Executive Chef:** Luciano Mulito. **Corporate Sales Executive/Assistant General Manager of Events:** Janelle Metzger. **HR Generalist:** Katherine Strehlow. **Assistant Box Office Manager:** Caleb Brock. **Brand Ambassador:** Althea Wagoner.

FIELD STAFF
Manager: Pete Zamora. **Hitting Coach:** Jed Morris. **Pitching Coach:** Thomas Eshelman.

GAME INFORMATION
Radio Announcer: TBD. **No. of Games Broadcast:** 66. **Flagship Station:** MiLB.com. **PA Announcer:** Dave McCrory. **Official Scorer:** Lloyd Nixon. **Stadium Name:** The Lake Elsinore Diamond Stadium. **Location:** From I-15, exit at Diamond Drive, west one mile to the stadium. **Standard Game Times:** TBD. **Ticket Price Range:** $9-$30. **Visiting Club Hotel:** TBD.

MODESTO NUTS

Office Address: 601 Neece Dr, Modesto, CA 95351.
Mailing Address: PO Box 883, Modesto, CA 95353.
Telephone: (209) 572-4487. **Fax:** (209) 572-4490
E-Mail Address: fun@modestonuts.com. **Website:** www.modestonuts.com.
Affiliation (first year): Seattle Mariners (2017). **Years in League:** 2021-

OWNERSHIP/MANAGEMENT
Operated by: Seattle Mariners.
General Manager: Veronica Hernandez. **Head Groundskeeper:** Alan Jones. **Director of Ticket Sales:** Chris Fleischmann. **Director of Corporate Partnerships:** Corey Gales. **Box Office Manager:** Kyler Brown. **Office Manager:** Rita McCay. **Food and Beverage Manager:** Shayla Parker. **Production & Creative Services Manager:** Chris Estrada. **Community Relations Manager:** Lesley Cantu. **Stadium Operations Manager:** Connor Skustad. **Director of Marketing and Broadcasting:** Tim Quitadamo. **Group Sales Representative:** Natali Gutierrez. **Group Sales Representative:** Tim Felix.

FIELD STAFF
Manager: Zach Vincej. **Hitting Coach:** Seth Mejias-Brean. **Pitching Coach:** Jake Witt. **Coach:** Hecmart Nieves. **Trainer:** Blake Wooten. **Strength and Conditioning Coach:** Jose Alcantara Beas.

GAME INFORMATION
Radio Announcer: Tim Quitadamo. **PA Announcer:** Mario Ramos. **Official Scorer:** Rotates. **Stadium Name:** John Thurman Field. **Location:** Highway 99 in southwest Modesto to Tuolumne Boulevard exit, west on Tuolumne for one block to Neece Drive, left for 1/4 mile to stadium. **Standard Game Times:** 7:05 pm, Sun. 2:05 pm/605 pm. **Ticket Price Range:** $8-16. **Visiting Club Hotel:** DoubleTree Modesto.

RANCHO CUCAMONGA QUAKES

Office Address: 8408 Rochester Ave., Rancho Cucamonga, CA 91730.
Mailing Address: P.O. Box 4139, Rancho Cucamonga, CA 91729.
Telephone: (909) 481-5000. **Fax:** (909) 481-5005.
E-Mail Address: info@rcquakes.com. **Website:** www.rcquakes.com.
Affiliation (first year): Los Angeles Dodgers (2011). **Years in League:** 2021-

OWNERSHIP/MANAGEMENT
Operated By: Bobby Brett. **Principal Owner:** Bobby Brett.
President: Brent Miles. **Vice President/General Manager:** Grant Riddle. **Group Sales & Hospitality Manager:** Jake Briones. **Vice President, Group Sales:** Kyle Burleson. **Assistant General Manager, Season Tickets/Operations:** Eric Jensen. **Sponsorship Account Executive:** Andrew Kestler. **"Voice of the Quakes"/Director of Public Relations:** Mike Lindskog. **Director of Ticket Operations/Group Sales:** Alec Maldonado. **Fan Engagement Manager:** Grace Mikuriya. **Group Sales & Hospitality Manager:** Kyle Olmsted. **Vice President, Ticket Sales:** Monica Ortega. **Vice President, Sponsorships:** Chris Pope. **Sponsorship Account Executive:** George Ruiz Jr. **Assistant General Manager, Fan Engagement:** Bobbi Salcido. **Office Manager:** Shelley Scebbi. **Sponsorship Service Manager:** Madison Smeathers. **Director of Accounting:** Denise Vasquez.

MINOR LEAGUES

FIELD STAFF
Manager: TBA. Hitting Coach: TBA. Pitching Coaches: TBA. Bench Coach: TBA.

GAME INFORMATION
Radio Announcer: Mike Lindskog. No. of Games Broadcast: 132. Flagship Station: iHeart Radio App / Tune-In Radio App. PA Announcer: Chris Albaugh. Official Scorer: Steve Wishek. Stadium Name: LoanMart Field. Location: I-10 to I-15 North, exit at Foothill Boulevard, left on Foothill, left on Rochester to Stadium. Standard Game Times: 6:30 pm; First Half Sundays (April through June) and Sept.11th at 2:00 pm; Second Half Sundays (July through August) 5:05 pm. Visiting Club Hotel: Best Western Heritage Inn, 8179 Spruce Ave, Rancho Cucamonga, CA 91730. Telephone: (909) 466-1111.

SAN JOSE GIANTS

Office Address: 588 E Alma Ave, San Jose, CA 95112.
Mailing Address: PO Box 21727, San Jose, CA 95151.
Telephone: (408) 297-1435. Fax: (408) 297-1453.
E-Mail Address: info@sjgiants.com. Website: www.sjgiants.com.
Affiliation (first year): San Francisco Giants (1988). Years in League: 2021-

OWNERSHIP/MANAGEMENT
Operated by: DBH San Jose, LLC. Ownership: Peter Freund.
General Manager: Ben Taylor. VP, Marketing: Matt Alongi. VP, Sales: Jeff Di Giorgio. Director, Broadcasting: Joe Ritzo. Director, Finance: Dave Satterfield. Senior Manager, Ticketing: Ryan Anthony. Senior Manager, Retail/Marketing: Sierra Hanley. Senior Manager, Marketing: Travis Ishikawa. Manager, Food and Beverage: Ramiro Mijares. Manager, Group Sales: Sam Martinez. Coordinator, Finance: Gina Gallego. Coordinator, Digital Media: Sam Barasch. Coordinator, Group Sales: Chris Colosi. Coordinator, Box Office: Heriberto Cortes-Torres. Groundskeeper: Kevin Tallman.

FIELD STAFF
Manager: Jeremiah Knackstedt. Hitting Coach: Travis Ishikawa. Pitching Coach: Dan Runzler. Fundamentals Coach: Ydwin Villegas. Athletic Trainer: Christian Fosler. Strength & Conditioning Coach: Michelle Kuda.

GAME INFORMATION
Radio Announcers: Joe Ritzo, Justin Allegri. No. of Games Broadcast: 132
Flagship: sjgiants.com. Television Announcers: Joe Ritzo, All home games on MiLB.TV. PA Announcer: Russ Call. Official Scorer: Mike Hohler. Stadium Name: Excite Ballpark. Location: South on I-280, Take 10th/11th Street Exit, turn right on 10th Street, turn left on Alma Ave. North on I-280, Take the 10th/11th Street Exit, Turn left on 10th Street, turn left on Alma Ave. Standard Game Times: Tue-Thur. 6:30 p.m, Fri. 7 p.m. Sat. 5 p.m (6 p.m. after June 1), Sun 1 p.m. (5 p.m. after June 1). Ticket Price Range: $5-29.

STOCKTON PORTS

Address: 404 W Fremont St, Stockton, CA 95203.
Telephone: (209) 644-1900. Fax: (209) 644-1931.
E-Mail Address: info@stocktonports.com. Website: www.stocktonports.com.
Affiliation (first year): Oakland Athletics (2005). Years in League: 2021-

OWNERSHIP/MANAGEMENT
Operated By: 7th Inning Stretch LLC.
President: Pat Filippone. General Manager: Jordan Feneck. Director of Baseball Communications: Chris Zavaglia. Senior Sales Manager: DeShon Beck. Stadium Operations & Special Events Manager: Kevin Blanc. Corporate Partnerships Manager: Calvin Chesler. Ticket Operations Manager: Christopher Dokken. Box Office Manager: Devin Nelson. Media Relations Manager: Lucy Carpenter. Community Relations Manager: James Cole. Broadcaster: Alex Jensen. Front Office Manager: Kay Lee. Business Operations Manager: Sarah Beasley. Bookkeeper: Lyla Jacobson.

FIELD STAFF
Manager: Gregorio Petit. Pitching Coach: Gabriel Ozuna. Hitting Coach: Kevin Kouzmanoff. Hitting Coach: Ruben Escalera. Trainer: Noah Huff. Sport Performance Coach: Nathaniel Penaranda.

GAME INFORMATION
Radio Announcer: Alex Jensen. No of Games Broadcast: 132. Flagship Station: TBD. PA Announcer: TBD. Official Scorer: Paul Muyskens. Stadium Name: Banner Island Ballpark. Location: From I-5/99, take Crosstown Freeway (Highway 4) exit El Dorado Street, north on El Dorado to Fremont Street, left on Fremont. Standard Game Times: 7:05 pm. Ticket Price Range: $10-$20.

MINOR LEAGUES

VISALIA RAWHIDE

Address: 300 N Giddings St, Visalia, CA 93291.
Telephone: (559) 732-4433. **Fax:** (559) 739-7732.
E-Mail Address: info@rawhidebaseball.com.
Website: www.rawhidebaseball.com.
Affiliation (first year): Arizona Diamondbacks (2007). **Years in League:** 2021-

OWNERSHIP/MANAGEMENT
Ownership: First Pitch Entertainment. **Team President:** Sam Sigal. **Co-General Managers:** Mike Candela and Julian Rifkind. **Assistant General Managers:** Brady Hochhalter and Markus Hagglund. **Director of Broadcasting & Media Relations:** Jill Gearin. **Director of Facilities & Grounds:** James Templeton. **Director of Entertainment and Community:** Joe Ross. **Ballpark Operations Assistant:** Robert Skipper. **Promotions & Community Engagement Manager:** Isabella Haberman. **Digital Content Creation Manager:** Dawson Wright. **Ticket Operations Manager:** Dalila Palacios.

FIELD STAFF
Manager: Darrin Garner. **Hitting Coach:** Kyle MacKinnon. **Pitching Coach:** Tyler Mark. **Coach:** Rolando Arnedo. **Trainer:** Connor Oates. **Strength & Conditioning Coach:** Nate Kolb.

GAME INFORMATION
Radio Announcers: Jill Gearin. **Broadcasts:** all home and road games. **Flagship Station:** MiLB.com.
PA Announcer: Brian Anthony. **Official Scorer:** Harry Kargenian and Mark "Scooter" Cossentine. **Stadium Name:** Valley Strong Ballpark. **Location:** From Highway 99, take 198 East to Mooney Boulevard exit, left at second signal on Giddings; four blocks to ballpark. **Standard Game Times:** 6:30pm, Sun. 1pm April-June and 6pm July-September.
Ticket Price Range: $13-30. **Visiting Club Hotel:** Quality Inn, 1010 E Prosperity Ave, Tulare, CA 93274.

MINOR LEAGUES

CAROLINA LEAGUE

STADIUM INFORMATION

Club	Stadium	Opened	LF	CF	RF	Capacity	2022 Att.
Augusta	SRP Park	2018	330	395	318	4,782	262,172
Carolina	Five County Stadium	1991	330	400	309	6,500	138,579
Charleston	Joseph P. Riley, Jr. Ballpark	1997	306	386	336	5,800	251,491
Columbia	Segra Park	2016	319	400	330	7,501	217,225
Delmarva	Arthur W. Perdue Stadium	1996	309	402	309	5,200	154,786
Down East	Grainger Stadium	1949	335	390	335	4,100	98,328
Fayetteville	SEGRA Stadium	2019	319	400	330	4,786	214,470
Fredericksburg	FredNats Ballpark	2020	326	402	327	7,000	260,546
Kannapolis	Atrium Health Ballpark	2020	325	400	315	4,930	192,161
Lynchburg	City Stadium	1939	325	390	325	4,000	91,232
Myrtle Beach	TicketReturn.com Field	1999	308	400	328	5,200	247,926
Salem	Salem Memorial Stadium	1995	325	401	325	6,415	181,287

AUGUSTA GREENJACKETS

Office Address: 187 Railroad Ave. North Augusta, SC 29841.
Mailing Address: 187 Railroad Ave. North Augusta, SC 29841.
Telephone: (803) 349-9467. **Fax:** (803) 349-9434.
E-Mail Address: info@greenjacketsbaseball.com. **Website:** www.greenjacketsbaseball.com.
Affiliation (first year): Atlanta Braves (2021). **Years in League:** 2021-

OWNERSHIP/MANAGEMENT
Ownership Group: Diamond Baseball Holdings, LLC.
President: Jeff Eiseman. **VP, Business Operations:** Missy Martin. **Vice President:** Tom Denlinger. **General Manager:** Brandon Greene. **Director, Ticket Sales:** Austin Lowndes. **Director, Finance & Administration:** Melinda Pohl. **Director, Operations:** Andrew Crawford. **Director, Marketing:** Catie Jagodzinski. **Senior Director, Corporate Sales:** Steven Elovich. **Director, Group Sales:** Yari Natal. **Senior Account Executive, Ticket Sales:** Jamie Martin. **Account Executive, Ticket Sales:** Jake Brock. **Account Executive, Ticket Sales:** Jack Smith. **Account Executive, Ticket Sales:** Melina Picciano. **Specialist, Stadium Operations:** Adam Pinckard. **Specialist, Event & Stadium Operations:** Mitch Harrington. **Specialist, Stadium Operations:** John Sparks. **Manager, Ticket Operations:** Tyler Henderson. **Manager, Retail Merchandise:** Adam Latta. **Coordinator, Marketing:** Caoilinn Gallagher. **Director, Food & Beverage:** John Schow. **Manager, Food & Beverage:** David Hutto. **Manager, Concessions & Kitchen:** Gerald Fickling. **Manager, Events & Services:** Alyson Schwartz. **Head Groundskeeper:** Darrell Lemmer.

FIELD STAFF
Manager: Nestor Perez Jr. **Hitting Coach:** Connor Narron. **Pitching Coach:** Michael Steed.

GAME INFORMATION
PA Announcer: Scott Skaden. **Stadium Name:** SRP Park. **Standard Game Times:** Mon.-Fri., 7:05 pm, Sat., 6:05 pm, Sun., 1:35 pm, Firework Sun. 6:05 pm. **Ticket Price Range:** $10-$29. **Visiting Club Hotel:** Comfort Suites, 2911 Riverwest Dr, Augusta, GA. **Telephone:** (706) 434-2540.

CAROLINA MUDCATS

Office Address: 1501 NC Hwy 39, Zebulon, NC 27597.
Mailing Address: PO Drawer 1218, Zebulon, NC 27597.
Telephone: (919) 269-2287.
E-Mail Address: muddy@carolinamudcats.com. **Website:** www.carolinamudcats.com.
Affiliation (first year): Milwaukee Brewers (2017-). **Years in League:** 2021-Present

OWNERSHIP/MANAGEMENT
Ownership: Milwaukee Brewers Baseball Club. **Operated by:** Milwaukee Brewers Baseball Club
General Manager, Baseball & Stadium Operations: Eric Gardner. **General Manager, Business Development & Brand Marketing:** David Lawrence. **Manager, Group Tickets & Premium Sales:** Megan Bloyd. **Manager, Box Office Operations & Season Tickets:** Jason Leone. **Associate, Ticket and Group Sales:** Nathan Cantrell. **Associate, Ticket and Group Sales:** Drew Garland. **Director, Food and Beverage:** Hugh Gallagher. **Personnel Manager, Food & Beverage:** Edith Crudup. **Director, Stadium Grounds:** John Packer. **Sr. Coordinator, Stadium Operations:** Justin Bose. **Sr. Coordinator, Stadium Operations:** Logan Clark. **Sr. Director, External Development, Broadcast & Media:** Greg Young. **Coordinator, Social Media/Marketing/Graphics:** Aaron Bayles. **Coordinator, Marketing & Promotions:** Samantha Micha. **Creative Services Associate:** Ryne Barnes. **Community Relations & Mascot Associate:** Jermaine Nix. **Merchandise Associate:** Dan Watson.

MINOR LEAGUES

FIELD STAFF
Manager: Victor Estevez. **Pitching Coach:** Michael O'Neal. **Hitting Coach:** JJ Reimer. **Development Coach:** David Valdez. **Athletic Trainer:** Myles Fish. **Strength Coach:** Jonah Mergen.

GAME INFORMATION
Radio Announcer: Greg Young. **No. of Games Broadcast:** 66 (home games). **Flagship Station:** carolinamudcats.com. **PA Announcer:** Hayes Permar. **Official Scorer:** Bill Woodward. **Stadium Name:** Five County Stadium. **Location:** From Raleigh, US 64 East to 264 East, exit at Highway 39 in Zebulon. **Standard Game Times:** 7:00 pm(Mon-Fri), 5:00 pm (Sat), 1:00 PM (Sun). **Ticket Price Range:** $11-$16. **Visiting Club Hotel:** Doubletree by Hilton Midtown, 2805 Highwoods Blvd, Raleigh, NC, 27604.

CHARLESTON RIVERDOGS

Office Address: 360 Fishburne St, Charleston, SC 29403.
Mailing Address: PO Box 20849, Charleston, SC 29403.
Telephone: (843) 723-7241. **Fax:** (843) 723-2641.
E-Mail Address: admin@riverdogs.com. **Website:** www.riverdogs.com.
Affiliation (first year): Tampa Bay Rays (2021). **Years in League:** 2021-

OWNERSHIP/MANAGEMENT
Operated by: The Goldklang Group/South Carolina Baseball Club LP.
Chairman: Marv Goldklang. **President:** Jeff Goldklang. **Club President/General Manager:** Dave Echols. **Executive Advisor to the Chairman:** Mike Veeck. **Director, Fun:** Bill Murray. **Co-Owners:** Peter Freund, Al Phillips. **Senior Vice President:** Ben Abzug. **VP, Corporate Sales:** Andy Lange. **Assistant GM:** Garret Randle. **Director, Marketing:** Michael Lopes. **Promotions Manager:** Jake Adams. **VP, Food/Beverage:** Josh Shea. **Director, Broadcasting and Media Relations:** Jason Kempf. **Video Production and Multimedia Manager:** Hannah Von Zup. **Ticket Operations Manager:** Tatum McQueen. **Group Sales Manager:** Savannah Bullins. **Community Relations Manager:** Amanda Najera. **Director, Operations:** Brandon Dunnam. **Director, Merchandise:** Cynthia Linhart. **Business Manager:** Dale Stickney. **Office Manager:** Traci Wilson. **Head Groundskeeper:** Kevin Coyne. **Director of Club Sales/Events:** Lance Fletcher. **Event Manager:** Terin Sims.

FIELD STAFF
Manager: Sean Smedley. **Hitting Coach:** Perry Roth. **Pitching Coach:** Levi Romero. **Bench Coach:** Ronnie Richardson.

GAME INFORMATION
Radio Announcer: Jason Kempf. **No. of Games Broadcast:** 132. **Flagship Station:** N/A. **PA Announcer:** Ken Carrington. **Official Scorer:** Mike Hoffman. **Stadium Name:** Joseph P. Riley, Jr. Park. **Location:** 360 Fishburne St, Charleston, SC 29403, From US 17, take Lockwood Dr. North, right on Fishburne St. **Standard Game Times:** Mon.-Fri., 7:05pm, Sat. 6:05 pm, Sun. 5:05 pm. **Ticket Price Range:** $8-20. **Visiting Club Hotel:** Courtyard by Marriott Charleston-North Charleston.

COLUMBIA FIREFLIES

Office Address: 1640 Freed Street, Columbia, SC 29201.
Mailing Address: 1640 Freed Street, Columbia, SC 29201.
Telephone: (803) 726-4487.
E-Mail Address: info@columbiafireflies.com. **Website:** www.columbiafireflies.com
Affiliation (first year): Kansas City Royals (2021). **Years in League:** 2021-

OWNERSHIP/MANAGEMENT
Operated By: Columbia Fireflies Baseball, LLC.
President: Brad Shank. **Chief Revenue Officer:** Kevin Duplaga. **Food & Beverage Director:** David Shroeder. **Vice President, Accounting & Baseball Operations:** Jonathan Mercier. **Director, Marketing:** Ashlie DeCarlo. **Executive Assistant, HR Manager:** Katie Maroney. **Director of Ticket Operations:** Ty Jamieson. **Director, Group Sales:** Nick Spano. **Ticket Account Managers:** Austin Blevins, Matt Chernesky, Aydan Fields and Conor Mitchum. **Activation Coordinator/Graphic Designer:** Casey Vecchio. **Promotions/Fan Engagement Manager:** John Oliver. **Video Production Manager:** Jack Novelli. **Merchandise Manager:** Kodie Wilson. **Executive Chef:** Bobby Hunter. **Premium Hospitality and Catering Manager:** Bethany Venable. **Commissary Manager:** Brycen Rogers. **Director of Stadium Operations:** Matt Lundquist. **Assistant Director of Stadium Operations:** Tyler Restrepo. **Head Groundskeeper:** Assistant Sports Turf Manager: Austin Medlock. **Corporate Partnerships Account Executive:** Jason Haller. **Director of Special Events:** Alyssa Stein. **Head of Venue Safety:** Mark Tubbs.

FIELD STAFF
Manager: Tony Pena Jr. **Hitting Coach:** Ari Adut. **Pitching Coach:** John Habyan. **Bench Coach:** Matt Schmidt.

GAME INFORMATION
Radio Announcer: John Kocsis Jr. **No. of Games Broadcast:** 70. **Flagship Station:** Unavailable. **PA Announcer:** Bryan Vacchio. **Official Scorer:** Bond Nickles. **Stadium Name:** Segra Park. **Location:** 1640 Freed Street, Columbia, SC 29201. **Standard Game Times:** Mon.-Fri., 7:05pm, Sat. 6:05pm, Sun. 5:05. **Ticket Price Range:** $5-$12.

MINOR LEAGUES

DELMARVA SHOREBIRDS

Office Address: 6400 Hobbs Rd, Salisbury, MD 21804.
Mailing Address: PO Box 1557, Salisbury, MD 21802.
Telephone: (410) 219-3112. **Fax:** (410) 219-9164.
E-Mail Address: info@theshorebirds.com. **Website:** www.theshorebirds.com.
Affiliation (first year): Baltimore Orioles (1997). **Years in League:** 2021-

OWNERSHIP/MANAGEMENT
Operated By: 7th Inning Stretch, LP. **Owner:** Tom Volpe. **President:** Pat Filippone. **General Manager:** Chris Bitters. **Assistant GM:** Jimmy Sweet. **Director of Marketing:** Ben Vigliarolo. **Director of Broadcasting & Communications:** Sam Jellinek. **Community Relations Manager:** Sam Lehman. **Director of Ticket & Merchandise Operations:** Benjamin Posner. **Director of Group Sales:** Joe DeLucia. **Group Event Coordinator:** Jennifer Atkinson. **Ticket Sales Account Executive:** Matt Bagrowski. **Director of Stadium Operations:** Erik Schumacher. **Head Groundskeeper:** Oscar Martinez. **Accounting Manager:** Matt Figard.

FIELD STAFF
Manager: Felipe Alou, Jr. **Pitching Coach:** Adam Bleday. **Hitting Coach:** Josh Bunselmeyer.

GAME INFORMATION
Radio: Internet Only. **No. of Games Broadcast:** 132. **Flagship Station:** N/A. **Stadium Name:** Arthur W. Perdue Stadium. **Location:** From US 50 East, right on Hobbs Rd; From US 50 West, left on Hobbs Road. **Standard Game Time:** 7:05 pm. **Ticket Price Range:** $14-$20. **Visiting Club Hotel:** TBD.

DOWN EAST WOOD DUCKS

Address: 400 East Grainger Avenue, Kinston, NC 28502
Telephone: (252) 686-5165
E-Mail Address: jbullock@woodducksbaseball.com. **Website:** woodducksbaseball.com
Affiliation (first year): Texas Rangers (2017). **Years in League:** 2021-

OWNERSHIP/MANAGEMENT
Operated By: Texas Rangers, LLC.
Vice President: Wade Howell. **General Manager:** Jon Clemmons. **Assistant GM, Operations:** Janell Fitch. **Marketing Manager:** Maddy Meehan. **Group Sales Executives:** Ben Tramontana, Shivar Person, Raeganne Sholar.

FIELD STAFF
Manager: Carlos Maldonado. **Hitting Coach:** Brian Pozos. **Pitching Coach:** Julio Valdez. **Development Coaches:** Nick Janssen, Ruben Sosa. **Trainer:** Neal Ori. **Strength & Conditioning Coach:** Brett Platts.

GAME INFORMATION
Radio Announcer: TBA. **PA Announcer:** TBA. **Stadium Name:** Grainger Stadium.
Standard Game Times: 7:00 (weekdays), 5:00 (Saturdays), 1:00 (Sundays). **Ticket Price Range:** $7-$14
Visiting Club Hotel: Mother Earth Motor Lodge, 501 N Heritage St., Kinston, NC 28501.

FAYETTEVILLE WOODPECKERS

Address: 460 Hay St., Fayetteville, NC 28301
Telephone: 910-339-1989.
E-Mail Address: Woodpeckers@astros.com. **Website:** fayettevillewoodpeckers.com.
Affiliation (first year): Houston Astros (2019). **Years in League:** 2021-

OWNERSHIP/MANAGEMENT
Principal Owner: Houston Astros
General Manager: TBD. **Director, Finance:** Jennifer Carpenter. **Director, Field Operations:** Alpha Jones. **Director, Ticket Sales & Service:** Gabe Evans. **Director, Marketing & Communications:** Ashlei Elise. **Manager, Sponsorship Strategy & Activation:** Brittany Tschida. **Manager, Baseball Operations:** Mike Montesino. **Manager, Events:** Rachel Smith. **Manager, Creative Services:** Ryan LeFevre. **Manager, Graphics & Video Production:** Tania Aho. **Coordinator, Social Media:** Andie Kruczkowski. **Manager, Community Relations & Media Relations:** Landrey Young. **Account Executive, Ticketing:** Maurice Spagatner. **Account Executive, Ticketing:** Jon Wingate. **Account Manager, Season Tickets:** Jackson Bingham. **Account Executive, Sponsorships:** TBD. **Manager, Retail:** TBD. **Director, Operations:** Matt Chappell. **Manager, Stadium Operations:** Mike Cipolla. **Coordinator, Ballpark Entertainment:** TBD. **Coordinator, Field Operations:** Eli Laney.

FIELD STAFF
Manager: Ricardo Rivera. **Hitting Coach:** Luis Reynoso. **Pitching Coach:** Zach Wilkins.

MINOR LEAGUES

GAME INFORMATION
Radio Announcer: Andrew Chapman. **No. of Games Broadcast:** 132. **Flagship Station:** N/A. **PA Announcer:** Ray Thomas. **Official Scorer:** TBD. **Stadium Name:** Segra Stadium. **Standard Game Times:** M-F 7:05pm, Sat. 5:05pm, Sun. 2:05pm. **Visiting Club Hotel:** Fairfield Inn. **Telephone:** 910-223-7867.

FREDERICKSBURG NATIONALS

Office Address: 42 Jackie Robinson Way, Fredericksburg, VA 22401
Mailing Address: 42 Jackie Robinson Way, Fredericksburg, VA 22401
Telephone: (540) 858-4242. **E-Mail Address:** info@frednats.com.
Website: www.frednats.com.
Affiliation (first year): Washington Nationals (2005). **Years in League:** 2021—

OWNERSHIP/MANAGEMENT
Operated By: SAJ Baseball LLC. **Principal Owner:** Art Silber.
President/COO: Lani Silber Weiss. **Executive VP/General Manager:** Nick Hall. **Vice President, Partnerships:** Tory Goodman. **Director, Business Development:** Charly Zuetlau. **Partnership Activation Manager:** Jimmy Burns. **Partnership Sales Manager:** Alex Sutor. **Vice President, Ticket Sales and Operations:** David Woodard. **Ticket Sales Account Executive:** Chris Borysewicz, Austin Byrd, Quentin Johnson Jr., Brian Lehman. **Box Office Manager:** Rich Crosslin. **Ticket Operations Coordinator:** Trey Pearsall. **Analytics Manager:** Sam Pawlik. **Special Events & Hospitality Manager:** Ally Chism. **Special Events & Hospitality Assistant:** Skyla Flock. **Vice President, Operations:** Eliot Williams. **Operations Manager:** Ty Smith. **Director, Merchandise:** McKenzie Goodman. **Assistant Manager, Merchandise:** Katie Dorrell. **Home Clubhouse Manager:** Zach Centrella. **Head Groundskeeper:** Eric Taylor. **Director, Accounting and Human Resources:** Ellen Ball. **Controller:** Rebecca Armstrong. **Office Manager:** Kelly Bond. **Assistant General Manager & Vice President of Creative Services:** Robert Perry. **Director of Design:** Alexis Deegan. **Director of Production:** Zhancheng Wu. **Community Relations Manager:** Adam Flock. **Broadcaster/Director of Media Relations:** Joey Zanaboni. **Director of Operations, Catering:** Dominic Derboghossian. **Food and Beverage Operations Manager:** Taylor Cornelius. **Catering Manager:** Jane Porcheddu.

FIELD STAFF
Manager: Jake Lowery. **Hitting Coach:** Delwyn Young. **Pitching Coach:** Justin Lord. **Developmental Coach:** Carmelo Jaime. **Athletic Trainer:** Jacob Meyer. **Strength & Conditioning Coach:** Nathan Sier.

GAME INFORMATION
Radio Announcer: Joey Zanaboni. **No. of Games Broadcast:** 132. **Flagship:** www.frednats.com. **PA Announcer:** Todd Pristas. **Official Scorers:** TBA. **Stadium Name:** FredNats Ballpark. **Location:** From I-95, take exit 130B onto VA-3W/Plank Road for 0.7 miles. Turn right onto Carl D. Silver Pkwy. Stay straight for 1.8 miles until you reach stadium parking lot. **Standard Game Times:** 7:05pm. **Ticket Price Range:** $10-$16. **Visiting Club Hotel:** Country Inn and Suites.

KANNAPOLIS CANNON BALLERS

Office Address: 216 West Ave. Kannapolis, NC 28081
Mailing Address: 216 West Ave. Kannapolis, NC 28081
Telephone: (704) 932-3267
Email Address: info@kcballers.com. **Website:** kcballers.com
Affiliation (first year): Chicago White Sox (2001). **Years in League:** 2021—

OWNERSHIP/MANAGEMENT
Operated by: Temerity Baseball Club, LLC. **Operating Partner:** Scotty Brown. **Chief Revenue Officer:** Vince Marcucci. **General Manager:** Matt Millward. **Ticket Sales Manager:** Walker Brooke. **Broadcasting & Media Relations Coordinator:** Dan Helotie. **Director of Retail Operations:** Brent Sneed. **Group Sales Manager:** Patrick Hicks. **Special Events Manager:** Abigail Miller. **Facility Operations Manager:** Austin McIntire. **Director of Social Media & Partnership Coordinator:** Blair Jewell. **Graphic Designer:** Trace Whitley. **Head Groundskeeper:** Tim Siegel. **Director of Video Production & Entertainment:** Melissa Clark. **Director of Food & Beverage Operations:** Don Petrere. **Ticket Sales Account Executive:** Brooke Royal. **Entertainment and Team Ambassador:** Trevor Wilt. **Clubhouse & Equipment Manager:** Chase Baumgardner. **Finance and HR Specialist:** Morgan Howden.

FIELD STAFF
Manager: Patrick Leyland. **Pitching Coach:** Blake Hickman. **Hitting Coach:** Charlie Romero. **Trainer:** AJ Smith. **Performance Coach:** Juan Maldonado.

GAME INFORMATION
Radio Announcer: Dan Helotie. **No. of Games Broadcast:** TBD. **Flagship Station:** MiLB.tv/kcballers.com. **PA Announcer:** Jordan Connell. **Official Scorer:** Jimmy Lewis. **Stadium Name:** Atrium Health Ballpark. **Location:** Exit 58 on I-85, turn west on to South Cannon Blvd., continue straight until left turn on Dale Earnhardt Blvd., take right on Vance, then left on West Ave. **Standard Game Times:** Tue-Sat, 7p.m./Sun, 1p.m. **Ticket Price Range:** $8-$22. **Visiting Club Hotel:** Holiday Inn Express & Suites Concord.

MINOR LEAGUES

LYNCHBURG HILLCATS

Address: 3180 Fort Avenue, Lynchburg, VA 24501
Telephone: 434-582-1144. Fax: 434-846-0768
E-mail: info@lynchburg-hillcats.com. Website: www.lynchburg-hillcats.com
Affiliation (first year): Cleveland Guardians (2015). Years in League: 2021-present

OWNERSHIP/MANAGEMENT
Operated by: Elmore Sports Group. President: Chris Jones. General Manager: Matt Ramstead. Assistant General Manager: Lincoln Evans. Director of Accounting & Finance: Dallas Mata. Director of Sales & Marketing: Rox Cruz. Director of Food & Beverage: DJ Rawls. Senior Account Executive: Hagen Allred. Clubhouse Manager: Ryan Henson. Director, Broadcasting/Media Relations: Jason Prill. Groundskeepers: Tyler Bergin, Matt Bergin.

FIELD STAFF
Manager: Jordan Smith. Hitting Coach: Ordomar Valdez. Pitching Coach: Tony Arnold. Bench Coach: Yan Rivera. Strength & Conditioning Coach: Luis Rios. Athletic Trainer: Franklin Sammons.

GAME INFORMATION
Radio Announcer: Jason Prill. No. of Games Broadcast: 132. Official Scorers: TBD. Stadium Name: Bank of the James Stadium. Location: US 29 Business South to Bank of the James Stadium (exit 6); US 29 Business North to Bank of the James Stadium (exit 4). Ticket Price Range: $8-16. Visiting Club Hotel: TBD.

MYRTLE BEACH PELICANS

Mailing Address: 1251 21st Avenue N. Myrtle Beach, SC 29577.
Telephone: (843) 918-6000. Fax: (843) 918-6001.
E-Mail Address: info@myrtlebeachpelicans.com. Website: myrtlebeachpelicans.com.
Affiliation: (first year): Chicago Cubs (2015). Years in League: 2021-

OWNERSHIP/MANAGEMENT
Owners, Greenberg Sports Group: Chuck Greenberg.
President: Ryan Moore. General Manager: Kristin Call. Sr. Director, Finance: Anne Frost. Administrative Assistant/Office Manager: Beth Freitas. AGM: Ryan Cannella. Director of Ticket Sales: Todd Chapman. Corporate Sales Manager: Eric Theiss. Box Office Manager: Shannon Barbee. Sponsorship Execution Coordinator: Cassie Wishner. AGM: Hunter Horenstein. Director of Operations: Dan Bailey. Merchandise Manager/Pro Shop: Dan Bailey. Director, Food & Beverage: Brad Leininger. Sports Turf Manager: Jordan Barr. Media Relations: Sam Weiderhaft.

FIELD STAFF
Manager: Buddy Bailey. Hitting Coach: Roberto Vaz. Pitching Coach: Bruce Billings. Trainer: Maggie Lowenhar. Strength Coach: Jesus De La Sancha.

GAME INFORMATION
Stadium Name: Pelicans Ballpark. Location: US Highway 17 Bypass to 21st Ave. North, half mile to stadium. Standard Game Times: 7:05 p.m. Ticket Price Range: $9-$15. Visiting Club Hotel: Doubletree Resorts, 3200 South Ocean Blvd., Myrtle Beach, S.C., 29577. Telephone: (843) 315-7100.

SALEM RED SOX

Office Address: 1004 Texas St., Salem, VA 24153.
Mailing Address: PO Box 842, Salem, VA 24153.
Telephone: (540) 389-3333. Fax: (540) 389-9710.
E-Mail Address: info@salemsox.com. Website: www.salemsox.com.
Affiliation (first year): Boston Red Sox (2009). Years in League: 2021-

OWNERSHIP/MANAGEMENT
Operated By: Carolina Baseball LLC/Fenway Sports Group. Managing Director: Dave Beeston. General Manager: Allen Lawrence. AGM/VP of Tickets: Blair Hoke. Head Groundskeeper: Will Cole. Senior Ticket Operations & Analytics Manager: Lior Bittan. Director of Food/Beverage: Helen Scholar. Bookkeeper: Barry Stephens. Video Production Manager: Steven Langdon. Merchandise & Special Events Director: Kayla Keegan. Facilities Manager: RJ Rorrer. Home Clubhouse Manager: Tom Wagner. Visiting Clubhouse Manager: Jonny Matos.

FIELD STAFF
Manager: Liam Carroll. Hitting Coach: Nelson Paulino. Pitching Coach: Jason Blanton. Bench Coach: Ozzie Chavez. Development Coach: Juan Rivera. Trainer: Jacob Loughman. Strength & Conditioning Coach: Spencer Ducheny.

GAME INFORMATION
Radio Announcer: Giovanni Heater & Tyler Katz. No. of Games Broadcast: 132. Flagship Station: None. PA Announcer: Deanna McNaughton. Official Scorer: Billy Wells. Stadium Name: Carilion Clinic Field at Salem Memorial Ballpark. Location: I-81 to exit 141 (Route 419), follow signs to Salem Civic Center Complex. Standard Game Times: 7:05 pm, Sat./Sun. 6:05/3:05. Ticket Price Range: $9-19. Visiting Club Hotel: Comfort Suites Ridgewood Farms, 2898 Keagy Rd., Salem, VA 24153. Telephone: (540) 375-4800.Center Complex. 6:05/4:05.

MINOR LEAGUES

FLORIDA STATE LEAGUE

STADIUM INFORMATION

Club	Stadium	Opened	LF	CF	RF	Capacity	2022 Att.
Bradenton	LECOM Park	1923	335	400	335	8,654	56,522
Clearwater	BayCare Ballkpark	2004	330	400	330	8,500	151,982
Daytona	Jackie Robinson Ballpark	1930	317	400	325	4,200	91,156
Dunedin	Florida Auto Exchange Stadium	1977	335	400	327	5,509	24,402
Fort Myers	Hammond Stadium	1991	330	405	330	7,900	86,987
Jupiter	Roger Dean Chevrolet Stadium	1998	330	400	325	6,871	42,156
Lakeland	Publix Field at Joker Marchant Stadium	1966	340	420	340	7,961	35,855
Palm Beach	Roger Dean Chevrolet Stadium	1998	330	400	325	6,871	36,880
St. Lucie	First Data Field	1988	338	410	338	7,000	71,213
Tampa	Steinbrenner Field	1996	318	408	314	10,270	46,627

BRADENTON MARAUDERS

Address: 1611 9th St. W., Bradenton, FL 34205.
Telephone: (941) 747-3031.
E-Mail Address: MaraudersInfo@pirates.com
Website: bradentonmarauders.com
Affiliation (first year): Pittsburgh Pirates (2010). **Years in League:** 2021-

OWNERSHIP/MANAGEMENT
Operated By: Pittsburgh Associates of Florida
VP, Florida & Dominican Republic Operations: Jeff Podobnik. **General Manager/Director of Sales & Marketing:** Craig Warzecha. **Assistant General Manager/Manager, Marketing & Game Presentation:** Rebekah Rivette. **Director, Florida Operations:** Ray Morris. **Manager, Ticket Sales & Service:** Nolan Bialek. **Coordinator, LECOM Park Operations:** Tyler Skipper. **Coordinator, Fan & Community Engagement:** Haley Diess. **Coordinator, Ticket Operations:** Tyler Gray. **Account Manager, Ticket Sales:** Travis Persinger. **Head Groundskeeper:** Joseph Knight.

FIELD STAFF
Manager: Jonathan Johnston. **Pitching Coach:** Matt Ford. **Hitting Coach:** Quentin Brown. **Integrated Baseball Performance Coach:** Casey Harms. **Development Coach:** Gustavo Omaña. **Trainer:** TBD. **Strength Coach:** TBD. **Athletic Training Coordinator:** Alexa Dehaeseleer.

GAME INFORMATION
PA Announcer: Jeff Phillips. **Official Scorer:** Dave Taylor. **Stadium Name:** LECOM Park. **Location:** I-75 to exit 220 (220B from I-75N) to SR 64 West/Manatee Ave, Left onto 9th St West, LECOM PARK on the left. **Standard Game Times:** 6:30 pm, Sun. 1:00 pm. **Ticket Price Range:** $8-16. **Visiting Club Hotel:** Holiday Inn Express West, 4450 47th St W, Bradenton, FL 34210. **Telephone:** (941) 747-3031.

CLEARWATER THRESHERS

Address: 601 N Old Coachman Road, Clearwater, FL 33765.
Telephone: (727) 712-4300. **Fax:** (727) 712-4498.
Website: www.threshersbaseball.com.
Affiliation (first year): Philadelphia Phillies (1985). **Years in League:** 2021-

OWNERSHIP/MANAGEMENT
Operated by: Philadelphia Phillies.
Director, Florida Operations: John Timberlake. **General Manager, Clearwater Threshers:** Jason Adams. **General Manager, BayCare Ballpark:** Doug Kemp. **Senior Manager, Corporate Partnerships:** Dan McDonough. **Assistant GM, Clearwater Threshers:** Dan Madden. **Manager, Business Operations:** Dianne Gonzalez. **Manager, Ticket Operations:** Patrick Prevelige. **Manager, Food and Beverage:** Justin Gunsaulus. **Manager, Community Engagement and Media:** Robert Stretch. **Manager, Promotions and Game Entertainment:** Dominic Repper. **Manager, Clubhouse:** Justin Glover. **Manager, Merchandise:** Shan Isett. **Manager, Facility Services:** Scott Kelyman. **Manager, Security Operations:** Tim Scott. **Corporate Sales Associate:** Cory Sipe. **Coordinator, Facility and Operations:** Sean McCarthy. **Coordinator, Concessions:** Alyssa Winans. **Coordinator, Graphic Design:** Jill Brush. **Coordinator, Warehouse:** Steve Piatek. **Assistant Manager, Food and Beverage:** Mike O'Soro. **Assistant Manager, Ticket Operations:** Shaylyn Edwards. **Assistant Manager, Merchandise:** Cara Christison. **Assistant Manager, Group Sales:** Victoria Phipps. **Assistant Manager, Business Operations:** Nick Kelly. **Operations Assistant:** Will Priest. **Operations Assistant:** Austin Joyce. **Executive Suites Chef:** Jim Blades. **Office Manager:** Leslie Henley. **Field Supervisor:** Ray Sayre. **Ground Crew:** Mikey Klinger. **Ground Crew:** Lance Weber.

MINOR LEAGUES

FIELD STAFF
Manager: Marty Malloy. **Hitting Coach:** Chris Heintz. **Pitching Coach:** Matt Hockenberry. **Position Coach:** Mycal Jones. **Athletic Trainer:** Samantha Jones. **Strength Coach:** Joseph Miranda.

GAME INFORMATION
PA Announcer: TBA. **Official Scorer:** Larry Wiederecht. **Stadium Name:** BayCare Ballpark. **Location:** US 19 North and Drew Street in Clearwater. **Standard Game Times:** Mon.-Sat. 6:30 pm, Sun. 12 p.m., most Wednesdays are day games. **Ticket Price Range:** $7-14. **Visiting Club Hotel:** TBA.

DAYTONA TORTUGAS

Address: 110 E Orange Ave, Daytona Beach, FL 32114.
Telephone: (386) 257-3172. **Fax:** (386) 523-9490.
E-Mail Address: info@daytonatortugas.com.
Website: www.daytonatortugas.com.
Affiliation (first year): Cincinnati Reds (2015). **Years in League:** 2021-

OWNERSHIP/MANAGEMENT
Operated By: Tortugas Baseball Club LLC.
Principal Owner/President: Reese Smith III. **Co-Owners:** Bob Fregolle, Rick French, Kyle McEwen. **General Manager:** Jim Jaworski. **Finance Manager:** Dan Smith. **Director, Ticket Operations:** Kristina Markus. **Manager, Ticket, and Group Sales:** Cameron Jefferson. **Senior Director, Corporate Sales:** Zack Hurst. **Manager, Corporate Sales:** Alexander Tarrant. **Manager, Community Relations, and Outside Events:** Rachel Morton. **Play-by-Play Broadcaster & Director of Media Relations:** Justin Rocke. **Director, Food & Beverage:** Angela Ford. **Stadium Operations and Grounds Manager:** TBA

FIELD STAFF
Manager: Julio Morillo. **Pitching Coach:** TBA. **Hitting Coach:** Jason Broussard. **Coach:** Lenny Harris. **Coach:** Dick Schofield. **Athletic Trainer:** Lauren Powers. **Performance Coach:** Conor Cantwell. **Video & Technology Specialist:** Andres Borges.

GAME INFORMATION
Radio Announcer: Justin Rocke. **No. of Games Broadcast:** 132. **Flagship Station:** MiLB First Pitch app & www.daytonatortugas.com. **PA Announcer:** Tim LeCras. **Official Scorer:** Don Roberts. **Stadium Name:** Jackie Robinson Ballpark. **Location:** I-95 to International Speedway Blvd Exit, east to Beach Street, south to Magnolia Ave east to ballpark; A1A North/South to Orange Ave west to ballpark. **Standard Game Time:** 6:35 p.m. (Mon-Sat); 5:35 p.m. (Sun). **Ticket Price Range:** $8-15. **Visiting Club Hotel:** Holiday Inn Resort Daytona Beach Oceanfront, 1615 S. Atlantic Ave Daytona Beach, FL 32118. **Telephone:** (386) 255-0921.

DUNEDIN BLUE JAYS

Address: 373 Douglas Ave Dunedin, FL 34698.
Telephone: (727) 733-9302. **Fax:** (727) 734-7661.
E-Mail Address: dunedin@bluejays.com. **Website:** dunedinbluejays.com.
Affiliation (first year): Toronto Blue Jays (1987). **Years in League:** 2021-

OWNERSHIP/MANAGEMENT
Director Florida Operations: Shelby Nelson. **General Manager:** Desiree Ellison. **Senior Manager, Security:** Jason Weaving. **Accounting Manager:** Gayle Gentry. **Head Superintendent:** Patrick Skunda.

FIELD STAFF
Manager: TBA. **Hitting Coach:** TBA. **Pitching Coach:** TBA. **Position Coach:** TBA. **Strength & Conditioning Coach:** TBA. **Athletic Trainer:** TBA.

GAME INFORMATION
PA Announcer: Bradley Keville. **Official Scorer:** Steven Boychuk. **Stadium Name:** TD Ballpark. **Location:** From I-275, north on Highway 19, exit on Drew Street, right on North Keene Road, left onto Union Street. Right onto Douglas Avenue and stadium is on the right. **Standard Game Times:** 6:30 pm, Sun. noon. **Ticket Price Range:** TBD. **Visiting Club Hotel:** TBD.

FORT MYERS MIGHTY MUSSELS

Address: 14400 Six Mile Cypress Pkwy, Fort Myers, FL 33912.
Telephone: (239) 768-4210. **Fax:** (239) 768-4211.
E-Mail Address: frontdesk@mightymussels.com.
Website: www.mightymussels.com.
Affiliation (first year): Minnesota Twins (1992). **Years in League:** 2021-

MINOR LEAGUES

OWNERSHIP/MANAGEMENT
Operated By: Kaufy Baseball, LLC. **Owner:** John Martin. **Partner:** Andrew Kaufmann, Alan Martin, Andy Jenks. **President:** Chris Peters. **General Manager:** Judd Loveland. **Vice President of Sales and Marketing:** Dan Lauer. **Business Director:** Tracy Bettermann. **Broadcast & Media Relations Manager:** John Vittas. **Marketing Manager:** Shannon Rankin. **Operations Coordinator:** Rachel Lane. **Director of Food & Beverage:** Loren Merrigan. **Merchandise Manager:** Lynn Izzo. **Sales Account Representatives:** Rosmy Cerdas, Austin Dutton, Claire Behan, Chloe Riley.

FIELD STAFF
Manager: Brian Meyer. **Pitching Coaches:** Richard Salazar, Jared Gaynor. **Hitting Coaches:** Rayden Sierra, Luis Reyes.

GAME INFORMATION
Radio Announcer: John Vittas. **No. of Games Broadcast:** 110. **Internet Broadcast:** www.mightymussels.com. **PA Announcer:** Tim Jacobson. **Official Scorer:** Benn Norton. **Stadium Name:** William H. Hammond Stadium at the CenturyLink Sports Complex. **Location:** Exit 131 off I-75, west on Daniels Parkway, left on Six Mile Cypress Parkway. **Standard Game Times:** Tue-Fri 7:00 pm, Sat 6:00pm, Sun. 12:00 pm. **Ticket Price Range:** $10-$15. **Visiting Club Hotel:** Fairfield Inn & Suites Fort Myers Cape Coral, 7090 Cypress Terrace, Fort Myers, FL 33907.

JUPITER HAMMERHEADS

Address: 4751 Main Street, Jupiter, FL 33458.
Telephone: (561) 775-1818. **Fax:** (561) 691-6886.
E-Mail Address: PalmBeachCardinals@rogerdeanchevroletstadium.com.
Affiliation (first year): Miami Marlins (1998). **Years in League:** 2021-

OWNERSHIP/MANAGEMENT
Owned By: Miami Marlins, Jupiter Stadium, LTD.
General Manager, Jupiter Stadium, LTD: Mike Bauer. **General Manager:** Nick Bernabe. **Executive Assistant:** Lynn Besaw. **Media Relations & Marketing Manager:** Ryer Gardenswartz. **Media Relations Assistant:** Reece Weiner. **Director of Accounting:** Pam Sartory. **Ticket Office Manager:** Amanda Seimer. **Director of Operations:** Andrew Seymour. **Corporate Partnerships Manager:** Rachel Duewer. **Marketing & Promotions Manager:** Taylor Burress. **Building Manager:** Walter Herrera. **Director, Grounds & Facilities:** Jordan Treadway. **Assistant Director, Grounds & Facilities:** Mitchell Moenster. **Event Operations Coordinator:** Justin Valverde. **Merchandise Manager:** Kimberley Emerick.

FIELD STAFF
Manager: TBA. **Pitching Coach:** TBA. **Hitting Coach:** TBA. **Strength & Conditioning Coach:** TBA. **Athletic Trainer:** TBA. **Defensive Coach:** TBA.

GAME INFORMATION
PA Announcers: John Frost, Jay Zeager. **Official Scorer:** Brennan McDonald. **Stadium Name:** Roger Dean Chevrolet Stadium. **Location:** I-95 to exit 83, east on Donald Ross Road for 1/4 mile, left on Parkside Dr. **Standard Game Times:** 6:30 pm, Sat. 6:00 pm, Sun. 12:00pm. **Ticket Price Range:** $6- $12. **Visiting Club Hotel:** Fairfield Inn by Marriott, 6748 Indiantown Road, Jupiter, FL 33458. **Telephone:** (561) 748-5252.

LAKELAND FLYING TIGERS

Address: 2301 Lakeland Hills Blvd., Lakeland, FL 33805.
Telephone: (863) 686-8075. **Fax:** (863) 687-4127.
Website: www.lakelandflyingtigers.com.
Affiliation (first year): Detroit Tigers (1967). **Years in League:** 2021-

OWNERSHIP/MANAGEMENT
Owned By: Detroit Tigers, Inc. **President and CEO:** Ilitch Holdings, Inc. **Chairman and CEO, Detroit Tigers:** Christopher Ilitch. **Vice President, Lakeland Business Operations:** Josh Bullock. **Director, Florida Operations:** Ron Myers. **General Manager:** Zach Burek. **Manager, Administration/Operations Manager:** Shannon Follett. **Security Operations Manager:** David Clark. **Ticket Manager:** Ryan Eason. **Sales Manager:** Shannon Dixie. **Sales Representative:** Aidan Starr. **Sales Representative:** Gracie Plair.

FIELD STAFF
Manager: Andrew Graham. **Hitting Coach:** C.J. Wamsley. **Pitching Coach:** Dean Stiles. **Bench Coach:** Rafael Gil. **Athletic Trainer:** Erick Flores. **Strength & Conditioning Coach:** Dax Fiore. **Clubhouse Manager:** Pete Mancuso.

GAME INFORMATION
PA Announcer: Unavailable. **Official Scorer:** Joe Falatek. **Stadium Name:** Publix Field at Joker Marchant Stadium. **Location:** Exit 33 on I-4 to 33 South (Lakeland Hills Blvd.), 1.5 miles on left. **Standard Game Times:** M-F 630 p.m., Sat 6:00 pm, Sun 1:00 pm. **Ticket Price Range:** $6-10. **Visiting Club Hotel:** TownePlace Suites by Marriott Lakeland, 3370 US Highway 98 North, Lakeland, FL 33805, 863-680-1115.

MINOR LEAGUES

PALM BEACH CARDINALS

Address: 4751 Main Street, Jupiter, FL 33458.
Telephone: (561) 775-1818. **Fax:** (561) 691-6886.
E-Mail Address: PalmBeachCardinals@rogerdeanchevroletstadium.com.
Affiliation (first year): St. Louis Cardinals (2003). **Years in League:** 2021-

OWNERSHIP/MANAGEMENT
Owned By: St. Louis Cardinals, Jupiter Stadium, LTD.
General Manager, Jupiter Stadium, LTD: Mike Bauer. **General Manager:** Andrew Seymour. **Executive Assistant:** Lynn Besaw. **Media Relations & Marketing Manager:** Ryer Gardenswartz. **Media Relations Assistant:** Reece Weiner. **Director of Accounting:** Pam Sartory. **Ticket Office Manager:** Amanda Seimer. **Director of Sales:** Nick Bernabe. **Corporate Partnerships Manager:** Rachel Duewer. **Marketing & Promotions Manager:** Taylor Burress. **Building Manager:** Walter Herrera. **Director, Grounds & Facilities:** Jordan Treadway. **Assistant Director, Grounds & Facilities:** Mitchell Moenster. **Event Operations Coordinator:** Justin Valverde. **Merchandise Manager:** Kimberley Emerick.

FIELD STAFF
Manager: Gary Kendall. **Hitting Coach:** Willi Martin. **Pitching Coach:** Giovanni Carrara. **Coach:** Bernard Gilkey. **Athletic Trainer:** Jeff Case. **S&C:** Campbell Quirk. **Affiliate Fellow:** Manaul Santamaria

GAME INFORMATION
PA Announcers: John Frost, Jay Zeager. **Official Scorer:** Lou Villano. **Stadium Name:** Roger Dean Chevrolet Stadium. **Location:** I-95 to exit 83, east on Donald Ross Road for 1/4 mile, left on Parkside Dr. **Standard Game Times: Tues:** 5:00 PM. **Wed-Fri:** 6:30. **Sun:** 12:00 PM. **Ticket Price Range:** $6- $12. **Visiting Club Hotel:** Fairfield Inn by Marriott, 6748 Indiantown Road, Jupiter, FL 33458. **Telephone:** (561) 748-5252.

ST. LUCIE METS

Address: 31 Piazza Drive, Port St Lucie, FL 34986.
Telephone: (772) 871-2100. **Fax:** (772) 878-9802.
Website: www.stluciemets.com.
Affiliation (first year): New York Mets (1988). **Years in League:** 2021-

OWNERSHIP/MANAGEMENT
Owner/Chairman/CEO: Steven A. Cohen. **Owner & President of Amazin' Mets Foundation:** Alexandra M. Cohen. **Vice Chairman:** Andrew B. Cohen. **President:** Sandy Alderson. **Vice President, Minor League Facilities:** Paul Taglieri. **General Manager:** Traer Van Allen. **Assistant General Manager, Team Operations & Ticketing:** Kyle Gleockler. **Assistant General Manager, Game Operations, Community Relations & Group Sales:** Kasey Blair. **Director, Sales/Corporate Partnerships:** Lauren DeAcetis. **Senior Manager, Multimedia:** Adam MacDonald. **Manager, Group Sales & Ticketing Operations:** Josh Sexton. **Manager, Fantasy Camp & Events:** Doug Dickey. **Manager, Sales & Corporate Partnerships:** Brett Bladergroen. **Senior Accountant:** Pamela Kuhnle. **Executive Assistant:** Mary O'Brien. **Maintenance:** Jeff Montpetit.

FIELD STAFF
Manager: Gilbert Gomez. **Pitching Coach:** TBA. **Hitting Coach:** TBA. **Bench Coach:** TBA. **Development Coach:** TBA. **Trainer:** TBA. **Performance Coach:** TBA.

GAME INFORMATION
PA Announcer: Evan Nine. **Official Scorer:** Bill Whitehead. **Stadium Name:** Clover Park. **Location:** Exit 121 (St Lucie West Blvd) off I-95, east 1/2 mile, left on NW Peacock Blvd. **Standard Game Times:** Tuesday-Saturday- 6:10; Sundays- 12:10. **Ticket Price Range:** $6-$14. **Visiting Club Hotel:** Holiday Inn Express & Suites, 1601 NW Courtyard Circle, Port St Lucie, FL 34986. **Telephone:** (772) 879-6565.

TAMPA TARPONS

Address: One Steinbrenner Drive, Tampa, FL 33614.
Telephone: (813) 875-7753. **Fax:** (813) 673-3186
E-Mail Address: info@tarponsbaseball.com. **Website:** tarponsbaseball.com
Affiliation (first year): New York Yankees (1994). **Years in League:** 2021-

OWNERSHIP/MANAGEMENT
Operated by: Florida Bomber Baseball LLC. **VP Business Operations and General Manager:** Vance Smith. **Assistant GM:** Jeremy Ventura. **Manager, Premium Surfaces:** Jennifer Magliocchetti. **Account Executives, Ticket Sales & Service:** Justin Lewis, Ashley Morris. **Scoreboard Control Room Director:** Eric Baio.

FIELD STAFF
Manager: Rachel Balkovec. **Pitching Coach:** Gerardo Casadiego. **Hitting Coach:** Rick Guarno. **Defensive Coaches:** Lino Diaz, Michel Hernandez. **Trainer:** Nori Subero. **Strength Coach:** Dylan Lidge. **Scouting Analyst:** Devin Clementi.

MINOR LEAGUES

GAME INFORMATION
Radio: TBD. **PA Announcer:** TBD. **Official Scorer:** Unavailable. **Stadium Name:** George M. Steinbrenner Field. **Location:** I-275 to Dale Mabry Hwy, North on Dale Mabry Hwy (Facility is at corner of West Martin Luther King Blvd/ Dale Mabry Hwy). **Standard Game Times:** Mon-Sat. 6:30pm, Sun 1:00 pm. **Ticket Price Range:** $7-12. **Visiting Club Hotel:** TBD.

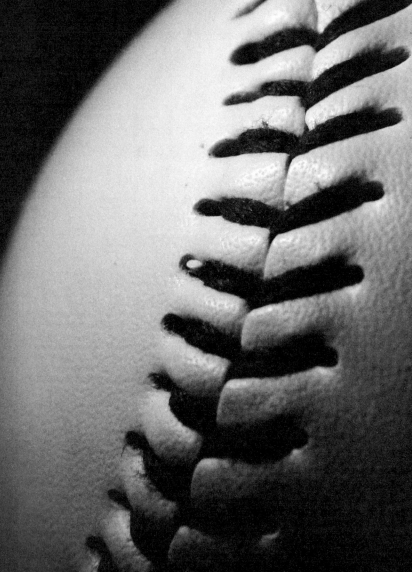

TEAM SCHEDULES

SCHEDULES

MAJORS

AMERICAN LEAGUE

BALTIMORE ORIOLES

MARCH
30 . . . . at Boston

APRIL
1-2 . . . . at Boston
4-5 . . . . at Texas
6-9 . . . . . . New York (AL)
10-13 . . . . Oakland
14-16 . . . .at Chicago (AL)
18-19 . . . . at Washington
21-23 . . . . Detroit
24-26 . . . . Boston
27-30 . . . . at Detroit

MAY
2-4 . . . . . . at Kansas City
5-7 . . . . at Atlanta
8-10 . . . . . . Tampa Bay
12-14 . . . . . . .Pittsburgh
15-18 . . .Los Angeles (AL)
19-21 . . . . . . at Toronto
23-25 . . at New York (AL)
26-28 . . . . Texas
29-31 . . . . Cleveland

JUNE
3-4 . . . . . at San Francisco
6-8 . . . . . . at Milwaukee
9-11 . . . . . . Kansas City
13-15 . . . . Toronto
16-18 . . .at Chicago (NL)
20-21 . . . .at Tampa Bay
23-25 . . . . Seattle
26-28 . . . . Cincinnati
30 . . . . .Minnesota

JULY
1-2 . . . . .Minnesota
3-6 . . . . at New York (AL)
8-9 . . . . at Minnesota
14-16 . . . . Miami
17-19 . . .Los Angeles (NL)
20-23 . . . .at Tampa Bay
24-26 . . .at Philadelphia
28-30 . . . . New York (AL)
31 . . . . at Toronto

AUGUST
1-3 . . . . at Toronto
4-6 . . . . . . New York (NL)
8-10 . . . . Houston
12-13 . . . . . . at Seattle
15-17 . . . at San Diego
19-20 . . . . . at Oakland
22-24 . . . . Toronto
25-27 . . . . . . .Colorado
28-30 . . . . . Chicago (AL)

SEPTEMBER
2-3 . . . . at Arizona
5-7 . . . . at Los Angeles (AL)
8-10 . . . . at Boston
11-13 . . . . St. Louis
14-17 . . . . . Tampa Bay
19-20 . . . . . at Houston
21-24 . . . . . at Cleveland
26-27 . . . .Washington
28-30 . . . . Boston

OCTOBER
1 . . . . Boston

BOSTON RED SOX

MARCH
30 . . . . Baltimore

APRIL
1-2 . . . . Baltimore
3-5 . . . . .Pittsburgh
6-9 . . . . at Detroit
10-13 . . . . . at Tampa Bay
14-17 . . .Los Angeles (AL)
18-20 . . . . . .Minnesota
22-23 . . . . . at Milwaukee
24-26 . . . . . .at Baltimore
28-30 . . . . Cleveland

MAY
1-4 . . . . Toronto
5-7 . . . . .at Philadelphia
9-10 . . . . . . at Atlanta
12-14 . . . . St. Louis
15-17 . . . . Seattle
20-21 . . . at San Diego
23-25 . . at Los Angeles (AL)
27-28 . . . . . . at Arizona
30-31 . . . . Cincinnati

JUNE
1 . . . . Cincinnati
2-4 . . . . Tampa Bay
6-8 . . . . at Cleveland
9-11 . . . . .at New York (AL)
12-14 . . . . .Colorado
16-18 . . . . . New York (AL)
19-22 . . . . . at Minnesota
24-25 . . . .at Chicago (AL)
27-29 . . . . Miami
30 . . . . at Toronto

JULY
1-2 . . . . at Toronto
4-6T . . . . .exas
7-9 . . . . Oakland
15-16 . . .at Chicago (NL)
18-19 . . . . at Oakland
21-23 . . . . . New York (AL)
25-26 . . . . Atlanta
29-30 . . . at San Francisco

AUGUST
1-2 . . . . at Seattle
4-6 . . . . Toronto
7-10 . . . . Kansas City

11-13 . . . . Detroit
15-17 . . . . . at Washington
18-20 . . .at New York (AL)
22-24 . . . . . . at Houston
25-27 . . . .Los Angeles (NL)
28-30 . . . . Houston

SEPTEMBER
2-3 . . . . . . at Kansas City
4-6 . . . . . .at Tampa Bay

CHICAGO WHITE SOX

MARCH
30 . . . . at Houston

APRIL
1-2 . . . . at Houston
3-6 . . . . . . .San Francisco
7-9 . . . . at Pittsburgh
10-12 . . . . at Minnesota
14-16 . . . . Baltimore
17-19 . . . . . Philadelphia
21-23 . . . .at Tampa Bay
24-26 . . . . . . at Toronto
27-30 . . . . . Tampa Bay

MAY
2-4 . . . . .Minnesota
5-7 . . . . . . at Cincinnati
8-11 . . . . at Kansas City
13-14 . . . . Houston
17-18 . . . . . Cleveland
20-21 . . . . Kansas City
22-24 . . . . at Cleveland
25-28 . . . . . . at Detroit
30-31 . . .Los Angeles (AL)

JUNE
3-4 . . . . Detroit
6-8 . . . .at New York (AL)
10-11 . . . . Miami
14-16 . . at Los Angeles (NL)
17-18 . . . . . at Seattle
20-22 . . . . Texas
24-25 . . . . Boston
27-29 . . at Los Angeles (AL)

CLEVELAND GUARDIANS

MARCH
31 . . . . at Seattle

APRIL
1-2 . . . . at Seattle
4-5 . . . . at Oakland
7-9 . . . . Seattle
10-12 . . . . . New York (AL)
14-16 . . . . at Washington
17-19 . . . . . . at Detroit
21-23 . . . . Miami
24-26 . . . . . .Colorado
28-30 . . . . at Boston

MAY
1-3 . . . .at New York (AL)
5-7 . . . . .Minnesota
8-10 . . . . Detroit

8-10 . . . . Baltimore
11-14 . . . . . New York (AL)
15-17 . . . . at Toronto
19-20 . . . . at Texas
22-24 . . . . . Chicago (AL)
26-27 . . . . . . Tampa Bay
28-30 . . . .at Baltimore

OCTOBER
1 . . . . .at Baltimore

JULY
1-2 . . . . at Oakland
5-7 . . . . Toronto
8-9 . . . . St. Louis
14-16 . . . . at Atlanta
18-20 . . .at New York (AL)
22-23 . . . . . at Minnesota
26-27 . . . . . Chicago (NL)
28-30 . . . . Cleveland

AUGUST
2-3 . . . . at Texas
4-6 . . . . . . at Cleveland
8-10 . . . . New York (AL)
12-13 . . . . . . Milwaukee
16-17 . . .at Chicago (NL)
19-20 . . . . . at Colorado
22-23 . . . . Seattle
25-27 . . . . Oakland
28-30 . . . .at Baltimore

SEPTEMBER
2-3 . . . . Detroit
5-7 . . . . at Kansas City
8-10 . . . . at Detroit
11-13 . . . . . Kansas City
14-17 . . . . . .Minnesota
18-20 . . . . at Washington
22-24 . . . . . at Boston
25-27 . . . . . .Arizona
29-30 . . . . . . San Diego

OCTOBER
1 . . . . San Diego

12-14 . . . .Los Angeles (AL)
17-18 . . .at Chicago (AL)
19-21 . . .at New York (NL)
22-24 . . . . Chicago (AL)
26-28 . . . . St. Louis
29-31 . . . .at Baltimore

JUNE
1-4 . . . . . . at Minnesota
6-8 . . . . Boston
9-11 . . . . Houston
14-16 . . . . at San Diego
17-18 . . . . at Arizona
20-22 . . . . Oakland
23-25 . . . . . . Milwaukee
28-29 . . . . at Kansas City
30 . . . . . .at Chicago (NL)

Baseball America 2023 Directory • **145**

SCHEDULES

JULY
1-2 . . . . . .at Chicago (NL)
3-5 . . . . Atlanta
6-9 . . . . Kansas City
15-16 . . . . at Texas
17-19 . . . . at Pittsburgh
21-23 . . . . . Philadelphia
24-26 . . . . . Kansas City
28-30 . . . . .at Chicago (AL)

AUGUST
1-2 . . . . at Houston
4-6 . . . . . . Chicago (AL)
7-10 . . . . Toronto
11-13 . . . . at Tampa Bay
15-16 . . . . at Cincinnati
17-20 . . . . Detroit
22-24 . . . .Los Angeles (NL)

25-27 . . . . at Toronto
28-30 . . . . . at Minnesota

SEPTEMBER
1-3 . . . . Tampa Bay
4-6 . . . . .Minnesota
8-10 . . . at Los Angeles (AL)
12-13 . . . . at San Francisco
15-17 . . . . Texas
18-20 . . . . at Kansas City
21-24 . . . . Baltimore
26-27 . . . . Cincinnati
29-30 . . . . at Detroit

OCTOBER
1 . . . . at Detroit

5-8 . . . . .at Toronto
9-11 . . . . at Cleveland
14-16 . . . . .Washington
17-18 . . . . . . Cincinnati
20-21 . . . New York (NL)
24-25 . . at Los Angeles (NL)
27-29 . . . . . . .at St. Louis

JULY
1-3 . . . . at Texas
4-5 . . . . .Colorado
7-9 . . . . Seattle
15-16 . . at Los Angeles (AL)
19 . . . . at Colorado
21-23 . . . . . . at Oakland
25-27 . . . . Texas
29-30 . . . . . . Tampa Bay

AUGUST
1-2 . . . . Cleveland
3-6 . . . . .at New York (AL)

8-10 . . . . .at Baltimore
12-13 . . . Los Angeles (AL)
14-16 . . . . at Miami
19-20 . . . . Seattle
22-24 . . . . Boston
25-27 . . . . at Detroit
28-30 . . . . at Boston

SEPTEMBER
2-3 . . . . New York (AL)
4-7 . . . . at Texas
9-10 . . . . . . San Diego
12-13 . . . . Oakland
16-17 . . . at Kansas City
19-20 . . . . Baltimore
23-24 . . . . . Kansas City
26-28 . . . . . . at Seattle
30 . . . . at Arizona

OCTOBER
1 . . . . at Arizona

DETROIT TIGERS

MARCH
30 . . . . at Tampa Bay

APRIL
1-2 . . . . at Tampa Bay
4-5 . . . . at Houston
6-9 . . . . Boston
11-13 . . . . . . .at Toronto
14-16 . . . .San Francisco
17-19 . . . . . Cleveland
21-23 . . . .at Baltimore
24 26 . . . . at Milwaukee
27-30 . . . . . Baltimore

MAY
2-4 . . . . . . New York (NL)
6-7 . . . . .at St. Louis
8-10 . . . . at Cleveland
12-14 . . . . Seattle
16-17 . . . . . .Pittsburgh
19-21 . . . at Washington
22-24 . . at Kansas City
25-28 . . . Chicago (AL)
29-31 . . . . Texas

JUNE
3-4 . . . . . .at Chicago (AL)
5-7 . . . . . .at Philadelphia
9-11 . . . . .Arizona
12-14 . . . . Atlanta
15-18 . . . at Minnesota
19-21 . . . . Kansas City
23-25 . . . .Minnesota
27-29 . . . . at Texas

JULY
1-2 . . . . .at Colorado
4-6 . . . . Oakland
7-9 . . . . Toronto
15-16 . . . . at Seattle
18-20 . . at Kansas City
21-23 . . . . .San Diego
25-27 . . .Los Angeles (AL)
28-30 . . . . at Miami

AUGUST
1-2 . . . . at Pittsburgh
4-6 . . . . Tampa Bay
7-10 . . . . .Minnesota
11-13 . . . . at Boston
15-16 . . . at Minnesota
17-20 . . . . at Cleveland
21-23 . . . . Chicago (NL)
25-27 . . . . Houston
28-31 . . . . . New York (AL)

SEPTEMBER
2-3 . . . . . .at Chicago (AL)
5-7 . . . . .at New York (AL)
8-10 . . . . . . Chicago (AL)
12-14 . . . . Cincinnati
16-17 . . at Los Angeles (AL)
19-21 . . at Los Angeles (NL)
22-24 . . . . . . at Oakland
26-28 . . . . . Kansas City
29-30 . . . . Cleveland

OCTOBER
1 . . . . Cleveland

KANSAS CITY ROYALS

MARCH
30 . . . . .Minnesota

APRIL
1-2 . . . . .Minnesota
3-6 . . . . Toronto
7-9 . . . . at San Francisco
11-13 . . . . at Texas
15-16 . . . . Atlanta
17-19 . . . . Texas
22-23 . . at Los Angeles (AL)
25-26 . . . . . . at Arizona
27-30 . . . . . at Minnesota

MAY
2-4 . . . . Baltimore
6-7 . . . . Oakland
8-11 . . . . . Chicago (AL)
13-14 . . . . .at Milwaukee
16-17 . . . . at San Diego
20-21 . . . . .at Chicago (AL)
22-24 . . . . Detroit
27-28 . . . . . .Washington
29-30 . . . . .at St. Louis

JUNE
3-4 . . . . .Colorado
5-7 . . . . at Miami
9-11 . . . . . .at Baltimore
13-15 . . . . . Cincinnati
17-18 . . . .Los Angeles (AL)
19-21 . . . . at Detroit
22-25 . . . . . .at Tampa Bay
28-29 . . . . Cleveland

JULY
1-2 . . . . .Los Angeles (NL)
3-5 . . . . . . .at Minnesota
6-9 . . . . at Cleveland
15-16 . . . . . Tampa Bay
18-20 . . . . .Detroit
21-23 . . . .at New York (AL)
24-26 . . . . at Cleveland
29-30 . . . . . .Minnesota

AUGUST
2-3 . . . . . . New York (NL)
4-6 . . . . . .at Philadelphia
7-10 . . . . at Boston
12 . . . . St. Louis
15-17 . . . . Seattle
18-20 . . .at Chicago (NL)
22-23 . . . . . . at Oakland
26-27 . . . . . at Seattle
29-31 . . . . . . .Pittsburgh

SEPTEMBER
2-3 . . . . Boston
5-7 . . . . Chicago (AL)
8-10 . . . . .at Toronto
11-13 . . . .at Chicago (AL)
16-17 . . . . Houston
18-20 . . . . . Cleveland
23-24 . . . . . at Houston
26-28 . . . . . . at Detroit
30 . . . . . . New York (AL)

OCTOBER
1 . . . . New York (AL)

HOUSTON ASTROS

MARCH
30 . . . . Chicago (AL)

APRIL
1-2 . . . . Chicago (AL)
4-5 . . . . Detroit
6-9 . . . . .at Minnesota
10-12 . . . . . at Pittsburgh
15-16 . . . . Texas
18-20 . . . . Toronto
21-23 . . . . . . at Atlanta
24-26 . . . . . at Tampa Bay
29-30 . . . Philadelphia

MAY
2-3 . . . . .San Francisco
6-7 . . . . at Seattle
9-10 . . . at Los Angeles (AL)
13-14 . . . .at Chicago (AL)
16-18 . . . Chicago (NL)
20-21 . . . . Oakland
22-24 . . . .at Milwaukee
27-28 . . . . at Oakland
29-31 . . . . . .Minnesota

JUNE
1 . . . . .Minnesota
2-4 . . . . .Los Angeles (AL)

SCHEDULES

LOS ANGELES ANGELS

MARCH
31 . . . . at Oakland

APRIL
1-2 . . . . at Oakland
4-5 . . . . at Seattle
8-9 . . . . Toronto
11-12 . . . . .Washington
14-17 . . . . . . at Boston
18-20 . . . .at New York (AL)
22-23 . . . . . Kansas City
25-27 . . . . . . Oakland
29-30 . . . . .at Milwaukee

MAY
2-4 . . . . .at St. Louis
6-7T . . . . .exas
9-10 . . . . Houston
12-14 . . . . . at Cleveland
15-18 . . . .at Baltimore
20-21 . . . . .Minnesota
23-25 . . . . . . Boston
27-28 . . . . . . Miami
30-31 . . . .at Chicago (AL)

JUNE
2-4 . . . . . . at Houston
7-9 . . . . . . Chicago (NL)
10-11 . . . . Seattle
13-16 . . . . . . at Texas
17-18 . . . . at Kansas City
21-22 . . .Los Angeles (NL)
24-25 . . . . . at Colorado
27-29 . . . . . Chicago (AL)

JULY
1-2 . . . . .Arizona
4-6 . . . . . . at San Diego
8-9 . . . at Los Angeles (NL)
15-16 . . . . Houston
18-19 . . . . New York (AL)
22-23 . . . . . . .Pittsburgh
25-27 . . . . . . at Detroit
28-30 . . . . . at Toronto
31 . . . . at Atlanta

AUGUST
1-2 . . . . at Atlanta
4-6 . . . . Seattle
8-10 . . . . . .San Francisco
12-13 . . . . . . at Houston
15-17 . . . . . . at Texas
19-20 . . . . . Tampa Bay
22-23 . . . . . . Cincinnati
25-27 . . .at New York (NL)
28-30 . . . . .at Philadelphia

SEPTEMBER
2-3 . . . . at Oakland
5-7 . . . . Baltimore
8-10 . . . . Cleveland
12-13 . . . . . . at Seattle
16-17 . . . . Detroit
19-21 . . . .at Tampa Bay
23-24 . . . .at Minnesota
26-28 . . . . Texas
30 . . . . Oakland

OCTOBER
1 . . . . Oakland

MINNESOTA TWINS

MARCH
30 . . . . . . at Kansas City

APRIL
1-2 . . . . . . at Kansas City
3-5 . . . . at Miami
6-9 . . . . Houston
10-12 . . . . . Chicago (AL)
13-16 . . at New York (AL)
18-20 . . . . . . at Boston
22-23 . . . . .Washington
24-26 . . . . New York (AL)
27-30 . . . . . Kansas City

MAY
2-4 . . . . . .at Chicago (AL)
5-7 . . . . at Cleveland
9-11 . . . . San Diego
13-14 . . . . . Chicago (NL)
16-17 . at Los Angeles (NL)
20-21 . at Los Angeles (AL)
22-24 . . . .San Francisco
27-28 . . . . . . Toronto
29-31 . . . . . . at Houston

JUNE
1 . . . . at Houston
1-4 . . . . Cleveland
6-8 . . . . . at Tampa Bay
9-11 . . . . . . at Toronto
13-14 . . . . . Milwaukee
15-18 . . . . Detroit
19-22 . . . . Boston
23-25 . . . . . at Detroit
26-28 . . . . . . at Atlanta
30 . . . . .at Baltimore

JULY
1-2 . . . . .at Baltimore
3-5 . . . . Kansas City
8-9 . . . . Baltimore
15-16 . . . . . . at Oakland
18-20 . . . . at Seattle
22-23 . . . . Chicago (AL)
24-26 . . . . Seattle
29-30 . . . . . at Kansas City

AUGUST
1-3 . . . . .at St. Louis
5-6 . . . . .Arizona
7-10 . . . . at Detroit
11-13 . . . .at Philadelphia
15-16 . . . . Detroit
19-20 . . . . .Pittsburgh
23 . . . . at Milwaukee
24-27 . . . . Texas
28-30 . . . . . . Cleveland

SEPTEMBER
2-3 . . . . at Texas
4-6 . . . . . . at Cleveland
9-10 . . . . . New York (NL)
11-13 . . . . . Tampa Bay
14-17 . . .at Chicago (AL)
18-20 . . . . . at Cincinnati
23-24 . . . .Los Angeles (AL)
26-28 . . . . Oakland
30 . . . . .at Colorado

OCTOBER
1 . . . . .at Colorado

NEW YORK YANKEES

MARCH
30 . . . . . . .San Francisco

APRIL
1-2 . . . . . . .San Francisco
3-5 . . . . . . Philadelphia
6-9 . . . . . .at Baltimore
10-12 . . . . at Cleveland
13-16 . . . . . .Minnesota
18-20 . . .Los Angeles (AL)
21-23 . . . . . . Toronto
24-26 . . . . at Minnesota
28-30 . . . . . at Texas

MAY
1-3 . . . . Cleveland
5-7 . . . . .at Tampa Bay
8-10 . . . . Oakland
11-14 . . . . . Tampa Bay
15-18 . . . . . at Toronto
19-21 . . . . . at Cincinnati
23-25 . . . . . Baltimore
26-28 . . . . .San Diego
30-31 . . . . . at Seattle

JUNE
1 . . . . at Seattle
3-4 . . . at Los Angeles (NL)
6-8 . . . . . . Chicago (AL)
9-11 . . . . Boston
13-14 . . .at New York (NL)
16-18 . . . . . . at Boston
20-22 . . . . Seattle
23-25 . . . . Texas
28-29 . . . . . . at Oakland

JULY
1-2 . . . . .at St. Louis
3-6 . . . . Baltimore
7-9 . . . . Chicago (NL)
15-16 . . . . . at Colorado
18-19 . . at Los Angeles (AL)
21-23 . . . . . . Kansas City
25-26 . . . . New York (NL)
28-30 . . . . . .at Baltimore
31 . . . . Tampa Bay

AUGUST
1-2 . . . . Tampa Bay
3-6 . . . . Houston
8-10 . . . . .at Chicago (AL)
11-13 . . . . at Miami
14-16 . . . . . . at Atlanta
18-20 . . . . Boston
22-24 . . . . .Washington
25-27 . . . at Tampa Bay
28-31 . . . . . at Detroit

SEPTEMBER
2-3 . . . . at Houston
5-7 . . . . Detroit
8-10 . . . . Milwaukee
11-14 . . . . . . at Boston
15-17 . . . at Pittsburgh
19-21 . . . . . . Toronto
22-24 . . . . . . .Arizona
26-28 . . . . . .at Toronto
30 . . . . . . at Kansas City

OCTOBER
1 . . . . at Kansas City

OAKLAND ATHLETICS

MARCH
31 . . . . .Los Angeles (AL)

APRIL
1-2 . . . .Los Angeles (AL)
4-5 . . . . Cleveland
7-9 . . . . . . .at Tampa Bay
10-13 . . . .at Baltimore
15-16 . . . . New York (NL)
18-19 . . . . Chicago (NL)
22-23 . . . . . . at Texas
25-27 . . at Los Angeles (AL)
29-30 . . . . Cincinnati

MAY
3-4 . . . . Seattle
6-7 . . . . at Kansas City
8-10 . . . .at New York (AL)
12-14 . . . . Texas
16-17 . . . . .Arizona
20-21 . . . . at Houston
23-26 . . . . . . at Seattle
27-28 . . . . . . Houston
30-31 . . . . . . .Atlanta

JUNE
2-4 . . . . at Miami
5-7 . . . . at Pittsburgh
10-11 . . . . . .at Milwaukee
13-15 . . . . . Tampa Bay
17-18 . . . . . Philadelphia
20-22 . . . . at Cleveland
23-25 . . . . . . .at Toronto
28-29 . . . . . New York (AL)

JULY
1-2 . . . . Chicago (AL)
4-6 . . . . at Detroit
7-9 . . . . at Boston
15-16 . . . . . . .Minnesota
18-19 . . . . Boston
21-23 . . . . Houston
26-27 . . . . at San Francisco
29-30 . . . . . . at Colorado

AUGUST
2-4 . . . . at Los Angeles (NL)
5-6 . . . . .San Francisco
8-9 . . . . Texas
11-13 . . . . . at Washington
14-16 . . . . . .at St. Louis
19-20 . . . . . . Baltimore
22-23 . . . . . . Kansas City
25-27 . . . .at Chicago (AL)
29-30 . . . . . . at Seattle

SEPTEMBER
2-3 . . . .Los Angeles (AL)
4-6 . . . . Toronto
9-10 . . . . at Texas
12-13 . . . . . . at Houston
16-17 . . . . . . .San Diego
19-20 . . . . Seattle
22-24 . . . . Detroit
26-28 . . . . . at Minnesota
30 . . . . at Los Angeles (AL)

OCTOBER
1 . . . . . at Los Angeles (AL)

SCHEDULES

SEATTLE MARINERS

MARCH
31 . . . . Cleveland

APRIL
1-2 . . . . Cleveland
4-5 . . . . . .Los Angeles (AL)
7-9 . . . . . . at Cleveland
10-12 . . .at Chicago (NL)
15-16 . . . . .Colorado
18-19 . . . . . . Milwaukee
22-23 . . . . St. Louis
25-27 . . . . .at Philadelphia
28-30 . . . . at Toronto

MAY
3-4 . . . . at Oakland
6-7 . . . . Houston
9-10 . . . . Texas
12-14 . . . . at Detroit
15-17 . . . . . . at Boston
19-21 . . . . . at Atlanta
23-26 . . . . Oakland
27-28 . . . . . .Pittsburgh
30-31 . . . . New York (AL)

JUNE
1 . . . . New York (AL)
3-4 . . . . at Texas
7 . . . . at San Diego
10-11 . . at Los Angeles (AL)
13-15 . . . . Miami
17-18 . . . . . Chicago (AL)
20-22 . . . .at New York (AL)
23-25 . . . . . .at Baltimore
27-28 . . . . . .Washington

JULY
1-2 . . . . Tampa Bay
4-6 . . . . . at San Francisco
7-9 . . . . at Houston
15-16 . . . . Detroit
18-20 . . . . . . .Minnesota
22-23 . . . . Toronto
24-26 . . . . . at Minnesota
29-30 . . . . at Arizona

AUGUST
1-2 . . . . Boston
4-6 . . . . at Los Angeles (AL)
9-10 . . . . San Diego
12-13 . . . . Baltimore
15-17 . . . . at Kansas City
19-20 . . . . . . at Houston
22-23 . . .at Chicago (AL)
26-27 . . . . . Kansas City
29-30 . . . . Oakland

SEPTEMBER
1-3 . . . .at New York (NL)
4-6 . . . . at Cincinnati
7-10 . . . . . .at Tampa Bay
12-13 . . .Los Angeles (AL)
16-17 . . .Los Angeles (NL)
19-20 . . . . . at Oakland
23-24 . . . . at Texas
26-28 . . . . Houston
29-30 . . . . Texas

OCTOBER
1 . . . . Texas

TAMPA BAY RAYS

MARCH
30 . . . . .Detroit

APRIL
1-2 . . . . .Detroit
3-5 . . . . . at Washington
7-9 . . . . Oakland
10-13 . . . . Boston
14-16 . . . . . . at Toronto
17-19 . . . . at Cincinnati
21-23 . . . . Chicago (AL)
24-26 . . . . Houston
27-30 . . . .at Chicago (AL)

MAY
2-4 . . . . .Pittsburgh
5-7 . . . . . . New York (AL)
8-10 . . . . . . .at Baltimore
11-14 . . . .at New York (AL)
16-18 . . . .at New York (NL)
19-21 . . . . . . Milwaukee
22-25 . . . . Toronto
26-28 . . .Los Angeles (NL)
29-31 . . . .at Chicago (NL)

JUNE
2-4 . . . . at Boston
6-8 . . . . .Minnesota
9-11 . . . . Texas
13-15 . . . . . . at Oakland
17-18 . . . . at San Diego
20-21 . . . . Baltimore
22-25 . . . . . Kansas City
28-29 . . . . . . at Arizona

JULY
1-2 . . . . at Seattle
4-6 . . . . Philadelphia
7-9 . . . . .Atlanta
15-16 . . . . at Kansas City
18-19 . . . . . . at Texas
20-23 . . . . Baltimore
25-26 . . . . Miami
29-30 . . . . . at Houston
31 . . . . .at New York (AL)

AUGUST
1-2 . . . .at New York (AL)
4-6 . . . . at Detroit
8-10 . . . . St. Louis
11-13 . . . . Cleveland
15-16 . . . at San Francisco
19-20 . . at Los Angeles (AL)
22-24 . . . . .Colorado
25-27 . . . . . New York (AL)
29-30 . . . . . . .at Miami

SEPTEMBER
1-3 . . . . at Cleveland
4-6 . . . . Boston
7-10 . . . . Seattle
11-13 . . . .at Minnesota
14-17 . . . . . .at Baltimore
19-21 . . .Los Angeles (AL)
22-24 . . . . Toronto
26-27 . . . . . at Boston
29-30 . . . . . . at Toronto

OCTOBER
1 . . . . .at Toronto

TEXAS RANGERS

MARCH
30 . . . . Philadelphia

APRIL
1-2 . . . . Philadelphia
4-5 . . . . Baltimore
7-9 . . . . . .at Chicago (NL)
11-13 . . . . . Kansas City
15-16 . . . . . at Houston
17-19 . . . . at Kansas City
22-23 . . . . Oakland
24-26 . . . . at Cincinnati
28-30 . . . . New York (AL)

MAY
3 . . . . .Arizona
6-7 . . . . at Los Angeles (AL)
9-10 . . . . . . at Seattle
12-14 . . . . . at Oakland
16-18 . . . . .Atlanta
20-21 . . . . . .Colorado
22-24 . . . . at Pittsburgh
26-28 . . . .at Baltimore
29-31 . . . . at Detroit

JUNE
3-4 . . . . Seattle
6-8 . . . . St. Louis
9-11 . . . . . .at Tampa Bay
13-16 . . . .Los Angeles (AL)
17-18 . . . . Toronto
20-22 . . . .at Chicago (AL)
23-25 . . . .at New York (AL)
27-29 . . . . Detroit

JULY
1-3 . . . . Houston
4-6 . . . . at Boston
7-9 . . . . . at Washington
15-16 . . . . Cleveland
18-19 . . . . . . Tampa Bay
22-23 . . .Los Angeles (NL)
25-27 . . . . . at Houston
29-30 . . . . at San Diego

AUGUST
2-3 . . . . Chicago (AL)
5-6 . . . . Miami
8-9 . . . . at Oakland
12-13 . . . . at San Francisco
15-17 . . .Los Angeles (AL)
19-20 . . . . . . Milwaukee
22-23 . . . . . at Arizona
24-27 . . . .at Minnesota
28-30 . . . .at New York (NL)

SEPTEMBER
2-3 . . . . .Minnesota
4-7 . . . . Houston
9-10 . . . . Oakland
11-14 . . . . . . .at Toronto
15-17 . . . . at Cleveland
19-20 . . . . Boston
23-24 . . . . Seattle
26-28 . at Los Angeles (AL)
29-30 . . . . . . at Seattle

OCTOBER
1 . . . . at Seattle

TORONTO BLUE JAYS

MARCH
30 . . . . .at St. Louis

APRIL
1-2 . . . . .at St. Louis
3-6 . . . . . at Kansas City
8-9 . . at Los Angeles (AL)
11-13 . . . . Detroit
14-16 . . . . . . Tampa Bay
18-20 . . . . . at Houston
21-23 . . .at New York (AL)
24-26 . . . . Chicago (AL)
28-30 . . . . Seattle

MAY
1-4 . . . . at Boston
5-7 . . . . . at Pittsburgh
9-10 . . . . .at Philadelphia
12-14 . . . . .Atlanta
15-18 . . . . New York (AL)
19-21 . . . . Baltimore
22-25 . . . . at Tampa Bay
27-28 . . . . at Minnesota
30-31 . . . . . Milwaukee

JUNE
1 . . . . Milwaukee
2-4 . . . .at New York (NL)
5-8 . . . . Houston
9-11 . . . . . . .Minnesota
13-15 . . . . . .at Baltimore
17-18 . . . . . at Texas
19-21 . . . . . . .at Miami
23-25 . . . . . . Oakland
27-29 . . . . .San Francisco
30 . . . . Boston

JULY
1-2 . . . . Boston
5-7 . . . . . .at Chicago (AL)
7-9 . . . . at Detroit
14-16 . . . . .Arizona
18-20 . . . . . . San Diego
22-23 . . . . . . at Seattle
25-26 . . at Los Angeles (NL)
28-30 . . . .Los Angeles (AL)
31 . . . . Baltimore

AUGUST
1-3 . . . . Baltimore
4-6 . . . . at Boston
7-10 . . . . . at Cleveland
11-13 . . . . Chicago (NL)
15-16 . . . . Philadelphia
18-20 . . . . at Cincinnati
22-24 . . . .at Baltimore
25-27 . . . . . Cleveland
28-30 . . . .Washington

SEPTEMBER
2-3 . . . . .at Colorado
4-6 . . . . at Oakland
8-10 . . . . . . Kansas City
11-14 . . . . Texas
15-17 . . . . Boston
19-21 . . .at New York (AL)
22-24 . . . .at Tampa Bay
26-28 . . . . New York (AL)
29-30 . . . . . . Tampa Bay

OCTOBER
1 . . . . Tampa Bay

148 • Baseball America 2023 Directory

BaseballAmerica.com

SCHEDULES

NATIONAL LEAGUE

ARIZONA DIAMONDBACKS

MARCH
31 . . . . at Los Angeles (NL)

APRIL
1-2. . . . at Los Angeles (NL)
4 . . . . at San Diego
7-9. . . . .Los Angeles (NL)
11-12 . . . . . . Milwaukee
14-16 . . . . .at Miami
17-19 . . . . . .at St. Louis
21-23 . . . . . . San Diego
25-26 . . . . . Kansas City
29-30 . . . . . . at Colorado

MAY
3 . . . . at Texas
6-7. . . . . . . .Washington
9-10. . . . . Miami
12-14 . . . . .San Francisco
16-17 . . . . . . at Oakland
19-21 . . . . . at Pittsburgh
22-24 . . . at Philadelphia
27-28 . . . . Boston
29-31 . . . . . . .Colorado

JUNE
.1 . . . . .Colorado
3-4. . . . . Atlanta
6-8. . . . at Washington
9-11 . . . . . . at Detroit
13-15 . . . . . Philadelphia
17-18 . . . . . . Cleveland
20-21 . . . .at Milwaukee
24-25 . . . at San Francisco
28-29 . . . . . . Tampa Bay

JULY
1-2. . . . at Los Angeles (AL)
4-7. . . . . . New York (NL)
8-9. . . . . .Pittsburgh
14-16 . . . . . . at Toronto
18-20 . . . . . . at Atlanta
21-23 . . . at Cincinnati
25-26 . . . . . . St. Louis
29-30 . . . . . . Seattle

AUGUST
1-3. . . . at San Francisco
5-6. . . . . . . at Minnesota
9-10. . . .Los Angeles (NL)
12-13 . . . . . . San Diego
15-16 . . . . . at Colorado
18-20 . . . . at San Diego
22-23 . . . . Texas
25-27 . . . . . Cincinnati
29-31 . . at Los Angeles (NL)

SEPTEMBER
2-3. . . . . Baltimore
4-6. . . . . .Colorado
7-10 . . . .at Chicago (NL)
11-14 . . .at New York (NL)
16-17 . . . . Chicago (NL)
20 . . . . . San Francisco
22-24 . . at New York (AL)
25-27 . . .at Chicago (AL)
30 . . . . Houston

OCTOBER
1 . . . . Houston

ATLANTA BRAVES

MARCH
30 . . . . . . at Washington

APRIL
1-2. . . . at Washington
3-5. . . . . . . .at St. Louis
6-9. . . . . . . San Diego
10-12 . . . . . . Cincinnati
15-16 . . . . at Kansas City
18-19 . . . at San Diego
21-23 . . . . . . Houston
24-27 . . . . Miami
28-30 . . .at New York (NL)

MAY
1 . . . . . .at New York (NL)
2-4. . . . . at Miami
5-7. . . . . Baltimore
9-10. . . . . Boston
12-14 . . . . . . at Toronto
16-18 . . . . . . at Texas
19-21 . . . . Seattle
22-24 . . . .Los Angeles (NL)
25-28 . . . Philadelphia
30-31 . . . . . . at Oakland

JUNE
3-4. . . . . at Arizona
6-8. . . . . New York (NL)
9-11 . . . . . .Washington
12-14 . . . . . . at Detroit
15-18 . . . . . . .Colorado
20-22 . . .at Philadelphia
23-25 . . . at Cincinnati
26-28 . . . . . .Minnesota
30 . . . . Miami

JULY
1-2. . . . . Miami
3-5. . . . . . . at Cleveland
7-9. . . . . .at Tampa Bay
14-16 . . . . Chicago (AL)
18-20 . . . . .Arizona
22-23 . . . . .at Milwaukee
25-26 . . . . . . at Boston
28-30 . . . . . . Milwaukee
31 . . . . .Los Angeles (AL)

AUGUST
1-2. . . . .Los Angeles (AL)
4-6. . . . . .at Chicago (NL)
7-10 . . . . . at Pittsburgh
11-13 . . .at New York (NL)
14-16 . . . . New York (NL)
18-20 . . . . .San Francisco
21-23 . . . . New York (NL)
26-27 . . . at San Francisco
29-31 . . . . . at Colorado

SEPTEMBER
1-3. . . . at Los Angeles (NL)
5-7. . . . . St. Louis
8-10. . . . . . . .Pittsburgh
12-14 . . . .at Philadelphia
15-17 . . . . . .at Miami
18-20 . . . . Philadelphia
21-24 . . . at Washington
26-28 . . . . Chicago (NL)
29-30 . . . . .Washington

OCTOBER
1 . . . . .Washington

CHICAGO CUBS

MARCH
30 . . . . Milwaukee

APRIL
1-2. . . . . . Milwaukee
3-5. . . . . at Cincinnati
7-9T . . . . .exas
10-12 . . . . . . Seattle
15-16 . . at Los Angeles (NL)
18-19 . . . . . . at Oakland
20-23 . . . .Los Angeles (NL)
25-27 . . . . . . San Diego
28-30 . . . . . . at Miami

MAY
1-4. . . . . . at Washington
5-7. . . . . Miami
8-10. . . . . St. Louis
13-14 . . . . . at Minnesota
16-18 . . . . . at Houston
19-21 . . . .at Philadelphia
23-25 . . . . New York (NL)
26-28 . . . . . Cincinnati
29-31 . . . . . Tampa Bay

JUNE
3-6. . . . . . at San Diego
7-9. . . . at Los Angeles (AL)
10-11 . . at San Francisco
14-16 . . . . .Pittsburgh
16-18 . . . . . Baltimore
19-21 . . . at Pittsburgh
24-25 . . . . .at St. Louis
28-30 . . . . . Philadelphia
30 . . . . Cleveland

JULY
1-2. . . . . Cleveland
3-6. . . . . . .at Milwaukee
7-9. . . . .at New York (AL)
15-16 . . . . Boston
18-20 . . . . . .Washington
21-23 . . . . . . St. Louis
26-27 . . . .at Chicago (AL)
27-30 . . . . . .at St. Louis

AUGUST
1-4. . . . . . . Cincinnati
4-6. . . . . Atlanta
7-9. . . .at New York (NL)
11-13 . . . . . at Toronto
16-17 . . . . Chicago (AL)
18-20 . . . . Kansas City
21-23 . . . . . at Detroit
24-27 . . . at Pittsburgh
29-30 . . . . . Milwaukee

SEPTEMBER
1-3. . . . . . . at Cincinnati
4-6. . . . . . .San Francisco
7-10 . . . . .Arizona
12-13 . . . . .at Colorado
16-17 . . . . at Arizona
19-21 . . . . .Pittsburgh
22-24 . . . . . .Colorado
26-28 . . . . at Atlanta
30 . . . . . . .at Milwaukee

OCTOBER
1 . . . . .at Milwaukee

CINCINNATI REDS

MARCH
30 . . . . .Pittsburgh

APRIL
1-2. . . . . .Pittsburgh
3-5C . . . . hicago (NL)
6-9. . . . . .at Philadelphia
10-12 . . . . . at Atlanta
13-16 . . . . Philadelphia
17-19 . . . . . Tampa Bay
20-23 . . . at Pittsburgh
24-26 . . . . Texas
29-30 . . . . . . at Oakland

MAY
2-3. . . . . . . at San Diego
5-7. . . . . . Chicago (AL)
9-11 . . . . . New York (NL)
12-14 . . . . . . at Miami
16-17 . . . . .at Colorado
19-21 . . . . New York (AL)
22-25 . . . . St. Louis
26-28 . . .at Chicago (NL)
30-31 . . . . at Boston

JUNE
1 . . . . at Boston
2-5. . . . . Milwaukee
6-8. . . .Los Angeles (NL)
10-11 . . . .at St. Louis
13-15 . . . . at Kansas City
17-18 . . . . . at Houston
19-21 . . . .Colorado
23-25 . . . . . . .Atlanta
26-28 . . . . . .at Baltimore
30 . . . . San Diego

JULY
1-2. . . . . San Diego
3-6. . . . . . at Washington
8-9. . . . . .at Milwaukee
14-16 . . . . . Milwaukee
17-20 . . . . .San Francisco
21-23 . . . . .Arizona
25-26 . . . at Milwaukee
29-30 . . at Los Angeles (NL)

AUGUST
1-4. . . . .at Chicago (NL)
4-6. . . . . . .Washington
7-9. . . . . Miami
11-13 . . . . at Pittsburgh
15-16 . . . . . Cleveland
18-20 . . . . . . Toronto
22-23 . . at Los Angeles (AL)
25-27 . . . . at Arizona
29-30 . . . at San Francisco

SEPTEMBER
1-3. . . . . . . Chicago (NL)
4-6. . . . . Seattle
8-10. . . . . St. Louis
12-14 . . . . . at Detroit
15-17 . . .at New York (NL)
18-20 . . . . . .Minnesota
22-24 . . . . . .Pittsburgh
26-27 . . . . at Cleveland
30 . . . . .at St. Louis

OCTOBER
1 . . . . .at St. Louis

BaseballAmerica.com

Baseball America 2023 Directory • **149**

SCHEDULES

COLORADO ROCKIES

MARCH
30 . . . . at San Diego

APRIL
1-2 . . . . . . at San Diego
4-5 . . . at Los Angeles (NL)
6-9 . . . . . . .Washington
11-12 . . . . . . St. Louis
15-16 . . . . at Seattle
18-19 . . . . . . .Pittsburgh
20-23 . . .at Philadelphia
24-26 . . . . . at Cleveland
29-30 . . . . .Arizona

MAY
3-4 . . . . Milwaukee
5-7 . . . . .at New York (NL)
8-10 . . . . . at Pittsburgh
13-14 . . . . . Philadelphia
16-17 . . . . . . Cincinnati
20-21 . . . . . . at Texas
23-25 . . . . Miami
27-28 . . . . New York (NL)
29-31 . . . . . at Arizona

JUNE
1 . . . . at Arizona
3-4 . . . . . at Kansas City
7-8 . . . . . .San Francisco
10-11 . . . . . San Diego
12-14 . . . . . at Boston
15-18 . . . . . at Atlanta
19-21 . . . . at Cincinnati
24-25 . . . .Los Angeles (AL)
28-30 . . . .Los Angeles (NL)

JULY
1-2 . . . . Detroit
4-5 . . . . at Houston
8-9 . . . . . at San Francisco
15-16 . . . . . New York (AL)
19 . . . . Houston
21-23 . . . . at Miami
24-26 . . . at Washington
29-30 . . . . Oakland

AUGUST
1-2 . . . . San Diego
5-6 . . . . .at St. Louis
8-9 . . . . . . .at Milwaukee
11-13 . . at Los Angeles (NL)
15-16 . . . . .Arizona
19-20 . . . . Chicago (AL)
22-24 . . . . at Tampa Bay
25-27 . . .at Baltimore
29-31 . . . . Atlanta

SEPTEMBER
2-3 . . . . Toronto
4-6 . . . . at Arizona
9-10 . . . . . at San Francisco
12-13 . . . . . Chicago (NL)
15-17 . . . . .San Francisco
19-20 . . . . at San Diego
22-24 . . .at Chicago (NL)
26-29 . . .Los Angeles (NL)
30 . . . . .Minnesota

OCTOBER
1 . . . . .Minnesota

MIAMI MARLINS

MARCH
30-31 . . . . . New York (NL)

APRIL
1-2 . . . . . . New York (NL)
3-5 . . . . . . .Minnesota
6-9 . . . . .at New York (NL)
10-12 . . .at Philadelphia
14-16 . . . . . . .Arizona
17-19 . . . . .San Francisco
21-23 . . . . at Cleveland
24-27 . . . . . at Atlanta
28-30 . . . . . Chicago (NL)

MAY
2-4 . . . . Atlanta
5-7 . . . . .at Chicago (NL)
9-10 . . . . . . at Arizona
12-14 . . . . . Cincinnati
16-18 . . . . . Washington
20-21 . . . at San Francisco
23-25 . . . . at Colorado
27-28 . . at Los Angeles (AL)
30-31 . . . . . San Diego

JUNE
1 . . . . San Diego
2-4 . . . . Oakland
5-7 . . . . . . Kansas City
10-11 . . .at Chicago (NL)
13-15 . . . . . at Seattle
16-18 . . . . at Washington
19-21 . . . . Toronto
22-25 . . . . . .Pittsburgh
27-29 . . . . at Boston
30 . . . . at Atlanta

JULY
1-2 . . . . at Atlanta
3-6 . . . . St. Louis
7-9 . . . . . Philadelphia
14-16 . . . .at Baltimore
17-19 . . . .at St. Louis
21-23 . . . . .Colorado
25-26 . . . at Tampa Bay
28-30 . . . . Detroit
31 . . . . . . Philadelphia

AUGUST
1-3 . . . . . . Philadelphia
5-6 . . . . at Texas
7-9 . . . . . at Cincinnati
11-13 . . . . New York (AL)
14-16 . . . . Houston
19-20 . . at Los Angeles (NL)
22-23 . . . . at San Diego
25-27 . . . . .Washington
29-30 . . . . . Tampa Bay
31 . . . . . . at Washington

SEPTEMBER
1-3 . . . . . at Washington
5-7 . . . . .Los Angeles (NL)
8-10 . . . . .at Philadelphia
11-14 . . . . at Milwaukee
15-17 . . . . .Atlanta
18-20 . . . New York (NL)
22-24 . . . . . Milwaukee
26-28 . . . .at New York (NL)
29-30 . . . . at Pittsburgh

OCTOBER
1 . . . . at Pittsburgh

LOS ANGELES DODGERS

MARCH
31 . . . . .Arizona

APRIL
1-2 . . . . .Arizona
4-5 . . . . .Colorado
7-9 . . . . at Arizona
11-13 . . . . at San Francisco
15-16 . . . . Chicago (NL)
18-19 . . . . New York (NL)
20-23 . . . .at Chicago (NL)
25-27 . . . . at Pittsburgh
29-30 . . . . . . St. Louis

MAY
2-3 . . . . Philadelphia
6-7 . . . . . . at San Diego
8-10 . . . . . .at Milwaukee
13-14 . . . . . San Diego
16-17 . . . . .Minnesota
18-21 . . . . . .at St. Louis
22-24 . . . . . . at Atlanta
26-28 . . . at Tampa Bay
30-31 . . . . . .Washington

JUNE
3-4 . . . . . . New York (AL)
6-8 . . . . . . at Cincinnati
9-11 . . . .at Philadelphia
14-16 . . . . . Chicago (AL)
17-18 . . . . .San Francisco
21-22 . . at Los Angeles (AL)
24-25 . . . . .Houston
28-30 . . . . . at Colorado

JULY
1-2 . . . . . . at Kansas City
4-7 . . . . .Pittsburgh
8-9 . . . . .Los Angeles (AL)
14-16 . . . .at New York (NI)
17-19 . . . .at Baltimore
22-23 . . . . at Texas
25-26 . . . . Toronto
29-30 . . . . Cincinnati

AUGUST
2-4 . . . . Oakland
5-7 . . . . . . at San Diego
9-10 . . . . at Arizona
11-13 . . . . .Colorado
16-18 . . . . . Milwaukee
19-20 . . . . Miami
22-24 . . . . at Cleveland
25-27 . . . . . at Boston
29-31 . . . . .Arizona

SEPTEMBER
1-3 . . . . .Atlanta
5-7 . . . . at Miami
8-10 . . . . . at Washington
12-14 . . . . . San Diego
16-17 . . . . . . at Seattle
19-21 . . . . Detroit
22-24 . . . .San Francisco
26-29 . . . . . . at Colorado
30 . . . . . . at San Francisco

OCTOBER
1 . . . . . . at San Francisco

MILWAUKEE BREWERS

MARCH
30 . . . . . .at Chicago (NL)

APRIL
1-2 . . . . . .at Chicago (NL)
3-5 . . . . . New York (NL)
8-9 . . . . St. Louis
11-12 . . . . . . at Arizona
14-16 . . . . . at San Diego
18-19 . . . . . at Seattle
22-23 . . . . Boston
24-26 . . . . . . .Detroit
29-30 . . . .Los Angeles (AL)

MAY
3-4 . . . . at Colorado
6-7 . . . . . at San Francisco
8-10 . . . .Los Angeles (NL)
13-14 . . . . . Kansas City
15-17 . . . . . .at St. Louis
19-21 . . . .at Tampa Bay
22-24 . . . . .Houston
25-28 . . . . .San Francisco
30-31 . . . . . . at Toronto

JUNE
1 . . . . .at Toronto
2-5 . . . . at Cincinnati
6-8 . . . . Baltimore
10-11 . . . . . . Oakland
13-14 . . . . . at Minnesota
17-18 . . . . . .Pittsburgh
20-21 . . . . . . .Arizona
23-25 . . . . . at Cleveland
26-29 . . . .at New York (NL)
30 . . . . at Pittsburgh

JULY
1-2 . . . . at Pittsburgh
3-6 . . . . Chicago (NL)
8-9 . . . . Cincinnati
14-16 . . . . . at Cincinnati
18-20 . . . .at Philadelphia
22-23 . . . . .Atlanta
25-26 . . . . . Cincinnati
28-30 . . . . . at Atlanta
31 . . . . . . at Washington

AUGUST
1-2 . . . . . . at Washington
3-6 . . . . .Pittsburgh
8-9 . . . . .Colorado
12-13 . . . .at Chicago (AL)
16-18 . . at Los Angeles (NL)
19-20 . . . . at Texas
23 . . . . .Minnesota
26-27 . . . . . . .San Diego
29-30 . . . .at Chicago (NL)

SEPTEMBER
2-3 . . . . Philadelphia
4-6 . . . . at Pittsburgh
8-10 . . . . .at New York (AL)
11-14 . . . . Miami
16-17 . . . . . .Washington
18-21 . . . . . at St. Louis
22-24 . . . . . . .at Miami
26-28 . . . . . . St. Louis
30 . . . . Chicago (NL)

OCTOBER
1 . . . . Chicago (NL)

150 · Baseball America 2023 Directory

BaseballAmerica.com

SCHEDULES

NEW YORK METS

MARCH
30-31 . . . . at Miami

APRIL
1-2 . . . . at Miami
3-5 . . . . .at Milwaukee
6-9 . . . . Miami
10-12 . . . . . . San Diego
15-16 . . . . . . at Oakland
18-19 . at Los Angeles (NL)
21-23 . . . at San Francisco
25-27 . . . . . .Washington
28-30 . . . . Atlanta

MAY
1 . . . . .Atlanta
2-4 . . . . at Detroit
5-7 . . . . .Colorado
9-11 . . . . at Cincinnati
12-15 . . . . at Washington
16-18 . . . . . . Tampa Bay
19-21 . . . . . Cleveland
23-25 . . .at Chicago (NL)
27-28 . . . . . at Colorado
30-31 . . . . . Philadelphia

JUNE
1 . . . . Philadelphia
2-4 . . . . Toronto
6-8 . . . . at Atlanta
9-11 . . . . . at Pittsburgh
13-14 . . . . New York (AL)
16-18 . . . . St. Louis
20-21 . . . . at Houston
23-25 . . . .at Philadelphia
26-29 . . . . . Milwaukee
30 . . . . . . .San Francisco

JULY
1-2 . . . . .San Francisco
4-7 . . . . at Arizona
8-9 . . . . at San Diego
14-16 . . . .Los Angeles (NL)
18-20 . . . . . Chicago (AL)
21-23 . . . . . at Boston
25-26 . . at New York (AL)
27-30 . . . . . .Washington

AUGUST
2-3 . . . . at Kansas City
4-6 . . . . .at Baltimore
7-9 . . . . Chicago (NL)
11-13 . . . . Atlanta
14-16 . . . . . . .Pittsburgh
17-20 . . . .at St. Louis
21-23 . . . . . . at Atlanta
25-27 . . .Los Angeles (AL)
28-30 . . . . Texas

SEPTEMBER
1-3 . . . . Seattle
5-6 . . . . . at Washington
9-10 . . . . . at Minnesota
11-14 . . . . .Arizona
15-17 . . . . . Cincinnati
18-20 . . . . . . at Miami
21-24 . . . .at Philadelphia
26-28 . . . . Miami
29-30 . . . . . Philadelphia

OCTOBER
1 . . . . Philadelphia

PITTSBURGH PIRATES

MARCH
30 . . . . at Cincinnati

APRIL
1-2 . . . . at Cincinnati
3-5 . . . . at Boston
7-9 . . . . . . Chicago (AL)
10-12 . . . . . . Houston
13-16 . . . . . .at St. Louis
18-19 . . . . at Colorado
20-23 . . . . . Cincinnati
25-27 . . .Los Angeles (NL)
28-30 . . . at Washington

MAY
2-4 . . . . .at Tampa Bay
5-7 . . . . Toronto
8-10 . . . . . .Colorado
12-14 . . . . .at Baltimore
16-17 . . . . . at Detroit
19-21 . . . . . . .Arizona
22-24 . . . . Texas
27-28 . . . . . . at Seattle
29-31 . . at San Francisco

JUNE
2-4 . . . . St. Louis
5-7 . . . . Oakland
9-11 . . . . . New York (NL)
14-16 . .at Chicago (NL)
17-18 . . . .at Milwaukee
19-21 . . . . . Chicago (NL)
22-25 . . . . . . at Miami
27-29 . . . . San Diego
30 . . . . Milwaukee

JULY
1-2 . . . . Milwaukee
4-7 . . . at Los Angeles (NL)
8-9 . . . . at Arizona
14-16 . . . . .San Francisco
17-19 . . . . . Cleveland
22-23 . at Los Angeles (AL)
25-26 . . . . . at San Diego
28-30 . . . . . Philadelphia

AUGUST
1-2 . . . . .Detroit
3-6 . . . . . . .at Milwaukee
7-10 . . . . .Atlanta
11-13 . . . . Cincinnati
14-16 . . .at New York (NL)
19-20 . . . . . . at Minnesota
21-23 . . . . St. Louis
24-27 . . . . Chicago (NL)
29-31 . . . . at Kansas City

SEPTEMBER
2-3 . . . . .at St. Louis
4-6 . . . . Milwaukee
8-10 . . . . at Atlanta
11-14 . . . . . . .Washington
15-17 . . . . New York (AL)
19-21 . . .at Chicago (NL)
22-24 . . . at Cincinnati
26-28 . . .at Philadelphia
29-30 . . . . Miami

OCTOBER
1 . . . . Miami

PHILADELPHIA PHILLIES

MARCH
30 . . . . at Texas

APRIL
1-2 . . . . at Texas
3-5 . . . . .at New York (AL)
6-9 . . . . Cincinnati
10-12 . . . . Miami
13-16 . . . . . at Cincinnati
17-19 . . .at Chicago (AL)
20-23 . . . . .Colorado
25-27 . . . . Seattle
29-30 . . . . . . at Houston

MAY
2-3 . . . . at Los Angeles (NL)
5-7 . . . . Boston
9-10 . . . . Toronto
13-14 . . . . . . at Colorado
16-17 . . at San Francisco
19-21 . . . . Chicago (NL)
22-24 . . . . .Arizona
25-28 . . . . . . at Atlanta
30-31 . . .at New York (NL)

JUNE
1 . . . . . . .at New York (NL)
2-4 . . . . . . at Washington
5-7 . . . . Detroit
9-11 . . . .Los Angeles (NL)
13-15 . . . . . . .at Arizona
17-18 . . . . . . at Oakland
20-22 . . . . . . .Atlanta
23-25 . . . . New York (NL)
28-30 . . . .at Chicago (NL)
30 . . . . .Washington

JULY
1-2 . . . . .Washington
4-6 . . . . . . .at Tampa Bay
7-9 . . . . at Miami
14-16 . . . . . . San Diego
18-20 . . . . . . Milwaukee
21-23 . . . . . at Cleveland
24-26 . . . . . . Baltimore
28-30 . . . . . . at Pittsburgh
31 . . . . at Miami

AUGUST
1-3 . . . . at Miami
4-6 . . . . Kansas City
7-10 . . . . . .Washington
11-13 . . . . . .Minnesota
15-16 . . . . at Toronto
18-20 . . . . at Washington
21-23 . . . . .San Francisco
25-27 . . . . St. Louis
28-30 . . . .Los Angeles (AL)

SEPTEMBER
2-3 . . . . at Milwaukee
4-6 . . . . at San Diego
8-10 . . . . Miami
12-14 . . . . Atlanta
16-17 . . . . . . .at St. Louis
18-20 . . . . . at Atlanta
21-24 . . . . New York (NL)
26-28 . . . . . . .Pittsburgh
29-30 . . . .at New York (NL)

OCTOBER
1 . . . . . .at New York (NL)

SAN DIEGO PADRES

MARCH
30 . . . . .Colorado

APRIL
1-2 . . . . .Colorado
4 . . . . .Arizona
6-9 . . . . at Atlanta
10-12 . . .at New York (NL)
14-16 . . . . . . Milwaukee
18-19 . . . . . . Atlanta
21-23 . . . . . . at Arizona
25-27 . . .at Chicago (NL)
29-30 . . . . .San Francisco

MAY
2-3 . . . . Cincinnati
6-7 . . . . .Los Angeles (NL)
9-11 . . . . . at Minnesota
13-14 . . at Los Angeles (NL)
16-17 . . . . . Kansas City
20-21 . . . . Boston
23-25 . . . . at Washington
26-28 . . .at New York (AL)
30-31 . . . . . . at Miami

JUNE
1 . . . . at Miami
3-6 . . . . Chicago (NL)
7 . . . . Seattle
10-11 . . . .at Colorado
14-16 . . . . . Cleveland
17-18 . . . . . . Tampa Bay
20-22 . . . at San Francisco
24-25 . . . . . .Washington
27-29 . . . . at Pittsburgh
30 . . . . at Cincinnati

JULY
1-2 . . . . at Cincinnati
4-6 . . . .Los Angeles (AL)
8-9 . . . . . . New York (NL)
14-16 . . . .at Philadelphia
18-20 . . . . . .at Toronto
21-23 . . . . . at Detroit
25-26 . . . . .Pittsburgh
29-30 . . . . Texas

AUGUST
1-2 . . . . .at Colorado
5-7 . . . . .Los Angeles (NL)
9-10 . . . . at Seattle
12-13 . . . . . . at Arizona
15-17 . . . . . . Baltimore
18-20 . . . . .Arizona
22-23 . . . . Miami
26-27 . . . . .at Milwaukee
28-30 . . . . .at St. Louis

SEPTEMBER
1-3 . . . . . .San Francisco
4-6 . . . . Philadelphia
9-10 . . . . . . at Houston
12-14 . at Los Angeles (NL)
16-17 . . . . . . at Oakland
19-20 . . . . . . .Colorado
23-24 . . . . . St. Louis
26-28 . . at San Francisco
29-30 . . .at Chicago (AL)

OCTOBER
1 . . . . . . .at Chicago (AL)

BaseballAmerica.com

Baseball America 2023 Directory • 151

SCHEDULES

SAN FRANCISCO GIANTS

MARCH
30 . . . . . . at New York (AL)

APRIL
1-2 . . . . . at New York (AL)
3-6 . . . . . .at Chicago (AL)
7-9 . . . . Kansas City
11-13 . . .Los Angeles (AL)
14-16 . . . . . . at Detroit
17-19 . . . . at Miami
21-23 . . . . . New York (NL)
25-27 . . . . St. Louis
29-30 . . . . . at San Diego

MAY
2-3 . . . . at Houston
6-7 . . . . Milwaukee
9-10 . . . . . .Washington
12-14 . . . . . at Arizona
16-17 . . . . . Philadelphia
20-21 . . . . Miami
22-24 . . . at Minnesota
25-28 . . . at Milwaukee
29-31 . . . . .Pittsburgh

JUNE
3-4 . . . . Baltimore
7-8 . . . . . . at Colorado
10-11 . . . . . Chicago (NL)
12-14 . . . . .at St. Louis
17-18 . . at Los Angeles (NL)
20-22 . . . . . . San Diego
24-25 . . . . .Arizona
27-29 . . . . . .at Toronto
30 . . . . . .at New York (NL)

JULY
1-2 . . . . . .at New York (NL)
4-6 . . . . Seattle
8-9 . . . . .Colorado
14-16 . . . . . at Pittsburgh
17-20 . . . . at Cincinnati
21-23 . . . at Washington
26-27 . . . . . . Oakland
29-30 . . . . Boston

AUGUST
1-3 . . . . .Arizona
5-6 . . . . at Oakland
8-10 . . . at Los Angeles (AL)
12-13 . . . . Texas
15-16 . . . . . Tampa Bay
18-20 . . . . . . at Atlanta
21-23 . . .at Philadelphia
26-27 . . . . .Atlanta
29-30 . . . . . Cincinnati

SEPTEMBER
1-3 . . . . . . at San Diego
4-6 . . . . .at Chicago (NL)
9-10 . . . . .Colorado
12-13 . . . . . Cleveland
15-17 . . . . . at Colorado
20 . . . . at Arizona
22-24 . . at Los Angeles (NL)
26-28 . . . . . . San Diego
30 . . . . . .Los Angeles (NL)

OCTOBER
1 . . . . . . .Los Angeles (NL)

ST. LOUIS CARDINALS

MARCH
30 . . . . Toronto

APRIL
1-2 . . . . Toronto
3-5 . . . . Atlanta
8-9 . . . . . . .at Milwaukee
11-12 . . . . . .at Colorado
13-16 . . . . .Pittsburgh
17-19 . . . . .Arizona
22-23 . . . . . . at Seattle
25-27 . . . . at San Francisco
29-30 . . at Los Angeles (NL)

MAY
2-4 . . . . . .Los Angeles (AL)
6-7 . . . . Detroit
8-10 . . . . . .at Chicago (NL)
12-14 . . . . . at Boston
15-17 . . . . . . Milwaukee
18-21 . . .Los Angeles (NL)
22-25 . . . . . at Cincinnati
26-28 . . . . . at Cleveland
29-30 . . . . . Kansas City

JUNE
2-4 . . . . at Pittsburgh
6-8 . . . . at Texas
10-11 . . . . Cincinnati
12-14 . . . . . .San Francisco
16-18 . . . .at New York (NL)
19-21 . . . at Washington
24-25 . . . . . Chicago (NL)
27-29 . . . . Houston

JULY
1-2 . . . . . . New York (AL)
3-6 . . . . .at Miami
8-9 . . . . .at Chicago (AL)
15-16 . . . . . .Washington
17-19 . . . . Miami
21-23 . . . .at Chicago (NL)
25-26 . . . . at Arizona
27-30 . . . . . Chicago (NL)

AUGUST
1-3 . . . . .Minnesota
5-6 . . . . .Colorado
8-10 . . . . . . .at Tampa Bay
12 . . . . . . at Kansas City
14-16 . . . . Oakland
17-20 . . . New York (NL)
21-23 . . . . . at Pittsburgh
25-27 . . . .at Philadelphia
28-30 . . . . . San Diego

SEPTEMBER
2-3 . . . . .Pittsburgh
5-7 . . . . at Atlanta
8-10 . . . . . . at Cincinnati
11-13 . . . . . .at Baltimore
16-17 . . . . . Philadelphia
18-21 . . . . . Milwaukee
23-24 . . . . . at San Diego
26-28 . . . . at Milwaukee
30 . . . . Cincinnati

OCTOBER
1 . . . . Cincinnati

WASHINGTON NATIONALS

MARCH
30 . . . . Atlanta

APRIL
1-2 . . . . Atlanta
3-5 . . . . Tampa Bay
6-9 . . . . at Colorado
11-12 . . at Los Angeles (AL)
14-16 . . . . Cleveland
18-19 . . . . Baltimore
22-23 . . . at Minnesota
25-27 . . . .at New York (NL)
28-30 . . . . .Pittsburgh

MAY
1-4 . . . . Chicago (NL)
6-7 . . . . at Arizona
9-10 . . . . . at San Francisco
12-15 . . . . New York (NL)
16-18 . . . . at Miami
19-21 . . . . . . .Detroit
23-25 . . . . . . San Diego
27-28 . . . at Kansas City
30-31 . . at Los Angeles (NL)

JUNE
2-4 . . . . Philadelphia
6-8 . . . . .Arizona
9-11 . . . . at Atlanta
14-16 . . . . . at Houston
16-18 . . . . . . Miami
19-21 . . . . . . St. Louis
24-25 . . . . at San Diego
27-28 . . . . . . at Seattle
30 . . . . at Philadelphia

JULY
1-2 . . . . . .at Philadelphia
3-6 . . . . Cincinnati
7-9 . . . . Texas
15-16 . . . . . .at St. Louis
18-20 . . .at Chicago (NL)
21-23 . . . .San Francisco
24-26 . . . . . .Colorado
27-30 . . . .at New York (NL)
31 . . . . Milwaukee

AUGUST
1-2 . . . . Milwaukee
4-6 . . . . . . at Cincinnati
7-10 . . . . . .at Philadelphia
11-13 . . . . Oakland
15-17 . . . . Boston
18-20 . . . . . . Philadelphia
22-24 . . . at New York (AL)
25-27 . . . . at Miami
28-30 . . . . . .at Toronto
31 . . . . Miami

SEPTEMBER
1-3 . . . . Miami
5-6 . . . . . . New York (NL)
8-10 . . . . .Los Angeles (NL)
11-14 . . . . at Pittsburgh
16-17 . . . . .at Milwaukee
18-20 . . . Chicago (NL)
21-24 . . . . .Atlanta
26-27 . . . . . .at Baltimore
29-30 . . . . . at Atlanta

OCTOBER
1 . . . . at Atlanta

152 · Baseball America 2023 Directory

BaseballAmerica.com

Schedules are subject to change. We would
suggest confirming dates and times with teams.

SCHEDULES

TRIPLE-A

INTERNATIONAL LEAGUE

BUFFALO BISONS

MARCH		JULY	
31 . . . . . at Scranton/WB		1-3 . . . . Worcester	
APRIL		4-9 . . . . . at Rochester	
1-2 . . . . . at Scranton/WB		14-16 . . . . Toledo	
4-9 . . . . Worcester		18-23 . . . . . at Syracuse	
11-16 . . . . . at Rochester		25-30 . . . . . Scranton/WB	
18-23 . . . . Iowa		**AUGUST**	
25-30 . . . . . at Gwinnett		1-6 . . . . at Lehigh Valley	
MAY		8-13 . . . . . . at Worcester	
2-7 . . . . . at Worcester		15-20 . . . . . . Rochester	
9-14 . . . . Syracuse		22-27 . . . . at Syracuse	
16-21 . . . . . Rochester		29-31 . . . . . Indianapolis	
23-28 . . . . at Lehigh Valley		**SEPTEMBER**	
30-31 . . . . St. Paul		1-3 . . . . . . Indianapolis	
JUNE		5-10 . . . . . . Lehigh Valley	
1-4 . . . . St. Paul		12-17 . . . at Scranton/WB	
6-11 . . . . at Toledo		19-24 . . . . Norfolk	
13-18 . . . . Syracuse			
20-25 . . . . at Scranton/WB			
28-30 . . . . Worcester			

CHARLOTTE KNIGHTS

MARCH		JULY	
31 . . . . Memphis		1-3 . . . . at Norfolk	
APRIL		4-9 . . . . . . Jacksonville	
1-2 . . . . Memphis		14-16 . . . . at Lehigh Valley	
4-9 . . . . . at Columbus		18-23 . . . . Memphis	
11-16 . . . . . Jacksonville		25-30 . . . . at Durham	
18-23 . . . . . at Louisville		**AUGUST**	
25-30 . . . . Norfolk		1-6 . . . . at Norfolk	
MAY		8-13 . . . . Gwinnett	
2-7 . . . . . . at Gwinnett		15-20 . . . . . . at Nashville	
9-14 . . . . Durham		22-27 . . . . Memphis	
16-21 . . . . . Scranton/WB		29-31 . . . . at Jacksonville	
23-28 . . . . at Jacksonville		**SEPTEMBER**	
30-31 . . . . . . Nashville		1-3 . . . . . at Jacksonville	
JUNE		5-10 . . . . Durham	
1-4 . . . . Nashville		12-17 . . . . . . Nashville	
6-11 . . . . . . at Gwinnett		19-24 . . . . . at Memphis	
13-18 . . . . . . at Durham			
20-25 . . . . . . Louisville			
28-30 . . . . . . at Norfolk			

COLUMBUS CLIPPERS

APRIL		JULY	
1-2 . . . . at Iowa		1-3 . . . . Toledo	
4-9 . . . . Charlotte		4-9 . . . . at Nashville	
11-16 . . . . . at Worcester		14-16 . . . . Iowa	
18-23 . . . . Toledo		18-23 . . . . . at Louisville	
25-30 . . . at Indianapolis		25-30 . . . . Omaha	
MAY		**AUGUST**	
2-7 . . . . Iowa		1-6 . . . . St. Paul	
9-14 . . . . . . at Louisville		8-13 . . . . at Toledo	
16-21 . . . . St. Paul		15-20 . . . . at Syracuse	
23-28 . . . . . Indianapolis		22-27 . . . . . Jacksonville	
30-31 . . . . at Iowa		30-31 . . . . . at St. Paul	
JUNE		**SEPTEMBER**	
1-4 . . . . at Iowa		1-3 . . . . . . at St. Paul	
6-11 . . . . Louisville		5-10 . . . . . Scranton/WB	
14-18 . . . . . . at Omaha		12-17 . . . . . . at Toledo	
20-25 . . . . at Indianapolis		19-24 . . . . Omaha	
28-30 . . . . Toledo			

DURHAM BULLS

MARCH		JULY	
31 . . . . Norfolk		1-3 . . . . . at Jacksonville	
APRIL		4-9 . . . . Norfolk	
1-2 . . . . Norfolk		15-16 . . . . . . at St. Paul	
4-9 . . . . . at Jacksonville		18-23 . . . . . at Rochester	
11-16 . . . . . Lehigh Valley		25-30 . . . . Charlotte	
18-23 . . . . . at Syracuse		**AUGUST**	
25-30 . . . . Memphis		1-6 . . . . at Nashville	
MAY		8-13 . . . . Memphis	
2-7 . . . . at Norfolk		15-20 . . . . Gwinnett	
9-14 . . . . . . at Charlotte		22-27 . . . . . . at Norfolk	
16-21 . . . . . . Nashville		29-31 . . . . . . Nashville	
23-28 . . . . . at Gwinnett		**SEPTEMBER**	
29-31 . . . . . Jacksonville		1-3 . . . . Nashville	
JUNE		5-10 . . . . . . at Charlotte	
1-4 . . . . . . Jacksonville		12-17 . . . . . . Louisville	
7-11 . . . . . at Memphis		19-24 . . . . . at Gwinnett	
13-18 . . . . . . Charlotte			
20-25 . . . . . . Syracuse			
28-30 . . . . at Jacksonville			

GWINNETT STRIPERS

MARCH		JULY	
31 . . . . Jacksonville		1-3 . . . . at St. Paul	
APRIL		4-9 . . . . Omaha	
1-2 . . . . . . Jacksonville		15-16 . . . . . at Memphis	
4-9 . . . . at Norfolk		18-23 . . . . Norfolk	
11-16 . . . . Memphis		25-30 . . . . at Jacksonville	
18-23 . . . . . . at Omaha		**AUGUST**	
25-30 . . . . Buffalo		1-6 . . . . . . Indianapolis	
MAY		8-13 . . . . . . at Charlotte	
2-7 . . . . Charlotte		15-20 . . . . . at Durham	
9-14 . . . . . at Nashville		22-27 . . . . Nashville	
16-21 . . . . . at Memphis		29-31 . . . . . at Memphis	
23-28 . . . . Durham		**SEPTEMBER**	
30-31 . . . . . . at Norfolk		2-3 . . . . at Memphis	
JUNE		5-10 . . . . Worcester	
1-4 . . . . at Norfolk		12-17 . . . . at Jacksonville	
6-11 . . . . Charlotte		19-24 . . . . Durham	
13-18 . . . . . at Nashville			
20-25 . . . . . Jacksonville			
28-31 . . . . . . at St. Paul			

INDIANAPOLIS INDIANS

MARCH		JULY	
31 . . . . Omaha		1-3 . . . . . . at Louisville	
APRIL		4-9 . . . . Memphis	
1-2 . . . . Omaha		15-16 . . . . . . at Omaha	
4-9 . . . . . . at Louisville		18-23 . . . . at Iowa	
11-16 . . . . St. Paul		25-30 . . . . . . Louisville	
18-23 . . . . . at Memphis		**AUGUST**	
25-30 . . . . Columbus		1-6 . . . . . . at Gwinnett	
MAY		8-13 . . . . Nashville	
2-7 . . . . at Toledo		16-20 . . . . . . at St. Paul	
9-14 . . . . . at St. Paul		22-27 . . . . Iowa	
16-21 . . . . Iowa		29-31 . . . . . . at Buffalo	
23-28 . . . . at Columbus		**SEPTEMBER**	
29-31 . . . . Toledo		1-3 . . . . at Buffalo	
JUNE		5-10 . . . . Toledo	
1-4 . . . . Toledo		12-17 . . . . . . at Omaha	
6-11 . . . . Omaha		19-24 . . . . . . Rochester	
13-18 . . . . . . at Iowa			
20-25 . . . . . Columbus			
28-30 . . . . at Louisville			

BaseballAmerica.com

Baseball America 2023 Directory • **153**

SCHEDULES

IOWA CUBS

APRIL
1-2	Columbus
4-9	at St. Paul
11-16	Omaha
18-23	at Buffalo
25-30	Louisville

MAY
2-7	at Columbus
9-14	Toledo
16-21	at Indianapolis
23-28	at Nashville
30-31	Columbus

JUNE
1-4	Columbus
7-11	at St. Paul
13-18	Indianapolis
20-25	Memphis
28-30	at Omaha

JULY
1-4	at Omaha
5-9	St. Paul
14-16	at Columbus
18-23	Indianapolis
26-30	at Memphis

AUGUST
1-6	Toledo
9-13	at Omaha
15-20	Louisville
22-27	at Indianapolis
29-31	at Toledo

SEPTEMBER
1-3	at Toledo
5-10	Omaha
12-17	St. Paul
19-24	at Louisville

JACKSONVILLE JUMBO SHRIMP

MARCH
31	at Gwinnett

APRIL
1-2	at Gwinnett
4-9	Durham
11-16	at Charlotte
18-23	Nashville
25-30	Lehigh Valley

MAY
2-7	at Memphis
9-14	Norfolk
16-21	at Louisville
23-28	Charlotte
29-31	at Durham

JUNE
1-4	at Durham
6-11	Nashville
13-18	Memphis
20-25	at Gwinnett
28-30	Durham

JULY
1-3	Durham
4-9	at Charlotte
14-16	Worcester
18-23	at Nashville
25-30	Gwinnett

AUGUST
2-6	at Memphis
8-13	Norfolk
15-20	at Lehigh Valley
22-27	at Columbus
29-31	Charlotte

SEPTEMBER
1-3	Charlotte
5-10	at Norfolk
12-17	Gwinnett
19-24	at Nashville

LEHIGH VALLEY IRONPIGS

MARCH
31	at Rochester

APRIL
1-2	at Rochester
4-8	Scranton/WB
11-16	at Durham
18-23	Worcester
25-30	at Jacksonville

MAY
2-7	at Syracuse
9-14	Memphis
16-21	at Worcester
23-28	Buffalo
30-31	Scranton/WB

JUNE
1-4	Scranton/WB
6-11	at Syracuse
13-18	Toledo
20-25	at Worcester
28-30	Rochester

JULY
1-3	Rochester
4-9	at Scranton/WB
14-16	Charlotte
18-23	at Toledo
25-30	Syracuse

AUGUST
1-6	Buffalo
8-13	at Rochester
15-20	Jacksonville
22-27	at Scranton/WB
29-31	Syracuse

SEPTEMBER
1-3	Syracuse
5-10	at Buffalo
12-17	at Rochester
19-24	Worcester

LOUISVILLE BATS

MARCH
31	at Nashville

APRIL
1-2	at Nashville
4-9	Indianapolis
11-16	at Toledo
18-23	Charlotte
25-30	at Iowa

MAY
2-7	at Omaha
9-14	Columbus
16-21	Jacksonville
23-28	at Syracuse
30-31	Worcester

JUNE
1-4	Worcester
6-11	at Columbus
13-18	St. Paul
20-25	at Charlotte
28-30	Indianapolis

JULY
1-3	Indianapolis
4-9	at Toledo
14-16	Nashville
18-23	Columbus
25-30	at Indianapolis

AUGUST
1-6	Omaha
9-13	at St. Paul
15-20	at Iowa
22-27	Toledo
29-31	at Omaha

SEPTEMBER
1-3	at Omaha
5-10	St. Paul
12-17	at Durham
19-24	Iowa

MEMPHIS REDBIRDS

MARCH
31	at Charlotte

APRIL
1-2	at Charlotte
4-9	Nashville
11-16	at Gwinnett
18-23	Indianapolis
25-30	at Durham

MAY
2-7	Jacksonville
9-14	at Lehigh Valley
16-21	Gwinnett
23-28	Norfolk
31	at Omaha

JUNE
1-4	at Omaha
7-11	Durham
13-18	at Jacksonville
20-25	at Iowa

29-30	Nashville

JULY
1-3	Nashville
4-9	at Indianapolis
15-16	Gwinnett
18-23	at Charlotte
26-30	Iowa

AUGUST
2-6	Jacksonville
8-13	at Durham
15-20	Norfolk
22-27	at Charlotte
29-31	Gwinnett

SEPTEMBER
2-3	Gwinnett
5-10	at Nashville
12-17	at Norfolk
19-24	Charlotte

NASHVILLE SOUNDS

MARCH
31	Louisville

APRIL
1-2	Louisville
4-9	at Memphis
11-16	Norfolk
18-23	at Jacksonville
25-30	Omaha

MAY
2-7	at St. Paul
9-14	Gwinnett
16-21	at Durham
23-28	Iowa
30-31	at Charlotte

JUNE
1-4	at Charlotte
6-11	at Jacksonville
13-18	Gwinnett
20-25	Norfolk
29-30	at Memphis

JULY
1-3	at Memphis
4-9	Columbus
14-16	at Louisville
18-23	Jacksonville
25-30	at Norfolk

AUGUST
1-6	Durham
8-13	at Indianapolis
15-20	Charlotte
22-27	at Gwinnett
29-31	at Durham

SEPTEMBER
1-3	at Durham
5-10	Memphis
12-17	at Charlotte
19-24	Jacksonville

SCHEDULES

NORFOLK TIDES

MARCH
31 . . . . at Durham

APRIL
1-2 . . . . at Durham
4-9 . . . . Gwinnett
11-16 . . . . . . at Nashville
18-23 . . . . Rochester
25-30 . . . . . . at Charlotte

MAY
2-7 . . . . Durham
9-14 . . . . . at Jacksonville
16-21 . . . . Syracuse
23-28 . . . . . . at Memphis
30-31 . . . . Gwinnett

JUNE
1-4 . . . . Gwinnett
6-11 . . . . at Scranton/WB
13-18 . . . . Worcester

20-25 . . . . . . at Nashville
28-30 . . . . Charlotte

JULY
1-3 . . . . Charlotte
4-9 . . . . at Durham
14-16 . . . . . Scranton/WB
18-23 . . . . . . at Gwinnett
25-30 . . . . Nashville

AUGUST
1-6 . . . . Charlotte
8-13 . . . . . at Jacksonville
15-20 . . . . . at Memphis
22-27 . . . . Durham
29-31 . . . . . at Worcester

SEPTEMBER
1-3 . . . . . . at Worcester
5-10 . . . . . Jacksonville
12-17 . . . . Memphis
19-24 . . . . . . at Buffalo

OMAHA STORM CHASERS

MARCH
31 . . . . . at Indianapolis

APRIL
1-2 . . . . at Indianapolis
4-9 . . . . Toledo
11-16 . . . . . . at Iowa
18-23 . . . . Gwinnett
25-30 . . . . . at Nashville

MAY
2-7 . . . . Louisville
9-14 . . . . at Scranton/WB
16-21 . . . . Toledo
23-28 . . . . . . at St. Paul
31 . . . . Memphis

JUNE
1-4 . . . . Memphis
6-11 . . . . at Indianapolis
14-18 . . . . Columbus

20-25 . . . . . at Rochester
28-30 . . . . Iowa

JULY
1-4 . . . . Iowa
4-9 . . . . . . at Gwinnett
15-16 . . . . . Indianapolis
18-23 . . . . St. Paul
25-30 . . . . at Columbus

AUGUST
1-6 . . . . . . at Louisville
9-13 . . . . Iowa
15-20 . . . . . . at Toledo
22-27 . . . . . . St. Paul
29-31 . . . . . . Louisville

SEPTEMBER
1-3 . . . . Louisville
5-10 . . . . at Iowa
12-17 . . . . . Indianapolis
19-24 . . . . at Columbus

ROCHESTER RED WINGS

MARCH
31 . . . . . . Lehigh Valley

APRIL
1-2 . . . . . Lehigh Valley
4-9 . . . . . at Syracuse
11-16 . . . . Buffalo
18-23 . . . . . . at Norfolk
25-30 . . . . St. Paul

MAY
2-7 . . . . at Scranton/WB
9-14 . . . . . . Worcester
16-21 . . . . . at Buffalo
23-28 . . . . . . at Toledo
29-31 . . . . . . Syracuse

JUNE
1-4 . . . . Syracuse
6-11 . . . . . . at Worcester
13-18 . . . . . Scranton/WB

20-25 . . . . Omaha
28-30 . . . at Lehigh Valley

JULY
1-3 . . . . at Lehigh Valley
4-9 . . . . Buffalo
14-16 . . . . . at Syracuse
18-23 . . . . . . Durham
25-30 . . . . at Worcester

AUGUST
1-6 . . . . at Scranton/WB
8-13 . . . . . Lehigh Valley
15-20 . . . . . at Buffalo
22-27 . . . . . Worcester
29-31 . . . . Scranton/WB

SEPTEMBER
1-3 . . . . . . Scranton/WB
5-10 . . . . . at Syracuse
12-17 . . . . Lehigh Valley
19-24 . . . at Indianapolis

SCRANTON/WILKES-BARRE RAILRIDERS

MARCH
31 . . . . Buffalo

APRIL
1-2 . . . . Buffalo
4-8 . . . . at Lehigh Valley
11-16 . . . . . . Syracuse
18-23 . . . . . at St. Paul
25-30 . . . . . at Worcester

MAY
2-7 . . . . Rochester
9-14 . . . . Omaha
16-21 . . . . at Charlotte
23-28 . . . . . . Worcester
30-31 . . . at Lehigh Valley

JUNE
1-4 . . . . at Lehigh Valley
6-11 . . . . Norfolk
13-18 . . . . . at Rochester

20-25 . . . . Buffalo
28-30 . . . . . at Syracuse

JULY
1-3 . . . . . at Syracuse
4-9 . . . . . Lehigh Valley
14-16 . . . . . at Norfolk
18-23 . . . . . Worcester
25-30 . . . . . at Buffalo

AUGUST
1-6 . . . . Rochester
8-13 . . . . . . Syracuse
15-20 . . . . at Worcester
22-27 . . . . Lehigh Valley
29-31 . . . . at Rochester

SEPTEMBER
1-3 . . . . . . at Rochester
5-10 . . . . at Columbus
12-17 . . . . Buffalo
19-24 . . . . at Syracuse

ST. PAUL SAINTS

MARCH
31 . . . . at Toledo

APRIL
1-2 . . . . at Toledo
4-9 . . . . Iowa
11-16 . . . . at Indianapolis
18-23 . . . . . Scranton/WB
25-30 . . . . . at Rochester

MAY
2-7 . . . . Nashville
9-14 . . . . . Indianapolis
16-21 . . . . at Columbus
23-28 . . . . . . Omaha
30-31 . . . . . . at Buffalo

JUNE
1-4 . . . . at Buffalo
7-11 . . . . Iowa
13-18 . . . . . at Louisville

20-25 . . . . at Toledo
28-30 . . . . Gwinnett

JULY
1-3 . . . . . . Gwinnett
5-9 . . . . at Iowa
15-16 . . . . . Durham
18-23 . . . . . at Omaha
26-30 . . . . Toledo

AUGUST
1-6 . . . . . at Columbus
9-13 . . . . . . Louisville
16-20 . . . . . Indianapolis
22-27 . . . . . at Omaha
30-31 . . . . . Columbus

SEPTEMBER
1-3 . . . . Columbus
5-10 . . . . . at Louisville
12-17 . . . . . . at Iowa
19-24 . . . . Toledo

SYRACUSE METS

MARCH
31 . . . . . . at Worcester

APRIL
1-2 . . . . . at Worcester
4-9 . . . . . . Rochester
11-16 . . . at Scranton/WB
18-23 . . . . Durham
25-30 . . . . . . at Toledo

MAY
2-7 . . . . . Lehigh Valley
9-14 . . . . . at Buffalo
16-21 . . . . . at Norfolk
23-28 . . . . . Louisville
29-31 . . . . at Rochester

JUNE
1-4 . . . . . . at Rochester
6-11 . . . . Lehigh Valley
13-18 . . . . . at Buffalo

20-25 . . . . . at Durham
28-30 . . . . Scranton/WB

JULY
1-3 . . . . . Scranton/WB
4-9 . . . . . at Worcester
14-16 . . . . . Rochester
18-23 . . . . . . Buffalo
25-30 . . . at Lehigh Valley

AUGUST
1-6 . . . . Worcester
8-13 . . . at Scranton/WB
15-20 . . . . Columbus
22-27 . . . . . . Buffalo
29-31 . . . at Lehigh Valley

SEPTEMBER
1-3 . . . . at Lehigh Valley
5-10 . . . . . . Rochester
12-17 . . . . at Worcester
19-24 . . . . Scranton/WB

SCHEDULES

TOLEDO MUD HENS

MARCH
31 . . . . St. Paul

APRIL
1-2 . . . . St. Paul
4-9 . . . . at Omaha
11-16 . . . . Louisville
18-23 . . . . . at Columbus
25-30 . . . . Syracuse

MAY
2-7 . . . . Indianapolis
9-14 . . . . at Iowa
16-21 . . . . at Omaha
23-28 . . . . Rochester
29-31 . . . . at Indianapolis

JUNE
1-4 . . . . . at Indianapolis
6-11 . . . . Buffalo
13-18 . . . . at Lehigh Valley

20-25 . . . . St. Paul
28-30 . . . . . at Columbus

JULY
1-3 . . . . . . at Columbus
4-9 . . . . Louisville
14-16 . . . . . . at Buffalo
18-23 . . . . . Lehigh Valley
26-30 . . . . at St. Paul

AUGUST
1-6 . . . . at Iowa
8-13 . . . . Columbus
15-20 . . . . Omaha
22-27 . . . . at Louisville
29-31 . . . . Iowa

SEPTEMBER
1-3 . . . . Iowa
5-10 . . . . . at Indianapolis
12-17 . . . . Columbus
19-24 . . . . at St. Paul

WORCESTER RED SOX

MARCH
31 . . . . Syracuse

APRIL
1-2 . . . . Syracuse
4-9 . . . . at Buffalo
11-16 . . . . Columbus
18-23 . . . . at Lehigh Valley
25-30 . . . . . Scranton/WB

MAY
2-7 . . . . Buffalo
9-14 . . . . . at Rochester
16-21 . . . . . Lehigh Valley
23-28 . . . . at Scranton/WB
30-31 . . . . . . at Louisville

JUNE
1-4 . . . . at Louisville
6-11 . . . . Rochester
13-18 . . . . at Norfolk
20-25 . . . . . Lehigh Valley

28-30 . . . . at Buffalo

JULY
1-3 . . . . at Buffalo
4-9 . . . . Syracuse
14-16 . . . . at Jacksonville
18-23 . . . . at Scranton/WB
25-30 . . . . Rochester

AUGUST
1-6 . . . . at Syracuse
8-13 . . . . Buffalo
15-20 . . . . . Scranton/WB
22-27 . . . at Rochester
29-31 . . . . Norfolk

SEPTEMBER
1-3 . . . . Norfolk
5-10 . . . . . . at Gwinnett
12-17 . . . . Syracuse
19-24 . . . . at Lehigh Valley

PACIFIC COAST LEAGUE

ALBUQUERQUE ISOTOPES

APRIL
1-2 . . . . . at Round Rock
5-9 . . . . Salt Lake
12-16 . . . . at El Paso
19-23 . . . . . . Okla. City
26-30 . . . . at Round Rock

MAY
3-7 . . . . Sugar Land
10-14 . . . . at Las Vegas
17-21 . . . . Tacoma
24-28 . . . . . Round Rock
31 . . . . at Salt Lake

JUNE
1-4 . . . . . . at Salt Lake
7-12 . . . . . . Sugar Land
13-18 . . . . at Tacoma
20-25 . . . . at Reno
29-29 . . . . El Paso

JULY
1-4 . . . . El Paso
5-9 . . . . . . at Okla. City
15-17 . . . . . . Salt Lake
18-23 . . . . at Sugar Land
26-31 . . . . . Sacramento

AUGUST
2-7 . . . . Las Vegas
9-13 . . . . . at Round Rock
16-20 . . . . El Paso
23-27 . . . . at Okla. City
30-31 . . . . . at Sacramento

SEPTEMBER
1-3 . . . . . . at Sacramento
6-10 . . . . Reno
13-17 . . . . . . at El Paso
20-24 . . . . Okla. City

EL PASO CHIHUAHUAS

APRIL
1-2 . . . . Sugar Land
5-9 . . . . . at Sacramento
12-16 . . . . . Albuquerque
19-23 . . . . . . at Tacoma
26-30 . . . . Salt Lake

MAY
3-7 . . . . Okla. City
9-14 . . . . . at Sugar Land
17-21 . . . . at Round Rock
24-29 . . . . Reno
31 . . . . at Las Vegas

JUNE
1-4 . . . . . . at Las Vegas
7-12 . . . . Okla. City
14-18 . . . . at Round Rock
21-26 . . . . Tacoma
29-29 . . . . at Albuquerque

JULY
1-4 . . . . at Albuquerque
5-10 . . . . Las Vegas
15-16 . . . . at Sugar Land
19-23 . . . . . at Okla. City
26-31 . . . . . Round Rock

AUGUST
2-6 . . . . at Salt Lake
9-14 . . . . Sugar Land
16-20 . . . at Albuquerque
23-28 . . . . . Sacramento
30-31 . . . . at Reno

SEPTEMBER
1-4 . . . . at Reno
6-11 . . . . . . Round Rock
13-17 . . . . . Albuquerque
19-24 . . . . at Sugar Land

156 · Baseball America 2023 Directory

BaseballAmerica.com

SCHEDULES

LAS VEGAS AVIATORS

MARCH
31 . . . . at Reno

APRIL
1-2 . . . . at Reno
5-9 . . . . Okla. City
12-16 . . . . Salt Lake
18-23 . . . . . at Sugar Land
26-30 . . . . Tacoma

MAY
3-7 . . . . . at Sacramento
10-14 . . . . Albuquerque
17-21 . . . . . . at Salt Lake
23-28 . . . . at Tacoma
31 . . . . El Paso

JUNE
1-4 . . . . El Paso
7-11 . . . . . at Sacramento
14-18 . . . . Reno
21-25 . . . . . at Okla. City
29-30 . . . . . Round Rock

JULY
1-4 . . . . . . Round Rock
5-10 . . . . at El Paso
15-17 . . . . Reno
19-24 . . . . . at Salt Lake
26-31 . . . . . . Sugar Land

AUGUST
2-7 . . . . at Albuquerque
9-14 . . . . . . Sacramento
16-20 . . . . at Reno
23-27 . . . . . . at Tacoma
30-31 . . . . Salt Lake

SEPTEMBER
1-4 . . . . Salt Lake
6-11 . . . . . . Sacramento
12-17 . . . . . at Round Rock
20-24 . . . . Reno

OKLAHOMA CITY DODGERS

APRIL
1-2 . . . . Tacoma
5-9 . . . . . at Las Vegas
11-16 . . . . . . Sugar Land
19-23 . . . . at Albuquerque
25-30 . . . . . . Sacramento

MAY
3-7 . . . . at El Paso
10-14 . . . . at Round Rock
17-21 . . . . . . Sugar Land
24-28 . . . . at Sacramento
31 . . . . Reno

JUNE
1-4 . . . . Reno
7-12 . . . . . . at El Paso
14-18 . . . . Salt Lake
21-25 . . . . Las Vegas
29-30 . . . . . at Sugar Land

JULY
1-3 . . . . . at Sugar Land
5-9 . . . . . Albuquerque
15-16 . . . . at Sacramento
19-23 . . . . El Paso
26-30 . . . . at Reno

AUGUST
2-6 . . . . . . Round Rock
8-13 . . . . at Tacoma
16-20 . . . . . . at Salt Lake
23-27 . . . . . Albuquerque
30-31 . . . . . Round Rock

SEPTEMBER
1-3 . . . . . . Round Rock
5-10 . . . . at Sugar Land
13-17 . . . . Tacoma
20-24 . . . . at Albuquerque

RENO ACES

MARCH
31 . . . . Las Vegas

APRIL
1-2 . . . . Las Vegas
5-9 . . . . . . at Tacoma
12-16 . . . . . Sacramento
19-23 . . . . . at Salt Lake
26-30 . . . . . . Sugar Land

MAY
3-7 . . . . . . Round Rock
10-14 . . . . . at Tacoma
16-21 . . . . . Sacramento
24-29 . . . . . . at El Paso
31 . . . . . . at Okla. City

JUNE
1-4 . . . . . . at Okla. City
7-11 . . . . Tacoma
14-18 . . . . . at Las Vegas
20-25 . . . . . Albuquerque
29-30 . . . . at Sacramento

JULY
1-4 . . . . . at Sacramento
5-9 . . . . Tacoma
15-17 . . . . . at Las Vegas
19-23 . . . . at Round Rock
26-30 . . . . Okla. City

AUGUST
2-6 . . . . . at Sacramento
9-13 . . . . Salt Lake
16-20 . . . . . . Las Vegas
22-27 . . . . at Sugar Land
30-31 . . . . El Paso

SEPTEMBER
1-4 . . . . El Paso
6-10 . . . . at Albuquerque
13-17 . . . . Salt Lake
20-24 . . . . . at Las Vegas

ROUND ROCK EXPRESS

APRIL
1-2 . . . . . . Albuquerque
4-9 . . . . . at Sugar Land
11-16 . . . . Tacoma
19-23 . . . . at Sacramento
26-30 . . . . . Albuquerque

MAY
3-7 . . . . at Reno
10-14 . . . . Okla. City
17-21 . . . . El Paso
24-28 . . . at Albuquerque
31 . . . . Sugar Land

JUNE
1-4 . . . . Sugar Land
7-11 . . . . . at Salt Lake
14-18 . . . . El Paso
21-25 . . . . . Sacramento
29-30 . . . . . at Las Vegas

JULY
1-4 . . . . . . at Las Vegas
4-9 . . . . Sugar Land
15-16 . . . . . . at Tacoma
19-23 . . . . Reno
26-31 . . . . at El Paso

AUGUST
2-6 . . . . . at Okla. City
9-13 . . . . . Albuquerque
15-20 . . . at Sugar Land
23-27 . . . . . Salt Lake
30-31 . . . . . at Okla. City

SEPTEMBER
1-3 . . . . . . at Okla. City
6-11 . . . . . . at El Paso
12-17 . . . . Las Vegas
20-24 . . . . . . at Tacoma

SACRAMENTO RIVER CATS

MARCH
31 . . . . at Salt Lake

APRIL
1-2 . . . . . . at Salt Lake
5-9 . . . . El Paso
12-16 . . . . at Reno
19-23 . . . . . Round Rock
25-30 . . . . . at Okla. City

MAY
3-7 . . . . Las Vegas
10-14 . . . . Salt Lake
16-21 . . . . at Reno
24-28 . . . . . Okla. City
31 . . . . at Tacoma

JUNE
1-4 . . . . at Tacoma
7-11 . . . . Las Vegas
14-18 . . . . at Sugar Land
21-25 . . . . . at Round Rock
29-30 . . . . Reno

JULY
1-4 . . . . Reno
5-9 . . . . at Salt Lake
15-16 . . . . Okla. City
19-23 . . . . Tacoma
26-31 . . . . at Albuquerque

AUGUST
2-6 . . . . Reno
9-14 . . . . . . at Las Vegas
16-20 . . . . . . Tacoma
23-28 . . . . . . at El Paso
30-31 . . . . . Albuquerque

SEPTEMBER
1-3 . . . . Albuquerque
6-11 . . . . . . at Las Vegas
13-17 . . . . . . Sugar Land
20-24 . . . . . . at Salt Lake

SCHEDULES

SALT LAKE BEES

MARCH	
31	Sacramento

APRIL	
1-2	Sacramento
5-9	at Albuquerque
12-16	at Las Vegas
19-23	Reno
26-30	at El Paso

MAY	
3-7	Tacoma
10-14	at Sacramento
17-21	Las Vegas
23-28	at Sugar Land
31	Albuquerque

JUNE	
1-4	Albuquerque
7-11	Round Rock
14-18	at Okla. City
21-25	Sugar Land
29-30	at Tacoma

JULY	
1-4	at Tacoma
5-9	Sacramento
15-17	at Albuquerque
19-24	Las Vegas
25-30	at Tacoma

AUGUST	
2-6	El Paso
9-13	at Reno
16-20	Okla. City
23-27	at Round Rock
30-31	at Las Vegas

SEPTEMBER	
1-4	at Las Vegas
6-10	Tacoma
13-17	at Reno
20-24	Sacramento

SUGAR LAND SPACE COWBOYS

APRIL	
1-2	at El Paso
4-9	Round Rock
11-16	at Okla. City
18-23	Las Vegas
26-30	at Reno

MAY	
3-7	at Albuquerque
9-14	El Paso
17-21	at Okla. City
23-28	Salt Lake
31	at Round Rock

JUNE	
1-4	at Round Rock
7-12	at Albuquerque
14-18	Sacramento
21-25	at Salt Lake
29-30	Okla. City

JULY	
1-3	Okla. City
4-9	at Round Rock
15-16	El Paso
18-23	Albuquerque
26-31	at Las Vegas

AUGUST	
2-6	Tacoma
9-14	at El Paso
15-20	Round Rock
22-27	Reno
30-31	at Tacoma

SEPTEMBER	
1-3	at Tacoma
5-10	Okla. City
13-17	at Sacramento
19-24	El Paso

TACOMA RAINIERS

APRIL	
1-2	at Okla. City
5-9	Reno
11-16	at Round Rock
19-23	El Paso
26-30	at Las Vegas

MAY	
3-7	at Salt Lake
10-14	Reno
17-21	at Albuquerque
23-28	Las Vegas
31	Sacramento

JUNE	
1-4	Sacramento
7-11	at Reno
13-18	Albuquerque
21-26	at El Paso
29-30	Salt Lake

JULY	
1-4	Salt Lake
5-9	at Reno
15-16	Round Rock
19-23	at Sacramento
25-30	Salt Lake

AUGUST	
2-6	at Sugar Land
8-13	Okla. City
16-20	at Sacramento
23-27	Las Vegas
30-31	Sugar Land

SEPTEMBER	
1-3	Sugar Land
6-10	at Salt Lake
13-17	at Okla. City
20-24	Round Rock

DOUBLE-A

EASTERN LEAGUE

AKRON RUBBERDUCKS

APRIL	
6-8	Erie
11-16	at Bowie
18-23	Harrisburg
25-30	at Binghamton

MAY	
2-7	Portland
9-14	at Altoona
16-21	at Richmond
23-28	Bowie
30-31	Hartford

JUNE	
1-4	Hartford
6-11	at Portland
13-18	at New Hampshire
20-25	Binghamton
28-30	at Erie

JULY	
1-3	at Erie
4-9	Harrisburg
14-16	at Bowie
18-23	Richmond
25-30	at Erie

AUGUST	
1-6	Somerset
8-13	at Harrisburg
15-20	Erie
22-27	at Altoona
29-31	Bowie

SEPTEMBER	
1-3	Bowie
5-10	at Richmond
12-17	Altoona

ALTOONA CURVE

APRIL	
6-8	New Hampshire
11-16	at Erie
18-23	Bowie
25-30	at Reading

MAY	
2-7	at Richmond
9-14	Akron
16-21	at Bowie
23-28	Hartford
30-31	Binghamton

JUNE	
1-4	Binghamton
6-11	at Richmond
13-18	at Somerset
20-25	Bowie
28-30	at Harrisburg

JULY	
1-3	at Harrisburg
4-9	Erie
14-16	at New Hampshire
18-23	Reading
25-30	at Harrisburg

AUGUST	
1-6	Richmond
8-13	Erie
15-20	at Bowie
22-27	Akron
29-31	at Erie

SEPTEMBER	
1-3	at Erie
5-10	Harrisburg
12-17	at Akron

158 · Baseball America 2023 Directory

BaseballAmerica.com

SCHEDULES

BINGHAMTON RUMBLE PONIES

APRIL
6-8 . . . . at Portland
11-16 . . . . Somerset
18-23 . . . . . . at Hartford
25-30 . . . . .Akron

MAY
2-7 . . . . .at Somerset
9-14 . . . . Hartford
16-21 . . at New Hampshire
23-28 . . . . . . .Richmond
30-31 . . . . . . .at Altoona

JUNE
1-4 . . . . .at Altoona
6-11 . . . . .at Reading
13-18 . . . . Portland
20-25 . . . . . . at Akron
28-30 . . . . Hartford

JULY
1-3 . . . . Hartford
4-9 . . . . at Portland
14-16 . . . . Somerset
18-23 . . . . Erie
25-30 . . . . . . .at Reading

AUGUST
1-6 . . . . . New Hampshire
8-13 . . . . . . .at Somerset
15-20 . . . . Portland
22-27 . . at New Hampshire
29-31 . . . . . . .Harrisburg

SEPTEMBER
1-3 . . . . .Harrisburg
5-10 . . . . . at Hartford
12-17 . . . . Reading

BOWIE BAYSOX

APRIL
6-8 . . . . at Hartford
11-16 . . . . .Akron
18-23 . . . . . . .at Altoona
25-30 . . . . Richmond

MAY
2-7 . . . . Erie
9-14 . . . . . . at Harrisburg
16-21 . . . . Altoona
23-28 . . . . . . at Akron
30-31 . . . . . . .Harrisburg

JUNE
1-4 . . . . .Harrisburg
6-11 . . . . at Erie
13-18 . . . . . . .Richmond
20-25 . . . . . . .at Altoona
28-30 . . . . Somerset

JULY
1-3 . . . . Somerset
4-9 . . . . . . at Richmond
14-16 . . . . .Akron
18-23 . . . . . . .Harrisburg
25-30 . . . . . .at Somerset

AUGUST
1-6 . . . . Portland
8-13 . . . . . . at Richmond
15-20 . . . . Altoona
22-27 . . . . at Erie
29-31 . . . . at Akron

SEPTEMBER
1-3 . . . . at Akron
5-10 . . . . . New Hampshire
12-17 . . . . . at Harrisburg

ERIE SEAWOLVES

APRIL
6-8 . . . . at Akron
11-16 . . . . Altoona
18-23 . . . . . . at Richmond
25-30 . . . . Portland

MAY
2-7 . . . . at Bowie
9-14 . . . . Richmond
16-21 . . . . . at Harrisburg
23-28 . . . . Somerset
30-31 . . . . . at Richmond

JUNE
1-4 . . . . at Richmond
6-11 . . . . .Bowie
13-18 . . . . at Harrisburg
20-25 . . . . . . at Hartford
28-30 . . . . .Akron

JULY
1-3 . . . . .Akron
4-9 . . . . .at Altoona
14-16 . . . . Hartford
18-23 . . . . .at Binghamton
25-30 . . . . .Akron

AUGUST
1-6 . . . . .Harrisburg
8-13 . . . . . . .at Altoona
15-20 . . . . . . at Akron
22-27 . . . . .Bowie
29-31 . . . . Altoona

SEPTEMBER
1-3 . . . . Altoona
5-10 . . . . . .at Somerset
12-17 . . . . Richmond

HARRISBURG SENATORS

APRIL
6-8 . . . . .at Somerset
11-16 . . . . . . .Richmond
18-23 . . . . at Akron
25-30 . . . . Somerset

MAY
2-7 . . at New Hampshire
9-14 . . . . .Bowie
16-21 . . . . Erie
23-28 . . . . . . .at Reading
30-31 . . . . . . at Bowie

JUNE
1-4 . . . . at Bowie
6-11 . . . . New Hampshire
13-18 . . . . Erie
20-25 . . . . . at Richmond
28-30 . . . . Altoona

JULY
1-3 . . . . Altoona
4-9 . . . . at Akron
14-16 . . . . . . .Richmond
18-23 . . . . . . .at Bowie
25-30 . . . . Altoona

AUGUST
1-6 . . . . at Erie
8-13 . . . . .Akron
15-20 . . . . at Richmond
22-27 . . . . Reading
29-31 . . . . .at Binghamton

SEPTEMBER
1-3 . . . . . .at Binghamton
5-10 . . . . .at Altoona
12-17 . . . . .Bowie

HARTFORD YARD GOATS

APRIL
6-8 . . . . .Bowie
11-16 . . . . .at Reading
18-23 . . . . . Binghamton
25-30 . . at New Hampshire

MAY
2-7 . . . . Reading
9-14 . . . .at Binghamton
16-21 . . . . Portland
23-28 . . . . . . .at Altoona
30-31 . . . . . . at Akron

JUNE
1-4 . . . . at Akron
6-11 . . . . Somerset
13-18 . . . . . .at Reading
20-25 . . . . Erie
28-30 . . . . .at Binghamton

JULY
1-3 . . . . . .at Binghamton
4-9 . . . . . New Hampshire
14-16 . . . . . . at Erie
18-23 . . . . Somerset
25-30 . . at New Hampshire

AUGUST
1-6 . . . . Reading
8-13 . . . . at Portland
15-20 . . . New Hampshire
22-27 . . . . . .at Somerset
29-31 . . . . Richmond

SEPTEMBER
1-3 . . . . .Richmond
5-10 . . . . . . Binghamton
12-17 . . . . . . at Portland

NEW HAMPSHIRE FISHER CATS

APRIL
6-8 . . . . .at Altoona
11-16 . . . . Portland
18-23 . . . . . .at Somerset
25-30 . . . . Hartford

MAY
2-7 . . . . .Harrisburg
9-14 . . . . . . .at Reading
16-21 . . . . . Binghamton
23-28 . . . . . . at Portland
30-31 . . . . Reading

JUNE
1-4 . . . . Reading
6-11 . . . . . at Harrisburg
13-18 . . . . .Akron
20-25 . . . . . .at Somerset
28-30 . . . . Portland

JULY
1-3 . . . . Portland
4-9 . . . . at Hartford
14-16 . . . . Altoona
18-23 . . . . . . at Portland
25-30 . . . . Hartford

AUGUST
1-6 . . . . . .at Binghamton
8-13 . . . . Reading
15-20 . . . . . . at Hartford
22-27 . . . . . Binghamton
29-31 . . . . . . .at Reading

SEPTEMBER
1-3 . . . . .at Reading
5-10 . . . . .at Bowie
12-17 . . . . Somerset

BaseballAmerica.com

Baseball America 2023 Directory • **159**

SCHEDULES

PORTLAND SEA DOGS

APRIL	
6-8	Binghamton
11-16	at New Hampshire
18-23	Reading
25-30	at Erie

MAY	
2-7	at Akron
9-14	Somerset
16-21	at Hartford
23-28	New Hampshire
30-31	at Somerset

JUNE	
1-4	at Somerset
6-11	Akron
13-18	at Binghamton
20-25	Reading
28-30	at New Hampshire

JULY	
1-3	at New Hampshire
4-9	Binghamton
14-16	at Reading
18-23	New Hampshire
25-30	at Richmond

AUGUST	
1-6	at Bowie
8-13	Hartford
15-20	at Binghamton
22-27	Richmond
29-31	Somerset

SEPTEMBER	
1-3	Somerset
5-10	at Reading
12-17	Hartford

READING FIGHTIN PHILS

APRIL	
7-9	at Richmond
11-16	Hartford
18-23	at Portland
25-30	Altoona

MAY	
2-7	at Hartford
9-14	New Hampshire
16-21	at Somerset
23-28	Harrisburg
30-31	at New Hampshire

JUNE	
1-4	at New Hampshire
6-11	Binghamton
13-18	Hartford
20-25	at Portland
28-30	Richmond

JULY	
1-3	Richmond
4-9	at Somerset
14-16	Portland
18-23	at Altoona
25-30	Binghamton

AUGUST	
1-6	at Hartford
8-13	at New Hampshire
15-20	Somerset
22-27	at Harrisburg
29-31	New Hampshire

SEPTEMBER	
1-3	New Hampshire
5-10	Portland
12-17	at Binghamton

RICHMOND FLYING SQUIRRELS

APRIL	
7-9	Reading
11-16	at Harrisburg
18-23	Erie
25-30	at Bowie

MAY	
2-7	Altoona
9-14	at Erie
16-21	Akron
23-28	at Binghamton
30-31	Erie

JUNE	
1-4	Erie
6-11	Altoona
13-18	at Bowie
20-25	Harrisburg
28-30	at Reading

JULY	
1-3	at Reading
4-9	Bowie
14-16	at Harrisburg
18-23	at Akron
25-30	Portland

AUGUST	
1-6	at Altoona
8-13	Bowie
15-20	Harrisburg
22-27	at Portland
29-31	at Hartford

SEPTEMBER	
1-3	at Hartford
5-10	Akron
12-17	at Erie

SOMERSET PATRIOTS

APRIL	
6-8	Harrisburg
11-16	at Binghamton
18-23	New Hampshire
25-30	at Harrisburg

MAY	
2-7	Binghamton
9-14	at Portland
16-21	Reading
23-28	at Erie
30-31	Portland

JUNE	
1-4	Portland
6-11	at Hartford
13-18	Altoona
20-25	New Hampshire
28-30	at Bowie

JULY	
1-3	at Bowie
4-9	Reading
14-16	at Binghamton
18-23	at Hartford
25-30	Bowie

AUGUST	
1-6	at Akron
8-13	Binghamton
15-20	at Reading
22-27	Hartford
29-31	at Portland

SEPTEMBER	
1-3	at Portland
5-10	Erie
12-17	at New Hampshire

SOUTHERN LEAGUE

BILOXI SHUCKERS

APRIL	
7-9	at Mississippi
11-16	Pensacola
18-23	at Rocket City
25-30	Mississippi

MAY	
2-7	at Montgomery
9-14	Rocket City
16-21	at Chattanooga
23-28	Montgomery
30-31	Pensacola

JUNE	
1-4	Pensacola
6-11	at Mississippi
13-18	at Montgomery
20-25	Chattanooga
28-30	Mississippi

JULY	
1-3	Mississippi
4-9	at Pensacola
14-16	Rocket City
18-23	at Montgomery
25-30	Birmingham

AUGUST	
1-6	at Pensacola
8-13	Tennessee
15-20	at Mississippi
22-27	Pensacola
29-31	at Tennessee

SEPTEMBER	
1-3	at Tennessee
6-10	at Birmingham
12-17	Montgomery

BIRMINGHAM BARONS

APRIL	
6-8	at Tennessee
12-16	Rocket City
18-23	at Pensacola
25-30	Tennessee

MAY	
2-7	at Chattanooga
9-14	Pensacola
16-21	at Rocket City
23-28	at Tennessee
31	Mississippi

JUNE	
1-4	Mississippi
6-11	at Chattanooga
14-18	Tennessee
20-25	at Mississippi
29-30	Rocket City

JULY	
1-3	Rocket City
4-9	at Tennessee
15-16	Pensacola
19-23	Chattanooga
25-30	at Biloxi

AUGUST	
2-6	Rocket City
8-13	at Montgomery
16-20	Chattanooga
22-27	at Rocket City
30-31	Montgomery

SEPTEMBER	
1-3	Montgomery
6-10	Biloxi
12-17	at Chattanooga

SCHEDULES

CHATTANOOGA LOOKOUTS

APRIL
6-8 . . . . . . .at Rocket City
11-16 . . . . . . .Mississippi
18-23 . . . . . at Tennessee
25-30 . . . . . . Rocket City

MAY
2-7 . . . . Birmingham
9-14 . . . . . at Mississippi
16-21 . . . . Biloxi
23-28 . . . . . .at Rocket City
29-31 . . . . . . at Tennessee

JUNE
1-4at . . . . . . .Tennessee
6-11 . . . . . . Birmingham
13-18 . . . . . . Rocket City
20-25 . . . . at Biloxi
28-30 . . . . . . .Tennessee

JULY
1-3 . . . . .Tennessee
4-9 . . . . . . .at Rocket City
14-16 . . . . . . .Mississippi
19-23 . . . . .at Birmingham
25-30 . . . . . . Montgomery

AUGUST
1-6 . . . . at Tennessee
8-13 . . . . Pensacola
16-20 . . . . .at Birmingham
22-27 . . . . . . .Tennessee
29-31 . . . . . at Pensacola

SEPTEMBER
1-3 . . . . at Pensacola
5-10 . . . . . at Montgomery
12-17 . . . . . . Birmingham

MISSISSIPPI BRAVES

APRIL
7-9 . . . . Biloxi
11-16 . . . . at Chattanooga
18-23 . . . . . Montgomery
25-30 . . . . at Biloxi

MAY
2-7 . . . . at Pensacola
9-14 . . . . . Chattanooga
16-21 . . . . at Montgomery
23-28 . . . . . . Pensacola
31 . . . . . . .at Birmingham

JUNE
1-4 . . . . . .at Birmingham
6-11 . . . . Biloxi
13-18 . . . . . at Pensacola
20-25 . . . . . Birmingham
28-30 . . . . at Biloxi

JULY
1-3 . . . . at Biloxi
4-9 . . . . Montgomery
14-16 . . . . at Chattanooga
18-23 . . . . . at Tennessee
25-30 . . . . Pensacola

AUGUST
1-6 . . . . Montgomery
8-13 . . . . . .at Rocket City
15-20 . . . . Biloxi
22-27 . . . . at Montgomery
29-31 . . . . . . Rocket City

SEPTEMBER
1-3 . . . . Rocket City
5-10 . . . . .Tennessee
12-17 . . . . . at Pensacola

MONTGOMERY BISCUITS

APRIL
7-9 . . . . at Pensacola
11-16 . . . . . . .Tennessee
18-23 . . . . . at Mississippi
25-30 . . . . Pensacola

MAY
2-7 . . . . Biloxi
9-14 . . . . . at Tennessee
16-21 . . . . . .Mississippi
23-28 . . . . at Biloxi
30-31 . . . . . . Rocket City

JUNE
1-4 . . . . Rocket City
6-11 . . . . . at Pensacola
13-18 . . . . Biloxi
20-25 . . .at Rocket City
28-30 . . . . Pensacola

JULY
1-3 . . . . Pensacola
4-9 . . . . . . .at Mississippi
14-16 . . . . .Tennessee
18-23 . . . . Biloxi
25-30 . . . . at Chattanooga

AUGUST
1-6 . . . . . . .at Mississippi
8-13 . . . . . . Birmingham
15-20 . . . . at Pensacola
22-27 . . . . . .Mississippi
30-31 . . . . .at Birmingham

SEPTEMBER
1-3 . . . . . .at Birmingham
5-10 . . . . . . Chattanooga
12-17 . . . . at Biloxi

PENSACOLA BLUE WAHOOS

APRIL
7-9 . . . . Montgomery
11-16 . . . . . . at Biloxi
18-23 . . . . . Birmingham
25-30 . . . at Montgomery

MAY
2-7 . . . . .Mississippi
9-14 . . . . . at Birmingham
16-21 . . . . . . .Tennessee
23-28 . . . at Mississippi
30-31 . . . . at Biloxi

JUNE
1-4 . . . . at Biloxi
6-11 . . . . . . Montgomery
13-18 . . . . . . .Mississippi
20-25 . . . . . at Tennessee
28-30 . . . . at Montgomery

JULY
1-3 . . . . at Montgomery
4-9 . . . . Biloxi
15-16 . . . .at Birmingham
18-23 . . . . . . Rocket City
25-30 . . . . . at Mississippi

AUGUST
1-6 . . . . Biloxi
8-13 . . . . at Chattanooga
15-20 . . . . . Montgomery
22-27 . . . . at Biloxi
29-31 . . . . . Chattanooga

SEPTEMBER
1-3 . . . . Chattanooga
5-10 . . . . . .at Rocket City
12-17 . . . . . . .Mississippi

ROCKET CITY TRASH PANDAS

APRIL
6-8 . . . . Chattanooga
12-16 . . . . .at Birmingham
18-23 . . . . Biloxi
25-30 . . . . at Chattanooga

MAY
2-7 . . . . .Tennessee
9-14 . . . . at Biloxi
16-21 . . . . . Birmingham
23-28 . . . . . Chattanooga
30-31 . . . . at Montgomery

JUNE
1-4 . . . . . at Montgomery
6-11 . . . . . . .Tennessee
13-18 . . . . at Chattanooga
20-25 . . . . . Montgomery
29-30 . . . . .at Birmingham

JULY
1-3 . . . . .at Birmingham
4-9 . . . . Chattanooga
14-16 . . . . . at Biloxi
18-23 . . . . at Pensacola
25-30 . . . . . . .Tennessee

AUGUST
2-6 . . . . . .at Birmingham
8-13 . . . . . .Mississippi
15-20 . . . . . at Tennessee
22-27 . . . . . Birmingham
29-31 . . . . .at Mississippi

SEPTEMBER
1-3 . . . . . . .at Mississippi
5-10 . . . . Pensacola
12-17 . . . . . at Tennessee

TENNESSEE SMOKIES

APRIL
6-8 . . . . Birmingham
11-16 . . . at Montgomery
18-23 . . . . . Chattanooga
25-30 . . . .at Birmingham

MAY
2-7 . . . . . . .at Rocket City
9-14 . . . . . . Montgomery
16-21 . . . at Pensacola
23-28 . . . . . Birmingham
29-31 . . . . . Chattanooga

JUNE
1-4 . . . . Chattanooga
6-11 . . . . . .at Rocket City
14-18 . . .at Birmingham
20-25 . . . . . . Pensacola
28-30 . . . . at Chattanooga

JULY
1-3 . . . . . at Chattanooga
4-9 . . . . . . Birmingham
14-16 . . . . at Montgomery
18-23 . . . . . . .Mississippi
25-30 . . . . .at Rocket City

AUGUST
1-6 . . . . Chattanooga
8-13 . . . . at Biloxi
15-20 . . . . . . Rocket City
22-27 . . . . at Chattanooga
29-31 . . . . Biloxi

SEPTEMBER
1-3 . . . . Biloxi
5-10 . . . . . .at Mississippi
12-17 . . . . . . Rocket City

SCHEDULES

TEXAS LEAGUE

AMARILLO SOD POODLES

APRIL
6-9 . . . . at Frisco
12-16 . . . . . Corpus Christi
19-23 . . . . at NW Arkansas
26-30 . . . . Frisco

MAY
2-7 . . . . . at Corpus Christi
9-14 . . . . Midland
16-21 . . . . at Frisco
24-28 . . . . at San Antonio
31 . . . . Springfield

JUNE
1-4 . . . . Springfield
6-11 . . . . at Midland
14-18 . . . . . San Antonio
20-25 . . . at Corpus Christi
29-30 . . . . Tulsa

JULY
1-3 . . . . Tulsa
4-9 . . . . at Springfield
15-16 . . . . Frisco
19-23 . . . . Wichita
25-30 . . . . . . at Midland

AUGUST
2-6 . . . . . . Corpus Christi
9-13 . . . . at Tulsa
16-20 . . . . Arkansas
23-27 . . . . at San Antonio
29-31 . . . . Midland

SEPTEMBER
2-3 . . . . Midland
5-10 . . . . . . at Arkansas
12-17 . . . . Frisco

ARKANSAS TRAVELERS

APRIL
7-9 . . . . . at Corpus Christi
11-16 . . . . Springfield
18-23 . . . . at Frisco
25-30 . . . . Tulsa

MAY
2-7 . . . . . . at Springfield
9-14 . . . . . . NW Arkansas
17-21 . . . . at Wichita
23-28 . . . . Frisco
30-31 . . . . Midland

JUNE
1-4 . . . . Midland
7-11 . . . . at Tulsa
13-18 . . . . Corpus Christi
21-25 . . . . . . at Wichita
28-29 . . . . . . Springfield

JULY
1-3 . . . . Springfield
5-9 . . . . . at NW Arkansas
15-16 . . . . Corpus Christi
18-23 . . . at Springfield
25-30 . . . . . NW Arkansas

AUGUST
1-6 . . . . San Antonio
8-13 . . . . at Midland
16-20 . . . . . . at Amarillo
22-27 . . . . Wichita
30-31 . . . . at Tulsa

SEPTEMBER
1-3 . . . . at Tulsa
5-10 . . . . Amarillo
13-17 . . . . at NW Arkansas

CORPUS CHRISTI HOOKS

APRIL
7-9 . . . . Arkansas
12-16 . . . . . . at Amarillo
18-23 . . . . . San Antonio
25-30 . . . . . . at Midland

MAY
2-7 . . . . Amarillo
10-14 . . . . at San Antonio
16-21 . . . . Tulsa
23-28 . . . . Midland
31 . . . . . at NW Arkansas

JUNE
1-4 . . . . . at NW Arkansas
6-11 . . . . Frisco
13-18 . . . . . . at Arkansas
20-25 . . . . . . Amarillo
28-30 . . . . . . at Midland

JULY
1-3 . . . . at Midland
4-9 . . . . San Antonio
15-16 . . . . at Arkansas
18-23 . . . . Midland
26-30 . . . . at San Antonio

AUGUST
2-6 . . . . at Amarillo
8-13 . . . . Frisco
15-20 . . . . . NW Arkansas
22-27 . . . . . at Springfield
30-31 . . . . at Frisco

SEPTEMBER
1-3 . . . . at Frisco
5-10 . . . . Wichita
12-17 . . . . at Tulsa

FRISCO ROUGHRIDERS

APRIL
6-9 . . . . Amarillo
12-16 . . . . at San Antonio
18-23 . . . . Arkansas
26-30 . . . . . . at Amarillo

MAY
2-7 . . . . at Midland
9-14 . . . . Wichita
16-21 . . . . Amarillo
23-28 . . . . . at Arkansas
31 . . . . San Antonio

JUNE
1-4 . . . . San Antonio
6-11 . . . . at Corpus Christi
14-18 . . . at NW Arkansas
20-25 . . . . . . Springfield
29-30 . . . . at San Antonio

JULY
1-3 . . . . at San Antonio
5-9 . . . . Midland
15-16 . . . . . . at Amarillo
19-23 . . . . San Antonio
26-30 . . . . at Wichita

AUGUST
2-6 . . . . Midland
8-13 . . . . at Corpus Christi
16-20 Tulsa
22-27 . . . . . . at Midland
30-31 . . . . Corpus Christi

SEPTEMBER
1-3 . . . . . . Corpus Christi
4-10 . . . . . . NW Arkansas
12-17 . . . . at Amarillo

MIDLAND ROCKHOUNDS

APRIL
7-8 . . . . . at NW Arkansas
11-16 . . . . Tulsa
18-23 . . . . . . at Springfield
25-30 . . . . . Corpus Christi

MAY
2-7 . . . . Frisco
9-14 . . . . at Amarillo
16-21 . . . . . San Antonio
23-28 . . . at Corpus Christi
30-31 . . . . at Arkansas

JUNE
1-4 . . . . at Arkansas
6-11 . . . . Amarillo
13-18 . . . . Wichita
21-2 . . . . . 5at San Antonio
28-30 . . . . . Corpus Christi

JULY
1-3 . . . . . Corpus Christi
5-9 . . . . at Frisco
15-16 . . . . Tulsa
18-23 . . . at Corpus Christi
25-30 . . . . Amarillo

AUGUST
2-6 . . . . at Frisco
8-13 . . . . Arkansas
16-20 . . . at San Antonio
22-27 . . . . Frisco
29-31 . . . . . . at Amarillo

SEPTEMBER
2-3 . . . . at Amarillo
5-10 . . . . . . San Antonio
13-17 . . . . at Wichita

NORTHWEST ARKANSAS NATURALS

APRIL
7-8 . . . . Midland
12-16 . . . . at Wichita
19-23 . . . . Amarillo
26-30 . . . . at San Antonio

MAY
2-7 . . . . Wichita
9-14 . . . . at Arkansas
16-21 . . . . . . Springfield
24-28 . . . . at Tulsa
31 . . . . . . Corpus Christi

JUNE
1-4 . . . . . Corpus Christi
6-11 . . . . at Springfield
14-18 . . . . Frisco
21-25 . . . . at Tulsa
29-30 . . . . . . at Wichita

JULY
1-3 . . . . at Wichita
5-9 . . . . Arkansas
15-16 . . . . at San Antonio
19-23 . . . . Tulsa
25-30 . . . . . . at Arkansas

AUGUST
1-6 . . . . . . at Springfield
9-13 . . . . Wichita
15-20 . . . at Corpus Christi
23-27 . . . . Tulsa
30-31 . . . . . . Springfield

SEPTEMBER
1-3 . . . . Springfield
4-10 . . . . at Frisco
13-17 . . . . Arkansas

162 · Baseball America 2023 Directory

BaseballAmerica.com

SCHEDULES

SAN ANTONIO MISSIONS

APRIL
7-9 . . . . .at Tulsa
12-16 . . . . .Frisco
18-23 . . . .at Corpus Christi
26-30 . . . . . . NW Arkansas

MAY
2-7 . . . . .at Tulsa
10-14 . . . . . Corpus Christi
16-21 . . . . at Midland
24-28 . . . . Amarillo
31 . . . . at Frisco

JUNE
1-4 . . . . at Frisco
7-11 . . . . .Wichita
14-18 . . . . . . at Amarillo
21-25 . . . . Midland
29-30 . . . . .Frisco

JULY
1-3 . . . . .Frisco
4-9 . . . . .at Corpus Christi
15-16 . . . . . NW Arkansas
19-23 . . . . at Frisco
26-30 . . . . Corpus Christi

AUGUST
1-6 . . . . at Arkansas
8-13 . . . . . .at Springfield
16-20 . . . . Midland
23-27 . . . . Amarillo
30-31 . . . . at Wichita

SEPTEMBER
1-3 . . . . at Wichita
5-10 . . . . at Midland
13-17 . . . . Springfield

TULSA DRILLERS

APRIL
7-9 . . . . San Antonio
11-16 . . . . . . at Midland
18-23 . . . . .Wichita
25-30 . . . . . . at Arkansas

MAY
2-7 . . . . San Antonio
10-14 . . . . . . Springfield
16-21 . . .at Corpus Christi
24-28 . . . . . NW Arkansas
31 . . . . at Wichita

JUNE
1-4 . . . . at Wichita
7-11 . . . . .Arkansas
13-18 . . . . .at Springfield
21-25 . . . . . NW Arkansas
29-30 . . . . . . at Amarillo

JULY
1-3 . . . . at Amarillo
4-9 . . . . .Wichita
15-16 . . . . . . at Midland
19-23 . . . . at NW Arkansas
26-30 . . . . . . Springfield

AUGUST
2-6 . . . . at Wichita
9-13 . . . . Amarillo
16-20 . . . . at Frisco
23-27 . . . . at NW Arkansas
30-31 . . . . .Arkansas

SEPTEMBER
1-3 . . . . .Arkansas
5-10 . . . . . .at Springfield
12-17 . . . . . Corpus Christi

SPRINGFIELD CARDINALS

APRIL
6-8 . . . . .Wichita
11-16 . . . . . . at Arkansas
18-23 . . . . Midland
26-30 . . . . at Wichita

MAY
2-7 . . . . .Arkansas
10-14 . . . . .at Tulsa
16-21 . . . . at NW Arkansas
23-28 . . . . .Wichita
31- . . . . at Amarillo

JUNE
1-4 . . . . at Amarillo
6-11 . . . . . . NW Arkansas
13-18 . . . . Tulsa
20-25 . . . . at Frisco
28-29 . . . . . . at Arkansas

JULY
1-3at . . . . .Arkansas
4-9 . . . . Amarillo
15-16 . . . . . . at Wichita
18-23 . . . . .Arkansas
26-30 . . . . .at Tulsa

AUGUST
1-6 . . . . NW Arkansas
8-13 . . . . . . San Antonio
16-20 . . . . . . at Wichita
22-27 . . . . Corpus Christi
30-31 . . . . at NW Arkansas

SEPTEMBER
1-3 . . . . . . at NW Arkansas
5-10 . . . . Tulsa
13-17 . . . . .at San Antonio

WICHITA WIND SURGE

APRIL
6-8 . . . . . . .at Springfield
12-16 . . . . . NW Arkansas
18-23 . . . . . . .at Tulsa
26-30 . . . . . . Springfield

MAY
2-7 . . . . . at NW Arkansas
9-14 . . . . at Frisco
17-21 . . . . . . .Arkansas
23-28 . . . . . .at Springfield
31 . . . . Tulsa

JUNE
1-4 . . . . Tulsa
7-11 . . . . .at San Antonio
13-18 . . . . . . at Midland
21-25 . . . . .Arkansas
29-30 . . . . . NW Arkansas

JULY
1-3 . . . . NW Arkansas
4-9 . . . . .at Tulsa
15-16 . . . . Springfield
19-23 . . . . . . at Amarillo
26-30 . . . . .Frisco

AUGUST
2-6 . . . . Tulsa
9-13 . . . . at NW Arkansas
16-20 . . . . . . Springfield
22-27 . . . . . . at Arkansas
30-31 . . . . . . San Antonio

SEPTEMBER
1-3 . . . . San Antonio
5-10 . . . .at Corpus Christi
13-17 . . . . Midland

BaseballAmerica.com

Baseball America 2023 Directory · **163**

SCHEDULES

HIGH-A

MIDWEST LEAGUE

BELOIT SKY CARP

APRIL	
7-9	Wisconsin
11-16	at South Bend
18-23	Cedar Rapids
25-30	at Wisconsin

MAY	
2-7	West Michigan
9-14	at Fort Wayne
16-21	South Bend
23-28	at Quad Cities
30-31	Great Lakes

JUNE	
1-4	Great Lakes
6-11	at Peoria
13-18	Quad Cities
20-25	at Cedar Rapids
28-30	South Bend

JULY	
1-3	South Bend
4-9	at Wisconsin
14-16	Cedar Rapids
18-23	Quad Cities
25-30	at Lake County

AUGUST	
1-6	at Dayton
8-13	Peoria
15-20	at Quad Cities
22-27	Lake County
29-31	Wisconsin

SEPTEMBER	
1-3	Wisconsin
5-10	at Peoria

CEDAR RAPIDS KERNELS

APRIL	
6-8	at Peoria
11-16	Quad Cities
18-23	at Beloit
25-30	West Michigan

MAY	
2-7	at South Bend
9-14	at Quad Cities
16-21	Peoria
23-28	Wisconsin
30-31	at Lansing

JUNE	
1-4	at Lansing
6-11	at Dayton
13-18	South Bend
20-25	Beloit
28-30	at Peoria

JULY	
1-3	at Peoria
4-9	Quad Cities
14-16	at Beloit
18-23	Peoria
25-30	at Wisconsin

AUGUST	
1-6	Lansing
8-13	at Quad Cities
15-20	Wisconsin
22-27	at South Bend
29-31	Lake County

SEPTEMBER	
1-3	Lake County
5-10	at Wisconsin

DAYTON DRAGONS

APRIL	
6-8	at Lake County
11-16	Great Lakes
18-23	at West Michigan
25-30	Lake County

MAY	
2-7	at Lansing
9-14	at Peoria
16-21	Fort Wayne
23-28	at South Bend
30-31	West Michigan

JUNE	
1-4	West Michigan
6-11	Cedar Rapids
13-18	at Fort Wayne
20-25	Lake County
27-30	at West Michigan

JULY	
1-2	at West Michigan
4-9	Great Lakes
14-16	at Lake County
18-23	Wisconsin
25-30	at Great Lakes

AUGUST	
1-6	Beloit
8-13	at Wisconsin
15-20	at Fort Wayne
22-27	Lansing
29-31	at Great Lakes

SEPTEMBER	
1-3	at Great Lakes
5-10	Fort Wayne

FORT WAYNE TINCAPS

APRIL	
6-8	at West Michigan
11-16	Lake County
18-23	at Peoria
25-30	Great Lakes

MAY	
2-7	at Lake County
9-14	Beloit
16-21	at Dayton
23-28	Lansing
30-31	South Bend

JUNE	
1-4	South Bend
6-11	at Quad Cities
13-18	Dayton
20-25	at South Bend
28-30	at Lake County

JULY	
1-3	at Lake County
4-9	West Michigan
14-16	at Great Lakes
18-23	Lake County
25-30	at West Michigan

AUGUST	
1-6	Great Lakes
8-13	at Lansing
15-20	Dayton
22-27	at Great Lakes
29-31	South Bend

SEPTEMBER	
1-3	South Bend
5-10	at Dayton

SCHEDULES

GREAT LAKES LOONS

APRIL
7-9 . . . . Lansing
11-16 . . . . at Dayton
18-23 . . . . . . South Bend
25-30 . . . . . at Fort Wayne

MAY
2-7 . . . . Quad Cities
9-14 . . . . . at Lake County
16-21 . . . . West Michigan
23-28 . . . . at Peoria
30-31 . . . . at Beloit

JUNE
1-4 . . . . at Beloit
6-11 . . . . . . Lake County
13-18 . . . . Wisconsin
20-25 . . . at West Michigan
28-30 . . . . Lansing

JULY
1-3 . . . . Lansing
4-9 . . . . at Dayton
14-16 . . . . . . Fort Wayne
18-23 . . . . . . at Lansing
25-30 . . . . Dayton

AUGUST
1-6 . . . . . at Fort Wayne
8-13 . . . . . West Michigan
15-20 . . . . . at Lansing
22-27 . . . . . . Fort Wayne
29-31 . . . . Dayton

SEPTEMBER
1-3 . . . . Dayton
5-10 . . . . at West Michigan

LAKE COUNTY CAPTAINS

APRIL
6-8 . . . . Dayton
11-16 . . . . at Fort Wayne
18-23 . . . . Lansing
25-30 . . . . at Dayton

MAY
2-7 . . . . Fort Wayne
9-14 . . . . Great Lakes
16-21 . . . . . . at Lansing
23-28 . . . at West Michigan
30-31 . . . . . . Quad Cities

JUNE
1-4 . . . . Quad Cities
6-11 . . . . . at Great Lakes
13-18 . . . . West Michigan
20-25 . . . . at Dayton
28-30 . . . . . . Fort Wayne

JULY
1-3 . . . . Fort Wayne
4-9 . . . . at Lansing
14-16 . . . . Dayton
18-23 . . . . at Fort Wayne
25-30 . . . . Beloit

AUGUST
1-6 . . . at West Michigan
8-13 . . . . South Bend
15-20 . . . . Peoria
22-27 . . . . at Beloit
29-31 . . . . at Cedar Rapids

SEPTEMBER
1-3 . . . . at Cedar Rapids
5-10 . . . . Lansing

LANSING LUGNUTS

APRIL
7-9 . . . . . . at Great Lakes
11-16 . . . . West Michigan
18-23 . . . . at Lake County
25-30 . . . . . . Quad Cities

MAY
2-7 . . . . Dayton
9-14 . . . at West Michigan
16-21 . . . . . Lake County
23-28 . . . . at Fort Wayne
30-31 . . . . . Cedar Rapids

JUNE
1-4 . . . . . . Cedar Rapids
6-11 . . . . at South Bend
13-18 . . . . Peoria
20-25 . . . . . at Wisconsin
28-30 . . . . at Great Lakes

JULY
1-3 . . . . . at Great Lakes
4-9 . . . . . . Lake County
14-16 . . . at West Michigan
18-23 . . . . . Great Lakes
25-30 . . . . at Quad Cities

AUGUST
1-6 . . . . at Cedar Rapids
8-13 . . . . Fort Wayne
15-20 . . . . . Great Lakes
22-27 . . . . . . at Dayton
29-31 . . . . West Michigan

SEPTEMBER
1-3 . . . . . West Michigan
5-10 . . . . at Lake County

PEORIA CHIEFS

APRIL
6-8 . . . . . . Cedar Rapids
11-16 . . . . at Wisconsin
18-23 . . . . . Fort Wayne
25-30 . . . . at South Bend

MAY
2-7 . . . . Wisconsin
9-14 . . . . Dayton
16-21 . . . at Cedar Rapids
23-28 . . . . . . Great Lakes
30-31 . . . . at Wisconsin

JUNE
1-4 . . . . . . at Wisconsin
6-11 . . . . Beloit
13-18 . . . . . at Lansing
20-25 . . . at Quad Cities
28-30 . . . . . Cedar Rapids

JULY
1-3 . . . . . . Cedar Rapids
4-9 . . . . . at South Bend
14-16 . . . . Wisconsin
18-23 . . . at Cedar Rapids
25-30 . . . . . . South Bend

AUGUST
1-6 . . . . Quad Cities
8-13 . . . . at Beloit
15-20 . . . . at Lake County
22-27 . . . . West Michigan
29-31 . . . . at Quad Cities

SEPTEMBER
1-3 . . . . . at Quad Cities
5-10 . . . . Beloit

QUAD CITIES RIVER BANDITS

APRIL
7-9 . . . . South Bend
11-16 . . . at Cedar Rapids
18-23 . . . . . Wisconsin
25-30 . . . . . at Lansing

MAY
2-7 . . . . . at Great Lakes
9-14 . . . . . Cedar Rapids
16-21 . . . . at Wisconsin
23-28 . . . . . . Beloit
30-31 . . . at Lake County

JUNE
1-4 . . . . at Lake County
6-11 . . . . . . Fort Wayne
13-18 . . . . . . at Beloit
20-25 . . . . Peoria
28-30 . . . . . . Wisconsin

JULY
1-3 . . . . Wisconsin
4-9 . . . . . at Cedar Rapids
14-16 . . . . . South Bend
18-23 . . . . . . at Beloit
25-30 . . . . Lansing

AUGUST
1-6 . . . . at Peoria
8-13 . . . . . Cedar Rapids
15-20 . . . . Beloit
22-27 . . . . . at Wisconsin
29-31 . . . . . . Peoria

SEPTEMBER
1-3 . . . . Peoria
5-10 . . . . at South Bend

SOUTH BEND CUBS

APRIL
7-9 . . . . . at Quad Cities
11-16 . . . . Beloit
18-23 . . . . at Great Lakes
25-30 . . . . Peoria

MAY
2-7 . . . . . . Cedar Rapids
9-14 . . . . . at Wisconsin
16-21 . . . . . . at Beloit
23-28 . . . . Dayton
30-31 . . . . at Fort Wayne

JUNE
1-4 . . . . . at Fort Wayne
6-11 . . . . Lansing
13-18 . . . at Cedar Rapids
20-25 . . . . . Fort Wayne
28-30 . . . . . . at Beloit

JULY
1-3 . . . . at Beloit
4-9 . . . . Peoria
14-16 . . . . at Quad Cities
18-23 . . . . West Michigan
25-30 . . . . . . at Peoria

AUGUST
1-6 . . . . Wisconsin
8-13 . . . . at Lake County
15-20 . . . at West Michigan
22-27 . . . . . Cedar Rapids
29-31 . . . . at Fort Wayne

SEPTEMBER
1-3 . . . . . at Fort Wayne
5-10 . . . . . . Quad Cities

SCHEDULES

WEST MICHIGAN WHITECAPS

APRIL
6-8 . . . . Fort Wayne
11-16 . . . . at Lansing
18-23 . . . . Dayton
25-30 . . . . at Cedar Rapids

MAY
2-7 . . . . at Beloit
9-14 . . . . Lansing
16-21 . . . . . at Great Lakes
23-28 . . . . . Lake County
30-31 . . . . at Dayton

JUNE
1-4 . . . . at Dayton
6-11 . . . . Wisconsin
13-18 . . . . at Lake County
20-25 . . . . . . Great Lakes
27-30 . . . . Dayton

JULY
1-2 . . . . Dayton
4-9 . . . . . at Fort Wayne
14-16 . . . . Lansing
18-23 . . . . at South Bend
25-30 . . . . . . Fort Wayne

AUGUST
1-6 . . . . . . Lake County
8-13 . . . . . at Great Lakes
15-20 . . . . . South Bend
22-27 . . . . at Peoria
29-31 . . . . at Lansing

SEPTEMBER
1-3 . . . . at Lansing
5-10 . . . . Great Lakes

WISCONSIN TIMBER RATTLERS

APRIL
7-9 . . . . at Beloit
11-16 . . . . Peoria
18-23 . . . . . at Quad Cities
25-30 . . . . Beloit

MAY
2-7 . . . . at Peoria
9-14 . . . . South Bend
16-21 . . . . . . Quad Cities
23-28 . . . . at Cedar Rapids
30-31 . . . . Peoria

JUNE
1-4 . . . . Peoria
6-11 . . . . at West Michigan
13-18 . . . . at Great Lakes
20-25 . . . . Lansing
28-30 . . . . . at Quad Cities

JULY
1-3 . . . . . at Quad Cities
4-9 . . . . Beloit
14-16 . . . . . . at Peoria
18-23 . . . . at Dayton
25-30 . . . . . Cedar Rapids

AUGUST
1-6 . . . . . . at South Bend
8-13 . . . . Dayton
15-20 . . . . at Cedar Rapids
22-27 . . . . . . Quad Cities
29-31 . . . . at Beloit

SEPTEMBER
1-3 . . . . at Beloit
5-10 . . . . Cedar Rapids

NORTHWEST LEAGUE

EUGENE EMERALDS

APRIL
8-9 . . . . at Everett
12-16 . . . . . . at Spokane
19-24 . . . . Hillsboro
26-30 . . . . . at Vancouver

MAY
3-8 . . . . Spokane
10-14 . . . . at Tri-City
17-21 . . . . Hillsboro
24-28 . . . . Everett
31 . . . . at Vancouver

JUNE
1-4 . . . . . . at Vancouver
7-11 . . . . Tri-City
14-18 . . . . . at Spokane
21-25 . . . . . . Vancouver
29-29 . . . . at Everett

JULY
1-4 . . . . at Everett
5-9 . . . . Tri-City
15-16 . . . . . at Vancouver
19-23 . . . . . at Hillsboro
26-30 . . . . Spokane

AUGUST
2-7 . . . . at Tri-City
9-13 . . . . Everett
16-20 . . . . . . Vancouver
23-27 . . . . . at Hillsboro
30-31 . . . . Tri-City

SEPTEMBER
1-3 . . . . Tri-City
5-10 . . . . at Everett

EVERETT AQUASOX

APRIL
8-9 . . . . Eugene
12-16 . . . . . . at Hillsboro
19-23 . . . . . . Vancouver
25-30 . . . . . . at Spokane

MAY
3-7 . . . . Tri-City
10-14 . . . . . at Vancouver
17-21 . . . . Spokane
24-28 . . . . . . at Eugene
30 . . . . Hillsboro

JUNE
1-4 . . . . Hillsboro
7-11 . . . . Vancouver
14-19 . . . . . . at Tri-City
21-25 . . . . . at Hillsboro
29-29 . . . . Eugene

JULY
1-4 . . . . Eugene
5-9 . . . . at Spokane
15-16 . . . . Hillsboro
19-23 . . . . Tri-City
26-30 . . . . . at Vancouver

AUGUST
2-6 . . . . Spokane
9-13 . . . . at Eugene
16-20 . . . . . . Hillsboro
23-28 . . . . . . at Tri-City
30-31 . . . . . . at Spokane

SEPTEMBER
1-4 . . . . at Spokane
5-10 . . . . Eugene

HILLSBORO HOPS

APRIL
7-9 . . . . at Tri-City
12-16 . . . . Everett
19-24 . . . . . . at Eugene
26-30 . . . . Tri-City

MAY
3-7 . . . . Vancouver
10-14 . . . . . at Spokane
17-21 . . . . . at Eugene
24-28 . . . . Tri-City
30 . . . . at Everett

JUNE
1-4 . . . . at Everett
7-11 . . . . Spokane
14-18 . . . . . at Vancouver
21-25 . . . . Everett
29-30 . . . . . . at Tri-City

JULY
1-4 . . . . at Tri-City
5-9 . . . . Vancouver
15-16 . . . . . . at Everett
19-23 . . . . Eugene
26-31 . . . . . . at Tri-City

AUGUST
2-6 . . . . Vancouver
9-13 . . . . . . at Spokane
16-20 . . . . . . at Everett
23-27 . . . . Eugene
30-31 . . . . . at Vancouver

SEPTEMBER
1-3 . . . . . . at Vancouver
6-10 . . . . Spokane

166 · Baseball America 2023 Directory

BaseballAmerica.com

SCHEDULES

SPOKANE INDIANS

APRIL
8-9 . . . . at Vancouver
12-16 . . . . Eugene
19-23 . . . . at Tri-City
25-30 . . . . Everett

MAY
3-8 . . . . at Eugene
10-14 . . . . Hillsboro
17-21 . . . . at Everett
23-28 . . . . . . Vancouver
31 . . . . at Tri-City

JUNE
1-4 . . . . at Tri-City
7-11 . . . . at Hillsboro
14-18 . . . . Eugene
21-25 . . . . Tri-City
28-30 . . . . . at Vancouver

JULY
1-2 . . . . at Vancouver
5-9 . . . . Everett
15-17 . . . . . . at Tri-City
19-23 . . . . . Vancouver
26-30 . . . . . . at Eugene

AUGUST
2-6 . . . . at Everett
9-13 . . . . Hillsboro
16-20 . . . . Tri-City
23-27 . . . . . at Vancouver
30-31 . . . . Everett

SEPTEMBER
1-4 . . . . Everett
6-10 . . . . . . at Hillsboro

TRI-CITY DUST DEVILS

APRIL
7-9 . . . . Hillsboro
12-16 . . . . . at Vancouver
19-23 . . . . . . Spokane
26-30 . . . . . at Hillsboro

MAY
3-7 . . . . at Everett
10-14 . . . . Eugene
17-21 . . . . . . Vancouver
24-28 . . . . at Hillsboro
31 . . . . Spokane

JUNE
1-4 . . . . Spokane
7-11 . . . . . . at Eugene
14-19 . . . . . . Everett
21-25 . . . . . at Spokane
29-30 . . . . . . Hillsboro

JULY
1-4 . . . . Hillsboro
5-9 . . . . at Eugene
15-17 . . . . . Spokane
19-23 . . . . . at Everett
26-31 . . . . . Hillsboro

AUGUST
2-7 . . . . Eugene
9-13 . . . . . at Vancouver
16-20 . . . . . at Spokane
23-28 . . . . . . Everett
30-31 . . . . . at Eugene

SEPTEMBER
1-3 . . . . at Eugene
6-11 . . . . . . Vancouver

VANCOUVER CANADIANS

APRIL
8-9 . . . . Spokane
12-16 . . . . Tri-City
19-23 . . . . . at Everett
26-30 . . . . . . Eugene

MAY
3-7 . . . . . . at Hillsboro
10-14 . . . . . . Everett
17-21 . . . . . at Tri-City
23-28 . . . . . at Spokane
31 . . . . Eugene

JUNE
1-4 . . . . Eugene
7-11 . . . . . . at Everett
14-18 . . . . . . Hillsboro
21-25 . . . . . at Eugene
28-30 . . . . . . Spokane

JULY
1-2 . . . . Spokane
5-9 . . . . . . at Hillsboro
15-16 . . . . . . Eugene
19-23 . . . . at Spokane
26-30 . . . . Everett

AUGUST
2-6 . . . . . . at Hillsboro
9-13 . . . . Tri-City
16-20 . . . . at Eugene
23-27 . . . . . Spokane
30-31 . . . . . Hillsboro

SEPTEMBER
1-3 . . . . Hillsboro
6-11 . . . . . . at Tri-City

SOUTH ATLANTIC LEAGUE

ABERDEEN IRONBIRDS

APRIL
6-8 . . . . Wilmington
11-16 . . at Hudson Valley
18-23 . . . . Jersey Shore
25-30 . . . . at Wilmington

MAY
2-7 . . . . at Brooklyn
9-14 . . . . . Hudson Valley
16-21 . . at Winston-Salem
23-28 . . . . . Jersey Shore
30-31 . . . at Hudson Valley

JUNE
1-4 . . . . at Hudson Valley
6-11 . . . . Asheville
13-18 . . . . . . Brooklyn
20-25 . . . . at Wilmington
27-30 . . . . Winston-Salem

JULY
1-2 . . . . . Winston-Salem
4-9 . . . . . at Greensboro
14-16 . . . . . . Wilmington
18-23 . . . . Bowling Green
25-30 . . . . at Jersey Shore

AUGUST
1-6 . . . . Hickory
8-13 . . . . at Brooklyn
15-20 . . . . . . Wilmington
22-27 . . at Hudson Valley
29-31 . . . . at Jersey Shore

SEPTEMBER
1-3 . . . . . at Jersey Shore
5-10 . . . . Greenville

ASHEVILLE TOURISTS

APRIL
6-8 . . . . . Bowling Green
11-16 . . . . at Greenville
18-23 . . . . Winston-Salem
25-30 . . . at Bowling Green

MAY
2-7 . . . . Greenville
9-14 . . . . at Rome
16-21 . . . . . Greensboro
23-28 . . . . . . at Hickory
30-31 . . . . . . Wilmington

JUNE
1-4 . . . . Wilmington
6-11 . . . . . . at Aberdeen
13-18 . . . at Winston-Salem
20-25 . . . . . . Hickory
28-30 . . . . Greenville

JULY
1-3 . . . . Greenville
4-9 . . . . at Bowling Green
14-16 . . . . Winston-Salem
18-23 . . . . . at Greenville
25-30 . . . . Rome

AUGUST
1-6 . . . . . at Greensboro
8-13 . . . . Hickory
15-20 . . at Jersey Shore
22-27 . . . . . . Brooklyn
29-31 . . . . Bowling Green

SEPTEMBER
1-3 . . . . . Bowling Green
5-10 . . . . at Rome

BOWLING GREEN HOT RODS

APRIL
6-8 . . . . at Asheville
11-16 . . . . Rome
18-23 . . . . . . at Hickory
25-30 . . . . Asheville

MAY
2-7 . . . . at Rome
9-14 . . . . Hickory
16-21 . . . . . at Greenville
23-28 . . . . at Greensboro
30-31 . . . . Rome

JUNE
1-4 . . . . Rome
6-11 . . . . Winston-Salem
13-18 . . . . at Hickory
20-25 . . . . . . Greenville
28-30 . . . . at Rome

JULY
1-3 . . . . at Rome
4-9 . . . . Asheville
14-16 . . . at Hudson Valley
18-23 . . . . . at Aberdeen
25-30 . . . . Greenville

AUGUST
1-6 . . . . at Winston-Salem
8-13 . . . . Wilmington
15-20 . . . . at Greensboro
22-27 . . . . Winston-Salem
29-31 . . . . . . at Asheville

SEPTEMBER
1-3 . . . . at Asheville
5-10 . . . . Greensboro

BaseballAmerica.com

Baseball America 2023 Directory • **167**

SCHEDULES

BROOKLYN CYCLONES

APRIL
7-9 . . . . . . Jersey Shore
11-16 . . . at Winston-Salem
18-23 . . . . Wilmington
25-30 . . . . at Jersey Shore

MAY
2-7 . . . . Aberdeen
9-14 . . . . at Wilmington
16-21 . . . at Hudson Valley
23-28 . . . . Winston-Salem
30-31 . . . . at Jersey Shore

JUNE
1-4 . . . . . at Jersey Shore
6-11 . . . . Greenville
13-18 . . . . . at Aberdeen
20-25 . . . . Hudson Valley
28-30 . . . . . . Jersey Shore

JULY
1-3 . . . . . . Jersey Shore
4-9 . . . . . at Wilmington
14-16 . . . . . . Greensboro
18-23 . . . at Hudson Valley
25-30 . . . Wilmington

AUGUST
1-6 . . . . . at Jersey Shore
8-13 . . . . Aberdeen
15-20 . . . . . Hudson Valley
22-27 . . . . . . at Asheville
29-31 . . . . . at Greenville

SEPTEMBER
1-3 . . . . at Greenville
5-10 . . . . Wilmington

GREENSBORO GRASSHOPPERS

APRIL
7-9 . . . . at Hudson Valley
11-16 . . . . at Jersey Shore
18-23 . . . . Greenville
25-30 . . . . Rome

MAY
2-7 . . . . at Winston-Salem
9-14 . . . . . Jersey Shore
16-21 . . . . . . at Asheville
23-28 . . . . Bowling Green
30-31 . . . at Winston-Salem

JUNE
1-4 . . . . at Winston-Salem
6-11 . . . . Wilmington
13-18 . . . . at Greenville
20-25 . . . Winston-Salem
27-30 . . . . at Hickory

JULY
1-2 . . . . at Hickory
4-9 . . . . Aberdeen
14-16 . . . . . . at Brooklyn
18-23 . . . . at Wilmington
25-30 . . . Winston-Salem

AUGUST
1-6 . . . . Asheville
8-13 . . . . . at Greenville
15-20 . . . Bowling Green
22-27 . . . . at Rome
29-31 . . . . Hickory

SEPTEMBER
1-3 . . . . Hickory
5-10 . . . at Bowling Green

GREENVILLE DRIVE

APRIL
6-8 . . . . at Rome
11-16 . . . . Asheville
18-23 . . . . at Greensboro
25-30 . . . . . Hudson Valley

MAY
2-7 . . . . at Asheville
9-14 . . . . Winston-Salem
16-21 . . . Bowling Green
23-28 . . . . at Rome
30-31 . . . . Hickory

JUNE
1-4 . . . . Hickory
6-11 . . . . . . at Brooklyn
13-18 . . . . . Greensboro
20-25 . . at Bowling Green
28-30 . . . . . . at Asheville

JULY
1-3 . . . . . at Asheville
4-9 . . . . Rome
14-16 . . . . . . at Hickory
18-23 . . . . Asheville
25-30 . . at Bowling Green

AUGUST
1-6 . . . . Rome
8-13 . . . . Greensboro
15-20 . . at Winston-Salem
22-27 . . . . . at Hickory
29-31 . . . . . . Brooklyn

SEPTEMBER
1-3 . . . . Brooklyn
5-10 . . . . . at Aberdeen

HICKORY CRAWDADS

APRIL
6-8 . . . . Winston-Salem
11-16 . . . . at Wilmington
18-23 . . . Bowling Green
25-30 . . . at Winston-Salem

MAY
2-7 . . . . . . Jersey Shore
9-14 . . . at Bowling Green
16-21 . . . . Rome
23-28 . . . . . . Asheville
30-31 . . . . . at Greenville

JUNE
1-4 . . . . at Greenville
6-11 . . . . at Rome
13-18 . . . Bowling Green
20-25 . . . . . . at Asheville
27-30 . . . . . Greensboro

JULY
1-2 . . . . . . Greensboro
4-9 . . . at Winston-Salem
14-16 . . . . . . Greenville
18-23 . . . . at Rome
25-30 . . . . Hudson Valley

AUGUST
1-6 . . . . . . at Aberdeen
8-13 . . . . . at Asheville
15-20 . . . . Rome
22-27 . . . . . . Greenville
29-31 . . . at Greensboro

SEPTEMBER
1-3 . . . . at Greensboro
5-10 . . . . Winston-Salem

HUDSON VALLEY RENEGADES

APRIL
7-9 . . . . . . Greensboro
11-16 . . . . Aberdeen
18-23 . . . . . . at Rome
25-30 . . . . . at Greenville

MAY
2-7 . . . . Wilmington
9-14 . . . . . at Aberdeen
16-21 . . . . . Brooklyn
23-28 . . . at Wilmington
30-31 . . . . . Aberdeen

JUNE
1-4 . . . . Aberdeen
6-11 . . . at Jersey Shore
13-18 . . . . Rome
20-25 . . . . at Brooklyn
28-30 . . . . . . Wilmington

JULY
1-3 . . . . . . Wilmington
4-9 . . . . at Jersey Shore
14-16 . . . Bowling Green
18-23 . . . . . . Brooklyn
25-30 . . . . . at Hickory

AUGUST
1-6 . . . . at Wilmington
8-13 . . . . . Jersey Shore
15-20 . . . . at Brooklyn
22-27 . . . . . Aberdeen
29-31 . . . . at Wilmington

SEPTEMBER
1-3 . . . . . at Wilmington
5-10 . . . . . Jersey Shore

JERSEY SHORE BLUECLAWS

APRIL
7-9 . . . . . . at Brooklyn
11-16 . . . . Greensboro
18-23 . . . . at Aberdeen
25-30 . . . . . Brooklyn

MAY
2-7 . . . . . . at Hickory
9-14 . . . at Greensboro
16-21 . . . . Wilmington
23-28 . . . . at Aberdeen
30-31 . . . . . Brooklyn

JUNE
1-4 . . . . Brooklyn
6-11 . . . . Hudson Valley
13-18 . . . at Wilmington
20-25 . . . . Rome
28-30 . . . . at Brooklyn

JULY
1-3 . . . . . at Brooklyn
4-9 . . . . . Hudson Valley
14-16 . . . . . at Rome
18-23 . . at Winston-Salem
25-30 . . . . . Aberdeen

AUGUST
1-6 . . . . . Brooklyn
8-13 . . . at Hudson Valley
15-20 . . . . . Asheville
22-27 . . at Wilmington
29-31 . . . . Aberdeen

SEPTEMBER
1-3 . . . . . . Aberdeen
5-10 . . . at Hudson Valley

SCHEDULES

ROME BRAVES

APRIL
6-8	Greenville
11-16	at Bowling Green
18-23	Hudson Valley
25-30	at Greensboro

MAY
2-7	Bowling Green
9-14	Asheville
16-21	at Hickory
23-28	Greenville
30-31	at Bowling Green

JUNE
1-4	at Bowling Green
6-11	Hickory
13-18	at Hudson Valley
20-25	at Jersey Shore
28-30	Bowling Green

JULY
1-3	Bowling Green
4-9	at Greenville
14-16	Jersey Shore
18-23	Hickory
25-30	at Asheville

AUGUST
1-6	at Greenville
8-13	Winston-Salem
15-20	at Hickory
22-27	Greensboro
29-31	at Winston-Salem

SEPTEMBER
1-3	at Winston-Salem
5-10	Asheville

WILMINGTON BLUE ROCKS

APRIL
6-8	at Aberdeen
11-16	Hickory
18-23	at Brooklyn
25-30	Aberdeen

MAY
2-7	at Hudson Valley
9-14	Brooklyn
16-21	at Jersey Shore
23-28	Hudson Valley
30-31	at Asheville

JUNE
1-4	at Asheville
6-11	at Greensboro
13-18	Jersey Shore
20-25	Aberdeen
28-30	at Hudson Valley

JULY
1-3	at Hudson Valley
4-9	Brooklyn
14-16	at Aberdeen
18-23	Greensboro
25-30	at Brooklyn

AUGUST
1-6	Hudson Valley
8-13	at Bowling Green
15-20	at Aberdeen
22-27	Jersey Shore
29-31	Hudson Valley

SEPTEMBER
1-3	Hudson Valley
5-10	at Brooklyn

WINSTON-SALEM DASH

APRIL
6-8	at Hickory
11-16	Brooklyn
18-23	at Asheville
25-30	Hickory

MAY
2-7	Greensboro
9-14	at Greenville
16-21	Aberdeen
23-28	at Brooklyn
30-31	Greensboro

JUNE
1-4	Greensboro
6-11	at Bowling Green
13-18	Asheville
20-25	at Greensboro
27-30	at Aberdeen

JULY
1-2	at Aberdeen
4-9	Hickory
14-16	at Asheville
18-23	Jersey Shore
25-30	at Greensboro

AUGUST
1-6	Bowling Green
8-13	at Rome
15-20	Greenville
22-27	at Bowling Green
29-31	Rome

SEPTEMBER
1-3	Rome
5-10	at Hickory

LOW-A

CALIFORNIA LEAGUE

FRESNO GRIZZLIES

APRIL
7-8	at San Jose
12-16	Stockton
18-23	at Rancho Cuca.
25-30	San Jose

MAY
3-7	at Stockton
9-14	Visalia
17-21	at Modesto
23-28	Stockton
29	at San Jose

JUNE
1-5	at San Jose
7-12	Lake Elsinore
14-19	Inland Empire
21-26	at Modesto
29-30	at Stockton

JULY
1-4	at Stockton
5-10	San Jose
15-16	at Lake Elsinore
19-24	Modesto
26-31	at Inland Empire

AUGUST
2-7	Rancho Cuca.
9-14	at San Jose
16-21	at Modesto
23-28	Stockton
30-31	at Visalia

SEPTEMBER
1-3	at Visalia
6-10	Modesto

INLAND EMPIRE 66ERS

APRIL
7-9	at Rancho Cuca.
12-16	Lake Elsinore
19-23	at San Jose
26-30	Rancho Cuca.

MAY
2-7	at Visalia
10-14	Modesto
17-21	at Lake Elsinore
24-28	Visalia
31	at Rancho Cuca.

JUNE
1-4	at Rancho Cuca.
7-12	Stockton
14-19	at Fresno
21-26	Visalia
27-30	at Lake Elsinore

JULY
1-3	at Lake Elsinore
5-10	Rancho Cuca.
15-17	at Stockton
19-23	at Visalia
26-31	Fresno

AUGUST
2-7	San Jose
9-14	at Rancho Cuca.
16-20	at Lake Elsinore
23-28	Visalia
30-31	at Modesto

SEPTEMBER
1-3	at Modesto
6-11	Lake Elsinore

LAKE ELSINORE STORM

APRIL
7-9	Visalia
12-16	at Inland Empire
19-23	Modesto
26-30	at Visalia

MAY
2-7	Rancho Cuca.
9-14	at San Jose
17-21	Inland Empire
24-28	at Rancho Cuca.
31	Visalia

JUNE
1-4	Visalia
7-12	at Fresno
14-18	Stockton
21-25	at Rancho Cuca.
27-30	Inland Empire

JULY
1-3	Inland Empire
5-9	at Visalia
15-16	Fresno
19-23	Rancho Cuca.
26-31	at Stockton

AUGUST
2-7	at Modesto
9-13	Visalia
16-20	Inland Empire
23-28	at Rancho Cuca.
30-31	San Jose

SEPTEMBER
1-3	San Jose
6-11	at Inland Empire

BaseballAmerica.com

Baseball America 2023 Directory • **169**

SCHEDULES

MODESTO NUTS

APRIL
7-9 . . . . at Stockton
12-16 . . . . San Jose
19-23 . . . at Lake Elsinore
26-30 . . . . Stockton

MAY
3-7 . . . . at San Jose
10-14 . . . at Inland Empire
17-21 . . . . Fresno
24-28 . . . . San Jose
30 . . . . at Stockton

JUNE
1-4 . . . . at Stockton
7-11 . . . . . Rancho Cuca.
14-18 . . . . . . at Visalia
21-26 . . . . Fresno
28-30 . . . . . . at San Jose

JULY
1-4 . . . . at San Jose
5-10 . . . . Stockton
15-17 . . . . at Rancho Cuca.
19-24 . . . . at Fresno
26-31 . . . . Visalia

AUGUST
2-7 . . . . . . Lake Elsinore
9-14 . . . . . . at Stockton
16-21 . . . . Fresno
23-28 . . . . . . at San Jose
30-31 . . . . . Inland Empire

SEPTEMBER
1-3 . . . . . Inland Empire
6-10 . . . . at Fresno

RANCHO CUCAMONGA QUAKES

APRIL
7-9 . . . . . Inland Empire
12-16 . . . . at Visalia
18-23 . . . . Fresno
26-30 . . . at Inland Empire

MAY
2-7 . . . . at Lake Elsinore
9-14 . . . . Stockton
17-21 . . . . . . at Visalia
24-28 . . . . . Lake Elsinore
31 . . . . . . Inland Empire

JUNE
1-4 . . . . . Inland Empire
7-11 . . . . at Modesto
14-18 . . . . at San Jose
21 25 . . . . Lake Elsinore
29-30 . . . . Visalia

JULY
1-4 . . . . Visalia
5-10 . . . . at Inland Empire
15-17 . . . . Modesto
19-23 . . . . at Lake Elsinore
26-31 . . . . San Jose

AUGUST
2-7 . . . . at Fresno
9-14 . . . . . Inland Empire
16-20 . . . . . . at Visalia
23-28 . . . . . Lake Elsinore
30-31 . . . . . . at Stockton

SEPTEMBER
1-4 . . . . . . at Stockton
6-10 . . . . Visalia

SAN JOSE GIANTS

APRIL
7-8 . . . . Fresno
12-16 . . . . . . at Modesto
19-23 . . . . Inland Empire
25-30 . . . . at Fresno

MAY
3-7 . . . . Modesto
9-14 . . . . . . Lake Elsinore
16-21 . . . . . at Stockton
24-28 . . . . . . at Modesto
29 . . . . Fresno

JUNE
1-5 . . . . Fresno
7-11 . . . . at Visalia
14-18 . . . . Rancho Cuca.
21-25 . . . . . . at Stockton
28-30 . . . . Modesto

JULY
1-4 . . . . Modesto
5-10 . . . . at Fresno
15-17 . . . . Visalia
19-24 . . . . Stockton
26-31 . . . . at Rancho Cuca.

AUGUST
2-7 . . . . at Inland Empire
9-14 . . . . Fresno
16-21 . . . . . at Stockton
23-28 . . . . Modesto
30-31 . . . . at Lake Elsinore

SEPTEMBER
1-3 . . . . . at Lake Elsinore
6-10 . . . . Stockton

STOCKTON PORTS

APRIL
7-9 . . . . Modesto
12-16 . . . . at Fresno
18-23 . . . . Visalia
26-30 . . . . . . at Modesto

MAY
3-7 . . . . Fresno
9-14 . . . . at Rancho Cuca.
16-21 . . . . San Jose
23-28 . . . . . . at Fresno
30 . . . . Modesto

JUNE
1-4 . . . . Modesto
7-12 . . . . at Inland Empire
14-18 . . . at Lake Elsinore
21-25 . . . . San Jose
29-30 . . . . Fresno

JULY
1-4 . . . . Fresno
5-10 . . . . at Modesto
15-17 . . . . Inland Empire
19-24 . . . . . . at San Jose
26-31 . . . . . Lake Elsinore

AUGUST
2-6 . . . . at Visalia
9-14 . . . . Modesto
16-21 . . . . San Jose
23-28 . . . . . . at Fresno
30-31 . . . . . Rancho Cuca.

SEPTEMBER
1-4 . . . . . Rancho Cuca.
6-10 . . . . at San Jose

VISALIA RAWHIDE

APRIL
7-9 . . . . . at Lake Elsinore
12-16 . . . . Rancho Cuca.
18-23 . . . . . . at Stockton
26-30 . . . . . Lake Elsinore

MAY
2-7 . . . . . Inland Empire
9-14 . . . . at Fresno
17-21 . . . . Rancho Cuca.
24-28 . . . at Inland Empire
31 . . . . . at Lake Elsinore

JUNE
1-4 . . . . at Lake Elsinore
7-11 . . . . San Jose
14-18 . . . . Modesto
21-26 . . . at Inland Empire
29-30 . . . . at Rancho Cuca.

JULY
1-4 . . . . at Rancho Cuca.
5-9 . . . . . . Lake Elsinore
15-17 . . . . . . at San Jose
19-23 . . . . . Inland Empire
26-31 . . . . at Modesto

AUGUST
2-6 . . . . Stockton
9-13 . . . . . at Lake Elsinore
16-20 . . . . . Rancho Cuca.
23-28 . . . at Inland Empire
30-31 . . . . Fresno

SEPTEMBER
1-3 . . . . Fresno
6-10 . . . . . at Rancho Cuca

170 · Baseball America 2023 Directory

BaseballAmerica.com

SCHEDULES

CAROLINA LEAGUE

AUGUSTA GREENJACKETS

APRIL
6-8 . . . . . . at Columbia
11-16 . . . . . . Down East
18-23 . . . . at Myrtle Beach
25-30 . . . . Columbia

MAY
2-7 . . . . . at Kannapolis
9-14 . . . . Charleston
16-21 . . at Myrtle Beach
23-28 . . . . . . Kannapolis
30-31 . . . . at Charleston

JUNE
1-4 . . . . . at Charleston
6-11 . . . . . . Myrtle Beach
13-18 . . . . . . Carolina
20-25 . . . . . at Delmarva
28-30 . . . . . at Columbia

JULY
1-3 . . . . . . at Columbia
4-9 . . . . . Myrtle Beach
14-16 . . . . at Fayetteville
18-23 . . . . Fredericksburg
25-30 . . . . at Charleston

AUGUST
1-6 . . . . Columbia
8-13 . . . . at Salem
15-20 . . at Fredericksburg
22-27 . . . . . Charleston
29-31 . . . . Salem

SEPTEMBER
1-3 . . . . Salem
5-10 . . . . . at Down East

CAROLINA MUDCATS

APRIL
7-9 . . . . . at Fayetteville
11-16 . . . . Salem
18-23 . . . . at Down East
25-30 . . . . . Kannapolis

MAY
2-7 . . . . . . at Delmarva
9-14 . . . . Fredericksburg
16-21 . . . . at Kannapolis
23-28 . . . . . Down East
30-31 . . . . at Lynchburg

JUNE
1-4 . . . . . at Lynchburg
6-11 . . . . . . Fayetteville
13-18 . . . . . at Augusta
20-25 . . . . . Lynchburg
28-30 . . . . at Down East

JULY
1-3 . . . . . at Down East
4-9 . . . . . . Fayetteville
14-16 . . . at Myrtle Beach
18-23 . . . . . Kannapolis
25-30 . . . . . at Columbia

AUGUST
1-6 . . . . . at Fayetteville
8-13 . . . . Delmarva
15-20 . . at Kannapolis
22-27 . . . . . . Columbia
29-31 . . . . . Down East

SEPTEMBER
1-3 . . . . . . Down East
5-10 . . . . at Salem

CHARLESTON RIVERDOGS

APRIL
6-8 . . . . . at Myrtle Beach
11-16 . . . . . . Columbia
18-23 . . . . at Kannapolis
25-30 . . . Myrtle Beach

MAY
2-7 . . . . Lynchburg
9-14 . . . . . . at Augusta
16-21 . . . . . . Delmarva
23-28 . . . . at Columbia
30-31 . . . . Augusta

JUNE
1-4 . . . . Augusta
6-11 . . . at Fredericksburg
13-18 . . . at Lynchburg
20-25 . . . . . Fayetteville
28-30 . . . . at Myrtle Beach

JULY
1-3 . . . . at Myrtle Beach
4-9 . . . . Columbia
14-16 . . . . at Down East
18-23 . . . . . at Delmarva
25-30 . . . . . . Augusta

AUGUST
1-6 . . . . . . Kannapolis
8-13 . . . . . at Columbia
15-20 . . . . . Down East
22-27 . . . . . at Augusta
29-31 . . . . Myrtle Beach

SEPTEMBER
1-3 . . . . . Myrtle Beach
5-10 . . . . . at Fayetteville

COLUMBIA FIREFLIES

APRIL
6-8 . . . . Augusta
11-16 . . . . at Charleston
18-23 . . . . . Fayetteville
25-30 . . . . . at Augusta

MAY
2-7 . . . . . . Myrtle Beach
9-14 . . . . at Salem
16-21 . . at Fredericksburg
23-28 . . . . . Charleston
30-31 . . . . at Down East

JUNE
1-4 . . . . . at Down East
6-11 . . . . Salem
13-18 . . . . at Fayetteville
20-25 . . . . Fredericksburg
28-30 . . . . Augusta

JULY
1-3 . . . . Augusta
4-9 . . . . . at Charleston
14-16 . . . . . Kannapolis
18-23 . . . at Myrtle Beach
25-30 . . . . Carolina

AUGUST
1-6 . . . . . . at Augusta
8-13 . . . . . . Charleston
15-20 . . . . Myrtle Beach
22-27 . . . . . at Carolina
29-31 . . . . . . Delmarva

SEPTEMBER
1-3 . . . . Delmarva
5-10 . . . . at Myrtle Beach

DELMARVA SHOREBIRDS

APRIL
6-8 . . . . at Salem
11-16 . . . . . . Kannapolis
18-23 . . . at Fredericksburg
25-30 . . . . Salem

MAY
2-7 . . . . Carolina
9-14 . . . . . at Down East
16-21 . . . at Charleston
23-28 . . . . . Lynchburg
30-31 . . . at Fredericksburg

JUNE
1-4 . . . at Fredericksburg
6-11 . . . . . . Down East
13-18 . . . . . . at Salem
20-25 . . . . Augusta
28-30 . . . . . at Lynchburg

JULY
1-3 . . . . . . at Lynchburg
4-9 . . . . . Fredericksburg
14-16 . . . . at Salem
18-23 . . . . . Charleston
25-30 . . . . at Kannapolis

AUGUST
1-6 . . . . Lynchburg
8-13 . . . . . . at Carolina
15-20 . . . . Salem
22-27 . . . at Lynchburg
29-31 . . . . . at Columbia

SEPTEMBER
1-3 . . . . at Columbia
5-10 . . . . . Fredericksburg

DOWN EAST WOOD DUCKS

APRIL
6-8 . . . . Kannapolis
11-16 . . . . . . at Augusta
18-23 . . . . . . Carolina
25-30 . . . . at Fayetteville

MAY
2-7 . . . . at Fredericksburg
9-14 . . . . Delmarva
16-21 . . . . . Fayetteville
23-28 . . . . . at Carolina
30-31 . . . . Columbia

JUNE
1-4 . . . . Columbia
6-11 . . . . . . at Delmarva
13-18 . . . . . Kannapolis
20-25 . . . . at Salem
28-30 . . . . Carolina

JULY
1-3 . . . . Carolina
4-9 . . . . . at Kannapolis
14-16 . . . . . . Charleston
18-23 . . . . Salem
25-30 . . . . at Fayetteville

AUGUST
1-6 . . . . . . Myrtle Beach
8-13 . . . . . at Kannapolis
15-20 . . . . at Charleston
22-27 . . . . . . Fayetteville
29-31 . . . . . . at Carolina

SEPTEMBER
1-3 . . . . at Carolina
5-10 . . . . Augusta

BaseballAmerica.com

Baseball America 2023 Directory • **171**

SCHEDULES

FAYETTEVILLE WOODPECKERS

APRIL
7-9	Carolina
11-16	Fredericksburg
18-23	at Columbia
25-30	Down East

MAY
2-7	at Salem
9-14	Kannapolis
16-21	at Down East
23-28	Myrtle Beach
29-31	at Kannapolis

JUNE
1-4	at Kannapolis
6-11	at Carolina
13-18	Columbia
20-25	at Charleston
28-30	Kannapolis

JULY
1-3	Kannapolis
4-9	at Carolina
14-16	Augusta
18-23	at Lynchburg
25-30	Down East

AUGUST
1-6	Carolina
8-13	at Myrtle Beach
15-20	Lynchburg
22-27	at Down East
29-31	at Kannapolis

SEPTEMBER
1-3	at Kannapolis
5-10	Charleston

FREDERICKSBURG NATIONALS

APRIL
7-9	Lynchburg
11-16	at Fayetteville
18-23	Delmarva
25-30	at Lynchburg

MAY
2-7	Down East
9-14	at Carolina
16-21	Columbia
23-28	at Salem
30-31	Delmarva

JUNE
1-4	Delmarva
6-11	at Charleston
13-18	at Myrtle Beach
20-25	at Columbia
28-30	Salem

JULY
1-3	Salem
4-9	at Delmarva
14-16	Lynchburg
18-23	at Augusta
25-30	Myrtle Beach

AUGUST
1-6	Salem
8-13	at Lynchburg
15-20	Augusta
22-27	at Salem
29-31	Lynchburg

SEPTEMBER
1-3	Lynchburg
5-10	at Delmarva

KANNAPOLIS CANNON BALLERS

APRIL
6-8	at Down East
11-16	at Delmarva
18-23	Charleston
25-30	at Carolina

MAY
2-7	Augusta
9-14	at Fayetteville
16-21	Carolina
23-28	at Augusta
29-31	Fayetteville

JUNE
1-4	Fayetteville
6-11	Lynchburg
13-18	at Down East
20-25	Myrtle Beach
28-30	at Fayetteville

JULY
1-3	at Fayetteville
4-9	Down East
14-16	at Columbia
18-23	at Carolina
25-30	Delmarva

AUGUST
1-6	at Charleston
8-13	Down East
15-20	Carolina
22-27	at Myrtle Beach
29-31	Fayetteville

SEPTEMBER
1-3	Fayetteville
5-10	at Lynchburg

LYNCHBURG HILLCATS

APRIL
7-9	at Fredericksburg
11-16	Myrtle Beach
18-23	at Salem
25-30	Fredericksburg

MAY
2-7	at Charleston
9-14	at Myrtle Beach
16-21	Salem
23-28	at Delmarva
30-31	Carolina

JUNE
1-4	Carolina
6-11	at Kannapolis
13-18	Charleston
20-25	at Carolina
28-30	Delmarva

JULY
1-3	Delmarva
4-9	Salem
14-16	at Fredericksburg
18-23	Fayetteville
25-30	at Salem

AUGUST
1-6	at Delmarva
8-13	Fredericksburg
15-20	at Fayetteville
22-27	Delmarva
29-31	at Fredericksburg

SEPTEMBER
1-3	at Fredericksburg
5-10	Kannapolis

MYRTLE BEACH PELICANS

APRIL
6-8	Charleston
11-16	at Lynchburg
18-23	Augusta
25-30	at Charleston

MAY
2-7	at Columbia
9-14	Lynchburg
16-21	Augusta
23-28	at Fayetteville
30-31	Salem

JUNE
1-4	Salem
6-11	at Augusta
13-18	Fredericksburg
20-25	at Kannapolis
28-30	Charleston

JULY
1-3	Charleston
4-9	at Augusta
14-16	Carolina
18-23	Columbia
25-30	at Fredericksburg

AUGUST
1-6	at Down East
8-13	Fayetteville
15-20	at Columbia
22-27	Kannapolis
29-31	at Charleston

SEPTEMBER
1-3	at Charleston
5-10	Columbia

SALEM RED SOX

APRIL
6-8	Delmarva
11-16	at Carolina
18-23	Lynchburg
25-30	at Delmarva

MAY
2-7	Fayetteville
9-14	Columbia
16-21	at Lynchburg
23-28	Fredericksburg
30-31	at Myrtle Beach

JUNE
1-4	at Myrtle Beach
6-11	at Columbia
13-18	Delmarva
20-25	Down East
28-30	at Fredericksburg

JULY
1-3	at Fredericksburg
4-9	at Lynchburg
14-16	Delmarva
18-23	at Down East
25-30	Lynchburg

AUGUST
1-6	at Fredericksburg
8-13	Augusta
15-20	at Delmarva
22-27	Fredericksburg
29-31	at Augusta

SEPTEMBER
1-3	at Augusta
5-10	Carolina

SCHEDULES

FLORIDA STATE LEAGUE

BRADENTON MARAUDERS

APRIL		JULY	
7-9	Clearwater	1-3	Clearwater
11-16	at Lakeland	4-9	at Daytona
18-23	Daytona	14-16	Dunedin
25-30	at Dunedin	18-23	Fort Myers
		25-30	at St. Lucie

MAY		AUGUST	
2-7	at Tampa	1-6	Tampa
9-14	Lakeland	8-13	at Fort Myers
16-21	at Clearwater	15-20	Lakeland
23-28	Jupiter	22-27	at Jupiter
30-31	at Tampa	29-31	Palm Beach

JUNE		SEPTEMBER	
1-4	at Tampa	1-3	Palm Beach
6-11	Dunedin	5-10	at Fort Myers
13-18	Fort Myers		
20-25	at Lakeland		
28-30	Clearwater		

CLEARWATER THRESHERS

APRIL		JULY	
7-9	at Bradenton	1-3	at Bradenton
11-16	Fort Myers	4-9	Palm Beach
18-23	at Tampa	14-16	at Fort Myers
25-30	St. Lucie	18-23	Tampa
		25-30	at Jupiter

MAY		AUGUST	
2-7	Lakeland	1-6	Lakeland
9-14	at Dunedin	8-13	at Tampa
16-21	Bradenton	15-20	Dunedin
23-28	at St. Lucie	22-27	at Lakeland
30-31	Dunedin	29-31	Fort Myers

JUNE		SEPTEMBER	
1-4	Dunedin	1-3	Fort Myers
6-11	at Fort Myers	5-10	at Palm Beach
13-18	Tampa		
20-25	at Dunedin		
28-30	at Bradenton		

DAYTONA TORTUGAS

APRIL		JULY	
7-9	at St. Lucie	1-3	at Tampa
11-16	Palm Beach	4-9	Bradenton
18-23	at Bradenton	14-16	at Palm Beach
25-30	Fort Myers	18-23	Jupiter
		25-30	at Lakeland

MAY		AUGUST	
2-7	at Palm Beach	1-6	St. Lucie
9-14	St. Lucie	8-13	at Jupiter
16-21	at Jupiter	15-20	Tampa
23-28	Lakeland	22-27	at Fort Myers
30-31	at Palm Beach	29-31	Dunedin

JUNE		SEPTEMBER	
1-4	at Palm Beach	1-3	Dunedin
6-11	at St. Lucie	5-10	at St. Lucie
13-18	Jupiter		
20-25	Palm Beach		
28-30	at Tampa		

DUNEDIN BLUE JAYS

APRIL		JULY	
6-8	at Fort Myers	1-3	at St. Lucie
11-16	Tampa	4-9	Tampa
18-23	at Palm Beach	14-16	at Bradenton
25-30	Bradenton	18-23	Lakeland
		25-30	at Tampa

MAY		AUGUST	
2-7	at Fort Myers	1-6	Fort Myers
9-14	Clearwater	8-13	at Lakeland
16-21	at Tampa	15-20	at Clearwater
23-28	Fort Myers	22-27	St. Lucie
30-31	at Clearwater	29-31	at Daytona

JUNE		SEPTEMBER	
1-4	at Clearwater	1-3	at Daytona
6-11	at Bradenton	5-10	Jupiter
13-18	Lakeland		
20-25	Clearwater		
28-30	at St. Lucie		

FORT MYERS MIGHTY MUSSELS

APRIL		JULY	
6-8	Dunedin	1-3	Lakeland
11-16	at Clearwater	4-9	at Jupiter
18-23	Jupiter	14-16	Clearwater
25-30	at Daytona	18-23	at Bradenton
		25-30	Palm Beach

MAY		AUGUST	
2-7	Dunedin	1-6	at Dunedin
9-14	Tampa	8-13	Bradenton
16-21	at Lakeland	15-20	at Palm Beach
23-28	at Dunedin	22-27	Daytona
30-31	St. Lucie	29-31	at Clearwater

JUNE		SEPTEMBER	
1-4	St. Lucie	1-3	at Clearwater
6-11	Clearwater	5-10	Bradenton
13-18	at Bradenton		
20-25	at Tampa		
28-30	Lakeland		

JUPITER HAMMERHEADS

APRIL		JULY	
6-8	at Palm Beach	1-3	at Palm Beach
11-16	St. Lucie	4-9	Fort Myers
18-23	at Fort Myers	14-16	at St. Lucie
25-30	Tampa	18-23	at Daytona
		25-30	Clearwater

MAY		AUGUST	
2-7	at St. Lucie	1-6	at Palm Beach
9-14	Palm Beach	8-13	Daytona
16-21	Daytona	15-20	at St. Lucie
23-28	at Bradenton	22-27	Bradenton
30-31	at Lakeland	29-31	Lakeland

JUNE		SEPTEMBER	
1-4	at Lakeland	1-3	Lakeland
6-11	Palm Beach	5-10	at Dunedin
13-18	at Daytona		
20-25	St. Lucie		
28-30	at Palm Beach		

BaseballAmerica.com

Baseball America 2023 Directory • **173**

SCHEDULES

LAKELAND FLYING TIGERS

APRIL
7-9	at Tampa
11-16	Bradenton
18-23	at St. Lucie
25-30	Palm Beach

MAY
2-7	at Clearwater
9-14	at Bradenton
16-21	Fort Myers
23-28	at Daytona
30-31	Jupiter

JUNE
1-4	Jupiter
6-11	Tampa
13-18	at Dunedin
20-25	Bradenton
28-30	at Fort Myers

JULY
1-3	at Fort Myers
4-9	St. Lucie
14-16	at Tampa
18-23	at Dunedin
25-30	Daytona

AUGUST
1-6	at Clearwater
8-13	Dunedin
15-20	at Bradenton
22-27	Clearwater
29-31	at Jupiter

SEPTEMBER
1-3	at Jupiter
5-10	Tampa

PALM BEACH CARDINALS

APRIL
6-8	Jupiter
11-16	at Daytona
18-23	Dunedin
25-30	at Lakeland

MAY
2-7	Daytona
9-14	at Jupiter
16-21	at St. Lucie
23-28	Tampa
30-31	Daytona

JUNE
1-4	Daytona
6-11	at Jupiter
13-18	St. Lucie
20-25	at Daytona
28-30	Jupiter

JULY
1-3	Jupiter
4-9	at Clearwater
14-16	Daytona
18-23	St. Lucie
25-30	at Fort Myers

AUGUST
1-6	Jupiter
8-13	at St. Lucie
15-20	Fort Myers
22-27	at Tampa
29-31	at Bradenton

SEPTEMBER
1-3	at Bradenton
5-10	Clearwater

ST. LUCIE METS

APRIL
7-9	Daytona
11-16	at Jupiter
18-23	Lakeland
25-30	at Clearwater

MAY
2-7	Jupiter
9-14	at Daytona
16-21	Palm Beach
23-28	Clearwater
30-31	at Fort Myers

JUNE
1-4	at Fort Myers
6-11	Daytona
13-18	at Palm Beach
20-25	at Jupiter
28-30	Dunedin

JULY
1-3	Dunedin
4-9	at Lakeland
14-16	Jupiter
18-23	at Palm Beach
25-30	Bradenton

AUGUST
1-6	at Daytona
8-13	Palm Beach
15-20	Jupiter
22-27	at Dunedin
29-31	at Tampa

SEPTEMBER
1-3	at Tampa
5-10	Daytona

TAMPA TARPONS

APRIL
7-9	Lakeland
11-16	at Dunedin
18-23	Clearwater
25-30	at Jupiter

MAY
2-7	Bradenton
9-14	at Fort Myers
16-21	Dunedin
23-28	at Palm Beach
30-31	Bradenton

JUNE
1-4	Bradenton
6-11	at Lakeland
13-18	at Clearwater
20-25	Fort Myers
28-30	Daytona

JULY
1-3	Daytona
4-9	at Dunedin
14-16	Lakeland
18-23	at Clearwater
25-30	Dunedin

AUGUST
1-6	at Bradenton
8-13	Clearwater
15-20	at Daytona
22-27	Palm Beach
29-31	St. Lucie

SEPTEMBER
1-3	St. Lucie
5-10	at Lakeland

174 · Baseball America 2023 Directory

BaseballAmerica.com

PARTNER/ INDEPENDENT LEAGUES

PARTNER/INDEPENDENT LEAGUES

AMERICAN ASSOCIATION

Mailing Address: PO Box 995, Moorhead, MN 56561-0995.
Telephone: (218) 512-0380.
Email: info@aabaseball.com
Websites: aabaseball.com, aabaseball.tv
Year Founded: 2005.
Commissioner: Joshua E. Schaub. **Deputy Commissioner:** Josh Buchholz. **Director of Umpires:** Ronnie Teague. **Director of Digital Media:** Jake Kranz. **Digital Content Host:** TBD. **League Historian:** Hoffman Wolff.
Board of Directors: Jim Abel (Lincoln), Mark Brandmeyer (Kansas City), Daryn Eudaly (Cleburne), Dr. Bob Froehlich (Kane County), Shawn Hunter (Chicago), Sam Katz (Winnipeg), Tom Kelenic (Lake Country), John Roost (Sioux City), Patrick Salvi (Gary SouthShore), Brian Slipka (Sioux Falls), Brad Thom (Fargo-Moorhead), Mike Zimmerman (Milwaukee).
Division Structure: East—Chicago Dogs, Cleburne Railroaders, Gary SouthShore RailCats, Kane County Cougars, Lake Country DockHounds, Milwaukee Milkmen. West—Fargo-Moorhead RedHawks, Kansas City Monarchs, Lincoln Saltdogs, Sioux City Explorers, Sioux Falls Canaries, Winnipeg Goldeyes.
Regular Season: 100 games. **Opening Date:** May 11. **Closing Date:** September 4.
Playoff Format: Top four teams in each division play in best-of-three series. Winners play in best-of-three Division Series. Winners play best-of-five American Association Finals.
Roster Limit: 25. **Player Eligibility Rule:** Minimum of five first-year players; maximum of six veterans (at least six or more years of professional service).
Brand of Baseball: Rawlings. **Statistician:** Pointstreak/Stack Sports, 5360 Legacy Drive, Suite #150, Plano, TX 75024.

STADIUM INFORMATION

Club	Stadium	Opened	LF	CF	RF	Capacity	2022 Att.
Chicago	Impact Field	2018	313	389	294	6,300	191,984
Cleburne	The Depot at Cleburne Station	2017	335	400	320	3,750	65,062
Fargo-Moorhead	Newman Outdoor Field	1996	314	408	318	4,172	147,073
Gary SouthShore	U.S. Steel Yard	2002	320	400	335	6,139	152,894
Kane County	Northwestern Medicine Field	1991	335	400	335	10,923	248,354
Kansas City	Legends Field	2003	300	396	328	6,270	105,302
Lake Country	Wisconsin Brewing Company Park	2022	325	400	325	3,641	93,711
Lincoln	Haymarket Park	2001	335	403	325	4,500	144,494
Milwaukee	Franklin Field	2019	330	407	330	4,000	86,028
Sioux City	Mercy Field at Lewis and Clark Park	1993	330	400	330	3,800	52,121
Sioux Falls	Sioux Falls Stadium	1964	313	410	312	4,462	59,425
Winnipeg	Shaw Park	1999	325	400	325	7,121	163,893

CHICAGO DOGS

Office Address: 9800 Balmoral Avenue, Rosemont, IL, 60018. **Telephone:** 847.636.5450.
E-mail: info@thechicagodogs.com. **Website:** thechicagodogs.com. **Owner:** Shawn Hunter.
Chief Operating Officer/Baseball Operations: Trish Zuro. **Corporate Sponsorships:** Chris Lennon. **Director of Sales:** Evan Gersonde. **Sales Managers:** Jon Ryan & Mackenzie Thomas. **Account Executives:** Robert Liable & Shaun Van Tholen. **Social Media and Game Entertainment:** Meredith Cavaleri. **Media Relations:** Alexandra Jakubiak. **Community Relations:** Daniela Barrios. **Broadcast and Media Relations Manager:** Sam Brief. **Website Design/Photographer:** Matt Zuro. **Director of Operations Food & Beverage:** Joe Costa.
Manager: Butch Hobson. **Pitching Coach:** Stu Cliburn. **Hitting Coach:** Joe Dominiak. **Clubhouse Manager:** Edgardo Lopez. **Head Groundskeeper:** Justin Spillman.

GAME INFORMATION
Broadcaster: Sam Brief. **Games Broadcast:** 100. **Stadium Name:** Impact Field, 9850 Balmoral Avenue, Rosemont, IL 60018.
Standard Game Times: Mon.-Fri.: 6:30 pm, Sat.: 6:00 pm, Sun.: 3:00 pm

CLEBURNE RAILROADERS

Address: 1906 Brazzle Boulevard, Cleburne, TX 76033. **Telephone:** (817) 945-8705.
Email: info@railroaderbaseball.com. **Website:** railroaderbaseball.com.
Co-Owner: Daryn Eudaly. **Co-Owner:** Collide Agency. **Co-Owner:** Top Tier Sports. **Co-Owner:** John Junker
General Manager: John Junker. **Business Manager:** Bill Adams. **Assistant General Manage/Sales:** Rory Niewenhous. **Ticket Sales:** Zack Gentry. **Broadcasting:** Brad Allred. **Media Relations and Social Media Manager:** Keaton Cordell. **Clubhouse Manager:** Cleo Welch.
Field Manager: Logan Watkins. **Hitting Coach:** Jose Amado. **Pitching Coach:** James Russell.

PARTNER/INDEPENDENT LEAGUES

GAME INFORMATION
Broadcaster: Brad Allred. **Games Broadcast:** 100. **Stadium Name:** The Depot at Cleburne Station. **Directions:** From Chisholm Trail Parkway (toll road) continue south across US HWY 67, turn left onto Cleburne Station Boulevard. From US HWY 67 South, exit Nolan River Road, turn left onto Nolan River Road, turn left onto Cleburne Station Boulevard. From US HWY 67 North, exit Nolan River Road, turn right onto Nolan River Road, turn left onto Cleburne Station Boulevard. **Standard Game Times:** Mon.-Sat., 7:06 pm, Sun., 6:00 pm.

FARGO-MOORHEAD REDHAWKS

Address: 1515 15th Ave N Fargo, ND 58102. **Telephone:** (701) 235-6161. **Fax:** (701) 297-9247.
Email: redhawks@fmredhawks.com, media@fmredhawks.com. **Website:** fmredhawks.com
Operated by: Fargo Baseball LLC.
Chairman of the Board: N. Bruce Thom. **President & CEO:** Brad Thom.
Vice President/General Manager: Matt Rau. **Vice President, Finance:** Rick Larson. **Vice President/Director of Promotions:** Karl Hoium. **Community Relations, Merchandise and Ticket Operations Director:** Ashley McCoy. **Stadium Superintendent/Head Groundskeeper:** Tom Drietz. **Box Office Manager:** Grant Langseth. **Group Sales Manager:** Teresa Mattson. **Food and Beverage Director:** Will Thom.
Field Manager: Chris Coste. **Hitting Coach:** Anthony Renz. **Pitching Coach:** Kevin McGovern. **Bullpen Coach:** Robbie Lopez. **Player Personnel Consultant:** Jeff Bittiger.

GAME INFORMATION
Radio Announcer: Jack Michaels. **Games Broadcast:** 100. **Flagship Station:** 740 THE FAN (KNFL-740AM, K297BW 107.3FM). **Stadium Name:** Newman Outdoor Field (1996). **Location:** I-29 North to exit 67, east on 19th Ave North, right on Albrecht Boulevard. **Standard Game Times:** M-F. 7:02 pm Sat.: 6:00 pm, Sun.: 1:00 pm.

GARY SOUTHSHORE RAILCATS

Address: One Stadium Plaza, Gary, IN 46402. **Telephone:** (219) 882-2255. **Fax:** (219) 882-2259.
Email Address: info@railcatsbaseball.com. **Website:** railcatsbaseball.com.
Operated by: Salvi Sports Enterprises.
Owner/CEO: Pat Salvi. **Owner:** Lindy Salvi.
President, Salvi Sports Enterprises: Brian Lyter. **General Manager:** Anthony Giammanco. **Assistant General Manager:** Noah Simmons. **Director of Marketing and Promotions:** Ashley Nylen. **Box Office Manager:** Matt Murphy. **Marketing Consultant:** Renee Connelly. **Head Groundskeeper:** Hunter Mihalic. **Manager of Hospitality & Special Events:** Taylor Campbell. **VP of Corporate Sponsorships, Salvi Sports Consulting:** David Kay.
Field Manager: Lamarr Rogers.

GAME INFORMATION
Broadcaster: Ryan Zimmerman. **Games Broadcast:** 100. **Flagship Station:** WEFM 95.9-FM. **Stadium Name:** Steel Yard. **Location:** Take I-65 North to end of highway at U.S. 12/20 (Dunes Highway). Turn left on U.S. 12/20 heading west for 1.5 miles (three stop lights). Stadium is on left side. **Standard Game Times:** Mon.-Fri.: 6:45 pm, Sat.: 4:00 pm, Sun.: 2:00 pm.

KANE COUNTY COUGARS

Address: 34W002 Cherry Lane, Geneva, IL 60134.
Telephone: (630) 232-8811. **Fax:** (630) 232-8815.
Email: info@kanecountycougars.com. **Website:** www.kccougars.com.
Operated By: Cougars Baseball Partnership/American Sports Enterprises, Inc.
Chairman/Chief Executive Officer/President: Dr. Bob Froehlich. **Owners:** Dr. Bob Froehlich, Cheryl Froehlich. **Board of Directors:** Dr. Bob Froehlich, Cheryl Froehlich, Stephanie Froehlich, Chris Neidhart, Marianne Neidhart.
Vice President/General Manager: Curtis Haug. **Director of Governmental & Business Relations:** John J. Louizos Esq. **Senior Director, Finance/Administration:** Douglas Czurylo. **Accounting:** Sally Sullivan. **Senior Director, Ticketing:** R. Michael Patterson. **Director, Ticket Operations:** Amy Mason. **Ticket Operations Coordinator:** Jeff Weaver. **Ticket Operations Intern:** Andrew Gambino. **Ballpark Event Coordinators:** Mackensi Karman, Lauren Paisker, Jake Zielinski. **Ticket Sales Interns:** Ryan Ashley, Michael Navigato, Tanner Tietz. **Sponsorship Liaison:** Steve Grzenia. **Director, Security:** TBD. **Director, Public Relations & Promotions:** Claire Jacobi. **Social Media Manager:** Jemea Green, **Design/Graphics:** Derek Murphy, Chris Wunnenberg. **Media Placement Coordinator:** Bill Baker. **Office Manager:** Sherri Johnson. **Video Director:** TBD. **Director, Food & Beverage:** Jon Nekolny. **Event & Coordinating Manager:** Cassidy Congdon. **Culinary Manager:** Ron Kludac. **Personnel Manager:** Jen Miller. **Director, Sales/Facilities:** Mike Klafehn. **Stadium Operations Manager:** Scott Anderson. **Director, Maintenance:** Jeff Snyder. **Head Groundskeeper:** Sean Ehlert.

PARTNER/INDEPENDENT LEAGUES

Field Manager: George Tsamis. **Hitting Coach:** Matt Passarelle. **Pitching Coach:** TBD. **Team Physician:** Dr. James Sostak. **Athletic Trainer:** TBD. **Clubhouse Manager:** TBD.

GAME INFORMATION
Radio Announcer: Joe Brand. **No. of Games Broadcast:** 50. **Flagship Station:** TBD. **Official Scorer:** Mike Haase. **Stadium Name:** Northwestern Medicine Field. **Location:** From east or west, (I-88 Ronald Reagan Memorial Tollway) to Farnsworth Ave. North exit, north five miles to Cherry Lane, left into stadium complex. From northwest, I-90 (Jane Addams Memorial Tollway) to Randall Rd. South exit, south 15 miles to Fabyan Parkway, east to Kirk Rd., north to Cherry Lane, left into stadium complex. **Standard Game Times:** Mon.-Sat.: 6:30 pm, Sun.: 1:00 pm.

KANSAS CITY MONARCHS

Address: 1800 Village West Parkway, Kansas City, KS 66111. **Telephone:** (913) 328-5618. **Email:** info@monarchsbaseball.com. **Web:** monarchsbaseball.com.
Operated by: Max Fun Entertainment, LLC.
Principal Owner: Mark Brandmeyer. **Partner/CEO:** Mark McKee.
President & General Manager: Jay S. Hinrichs. **Vice President, Hospitality:** Jim Cundiff.
Chief Financial Officer: Tom Ross. **Manager, Group Sales:** Nick Restivo. **Manager, Ticket Operations:** Kacy Muller. **Information Technology:** David Chick. **Manager, Hospitality:** Monica Garcia. **Manager, Production & Digital Assets:** Morgan Kolenda. **Uniform and Retail Production:** Pat Bachofer. **Host Family Coordinator:** Cheryl Reitmeyer. **Facility Maintenance:** Abraham Mercado. **Groundskeeper:** Nick Marquez. **Business Development:** Steven Como. **Graphics:** Tyson Moyer.
Team Physician: Dr. Michael Dempewolf, Sanos Orthopedics. **Certified Athletic Trainer:** Jared Bashaw.
Field Manager: Joe Calfapietra. **Coaches:** Frank White, Bill Sobbe. **Equipment Manager:** John West.

GAME INFORMATION
Radio Announcer: Carter Woodiel. **Games broadcast:** 100. **Site:** www.monarchsbaseball.com. **Public Address Announcer:** Nate Herron. **Game Day Production:** Kevin Schulmeister & Brad Zimmerman.
Stadium Name: Legends Field. **Location:** State Avenue West off I-435 Kansas City, Kansas. **Standard Game Times:** Mon.-Fri.: 7:00 pm, Sat.: 6:00 pm, Sun.: 1:00 pm.

LAKE COUNTRY DOCKHOUNDS

Address: 1011 Blue Ribbon Circle N, Oconomowoc, WI 53066. **Telephone:** (262) 468-7750
Email: info@lakecountry-live.com. **Website:** dockhounds.com
Managing Partners: Tony Bryant, Sonny Bando, Tom Kelenic, Tim Neubert
COO: Lisa Kelenic. **General Manager:** Trish Rasberry. **Stadium Operations Manager:** Zach Naatz. **Entertainment & Fan Experience Manager:** Lauren Huettner. **Marketing & Communications Manager:** Bryan Giese. **Group Sales Managers:** Justin Hunt & Tristan Kaufmann.
Field Manager: Jim Bennett. **Pitching Coach:** Paul Wagner. **Hitting Coach:** Bruce Hines. **Bench Coach:** Mike Couchee.

GAME INFORMATION
Broadcaster: Dominic Stearn. **Games Broadcast:** 100. **Stadium Name:** Wisconsin Brewing Company Park. **Location:** 1011 Blue Ribbon Circle N, Oconomowoc, WI 53066.
Standard Game Times: Mon.-Fri.: 6:35 pm, Sat.: 6:05 pm, Sun.: 1:35pm.

LINCOLN SALTDOGS

Address: 403 Line Drive Circle, Suite A, Lincoln, NE 68508. **Telephone:** (402) 474-BALL (2255). **Fax:** (402) 474-2254.
Email Address: info@saltdogs.com. **Website:** saltdogs.com.
Chairman: Jim Abel. **President:** Charlie Meyer. **General Manager:** Shane Tritz.
Director, Broadcasting/Communications: Michael Dixon. **Director, Stadium Operations:** Dave Aschwege. **Director, Video Production:** Michael Klein. **Assistant Director, Stadium Operations:** Brenden Gerlach. **Manager, Ticket Sales:** Kanai Kuhnel. **Group Sales Executive:** Alex Farrens. **Athletic Turf Manager:** Kyle Trewhitt. **Assistant Turf Manager:** Kyle Lengfelder. **Assistant Turf Manager:** Robyn Sullivan. **Office Manager:** Nikki Chipps. **Director of Operations, Concessions:** Steve Deriese. **Director, Kitchen Operations:** Katie Wilkinson.
Field Manager: Brett Jodie. **Coaches:** T.J. Zarewicz & Adam Donachie.

GAME INFORMATION
Public Address Announcer: Heath Kramer. **Broadcast Team:** Jeff Briden & Connor Clark. **No. of Games Broadcast:** 100. **Flagship Station:** KLMS 1480AM & ESPN101.5 FM. **Stadium Name:** Haymarket Park. **Location:** I-80 to Cornhusker Highway West, left on First Street, right on Sun Valley Boulevard, left on Line Drive. **Standard Game Times:** Mon.-Fri.: 7:05 pm, Sat.: 6:05 pm, Sun.: 1:05 pm.

PARTNER/INDEPENDENT LEAGUES

MILWAUKEE MILKMEN

Address: 7044 S. Ballpark Drive, Ste 300, Franklin WI 53132. **Telephone:** (414) 224-9823
Website: milwaukeemilkmen.com
Owner: Michael Zimmerman. **General Manager:** Dan Kuenzi. **Senior VP of Ticketing & Corporate Partnership:** Mike Doyle. **Director, Production & Entertainment:** Paul Cimoch.
CFO: Tom Johns. **Medical Staff:** Midwest Orthopedic Specialty Hospital.
Field Manager: Anthony Barone. **Hitting Coach:** DJ Boston. **Pitching Coach:** Jose Rodriguez

GAME INFORMATION
Stadium Name: Franklin Field. **Location:** 7035 S. Ballpark Drive, Franklin, WI 53132. **Standard Game Times:** Mon.-Fri.: 6:35 pm. Sat.: 6:00 pm. Sun.: 1:00 pm.

SIOUX CITY EXPLORERS

Address: 3400 Line Drive, Sioux City, IA 51106. **Telephone:** (712) 277-9467. **Fax:** (712) 277-9406.
Email Address: promotions@xsbaseball.com. **Website:** www.xsbaseball.com.
Owner: John Roost.
AGM: Cheyenne Anderson. **Director, Stadium Operations & Baseball Operation:** Chris Hasskarl. **Director, Sales:** Tara Rethman. **Director, Media Relations/Radio Broadcaster:** Zach Berman
Field Manager: Steve Montgomery. **Pitching Coach:** Bobby Post. **Athletic Trainer:** Bruce Fischbach. **Clubhouse Manager:** TBD.

GAME INFORMATION
Radio Announcer: Zach Berman. **No. of Games Broadcast:** 100. **Flagship Station:** KSCJ 1360-AM. **Webcast Address:** www.xsbaseball.com. **Stadium Name:** Mercy Field at Lewis and Clark Park. **Location:** I-29 to Singing Hills Blvd North, right on Line Drive. **Standard Game Times:** Mon.-Fri.: 7:05 pm, Sat.: 6:05 pm, Sun.: 4:00 pm.

SIOUX FALLS CANARIES

Office Address: 1001 N West Ave, Sioux Falls, SD 57104. **Telephone:** (605) 336-6060.
Email Address: info@sfcanaries.com. **Website:** sfcanaries.com.
Operated by: True North Sports, LLC.
Managing Partner/Co-Owner: Brian Slipka. **Co-Owner:** Anthony Albanese. **President:** Brian Jamros. **General Manager:** Duell Higbe. **External Operations & Gameday Manager:** Ali Lindner. **Community Relations & Special Events Coordinator:** Whitney Sitzman. **Food & Beverage Director:** Jess Blodgett. **Sales Manager:** Preston Kern. **Sales:** Jack Lust, Jakob Fritsch and Bailey Fey
Field Manager: Mike Meyer.

GAME INFORMATION
Radio Announcer: Tanner Hoops. **Public Address Announcer:** Randy Preston. **Game Entertainment:** John Gaskins. **No. of Games Broadcast:** 100. **Flagship Station:** FOX Sports KWSN 98.1FM/1230AM. **Webcast Address:** www.kwsn.com. **Stadium Name:** Sioux Falls Stadium. **Location:** I-29 to Russell Street, east one mile, south on West Avenue. **Standard Game Times:** Mon.-Fri.: 6:35 pm, Sat.: 5:35 pm, Sun.: 12:05 pm.

WINNIPEG GOLDEYES

Office Address: One Portage Ave E, Winnipeg, Manitoba R3B 3N3. **Telephone:** (204) 982-2273. **Fax:** (204) 982-2274.
Email: contact@goldeyes.com. **Website:** www.goldeyes.com.
Operated by: Winnipeg Goldeyes Baseball Club, Inc.
Principal Owner/President: Sam Katz.
General Manager: Andrew Collier. **Vice President & COO:** Regan Katz. **CFO:** Jason McRae-King. **Director, Sales/Marketing:** Dan Chase. **Manager, Ticket Office:** Paul Duque. **Coordinator, Food/Beverage:** Melissa Schlichting. **Account Executives:** Mike Holmes, Will Sutton, Sylvia Boslovitch. **Group Sales and Game Presentation:** Ed Doiron. **Digital Media Manager:** Jason Young. **Manager, Retail:** Alex Baronins. **Controller:** TJ Singh. **Facility Manager:** Don Ferguson. **Front Office Reception:** Lindsay Jestin.
Field Manager/Director, Player Procurement: Greg Tagert. **Hitting Coach:** Amos Ramon. **Pitching Coach:** Tom Thornton. **Clubhouse Manager:** Jamie Samson. **Athletic Therapist:** Ty Hassel.

GAME INFORMATION
No. of Games Broadcast: 100. **Flagship Station:** CJNU 93.7 FM. **Stadium Name:** Shaw Park. **Location:** North on Pembina Highway to Broadway, East on Broadway to Main Street, North on Main Street to Water Avenue, East on Water Avenue to Westbrook Street, North on Westbrook Street to Lombard Avenue, East on Lombard Avenue to Mill Street, South on Mill Street to ballpark. **Standard Game Times:** Mon.-Fri.: 6:30 pm, Sat.: 6:00 pm, Sun.: 1:00 pm.

PARTNER/INDEPENDENT LEAGUES

ATLANTIC LEAGUE

Mailing Address: PO Box 5190, Lancaster, Pa., 17606.
Telephone: (303) 915-8414 or (978) 790-5421.
Email Address: suggestions@atlanticleague.com. **Website:** www.atlanticleague.com.
Year Founded: 1998.
Founder/Chairman: Frank Boulton.
Board of Directors: Brandon Bellamy, Frank Boulton, Jack Lavoie, Susan Martinelli Shea, Andy Shea, Bill Shipley, Eric Shuffler, Coy Williard, Jr., Bob Zuckerman.
President: Rick White.
League Administrator: Emily Merrill. **Director of Communications:** Steve Shutt. **Director of Social Media:** Andrew Bandstra. **Director of Umpire Development:** Kevin Winn.
Division Structure: North—Lancaster, Long Island, Southern Maryland, Staten Island, York. **South**—Charleston, Frederick, Gastonia, High Point, Lexington.
Regular Season: 126 games (split-season).
2023 Opening Date: April 28. **Closing Date:** Sept. 17.
Playoff Format: First-half division winners meet second-half winners in best-of-five series; Winners meet in best-of-five final for league championship.
Roster Limit: 27. **Eligibility Rule:** No restrictions; MLB and MiLB suspensions honored.
Brand of Baseball: Drake. **Statistical Service:** Major League Baseball.

STADIUM INFORMATION

Club	Stadium	Opened	LF	CF	RF	Capacity	2022 Att.
Charleston	GoMart BallPark	2005	330	400	320	4,300	119,598
Gastonia	CaroMont Health Park	2021	315	400	325	5,000	101,471
High Point	Truist Point	2019	336	400	339	4,024	124,010
Frederick	Nymeo Field at Harry Grove Stadium	1990	325	400	325	6,033	N/A
Lancaster	Clipper Magazine Stadium	2005	320	400	300	6,250	222,167
Lexington	Wild Health Field	2001	320	401	318	7,800	150,392
Long Island	Fairfield Properties Ballpark	2000	325	400	325	6,002	285,888
Staten Island	Community Park	2001	320	390	318	8,500	76,759
So. Maryland	Regency Furniture Stadium	2008	310	400	325	6,000	174,293
York	PeoplesBank Park	2007	300	405	325	7,312	172,519

CHARLESTON DIRTY BIRDS

Address: 601 Morris St., Charleston, WV 25301. **Telephone:** (304) 344-2287
E-Mail: info@dirtybirdsbaseball.com. **Website:** www.dirtybirdsbaseball.com
Years In League: 2021-
Operated By: Andy Shea. **President/CEO:** Andy Shea
General Manager: Jeremy Taylor. **Business Manager:** Ben Blum. **Player Personnel Director:** Andrew Thompson. **Manager of Ticketing/Box Office Operations:** Mackenzie Brown. **Director of Corporate and Group Sales:** George Levandoski. **Group Sales:** Blaine Smith. **Suite Manager:** Nathan Richard. **Promotions/Community Relations/Communications:** Eden Douglas. **Merchandise Manager:** Jessica Swartz. **Special Events:** Blaine Smith.
Field Manager: Billy Horn. **Pitching Coach:** Joe Testa. **Bench Coach:** Anthony Coromato. **Bullpen Coach:** Eddy Milian.

GAME INFORMATION

Flagship Station/Streaming Platform: YouTube.com. **Ballpark:** GoMart Ballpark. **Location:** I-77 South to Capitol Street exit, left on Lee Street, left on Brooks Street.

FREDERICK BASEBALL CLUB

Address: 21 Stadium Drive, Frederick, MD 21703.
Telephone: : (301) 662-0013. **E-Mail:** info@frederickatlanticleague.com.
Website: www.frederickatlanticleague.com. **Years In League:** 2023-
Owner/CEO: Greg Baroni. **Owner/President:** Rich Roberts
Senior Vice President of Baseball Operations: Chuck Domino. **Executive Director of Baseball Operations:** Mary Nixon. **General Manager:** Andrew Klein. **Assistant General Manager:** Kari Collins. **Director of Marketing:** Branden McGee. **Director of Client Services:** Patrick Koogle/ **Box Office Manager:** Darin Cline. **Account Executive:** Chris Moore. **Head Groundskeeper:** Mike Dunn. **Food & Beverage Manager:** Erik Schneidhauer.
Manager: Mark Minicozzi. **Pitching Coach:** TBA. **Hitting Coach:** TBA. **Bench Coach:** TBA. **Trainer:** TBA. **Clubhouse Manager:** Brady Woods.

GAME INFORMATION

Radio Announcer: TBA. **Ballpark:** Nymeo Field at Harry Grove Stadium. **Location:** 21 Stadium Drive, Frederick, MD 21703.

PARTNER/INDEPENDENT LEAGUES

GASTONIA HONEY HUNTERS

Address: 800 West Franklin Blvd., Gastonia, NC 28052. **Telephone:** (704) 874-1810.
E-Mail: : info@gohoneyhunters.com. **Website:** www.gohoneyhunters.com.
Years In League: 2021-
Owner: Brandon Bellamy. **COO/GM:** Veronica Jeon. **General Manager:** David Martin.
Assistant General Manager: Brady Salisbury. **Box Office Manager:** Lauren Teer. **Senior Operations Manager:** Brian Fisher. **Box Office Manager:** Lauren Teer. **Sales Manager:** Payne Yoder. **Account Executives:** Butch Cox, Kyle Barry, Paige Miller. **Digital Marketing Coordinator:** Maddie Welch. **PR & Community Relations Coordinator:** Madison Hyleman. **Senior Manager, Sports & Entertainment Events:** Alexis Gray.
Manager: Mauro "Goose" Gozzo. **Hitting Coach:** Chuck Stewart. **Pitching Coach:** TBA. **Trainer:** Anna McCraw

GAME INFORMATION
Flagship Station/Streaming Platform: Youtube.com/honeyhuntersmedia. **Ballpark:** Caromont Health Park. **Location:** 800 W. Franklin Blvd, Gastonia.

HIGH POINT ROCKERS

Office Address: 301 N. Elm Street, High Point, NC 27262. **Telephone:** (336) 888-1000.
E-Mail Address: info@highpointrockers.com.
Website: www.HighPointRockers.com. ›**Years In League:** 2019-
Operated by: High Point Baseball, Inc.
Chairman, Board of Directors: Coy Williard. **President:** Pete Fisch.
Box Office Manager: Kaitlyn Camp. **Facilities Operations Manager:** Shane Poling. **Sales Executive:** J.P. Rooney. **Account Executive:** Garrett Allen. **Fan Experience & Promotions Coordinator:** Alicia Marcotte. **Special Events Coordinator:** Alex Mendenhall. **Director of Corporate Sales/Merchandise:** Caroline Cooling. **Business Manager:** Sherrie Poplin. **Concessions Manager:** Tyler Runyon. **Director of Communications:** Steve Shutt. **Community Relations & Social Media Manager:** Tanner Smith
Manager: Jamie Keefe. **Pitching Coach:** Frank Viola. **Bench Coach/Player Personnel:** Albert Gonzalez. **Trainer:** Joe Geck

GAME INFORMATION
Radio Announcer: Kendrick Fruits. **Flagship Station/Streaming Platform:** YouTube/High Point Rockers Baseball. **Ballpark:** Truist Point. **Location:** 301 N. Elm Street, High Point, NC 27262.

LANCASTER BARNSTORMERS

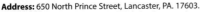

Address: 650 North Prince Street, Lancaster, PA. 17503.
Telephone: (717) 509-4487. **E-Mail:** info@lancasterbarnstormers.com.
Website: www.LancasterBarnstormers.com. **Years In League:** 2005-
Operated By: Lancaster Baseball Club, LLC.
Partners: Bob Zuckerman, Ian Ruzow, Steve Zuckerman, Rob Liss. **President/GM:** Michael Reynolds. **VP, Sales/Marketing:** Kristen Simon. **VP, Corporate Partnerships:** Melissa Tucker. **CFO:** Pam Raffensberger. **Box Office Manager/Ticket Sales:** Adam Smith. **Corporate Sponsorships:** Melissa Tucker. **Promotions:** Alex Bunn. **Community Relations:** Maureen Wheeler. **Marketing:** Lauren Zuckerman. **Special Events:** Sarah Weisenfluh. **Fan Engagement:** Ryan Cortazzo. **Director of Culinary Operations:** Mike White. **Social Media Director:** Laura Flowers. **Merchandise:** Samantha Biastre.
Manager: Ross Peeples. **Hitting Coach:** TBD. **Bench Coach:** Troy Steffy. **Trainer:** TBD. **Clubhouse Manager:** TBD.

GAME INFORMATION
Radio Announcer: Dave Collins. **Flagship Station/Streaming Platform:** YouTube.com. **Ballpark:** Clipper Magazine Stadium. **Location:** 650 N. Prince St, Lancaster, PA.

LEXINGTON LEGENDS

Address: 207 Legends Lane, Lexington, KY 40505. **Telephone:** (859) 252-4487. **Website:** www.lexingtonlegends.com. **Years In League:** 2021-
Owner: Nathan Lyons. **President/CEO:** Justin Ferrarell. **Organizational Development Director:** Whitney Penny. **Business Manager:** Heather Lowder. **Sales & Marketing Consultant:** Mike Allison. **Ticket Operations Manager:** Kade Sword. **Corporate Sales Executive:** Landon Cochran. **Sr. Account Executive-Ticket Sales:** Robby Drakeford
Manager: Barry Lyons. **Pitching Coach:** Cameron Roth. **Hitting Coach:** Enohel Polanco. **Bench Coach:** Bryan Swalley. **Trainer:** Joseph Holstedt.

GAME INFORMATION

Radio Announcer: TBA. **Flagship Station/Streaming Platform:** YouTube.com/Lexington Legends. **Ballpark:** Wild Health Field. **Location:** 207 Legends, Lane, Lexington, KY.

PARTNER/INDEPENDENT LEAGUES

LONG ISLAND DUCKS

Address: Fairfield Properties Ballpark, 3 Court House Dr, Central Islip, NY 11722.
Telephone: (631) 940-3825. **E-Mail:** info@liducks.com. **Website:** www.liducks.com.
Years In League: 2000-
Founder/CEO: Frank Boulton. **Owner/Chairman:** Seth Waugh. **President/General Manager:** Michael Pfaff.
Assistant GM/Senior VP, Sales: Doug Cohen. **VP, Box Office:** Brad Kallman. **VP, Communications:** Michael Polak.
Controller: AnnMarie DeMasi. **Dir., Group Sales:** Sean Smith. **Dir., Stadium Operations:** Anthony Polito. **Stadium Operations Coordinator:** Jake Hunter. **Human Resources/Office Manager:** Christine Blumenauer. **Merchandise Manager:** Michelle Jensen.
Executives: Matt Heilbrunn, Harrison Nolan, Justice Lallier. **Head Groundskeeper:** Dakota Smothergill. **Administrative Coordinator:** Glenn Newsome. **GM, Food & Beverage:** Alan Goodman.
Manager: Wally Backman. **Hitting Coach:** TBA. **Pitching Coach:** TBA. **Director, Sports Medicine:** TBA. **Head Athletic Trainer:** TBA. **Clubhouse Manager:** Emil Coccaro

GAME INFORMATION
Radio Announcers: Michael Mohr, Chris King, David Weiss. **Flagship Station/Streaming Platform:** LIDucks.com; Facebook.com/liducks; YouTube.com/ducksbaseball. **Ballpark:** Fairfield Properties Ballpark. **Location:** 3 Court House Dr, Central Islip, NY.

SOUTHERN MARYLAND BLUE CRABS

Address: 11765 St. Linus Drive, Waldorf, Maryland 20602.
Telephone: (301) 638-9788. **E-Mail:** info@somdbluecrabs.com.
Website: www.somdbluecrabs.com. **Years In League:** 2008-
Operated By: Crabs On Deck, LLC. **General Manager:** Courtney Knichel. **Assistant General Manager:** Trevor Lakins. **Promotions & Media Relations Manager:** Steve Bowen. **Community Relations Manager:** Jacob Dunaway. **Partnership Marketing Manager:** Chris Morris. **Sales Account Executive:** Jordan Beslow. **Director of Corporate Sponsorships:** Matt Hoepfl. **Stadium Operations:** Sheila Wilkerson. **Concessions:** Carousel Hospitality.
Groundskeeper: Ken Brooks.
Manager: Stan Cliburn. **Bench Coach:** Ray Ortega. **Pitching Coach:** Daryl Thompson. **Hitting Coach:** Braxton Lee. **Trainer:** Lauren Eck.

GAME INFORMATION
Radio Announcer: Andrew Mild. **Ballpark:** Regency Furniture Stadium. **Location:** 11765 St. Linus Drive, Waldorf, MD.

STATEN ISLAND FERRYHAWKS

Address: 75 Richmond Terrace, Staten Island, NY 10301. **E-Mail:** fun@ferryhawks.com.
Website: www.ferryhawks.com. **Years In League:** 2022-
Operated By: Staten Island Entertainment, LLC.
Owner/Chairman: John Catsimatidis. **Owner/President/CEO:** Eric Shuffler. **General Manager:** Gary Perone. **Chief Operating Officer/Chief Financial Officer:** Katie Mahoney-Vinson. **General Manager of Facility Operations:** Ray Irizarry. **VP Community Engagement:** Flynn Ferguson. **VP Ticket Sales and Services:** Jason Velez.
Box Office Manager: Scott McKinley. **Group Sales/Suite Manager:** Jason Velez. **Group Sales Representatives:** Joseph Gitto, Michael Goldberg, Pierceton Agdamag. **Corporate Sponsorships:** Kevin Brown. **Promotions:** Chelsea Ortiz. **Merchandise:** David Markowitz. **Marketing & Sponsorship Coordinator:** Mike Crescente. **Graphic Design/Creative Services Manager:** Trish Konczynski. **Concessions:** Scott Cruz.
Manager: Homer Bush. **Hitting Coach:** TBA. **Pitching Coach:** TBA. **Trainer:** Julianna Mangano.

GAME INFORMATION
Ballpark: Staten Island University Hospital "Community Park.". **Location:** 75 Richmond Terrace, Staten Island, NY.

YORK REVOLUTION

Address: 5 Brooks Robinson Way, York, PA 17401.
Telephone: (717) 801-4487. **Email:** info@yorkrevolution.com.
Website: www.yorkrevolution.com. **Years In League:** 2007-
Operated by: York Professional Baseball Club, LLC.
Owner: Bill Shipley. **President:** Eric Menzer. **General Manager/Vice President, Operations:** John Gibson. **VP, Business Development:** Nate Tile. **Director, Marketing/Communications:** Doug Eppler. **Director of Ticket & Retail Operations:** Cindy Brown. **Finance Coordinator:** Kendall Menzer. **Director of Group Sales:** Brandon Tesluk. **Director**

PARTNER/INDEPENDENT LEAGUES

of Partnerships and Promotions: Sarah Dailey. **Creative Director:** Cody Bannon. **Director of Operations:** David Dicce. **Director of Grounds & Field Operations:** Chris Carbaugh. **Creative Director:** Cody Bannon. **Event Sales Coordinator:** Brandi Snyder. **Community Engagement Manager:** Brianna Klinger. **Account Executives:** Kenton Meckley, Maggie Foster, Reese Jackson, Sean Davidson. **Ticket & Retail Manager:** Trevor Moulton. **Marketing Manager:** Taylor Harris.

    Manager: Rick Forney. **Hitting/Third Base Coach:** Derek Wolfe. **Pitching Coach:** Joe Harris. **Trainer:** Meg Haas.

GAME INFORMATION

    Radio Announcer: Darrell Henry. **Flagship Station/Streaming Platform:** WOYK 98.9 FM/1350 AM; YouTube.com/York Revolution. **Ballpark:** PeoplesBank Park. **Location:** 5 Brooks Robinson Way, York, PA.

PARTNER/INDEPENDENT LEAGUES

FRONTIER LEAGUE

Office Address: 2009 Baseball Blvd, Avon, OH 44011-1054.
Telephone: (812) 437-8709. **Fax:** (708) 286-6481
Email Address: office@frontierleague.com. **Website:** www.frontierleague.com.
Year Founded: 1993.
President: Eric Krupa
Commissioner Emeritus: Bill Lee.
Deputy Commissioner: Steve Tahsler.
Umpire Supervisor: Deron Brown
President, Board of Directors: Al Dorso (Sussex County). **Vice Presidents:** Tom Kramig (Lake Erie), Michel Laplante (Québec), Nick Semaca (Joliet).
Board of Directors: John Stanley (Evansville), David DelBello (Florence), Rich Sauget Jr. (Gateway), Mike Dorso (New Jersey), Rob Janetschek (New York), Regan Katz (Ottawa), Rick Murphy (Tri-City), Rene Martin (Trois-Rivières), Stu Williams (Washington), Mike VerSchave (Windy City).
Division Structure: East—Empire State, New Jersey, New York, Ottawa, Québec, Sussex County, Tri-City, Trois-Rivières. **West**— Evansville, Florence, Gateway, Joliet, Lake Erie, Schaumburg, Washington, Windy City.
Regular Season: 96 games. **2023 Opening Date:** May 12. **Closing Date:** Sept 4.
All-Star Game: July 11 at Windy City.
Playoff Format: 2nd place team vs. 1st place team in best-of-five Divisional Series. Winners advance to best-of-five Championship Series.
Roster Limit: 24. **Eligibility Rule:** Minimum of ten Rookie 1/Rookie 2 players. Maximum of four players born before October 1, 1994. **Brand of Baseball:** Rawlings.
Statistician: PrestoSports

STADIUM INFORMATION

Club	Stadium	Opened	LF	CF	RF	Capacity	2022 Att.
Evansville	Bosse Field	1915	315	415	315	5,110	122,516
Florence	Thomas More Stadium	2004	325	395	325	4,200	107,877
Gateway	GCS Ballpark	2002	318	395	325	5,500	76,864
Joliet	DuPage Medical Group Field	2002	330	400	327	6,229	137,988
Lake Erie	Mercy Health Stadium	2009	325	400	325	5,000	99,656
New Jersey	Hinchliffe Stadium	1998	320	390	323	7,800	52,086
New York	Clover Stadium	2011	323	403	313	4,750	139,628
Ottawa	Ottawa Stadium	1993	325	404	325	10,332	64,979
Québec	Stade Canac	1938	315	385	315	4,500	145,697
Schaumburg	Wintrust Field	1999	355	400	353	8,107	210,115
Sussex County	Skylands Stadium	1994	330	392	330	4,200	78,737
Tri-City	Joseph L. Bruno Stadium	2002	325	400	325	4,500	134,617
Trois-Rivières	Stade Quillorama	1938	342	372	342	4,500	67,419
Washington	Wild Things Park	2002	325	400	325	3,200	106,043
Windy City	Ozinga Field	1999	335	390	335	2,598	84,564

EVANSVILLE OTTERS

Mailing Address: 23 Don Mattingly Way, Evansville, IN 47711. **Telephone:** (812) 435-8686.
Website: www.evansvilleotters.com. **Facebook**—Evansville Otters, **Twitter**—@EvilleOtters, **Instagram**—@evansvilleotters
Operated by: Evansville Baseball, LLC.
Owner: Bussing family. **President:** John Stanley. **Vice President, Sales:** Joel Padfield. **General Manager:** Travis Painter. **Assisstant General Manager:** Nolan Vandergriff. **Director of Communications:** Matthew Will. **Director of Group Sales:** Keith Millikan. **PA Announcer:** Zane Clodfelter.
Field Manager: Andy McCauley.

GAME INFORMATION
No. of Games Broadcast: Home-51, Away-45. **Radio/Video Stream:** evansvilleotters.com (Otters Digital Network). **Stadium Name:** Bosse Field (Opened in 1915). **Directions:** US 41 to Lloyd Expressway West (IN-62), Main St Exit, Right on Main St, ahead 1 mile to Bosse Field. **Standard Game Times:** Mon.-Sat., 6:35pm, Sun., 1235pm-505pm.
Doubleheaders: 5:35 p.m. **Visiting Club Hotel:** The Comfort Inn & Suites, 3901 Highway 41 North, Evansville, IN 47711. Phone 812-423-5818.

PARTNER/INDEPENDENT LEAGUES

FLORENCE YALLS

Mailing Address: 7950 Freedom Way, Florence, Ky 41042. **Telephone:** (859) 594-4487. **Website:** www.florenceyalls.com.
President: David DelBello. **General Manager:** Max Johnson. **Media Relations Manager:** Anthony Mazzini. **Director of Stadium Operations:** Brennan Hatten. **Creative Director:** Nick Theuerling. **Field Manager:** Chad Roades. **Pitching Coach:** Karl Craigie. **Coach:** David Heilbrunn.

GAME INFORMATION
Stadium Name: Thomas More Stadium.

GATEWAY GRIZZLIES

Telephone: (618) 337-3000. **Email Address:** info@gatewaygrizzlies.com. **Website:** www.gatewaygrizzlies.com.
Owner: Annie Sauget-Miller.
General Manger: Kurt Ringkamp. **Box Office Manager:** TJ Zobrist. **Director of In-Game Entertainment:** Nate Owens. **Marketing Manager:** Becky Wuest. **Business Development Manager:** Brandon Carbray. **Promotions Director:** Hannah Radden. **Director of Food and Beverage:** Christian Schaub. **Merchandising and Hospitality:** Garret Murphy. **Director of Group Sales:** Nick Clemens. **Director of Stadium Operations and Events:** Sam Kehrer. **Stadium Operations Assistant:** Jacob Vogel.
Manager: Steve Brook. **Pitching Coach:** Nick Kennedy. **Bench Coach:** TBD. **Assistant Coach:** TBD.

GAME INFORMATION
No. of Games Broadcast: Home-48, Away-48. **PA Announcer:** Tom Calhoun. **Broadcaster:** Jason Guerrette **Stadium Name:** GCS Credit Union Ballpark. **Location:** I-255 at exit 15 (Mousette Lane).

JOLIET SLAMMERS

Office Address: 1 Mayor Art Schultz Dr, Joliet, IL 60432. **Telephone:** (815) 722-2677
E-Mail Address: info@jolietslammers.com. **Website:** www.jolietslammers.com.
Owner: Joliet Community Baseball & Entertainment, LLC.
Chief Financial Officer/General Manager: Heather Mills. **Director of Food & Beverage:** Joel Sigel. **Director of Community Relations:** Ken Miller. **Assistant General Manager:** Lauren Rhodes. **Director of Marketing and Corporate Services:** Lauren Baca. **Corporate Sales Account Executive:** Rick Wolf. **Stadium Operations Manager:** Dustin Saunders
Field Manager: Dan Schlereth.

GAME INFORMATION
No. of Games Broadcast: 96. **Flagship Station:** www.jolietslammers.com. **Stadium Name:** Duly Health and Care Field. **Location:** 1 Mayor Art Schultz Drive, Joliet, IL 60432. **Standard Game Times:** Mon.-Fri., 6:35 pm, Sat., 6:05 pm., Sun., 1:05 pm..

LAKE ERIE CRUSHERS

Address: 2009 Baseball Boulevard. Avon, Ohio 44011. **Telephone:** 440-934-3636.
Website: www.lakeeriecrushers.com. **Operated by:** Blue Dog Baseball, LLC.
Managing Officer: Tom Kramig. **Sr. Advisor:** Ron Way. **Asst. GM/Director of Sales & Marketing:** Bryan Ralston. **Account Executives:** Andrew Fish, Tanner Carlson. **Box Office Manager:** Hunter Alexander. **Corporate Sales Account Executives:** Jarrett Griebeler. **Director of Stadium Operations:** Joe Juda. **Business Manager:** Brian Wentzel. **Director, Concessions/Catering:** Branden Hyde. **Digital Marketing Manager:** Alyssa Bozin. **Promotions Manager:** Mackenzie Jameson.
Field Manager: Jared Lemieux.

GAME INFORMATION
Stadium Name: Mercy Health Stadium. **Location:** Intersection of I-90 and Colorado Ave in Avon, OH. **Standard Game Times:** Mon.-Fri., 7:05 pm, Sat., 6:05 pm, Sun., 2:05 pm.

PARTNER/INDEPENDENT LEAGUES

NEW JERSEY JACKALS

Office Address: 535 U.S. Highway 46 East, Little Falls, NJ, 07424. **Email Address:** contact@jackals.com. **Website:** jackals.com
Owner/President: Al Dorso **President, Baseball Operations:** Bobby Jones.
Sr. Vice President, Operations: Al Dorso Jr. **Vice President, Marketing:** Mike Dorso.
General Manager: N/A. **Director, Creative Services:** William Romano. **Public Relations:** Chris Faust / Reed Keller.
Field Manager: P.J. Phillips

GAME INFORMATION
Number of Games Broadcast: 96. **Webcast Address:** njjackals.mixlr.com/.
Stadium Name: Hinchliffe Stadium. **Location:** Liberty and Maple Streets, Paterson, NJ, 07522. **Directions:** Route 80 to Exit 56B, take Squirrelwood Rd/Nagle St to McBride Ave., make a right turn and continue on McBride Ave. until the Wayne Ave./Spruce St. stoplight. Turn left over the Passaic River and make the first right onto Maple St.

NEW YORK BOULDERS

Team President/GM: Shawn Reilly. **EVP:** Rob Janetschek.
Assistant General Manager/Box Office Manager/Ticket Sales Manager: Jessica Wilson. **VP of Business Development:** Seth Cantor. **Director of Finance:** Michele Almash. **Promotions Coordinator & Social Media:** Sara Bayles. **Account Executive:** Tyler Metcalf. **Facilities and Operations Coordinator:** Dan Blake. **Educational Director:** Gail Gultz. **PR & Media Coordinator & Relations:** Steve Balsan. **Palisades Food Service Manager:** Brenda Richter.
Field Manager: TJ Stanton. **Player Procurement/Scouting:** Kevin Tuve

GAME INFORMATION
Stadium Name: Clover Stadium. **Location:** 1 Phil Tisi Way Pomona, NY 10970. **Standard Game Times:** Mon.-Fri. 7 p.m., Sat. 6:30 p.m. Sun. May/June. 1:30 p.m. July/August. 5 p.m.

OTTAWA TITANS

Mailing Address: 300 Coventry Road, Ottawa, ON, K1K 4P5. **Telephone:** (343) 633-2273. **Fax:** (343) 633-2274.
Website: www.ottawatitans.com. **E-Mail:** . contact@ottawatitans.com
Founded: 2020. **First Year In League:** 2022.
Operated by: Ottawa Titans Baseball Club Inc.
Principal Owner/President/CEO: Sam Katz
Co-Owners: Ottawa Sports & Entertainment Group, Jacques J.M. Shore
Vice President/COO: Regan Katz. **CFO:** Jason McRae-King. **General Manager:** Martin Boyce. **Assistant General Manager:** Sebastien Boucher.
Media Manager/Broadcaster: Davide Disipio. **Box Office Manager:** Adam Donovan.. **Food & Beverage Manager:** AJ Scarcella. **Administrative/Social Media Coordinator:** Eddy O'Grady. **Business Development:** Melissa Schlichting. **IT & Misc.:** Jason Young, Ed Doiron. **Accountant:** TJ Singh. **Clubhouse Manager:** Marc Leduc.
Field Manager & Director of Baseball Operations: Bobby Brown. **Pitching Coach:** Tom Carcione. **Hitting Coach:** Anthony Markle. **Athletic Therapist:** Landon Veenstra.

GAME INFORMATION
Stadium: Ottawa Stadium. **Year Opened:** 1993. **Official Scorer:** Monique St-Laurent, Francine Marleau, Denis Viau.
English Announcer: Davide Disipio. **French Announcer:** Mikael Lafleur. **Standard Game Times:** M-F: 6:30 p.m.; **Saturday:** 6:00 p.m.; **Sunday:** 1:00 pm.

QUEBEC CAPITALES

Owners: Jean Tremblay, Pierre Tremblay, Michel Laplante
President: Michel Laplante. **General Manager:** Charles Demers. **Assistant General Manager:** Jean Grignon-Francke. **Assistant General Manager:** Daniel Fleury. **Human Resources Director:** Janel Laplante. **Sales Director:** Denis Desbiens. **Ticketing and group sales director:** Félix Gagnon. **Partnership Coordinator:** Francine Gendron. **Administrative director and accounting :** Béatrice Desbiens. **Consultant:** Frédéric Gariépy. **Marketing coordinator :** Xavier Samuel. **Graphic Designer:** Jade Harnish. **Administrative agent:** Nathalie Tremblay & Alie-Anne Laplante. **Gift Shop Manager:** Marc-André Langlois.**Field Manager:** Patrick Scalabrini

GAME INFORMATION
Stadium Name: Stade Canac. **Location:** 100 Cardinal Maurice-Roy, Quebec, QC, G1K 8Z1. **Standard Game Times:** Tue.-Fri. 7:05 pm, Sat., 7:05 pm, Sun., 5:05 pm.

PARTNER/INDEPENDENT LEAGUES

SCHAUMBURG BOOMERS

Office Address: 1999 Springinsguth Road, Schaumburg, IL 60193
Email Address: info@boomersbaseball.com. **Website:** www.boomersbaseball.com.
Owned by: Pat and Lindy Salvi.
Executive Vice President & General Manager: Michael Larson
Director of Facilities: Mike Tlusty. **Director Food/Beverage:** Julia Fasiang. **Director of Tickets & Hospitality:** Christopher Salazar. **Broadcaster:** Tim Calderwood. **Director of Promotions:** Lexi Fiolka
Director of Baseball Operations: Peter Long. **Director of Stadium Operations:** Jack McCoy. **Box Office Manager:** Abigail Vito. **Head Chef:** Kyle Miller
Field Manager: Jamie Bennett.

GAME INFORMATION
Broadcaster: Tim Calderwood. **No. of Games Broadcast:** Home-48, Away-48. **Flagship Station:** WRMN 1410 AM Elgin. **Stadium:** Wintrust Field. **Location:** I-290 to Thorndale Ave Exit, head West on Elgin-O'Hare Expressway until Springinsguth Road Exit, second left at Springinsguth Road (shared parking lot with Schaumburg Metra Station). **Visiting Club Hotel:** SpringHill Suites 1550 McConnor Pkwy, Schaumburg, IL 60173

SUSSEX COUNTY MINERS

Owner, President: Al Dorso Sr. **Owner, Vice President:** Al Dorso Jr. **Owner, Vice President:** Michael Dorso.
Corporate Partnerships: Joann Ciancitto, **Director of Sales & Community Engagement:** Kim Eid, **Sales & Social Media Coordinator:** Jake Hildreth, **Director, Broadcasting and Media Relations:** Bret Leuthner. Broadcasting, PXP, & **Media Relations:** Sean Bretherick. **Senior Graphic Design:** Will Romano. **Head Groundskeeper:** L.J. Black.
Field Manager: Chris Widger..

GAME INFORMATION
Broadcaster: Bret Leuthner. **No. of Games Broadcast:** 100. **Webcast Address:** www.scminers.com.
Stadium Name: Skylands Stadium. **Location:** In New Jersey, I-80 to exit 34B (Route 15 North) to Route 565 North; From Pennsylvania, I-84 to Route 6 (Matamoras) to Route 206 North to Route 565 North. **Standard Game Times:** Mon.-Fri., 7:05 pm, Sat., 6:05 pm, Sun., 2:05 pm.

TRI-CITY VALLEYCATS

Office Address: Joseph L Bruno Stadium, 80 Vandenburgh Ave, Troy, NY 12180.
Mailing Address: PO Box 694, Troy, NY 12181.
Telephone: (518) 629-2287. **Fax:** (518) 629-2299. **E-Mail Address:** info@tcvalleycats.com. **Website:** www.tcvalleycats.com
Operated By: Tri-City ValleyCats Inc. **Principal Owners:** Martin Barr, Jane Burton, Doug Gladstone, Rick Murphy, Stephen Siegel. **President:** Rick Murphy. **Vice President/General Manager:** Matt Callahan. **Assistant GM:** Michelle Skinner. **Ticket Sales and Operations Manager:** Jessica Guido. **Food & Beverage Manager:** Missy Henry. **Stadium Operations Manager:** Ed Krajewski. **Media Relations & Production Manager:** Jacob LaChapelle. **Account Executive:** Nick Rumsey.
Manager: Pete Incaviglia. **Bench Coach:** Thomas Incaviglia. **Pitching Coach:** Brooks Carey

GAME INFORMATION
Radio Announcer: TBD. **No. of Games Broadcast:** 51. **Flagship Station:** FloSports. **PA Announcer:** Anthony Pettograsso. **Official Scorer:** Patrick Barry. **Stadium Name:** Joseph Bruno Stadium. **Location:** From north, I-87 to exit 7 (Route 7), go east 1 1/2 miles to I-787 South, to Route 378 East, go over bridge to Route 4, right to Route 4 South, one mile to Hudson Valley Community College campus on left; From south, I-87 to exit 23 (I-787), I-787 north six miles to exit for Route 378 east, over bridge to Route 4, right to Route 4 South, one mile to campus on left; From east, Massachusetts Turnpike to exit B-1 (I-90), nine miles to Exit 8 (Defreestville), left off ramp to Route 4 North, five miles to campus on right; From west, I-90 to exit 24 (I-90 East), I-90 East for six miles to I-787 North (Troy), 2.2 miles to exit for Route 378 East, over bridge to Route 4, right to Route 4 south for one mile to campus on left. **Standard Game Times:** Mon. - Sat. 630pm, Sun. 5 pm. **Ticket Price Range:** $6.00-$14.00. **Visiting Club Hotel:** The Desmond Hotel Albany, 660 Albany-Shaker Road, Albany, NY 12211. **Telephone:** (518) 869-8100.

PARTNER/INDEPENDENT LEAGUES

TROIS-RIVIÈRES AIGLES

Office Address: 1760 Avenue Gilles-Villeneuve, Trois-Rivières, QC G9A 5K8.
Telephone: (819) 379-0404. **Email Address:** info@lesaiglestr.com.
Website: www.lesaiglestr.com
Owners: Côté-Reco Group and Vertdure Group. **President:** René Martin. **General Manager:** Jerome Duchesneau. **Chief Operation Officer:** Frederik Belanger. **Vice President, Special Projects:** Marc-Andre Marineau. **Communications Coordinator:** Vincent Gauthier.

GAME INFORMATION
No. of Games Broadcast: 51. **Webcast Address:** www.cfou.ca/direct.php.
Stadium Name: Stade Quillorama. **Location:** Take Hwy 40 West, exit Boul. des Forges/Centre-ville, keep right, turn right at light, turn right at stop sign.

WASHINGTON WILD THINGS

Office Address: One Washington Federal Way, Washington, PA 15301. **Telephone:** (724) 250-9555. **Fax:** (724) 250-2333.
Email Address: info@washingtonwildthings.com. **Website:** washingtonwildthings.com
Owned by: Sports Facility, LLC. **Operated by:** Washington Frontier League Baseball, LLC
Managing Partners: Stu Williams, Francine W. Williams. **President and General Manager:** Tony Buccilli Steve Zavacky. **Vice President:** Christine Blaine. **Assistant General Manager, Facility Ops:** Travis Pettit. **Assistant General Manager, Baseball Ops & Broadcaster:** Kyle Dawson. **Ticket Account Executive:** Erik Stouter. **Ticket Account Executive:** Jeff Fry. **Community Relations and Promotions Manager:** Stephanie Keller.
Field Manager: Tom Vaeth

GAME INFORMATION
Stadium Name: Wild Things Park
Location: I-70 to exit 15 (Chestnut Street), right on Chestnut Street to Washington Crown Center Mall, right at mall entrance, right on to Mall Drive to stadium
Standard Game Times: Tuesday, Thursday-Saturday, 7:05 p.m., Wednesday, 6:05 p.m., Sunday, 5:35 p.m.

WINDY CITY THUNDERBOLTS

Office Address: 14011 South Kenton Avenue, Crestwood, IL 60418
Telephone: (708) 489-2255. **Fax:** (708) 489-2999.
Email Address: info@wcthunderbolts.com. **Website:** www.wcthunderbolts.com.
Owned by: Franchise Sports, LLC.
General Manager: Mike VerSchave. **Assistant GM:** Bill Waliewski. **Director, Community Relations:** Johnny Sole. **Director, Not-For-Profit Events:** Karen Engel. **Director, Operations:** Chris Koll. **Director, Media Relations:** Terry Bonadonna.
Field Manager: Richie Sexson. **Hitting Coach:** Jaret Wright. **3rd Base Coach/Infield Coordinator:** Chris Coleman.

GAME INFORMATION
No. of Games Broadcast: 96. **Flagship Station:** WXAV, 88.3 FM. **Official Scorer:** Chris Gbur. **Stadium Name:** Ozinga Field. **Location:** I-294 to South Cicero Ave, exit (Route 50), south for 1 1/2 miles, left at Midlothian Turnpike, right on Kenton Ave; I-57 to 147th Street, west on 147th to Cicero, north on Cicero, right on Midlothian Turnpike, right on Kenton. **Standard Game Times:** Mon.-Fri., 6:35 pm, Sat., 6:05 pm, Sun., 1:05 pm.

PARTNER/INDEPENDENT LEAGUES

PIONEER BASEBALL LEAGUE

Office Address: 1111 Diamond Valley Rd, Suite 105 Windsor, CO 80550.
Telephone: 509-456-7615.
E-Mail Address: fanmail@pioneerleague.com.
Website: www.pioneerleague.com.
Years League Active: 1939-42, 1946-
President: Mike Shapiro. **Execuive Vice President:** Henry Hunter. **Director of Communications:** Jackson Shapiro. **Director of Baseball Administration:** Mathias Altman-Kurosaki. **Director of Marketing:** Tate Jordan.
Directors: Dave Baggott (Ogden), Peter C. Davis (Missoula), DG Elmore (Rocky Mountain), Gant Elmore (Idaho Falls), Mike Tollin (Grand Junction), Vinny Purpura (Great Falls), Dave Heller (Billings), Jeff Eiseman (Boise), Marty Kelly (Glacier) and Jeff Katofsky (Northern Colorado).
Regular Season: 96 games (split schedule). **2023 Opening Date:** May 23. **Closing Date:** Sept. 9.
Playoff Format: Three-game divisional playoffs. Winners meet in best-of-three series for league championship. **Roster Limit:** 25 active, minimum of 22 dressed for each game. **Player Eligibility Rule:** The players on a Member Club's Active Roster may have played professional baseball for three (3) or fewer years.

STADIUM INFORMATION

Club	Stadium	Opened	LF	CF	RF	Capacity	2022 Att.
Billings	Dehler Park	2008	329	410	350	3,071	94,563
Boise	Memorial Stadium	1989	335	400	335	3,426	160,582
Glacier	Flathead Field	2022					83,217
Grand Junction	Sam Suplizio Field	1949	302	400	333	7,014	73,277
Great Falls	Centene Stadium at Legion Park	1956	335	414	335	3,800	83,826
Idaho Falls	Melaleuca Field	1976	340	400	350	3,400	81,870
Missoula	Ogren Park at Allegiance Field	2004	309	398	287	3,500	87,981
Northern Colorado	TicketSmarter Stadium	2023				6,500	N/A
Ogden	Lindquist Field	1997	335	396	334	5,000	88,751
Rocky Mountain	Security Service Field	1988	350	410	350	8,500	88,112

BILLINGS MUSTANGS

Office Address: Dehler Park, 2611 9th Avenue North, Billings, MT 59101.
Mailing Address: PO Box 1553, Billings, MT 59103-1553.
Telephone: (406) 252-1241. **Fax:** (406) 252-2968.
E-Mail Address: mustangs@billingsmustangs.com. **Website:** billingsmustangs.com.
Years in League: 1948-63, 1969-

OWNERSHIP/MANAGEMENT
Operated By: Mustangs Baseball LLC.
President/CEO: Dave Heller. **General Manager:** Matt Allen. **Director, Ballpark Operations:** Matt Schoonover. **Director, Broadcasting/Media Relations:** Brennan Mense. **Director, Food and Beverage Services:** Curt Prchal. **Director, Field Operations:** Sam Sheets. **Directory, Gameday Operations:** Bryce Peterson.

FIELD STAFF
Manager: Billy Horton. **Athletic Trainer:** Tori Atencio.

GAME INFORMATION
Stadium Name: Dehler Park. **Location:** I-90 to Exit 450, north on 27th Street North to 9th Avenue North. **Standard Game Times:** Mon.–Sat., 6:35 pm, Sun., 1:05 pm.

BOISE HAWKS

Address: 5600 N. Glenwood St. Boise, ID 83714.
Telephone: (208) 322-5000. **Fax:** (208) 322-6846.
Website: www.boisehawks.com. **Years in League:** 1975-76, 1978, 1987-Present.

OWNERSHIP/MANAGEMENT
Operated by: Boise Professional Baseball LLC. **President:** Jeff Eiseman. **HR & Operations:** Missy Martin. **Vice President/General Manager:** Mike Van Hise. **Assistant GM of Facility Operations:** Jake Lusk. **Manager, Accounting/Office:** Judy Peterson. **Ticket Sales Manager:** Kristi Croteau. **Group Event Executive:** Colton Hampson. **Account Executive:** Dalton Schutz. **Assistant Director, Stadium Operations:** Christian Lomeli. **Media Relations/Marketing Manager:** Paige Plotzke. **Head Groundskeeper:** John Gides.

FIELD STAFF
Manager: Gary Van Tol. **Hitting Coach:** Aaron Sutton. **Pitching Coach:** Michiel van Kampen. **Director of Scouting:** Jimmy Johnson. **Athletic Trainer:** Shane Nelson. **Mental Skills Coordinator:** Coleman Evans.

GAME INFORMATION
Stadium Name: Memorial Stadium. **Location:** I-84 to Cole Rd., north to Western Idaho Fairgrounds at 5600 North

PARTNER/INDEPENDENT LEAGUES

Glenwood St.

GLACIER RANGE RIDERS

Address: 75 McDermott Lane Kalispell, MT 59901
Website: gorangeriders.com
E-mail: information@gorangeriders.com. **Years in League:** 2022-

OWNERSHIP/MANAGEMENT
Operated by: Ridge Run Enterprises, LLC. **Principal Owner:** Marty Kelly. **Vice President:** Chris Kelly. **GM:** Erik Moore. **Marketing & Entertainment:** Taylor Huntman. **Sales & Marketing:** Leo Kelly.

FIELD STAFF
Manager: Stu Pederson. **Special Advisors to the GM:** Todd Pratt and Jesse Crain. **Head Athletic Trainer:** Sam Konrath.

GAME INFORMATION
No. of Games Broadcast: 96.

GRAND JUNCTION JACKALOPES

Address: 1315 North Ave., Grand Junction, CO, 81501
Telephone: (970) 255-7625. **Fax:** (970) 241-2374
Email: mritter@gjrockies.com. **Website:** www.gjrockies.com
Years in League: 2001–

OWNERSHIP/MANAGEMENT
President: Mick Ritter. **Director of Broadcasting and Sales:** Ethan Jordan.

FIELD STAFF
Manager: James Frisbie. **Hitting Coach:** TBA. **Pitching Coach:** TBA.

GAME INFORMATION
Radio Announcer: Ethan Jordan. **No. of Games Broadcast:** 96. **Flagship Station:** TBA, gjrockies.com. **Television Announcer:** Ethan Jordan. **No. of Games Televised:** 48. **Flagship:** KGJT, My Network, Dish Network. **Produced by:** Colorado Mesa University. **PA Announcer:** Tim Ray. **Official Scorers:** Unknown. **Stadium Name:** Suplizio Field. **Location:** 1315 North Ave. Grand Junction, CO 81501.

GREAT FALLS VOYAGERS

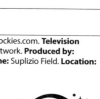

Address: 1015 25th St N, Great Falls, MT 59401.
Telephone: (406) 452-5311. **Fax:** (406) 454-0811.
E-Mail Address: voyagers@gfvoyagers.com. **Website:** www.gfvoyagers.com.
Years in League: 1948-1963, 1969-

OWNERSHIP/MANAGEMENT
Operated By: Great Falls Baseball Club.
Owner/CEO: Vinny Purpura. **President:** Scott Reasoner. **General Manager:** John Burks. **Assistant General Manager:** Logan Jacobson. **Director of Operations/Grounds:** Nick Blakley.

FIELD STAFF
Manager: Tommy Thompson.

GAME INFORMATION
No. of Games Broadcast: 96. **Stadium Name:** Centene Stadium. **Location:** From I-15 to exit 281 (10th Ave S), left on 26th, left on Eighth Ave North, right on 25th, ballpark on right, past railroad tracks.

IDAHO FALLS CHUKARS

Office Address: 900 Jim Garchow Way, Idaho Falls, ID 83402.
Mailing Address: PO 2183, Idaho, ID 83403. **Telephone:** (208) 522-8363. **Fax:** (208) 522-9858.
E-Mail Address: chukarsbaseball@gmail.com. **Website:** www.ifchukars.com.
Years in League: 1940-42, 1946-

OWNERSHIP/MANAGEMENT
Operated By: The Elmore Sports Group. **Principal Owner:** David Elmore. **President/General Manager:** Kevin Greene. **Vice President:** Paul Henderson. **Assistant GM:** Chris Hall. **Account Executives:** Cody Haggerton and Hunter Blackmon.

PARTNER/INDEPENDENT LEAGUES

Bookkeeper: Anna Meyer.

FIELD STAFF
Manager: TBA. **Hitting Coach:** TBA. **Pitching Coach:** Bob Milacki.

GAME INFORMATION
Stadium Name: Melaleuca Field. **Location:** I-15 to West Broadway exit, left onto Memorial Drive, right on Mound Avenue, 1/4 mile to the stadium. **Standard Game Times:** Mon.-Sat., 7:15 pm, Sun., 4:00 pm.

MISSOULA PADDLEHEADS

Address: 140 N Higgins, Suite 201, Missoula, MT 59802. **Telephone:** (406) 543-3300. **E-Mail Address:** mellis@gopaddleheads.com. **Website:** www.gopaddleheads.com.
Years in League: 1956-60, 1999-.

OWNERSHIP/MANAGEMENT
Operated By: Big Sky Professional Baseball LLC. **Co-Chairs:** Peter & Susan Crampton Davis. **President:** Matt Ellis. **Senior Director of Sales and Retail:** Kim Klages Johns. **Director of Creative Content Manager:** Wesley Harton. **Director of Wow:** Sam Boyd. **Retail Manager:** Dawna Kulaski. **Group Sales Manager:** Matt Zaleski. **Administration & eCommerce Specialist:** Jeanie Leidholt. **Accounting Director:** Rebecca Anciaux.

FIELD STAFF
Manager: Michael Schlact. **Hitting Coach:** Jeff Lyle. **Pitching Coach:** TBA. **Assistant Coach:** Brandon Riley. **Athletic Trainer:** TBA. **Strength & Conditioning Coach:** TBA.

GAME INFORMATION
Stadium Name: Ogren Park Allegiance Field. **Location:** 700 Cregg Lane, Missoula MT 59801. **Directions:** Take Orange Street to Cregg Lane, west on Cregg Lane, stadium west of McCormick Park past railroad trestle.

NORTHERN COLORADO OWLZ

Address: 1801 Diamond Valley Drive Windsor, CO 80550. **Telephone:** 970-460-0151. **E-Mail Address:** info@futurelegendscomplex.com. **Website:** www.nocoowlz.com. **Years in League:** 2022-.

OWNERSHIP/MANAGEMENT
Principal Owner: Jeff Katofsky. **General Manager:** Jason Ficca. **Assistant General Manager:** Harrison Shapiro. **Pro Sports Communications Manager:** Blake Baker. **Director of Marketing and Communications:** Jackie Keesling. **Digital Media Manager:** Nate Martinez. **Ticketing Manager:** Jacob Nemitz.

FIELD STAFF
Manager: Frank Gonzales.

GAME INFORMATION
No. of Games Broadcast: 96.

OGDEN RAPTORS

Address: 2330 Lincoln Ave, Ogden, UT 84401. **Telephone:** (801) 393-2400. **Fax:** (801) 393-2473.
E-Mail Address: homerun@ogden-raptors.com. **Website:** www.ogden-raptors.com.
Years in League: 1939-42, 1946-55, 1966-74, 1994-Present

OWNERSHIP/MANAGEMENT
Operated By: Ogden Professional Baseball, Inc. **Principal Owners:** Dave Baggott, John Lindquist.
President/General Manager: Dave Baggott. **General Manager:** Trever Wilson. **Assistant Director of Game Day Operations:** Richard Armstrong. **Director, Social Media:** Kevin Johnson. **Director, Information Technology:** Chris Greene. **Groundskeeper:** Kenny Kopinski. **Official Scorer:** Dennis Kunimura.

FIELD STAFF
Manager: Kash Beauchump. **Hitting Coach:** TBA. **Clubhouse Manager:** Dave "MacGyver" Ackerman.

GAME INFORMATION
Stadium Name: Lindquist Field. **Location:** I-15 North to 21th Street exit, east to Lincoln Avenue, south three blocks to park.

PARTNER/INDEPENDENT LEAGUES

ROCKY MOUNTAIN VIBES

Address: 4385 Tutt Blvd., Colorado Springs, CO 80922.
Telephone: (719) 597-1449. **Fax:** (719) 597-2491.
E-Mail Address: info@vibesbaseball.com. **Website:** www.vibesbaseball.com.
Years in League: 2019-

OWNERSHIP/MANAGEMENT
Operated By: Rocky Mountain Vibes. **Principal Owner:** Dave Elmore. **President/General Manager:** Chris Jones. **Assistant GM:** Aaron Griffith. **Director of Finance:** Donny Bailey. **Director of Sales and Hospitality:** Jake Hathaway. **Director of Marketing:** Kay Goodell. **Group Sales Manager:** Dean McKissock. **Ticket & Merchandise Manager:** Jacob Nemitz. **Head Groundskeeper:** Collin Tyzinski. **Director of Baseball & Media Operations:** Tyler Peterson. **Clubhouse Manager:** Presley Greier. **Assistant Food and Beverage Director:** Josh Nuding.

FIELD STAFF
Manager: Les Lancaster.

GAME INFORMATION
Broadcaster: Tyler Peterson. **No. of Games Broadcast:** 96. **Flagship Station:** TuneIn. **PA Announcer:** TBD. **Official Scorer:** TBD. **Stadium Name:** UCHealth Park. **Location:** I-25 South to Woodmen Road exit, east on Woodmen to Powers Blvd., right on Powers to Barnes Road.

INDEPENDENT LEAGUES

PECOS LEAGUE
Website: www.PecosLeague.com. **Address:** PO Box 271489, Houston, TX 77277. **Telephone:** (575) 680-2212. **E-mail:** info@pecosleague.com.
Commissioner: Andrew Dunn.
Pacific Division: Bakersfield Train Robbers, Lancaster Sound Breakers, Marysville Drakes, Santa Rosa Scuba Divers, San Rafael Pacifics, Vallejo Seaweed, Martinez Sturgeon, Monterey Amberjacks.
Mountain Division: Roswell Invaders, Alpine Cowboys, Austin Weirdos, Blackwell FlyCatchers, Santa Fe Fuego, Trinidad Triggers, Garden City Wind and Tucson Saguaros.
Year Founded: 2010.
Regular Season: 50 games. **Start Date:** June 1. **Finish Date:** Aug. 11.
Eligibility Rules: 25 and under. 22-player rosters.
Brand of Baseball: Rawlings.

UNITED SHORE PROFESSIONAL BASEBALL LEAGUE
Location: Jimmy Johns Field. 7171 Auburn Rd, Utica, MI. 48317. **Telephone:** (248) 601-2400. **Email:** baseballoperations@uspbl.com. **Website:** www.uspbl.com
Owner and CEO: Andy Appleby. **President:** Dana Schmitt. **Senior Vice President, Client Services:** Jeremiah Hergott. **Director of Baseball Operations:** Shane McCatty. **Vice President, Tickets & Premium Sales:** Dan Griesbaum Jr. **Senior Director of Baseball Administration:** Mike Zielinski. **Director of Finance & Accounting:** Nick Cowles. **Finance Assistant:** Ryan Porath. **Corporate Partnership Services Manager:** Dan Veit. **Director of Food & Beverage:** Azaria Ali. **Assistant Director of Food & Beverage:** Ronald Johnson. **Senior Director of Ballpark Operations:** Dillon DuBois. **Assistant Director of Ballpark Operations:** Landon Danks. **Merchandise Manager:** Abbey Robinson. **Senior Director of Marketing & Public Relations:** Katie Page. **Graphic Designer:** Kristen Soullier. **Director of Premium Sales & Service:** Adam Lewis. **Senior Director of Ticket Operations:** Brian Piper. **Community Relations Coordinator:** Noah Theiler. **Promotions Manager:** Monica Kurjan. **Assistant to the President:** Maddie Quick. **Sales Account Executive:** Owen Gretkierewicz. **Sales Account Executive:** David Acord. **Sales Account Executive:** Cameron Mercer.
Teams: Birmingham-Bloomfield Beavers, Eastside Diamond Hoppers, Utica Unicorns, Westside Woolly Mammoths.
Managers: Birmingham: Von Joshua. **Birmingham Assistant Manager:** Josh Hinz. **Eastside:** Ryan Kotke/John Dombrowski. **Utica:** Jim Essian. **Utica Assistant Manager:** Adrian Guzman. **Westside:** Taylor Grzelakowski. **Westside Assistant Manager:** Justin Karn. **Field Coordinator:** Paul Noce. **DVS Consultant:** Justin Orenduff. **Pitching Coordinator:** Mitch Aker. **Developmental Scout and Coach:** Josh Simmons. **Assistant Scouting Director:** Rye Pothakos.
Roster Limit: 20. **Eligibility Rules:** Players must be between 18 and 26 years old.
2023 Start Date: May 19th. **End Date:** Sept. 9. **All-Star Game:** July 8. **Playoffs:** Sept. 7-9.
Season length: 50 games per team. **Playoff Format:** Single-game elimination.

INTERNATIONAL

INTERNATIONAL LEAGUES

AMERICAS

MEXICO
MEXICAN LEAGUE

Address: Avenida Insurgentes Sur #797 Interior 3 y 4. Col. Nápoles. C.P. 03810, Benito Juárez, Ciudad de México. **Telephone:** 52-5557-1007. **E-Mail Address:** oficina@lmb.com.mx. **Website:** milb.com/mexican

Years League Active: 1955-
President: Horacio De la Vega Flores. **Sports Director:** Gabriel Medina Espinosa.

Division Structure. North Division: Acereros del Norte; Algodoneros Unión Laguna; Generales de Durango; Mariachis de Guadalajara; Rieleros de Aguascalientes; Saraperos de Saltillo; Sultanes de Monterrey; Tecolotes de los Dos Laredos; Toros de Tijuana. **South Division**: Bravos de León; Diablos Rojos del México; El Aguila de Veracruz; Guerreros de Oaxaca; Leones de Yucatán; Olmecas de Tabasco; Pericos de Puebla; Piratas de Campeche; Tigres de Quintana Roo.

Regular Season: 90 games (split-schedule).
2023 Opening Date: April 20. **Closing Date:** Aug. 6.

Playoff Format: Five teams from each division qualify for a four-round playoff. Championship round is best-of-seven series.

Roster Limit: 28. **Roster Limit, Imports:** 7.

AGUASCALIENTES RIELEROS
Office Address: Andador Manuel Madrigal 102 Héroes 20190 Aguascalientes. **Telephone:** 01 449 915 15 96 y 97. **E-Mail Address:** hola@rielerosags.com. **Website:** rielerosags.com.

CAMPECHE PIRATAS
Office Address: Calle Filiberto Qui Farfan No. 2, Col. Camino Real, CP 24020, Campeche, Campeche. **Telephone:** (52) 981-827-4759. **E-Mail Address:** http://www.piratasdecampeche.mx/contacto/ **Website:** piratasdecampeche.mx.

DOS LAREDOS TECOLOTES
Office Address: Reforma 4310, Col. México, Nuevo Laredo, Tamps. **Telephone:** (52) 1 867 279 8519. **E-Mail Address:** contacto@tecolotes2laredos.com. **Website:** tecolotes2laredos.com.

DURANGO GENERALES
Office Address: De Los Deportes, Unidad Deportiva, 98065_00 Zacatecas, ZAC. **Telephone:** (52) 618-196-4267. **E-Mail Address:** info@generalesdedurango.com. **Website:** generalesdedurango.com.

GUADALAJARA MARIACHIS
Office Address: Santa Lucia #373 Colonia Tepeyac, Zapopan, Jalisco C.P 45150. **Telephone:** (52) 333-037-7969. **Website:** mismariachis.com.mx.

LAGUNA ALGODONEROS
Office Address: Algodoneros Unión Laguna Juan Gutemberg s/n C.P. 27000 Torreón, Coah. Estadio Revolución. **Telephone:** (52) 871-718-5515. **E-Mail Address:** info@unionlaguna.mx. **Website:** unionlaguna.mx.

LEON BRAVES
Office Address: Estadio Domingo Santana Boulevard Congreso de Chilpancingo 803, Unidad Deportiva. León Guanajuato, México. CP 37237. **Telephone:** (52) 477-272-8675. **E-Mail Address:** contacto@bravosdeleon.mx. **Website:** bravosdeleon.com.

MEXICO CITY DIABLOS ROJOS
Office Address: Av río Churubusco #1001, Colonia ex-ejidos de la Magdalena Mixhuca, Alcaldía Iztacalco, C.P. 08010 CDMX. **Telephone:** (56) 91-28-72-92. **E-Mail Address:** contacto@diablos-rojos.com. **Website:** diablos.com.mx.

MONCLOVA ACEREROS DEL NORTE
Office Address: Cuauhtemoc #299, Col Ciudad Deportiva, CP 25750, Monclova, Coahuila. **Telephone:** (52) 866-636-2650. **E-Mail Address:** contacto@acereros.com.mx. **Website:** acereros.com.mx.

MONTERREY SULTANES
Office Address: Estadio de Béisbol Monterrey, en Av. Manuel L. Barragán S/N, Col. Regina, CP. 64290 Monterrey, N.L. **Telephone:** (52) 81-2270-2000. **E-Mail Address:** info@sultanes .com.mx. **Website:** sultanes.com.mx.

OAXACA GUERREROS
Office Address: Calz. Héroes de Chapultepec S.N. esq calle de los Derechos Humanos Col. Centro, Oaxaca de Juárez. **Telephone:** (52) 951-515-5522. **E-Mail Address:** contacto@guerreros.mx. **Website:** guerreros.mx.

PUEBLA PERICOS
Office Address: Calz. Ignacio Zaragoza 666, Maravillas. 72220 Puebla, Mexico. **E-Mail Address:** contacto@pericosdepuebla.com. **Website:** pericosdepuebla.com.

QUINTANA ROO TIGRES
Office Address: SM 21, 21, 77500 Cancún, Quintana Roo. Telephone: (52) 998-887-3108. **E-Mail Address:** medios@tigresqroo.com. **Website:** tigresqroo.com.

SALTILLO SARAPEROS
Office Address: Blvd. Nazario Ortiz S/N Col. Ciudad Deportiva CP. 25284 Saltillo, Coahulia. Telephone: (52) 844-416-9455. **E-Mail Address:** contacto@saraperos.com.mx. **Website:** saraperos.com.mx.

TABASCO OLMECAS
Office Address: Avenida Velodromo de la Ciudad Deportiva S/N, Atasta, 86100 Villahermosa, Tabasco. Telephone: (52) 993-352-2787. **E-Mail Address:** hola@olmecastabasco.mx. **Website:** olmecastabasco.mx.

TIJUANA TOROS
Office Address: Mision de Santo Tomas Rio Eufrates con, Col. Infonavit Capistrano, 22223 Tijuana, B.C., Mexico. **Telephone:** (52) 664-635-5600. **E-Mail Address:** contacto@torosdetijuana.com. **Website:** torosdetijuana.com.

VERACRUZ AGUILA
Office Address: Paseo Jacarandas 224 B, Virginia, 94294, Boca del Río, Veracruz. **E-Mail Address:** contacto@elaguiladeveracruz.com. **Website:** elaguiladeveracruz.com.

YUCATAN LEONES
Office Address: Calle 6 Nº315 x 35, Col. Morelos Oriente, Mérida, Yucatán. C.P. 97174. **Telephone:** (52) 999-432-0655. **E-Mail Address:** contacto@leones.mx. **Website:** leones.mx.

MEXICAN ACADEMY

Rookie Classification
Mailing Address: Ubicación: Av. El Fundador #100, Col. San Miguel, El Carmen N.L., C.P. 66550. **Telephone:** (81) 8158-7900. Fax: (52) 555-395-2454. **E-Mail Address:** pgarza@academia-lmb.com. **Website:** academia-lmb.com.

194 · Baseball America 2023 Directory

INTERNATIONAL LEAGUES

Director General: Salvador Viera Higuera.
Communications: Pablo Garza Garcia.
Regular Season: 50 games.

DOMINICAN REPUBLIC
DOMINICAN SUMMER LEAGUE

**Member, National Association
Rookie Classification**
Mailing Address: Calle Segunda No 64, Reparto Antilla, Santo Domingo, Dominican Republic. **Telephone:** (809) 532-3619. **Website:** dominicansummerleague.com. **E-Mail Address:** ligadeverano@codetel.net.do.
Years League Active: 1985-.
President: Orlando Diaz.
Member Clubs/Division Structure: Baseball City—Baltimore Black, Baltimore Orange, Blue Jays, D-backs Black, D-backs Red, Padres, Reds. **North**—Boston Blue, Boston Red, Cleveland Blue, Cleveland Red, Houston Blue, Houston Orange, Kansas City Glass, Kansas City Stewart.

Northeast—Cubs Blue, Cubs Red, Mets 1, Mets 2, NYY Bombers, NYY Yankees, Pittsburgh Black, Pittsburgh Gold.
Northwest—Athletics, Braves, Dodgers Bautista, Dodgers Mega, Marlins, Miami, Rays, Tampa Bay. **San Pedro**—Brewers 1, Brewers 2, Phillies Red, Phillies White, Texas Blue, Texas Red, Tigers 1, Tigers 2, White Sox. **South**—Angels, Cardinals, Colorado, Giants Black, Giants Orange, Mariners, Nationals, Rockies, Twins.
Regular Season: 72 games. **Opening Date:** Unavailable. **Closing Date:** Unavailable.
Playoff Format: Six teams qualify for playoffs, including four division winners and two wild-card teams. Teams with two best records receive a bye to the semifinals; four other playoff teams play best-of-three series. Winners advance to best-of-three semifinals. Winners advance to best-of-five championship series.
Roster Limit: 35 active. **Player Eligibility Rule:** No player may have four or more years of prior minor league service. No draft-eligible player from the U.S. or Canada (not including players from Puerto Rico) may participate in the DSL. No age limits apply.

JAPAN
Mailing Address: Mita Belljiu Building, 11th Floor, 5-36-7 Shiba, Minato-ku, Tokyo 108-0014. **Telephone:** 03-6400-1189. **Fax:** 03-6400-1190.
Website: npb.jp, npb.jp/eng
Commissioner: Sadayuki Sakakibara.
Secretary General: Atsushi Ihara. **Executive Director, Baseball Operations:** Minoru Hata. **Executive Director, NPB Rules & Labor:** Nobuhisa "Nobby" Ito.
Executive Director, Central League Operations: Kazuhide Kinefuchi. **Executive Director, Pacific League Operations:** Kazuo Nakano.
Nippon Series: Best-of-seven series between Central and Pacific League champions, begins Oct. 28.
All-Star Series: July 19 at Vantelin Dome in Nagoya; July 20 at Mazda Zoom-Zoom Stadium in Hiroshima.
Roster Limit: 70 per organization (one major league club, one minor league club). Major league club is permitted to register 28 players at a time, though just 25 may be available for each game.
Roster Limit, Imports: Four in majors (no more than three position players or pitchers); unlimited in minors.

CENTRAL LEAGUE
Regular Season: 143 games.
2023 Opening Date: March 31. **Climax Series:** Oct. 14.
Playoff Format: Second-place team meets third-place team in best-of-three series. Winner meets first-place team in best-of-seven series to determine representative in Japan Series (first-place team has one-game advantage to begin series).

CHUNICHI DRAGONS
Mailing Address: Chunichi Bldg 6F, 4-1-1 Sakae, Naka-ku, Nagoya 460-0008. **Telephone:** 052-261-8811.
Field Manager: Kazuyoshi Tatsunami.

HANSHIN TIGERS
Mailing Address: 2-33 Koshien-cho, Nishinomiya-shi, Hyogo-ken 663-8152. **Telephone:** 0798-46-1515.
Field Manager: Akinobu Okada.

HIROSHIMA TOYO CARP
Mailing Address: 2-3-1 Minami Kaniya, Minami-ku, Hiroshima 732-8501. **Telephone:** 082-554-1000.
Field Manager: Fujiii Akihito.

TOKYO YAKULT SWALLOWS
Mailing Address: Seizan Bldg, 4F, 2-12-28 Kita Aoyama, Minato-ku, Tokyo 107-0061. **Telephone:** 03-3405-8960.
Field Manager: Shingo Takatsu.

YOKOHAMA DENA BAYSTARS
Mailing Address: Kannai Arai Bldg, 7F, 1-8 Onoe-cho, Naka-ku, Yokohama 231-0015. **Telephone:** 045-681-0811.
Field Manager: Daisuke Miura.

YOMIURI GIANTS
Mailing Address: Yomiuri Shimbun Bldg, 26F, 1-7-1 Otemachi, Chiyoda-ku, Tokyo 100-8151. **Telephone:** 03-3246-7733. **Fax:** 03-3246-2726.
Manager: Tatsunori Hara.

PACIFIC LEAGUE
Regular Season: 143 games.
2023 Opening Date: March 30. **Climax Series:** Oct. 14. **Playoff Format:** Second-place team meets third-place team in best-of-three series. Winner meets first-place team in best-of-seven series to determine league's representative in Japan Series (first-place team has one-game advantage to begin series).

CHIBA LOTTE MARINES
Mailing Address: 1 Mihama, Mihama-ku, Chiba-shi, Chiba-ken 261-8587. **Telephone:** 03-5682-6341.
Field Manager: Rihito Yoshii.

FUKUOKA SOFTBANK HAWKS
Mailing Address: Fukuoka Yahuoku Japan Dome, Hawks Town, 2-2-2 Jigyohama, Chuo-ku, Fukuoka 810-0065. **Telephone:** 092-847-1006. **Owner:** Masayoshi Son.
Field Manager: Hiroshi Fujimoto.

HOKKAIDO NIPPON HAM FIGHTERS
Mailing Address: 1 Hitsujigaoka, Toyohira-ku, Sapporo 062-8655. **Telephone:** 011-857-3939.
Field Manager: Tsuyoshi Shinjo.

INTERNATIONAL LEAGUES

ORIX BUFFALOES
Mailing Address: 3-Kita-2-30 Chiyozaki, Nishi-ku, Osaka 550-0023. **Telephone:** 06-6586-0221. **Fax:** 06-6586-0240.
Field Manager: Satoshi Nakajima.

SAITAMA SEIBU LIONS
Mailing Address: 2135 Kami-Yamaguchi, Tokorozawa-shi, Saitama-ken 359-1189. **Telephone:** 04-2924-1155. **Fax:** 04-2928-1919.
Field Manager: Hatsuhiko Tsuji.

TOHOKU RAKUTEN GOLDEN EAGLES
Mailing Address: 2-11-6 Miyagino, Miyagino-ku, Sendai-shi, Miyagi-ken 983-0045. **Telephone:** 022-298-5300. **Fax:** 022-298-5360.
Field Manager: Kazuhisa Ishii.

KOREA

KOREA BASEBALL ORGANIZATION
Mailing Address: 278 Gangnam-daero, Seoul, Korea 06258. **Telephone:** (02) 3460-4600.
Years League Active: 1982-.
Website: koreabaseball.com.
Commissioner: Heo Koo-youn. **Secretary General:** Yang Hae-Young.
Member Clubs: Doosan Bears, Hanwha Eagles, Kia Tigers, KT Wiz, LG Twins, Lotte Giants, NC Dinos, Kiwoom Heroes, Samsung Lions, SSG Landers.
Regular Season: 144 games. **2023 Opening Date:** April 1.
Playoffs: Third- and fourth-place teams meet in best-of-three series: winner advances to meet second-place team in best-of-five series; winner meets first-place team in best-of-seven Korean Series for league championship.
Roster Limit: 26 active through Sept 1, when rosters expand to 31. **Imports:** Two active.

TAIWAN

CHINESE PROFESSIONAL BASEBALL LEAGUE
Mailing Address: 2F, No 32, Pateh Road, Sec 3, Taipei, Taiwan 10559. **Telephone:** 886-2-2577-6992. **Website:** cpbl.com.tw.
Years League Active: 1990-.
Commissioner: Chi-Chang Tsai.
Member Clubs: Chinatrust Brothers, Fubon Guardians, Rakuten Monkeys, Uni-President 7-Eleven Lions, Weichuan Dragons.
Regular Season: 120 games. Each team plays 60 games in the first and second halves of the season.
Player Limits: 25 active players. Three foreign players and no more than two foreign players on the field per team at any time.
2023 Opening Date: April 1. **All-Star Game:** July 29-30.
Playoffs: Half-season winners are eligible for the postseason. If a non-half-season winner team possesses a higher overall winning percentage than any other half-season winner, then this team gains a wild card and will play a best-of-five series against the half-season winner with the lower winner percentage. The winner of the playoff series advances to Taiwan Series (best-of-seven). If the same team clinches both first- and second-half seasons, then that team is awarded one win to start the Taiwan Series.

INTERNATIONAL LEAGUES

EUROPE

NETHERLANDS
DUTCH MAJOR LEAGUE CLUBS

Mailing Address: Koninklijke Nederlandse Baseball en Softball Bond (Royal Dutch Baseball and Softball Association), Postbus 2650, 3430 GB Nieuwegein, Holland. **Telephone:** 31-30-202-0100. **Website:** www.knbsb.nl. **Chairman:** Mark Herbold. **Legal Affairs:** Peter van der Aart. **National Teams and Talent Development:** Job van Beekhoven. **Treasurer:** Remko de Bie. **Marketing, Communications and Commerce:** Gerald Smith.

QUICK AMERSFOORT
Mailing Address: Postbus 780, 3800 AT Amersfoort. **Telephone:** +31 (0) 33-461-1914. **Website:** www.bsc-quick.nl

L&D AMSTERDAM PIRATES
Mailing Address: Herman Bonpad 5, 1067 SN Amsterdam. **Telephone:** +31 (0) 20-616-2151. **Website:** www.amsterdampirates.nl

CURACAO NEPTUNE
Mailing Address: Abraham van Stolkweg 31, 3041 JA Rotterdam. **Telephone:** +31 (0) 10-737-5369. **Website:** neptunussport.com

DSS/KINHEIM
Mailing Address: Rijksstraatweg 206, 2022 DH Haarlem. **Telephone:** +31 (0) 23-527-2678. **Website:** www.dss-honksoftbal.nl

UVV UTRECHT
Mailing Address: Parkzichtlaan 201, 3451 GX Vlueten. **Telephone:** +31 (0) 30-293-2702. **Website:** hsvuvv.nl

HCAW
Mailing Address: Zanderijweg 4-6, 1403 XV Bussum. **Telephone:** +31 (0) 35-693-1430. **Website:** www.hcaw.nl

HOOFDDORP PIONIERS
Mailing Address: Postbus 475, 2130 AL Hoofddorp. **Telephone:** +31 (0) 23-561-3557. **Website:** www.hoofddorp-pioniers.nl

OOSTERHOUT TWINS
Mailing Address: Postbus 4085, 4900 CB Oosterhout NB. **Telephone:** +31 (0) 162-433-760. **Website:** www.twins-sc.com

RCH MEMORIAL JEWELRY PINGUINS
Mailing Address: Ringvaartlaan 4 2103 XW Heemstede. **Telephone:** +31 (0) 023-528-4388. **Website:** www.rch-pinguins.nl

ITALY
ITALIAN BASEBALL LEAGUE CLUBS

Mailing Address: Federazione Italiana Baseball Softball, Viale Tiziano 74, 00196 Roma, Italy. **Telephone:** 39-06-32297201. **FAX:** 39-06-01902684. **Website:** www.fibs.it
President: Marco Landi.
Teams: Group A—Cagliari, Campidonico Grizzlies Torino, Ciemme Oltretorrente, Ecotherm Brescia, Parmaclima, Platform-Tmc Poviglio, Senago, Settimo. Group C—Comcor - Champion Modena, Farma Crocetta, Fontana Ermes Sala Baganza, Hort@Godo, Longbridge 2000 Bologna, Mediolanum New Rimini, San Marino, Torre Pedrera Falcons, Group B—Camec Collecchio, Itas Mutua Rovigo, Metalco Dragons Castelfranco Veneto, New Black Panthers Ronchi Dei Legionari, Padova, Sultan Allestimenti Navali Cervignano, Tecnovap Verona, Unipolsai Fortitudo Bologna. Group D—Academy Of Nettuno, Big Mat Grosseto 1952, Hotsand Macerata, Nettuno 1945, O.M. Valpanaro Athletics Bologna, Spirulina Becagli Grosseto.

WINTER BASEBALL

CARIBBEAN BASEBALL CONFEDERATION
Mailing Address: Frank Feliz Miranda No 1 Naco, Santo Domingo, Dominican Republic. **Telephone:** (809) 381-2643. **Fax:** (809) 565-4654.
Commissioner: Juan Francisco Puello. **Secretary:** Benny Agosto.
Member Countries: Cuba, Colombia, Dominican Republic, Mexico, Panama, Puerto Rico, Venezuela.
2024 Caribbean Series: Miami, Fla., February.

DOMINICAN LEAGUE

Office Address: Ave. Tiradentes, Ensanche La Fé, Estadio Quisqueya, Santo Domingo, Dominican Republic. **Telephone:** (809) 567-6371. **Fax:** (809) 567-5720. **E-Mail Address:** ligadom@hotmail.com. **Website:** lidom.com.
Years League Active: 1951-.
President: Vitelio Mejía Ortiz. **Vice President:** Winston Llenas Davila.
Member Clubs: Aguilas Cibaenas, Estrellas de Oriente, Gigantes del Cibao, Leones del Escogido, Tigres del Licey,

Toros del Este.
Regular Season: 50 games.
Playoff Format: Top four teams meet in 18-game round-robin. Top two teams advance to best-of-nine series for league championship. Winner advances to Caribbean Series.
Roster Limit: 30. **Imports:** 7.

MEXICAN PACIFIC LEAGUE

Mailing Address: Ave. Américas No. 1905, 5to. Piso, Col. Colomos Providencia, Guadalajara, Jalisco. **Telephone:** (52) 33 38 17 07 68. **E-Mail Address:** medios@lmp.mx. **Website:** lmp.mx.
Years League Active: 1958-.
President: Carlos Manrique Gonzalez. **General Manager:** Christian Veliz Valencia.
Member Clubs: Culiacan Tomateros, Guasave Algodoneros, Hermosillo Naranjeros, Jalisco Charros, Los Mochis Cañeros, Mazatlan Venados, Mexicali Aguilas, Monterrey Sultanes, Navojoa Mayos, Obregon Yaquis.
Regular Season: 68 games.
Playoff Format: Six teams advance to best-of-seven

INTERNATIONAL LEAGUES

quarterfinals. Three winners and losing team with best record advance to best-of-seven semifinals. Winners meet in best-of-seven series for league championship. Winner advances to Caribbean Series.

Roster Limit: 30. **Imports:** 5.

PUERTO RICAN LEAGUE

Office Address: Avenida Munoz Rivera 1056, Edificio First Federal, Suite 501, Rio Piedras, PR 00925. **Mailing Address:** PO Box 191852 San Juan, PR 00919—1852. **Telephone:** (786) 244-1146. **Website:** ligapr.com. **E-mail address:** info@ligapr.com

Years League Active: 1938-2007; 2008-

President: Juan Flores Galarza. **Operations Director:** Carlos J. Berroa Puertas. **Press Director:** Edna Garcia.

Member Clubs: Caguas Criollos, Carolina Gigantes, Mayaguez Indios, Ponce Leones, RA12, Santurce Cangrejeros.

Regular Season: 40 games.

Playoff Format: Top four teams meet in round robin series, with top two teams advancing to best-of-seven final. Winner advances to Caribbean Series.

Roster Limit: 30. **Imports:** 5.

VENEZUELAN LEAGUE

Mailing Address: Avenida Casanova, Centro Comercial "El Recreo," Torre Sur, Piso 3, Oficinas 6 y 7, Sabana Grande, Caracas, Venezuela. **Telephone:** (58) 212-761-6408. **Website:** lvbp.com.

Years League Active: 1946-.

Commissioner: Juan Francisco Puello Herrera. Member Clubs: Anzoategui Caribes, Aragua Tigres, Caracas Leones, La Guaira Tiburones, Lara Cardenales, Magallanes Navegantes, Margarita Bravos, Zulia Aguilas.

Regular Season: 64 games.

Playoff Format: Top two teams in each division, plus a wild-card team, meet in 16-game round-robin series. Top two finishers meet in best-of-seven series for league championship. Winner advances to Caribbean Series.

Roster Limit: 26. **Imports:** 7.

COLOMBIAN LEAGUE

Office/Mailing Address: Hotel Eslait Cra 53 No. 72-27 2do piso, Baranquilla. **Telephone:** (57) 368-6561. **E-mail Address:** r.mendoza@diprobeisbol.com. **Website:** lpbcol.com.

President: Pedro Salzedo Salom. **Director, Operations:** Kodiro Miranda. **Director, Communications:** Ricardo Mendoza Puccini.

Member Clubs: Barranquilla Caimanes, Barranquilla Gigantes, Cartagena Tigres, Monteria Vaqueros, Santa Marta Leones, Sincelejo Toros.

Regular season: 42 games.

Playoff Format: Best-of-five semifinals, Best-of-seven championship series.

AUSTRALIA

AUSTRALIAN BASEBALL LEAGUE

Address: Suite 3.03 (Level 3) 88 Albert Road South Melbourne, VIC 3205. **Telephone:** (61) 3 9915 9900. **E-Mail Address:** playbaseball@baseball.com.au. **Website:** theabl.com.au. **CEO:** Glenn Williams. **General Manager:** Shane Tonkin. **Marketing, Media and Communications:** Kaitlin Mason. **Events and Competitions Manager:** Sharon Butty.

Teams: Adelaide Giants, Auckland Tautara, Brisbane Bandits, Canberra Cavalry, Geelong-Korea, Melbourne Aces, Perth Heat, Sydney Blue Sox.

Opening Date: Play usually opens in November with playoffs in February.

Playoff Format: The teams with the best four records qualify for the playoffs. Teams are seeded 1-4, with the top two seeds hosting all three games of the best-of-three semifinal series. Winners advance to a best-of-three championship series.

DOMESTIC LEAGUE

ARIZONA FALL LEAGUE

Mailing Address: Arizona Fall League C/O Salt River Fields - Centerfield Office 7555 North Pima Road Scottsdale, AZ 85258. **Telephone:** (480)-990-1005. **E-Mail Address:** arizonafallleague@mlb.com. **Website:** mlb.com/arizona-fall-league. **Years League Active:** 1992-.

Operated by: Major League Baseball.

Communications: Chuck Fox.

Teams: Glendale Desert Dogs, Mesa Solar Sox, Peoria Javelinas, Salt River Rafters, Scottsdale Scorpions, Surprise Saguaros.

Regular season: 32 games. **Playoff Format:** Three teams advance to championship series. No. 2 plays No. 3 in one-game with winner advancing to face No. 1 team for title.

Roster Limit: 35 players per team plus a "taxi squad" of reserve players. Each major-league organization is required to provide seven players. Triple-A and Double-A players are eligible provided they are on Double-A or Triple-A rosters no later than August 15. Each organization is permitted to send two high Class A level players and two players below high Class A. No players with more than one year active or two years total of credited major-league service as of August 31 (including major league disabled list time) are eligible. Each team is allotted 20 pitchers but only 15 are designated "active" each game day.

198 · Baseball America 2023 Directory

BaseballAmerica.com

COLLEGES

COLLEGE

COLLEGE ORGANIZATIONS

NATIONAL COLLEGIATE ATHLETIC ASSOCIATION

Mailing Address: 700 W. Washington Street, PO Box 6222, Indianapolis, IN 46206. **Telephone:** (317) 917-6222. **Fax:** (317) 917-6826 (championships), (317) 917-6710 (baseball).

E-mail Addresses: Division I Championship: aholman@ncaa.org (Anthony Holman), rlburhr@ncaa.org (Randy Buhr), ctolliver@ncaa.org (Chad Tolliver), thalpin@ncaa.org (Ty Halpin), kgiles@ncaa.org (Kim Giles). **Division II Championship:** ebreece@ncaa.org (Eric Breece). **Division III:** jpwilliams@ncaa.org (J.P. Williams).

Websites: www.ncaa.org, www.ncaa.com.

President: Dr. Mark Emmert. **Managing director, Division I Championships/Alliances:** Anthony Holman. **Director, Division I Championships/Alliances:** Randy Buhr. **Associate Director, Championships/ Alliances:** Chad Tolliver. **Division II Assistant Director, Championships/Alliances:** Eric Breece. **Division III Assistant Director, Championships/Alliances:** J.P. Williams. **Media Contact, Division I Championships, Alliances/College World Series:** Jeff Williams. **Playing Rules Contact:** Ty Halpin. **Statistics Contacts:** Jeff Williams (Division I and RPI); Mark Bedics (Division II); Sean Straziscar (Division III).

Chairman, Division I Baseball Committee: Mike Buddie (Director of Athletics, Army).

Division I Baseball Committee: Jeff Altier (Director of Athletics, Stetson); Jay Artigues (Director of Athletics, Southeastern Louisiana); Sherard Clinkscales (Director of Athletics, Indiana State); Jennifer Cohen (Director of Athletics, Washington); John Cohen (Director of Athletics, Mississippi State); Kirby Hocutt (Director of Athletics, Texas Tech); Matthew Hogue (Director of Athletics, Coastal Carolina); Bob Moosburger (Director of Athletics, Bowling Green State); Eddie Nunez (Director of Athletics, New Mexico).

Chairman, Division II Baseball Committee: Todd Resser (Director of Athletics, Columbus State). **Chairman, Division III Baseball Committee:** Michael Lindberg (Director of Athletics, Wells, N.Y.).

2023 National Convention: Jan. 11-14 at San Antonio.

2023 CHAMPIONSHIP TOURNAMENTS

NCAA DIVISION I
College World Series: Omaha, June 16-26
Super Regionals (8): Campus sites, June 10-12
Regionals (16): Campus sites, June 3-6

NCAA DIVISION II
World Series: USA Baseball National Training Complex, Cary, N.C. June 3-10.

NCAA DIVISION III
World Series: Veterans Memorial Stadium, Cedar Rapids, Iowa, June 2-8

NATIONAL JUNIOR COLLEGE ATHLETIC ASSOCIATION

Mailing Address: 8801 JM Keynes Drive, Suite 450, Charlotte, NC 28262. **Telephone:** (719) 590-9788. **Fax:** (719) 590-7324. **E-Mail Address:** mgarrison@njcaa.org. **Website:** www.njcaa.org.

Executive Director: Christopher Parker. **Director, Division I Baseball Tournament:** Rod Lovett. **Director, Division II Baseball Tournament:** Angelo Maltese. **Director, Division III Baseball Tournament:** Antonio Cannavaro. **Director, Media Relations:** McKenzie Garrison.

2023 CHAMPIONSHIP TOURNAMENTS

DIVISION I
World Series: Grand Junction, CO, May 27-June 2/3.

DIVISION II
World Series: Enid, OK, May 27-June 2/3.

DIVISION III
World Series: Greeneville, TN, May 27-June 1.

CALIFORNIA COMMUNITY COLLEGE ATHLETIC ASSOCIATION

Mailing Address: 2017 O St., Sacramento, CA 95811. **Telephone:** (916) 444-1600. **Fax:** (916) 444-2616. **E-Mail Addresses:** ccarter@cccaasports.org, jboggs@cccaasports.org. **Website:** www.cccaasports.org.

Executive Director: Jennifer Cardone, Interim. **Director, Championships:** George Mategakis. **Administrative Assistant:** Rima Trotter, rtrotter@cccaasports.org.

2023 CHAMPIONSHIP TOURNAMENT

State Championship: May 27-29, Folsom Lake (Calf.) College.

NORTHWEST ATHLETIC CONFERENCE

Mailing Address: Clark College TGB 121, 1933 Fort Vancouver Way, Vancouver, WA 98663. **Telephone:** (360) 992-2833. **Fax:** (360) 696-6210. **E-Mail Address:** nwaacc@clark.edu. **Website:** www.nwacsports.org.

Executive Director: Marco Azurdia. **Executive Assistant:** Shelly Grothe. **Sports Information Director:** Iain Dexter. **Director, Operations:** Alli Young.

2023 CHAMPIONSHIP TOURNAMENT

NWAC Championship: David Story Field, Lower Columbia (Wash.) JC, May 25-29.

AMERICAN BASEBALL COACHES ASSOCIATION

Office Address: 4101 Piedmont Parkway, Greensboro, NC 27410. **Telephone:** (336) 821-3140. **Fax:** (336) 886-0000. **E-Mail Address:** abca@abca.org. **Website:** www.abca.org. **Executive Director:** Craig Keilitz. **Deputy Executive Director:** Jon Litchfield. **Asst. Executive Director, Trade Show:** Juahn Clark. **Asst. Executive Director, Convention/Marketing:** Zach Haile. **Asst. Executive Director, Coaching Outreach:** Ryan Brownlee. **Chairman:** Keith Madison. **President:** Jim Schlossnagle (Texas A&M University).

2024 National Convention: Jan. 4-7 in Dallas..

200 · Baseball America 2023 Directory

BaseballAmerica.com

NCAA DIVISION I CONFERENCES
AMERICA EAST CONFERENCE

Mailing Address: 451 D Street, Suite 702, Boston, MA 02127. **Telephone:** (617) 695-6369. **Website:** www.americaeast.com. **Baseball Members (First Year):** Albany (2002), Binghamton (2002), Maine (1990), Maryland-Baltimore County (2004), Massachusetts-Lowell (2014), New Jersey Tech (2021). **2023 Tournament:** Four teams, double-elimination, May 25-28 at Mahaney Diamond, Orono, Maine.

AMERICAN ATHLETIC CONFERENCE

Mailing Address: 545 E. John Carpenter Freeway, Third Floor, Irving, TX 75062. **Telephone:** (469) 284-5167. **E-Mail Address:** csullivan@theamerican.org. **Website:** www.theamerican.org. **Baseball Members:** (First Year): Central Florida (2014), Cincinnati (2014), East Carolina (2015), Houston (2014), Memphis (2014), South Florida (2014), Tulane (2015), Wichita State (2018). **Director, Communications:** Chuck Sullivan. **2023 Tournament:** Eight teams, double-elimination, May 23-28 at BayCare Ballpark, Clearwater, Fla.

ATLANTIC COAST CONFERENCE

Mailing Address: 4512 Weybridge Ln., Greensboro, NC 27407. **Telephone:** (336) 851-6062. **Fax:** (336) 854-8797. **E-Mail Address:** sphillips@theacc.org. **Website:** www.theacc.com. **Baseball Members (First Year):** Boston College (2006), Clemson (1954), Duke (1954), Florida State (1992), Georgia Tech (1980), Miami (2005), North Carolina (1954), North Carolina State (1954), Notre Dame (2014), Louisville (2015), Pittsburgh (2014), Virginia (1955), Virginia Tech (2005), Wake Forest (1954). **Associate Director, Communications:** Steve Phillips. **2023 Tournament:** 12 teams, group play followed by single-elimination semifinals and finals. May 23-28 at Durham Bulls Athletic Park, Durham, NC.

ASUN CONFERENCE

Mailing Address: 3301 Windy Ridge Parkway SE, Suite 350, Atlanta, GA 30339. **E-Mail Addresses:** greg.mette@asunsports.org. **Website:** www.asunsports.org. **Baseball Members:** (First Year): Austin Peay (2023), Bellarmine (2021), Central Arkansas (2022), Eastern Kentucky (2022), Florida Gulf Coast (2008), Jacksonville (1999), Jacksonville State (2022), Kennesaw State (2006), Liberty (2019), Lipscomb (2004), North Alabama (2019), North Florida (2006), Queens (N.C.) (2023), Stetson (1986). **Director, Sports Information:** Mike DeVader. **2023 Tournament:** Eight teams, double-elimination, May 23-27 at Melching Field at Conrad Park (Stetson).

ATLANTIC 10 CONFERENCE

Mailing Address: 11827 Canon Blvd., Suite 200, Newport News, VA 23606. **Telephone:** (757) 706-3059. **E-Mail Address:** twaterman@atlantic10.org. **Website:** www.atlantic10.com. **Baseball Members:** (First Year): Davidson (2015), Dayton (1996), Fordham (1996), George Mason (2014), George Washington (1977), Massachusetts (1977), Rhode Island (1981), Richmond (2002), St. Bonaventure (1980), Saint Joseph's (1983), Saint Louis (2006), Virginia Commonwealth (2013). **Director, Communications:** Tom Waterman. **2023 Tournament:** Seven teams, double elimination. May 23-27 at The Diamond, Richmond, Va.

BIG EAST CONFERENCE

Mailing Address: BIG EAST Conference, 655 3rd Avenue, 7th Floor, New York, NY 10017. **Telephone:** (212) 969-3181. **Fax:** (212) 969-2900. **E-Mail Address:** kquinn@bigeast.com. **Website:** www.bigeast.com. **Baseball Members:** (First Year): Butler (2014), Connecticut (1979-2013, 2021), Creighton (2014), Georgetown (1985), St. John's (1985), Seton Hall (1985), Villanova (1985), Xavier (2014). **Director Olympic Sports/Marketing Communications:** Kevin Ivany. **2023 Tournament:** Four teams, modified double-elimination. May 25-28 at Prasco Park, Mason, Ohio.

BIG SOUTH CONFERENCE

Mailing Address: 7233 Pineville-Matthews Rd., Suite 100, Charlotte, NC 28226. **Telephone:** (704) 341-7990. **Fax:** (704) 341-7991. **E-Mail Address:** jordanp@bigsouth.org. **Website:** www.bigsouthsports.com. **Baseball Members (First Year):** Campbell (2012), Charleston Southern (1983), Gardner-Webb (2009), High Point (1999), Longwood (2013), UNC Asheville (1985), Presbyterian (2009), Radford (1983), South Carolina-Upstate (2019), Winthrop (1983). **Director of Communications:** Jordan Parry. **2023 Tournament:** Four teams.. May 25-27, at Truist Point, High Point, N.C.

BIG TEN CONFERENCE

Mailing Address: 5440 Park Place, Rosemont, IL 60018. **Telephone:** (847) 696-1010. **Website:** www.big-ten.org. **Baseball Members (First Year):** Illinois (1896), Indiana (1906), Iowa (1906), Maryland (2015), Michigan (1896), Michigan State (1950), Minnesota (1906), Nebraska (2012), Northwestern (1898), Ohio State (1913), Penn State (1992), Purdue (1906), Rutgers (2015). Director, Communications: Megan Althoff. **2023 Tournament:** Eight teams, double-elimination, May 24-28, Charles Schwab Field Omaha.

BIG 12 CONFERENCE

Mailing Address: 400 E. John Carpenter Freeway, Irving, TX 75062. **Telephone:** (469) 524-1009. **E-Mail Address:** dwaxman@big12sports.com. **Website:** www.big12sports.com. **Baseball Members (First Year):** Baylor (1997), Kansas (1997), Kansas State (1997), Oklahoma (1997), Oklahoma State (1997), Texas Christian (2013), Texas (1997), Texas Tech (1997), West Virginia (2013). **Assistant Director, Media Relations:** David Waxman. **2022 Tournament:** Eight teams, double-elimination. May 24-28 at Globe Life Field, Arlington, Texas.

BIG WEST CONFERENCE

Mailing Address: 100 Spectrum Center Dr., Suite 420, Irvine, CA 92618. **Telephone:** (949) 261-2525. **Fax:** (949) 261-2528. **E-Mail Address:** jstcyr@bigwest.org. **Website:** www.bigwest.org. **Baseball Members (First Year):** Cal Poly (1997), UC Davis (2008), UC Irvine (2002), UC Riverside (2002), UC San Diego (2021), UC Santa Barbara (1970), Cal State Bakersfield (2021), Cal State Fullerton (1975), Cal State Northridge (2001), Hawaii (2013), Long Beach State (1970). **2023 Tournament:** None.

COLLEGE

COLONIAL ATHLETIC ASSOCIATION

Mailing Address: 8625 Patterson Ave., Richmond, VA 23229. **Telephone:** (804) 754-1616. **Fax:** (804) 754-1973. **E-Mail Address:** rwashburn@caasports.com. **Website:** www.caasports.com. **Baseball Members (First Year):** College of Charleston (2014), Delaware (2002), Elon (2015), Hofstra (2002), Monmouth (2023), North Carolina A&T (2023), James Madison (1986), UNC Wilmington (1986), Northeastern (2006), Stony Brook (2023), Towson (2002), North Carolina-Wilmington (2023), William & Mary (1986). **Associate Commissioner/Communications:** Rob Washburn. **2023 Tournament:** Six teams, double-elimination. May 25-29 at Latham Park, Elon, NC.

CONFERENCE USA

Mailing Address: 5201 N. O'Connor Blvd., Suite 300, Irving, TX 75039. **Telephone:** (214) 774-1300. **Fax:** (214) 496-0055. **E-Mail Address:** jstepp@c-usa.org. **Website:** www.conferenceusa.com. **Baseball Members (First Year):** Alabama-Birmingham (1996), Charlotte (2014), Dallas Baptist (2023) Florida Atlantic (2014), Florida International (2014), Louisiana Tech (2014), Middle Tennessee State (2014), Southern Mississippi (1996), Texas-San Antonio (2014), Western Kentucky (2015). **Assistant Commissioner, Communications:** Jordan Stepp. **2023 Tournament:** Eight teams, double-elimination. May 24-28 in Houston, hosted by Rice.

HORIZON LEAGUE

Mailing Address: 129 E. Market Street, Suite 900, Indianapolis, IN 46204. **Telephone:** (317) 237 5622. **Fax:** (317) 237-5620. **E-Mail Address:** dgliot@horizonleague.org. **Website:** www.horizonleague.org. **Baseball Members (First Year):** Illinois-Chicago (1994), Northern Kentucky (2016), Oakland (1994), Purdue-Fort Wayne (2021), Wright State (1994), Wisconsin-Milwaukee (1994), Youngstown State (2002). **Director, Communications and Digital Media Strategy:** Dan Gliot. **2023 Tournament:** Six teams, modified double-elimination. May 24-27, hosted by No. 1 seed.

IVY LEAGUE

Mailing Address: 228 Alexander Rd., Second Floor, Princeton, NJ 08544. **Telephone:** (609) 258-6426. **E-Mail Address:** jjr@ivyleaguesports.com. **Website:** www.ivyleaguesports.com. **Baseball Members (First Year):** Brown (1948), Columbia (1930), Cornell (1930), Dartmouth (1930), Harvard (1948), Pennsylvania (1930), Princeton (1930), Yale (1930). **Assistant Executive Director, Communications/Championships:** JJ Klein. **2023 Tournament:** May 19-22, hosted by No. 1 seed.

METRO ATLANTIC ATHLETIC CONFERENCE

Mailing Address: 712 Amboy Ave., Edison, NJ 08837. **Telephone:** (732) 738-5455. **E-Mail Address:** sam.watkins@maac.org. **Website:** www.maacsports.com. **Baseball Members (First Year):** Canisius (1990), Fairfield (1982), Iona (1982), Manhattan (1982), Marist (1998),Mount St. Mary's (2023), Niagara (1990), Quinnipiac (2014), Rider (1998), Siena (1990). **Director, New Media:** Samuel Watkins Jr. **2023 Tournament:** Six teams, double elimination, May 24-27 at Clover Stadium, Pomona, N.Y.

MID-AMERICAN CONFERENCE

Mailing Address: 24 Public Square, 15th Floor, Cleveland, OH 44113. **Telephone:** (216) 566-4622. **Fax:** (216) 858-9622. **E-Mail Address:** jguy@mac-sports.com. **Website:** www.getmesomemaction.com. **Baseball Members (First Year):** Akron (2020), Ball State (1973), Bowling Green State (1952), Central Michigan (1971), Eastern Michigan (1971), Kent State (1951), Miami (1947), Northern Illinois (1997), Ohio (1946), Toledo (1950), Western Michigan (1947). **Assistant Commissioner, Communications and Social Media:** Jeremy Guy. **2023 Tournament:** Six teams, double-elimination, hosted by No. 1 seed.

MISSOURI VALLEY CONFERENCE

Mailing Address: 1818 Chouteau Ave., St. Louis, MO 63103. **Telephone:** (314) 444-4300. **Fax:** (314) 444-4333. **E-Mail Address:** davis@mvc.org. **Website:** www.mvc-sports.com. **Baseball Members (First Year):** Belmont (2023), Bradley (1955), Evansville (1994), Illinois Chicago (2023), Illinois State (1980), Indiana State (1976), Missouri State (1990), Murray State (2023), Southern Illinois (1974), Valparaiso (2019). **Assistant Commissioner, Communications:** Ryan Davis. **2023 Tournament:** Eight teams, double-elimination, May 23-27 at Terre Haute, Ind.

MOUNTAIN WEST CONFERENCE

Mailing Address: 10807 New Allegiance Dr., Suite 250, Colorado Springs, CO 80921. **Telephone:** (719) 488-4052. **Fax:** (719) 487-7241. **E-Mail Address:** sbuchanan@themw.com. **Website:** www.themw.com. **Baseball Members (First Year):** Air Force (2000), Fresno State (2013), Nevada (2013), Nevada-Las Vegas (2000), New Mexico (2000), San Diego State (2000), San Jose State (2014). **Director, Strategic Communication:** Stuart Buchanan. **2023 Tournament:** May 25-28 at Fresno State.

NORTHEAST CONFERENCE

Mailing Address: 200 Cottontail Lane, Vantage Court South, Somerset, NJ 08873. **Telephone:** (732) 469 0440. **Fax:** (732) 469-0744. **E-Mail Address:** abarajas@northeastconference.org. **Website:** www.northeastconference.org. **Baseball Members (First Year):** Bryant (2010), Central Connecticut State (1999), Coppin State (2023), Delaware State (2023), Fairleigh Dickinson (1981), Long Island (1981), Maryland Eastern Shore (2023), Merrimack (2020), Mount St. Mary's (1989), Norfolk State (2023), Sacred Heart (2000), Stonehill (2023), Wagner (1981). **Communications Assistant:** Adrian Barajas. **2023 Tournament:** May 24-28 at Dutchess Stadium, Wappingers Falls, NY.

OHIO VALLEY CONFERENCE

Mailing Address: 215 Centerview Dr., Suite 115, Brentwood, TN 37027. **Telephone:** (615) 371-1698. **Fax:** (615) 891-1682. **E-Mail Address:** kschwartz@ovc.org. **Website:** www.ovcsports.com. **Baseball Members (First Year):** Arkansas-Little Rock (2023), Eastern Illinois (1996), Linderwood (2023), Morehead State (1948), Murray State (1948), Southeast Missouri State (1991), Southern Illinois-Edwardsville (2012), Southern Indiana (2023), Tennessee-Martin (1992), Tennessee Tech (1949). **Assistant Commissioner:** Kyle Schwartz. **2023 Tournament:** Eight teams, double-elimination, May 24-27 in Marion, Ill.

202 · Baseball America 2023 Directory

BaseballAmerica.com

COLLEGE

PACIFIC-12 CONFERENCE

Mailing Address: Pac-12 Conference 360 3rd Street, 3rd Floor San Francisco, CA 94107. **Telephone:** (415) 580-4200. **Website:** www.pac-12.com. **Baseball Members (First Year):** Arizona (1979), Arizona State (1979), California (1916), UCLA (1928), Oregon (2009) Oregon State (1916), Southern California (1923), Stanford (1918), Utah (2012), Washington (1916), Washington State (1919). **2023 Tournament:** Eight teams, double-elimination, May 23-27 at Scottsdale Stadium, Scottsdale, Ariz.

PATRIOT LEAGUE

Mailing Address: 3773 Corporate Pkwy., Suite 190, Center Valley, PA 18034. **Telephone:** (610) 289-1950. **Fax:** (610) 289-1951. **E-Mail Address:** rsakamoto@patriot-league.com. **Website:** www.patriotleague.org. **Baseball Members (First Year):** Army (1993), Bucknell (1991), Holy Cross (1991), Lafayette (1991), Lehigh (1991), Navy (1993). **Assistant Commissioner, Communications:** Ryan Sakamoto. **2023 Tournament:** four teams, two rounds of best-of-three series, hosted at campus sites, May 13-21, May 20-22.

SOUTHEASTERN CONFERENCE

Mailing Address: 2201 Richard Arrington Blvd. N., Birmingham, AL 35203. **Telephone:** (205) 458-3000. **Fax:** (205) 458-3030. **E-Mail Address:** scartell@sec.org. **Website:** www.secsports.com. **Baseball Members (First Year): East Division—**Florida (1933), Georgia (1933), Kentucky (1933), Missouri (2013), South Carolina (1992), Tennessee (1933), Vanderbilt (1933). **West Division—**Alabama (1933), Arkansas (1992), Auburn (1933), Louisiana State (1933), Mississippi (1933), Mississippi State (1933), Texas A&M (2013). **Director, Communications:** Chuck Dunlap. **2023 Tournament:** 12 teams, modified single/double-elimination. May 23-28 at Hoover Metropolitan Stadium, Hoover, Ala.

SOUTHERN CONFERENCE

Mailing Address: 702 N. Pine St., Spartanburg, SC 29303. **Telephone:** (864) 591-5100. **Fax:** (864) 591-3448. **E-Mail Address:** rwardlaw@socon.org. **Website:** www. soconsports.com. **Baseball Members (First Year):** The Citadel (1937), East Tennessee State (1979-2005, 2015), Mercer (2015), UNC Greensboro (1998), Samford (2009), VMI (1925-2003, 2015), Western Carolina (1977), Wofford (1998). **Media Relations Assistant:** Ralan Wardlaw. **2023 Tournament:** May 24-28 at Fluor Field, Greenville, S.C.

SOUTHLAND CONFERENCE

Mailing Address: 2600 Network Blvd, Suite 150, Frisco, Texas 75034. **Telephone:** (972) 422-9500. **Website:** southland.org. **Baseball Members (First Year):** Houston Christian (2014), Incarnate Word (2014), McNeese State (1973), New Orleans (2014), Nicholls State (1992), Northwestern State (1988), Southeastern Louisiana (1998), Texas A&M-Corpus Christi (2007). **2023 Tournament:** May 24-27 at McNeese State.

SOUTHWESTERN ATHLETIC CONFERENCE

Mailing Address: 1101 22nd Street South, Birmingham, AL 35205. **Telephone:** (205) 251-7573. **Fax:** (205) 297-9820. **E-Mail Address:** a.roberts@swac.org. **Website:** www.swac. org. **Baseball Members (First Year): East Division—**Alabama A&M (2000), Alabama State (1982), Bethune-Cookman (2022), Florida A&M (2022), Jackson State (1958),

Mississippi Valley State (1968). **West Division—** Alcorn State (1962), Arkansas-Pine Bluff (1999), Grambling State (1958), Prairie View A&M (1920), Southern (1934), Texas Southern (1954). **Asst. Commissioner, Communications:** Andrew Roberts. **2023 Tournament:** Eight teams, double-elimination. May 24-28 at Russ Chandler Stadium, Atlanta.

SUMMIT LEAGUE

Mailing Address: 340 W. Butterfield Rd., Suite 3D, Elmhurst, IL 60126. **Telephone:** (630) 516-0661. **Fax:** (630) 516-0673. **E-Mail Address:** powell@thesummitleague.org. **Website:** www.thesummitleague.org. **Baseball Members (First Year):** Nebraska-Omaha (2013), North Dakota State (2008), Northern Colorado (2022), Oral Roberts (1998), St. Thomas (2022), South Dakota State (2008), Western Illinois (1984). **Associate Commissioner, Communications:** Ryan Powell. **2023 Tournament:** May 24-27 at Newman Outdoor Field, Fargo, N.D..

SUN BELT CONFERENCE

Mailing Address: 1500 Sugar Bowl Dr., New Orleans, LA 70112. **Telephone:** (504) 556-0884. **Fax:** (504) 299-9068. **E-Mail Address:** sam@sunbeltsports.org. **Website:** www.sunbeltsports.org. **Baseball Members (First Year):** Appalachian State (2015), Arkansas State (1991), Coastal Carolina (2017), Georgia Southern, (2015), Georgia State (2014), James Madison (2023), Louisiana-Lafayette (1991), Louisiana-Monroe (2007), Marshall (2023), Old Dominion (2023), South Alabama (1976), Southern Mississippi (2023), Troy (2006),Texas State (2014). **Asst. Commissioner, Digital & Creative Services:** Sam Knehans. **2023 Tournament:** Eight teams, double-elimination. May 23-28 at Riverwalk Stadium, Montgomery, Ala.

WESTERN ATHLETIC CONFERENCE

Mailing Address: 9250 East Costilla Ave., Suite 300, Englewood, CO 80112. **Telephone:** (303) 799-9221. **Website:** www.wacsports.com. **Baseball Members (First Year):** Abilene Christian (2022), California Baptist (2019), Grand Canyon (2014), New Mexico State (2006),Sacramento State (2023), Sam Houston State (2022), Seattle (2023), Stephen F. Austin (2022), Tarleton State (2022), Texas-Arlington (2023), Texas-Rio Grande Valley (2014), Utah Tech (2021), Utah Valley (2014). **2023 Tournament:** May 23-27 at Hohokam Stadium, Mesa, Ariz.

WEST COAST CONFERENCE

Mailing Address: 951 Mariners Island Blvd., Third Floor, San Mateo, CA 94404. **Telephone:** (650) 873-8622. **Website:** www.wccsports.com. **Baseball Members (First Year):** Brigham Young (2012), Gonzaga (1996), Loyola Marymount (1968), Pacific (2014), Pepperdine (1968), Portland (1996), Saint Mary's (1968), San Diego (1979), San Francisco (1968), Santa Clara (1968). **2023 Tournament:** Four teams, double-elimination, May 24-27 at Banner Island Ballpark, Stockton, Calif.

COLLEGE

NCAA DIVISION I TEAMS
* Denotes recruiting coordinator

ABILENE CHRISTIAN WILDCATS

Conference: Western Athletic. **Mailing Address:** 1600 Campus Ct., Abilene, TX 79601. **Website:** www.acusports. com. **Head Coach:** Rick McCarty. **Telephone:** (325) 674-2817. **Baseball SID:** Zach Carlyle. **Assistant Coaches:** Blaze Lambert, Casey Demko, Daniel Furuto. **Telephone:** (325) 674-2817. **Home Field:** Crutcher Scott Field. **Seating Capacity:** 4,000. **Outfield Dimension: LF**—333, **CF**—381, **RF**—303.

AIR FORCE

Conference: Mountain West.
Mailing Address: 2169 Field House Dr. Air Force Academy, CO 80840-9500. **Website:** www.goairforce-falcons.com. **Head Coach:** Mike Kazlausky. **Telephone:** (719) 333-0835. **Baseball SID:** Nick Cicere. **Telephone:** (719) 333-3950. **Assistant Coaches:** Ryan Forrest, Jimmy Roesinger. **Telephone:** (719) 333-7539. **Home Field:** Falcon Field. **Seating Capacity:** 1,000. **Outfield Dimension: LF**—349, **CF**—400, **RF**—316

AKRON

Conference: Mid-American. **Address:** 373 Carroll St. Akron, OH 44325. **Website:** www.gozips.com.
Head Coach: Greg Beals. **Baseball SID:** Brian Dennison. **Assistant Coaches:** Tim Donnelly*, Blair Everhart.
Home Field: Skeeles Field. **Capacity:** 1500. **Outfield Dimensions:** LF-320 CF-390 RF-310.

ALABAMA

Conference: SEC.
Address: 1201 Coliseum Drive, Coleman Colsiseum, Tuscaloosa, AL 35401. **Website:** www.RollTide.com.
Head Coach: Brad Bohannon. **Telephone:** 205-348-4029.
Baseball SID: Alex Thompson. **Assistant Coaches:** Matt Reida*, Jason Jackson.
Home Field: Sewell-Thomas Stadium. **Capacity:** 5,867+. **Outfield Dimensions:** LF-320 CF-390 RF-320.

ALABAMA A&M

Conference: Southwestern.
Mailing Address: 4900 Meridian Street, PO Box 1597, Normal, AL 35762. **Website:** www.aamusports.com.
Head Coach: Elliott Jones. **Telephone:** (256) 372-7213. **Baseball SID:** Terissa Mark. **Telephone:** (256) 372-5880.
Assistant Coaches: Corben Green, Ashanti Wheatley, Louis Whitlow. **Home Field:** Bulldog Baseball Field. **Seating Capacity:** 500. **Outfield Dimension: LF**—330, **CF**—402, **RF**—318

ALABAMA STATE

Conference: Southwestern Athletic. **Address:** 915 S Jackson St., Montgomery, AL 36104. **Website:** www. bamastatesports.com.
Head Coach: Jose Vazquez. **Telephone:** 334-229-5600. **Baseball SID:** Fred Sington. **Assistant Coaches:** Drew Clark*, Branch Kloess.
Home Field: Wheeler-Watkins Baseball Complex. **Capacity:** 500. **Outfield Dimensions: LF**—330, **CF**—400 **RF**—330.

ALABAMA-BIRMINGHAM

Conference: Conference USA.
Mailing Address: 1720 2nd Ave. S, Bartow Arena, Birmingham, AL 35294-1160. **Website:** uabsports.com.
Head Coach: Casey Dunn. **Baseball SID:** Hailee Roe. **Telephone:** (205) 934-0722.
Assistant Coaches: BJ Green, Alan Kunkel.
Home Field: Regions Field. **Seating Capacity:** 8,500. **Outfield Dimension: LF**—320, **CF**—400, **RF**—325.

ALBANY

Conference: America East.
Address: 1400 Washington Avenue Albany, NY 12222. **Website:** ualbanysports.com.
Head Coach: Jon Mueller.
Baseball SID: Taylor O'Connor. **Assistant Coaches:** Jeff Kaier*, Dave Ames.
Home Field: Varsity Field.

ALCORN STATE

Conference: Southwestern.
Mailing Address: 1000 ASU Drive #510 Lorman, MS 39096. **Website:** www.alcornsports.com.
Head Coach: Reginald Williams. **Telephone:** (601) 877-4090. **Baseball SID:** Dahkeem Williams.
Assistant Coaches: Kirt Cormier.
Home Field: William "Bill" Foster Field at Willie E. "Rat" McGowan Stadium.

APPALACHIAN STATE

Conference: Sun Belt.
Mailing Address: Bodenheimer Dr, ASU Box 32153, Boone, NC 28607. **Website:** www.appstatesports.com.
Head Coach: Kermit Smith. **Baseball SID:** Shane Harvell.
Assistant Coaches: Britt Johnson, Justin Aspegren. **Telephone:** (828) 262-8664.
Home Field: Jim and Bettie Smith Stadium. **Seating Capacity:** 827. **Outfield Dimension: LF**—335, **CF**—400, **RF**—330

ARIZONA

Conference: Pac-12.
Address: The University of Arizona Athletics McKale Center 1 National Championship Drive P.O. Box 210096 Tucson, AZ 85721-0096. **Website:** ArizonaWildcats.com.
Head Coach: Chip Hale. **Telephone:** N/A.
Baseball SID: Brett Gleason. **Assistant Coaches:** Trip Couch*, Dave Lawn.
Home Field: Hi Corbett Field. **Capacity:** 9,000. **Outfield Dimensions:** LF-366 CF-392 RF-349.

ARIZONA STATE

Conference: Pac-12.
Mailing Address: Carson Center, PO Box 872505, Tempe, AZ 85287-2505. **Website:** www.thesundevils.com.
Head Coach: Willie Bloomquist. **Telephone:** (480) 965-3677. **Baseball SID:** Jeremy Hawkes. **Telephone:** (480) 965-9544.
Assistant Coaches: Travis Buck, Mike Goff.
Home Field: Phoenix Municipal Stadium. **Seating Capacity:** 8,775. **Outfield Dimension: LF**—345, **CF**—410, **RF**—345.

204 · Baseball America 2023 Directory

BaseballAmerica.com

COLLEGE

ARKANSAS

Conference: Southeastern.
Mailing Address: 1255 S. Razorback Rd, Fayetteville, AR 72701. **Website:** www.arkansasrazorbacks.com.
Head Coach: Dave Van Horn. **Baseball SID:** Oliver Grigg.
Assistant Coaches: Nate Thompson, Matt Hobbs, Bobby Wernes.
Home Field: Baum-Walker Stadium. **Seating Capacity:** 11,084. **Outfield Dimension:** LF—320, CF—400, RF—320.

ARKANSAS STATE

Conference: Sun Belt. **Address:** 217 Olympic Drive Jonesboro, AR 72401. **Website:** www.astateredwolves.com. **Head Coach:** Tommy Raffo. **Telephone:** . **Baseball SID:** Caleb Garner. **Assistant Coaches:** Drew LaBounty*, Alan Dunn. **Home Field:** Tomlinson Stadium/Kell Field. **Capacity:** 1,200. **Outfield Dimensions:** LF—335, CF—400, RF—335.

ARKANSAS-LITTLE ROCK

Conference: Sun Belt.
Mailing Address: 2801 South University Ave. Little Rock, AR 72204. **Website:** www.lrtrojans.com.
Head Coach: Chris Curry. **Baseball SID:** Rand Champion.
Assistant Coaches: Brady Cox.
Home Field: Gary Hogan Field. **Seating Capacity:** 2,500. **Outfield Dimension:** LF—335, CF—390, RF—305.

ARKANSAS-PINE BLUFF

Conference: Southwestern.
Mailing Address: 1200 North University Drive, Mail Slot 4891, Pine Bluff, AR 71601. **Website:** www.uapblionsroar.com.
Head Coach: Carlos James. **Telephone:** (870) 575-8995. **Baseball SID:** Cameo Stokes. **Telephone:** (870) 575-7955.
Assistant Coaches: Roger Mallison, Shane Youman-Osuoha. **Telephone:** (870) 575-8995.
Home Field: Torii Hunter Baseball Complex. **Seating Capacity:** 1,000. **Outfield Dimension:** LF—331, CF—401, RF—331

ARMY

Conference: Patriot League.
Mailing Address: United States Military Academy, Army West Point Athletics, 639 Howard Rd., West Point, NY 10996. **Website:** www.goarmywestpoint.com.
Head Coach: Chris Tracz. **Telephone:** (845) 938-4938. **Baseball SID:** Meg Ellis. **Telephone:** (845) 938-4090.
Assistant Coaches: Mike Cole, Jeremy Hileman.
Home Field: Johnson Stadium at Doubleday Field. **Seating Capacity:** 880. **Outfield Dimension:** LF—327, CF—400, RF—327.

AUBURN

Conference: Southeatern.
Address: 392 S Donahue Drive, Auburn, AL 36849. **Website:** auburntigers.com.
Head Coach: Butch Thompson. **Telephone:** (334) 844-4990.
Baseball SID: George Nunnelley. **Assistant Coaches:** Karl Nonemaker*, Gabe Gross.
Home Field: Plainsman Park. **Capacity:** 4,096. **Outfield Dimensions:** LF-315 CF-385 RF-331.

AUSTIN PEAY STATE

Conference: Atlantic Sun.
Address: 601 College Street, Clarksville, TN 37040. **Website:** www.LetsGoPeay.com.
Head Coach: Roland Fanning. **Telephone:** 931-221-6266. **Baseball SID:** Cody Bush. **Assistant Coaches:** Keirce Kimbel*, Jake Hendrick.
Home Field: Raymond C. Hand Park. **Capacity:** 777. **Outfield Dimensions:** LF-319 CF-380 RF-300.

BALL STATE

Conference: Mid-American.
Mailing Address: Ball State Athletics, HP 260, Muncie, IN 47306-0929. **Website:** www.ballstatesports.com.
Head Coach: Rich Maloney. **Telephone:** (765) 285-1425. **Baseball SID:** Chad Smith. **Telephone:** (765) 285-8242. **Assistant Coaches:** Alex Maloney, Larry Scully. **Telephone:** (765) 285-8226.
Home Field: Ball Diamond at First Merchants Ballpark Complex. **Seating Capacity:** 1,500. **Outfield Dimension:** LF—325, CF—400, RF—325.

BAYLOR

Conference: Big 12.
Mailing Address: 1500 South University Parks Dr., Waco, TX 76706. **Website:** www.baylorbears.com.
Head Coach: Mitch Thompson. **Telephone:** (254) 710-3029. **Baseball SID:** Max Calderon. **Telephone:** (254) 710-3073. **Assistant Coaches:** James Leverton, Zach Dillon. **Telephone:** (254) 710-3041.
Home Field: Baylor Ballpark. **Seating Capacity:** 5,000. **Outfield Dimension:** LF—330, CF—400, RF—300.

BELLARMINE

Conference: ASUN.
Mailing Address: 2001 Newburg Road, Louisville, KY 40205. **Website:** www.athletics.bellarmine.edu.
Head Coach: Chris Dominguez. **Telephone:** (502) 272-8278. **Baseball SID:** Natalie Cousin. **Telephone:** (502) 272-8217.
Assistant Coaches: Ross Spurgeon, Cody Williams, Adam Elliott. **Telephone:** (502) 272-8278.
Home Field: Knights Field. **Outfield Dimension:** LF—335, CF—380, RF—335.

BELMONT

Conference: Ohio Valley.
Mailing Address: 1900 Belmont Blvd, Nashville, TN, 37212 . **Website:** www.belmontbruins.com.
Head Coach: Dave Jarvis. **Telephone:** (615) 460-6166. **Baseball SID:** Noah Syverson.
Assistant Coaches: Aaron Smith, AJ Gaura. **Telephone:** (615) 460-6165.
Home Field: E.S. Rose Park. **Outfield Dimension:** LF—330, CF—400, RF—330.

BETHUNE-COOKMAN

Conference: Southwestern.
Mailing Address: 640 Dr. Mary McLeod Bethune Boulevard, Daytona Beach, FL 32114. **Website:** www.bcuathletics.com.
Head Coach: Jonathan Hernandez. **Telephone:** (386) 481-2224. **Baseball SID:** Bryce Hoynoski. **Telephone:** (386) 481-2278.
Assistant Coaches: Jose Carballo, Joel Sanchez.
Home Field: Jackie Robinson Ballpark. **Seating Capacity:** 4,200. **Outfield Dimension:** LF—317, CF—400, RF—325.

BaseballAmerica.com

Baseball America 2023 Directory · **205**

COLLEGE

BINGHAMTON

Conference: America East.
Mailing Address: 4400 Vestal Parkway East, Binghamton, NY 13902. **Website:** www.bubearcats.com.
Head Coach: Tim Sinicki. **Telephone:** (607) 777-2525.
Baseball SID: John Hartrick. **Telephone:** (607) 777-6800.
Assistant Coaches: Ryan Hurba, Mike Folli. **Telephone:** (607) 777-5808.
Home Field: Bearcats Baseball Complex. **Seating Capacity:** 2,500. **Outfield Dimension:** LF—325, **CF**—390, **RF**—325.

BOSTON COLLEGE

Conference: Atlantic Coast.
Mailing Address: 140 Commonwealth Ave, Chestnut Hill, MA 02467. **Website:** www.bceagles.com.
Head Coach: Mike Gambino. **Baseball SID:** Brendan Flynn.
Assistant Coaches: Kevin Vance, Tyler Holt.
Home Field: Harrington Athletics Village. **Seating Capacity:** 1,000. **Outfield Dimension:** LF—330, **CF**—403, **RF**—330.

BOWLING GREEN STATE

Conference: Mid-American.
Address: 1600 Stadium Drive; Bowling Green, OH 43403. **Website:** https://bgsufalcons.com/sports/baseball.
Head Coach: Kyle Hallock. **Telephone:** .
Baseball SID:: Kyle Edmond. **Assistant Coaches:** Matt Rembielak*, Joey Gamache.
Home Field: Steller Field. **Capacity:** . **Outfield Dimensions:** LF-345 CF-400 RF-345.

BRADLEY

Conference: Missouri Valley.
Address: 1501 W Bradley Ave, Peoria, IL 61625.
Website: www.bradleybraves.com.
Head Coach: Elvis Dominguez.
Baseball SID:: NA. **Assistant Coaches:** Kyle Trewyn*, Andrew Werner.
Home Field: Dozer Park. **Capacity:** 7,500. **Outfield Dimensions:** LF-310 CF-400 RF-310.

BRIGHAM YOUNG

Conference: West Coast.
Mailing Address: 111 MLRP, Provo UT 84094.
Website: www.byucougars.com.
Head Coach: Trent Pratt. **Telephone:** (801) 422-5049.
Baseball SID: Duff Tittle. **Telephone:** (801) 422-5048.
Assistant Coaches: Brent Haring. **Telephone:** (801) 422-4910.
Home Field: Miller Park. **Seating Capacity:** 2,200. **Outfield Dimension:** LF—347, **CF**—402, **RF**—343

BROWN

Conference: Ivy League.
Mailing Address: 233 Hope St Providence, RI 02912.
Website: www.brownbears.com.
Head Coach: Grant Achilles. **Telephone:** (401) 863-3090. **Baseball SID:** Tim Geer. **Telephone:** (401) 863-7014.
Assistant Coaches: Christopher Tilton, Zach Hubbard.
Home Field: Attanasio Family Field at Murray Stadium. **Seating Capacity:** 1,000.

BRYANT

Conference: Northeast.
Mailing Address: 1150 Douglas Pike, Smithfield, R.I. 02917. **Website:** www.bryantbulldogs.com.
Head Coach: Ryan Klosterman. **Telephone:** (401) 232-6397. **Baseball SID:** Tristan Hobbes. **Telephone:** (401) 232-6558.
Assistant Coaches: Eric Pelletier, Ted Hurvul, Alex Denoyelle.
Home Field: Conaty Park. **Seating Capacity:** 500.
Outfield Dimension: LF—330, **CF**—400, **RF**—330.

BUCKNELL

Conference: Patriot League.
Mailing Address: Kenneth Langone Athletics & Recreation Center, Bucknell University, One Dent Drive, Lewisburg, PA 17837. **Website:** www.bucknellbison.com.
Head Coach: Scott Heather. **Telephone:** (570) 577-3593. **Baseball SID:** Cole Cloonan. **Telephone:** (570) 577-1227.
Assistant Coaches: Jason Neitz, Brett Smith, Josh Kieffer. **Telephone:** (570) 577-1059.
Home Field: Depew Field. **Seating Capacity:** 1,000.
Outfield Dimension: LF—330, **CF**—400, **RF**—330.

BUTLER

Conference: Big East.
Mailing Address: Butler University Athletics 510 W. 49th Street Indianapolis, IN 46208. **Website:** www.butlersports.com.
Head Coach: Blake Beemer. **Telephone:** (317) 940-9721. **Baseball SID:** Kit Stetzel. **Telephone:** (317) 940-9994.
Assistant Coaches: Ross Learnard, Bladen Bales. **Telephone:** (317) 940-6536.
Home Field: Bulldog Park. **Seating Capacity:** 500.
Outfield Dimension: LF—330, **CF**—400, **RF**—330.

CALIFORNIA

Conference: Pac-12.
Address: 115 Haas Pavilion Berkeley, CA 94720.
Website: calbears.com.
Head Coach: Mike Neu. **Telephone:** 510-642-9026.
Baseball SID:: Matt Fontenot. **Assistant Coaches:** Noah Jackson*, Matt Flemer.
Home Field: Stu Gordon Stadium . **Capacity:** 2,500.
Outfield Dimensions: LF-320 CF-400 RF-320.

CAL BAPTIST

Conference: Western Athletic.
Address: 8432 Magnolia Avenue, Riverside, CA 92504.
Website: cbulancers.com.
Head Coach: Gary Adcock. **Telephone:** 951-343-4382.
Baseball SID:: Daniel Cook. **Assistant Coaches:** Andrew M Brasington*, Tyler Nordgren.
Home Field: Totman Stadium. **Capacity:** 1300.
Outfield Dimensions: LF-331 CF-406 RF-317.

CAL POLY

Conference: Big West.
Address: Cal Poly Athletics, 1 Grand Avenue, San Luis Obispo, CA 93407-0388. **Website:** GoPoly.com.
Head Coach: Larry Lee. **Telephone:** 805-459-0422.
Baseball SID:: Eric Burdick. **Assistant Coaches:** Matt Fonteno*, Seth Moir.
Home Field: Baggett Stadium. **Capacity:** 3,032.
Outfield Dimensions: LF—335, **CF**—405, **RF**—335.

COLLEGE

CAL STATE BAKERSFIELD

Conference: Big West.
Mailing Address: 9001 Stockdale Hwy, 8 GYM, Bakersfield, CA 93311-1022. **Website:** www.gorunners.com.
Head Coach: Jeremy Beard. **Telephone:** (509) 430-5354. **Baseball SID:** Dan Sperl.
Assistant Coaches: Quinn Hawksworth, David Tillotson.
Home Field: Hardt Field. **Seating Capacity:** 1,500. **Outfield Dimension: LF**—325, **CF**—390, **RF**—325.

CAL STATE FULLERTON

Address: 800 N. State College Blvd. Fullerton, Calif. 92831. **Website:** FullertonTitans.com.
Head Coach: Jason Dietrich. **Telephone:** (657) 278-2200.
Baseball SID:: Bryant Freese. **Assistant Coaches:** Josh Belovsky*, Neil Walton.
Home Field: Goodwin Field. **Capacity:** 3,500. **Outfield Dimensions:** LF-330 CF-400 RF-330.

CAL STATE NORTHRIDGE

Conference: Big West.
Address: 18111 Nordhoff St Northridge, CA 91330. **Website:** Gomatadors.com.
Head Coach: Eddie Cornejo . **Telephone:** (818) 677-3208.
Baseball SID:: Nick Bocanegra . **Assistant Coaches:** Bobby Andrews*, Elliot Surrey.
Home Field: Matador Field. **Capacity:** 1,200. **Outfield Dimensions:** LF-325 CF-390 RF-325.

CAMPBELL

Conference: Big South.
Mailing Address: 76 Upchurch Lane Lillington, NC 27546. **Website:** www.gocamels.com.
Head Coach: Justin Haire. **Baseball SID:** Davis Dupree.
Assistant Coaches: Joey Holcomb, Tyler Robinson.
Home Field: Jim Perry Stadium. **Seating Capacity:** 1,250. **Outfield Dimension: LF**—337, **CF**—395, **RF**—328.

CANISIUS

Conference: Metro Atlantic.
Mailing Address: 2001 Main Street, Buffalo, N.Y., 14208. **Website:** www.gogriffs.com.
Head Coach: Matt Mazurek. **Baseball SID:** Marshall Haim.
Assistant Coaches: Mason Sherrill.
Home Field: Demske Sports Complex.

CENTRAL ARKANSAS

Conference: ASUN.
Mailing Address: 201 Donaghey Ave., Bear Hall - 4th Floor, Conway, AR 72035. **Website:** www.ucasports.com.
Head Coach: Nick Harlan. **Telephone:** (402) 366-5948. **Baseball SID:** Steve East. **Telephone:** (501) 450-5743.
Assistant Coaches: Cody Davenport, Hayden Simpson, Curtis Kellogg.
Home Field: Bear Stadium.

CENTRAL CONNECTICUT STATE

Conference: Northeast.
Address: 1615 Stanley Street, New Britain, CT 06050. **Website:** www.CCSUBlueDevils.com.
Head Coach: Charlie Hickey. **Telephone:** (860) 832-3074.
Baseball SID:: Jeff Mead. **Assistant Coaches:** Pat Hall*, Rob Bono.
Home Field: CCSU Baseball Field. **Capacity:** . **Outfield Dimensions:** LF-330 CF-400 RF-310.

CENTRAL FLORIDA

Conference: American Athletic.
Address: 4000 Central Florida Blvd. Orlando, FL 32816. **Website:** www.ucfknights.com.
Head Coach: Greg Lovelady.
Baseball SID: Alex Funderburke. **Assistant Coaches:** Ted Tom*, .
Home Field: John Euliano Park. **Capacity:** 3,841. **Outfield Dimensions:** LF-320 CF-390 RF-320.

CENTRAL MICHIGAN

Conference: Mid-American.
Address: 100 Rose Center, Mt. Pleasant, MI 48859. **Website:** cmuchippewas.com.
Head Coach: Jordan Bischel.
Baseball SID:: Andy Sneddon. **Assistant Coaches:** Tony Jandron*, Kyle Schroeder.
Home Field: Theunissen Stadium. **Capacity:** 2000. **Outfield Dimensions:** LF-330 CF-395 RF-330.

CHARLESTON SOUTHERN

Conference: Big South.
Mailing Address: 9200 University Blvd., Charleston, S.C. 29406. **Website:** www.csusports.com.
Head Coach: Marc MacMillan. **Baseball SID:** Taylor Chitwood. **Telephone:** (843) 863-7433.
Assistant Coaches: Jordon Twohig, Karl Kuhn.
Home Field: Nielsen Field at CSU Ballpark. **Seating Capacity:** 1,000. **Outfield Dimension: LF**—330, **CF**—400, **RF**—330.

CHARLOTTE

Conference: Conference USA.
Address: 9201 University City Boulevard Charlotte, NC 28223. **Website:** https://charlotte49ers.com/.
Head Coach: Robert Woodard. **Telephone:** 704-687-0726.
Baseball SID:: Joe Templin. **Assistant Coaches:** Toby Bicknell*, Phil Cebuhar.
Home Field: Robert and Mariam Hayes Stadium. **Capacity:** 3,000. **Outfield Dimensions:** LF-335 CF-395 RF-315.

CINCINNATI

Conference: American Athletic.
Mailing Address: Richard E. Lindner Center 2751 O'Varsity Way, Cincinnati, Ohio 45221-0021. **Website:** www.gobearcats.com.
Head Coach: Scott Googins. **Telephone:** (513) 556-0566. **Baseball SID:** Alex Pepke. **Telephone:** (412) 996-5598.
Assistant Coaches: JD Heilmann, Kyle Sprague. **Telephone:** (513) 556-0565.
Home Field: UC Baseball Stadium. **Seating Capacity:** 3,085. **Outfield Dimension: LF**—325, **CF**—400, **RF**—325.

COLLEGE

CITADEL

Conference: Southern.
Mailing Address: 171 Moultrie Street, Charleston, SC 29409. **Website:** www.citadelsports.com.
Head Coach: Tony Skole. **Baseball SID:** John Brush.
Assistant Coaches: Zach Lucas, Blake Cooper.
Home Field: Joe Riley Park. **Seating Capacity:** 7,500.
Outfield Dimension: LF—305, **CF**—398, **RF**—337.

CLEMSON

Conference: ACC.
Address: 100 Perimeter Road, Clemson, SC. 29633.
Website: ClemsonTigers.com.
Head Coach: Erik Bakich. **Telephone:** 864-656-1947.
Baseball SID: Brian Hennessy. **Assistant Coaches:** Nick Schnabel*, Jimmy Belanger.
Home Field: Doug Kingsmore Stadium. **Capacity:** 6,272. **Outfield Dimensions: LF**—310, **CF**—390, **RF**—320.

COASTAL CAROLINA

Conference: Sun Belt.
Mailing Address: 965 One Landon Loop, Conway, S.C. 29526. **Website:** www.goccusports.com.
Head Coach: Gary Gilmore. **Telephone:** (843) 349-2524. **Baseball SID:** Kevin Davis. **Telephone:** (843) 349-2822.
Assistant Coaches: Kevin Schnall, Jason Beverlin. **Telephone:** (843) 349-3460.
Home Field: Springs Brooks Stadium. **Seating Capacity:** 2,500. **Outfield Dimension: LF**—320, **CF**—390, **RF**—320.

COLLEGE OF CHARLESTON

Conference: Colonial.
Mailing Address: 301 Meeting Street Charleston, SC 29401. **Website:** www.cofcsports.com.
Head Coach: Chad Holbrook. **Telephone:** (803) 622-0053. **Baseball SID:** Whitney Noble. **Telephone:** (843) 953-3683.
Assistant Coaches: Adam Brown, Will Dorton. **Telephone:** (843) 940-0868.
Home Field: Patriots Point. **Seating Capacity:** 2,000.
Outfield Dimension: LF—300, **CF**—400, **RF**—330.

COLUMBIA

Conference: Ivy League.
Address: 505 West 218th Street New York, N.Y. 10034.
Website: gocolumbialions.com.
Head Coach: Brett Boretti.
Baseball SID:: Mike Kowalsky. **Assistant Coaches:** Dan Tischler*, Tom Carty.
Home Field: Robertson Field at Satow Stadium.

CONNECTICUT

Conference: Big East.
Mailing Address: 2111 Hillside Rd., Storrs, CT 06268.
Website: www.uconnhuskies.com.
Head Coach: Jim Penders. **Telephone:** (860) 208-9140.
Baseball SID: Chris Jones. **Telephone:** (860) 938-6191.
Assistant Coaches: Joshua MacDonald, Jeff Hourigan. **Telephone:** (860) 465-6088.
Home Field: Elliot Ballpark. **Seating Capacity:** 2,000.
Outfield Dimension: LF—330, **CF**—400, **RF**—330.

COPPIN STATE

Conference: Northeast.
Address: 2500 West North. **Website:** coppinstatesports.com.
Head Coach: Sherman Reed, Sr.. **Telephone:** 410-951-3723.
Baseball SID:: Steve Kramer. **Assistant Coaches:** Sean Repay*, Colin Dower.
Home Field: Joe Cannon Stadium. **Seating Capacity:** 1,500. **Outfield Dimension: LF**—310, **CF**—425, **RF**—310.

CORNELL

Conference: Ivy League.
Mailing Address: Cornell University Athletics, Teagle Hall, 512 Campus Road, Ithaca, N.Y. 14853. **Website:** www.cornellbigred.com.
Head Coach: Dan Pepicelli. **Baseball SID:** Brandon Thomas. **Telephone:** (607) 255-5627.
Assistant Coaches: Tom Ford, John Toppa. **Telephone:** (908) 868-1392.
Home Field: Hoy Field. **Seating Capacity:** 500.

CREIGHTON

Conference: Big East.
Address: 2400 California Plaza Omaha,NE 68178.
Website: gocreighton.com.
Head Coach: Ed Servais. **Telephone:** 402-660-5846.
Baseball SID:: Glen Sisk. **Assistant Coaches:** Connor Gandossy*, Mitch Mormann.
Home Field: Charles Schwab Field. **Capacity:** 25,000.
Outfield Dimensions: LF-330 CF-408 RF-330.

DALLAS BAPTIST

Conference: Conference USA.
Address: 3000 Mountain Creek Parkway. **Website:** dbupatriots.com/sports/baseball.
Head Coach: Dan Heefner.
Baseball SID: Nate Frieling . **Assistant Coaches:** Cliff Pennington*, Micah Posey.
Home Field: Horner Ballpark. **Seating Capacity:** 2,000. **Outfield Dimension: LF**—330, **CF**—390, **RF**—330.

DARTMOUTH

Conference: Ivy League.
Mailing Address: Dartmouth Athletics, 6083 Alumni Gym, Hanover, N.H. 03755. **Website:** dartmouthsports.com.
Head Coach: Bob Whalen. **Telephone:** (603) 646-2477.
Baseball SID: Rick Bender. **Telephone:** (603) 646-1030.
Assistant Coaches: Blake McFadden, Chris Bosco, Jacob Biller. **Telephone:** (603) 646-9775.
Home Field: Red Rolfe Field at Biondi Park. **Seating Capacity:** 1,000.

DAVIDSON

Conference: Atlantic 10.
Mailing Address: 200 Baker Drive, Davidson NC 28035. **Website:** www.davidsonwildcats.com.
Head Coach: Rucker Taylor. **Telephone:** (704) 894-2772. **Baseball SID:** Justin Parker. **Telephone:** (704) 894-2931.
Assistant Coaches: Todd Miller, Bobby Hearn. **Telephone:** (704) 894-2002.
Home Field: Wilson Field. **Seating Capacity:** 700.
Outfield Dimension: LF—320, **CF**—385, **RF**—330.

208 · Baseball America 2023 Directory

BaseballAmerica.com

COLLEGE

DAYTON

Conference: Atlantic 10.
Address: University of Dayton 300 College Park, Dayton, OH 45469. **Website:** www.daytonflyers.com.
Head Coach: Jayson King. **Telephone:** 603-381-1279.
Baseball SID: Ross Bagienski. **Assistant Coaches:** Travis Ferrick*, Kyle Decker.
Home Field: Woerner Field at AES Ohio Stadium. **Capacity:** 2,000. **Outfield Dimensions:** LF-330 CF-400 RF-330.

DELAWARE

Conference: Colonial.
Address: South College Ave., Newark, DE 19716. **Website:** bluehens.com/sports/baseball.
Head Coach: Greg Mamula. **Telephone:** 302-831-8596.
Baseball SID: tbd. **Assistant Coaches:** Chris Collazo*, Casey Kulina.
Home Field: Bob Hannah Stadium. **Capacity:** 1300. **Outfield Dimensions:** LF-320 CF-410 RF-330.

DELAWARE STATE

Conference: Mid-Eastern.
Mailing Address: 1200 N. DuPont Highway, Dover, DE 19901. **Website:** www.dsuhornets.com.
Head Coach: JP Blandin. **Telephone:** (302) 857-6035.
Baseball SID: Dennis Jones. **Telephone:** (302) 857-6068.
Assistant Coaches: Stephen Baughan. **Telephone:** (302) 857-7809.
Home Field: Soldier Field. **Seating Capacity:** 500.

DUKE

Conference: ACC.
Address: 367 Scott Family Athletics Performance Center, Durham, NC 27708. **Website:** GoDuke.com.
Head Coach: Chris Pollard.
Baseball SID: Aaron Socha. **Assistant Coaches:** Ty Blankmeyer*, Brady Kirkpatrick.
Home Field: Durham Bulls Athletic Park. **Seating Capacity:** 10,000. **Outfield Dimension:** LF—305, CF—400, RF—327.

EAST CAROLINA

Conference: American Athletic.
Address: East Carolina Athletics Ward Sports Medicine Building 1 Ficklen Drive Mail Stop 158 Greenville, NC 27858. **Website:** www.ecupirates.com.
Head Coach: Cliff Godwin. **Telephone:** (252) 737-1985.
Baseball SID: Chip Welch. **Assistant Coaches:** Jeff Palumbo*, Austin Knight.
Home Field: Clark-LeClair Stadium. **Capacity:** 5,000. **Outfield Dimensions:** LF-320 CF-400 RF-320.

EAST TENNESSEE STATE

Conference: Southern.
Mailing Address: ETSU Athletics, PO Box 70707, Johnson City, TN 37614. **Website:** www.etsubucs.com.
Head Coach: Joe Pennucci. **Telephone:** (423) 439-4496. **Baseball SID:** Thomas Arteaga.
Assistant Coaches: Jamie Pinzino, Chad Marshall.
Home Field: Thomas Stadium. **Seating Capacity:** 1,000. **Outfield Dimension:** LF—325, CF—400, RF—325.

EASTERN ILLINOIS

Conference: Ohio Valley.
Address: 600 Lincoln Ave. Charleston, IL 61920. **Website:** eiupanthers.com.
Head Coach: Jason Anderson.
Baseball SID: Rich Moser. **Assistant Coaches:** Derek Francis*.
Home Field: Coaches Stadium. **Capacity:** 550. **Outfield Dimensions:** LF-340 CF-390 RF-340.

EASTERN KENTUCKY

Conference: ASUN.
Mailing Address: 521 Lancaster Avenue, 115 Alumni Coliseum, Richmond, KY 40475. **Website:** www.ekusports.com.
Head Coach: Chris Prothro. **Telephone:** (859) 622-2128. **Baseball SID:** Kevin Britton. **Telephone:** (859) 622-2006.
Assistant Coaches: Walt Jones, Tyler Anderson. **Telephone:** (859) 622-8295.
Home Field: Turkey Hughes Field at Earle Combs Stadium. **Seating Capacity:** 1,000. **Outfield Dimension:** LF—340, CF—410, RF—330.

EASTERN MICHIGAN

Conference: Mid-American.
Mailing Address: 799 N Hewitt Rd Ypsilanti MI 48197. **Website:** www.emueagles.com.
Head Coach: Eric Roof. **Telephone:** (734) 487-1985.
Baseball SID: Alex Jewell.
Assistant Coaches: Aaron Hilt, Jonathan Roof.
Home Field: Oestrike Stadium. **Seating Capacity:** 2,500.

ELON

Conference: Colonial.
Address: 543 N. Williamson Ave. Elon, N.C. 27244. **Website:** https://elonphoenix.com/index.aspx.
Head Coach: Mike Kennedy. **Telephone:** 336-278-6741.
Baseball SID: Pat James. **Assistant Coaches:** Robbie Huffstetler*, Jerry Oakes.
Home Field: Walter C. Latham Park. **Capacity:** 5,100. **Outfield Dimensions:** LF-325 CF-385 RF-325.

EVANSVILLE

Conference: Missouri Valley.
Mailing Address: 1800 Lincoln Ave, Evansville,IN 47714. **Website:** www.gopurpleaces.com.
Head Coach: Wes Carroll. **Baseball SID:** Michael Robertson.
Assistant Coaches: Matt Wollenzin, Tyler Shipley. **Telephone:** (812) 488-2764.
Home Field: German American Bank Field at Charles H. Braun Stadium. **Seating Capacity:** 1,200.

FAIRFIELD

Conference: Metro Atlantic.
Address: 1073 N Benson Rd Fairfield CT. **Website:** fairfieldstags.com/sports/baseball?path=baseball.
Head Coach: Bill Currier.
Baseball SID: Ivey Speight. **Assistant Coaches:** Brian Fay*, Dave Swanson.
Home Field: Alumni Diamond. **Capacity:** 400. **Outfield Dimension:** LF—330, CF—400, RF—330.

COLLEGE

FAIRLEIGH DICKINSON

Conference: Northeast.
Address: 1000 River Road, Teaneck, NJ 07666.
Website: fduknights.com/sports/baseball?path=baseball.
Head Coach: Manny Roman.
Baseball SID: Nick Sconzo. **Assistant Coaches:** Ethan Newton*.
Home Field: Naimoli Family Baseball Complex.
Seating Capacity: 500. **Outfield Dimension: LF**—318, **CF**—380, **RF**—315.

FLORIDA

Conference: SEC.
Address: University Athletic Association P.O. Box 14485 Gainesville, FL 32604. **Website:** FloridaGators.com.
Head Coach: Kevin O'Sullivan. **Telephone:** (352) 375-4683 ext. 4457.
Baseball SID: Sulivan Bortner. **Assistant Coaches:** Chuck Jeroloman (Co-Recruiting Coordinator)*, Taylor Black (Co-Recruiting Coordinator).
Home Field: Condron Family Ballpark. **Capacity:** 7,000 (expandable to 10,000). **Outfield Dimensions:** LF-330 CF-400 RF-330.

FLORIDA ATLANTIC

Conference: Conference USA.
Mailing Address: 777 Glades Road, Boca Raton FL, 33431. **Website:** www.fausports.com.
Head Coach: John McCormack. **Baseball SID:** Jonathan Fraysure.
Assistant Coaches: Jordan Tabakman, Michael Cleary, Ricky Santiago.
Home Field: FAU Baseball Stadium. **Seating Capacity:** 1,718. **Outfield Dimension: LF**—330, **CF**—400, **RF**—330.

FLORIDA GULF COAST

Conference: ASUN.
Mailing Address: 10501 FGCU Boulevard South, Fort Myers, FL 33965. **Website:** www.fgcuathletics.com.
Head Coach: Dave Tollett. **Telephone:** (239) 590-7051. **Baseball SID:** Adam Grossman.
Assistant Coaches: Brandon Romans, Matt Reid.
Home Field: Swanson Stadium. **Seating Capacity:** 1,500. **Outfield Dimension: LF**—325, **CF**—400, **RF**—325.

FLORIDA INTERNATIONAL

Conference: Conference USA.
Mailing Address: FIU Athletics, 11200 SW 8th Street, Miami, FL 33199. **Website:** www.fiusports.com.
Head Coach: Rich Witten. **Baseball SID:** Tyler Brain. **Telephone:** (305) 348-2084.
Assistant Coaches: Sean Thompson, Brian Jeroloman. **Telephone:** (305) 348-7403.
Home Field: FIU Baseball Stadium. **Seating Capacity:** 2,000. **Outfield Dimension: Outfield Dimensions: LF**—325, **CF**—400, **RF**—325.

FLORIDA STATE

Conference: Atlantic Coast.
Mailing Address: 403 W. Stadium Dr., Tallahassee, FL, 32306. **Website:** www.seminoles.com.
Head Coach: Link Jarrett. **Baseball SID:** Steven McCartney.
Assistant Coaches: Chuck Ristano, Rich Wallace.
Home Field: Mike Martin Field at Dick Howser Stadium. **Seating Capacity:** 6,700. **Outfield Dimension: LF**—340, **CF**—400, **RF**—320.

FORDHAM

Conference: Atlantic 10.
Address: 441 E. Fordham Rd. Bronx, NY 10458.
Website: fordhamsports.com/sports/baseball.
Head Coach: Kevin Leighton.
Baseball SID: Scott Kwiatkowski. **Assistant Coaches:** Elliot Glynn*, Pat Porter.
Home Field: Houlihan Park. **Capacity:** 1,400. **Outfield Dimensions:** LF-338 CF-395 RF-325.

FRESNO STATE

Conference: Mountain West.
Address: 1620 East Bulldog Lane OF 87. **Website:** www.gobulldogs.com.
Head Coach: Mike Batesole.
Baseball SID: Travis Blanshan.
Home Field: Pete Beiden Field at Bob Bennett Stadium. **Seating Capacity:** 5,757. **Outfield Dimension: LF**—330, **CF**—400, **RF**—330.

GARDNER-WEBB

Conference: Big South.
Address: 110 South Main Street, Boiling Springs, NC 28017. **Website:** gwusports.com.
Head Coach: Jim Chester. **Telephone:** (704) 406-4421.
Baseball SID: Marc Rabb. **Assistant Coaches:** Ryan Sloniger*, Anthony Marks.
Home Field: John Henry Moss Stadium/Bill Masters Field. **Capacity:** 600. **Outfield Dimension: LF**—330, **CF**—385, **RF**—330.

GEORGE MASON

Conference: Atlantic 10.
Address: 4501 University Dr, Fairfax, VA 22030.
Website: gomason.com.
Head Coach: Shawn Camp.
Baseball SID: Steve Kolbe. **Assistant Coaches:** Ryan Terrill*, Ryan Ricci.
Home Field: Raymond H. "Hap" Sphuler Field.
Capacity: 900. **Outfield Dimensions:** LF-320 CF-400 RF-320.

GEORGE WASHINGTON

Conference: Atlantic 10.
Mailing Address: 4200 S Four Mile Run Dr, Arlington, VA 22206. **Website:** www.gwsports.com.
Head Coach: Gregory Ritchie. **Telephone:** (202) 994-7399. **Baseball SID:** Julian Coltre. **Telephone:** (202) 994-8604.
Assistant Coaches: Tyler Kavanaugh, Chris O'Neill. **Telephone:** (202) 994-7399.
Home Field: Tucker Field. **Seating Capacity:** 500. **Outfield Dimension: LF**—330, **CF**—380, **RF**—330.

GEORGETOWN

Conference: Big East.
Mailing Address: McDonough Arena Washington, DC 20057. **Website:** www.gohoyas.com.
Head Coach: Edwin Thompson. **Baseball SID:** Dylan Smith.
Assistant Coaches: Julius McDougal, George Capen.
Home Field: Shirley Povich Field. **Seating Capacity:** 1,500. **Outfield Dimension: LF**—330, **CF**—375, **RF**—330.

210 · Baseball America 2023 Directory

COLLEGE

GEORGIA

Conference: SEC.
Address: P.O. Box 1472, Athens, Ga. 30602. **Website:** georgiadogs.com.
Head Coach: Scott Stricklin. **Telephone:** (706) 542-7971.
Baseball SID: Christopher Lakos. **Assistant Coaches:** Scott Daeley*, Sean Kenny.
Home Field: Foley Field. **Capacity:** 3,000. **Outfield Dimensions:** LF-350 CF-404 RF-314.

GEORGIA SOUTHERN

Conference: Sun Belt.
Address: 1332 Southern Dr, Statesboro, GA 30458. **Website:** GSEagles.com / georgiasouthern.edu.
Head Coach: Rodney Hennon. **Telephone:** 912-478-7360.
Baseball SID: Graham Cooper. **Assistant Coaches:** A.J. Battisto*, Cody Wofford.
Home Field: J.I. Clements Stadium. **Capacity:** 3,000. **Outfield Dimensions:** LF-335 CF-390 RF-329.

GEORGIA STATE

Conference: Sun Belt.
Address: 755 Hank Aaron Drive, Atlanta, GA 30315. **Website:** GeorgiaStateSports.com.
Head Coach: Brad Stromdahl.
Baseball SID: Allison George. **Assistant Coaches:** Niko Buentello*, Lars Davis.
Home Field: GSU Baseball Complex. **Capacity:** 1000. **Outfield Dimensions:** LF-334 CF-385 RF-338.

GEORGIA TECH

Conference: Atlantic Coast.
Mailing Address: 150 Bobby Dodd Way, Atlanta, GA 30332. **Website:** www.ramblinwreck.com.
Head Coach: Danny Hall. **Baseball SID:** Andrew Clausen.
Assistant Coaches: James Ramsey, Danny Borrell.
Home Field: Mac Nease Baseball Park at Russ Chandler Stadium. **Seating Capacity:** 3,600. **Outfield Dimension:** LF—328, CF—400, RF—334.

GONZAGA

Conference: West Coast.
Mailing Address: 502 E. Boone Ave; Spokane, WA 99258. **Website:** www.gozags.com.
Head Coach: Mark Machtolf. **Baseball SID:** Connor Gilbert. **Telephone:** (509) 313-6373.
Assistant Coaches: Danny Evans, Sean Winston, Antonio Garcia.
Home Field: Patterson Ballpark and Steve Hertz Field. **Seating Capacity:** 2,000. **Outfield Dimension:** LF—328, CF—390, RF—328.

GRAMBLING STATE

Conference: Southwestern Athletic.
Address: 403 Main St. PO BOX 4252 Grambling, La 71245. **Website:** gsutigers.com.
Head Coach: Davin Pierre. **Telephone:** 318-274-2416.
Baseball SID: Curtis Ford. **Assistant Coaches:** Davin Pierre*, Perez Knowles.
Home Field: R.W.E. Jones Park Ellis Field . **Capacity:** 2,000. **Outfield Dimensions:** LF-315 CF-400 RF-350.

GRAND CANYON

Conference: Western Athletic.
Address: 3300 W Camelback Road, Phoenix, AZ 85017. **Website:** GCULopes.com.
Head Coach: Gregg Wallis. **Telephone:** 602-639-7676.
Baseball SID: Josh Hauser. **Assistant Coaches:** Jack Wilson, Nathan Bannister.
Home Field: Brazell Field at GCU Ballpark. **Capacity:** 4,000. **Outfield Dimensions:** LF—320, CF—375, RF—330.

HARTFORD

Conference: America East.
Mailing Address: 200 Bloomfield Avenue West Hartford CT, 06117. **Website:** www.hartfordhawks.com.
Head Coach: Steve Malinowski. **Telephone:** (860) 768-4656. **Baseball SID:** Dan Szewczak. **Telephone:** (860) 768-7785.
Assistant Coaches: TJ Ward, John Slusarz. **Telephone:** (860) 768-4972.
Home Field: Fiondella Field. **Seating Capacity:** 1,200. **Outfield Dimension:** LF—325, CF—400, RF—325.

HARVARD

Conference: Ivy League.
Mailing Address: 65 North Harvard St., Boston, MA 02163. **Website:** www.gocrimson.com.
Head Coach: Bill Decker. **Telephone:** (617) 496-2629. **Baseball SID:** Nick Dow. **Telephone:** (617) 496-1379.
Assistant Coaches: Bryan Stark, Nate Cole. **Telephone:** (617) 496-1435.
Home Field: O'Donnell Field. **Seating Capacity:** 1,600. **Outfield Dimension:** LF—335, CF—415, RF—335.

HAWAII

Conference: Big West.
Address: 1337 Lower Campus Rd., Honolulu HI, 96822. **Website:** hawaiiathletics.com.
Head Coach: Rich Hill. **Telephone:** (808) 956-6247.
Baseball SID: Derren Iha. **Assistant Coaches:** Dan Cox*, Dave Nakama.
Home Field: Les Murakami Stadium. **Capacity:** 4,312. **Outfield Dimensions:** LF—325, CF—385, RF—325

HIGH POINT

Conference: Big South.
Mailing Address: One University Parkway, High Point, N.C. 27268. **Website:** www.highpointpanthers.com.
Head Coach: Joey Hammond. **Baseball SID:** Sarah Duysen. **Telephone:** (336) 841-4638.
Assistant Coaches: Miles Miller, Mickey Williard.
Home Field: Williard Stadium. **Seating Capacity:** 501.

HOFSTRA

Conference: Colonial.
Mailing Address: 230 Hofstra University, PFC 232, Hempstead NY 11549. **Website:** www.gohofstra.com.
Head Coach: Frank Catalanotto. **Telephone:** (516) 463-3759. **Baseball SID:** Len Skoros. **Telephone:** (516) 463-4602.
Assistant Coaches: Jimmy Goelz, Chris Rojas, Reid Gorecki. **Telephone:** (516) 463-5065.
Home Field: University Field. **Seating Capacity:** 600. **Outfield Dimension:** LF—322, CF—382, RF—337.

BaseballAmerica.com

Baseball America 2023 Directory • **211**

COLLEGE

HOLY CROSS

Conference: Patriot League.
Mailing Address: 1 College St. Worcester, MA 01610.
Website: www.goholycross.com.
Head Coach: Ed Kahovec. **Telephone:** (508) 793-2753.
Baseball SID: Sarah Kirkpatrick. **Telephone:** (508) 793-2780.
Assistant Coaches: Sam Tinkham, Michael Slattery.
Telephone: (508) 793-3406.
Home Field: Hanover Insurance Park at Fitton Field.
Seating Capacity: 3,000. **Outfield Dimension:** LF—332, CF—385, RF—313.

HOUSTON

Conference: American Athletic.
Mailing Address: 3204 Cullen Blvd., Houston, TX 77004. **Website:** www.uhcougars.com.
Head Coach: Todd Whitting. **Baseball SID:** Andrew Pate.
Assistant Coaches: Ross Kivett, Kyle Bunn, Tyler Bielamowicz.
Home Field: Darryl & Lori Schroeder Park. **Seating Capacity:** 3,500. **Outfield Dimension:** LF—330, CF—390, RF—330.

HOUSTON CHRISTIAN

Conference: Southland.
Mailing Address: 7502 Fondren Blvd. Houston, Tx 77074. **Website:** www.hbuhuskies.com.
Head Coach: Lance Berkman. **Telephone:** (281) 649-3000. **Baseball SID:** Russ Reneau. **Telephone:** (281) 649-3098.
Assistant Coaches: Tyler Bremer, Clayton VanderLaan.
Telephone: (281) 649-3000.
Home Field: Husky Field. **Seating Capacity:** 500.
Outfield Dimension: LF—330, CF—406, RF—330.

ILLINOIS

Conference: Big Ten.
Mailing Address: 601 E. Kirby Avenue Champaign, Ill., 61820. **Website:** www.fightingillini.com
Head Coach: Dan Hartleb. **Baseball SID:** John Peterson.
Assistant Coaches: Adam Christ, Mark Allen.
Home Field: Illinois Field. **Seating Capacity:** 1,500.
Outfield Dimension: LF—330, CF—400, RF—330.

ILLINOIS-CHICAGO

Conference: Missouri Valley.
Address: 901 West Roosevelt Road, Chicago, IL 60608.
Website: uicflames.com.
Head Coach: Sean McDermott. **Telephone:** 312-355-1757.
Baseball SID: AJ Schraffenberger. **Assistant Coaches:** John Flood*, Brendon Hayden.
Home Field: Les Miller Field at Curtis Granderson Stadium. **Capacity:** 1800. **Outfield Dimensions:** LF-320 CF-400 RF-325.

ILLINOIS STATE

Conference: Missouri Valley.
Mailing Address: 100 North University St. Normal, IL 61761. **Website:** www.goredbirds.com.
Head Coach: Steve Holm. **Baseball SID:** Scott Beaton.
Assistant Coaches: Wally Crancer, RD Spiehs, Derek Parola.
Home Field: Duffy Bass Field. **Seating Capacity:** 2,500. **Outfield Dimension:** LF—330, CF—400, RF—330.

INCARNATE WORD

Conference: Southland.
Mailing Address: 4301 Broadway, CPO 288, San Antonio, TX 78209. **Website:** www.uiwcardinals.com.
Head Coach: Ryan Shotzberger. **Baseball SID:** Alexa Low. **Telephone:** (210) 829-6048.
Assistant Coaches: Greg Evans, Kyle Simonds.
Home Field: Daniel Sullivan Field. **Seating Capacity:** 1,000. **Outfield Dimension:** LF—335, CF—407, RF—335.

INDIANA

Conference: Big Ten.
Address: 1873 N Fee Ln Bloomington, IN 47408 United States. **Website:** IU Hoosiers.com/baseball.
Head Coach: Jeff Mercer.
Baseball SID: Greg Campbell. **Assistant Coaches:** Derek Simmons*, Dustin Glant.
Home Field: Bart Kaufman. **Capacity:** 4,000.. **Outfield Dimension:** LF—330, CF—400, RF—340.

INDIANA STATE

Conference: Missouri Valley.
Mailing Address: 401 North 4th Street, Terre Haute, IN, 47809. **Website:** www.gosycamores.com.
Head Coach: Mitch Hannahs. **Telephone:** (812) 237-4051. **Baseball SID:** Seth Montgomery. **Telephone:** (812) 237-4073.
Assistant Coaches: Brian Smiley, Justin Hancock.
Home Field: Bob Warn Field. **Seating Capacity:** 2,500.
Outfield Dimension: LF—340, CF—402, RF—340.

IONA

Conference: Metro Atlantic.
Mailing Address: 715 North Ave, New Rochelle NY, 10801. **Website:** www.icgaels.com.
Head Coach: Conor Burke. **Baseball SID:** Jack Ravitz.
Assistant Coaches: Mike Sciamanico, Tyler Caserta, Alex Fishberg.
Home Field: City Park. **Outfield Dimensions:** LF—355, CF—385, RF—330.

IOWA

Conference: Big Ten.
Address: 930 Evashevski Dr., Iowa City, IA 52242.
Website: www.hawkeyesports.com/base.
Head Coach: Rick Heller. **Telephone:** 319-335-9259.
Baseball SID: Sam Basler. **Assistant Coaches:** Marty Sutherland*, Sean McGrath.
Home Field: Duane Banks Field. **Capacity:** 3,000.
Outfield Dimensions: LF-329 CF-395 RF-329.

JACKSON STATE

Conference: Southwestern.
Mailing Address: 1400 N Lynch Street Jackson, MS 39217. **Website:** www.gojsutigers.com.
Head Coach: Omar Johnson. **Telephone:** (601) 979-3930. **Baseball SID:** Evan Murry. **Telephone:** (601) 979-0849.
Assistant Coaches: Chandler Dillard.
Home Field: Braddy Field. **Seating Capacity:** 800.

JACKSONVILLE

Conference: ASUN.
Mailing Address: 2800 University Blvd N, Jacksonville, FL, 32211. **Website:** www.judolphins.com.
Head Coach: Chris Hayes. **Baseball SID:** Scott Manze.
Telephone: (904) 256-7402.

212 · Baseball America 2023 Directory

BaseballAmerica.com

COLLEGE

Assistant Coaches: Jerry Edwards. **Home Field:** John Sessions Stadium. **Seating Capacity:** 1,750. **Outfield Dimension: LF**—340, **CF**—405, **RF**—340.

JACKSONVILLE STATE

Conference: ASUN.
Mailing Address: 700 Pelham Rd N Jacksonville, AL 36265. **Website:** www.jsugamecocksports.com.
Head Coach: Jim Case. **Baseball SID:** Tony Schmidt. **Telephone:** (256) 782-5377.
Assistant Coaches: Mike Murphree, Evan Bush.
Home Field: Rudy Abbott Field at Jim Case Stadium.
Seating Capacity: 2,020. **Outfield Dimension: LF**—330, **CF**—403, **RF**—335.

JAMES MADISON

Conference: Sun Belt.
Address: 800 S Main Street, Harrisonburg, VA 22807. **Website:** JMUSports.com.
Head Coach: Marlin Ikenberry. **Telephone:** 540-568-3932.
Baseball SID: Christian Howe.
Home Field: Eagle Field at Veterans Memorial Park. **Capacity:** 1,200. **Outfield Dimensions:** LF-340 CF-400 RF-320.

KANSAS

Conference: Big 12.
Mailing Address: 1651 Naismith Dr Lawrence, KS 66045. **Website:** www.kuathletics.com.
Head Coach: Dan Fitzgerald. **Baseball SID:** Brandon Perel. **Assistant Coaches:** Brandon Scott, Tyler Hancock, Jon Coyne.
Home Field: Hoglund Ballpark. **Seating Capacity:** 2,500. **Outfield Dimension:** LF–330, **CF**—400, **RF**—330.

KANSAS STATE

Conference: Big 12.
Mailing Address: 1800 College Ave. Manhattan KS 66502. **Website:** www.kstatesports.com.
Head Coach: Pete Hughes. **Baseball SID:** Christopher Brown. **Assistant Coaches:** Rudy Darrow, Austin Wates, Thomas Hughes.
Home Field: Tointon Family Stadium. **Seating Capacity:** 2,344. **Outfield Dimension: LF**—325, **CF**—390, **RF**—320.

KENNESAW STATE

Conference: Atlantic Sun.
Address: 1000 Chastain Rd NW, Kennesaw, GA 30144. **Website:** ksuowls.com.
Head Coach: Ryan Coe.
Baseball SID: Michael Goss. **Assistant Coaches:** Matthew Passauer*, Brad Tyler.
Home Field: Fred Stillwell Stadium. **Capacity:** 900. **Outfield Dimensions:** LF-331 CF-400 RF-330.

KENT STATE

Conference: Mid-American.
Mailing Address: MAC Center, PO Box 5190, Kent, OH 44242. **Website:** www.kentstatesports.com.
Head Coach: Jeff Duncan. **Telephone:** (330) 672-8432.
Baseball SID: Dan Griffin. **Telephone:** (330) 672-8468.
Assistant Coaches: Mike Birkbeck, Barrett Serrato. **Telephone:** (330) 672-8433.
Home Field: Olga A. Mural Field at Schoonover Stadium. **Seating Capacity:** 500.

KENTUCKY

Conference: SEC.
Address: 510 Wildcat Court, Lexington, KY. **Website:** www.ukathletics.com.
Head Coach: Nick Mingione.
Baseball SID: Matt May. **Assistant Coaches:** Will Coggin*, Dan Roszel.
Home Field: Kentucky Proud Park. **Capacity:** 5000.
Outfield Dimensions: LF-335 CF-400 RF-320.

LAFAYETTE

Conference: Patriot.
Address: 730 High St, Easton, PA 18042. **Website:** Goleopards.com.
Head Coach: A.J. Miller. **Telephone:** 610-330-5945.
Baseball SID: Noah Sparandeo. **Assistant Coaches:** Ryan Luke*, Scott Boches.
Home Field: Hilton Rahn '51 Field at Kamine Stadium. **Capacity:** 500. **Outfield Dimensions:** LF-332 CF-403 RF-335.

LAMAR

Conference: Southland.
Address: 211 Redbird Lane Beaumont, TX 77710. **Website:** www.lamarcardinals.com.
Head Coach: Will Davis. **Telephone:** 2258023784.
Baseball SID: James Dixon. **Assistant Coaches:** Scott Hatten*, Sean Snedeker.
Home Field: Vincent-Beck Stadium. **Capacity:** 3,600.
Outfield Dimensions: LF-325 CF-380 RF-325.

LEHIGH

Conference: Patriot League.
Mailing Address: 27 Memorial Dr W, Bethlehem, PA 18015. **Website:** www.lehighsports.com.
Head Coach: Sean Leary. **Telephone:** (610) 758-4315.
Baseball SID: Josh Liddick.
Assistant Coaches: Pat Knight, Tyler Nelin, Trey Durrah. **Telephone:** (610) 758-4315.
Home Field: J. David Walker Field. **Outfield Dimension: LF**—320, **CF**—400, **RF**—320.

LIBERTY

Conference: Atlantic Sun.
Address: 1971 University Blvd, Lynchburg, VA 24515. **Website:** .
Head Coach: Scott Jackson.
Baseball SID: Ryan Bomberger. **Assistant Coaches:** Matt Williams*, Tyler Cannon.
Home Field: Worthington Field at Liberty Baseball Stadium. **Capacity:** 4000. **Outfield Dimensions:** LF-325 CF-395 RF-325.

LIPSCOMB

Conference: ASUN.
Mailing Address: One University Park Drive, Nashville, TN 37204-3951. **Website:** www.lipscombsports.com.
Head Coach: Jeff Forehand. **Telephone:** (615) 966-5716. **Baseball SID:** Hannah Jo Riley. **Telephone:** (270) 227-6485.
Assistant Coaches: Ryan Price, Adam Wyse.
Home Field: Ken Dugan Field at Stephen Lee Marsh Stadium. **Seating Capacity:** 1,500. **Outfield Dimension: LF**—330, **CF**—405, **RF**—330.

COLLEGE

LONG BEACH STATE

Conference: Big West.
Address: 1250 Bellflower Blvd Long Beach, CA 90840.
Website: longbeachstate.com.
Head Coach: Eric Valenzuela. **Telephone:** (562)985-8215.
Baseball SID: Collin Robinson. **Assistant Coaches:** Daniel Costanza*, Bryan Peters.
Home Field: Bohl Diamond at Blair Field. **Capacity:** 3,000. **Outfield Dimensions:** LF-335 CF-395 RF-330.

LONG ISLAND

Conference: Northeast.
Mailing Address: 720 Northern Blvd., Brookville, N.Y. 11548. **Website:** www.liuathletics.com.
Head Coach: Dan Pirillo. **Telephone:** (516) 299-2939.
Baseball SID: Casey Snedecor. **Telephone:** (718) 488-1307.
Assistant Coaches: Holden Capps, Kyle Strovink. **Telephone:** (516) 299-3985.
Home Field: LIU Baseball Stadium. **Outfield Dimension:** LF-330, CF-400, RF-330.

LONGWOOD

Conference: Big South.
Mailing Address: 201 High Street Farmville, VA 23909.
Website: www.longwoodlancers.com.
Head Coach: Chad Oxendine. **Baseball SID:** Sam Hovan. **Telephone:** (434) 395-2345.
Assistant Coaches: Brad Mincey, Mickey Beach. **Telephone:** (434) 395-2351.
Home Field: Buddy Bolding Stadium. **Seating Capacity:** 500. **Outfield Dimension:** LF-330, CF-390, RF-330.

LOUISIANA-LAFAYETTE

Conference: Sun Belt.
Mailing Address: 201 Reinhardt Drive, Lafayette, LA, 70506. **Website:** www. ragincajuns.com
Head Coach: Matt Deggs. **Baseball SID:** Matt Sullivan. **Telephone:** (337) 482-6331.
Assistant Coaches: Jake Wells, Seth Thibodeaux, Zach LaFleur.
Home Field: M.L. "Tigue" Moore Field at Russo Park. **Seating Capacity:** 6,015. **Outfield Dimension:** LF-330, CF-400, RF-330.

LOUISIANA-MONROE

Conference: Sun Belt.
Address: 700 University Ave. Monroe, LA.
Website: ulmwarhawks.com/sports/baseball.
Head Coach: Michael Federico.
Baseball SID: Mike Hammett. **Assistant Coaches:** Ryan McClaran*, Matt Collins.
Home Field: Lou St. Amant Field. **Capacity:** 5000.
Outfield Dimensions: LF-330 CF-405 RF-330.

LOUISIANA STATE

Conference: Southeastern.
Mailing Address: Nicholson Dr. at N. Stadium Dr., Baton Rouge, LA 70803. **Website:** www.lsusports.net.
Head Coach: Jay Johnson. **Telephone:** (225) 578-4148. **Baseball SID:** Bill Franques. **Telephone:** (225) 578-8226.
Assistant Coaches: Wes Johnson, Josh Jordan, Marc Wanaka. **Telephone:** (225) 578-4148.

Home Field: Alex Box Stadium. **Seating Capacity:** 10,326. **Outfield Dimension:** LF-330, CF-405, RF-330.

LOUISIANA TECH

Conference: Conference USA.
Mailing Address: Thomas Assembly Center 1650 West Alabama Ruston, La. 71270. **Website:** www.latechsports.com.
Head Coach: Lane Burroughs. **Baseball SID:** Patrick Davis. **Telephone:** (318) 257-5071.
Assistant Coaches: Mitch Gaspard, Cooper Fouts, Matt Miller.
Home Field: J.C. Love Field at Pat Patterson Park. **Seating Capacity:** 2,100. **Outfield Dimension:** LF-315, CF-380, RF-325.

LOUISVILLE

Conference: ACC.
Address: 215 Central Ave. **Website:** www.GoCards.com.
Head Coach: Dan McDonnell. **Telephone:** 502-852-0103.
Baseball SID: Stephen Williams. **Assistant Coaches:** Eric Snider*, Roger Williams.
Home Field: Jim Patterson Stadium. **Capacity:** 4,000. **Outfield Dimensions:** LF-330 CF-402 RF-330.

LOYOLA MARYMOUNT

Conference: West Coast.
Address: 1 Loyola Marymount University Dr. Los Angeles, CA 90045. **Website:** .
Head Coach: Nathan Choate.
Baseball SID: Quinn Ireland. **Assistant Coaches:** Mitchell Holland*, Eric Hutting.
Home Field: Page Stadium. **Capacity:** . **Outfield Dimensions:** LF-320 CF-406 RF-325.

MAINE

Conference: America East.
Address: 5747 Memorial Gym, Orono, Maine, 04469.
Website: goblackbears.com.
Head Coach: Nick Derba. **Telephone:** 207-581-1090.
Baseball SID: Kyle Emerson. **Assistant Coaches:** Scott Heath.
Home Field: Mahaney Diamond. **Seating Capacity:** 3,000. **Outfield Dimension:** LF-330, CF-400, RF-330.

MANHATTAN

Conference: Metro Atlantic.
Mailing Address: 4513 Manhattan College Parkway, Riverdale, N.Y. 10471. **Website:** www.gojaspers.com.
Head Coach: Dave Miller. **Telephone:** (718) 862-7821.
Baseball SID: Cooper Hayes. **Telephone:** (718) 862-7534.
Assistant Coaches: Steven Rosen, David Vandercook.
Home Field: Van Cortlandt Park.

MARIST

Conference: Metro Atlantic.
Mailing Address: McCann Center, 3399 North Road, Poughkeepsie, N.Y. 12601. **Website:** www.goredfoxes.com.
Head Coach: Lance Ratchford. **Telephone:** (845) 575-3000. **Baseball SID:** Kenny McGovern.
Assistant Coaches: Mike Coss*, Adam Chase.
Home Field: McCann Baseball Field. **Seating Outfield Dimension:** LF-320, CF-390, RF-320.

COLLEGE

MARSHALL

Conference: Sun Belt..
Mailing Address: Marshall Athletics Department.
Website: www.herdzone.com.
Head Coach: Greg Beals. **Telephone:** (304) 696-6454.
Baseball SID: Cody Linn. **Telephone:** (304) 696-2418.
Assistant Coaches: Taylor Sandefur, Cameron Coons.
Telephone: (304) 696-7146.
Home Field: Kennedy Center YMCA.

MARYLAND

Conference: Big Ten.
Address: 8500 Paint Branch Dr. College Park, MD
20742. **Website:** www.umterps.com.
Head Coach: Rob Vaughn.
Baseball SID: Sam Allard. **Assistant Coaches:**
Anthony Papio*, Matt Swope.
Home Field: Bob "Turtle" Smith Stadium. **Outfield
Dimension: LF**—320, **CF**—380, **RF**—325.

MARYLAND-BALTIMORE COUNTY

Conference: America East.
Mailing Address: 1000 Hilltop Cir, Baltimore, MD
21250. **Website:** www.umbcretrievers.com.
Head Coach: Liam Bowen. **Baseball SID:** Zach Seidel.
Assistant Coaches: Phil Disher*, Rory Costello.
Home Field: Alumni Field. **Seating Capacity:** 1,000.
Outfield Dimension: LF—340, **CF**—360, **RF**—340.

MARYLAND-EASTERN SHORE

Conference: Northeast.
Address: W.P. Hytche Athletic Center. **Website:** www.
easternshorehawks.com.
Head Coach: Brian Hollamon.
Baseball SID: Justin Odendhal. **Assistant Coaches:**
Shawn Phillips*, .
Home Field: Perdue Stadium. **Capacity: 5200.**
Outfield Dimension: LF—309, **CF**—402, **RF**—309.

MASSACHUSETTS

Conference: Atlantic 10.
Mailing Address: 200 Commonwealth Avenue, 3rd
Floor, Amherst, MA 01003. **Website:** www.umassathlet-
ics.com.
Head Coach: Matt Reynolds. **Telephone:** (413) 545-
3120. **Baseball SID:** Hana Johnson.
Assistant Coaches: Mark Royer, Brandon Shilekis.
Telephone: (703) 346-8571.
Home Field: Earl Lorden Field. **Outfield Dimension:**
LF—330, **CF**—400, **RF**—330.

MASSACHUSETTS-LOWELL

Conference: America East.
Mailing Address: 1 University Ave, Lowell, MA 01854.
Website: www.goriverhawks.com.
Head Coach: Ken Harring. **Telephone:** (978) 934-2344.
Baseball SID: Dan Kastner. **Telephone:** (978) 934-6685.
Assistant Coaches: Nick Barese, Joe Consolmagno.
Home Field: LeLacheur Park. **Seating Capacity:** 4,797.
Outfield Dimension: LF—337, **CF**—400, **RF**—301.

MCNEESE STATE

Address: 4205 Ryan St Lake Charles, LA 70605.
Website: mcneesesports.com.
Head Coach: Justin Hill. **Telephone:** (337) 475-5484.
Baseball SID: Jared Morris. **Assistant Coaches:** Jimmy

Ricklefsen*, Nick Zaleski.
Home Field: Joe Miller Ballpark. **Capacity:** 2000.
Outfield Dimensions: LF-330 CF-400 RF-330.

MEMPHIS

Conference: American Athletic.
Address: 1181-1191 E Getwell Loop Memphis, TN
38111. **Website:** gotigersgo.com.
Head Coach: Kerrick Jackson.
Baseball SID: Brock Busic. **Assistant Coaches:** Julian
Henson*, Tim Jamieson.
Home Field: FedEx Park.. **Seating Capacity:** 2,000.
Outfield Dimension: LF—318, **CF**—380, **RF**—317.

MERCER

Conference: SoCon.
Address: 1501 Mercer University Dr. **Website:** www.
mercerbears.com.
Head Coach: Craig Davis Gibson. **Telephone:** (478)
301-2396.
Baseball SID: Amanda Cover. **Assistant Coaches:**
Willie Stewart*, Cory Barton.
Home Field: Ortho GA Park @ Claude Smith Field.
Capacity: 1500. **Outfield Dimensions:** LF-335 CF-400
RF-320.

MERRIMACK

Conference: Northeast.
Mailing Address: 315 Turnpike Street, North Andover,
MA 01845. **Website:** www.merrimackathletics.com.
Head Coach: Brian Murphy. **Baseball SID:** Nick
Penkala. **Telephone:** (978) 837-5053.
Assistant Coaches: Patrick McKenna, Charlie Fletcher.
Home Field: Warrior Baseball Diamond. **Outfield
Dimension: LF**—335, **CF**—390, **RF**—335.

MIAMI

Conference: ACC.
Address: 5821 San Amaro Drive, Coral Gables, FL,
33146. **Website:** miamihurricanes.com.
Head Coach: Gino DiMare. **Telephone:** 305-284-4171.
Baseball SID: Josh White. **Assistant Coaches:** Jeff
Opalewski, Bailey Montgomery.
Home Field: Alex Rodriguez Park at Mark Light Field.
Capacity: 3,552. **Outfield Dimensions:** LF-330 CF-400
RF-330.

MIAMI (OHIO)

Conference: Mid-American.
Mailing Address: 550 E Withrow Street, Oxford, OH
45056. **Website:** www.miamiredhawks.com.
Head Coach: Danny Hayden. **Baseball SID:** Cole
Neelon. **Telephone:** (513) 529-0402. **Baseball SID:** Pearl
Zajbel.
Assistant Coaches: Bailey Montgomery, Jeff
Opalewski.
Home Field: McKie Field at Hayden Park. **Seating
Capacity:** 600. **Outfield Dimension: LF**—332, **CF**—400,
RF—341.

MICHIGAN

Conference: Big Ten.
Address: 1114 S State St, Ann Arbor, MI 48104.
Website: mgoblue.com.
Head Coach: Tracy Smith.
Baseball SID: Conor Stemme. **Assistant Coaches:** Ben
Greenspan*, Brock Huntzinger.

BaseballAmerica.com

Baseball America 2023 Directory • **215**

COLLEGE

Home Field: Ray Fisher Stadium. **Capacity:** 3,500.
Outfield Dimensions: LF-312 CF-395 RF-320.

MICHIGAN STATE

Conference: Big Ten.
Mailing Address: Room 304, Jenison Field House, 223 Kalamazoo Street, East Lansing, MI 48824-1025. **Website:** www.msuspartans.com.
Head Coach: Jake Boss. **Telephone:** (517) 355-4486.
Baseball SID: Zach Fisher. **Telephone:** (517) 355-2271.
Assistant Coaches: Mark Van Ameyde, Graham Sikes*. **Telephone:** (517) 355-3419.
Home Field: McLane Baseball Stadium at Kobs Field. **Seating Capacity:** 2,500.

MIDDLE TENNESSEE STATE

Conference: Conference USA.
Mailing Address: 1672 Greenland Drive, Murfreesboro, TN 37132. **Website:** www.goblueraiders. com.
Head Coach: Jerry Myers. **Telephone:** (615) 898-2961.
Baseball SID: Austin Pert. **Telephone:** (615) 473-4744.
Assistant Coaches: Jason Stein*, Kevin Nichols.
Home Field: Reese Smith, Jr. Field. **Seating Capacity:** 2,600. **Outfield Dimension: LF**—330, **CF**—390, **RF**—330.

MINNESOTA

Conference: Big Ten.
Address: 1425 15th Ave. SE. **Website:** gophersports. com.
Head Coach: John Anderson. **Telephone:** xx
Baseball SID: E.J. Stevens. **Assistant Coaches:** Packy Casey*, Ty McDevitt.
Home Field: Siebert Field. **Capacity:** 1,420. **Outfield Dimensions:** LF-330 CF-380 RF-330.

MISSISSIPPI

Conference: SEC.
Address: 908 All-American Drive University, MS 38677. **Website:** olemisssports.com.
Head Coach: Mike Bianco. **Telephone:** 662-915-6643.
Baseball SID: Kyle Birnbrauer. **Assistant Coaches:** Carl Lafferty*, Mike Clement.
Home Field: Swayze Field. **Capacity:** 11,477. **Outfield Dimensions:** LF-330 CF-390 RF-330.

MISSISSIPPI STATE

Conference: SEC.
Address: 110 Coliseum Circle, Mississippi State, MS 39762. **Website:** www.HailState.com.
Head Coach: Chris Lemonis. **Telephone:** 662-325-3597.
Baseball SID: Travis Rae.
Home Field: Dudy Noble Field/Polk-Dement STadium. **Capacity:** 15,000. **Outfield Dimensions:** LF-330 CF-400 RF-305.

MISSISSIPPI VALLEY STATE

Conference: Southwestern.
Mailing Address: 14000 Highway 82 West, Box 7246, Itta Bena, MS 38941. **Website:** www.mvsusports.com.
Head Coach: Milton Barney. **Baseball SID:** Brian Baublitz, Jr. **Telephone:** (662) 254-3011.
Assistant Coaches: Jaylan Bledsoe*, Kenny Hudson.
Home Field: Magnolia Field. **Seating Capacity:** 120.
Outfield Dimension: LF—313, **CF**—394, **RF**—315.

MISSOURI

Conference: Southeastern.
Mailing Address: 1 Champions Drive, Suite 200, Columbia, MO 65211. **Website:** www.mutigers.com.
Head Coach: Steve Bieser. **Baseball SID:** Ryan Koslen.
Assistant Coaches: Jason Hagerty, Ricky Meinhold.
Home Field: Taylor Stadium. **Seating Capacity:** 3,031.
Outfield Dimension: LF—340, **CF**—400, **RF**—340.

MISSOURI STATE

Conference: Missouri Valley.
Address: 901 S National Ave, Springfield, MO 65810.
Website: https://missouristatebears.com/.
Head Coach: Keith Guttin. **Telephone:** 417-836-4497.
Baseball SID: Ben Adamson. **Assistant Coaches:** Joey Hawkins*, Nick Petree.
Home Field: Hammons Field. **Capacity:** 8000.
Outfield Dimensions: LF-315 CF-400 RF-330.

MONMOUTH

Conference: Metro Atlantic.
Mailing Address: 400 Cedar Ave, West Long Branch, NJ 07764. **Website:** www.monmouthhawks.com.
Head Coach: Dean Ehehalt. **Baseball SID:** Gary Kowal.
Assistant Coaches: Kyle Norman, Mike Russo.
Home Field: Monmouth Baseball Field. **Seating Capacity:** 1,000. **Outfield Dimension: LF**—330, **CF**—400, **RF**—330.

MOREHEAD STATE

Conference: Ohio Valley.
Address: 1 Playforth Place Morehead, KY 40351.
Website: https://msueagles.com/sports/baseball.
Head Coach: Mik Aoki.
Baseball SID: Matt Schabert. **Assistant Coaches:** Brady Ward*, Tyler Jackson.
Home Field: Allen Field. **Capacity:** 1000. **Outfield Dimensions:** LF-328 CF-360 RF-324.

MOUNT ST. MARY'S

Conference: Metro Atlantic.
Address: 16300 Old Emmitsburg Rd, Emmitsburg, MD 21727. **Website: https://mountathletics.com/sports/baseball.**
Head Coach: Frank Leoni. **Telephone:** 301-447-3806.
Baseball SID: Cody Stahley. **Assistant Coaches:** Cullen Moore*, Aaron Tarr.
Home Field: E.T. Straw Stadium. **Capacity:** 500.
Outfield Dimensions: LF-330 CF-385 RF-315.

MURRAY STATE

Conference: Ohio Valley.
Mailing Address: 217 Stewart Stadium, Murray, KY, 42071. **Website:** www.goracers.com.
Head Coach: Dan Skirka. **Telephone:** (270) 809-4892.
Baseball SID: Clay Wagoner. **Telephone:** (270) 809-7051.
Assistant Coaches: Steve Adkins, Cooper Goen.
Home Field: Johnny Reagan. **Outfield Dimension: LF**—330, **CF**—400, **RF**—330.

NAVY

Conference: Patriot.
Address: Ricketts Hall 566 Brownson Rd. Annapolis, MD 21402. **Website: https://navysports.com/.**
Head Coach: Paul Kostacopoulos. **Telephone:** 410-293-5571.

COLLEGE

Baseball SID: Marshal Filipowicz. **Assistant Coaches:** Jeff Kane*, Tim Reilly.
Home Field: Terwilliger Brothers Field at Max Bishop Stadium. **Capacity:** 1,500. **Outfield Dimensions:** LF-318 CF-390 RF-300.

NEBRASKA

Conference: Big Ten.
Address: One Memorial Stadium 800 Stadium Dr. Lincoln, NE 68588. **Website:** www.huskers.com.
Head Coach: Will Bolt. **Telephone:** (402) 472-2269.
Baseball SID: Jared Meister. **Assistant Coaches:** Lance Harvell*, Jeff Christy.
Home Field: Hawks Field at Haymarket Park. **Capacity:** 8,486. **Outfield Dimensions:** LF-335 CF-395 RF-325.

NEBRASKA-OMAHA

Conference: Summit League.
Mailing Address: 6001 Dodge Street, Omaha, NE, 68182. **Website:** www.omavs.com.
Head Coach: Evan Porter. **Baseball SID:** Zach Levine.
Assistant Coaches: Brian Strawn, Payton Kinney.
Home Field: Tal Anderson Field. **Seating Capacity:** 1,500. **Outfield Dimension:** LF—330, **CF**—410, **RF**—330.

NEVADA

Conference: Mountain West.
Mailing Address: 1664 N. VIrginia Street, Legacy Hall/ MS 232, Reno, NV 89557-0232. **Website:** www.nevada-wolfpack.com.
Head Coach: Jake McKinley. **Baseball SID:** Aaron Juarez. **Telephone:** (208) 982-0040.
Assistant Coaches: Mark Moriarty, Jordan Getzelman*.
Home Field: Don Weir Field at Peccole Park. **Seating Capacity:** 3,000. **Outfield Dimension:** LF—340, **CF**—401, **RF**—340.

NEVADA-LAS VEGAS

Conference: Mountain West.
Address: 4505 S Maryland Pkwy, Las Vegas, NV 89154. **Website:** https://unlvrebels.com/.
Head Coach: Stan Stolte. **Telephone:** n/a.
Baseball SID: Kelsey Olson. **Assistant Coaches:** Cory Vanderhook*, Kevin Higgins.
Home Field: Earl E. Wilson. **Capacity:** 3,000. **Outfield Dimensions:** LF-335 CF-400 RF-335.

NEW JERSEY TECH

Conference: America East.
Address: 323 Dr Martin Luther King Jr Blvd, Newark, NJ 07102. **Website: https://njithighlanders.com/sports/ baseball?path=baseball.**
Head Coach: Robbie McClellan.
Baseball SID: Myles Rudnick. **Assistant Coaches:** Matt Greely*, Anthony **Deleo.Home Field:** Jim Hynes Stadium. **Seating Capacity:** 700.

NEW MEXICO

Conference: Mountain West.
Address: 1414 University Drive Albuquerque, NM 87109. **Website:** www.golobos.com.
Head Coach: Tod Brown. **Telephone:** 505-925-5500.
Baseball SID: Evan O'Kelly. **Assistant Coaches:** Nate Causey*, Michael Lopez.
Home Field: Santa Ana Star Field. **Capacity:** . **Outfield Dimensions:** LF-330 CF-413 RF-330.

NEW MEXICO STATE

Conference: Western Athletic.
Mailing Address: Fulton Center, 1815 Wells Street, Las Cruces, N.M. 88003-8001. **Website:** www.nmstatesports.com.
Head Coach: Mike Kirby. **Telephone:** (575) 646-7693.
Baseball SID: Jon Opiela.
Assistant Coaches: Brandon Van Horn, Keith Zuniga*. **Telephone:** (575) 646-2739.
Home Field: Presley Askew Field. **Seating Capacity:** 1,000. **Outfield Dimension:** LF—345, **CF**—400, **RF**—345.

NEW ORLEANS

Conference: Southland.
Mailing Address: 2000 Lakeshore Dr. New Orleans, LA 70148. **Website:** www.unoprivateers.com.
Head Coach: Blake Dean. **Baseball SID:** Emanuel Pepis.
Assistant Coaches: Phillip Hurst*, Dax Norris.
Home Field: Maestri Field at Privateer Park. **Seating Capacity:** 2,900. **Outfield Dimension:** LF—330, **CF**—405, **RF**—330.

NIAGARA

Conference: Metro Atlantic.
Mailing Address: Upper Level Gallagher Center, PO Box 2009, Niagara University, N.Y., 14109. **Website:** www.purpleeagles.com.
Head Coach: Rob McCoy. **Telephone:** (716) 286-7361.
Baseball SID: Dan Richeal. **Telephone:** (716) 286-8586.
Assistant Coaches: Matt Spatafora*. **Telephone:** (716) 286-8624.
Home Field: Bobo Field. **Outfield Dimension:** LF—327, **CF**—394, **RF**—315.

NICHOLLS STATE

Conference: Southland.
Mailing Address: PO Box 2032, Thibodaux, LA 70310. **Website:** www.geauxcolonels.com.
Head Coach: Mike Silva. **Baseball SID:** Jamie Bustos. **Telephone:** (985) 448-4281.
Assistant Coaches: Ladd Rhodes*, Cody Livingston.
Home Field: Ben Meyer Diamond at Ray E. Didier Field. **Seating Capacity:** 3,200. **Outfield Dimension:** LF—331, **CF**—400, **RF**—331.

NORFOLK STATE

Conference: Mid-Eastern.
Mailing Address: 700 Park Avenue, Norfolk, VA 23504. **Website:** www.nsuspartans.com.
Head Coach: Keith Shumate. **Telephone:** (757) 823-8196. **Baseball SID:** Alex Lehmbeck. **Telephone:** (757) 823-2628.
Assistant Coaches: Matt Rein, Matthew Owens. **Telephone:** (757) 823-8196.
Home Field: Marty L. Miller Field. **Seating Capacity:** 1,500. **Outfield Dimension:** LF—330, **CF**—402, **RF**—318.

NORTH CAROLINA

Conference: ACC.
Address: 235 Ridge Rd. **Website:** GoHeels.com.
Head Coach: Scott Forbes.
Baseball SID: Jody Jones. **Assistant Coaches:** Bryant Gaines*, Jesse Wierzbicki.
Home Field: Boshamer Stadium. **Capacity:** 4100. **Outfield Dimension:** LF—335, **CF**—400, **RF**—340.

BaseballAmerica.com

Baseball America 2023 Directory • **217**

COLLEGE

NORTH CAROLINA STATE

Conference: ACC.
Address: 1081 Varsity Drive Raleigh, NC 27695.
Website: gopack.com.
Head Coach: Elliott Avent.
Baseball SID: Tyler Hotz. **Assistant Coaches:** Chris Hart*, Clint Chysler.
Home Field: Doak Field at Dail Park. **Capacity:** 3500.
Outfield Dimensions: LF-328 CF-400 RF-330

NORTH DAKOTA STATE

Conference: Summit.
Address: Dept 1200 PO Box 6050 Fargo, ND 58108.
Website: www.gobison.com.
Head Coach: Tyler Oakes.
Baseball SID: Myles Johnson. **Assistant Coaches:** Brandon Hunt*, Tanner Neale.
Home Field: Newman Outdoor Field. **Capacity:** 4,**500.**
Outfield Dimension: LF—318, **CF**—408, **RF**—314.

NORTH FLORIDA

Conference: Atlantic Sun.
Address: 1 UNF Drive UNF Arena. **Website:** www.unfospreys.com.
Head Coach: Tim Parenton. **Telephone:** 904-420-4029.
Baseball SID: Brock Borgeson. **Assistant Coaches:** Brady Bogart*, Kyle Brooks.
Home Field: Harmon Stadium. **Capacity:** 1000.
Outfield Dimensions: LF-335 CF-400 RF-335.

NORTHEASTERN

Conference: Colonial.
Address: 360 Huntington Avenue Boston, Mass. 02115. **Website:** nuhuskies.com.
Head Coach: Mike Glavine. **Telephone:** (617)-373-3657 .
Baseball SID: Brandon Poli. **Assistant Coaches:** Kevin Cobb*, Nick Puccio.
Home Field: Friedman Diamond. **Capacity:** 2500.
Outfield Dimensions: LF-326 CF-400 RF-342.

NORTHERN COLORADO

Conference: Summit.
Mailing Address: 270D Butler-Hancock Athletic Center. **Website:** www.uncbears.com.
Head Coach: Mike Anderson. **Telephone:** (970) 351-1714. **Baseball SID:** Ross LaDue.
Assistant Coaches: Shane Opitz, Pablo Ortiz. **Telephone:** (970) 351-1203.
Home Field: Jackson Field. **Seating Capacity:** 1,500.
Outfield Dimension: LF—349, **CF**—416, **RF**—356.

NORTHERN ILLINOIS

Conference: Mid-American.
Mailing Address: Intercollegiate Athletics, Convocation Center (CV), DeKalb, IL 60115. **Website:** www.niuhuskies.com.
Head Coach: Mike Kunigonis. **Telephone:** (815) 753-0147. **Baseball SID:** Nick Shammas. **Telephone:** (815) 753-3706.
Assistant Coaches: Luke Stewart*, Josh Pethoud. **Telephone:** (815) 753-0147.
Home Field: Ralph McKinzie Field. **Seating Capacity:** 1,500. **Outfield Dimension: LF**—312, **CF**—395, **RF**—322.

NORTHERN KENTUCKY

Conference: Horizon League.
Mailing Address: 500 Nunn Drive Highland Heights, KY 41099. **Website:** www.nkunorse.com.
Head Coach: Dizzy Peyton. **Telephone:** (859) 572-5940. **Baseball SID:** Devon Lucal. **Telephone:** (859) 572-7659.
Assistant Coaches: Connor Walsh, Steve Dintaman*.
Home Field: Bill Aker Baseball Complex. **Seating Capacity:** 500. **Outfield Dimension: LF**—320, **CF**—365, **RF**—320.

NORTHWESTERN

Conference: Big Ten.
Mailing Address: 1501 Central Street, Evanston, IL 60208. **Website:** www.nusports.com.
Head Coach: Jim Foster. **Baseball SID:** Shealyn Abbott.
Assistant Coaches: Dusty Napoleon*, Jon Strauss.
Home Field: Rocky & Berenice Miller Park. **Seating Capacity:** 1,500. **Outfield Dimension: LF**—326, **CF**—401, **RF**—310.

NORTHWESTERN STATE

Conference: Southland.
Mailing Address: 468 Caspari Drive, Natchitoches, LA 71497. **Website:** www.nsudemons.com.
Head Coach: Bobby Barbier. **Telephone:** (318) 357-4139. **Baseball SID:** Jason Pugh. **Telephone:** (318) 357-6468.
Assistant Coaches: Spencer Goodwin*, Chris Bertrand. **Telephone:** (318) 357-4134.
Home Field: Brown-Stroud Field. **Seating Capacity:** 1,200. **Outfield Dimension: LF**—320, **CF**—400, **RF**—325.

NOTRE DAME

Conference: Atlantic Coast.
Mailing Address: University of Notre Dame Notre Dame, IN 46556. **Website:** www.und.com.
Head Coach: Shawn Stiffler. **Baseball SID:** Alyson Prigge.
Assistant Coaches: Logan Robins, Seth Voltz.
Home Field: Frank Eck Stadium. **Seating Capacity:** 2,500. **Outfield Dimension: LF**—330, **CF**—405, **RF**—330.

OAKLAND

Conference: Horizon League.
Mailing Address: 318 Meadow Brook Road, Rochester, MI 48309. **Website:** www.goldengrizzlies.com.
Head Coach: Jordon Banfield. **Baseball SID:** Teddy Rydquist.
Assistant Coaches: Brian Nelson. **Telephone:** (512) 468-7540.
Home Field: Oakland Baseball Field. **Seating Capacity:** 500. **Outfield Dimension: LF**—333, **CF**—380, **RF**—320.

OHIO

Conference: Mid-American.
Mailing Address: 95 Richland Ave, Athens, OH 45701. **Website:** www.ohiobobcats.com.
Head Coach: Craig Moore. **Baseball SID:** Sarah Newgarde.
Assistant Coaches: Kirby McGuire, Tim Brown.
Home Field: Bob Wren Field. **Seating Capacity:** 4,000. **Outfield Dimension: LF**—340, **CF**—405, **RF**—340.

COLLEGE

OHIO STATE

Conference: Big Ten.
Mailing Address: 2400 Olentangy River Road, Columbus, OH 43210. **Website:** www.ohiostatebuckeyes.com.
Head Coach: Bill Mosiello. **Telephone:** (614) 292-1075. **Baseball SID:** Breanna Jacobs. **Telephone:** (614) 292-3270
Assistant Coaches: Sean Allen, Andrew See*.
Home Field: Bill Davis Stadium. **Seating Capacity:** 4,450. **Outfield Dimension: LF**—330, **CF**—400, **RF**—330.

OKLAHOMA

Conference: Big 12.
Address: 180 W. Brooks St., Norman, OK 73019.
Website: SoonerSports.com.
Head Coach: Skip Johnson. **Telephone:** (405) 325-8354.
Baseball SID: Eric Hollier. **Assistant Coaches:** Clay Overcash*, Reggie Willits.
Home Field: L. Dale Mitchell Park. **Capacity:** 3,180.
Outfield Dimensions: LF-335-385 CF-411 RF-335-385.

OKLAHOMA STATE

Conference: Big 12.
Address: 103 N Bellis St, Stillwater Oklahoma.
Website: Okstate.Com.
Head Coach: Josh Holliday.
Baseball Sid: Wade Mcwhorter. **Assistant Coaches:** Justin Seely*, Rob Walton.
Home Field: O'Brate Stadium. **Seating Capacity:** 8,000. **Outfield Dimension: LF**—330, **CF**—402, **RF**—320.

OLD DOMINION

Conference: Conference USA.
Mailing Address: 4500 Parker Ave, Norfolk VA 23508.
Website: www.odusports.com.
Head Coach: Chris Finwood. **Telephone:** (757) 683-4230. **Baseball SID:** Pierce Yarberry. **Telephone:** (757) 683-3395.
Assistant Coaches: Jonathan Hadra, Mike Marron.
Telephone: (757) 683-4230.
Home Field: Bud Metheny Baseball Complex.
Seating Capacity: 2,500. **Outfield Dimension: LF**—325, **CF**—395, **RF**—325.

ORAL ROBERTS

Conference: Summit.
Address: 7777 S Lewis Ave, Tulsa, OK 74171. **Website:** oruathletics.com.
Head Coach: Ryan Folmar. **Telephone:** 918-495-7639.
Baseball SID: Kyle Stafford. **Assistant Coaches:** Ryan Neill*, Wes Davis.
Home Field: J.L. Johnson Stadium. **Capacity:** 2,418.
Outfield Dimensions: LF-330 CF-400 RF-330.

OREGON

Conference: Pac-12.
Address: 2727 Leo Harris Parkway; Eugene, OR 97401.
Website: GoDucks.com.
Head Coach: Mark Wasikowski. **Telephone:** 541-346-5235.
Baseball SID: Todd Miles. **Assistant Coaches:** Jack Marder*, Jake Angier.
Home Field: PK Park. **Capacity:** 4,000. **Outfield Dimensions:** LF-335 CF-390 RF-325.

OREGON STATE

Conference: Pac-12.
Address: 107 Gill Coliseum Corvallis OR 97331.
Website: .
Head Coach: Mitch Canham.
Baseball SID: Hank Hager. **Assistant Coaches:** Rich Dorman*, Ryan Gipson.
Home Field: Goss Stadium. **Seating Capacity:** 4,000.
Outfield Dimension: LF—330, **CF**—400, **RF**—330.

PACIFIC

Conference: West Coast.
Address: 3601 Pacific Ave, Stockton, Ca, 95211.
Website: https://pacifictigers.com/sports/baseball.
Head Coach: Chris Rodriguez. **Telephone:** 209-946-2709.
Baseball SID: Zach Karbach. **Assistant Coaches:** Elliott Cribby*, Ben Buechner.
Home Field: Klein Family Field. **Capacity:** 2500.
Outfield Dimensions: LF-317 CF-400 RF-325.

PENN STATE

Conference: Big Ten.
Address: 112 Medlar Field at Lubrano Park, University Park, PA 16802. **Website:** gopsusports.com.
Head Coach: Rob Cooper.
Baseball SID: Paul Marboe. **Assistant Coaches:** Sean Moore*, Josh Newman.
Home Field: Medlar Field at Lubrano Park. **Capacity:** 5,406. **Outfield Dimensions:** LF-325 CF-399 RF-320.

PENNSYLVANIA

Conference: Ivy League.
Mailing Address: Weightman Hall, 235 S. 33rd Street, Philadelphia, PA 19104. **Website:** www.pennathletics.com.
Head Coach: John Yurkow. **Telephone:** (215) 898-6282. **Baseball SID:** Adam Reiter. **Telephone:** (215) 898-6128.
Assistant Coaches: Mike Santello, Josh Schwartz.
Telephone: (215) 746-2325.
Home Field: Meiklejohn Stadium. **Seating Capacity:** 856. **Outfield Dimension: LF**—330, **CF**—380, **RF**—330.

PEPPERDINE

Conference: West Coast.
Address: 24255 Pacific Coast Highway. **Website:** .
Head Coach: Rick Hirtensteiner. **Telephone:** 13108049157.
Baseball SID: Kaitlyn Amaral. **Assistant Coaches:** Danny Worth*, Cameron Rowland.
Home Field: Eddy D. Field Stadium. **Seating Capacity:** 1,800. **Outfield Dimension: LF**—330, **CF**—400, **RF**—330.

PITTSBURGH

Conference: ACC.
Address: 395 Robinson Street Pittsburgh, PA 15261.
Website: www.pittsburghpanthers.com.
Head Coach: Mike Bell.
Baseball SID: Mike Ashcraft. **Assistant Coaches:** Ty Megahee*, Joe Mercadante.
Home Field: Charles Cost Field. **Capacity:** 1500.
Outfield Dimensions: LF-325 CF-390 RF-330.

COLLEGE

PORTLAND

Conference: West Coast.
Mailing Address: 5000 N. Willamette Blvd., Portland, OR 97203-5798. **Website:** www.portlandpilots.com.
Head Coach: Geoff Loomis. **Telephone:** (503) 943-7707. **Baseball SID:** Kyle Garcia.
Assistant Coaches: Trey Watt, Connor Lambert. **Telephone:** (503) 943-7732.
Home Field: Joe Etzel Field. **Seating Capacity:** 1,300. **Outfield Dimension: LF**—325, **CF**—388, **RF**—325.

PRAIRIE VIEW A&M

Conference: Southwestern.
Mailing Address: P.O.Box 519, MS 1500, Prairie View, TX 77446. **Website:** www.pvpanthers.com.
Head Coach: Auntwan Riggins. **Telephone:** (936) 261-3955. **Baseball SID:** La Tonia Thirston.
Assistant Coaches: Brian White, Anthony Macon. **Telephone:** (936) 261-3955.
Home Field: Tankersley Field. **Seating Capacity:** 800. **Outfield Dimension: LF**—327, **CF**—400, **RF**—327.

PRESBYTERIAN

Conference: Big South.
Address: 503 S. Broad Streat, Clinton, SC 29325. **Website:** www.gobluehose.com.
Head Coach: Elton Pollock. **Telephone:** 8648338323.
Baseball SID: Greg Hartlage. **Assistant Coaches:** John O'Neil*, Blake Miller.
Home Field: PC Baseball Complex/Elton Pollock Field. **Capacity:** 500. **Outfield Dimensions:** LF-325 CF-400 RF-325.

PRINCETON

Conference: Ivy League.
Mailing Address: Bill Clarke Field, Princeton University, Princeton, N.J. 08544. **Website:** www.goprincetontigers.com.
Head Coach: Scott Bradley. **Baseball SID:** Warren Croxton.
Assistant Coaches: Joe Haumacher, Alex Jurczynski*.
Home Field: Bill Clarke Field. **Seating Capacity:** 850.
Outfield Dimension: LF—325, **CF**—400, **RF**—315.

PURDUE

Conference: Big 10.
Address: 1225 Northwestern Avenue, West Lafayette, IN 47907. **Website:** PurdueSpors.com.
Head Coach: Greg Goff. **Telephone:** 765-494-7639.
Baseball SID: Ben Turner. **Assistant Coaches:** Terry Rooney*, Chris Marx.
Home Field: Alexander Field. **Capacity:** 2500.
Outfield Dimensions: LF-340 CF-408 RF-330.

PURDUE-FORT WAYNE

Conference: Horizon League.
Mailing Address: 2101 E. Coliseum Blvd., Fort Wayne, IN 46805-1499. **Website:** www.gomastodons.com.
Head Coach: Doug Schreiber. **Baseball SID:** Derrick Sloboda. **Telephone:** (260) 481-0729.
Assistant Coaches: Brent McNeil, Ken Jones. **Telephone:** (260) 481-5455.
Home Field: Mastodon Field. **Seating Capacity:** 200. **Outfield Dimension: LF**—330, **CF**—400, **RF**—330.

QUINNIPIAC

Conference: Metro Atlantic.
Mailing Address: 275 Mt Carmel Ave. Hamden CT 06518. **Website:** www.gobobcats.com.
Head Coach: John Delaney. **Baseball SID:** Tyler Walden-Martin.
Assistant Coaches: Trey Stover*, Rich Cesca. **Telephone:** (203) 582-6571.
Home Field: Bobcats Field. **Outfield Dimension: LF**—315, **CF**—405, **RF**—310.

RADFORD

Conference: Big South.
Mailing Address: 801 E Main St, Radford, VA 24142. **Website:** www.radfordathletics.com.
Head Coach: Alex Guerra. **Baseball SID:** Shelton Moss. **Telephone:** (540) 831-5726.
Assistant Coaches: Christian Bourne, Billy Funk, Seth Lancaster. **Telephone:** (540) 831-6513.
Home Field: Sherman Carter Memorial Stadium. **Seating Capacity:** 800. **Outfield Dimension: LF**—330, **CF**—400, **RF**—330.

RHODE ISLAND

Conference: Atlantic 10.
Address: 3 Keaney Rd Kingston, RI. **Website:** www.gorhody.com.
Head Coach: Raphael Cerrato. **Telephone:** 401-874-4888.
Baseball SID: Shane Donaldson. **Assistant Coaches:** Sean O'Brien*, David Fischer.
Home Field: Bill Beck Field. **Capacity:** 500. **Outfield Dimensions:** LF-330 CF-400 RF-330.

RICE

Conference: Conference USA.
Mailing Address: Department of Athletics, MS 548, 6100 Main Street, Houston, TX 77005. **Website:** www riceowls.com.
Head Coach: Jose Cruz, Jr.. **Baseball SID:** Chuck Pool. **Telephone:** (713) 348-5775.
Assistant Coaches: Paul Janish, Parker Bangs, Rob Hardy. **Telephone:** (713) 348-8859.
Home Field: Reckling Park. **Seating Capacity:** 7,000. **Outfield Dimension: LF**—330, **CF**—400, **RF**—330.

RICHMOND

Conference: Atlantic 10.
Address: 365 College Road University of Richmond, Va. 23173. **Website:** www.richmondspiders.com.
Head Coach: Tracy Woodson. **Telephone:** 804-289-8391.
Baseball SID: Bridgette Robles. **Assistant Coaches:** Nate Mulberg*, Josh Epstein.
Home Field: Pitt Field. **Capacity:** 600. **Outfield Dimensions:** LF-328 CF-390 RF-328.

RIDER

Conference: Metro Atlantic.
Address: 2083 Lawrenceville Rd. Lawrenceville NJ, 08536. **Website:** www.gobroncs.com.
Head Coach: Barry Davis.
Baseball SID: Norm Yacko. **Assistant Coaches:** Lee Lipinski*, Mike Petrowski.
Home Field: Sonny Pittaro Field. **Capacity:** 2,000. **Outfield Dimensions:** LF-330 CF-405 RF-330.

COLLEGE

RUTGERS

Conference: Big Ten.
Mailing Address: 83 Rockafeller Road, Piscataway, NJ 08854. **Website:** www.scarletknights.com.
Head Coach: Steve Owens. **Telephone:** (732) 445-7834. **Baseball SID:** Griffin Whitmer. **Telephone:** (732) 447-0783.
Assistant Coaches: Brendan Monaghan, Kyle Pettoruto, Mike Garza. **Telephone:** (732) 445-7746.
Home Field: Bainton Field. **Seating Capacity:** 1,500.
Outfield Dimension: LF—329, **CF**—392, **RF**—324.

SACRAMENTO STATE

Conference: Big Sky.
Mailing Address: 6000 J St., Sacramento, CA 95819. **Website:** www.hornetsports.com.
Head Coach: Reggie Christiansen. **Telephone:** (916) 278-4036. **Baseball SID:** Jason Spencer. **Telephone:** (916) 278-6896.
Assistant Coaches: Joe Wente, David Flores. **Telephone:** (916) 278-2017.
Home Field: John Smith Field. **Seating Capacity:** 1,200. **Outfield Dimension: LF**—333, **CF**—400, **RF**—333.

SACRED HEART

Conference: Northeast.
Mailing Address: William H. Pitt Center, 5151 Park Avenue, Fairfield, CT 06825. **Website:** www.sacredheart-pioneers.com.
Head Coach: Pat Egan. **Telephone:** (203) 365-7632. **Baseball SID:** Matthew Janik. **Telephone:** (203) 365-4464.
Assistant Coaches: TK Kiernan*, Isiah Daubon. **Telephone:** (203) 260-4932.
Home Field: Veteran's Park. **Seating Capacity:** 500.

ST. BONAVENTURE

Conference: Atlantic 10.
Address: St. Bonaventure, N.Y.. **Website:** GoBonnies.com.
Head Coach: Jason Rathbun. **Telephone:** 716-375-2641.
Baseball SID: Scott Eddy. **Assistant Coaches:** *, BJ Salerno.
Home Field: Fred Handler Park at McGraw-Jennings Field.
Outfield Dimension: LF—330, **CF**—403, **RF**—330.

ST. JOHN'S

Conference: Big East.
Mailing Address: 8000 Utopia Pkwy., Jamaica, NY 11439. **Website:** www.redstormsports.com.
Head Coach: Mike Hampton. **Telephone:** (718) 990-6148. **Baseball SID:** Andrew O'Connell. **Telephone:** (718) 990-1522.
Assistant Coaches: Danny Bethea, George Brown.
Home Field: Jack Kaiser Stadium. **Seating Capacity:** 3,500. **Outfield Dimension: LF**—325, **CF**—390, **RF**—325.

ST. JOSEPH'S

Conference: Atlantic 10.
Mailing Address: 5600 City Avenue, Philadelphia, PA 19131. **Website:** www.sjuhawks.com.
Head Coach: Fritz Hamburg. **Telephone:** (610) 660-1718. **Baseball SID:** Joe Greenwich. **Telephone:** (610) 660-1738.

Assistant Coaches: Ryan Wheeler, Pat Brown.
Telephone: (610) 660-2592.
Home Field: John W. Smithson Field. **Seating Capacity:** 400. **Outfield Dimension: LF**—327, **CF**—400, **RF**—330.

ST. PETER'S

Conference: Metro Atlantic.
Mailing Address: 2641 John F. Kennedy Blvd., Jersey City, N.J. 07306. **Website:** www.saintpeterspeacocks.com.
Head Coach: Grant Neary. **Telephone:** (201) 761-7319.
Baseball SID: Trevor Clifton. **Telephone:** (201) 761-7322.
Assistant Coaches: Eddie Cribby.
Home Field: Joseph J. Jaroschak Field. **Seating Capacity:** 500.

SAINT LOUIS

Conference: Atlantic 10.
Address: 3330 Laclede Ave., St. Louis, MO 63116. **Website:** slubillikens.com.
Head Coach: Darin Hendrickson. **Telephone:** 3149773172.
Baseball SID: Nick Rettig. **Assistant Coaches:** Adam Revelette*, Logan Moon.
Home Field: Billiken Sports Center. **Capacity:** 500. **Outfield Dimensions:** LF-330 CF-403 RF-330.

SAINT MARY'S

Conference: West Coast.
Mailing Address: 1928 St. Mary's Road, Moraga, CA 94575. **Website:** www.smcgaels.com.
Head Coach: Greg Moore. **Baseball SID:** Tim Fitzgerald. **Telephone:** (925) 631-4383.
Assistant Coaches: Josh Nashed, Jack Meggs.
Home Field: Louis Guisto Field. **Seating Capacity:** 1,100. **Outfield Dimension: LF**—330, **CF**—400, **RF**—330.

ST. THOMAS

Conference: Summit League.
Mailing Address: 2115 Summit Ave, St. Paul, MN, 55105. **Website:** www.tommiesports.com.
Head Coach: Chris Olean. **Telephone:** (651) 962-5924.
Baseball SID: Gene McGivern.
Assistant Coaches: Tanner Vavra, Neal Kunik.
Home Field: Koch Diamond. **Seating Capacity:** 400. **Outfield Dimension: LF**—315, **CF**—455, **RF**—330.

SAM HOUSTON STATE

Conference: Western Athletic.
Address: 1905 University Ave, Huntsville, TX 77340. **Website:** gobearkats.com.
Head Coach: Jay Sirianni.
Baseball SID: Hiring process . **Assistant Coaches:** Fuller Smith*, Shane Wedd.
Home Field: Don Sanders Stadium. **Capacity:** 1,164. **Outfield Dimensions:** LF-330, CF-400, RF-330..

SAMFORD

Conference: Southern.
Mailing Address: 800 Lakeshore Drive, Birmingham, AL 35229. **Website:** www.samfordsports.com.
Head Coach: Tony David. **Telephone:** (205) 726-4294.
Baseball SID: Joey Mullins. **Telephone:** (205) 726-2799.
Assistant Coaches: Tyler Shrout, Brad Moss. **Telephone:** (205) 726-4095.
Home Field: Joe Lee Griffin Field. **Seating Capacity:** 1,000. **Outfield Dimension: LF**—330, **CF**—399, **RF**—335.

BaseballAmerica.com

Baseball America 2023 Directory • **221**

COLLEGE

SAN DIEGO

Conference: West Coast.
Address: 5998 Alcala Park, San Diego, CA 92110.
Website: https://usdtoreros.com/sports/baseball.
Head Coach: Brock Ungricht.
Baseball SID: Anderson Haigler. **Assistant Coaches:** Matt Florer*, Erich Pfohl.
Home Field: Fowler Park. **Capacity:** 1800. **Outfield Dimensions:** LF-312 CF-393 RF-322.

SAN DIEGO STATE

Conference: Mountain West.
Mailing Address: 5500 Campanile Dr. San Diego, CA 92182. **Website:** www.goaztecs.com.
Head Coach: Mark Martinez. **Telephone:** (619) 594-1818. **Baseball SID:** Jim Solien. **Telephone:** (619) 594-2576. **Assistant Coaches:** Ryan Kirby, Shaun Cole. **Telephone:** (619) 594-6889.
Home Field: Tony Gwynn Stadium. **Seating Capacity:** 3,000. **Outfield Dimension: LF**—340, **CF**—410, **RF**—340.

SAN FRANCISCO

Conference: West Coast.
Address: 2130 Fulton St, San Francisco, CA 94117. **Website:** usfdons.com.
Head Coach: Rob DiToma.
Baseball SID: Christ Fortney. **Assistant Coaches:** Erik Supplee*, Kyle Hunt.
Home Field: Benedetti Diamond. **Capacity:** 1000. **Outfield Dimensions:** LF-330 CF-405 RF-300.

SAN JOSE STATE

Conference: Mountain West.
Mailing Address: 1 Washington Sq, San Jose, CA 95192. **Website:** www.sjsuspartans.com.
Head Coach: Brad Sanfilippo. **Baseball SID:** Sky Kerstein.
Assistant Coaches: Thomas Walker, Seth Moir.
Home Field: Excite Ballpark. **Seating Capacity:** 4,200. **Outfield Dimension: LF**—320, **CF**—390, **RF**—320.

SANTA CLARA

Conference: West Coast.
Address: 443 El Camino Real, Santa Clara, CA 95050. **Website:** https://www.santaclarabroncos.com/sports/m-basebl/index.
Head Coach: Rusty Filter.
Baseball SID: Joey Karp. **Assistant Coaches:** Jon Karcich*, Jay Brossman. **Home Field:** Stephen Schott Stadium. **Seating Capacity:** 1,500. **Outfield Dimension: LF**—340, **CF**—402, **RF**—335.

SEATTLE

Conference: Western Athletic.
Mailing Address: 901 12th Avenue, PO Box 222000, Seattle, WA 98122. **Website:** www.goseattleu.com.
Head Coach: Donny Harrel. **Telephone:** (206) 398-4399. **Baseball SID:** Russell Brown.
Assistant Coaches: Millard Dawson, Carter Capps.
Home Field: Bannerwood Park. **Seating Capacity:** 300.

SETON HALL

Conference: Big East.
Mailing Address: 400 South Orange Ave, South Orange, NJ 07079. **Website:** www.shupirates.com.
Head Coach: Robert Sheppard. **Telephone:** (973) 761-9557. **Baseball SID:** Peter Long. **Telephone:** (973) 761-9493.
Assistant Coaches: Giuseppe Papaccio, Jimmy Moran. **Telephone:** (732) 757-9534.
Home Field: Mike Sheppard Stadium. **Seating Capacity:** 1,000. **Outfield Dimension: LF**—315, **CF**—380, **RF**—330.

SIENA

Conference: Metro Atlantic.
Address: 515 Loudon Rd., Loudonville, NY 12211. **Website:** sienasaints.com.
Head Coach: Tony Rossi. **Telephone:** 15187865044.
Baseball SID: Mike Demos. **Assistant Coaches:** Joe Sheridan*, Bobby Bordieri.
Home Field: Connors Park. **Capacity:** 1000. **Outfield Dimensions:** LF-300 CF-400 RF-325.

SOUTH ALABAMA

Conference: Sun Belt.
Mailing Address: 300 Joseph E. Gottfried Drive, Mobile, AL 36688. **Website:** www.usajaguars.com.
Head Coach: Jad Prachniak. **Telephone:** (251) 414-8243. **Baseball SID:** Charlie Nichols. **Telephone:** (251) 414-8017. **Assistant Coaches:** Chris Blakey, Nick Patten. **Telephone:** (251) 460-6876.
Home Field: Stanky Field. **Seating Capacity:** 3,775. **Outfield Dimension: LF**—330, **CF**—400, **RF**—330.

SOUTH CAROLINA

Conference: SEC.
Address: 431 Williams Street, Columbia, SC. 29201. **Website:** GamecocksOnline.com.
Head Coach: Mark Kingston. **Telephone:** 803-777-7808.
Baseball SID: Kent Reichert. **Assistant Coaches:** Monte Lee*, Justin Parker.
Home Field: Founders Park. **Capacity:** 8,242. **Outfield Dimensions:** LF-325 CF-400 RF-325.

SOUTH CAROLINA-UPSTATE

Conference: Big South.
Mailing Address: 800 University Way, Spartanburg, SC 29303. **Website:** www.upstatespartans.com.
Head Coach: Mike McGuire. **Telephone:** (803) 629-5093. **Baseball SID:** Ryan Fry. **Telephone:** (864) 503-5129.
Assistant Coaches: Jacob Condra-Bogan, Kane Sweeney. **Telephone:** (864) 503-5176.
Home Field: Cleveland S. Harley Park. **Seating Capacity:** 800. **Outfield Dimension: LF**—335, **CF**—402, **RF**—335.

SOUTH DAKOTA STATE

Conference: Summit League.
Mailing Address: 2820 Marshall Center Brookings, SD. 57007. **Website:** www.gojacks.com.
Head Coach: Rob Bishop. **Telephone:** (605) 688-5625. **Baseball SID:** Jason Hove. **Telephone:** (605) 688-4623.
Assistant Coaches: Brian Grunzke, Connor Faix. **Telephone:** (605) 688-5625.
Home Field: Erv Huether Field. **Seating Capacity:** 600. **Outfield Dimension: LF**—330, **CF**—390, **RF**—330.

222 · Baseball America 2023 Directory

BaseballAmerica.com

COLLEGE

SOUTH FLORIDA

Conference: American Athletic.
Mailing Address: 4202 E. Fowler Ave Tampa FL 33620.
Website: www.gousfbulls.com.
Head Coach: Billy Mohl. **Telephone:** (813) 974-2504.
Baseball SID: Dave Albrecht.
Assistant Coaches: Bo Durkac, Karsten Whitson.
Home Field: USF Baseball Stadium. **Seating Capacity:** 3,211. **Outfield Dimension: LF**—325, **CF**—400, **RF**—330.

SOUTHEAST MISSOURI STATE

Conference: Ohio Valley.
Mailing Address: 1 University Plaza, Cape Girardeau, MO 63701. **Website:** www.semoredhawks.com.
Head Coach: Andy Sawyers. **Baseball SID:** Jeff Honza. **Telephone:** (573) 651-2933.
Assistant Coaches: Matthew Kinney, Trevor Ezell.
Home Field: Capaha Park. **Seating Capacity:** 2,000.
Outfield Dimension: LF—330, **CF**—400, **RF**—300.

SOUTHEASTERN LOUISIANA

Conference: Southland.
Mailing Address: SLU 10309, Hammond, LA 70402.
Website: www.lionsports.net.
Head Coach: Matt Riser. **Telephone:** (985) 549-5130.
Baseball SID: Damon Sunde. **Telephone:** (985) 549-3774.
Assistant Coaches: Ford Pemberton, Gerry Salisbury, Derrick Mount.
Home Field: Pat Kenelly Diamond at Alumni Field.
Outfield Dimension: LF—330, **CF**—400, **RF**—330.

SOUTHERN

Conference: Southwestern.
Mailing Address: A.W. Mumford Fieldhouse, PO Box 9942, Baton Rouge, LA 70813. **Website:** www.gojag-sports.com.
Head Coach: Chris Crenshaw. **Telephone:** (225) 771-3882. **Baseball SID:** Rodney Kirschner. **Telephone:** (225) 771-5609.
Assistant Coaches: Daniel Dulin, TJ Perkins.
Home Field: Lee-Hines Field. **Seating Capacity:** 1,500.

SOUTHERN CALIFORNIA

Conference: Pac-12.
Mailing Address: 3501 Watt Way, Los Angeles, CA 90089. **Website:** www.usctrojans.com.
Head Coach: Andy Stankiewicz. **Telephone:** (213) 740-8446. **Baseball SID:** Jacob Breems. **Telephone:** (213) 740-3809.
Assistant Coaches: Travis Jewett, Seth Etherton, Andy Jenkins. **Telephone:** (213) 740-8447.
Home Field: Dedeaux Field. **Seating Capacity:** 2,500.
Outfield Dimension: LF—335, **CF**—395, **RF**—335.

SOUTHERN ILLINOIS

Conference: Missouri Valley.
Address: 1263 Lincoln Dr, Carbondale, IL 62901.
Website: https://siusalukis.com/sports/baseball.
Head Coach: Lance Rhodes. **Telephone:** 618-453-3794.
Baseball SID: Tim McCaughan. **Assistant Coaches:** Brett Peel*, Austin Tribby.
Home Field: Itchy Jones Stadium at Abe Martin Field.
Capacity: 2,000. **Outfield Dimensions:** LF-330 CF-390 RF-330.

SOUTHERN ILLINOIS-EDWARDSVILLE

Conference: Ohio Valley.
Mailing Address: 1 Hairpin Dr, Edwardsville, IL 62026.
Website: www.siuecougars.com.
Head Coach: Sean Lyons. **Telephone:** (618) 650-2032.
Baseball SID: Joe Pott. **Telephone:** (618) 650-2860.
Assistant Coaches: Joe Kelch, Bailey Vuylsteke, Adam Vasil. **Telephone:** (618) 650-2032.
Home Field: Roy E. Lee Field at Simmons Baseball Complex. **Seating Capacity:** 1,000. **Outfield Dimension: LF**—330, **CF**—390, **RF**—330.

SOUTHERN MISSISSIPPI

Conference: Sun Belt.
Address: 190 College Dr. Hattiesburg, MS 39402.
Website: .
Head Coach: Scott Berry.
Baseball SID: Jack Duggan. **Assistant Coaches:** Travis Creel*, Christian Ostrander.
Home Field: Pete Taylor Park. **Capacity:** 5500.
Outfield Dimensions: LF-340 CF-400 RF-340.

STANFORD

Conference: Pac-12.
Address: 641 Campus Drive, Stanford, CA 94305.
Website: www.gostanford.com/bsb.
Head Coach: David Esquer. **Telephone:** 650-723-4528.
Baseball SID: Tyler Geivett. **Assistant Coaches:** Thomas Eager*, Steve Rodriguez.
Home Field: Klein Field at Sunken Diamond.
Capacity: 4,000. **Outfield Dimensions:** LF-335 CF-400 RF-335.

STEPHEN F. AUSTIN

Conference: Western Athletic.
Mailing Address: PO Box 13010, SFA Station, Nacogdoches, TX 75962. **Website:** www.sfajacks.com.
Head Coach: Johnny Cardenas. **Baseball SID:** Chelsea Groves. **Telephone:** (936) 468-2606.
Assistant Coaches: Dylan Belanger, Caleb Clowers. **Telephone:** (936) 468-7796.
Home Field: Jaycees Field. **Seating Capacity:** 740.
Outfield Dimension: LF—320, **CF**—390, **RF**—320.

STETSON

Conference: ASUN.
Mailing Address: 421 N. Woodland Blvd., Unit 8359, DeLand, FL 32723. **Website:** www.gohatters.com.
Head Coach: Steve Trimper. **Telephone:** (386) 822-8106. **Baseball SID:** Ricky Hazel. **Telephone:** (386) 822-8130.
Assistant Coaches: Shane Gierke, Daniel Latham. **Telephone:** (386) 822-8730.
Home Field: Melching Field at Conrad Park. **Seating Capacity:** 2,500. **Outfield Dimension: LF**—335, **CF**—403, **RF**—335.

STONEHILL COLLEGE

Conference: Northeast.
Address: 320 Easton Street Easton, Mass. 02356.
Website: www.stonehillskyhawks.com/.
Head Coach: Pat Boen. **Telephone:** (508) 565-1351.
Baseball SID: James Wouralis. **Assistant Coaches:** Zach Sultar*, Lou Proietti.
Home Field: Lou Gorman Field. **Outfield Dimensions: LF**—325, **CF**—390, **RF**—325

BaseballAmerica.com

Baseball America 2023 Directory • **223**

COLLEGE

STONY BROOK

Conference: America East.
Mailing Address: 100 Nicolls Road, Stony Brook, NY 11794. **Website:** www.stonybrookathletics.com.
Head Coach: Matt Senk. **Telephone:** (631) 632-9226.
Baseball SID: Cameron Boon. **Telephone:** (631) 632-7289. **Assistant Coaches:** Jim Martin, Alex Brosnan. **Telephone:** (631) 632-9226.
Home Field: Joe Nathan Field. **Seating Capacity:** 1,500. **Outfield Dimension: LF**—330, **CF**—390, **RF**—330.

TARLETON STATE

Conference: Western Athletic.
Address: 1033 W Washington St. Stephenville, Tx 76401. **Website:** TarletonSports.com.
Head Coach: Aaron Meade. **Telephone:** 254.968.1666.
Baseball SID: Trey Burnett. **Assistant Coaches:** Dallas Reed*, Wes Hunt.
Home Field: Tarleton Baseball Complex . **Capacity:** 1,500. **Outfield Dimensions:** LF-320 CF-400 RF-320.

TENNESSEE

Conference: SEC.
Address: 1511 Pat Head Summitt St., Knoxville, TN, 37996. **Website:** UTSports.com.
Head Coach: Tony Vitello. **Telephone:** 865-974-2057.
Baseball SID: Sean Barows. **Assistant Coaches:** Josh Elander*, Frank Anderson.
Home Field: Lindsey Nelson Stadium. **Capacity:** 4,045.
Outfield Dimensions: LF—320, **CF**—390, **RF**—320.

TENNESSEE-MARTIN

Conference: Ohio Valley.
Mailing Address: 554 University Street, Martin, TN, 38237. **Website:** www.utmsports.com.
Head Coach: Ryan Jenkins. **Telephone:** (731) 881-3691. **Baseball SID:** Brandon Burke. **Telephone:** (731) 881-7694.
Assistant Coaches: Bill White, Pat Cottrell.
Home Field: Skyhawk Baseball Field. **Seating Capacity:** 500. **Outfield Dimension: LF**—330, **CF**—385, **RF**—330.

TENNESSEE TECH

Conference: Ohio Valley.
Mailing Address: 1100 McGee Blvd. Cookeville TN 38501. **Website:** www.ttusports.com.
Head Coach: Matt Bragga. **Telephone:** (931) 372-3853. **Baseball SID:** Mike Lehman. **Telephone:** (931) 372-3088.
Assistant Coaches: Jim Miksis, Mikey White. **Telephone:** (931) 372-3853.
Home Field: Quillen Field at Bush Stadium at the Averitt Express Baseball Complex. **Seating Capacity:** 1,100. **Outfield Dimension: LF**—329, **CF**—405, **RF**—330.

TEXAS

Conference: Big 12.
Mailing Address: PO Box 7399, Austin, TX 78713-7399. **Website:** www.texassports.com.
Head Coach: David Pierce. **Telephone:** (512) 471-5732. **Baseball SID:** Kevin Rodriguez. **Telephone:** (512) 471-2078.
Assistant Coaches: Steve Rodriguez, Woody Williams, Caleb Longley.
Home Field: UFCU Disch-Falk Field. **Seating Capacity:** 6,649. **Outfield Dimension: LF**—340, **CF**—400, **RF**—325.

TEXAS A&M

Conference: SEC.
Address: 756 Houston Ave.; Kyle Field Room W127; College Station, TX 77840. **Website:** 12thman.com.
Head Coach: Jim Schlossnagle. **Baseball SID:** Ben Rikard. **Assistant Coaches:** Nolan Cain*, Nate Yeskie.
Home Field: Olsen Field at Blue Bell Park.
Capacity: 6,100.
Outfield Dimensions: LF—330, **CF**—400, **RF**—375.

TEXAS A&M-CORPUS CHRISTI

Conference: Southland.
Address: 6300 Ocean Dr, Corpus Christi, TX 78412.
Website: https://goislanders.com/.
Head Coach: Scott Malone. **Telephone:** 3618253720.
Baseball SID: Taylor Riemersma. **Assistant Coaches:** Matt Parker (Asst. Coach)*, Scott Kelly (Asst. Coach 2).
Home Field: Chapman Field. **Capacity:** 750. **Outfield Dimensions: LF**—330, **CF**—404, **RF**—330.

TEXAS-ARLINGTON

Conference: Sun Belt.
Mailing Address: Gilstrap Athletic Center, 1309 W. Mitchell Street, Arlington, TX 76019-0079.
Website: www.utamavs.com.
Head Coach: Clay Van Hook. **Telephone:** (817) 272-9744. **Baseball SID:** Ian Applegate. **Telephone:** (817) 272-9610.
Assistant Coaches: Mike Trapasso, Mike Taylor. **Telephone:** (817) 272-7170.
Home Field: Clay Gould Ballpark. **Seating Capacity:** 1,600. **Outfield Dimension: LF**—330, **CF**—400, **RF**—330.

TEXAS-RIO GRANDE VALLEY

Conference: Western Athletic.
Address: 1201 W. University Dr. Edinburg, TX 78539.
Website: GoUTRGV.com,
Head Coach: Derek Matlock. **Telephone:** 956-665-2235.
Baseball SID: Jonah Goldberg. **Assistant Coaches:** Robert Martinez*, Kyle Kilgo.
Home Field: UTRGV Baseball Stadium. **Capacity:** 5,000. **Outfield Dimensions: LF**—325, **CF**—410, **RF**—325.

TEXAS-SAN ANTONIO

Conference: Conference USA.
Head Coach: Patrick Hallmark. **Telephone:** 12105803848.
Baseball SID: Alma Solis. **Assistant Coaches:** Ryan Aguayo*, Zach Butler.
Home Field: Roadrunner Field. **Capacity:** 2000.
Outfield Dimensions: LF-340 CF-400 RF-340.

TEXAS CHRISTIAN

Conference: Big 12.
Mailing Address: TCU Athletics Department, TCU Box 297600, Fort Worth, TX 76129. **Website:** www.gofrogs.com.
Head Coach: Kirk Saarloos. **Baseball SID:** Brandie Davidson. **Telephone:** (817) 257-7479.
Assistant Coaches: TJ Bruce, John DiLaura.
Home Field: Charlie and Marie Lupton Baseball Stadium at Williams-Reilly Field. **Seating Capacity:** 4,500.
Outfield Dimensions: LF—330, **CF**—400, **RF**—330.

COLLEGE

TEXAS SOUTHERN

Conference: Southwestern.
Mailing Address: Texas Southern Athletics, 3100 Cleburne Street, Houston, TX 77004. **Website:** www.tsusports.com.
Head Coach: Michael Robertson. **Telephone:** (713) 313-4315. **Baseball SID:** Ryan McGinty. **Telephone:** (713) 313-6829.
Assistant Coaches: Ricky Urbano.
Home Field: MacGregor Park.

TEXAS STATE

Conference: Sun Belt.
Mailing Address: Texas State University Department of Athletics Darren B. Casey Athletic Administration Complex 601 University Drive San Marcos Texas 78666. **Website:** www.txstatebobcats.com.
Head Coach: Steven Trout. **Telephone:** (512) 245-3383. **Baseball SID:** Phillip Pongratz. **Telephone:** (512) 245-4692.
Assistant Coaches: Josh Blakley, Chad Massengale. **Telephone:** (512) 245-3383.
Home Field: Bobcat Ballpark. **Seating Capacity:** 2,500. **Outfield Dimension: LF**—330, **CF**—405, **RF**—330.

TEXAS TECH

Conference: Big 12.
Mailing Address: 2901 Drive of Champions Ste. 200 Lubbock, TX 79409. **Website:** www.texastech.com.
Head Coach: Tim Tadlock. **Telephone:** (806) 834-4646. **Baseball SID:** Matt Burkholder.
Assistant Coaches: J-Bob Thomas, Matt Gardner.
Home Field: Dan Law Field at Rip Griffin Park.
Seating Capacity: 4,432. **Outfield Dimension: LF**—327, **CF**—402, **RF**—327.

TOLEDO

Conference: Mid-American.
Address: 2801 W Bancroft Street. **Website:** utrockets.com.
Head Coach: Rob Reinstetle. **Telephone:** 4195306263. **Baseball SID:** Chris Cullum. **Assistant Coaches:** Nick McIntyre*, John Sheehan.
Home Field: Scott Park. **Capacity:** 1,000. **Outfield Dimensions:** LF-330 CF-400 RF-300.

TOWSON

Conference: Colonial.
Mailing Address: John B. Schuerholz Park - 8000 York Road - Towson, MD 21204. **Website:** www.towsontigers.com.
Head Coach: Matt Tyner. **Telephone:** (410) 704-2646. **Baseball SID:** David Vatz. **Telephone:** (410) 704-3102.
Assistant Coaches: Tanner Biagini, Mike Ruppenthal. **Telephone:** (410) 704-2646.
Home Field: John B. Schuerholz Park. **Seating Capacity:** 1,000. **Outfield Dimension: LF**—312, **CF**—424, **RF**—301.

TROY

Conference: Sun Belt.
Mailing Address: 5000 Veterans Memorial Drive Troy , AL 36082. **Website:** www.troytrojans.com.
Head Coach: Skylar Meade. **Baseball SID:** Brandon Mostyn.
Assistant Coaches: Adam Godwin.

Telephone: (217) 260-2069.
Home Field: Riddle-Pace Field. **Seating Capacity:** 2,500. **Outfield Dimension: LF**—340, **CF**—400, **RF**—310.

TULANE

Conference: American Athletic.
Mailing Address: 333 Ben Weiner Drive, New Orleans, LA 70118. **Website:** www.tulanegreenwave.com.
Head Coach: Jay Uhlman. **Telephone:** (504) 862-8216. **Baseball SID:** Tom Symonds. **Telephone:** (504) 862-8249.
Assistant Coaches: Justin Bridgman. **Telephone:** (504) 314-7203.
Home Field: Greer Field at Turchin Stadium. **Seating Capacity:** 5,000. **Outfield Dimension: LF**—325, **CF**—400, **RF**—325.

UC DAVIS

Conference: Big West.
Mailing Address: Hickey Gym 264, One Shields Ave., Davis, CA 95616. **Website:** www.ucdavisaggies.com.
Head Coach: Tommy Nicholson. **Baseball SID:** Matt Murphy. **Telephone:** (530) 752-8050.
Assistant Coaches: Andrew Ayers, Zack Thornton.
Home Field: Phil Swimley Field at Dobbins Stadium.
Seating Capacity: 3,500. **Outfield Dimension: LF**—310, **CF**—410, **RF**—310.

UC IRVINE

Conference: Big West.
Address: Anteater Ballpark. **Website:** ucirvinesports.com.
Head Coach: Ben Orloff.
Baseball SID: Alex Croteau. **Assistant Coaches:** JT Bloodworth*, Danny Bibona.
Home Field: Anteater Ballpark. **Seating Capacity:** 1,500. **Outfield Dimension: LF**—335, **CF**—408, **RF**—335.

Conference: Pac-12.
Address: UCLA. **Website:** UCLABruins.com.
Head Coach: John Savage.
Baseball SID: Andrew Wagner. **Assistant Coaches:** Bryant Ward*, Niko Gallego.
Home Field: Jackie Robinson Stadium. **Capacity:** 1,838. **Outfield Dimensions:** LF-330 CF-390 RF-330.

UC RIVERSIDE

Conference: Big West.
Address: 900 university ave riverside ca 92507. **Website:** gohighlanders.com.
Head Coach: Justin Johnson .
Baseball SID: Chelsea Pfohl . **Assistant Coaches:** Lloyd Acosta *, Mike Burns .
Home Field: Riverside Sports Complex. **Outfield Dimension: LF**—330, **CF**—400, **RF**—330.

UC SAN DIEGO

Conference: Big West.
Mailing Address: 9500 Gilman Drive, RIMAC 4th Floor, La Jolla, CA 92093-0531. **Website:** www.ucsdtritons.com.
Head Coach: Eric Newman. **Telephone:** (858) 534-8162. **Baseball SID:** Kendrick Mooney. **Telephone:** (858) 534-8451.
Assistant Coaches: Bryson LeBlanc, Matt Harvey. **Telephone:** (858) 246-1648.
Home Field: Triton Ballpark. **Seating Capacity:** 500. **Outfield Dimension: LF**—330, **CF**—400, **RF**—330.

Baseball America 2023 Directory • **225**

COLLEGE

UC SANTA BARBARA

Conference: Big West.
Mailing Address: ICA Building Santa Barbara, CA 93106-5200. **Website:** www.ucsbgauchos.com.
Head Coach: Andrew Checketts. **Telephone:** (805) 893-3690. **Baseball SID:** Daniel Moebus-Bowles. **Telephone:** (805) 893-8603.
Assistant Coaches: Dylan Jones, Donegal Fergus. **Telephone:** (805) 893-3690.
Home Field: Caesar Uyesaka Stadium. **Seating Capacity:** 1,000. **Outfield Dimension: LF**—335, **CF**—400, **RF**—335.

UNC ASHEVILLE

Conference: Big South.
Mailing Address: 1 University Heights, Asheville, NC 28804. **Website:** www.uncabulldogs.com.
Head Coach: Scott Friedholm. **Telephone:** (828) 251-6920. **Baseball SID:** Andy Fisher. **Telephone:** (828) 251-6931.
Assistant Coaches: Chris Bresnahan, Kyle Ward. **Telephone:** (828) 250-2309.
Home Field: Greenwood Field. **Seating Capacity:** 1,000. **Outfield Dimension: LF**—320, **CF**—390, **RF**—330.

UNC GREENSBORO

Conference: Southern.
Mailing Address: 1400 Spring Garden St, Greensboro, NC 27412. **Website:** www.uncgspartans.com.
Head Coach: Billy Godwin. **Baseball SID:** Jesika Moore. **Assistant Coaches:** Greg Starbuck, Cody Ellis.
Home Field: UNCG Baseball Stadium. **Seating Capacity:** 3,500. **Outfield Dimension: LF**—340, **CF**—405, **RF**—340.

UNC WILMINGTON

Conference: Colonial.
Address: 610 S. College Road, Wilmington, NC 28403. **Website:** www.uncwsports.com.
Head Coach: Randy Hood. **Telephone:** 9109623793. **Baseball SID:** Tom Riordan. **Assistant Coaches:** Chris Moore*, Kelly Secrest.
Home Field: Brooks Field. **Capacity:** 3500. **Outfield Dimensions:** LF-340 CF-390 RF-340.

UTAH

Conference: Pac-12.
Mailing Address: 1825 E South Campus Drive, Salt Lake City UT, 84112. **Website:** www.utahutes.com.
Head Coach: Gary Henderson. **Baseball SID:** Ryan Gallant.
Assistant Coaches: Mike Brown, Todd Guilliams.
Home Field: Smith's Ballpark. **Seating Capacity:** 14,511. **Outfield Dimension: LF**—345, **CF**—420, **RF**—315.

UTAH TECH

Conference: Western Athletic.
Address: 225 S. 700 E., St. George, UT 84770. **Website:** utahtechtrailblazers.com/.
Head Coach: Chris Pfatenhauer. **Telephone:** 435-652-7530.
Baseball SID: Steve Johnson. **Assistant Coaches:** Bobby Rinard*, Justin Hixson.
Home Field: Bruce Hurst Field. **Capacity:** 2500. **Outfield Dimensions:** LF-325 CF-380 RF-335.

UTAH VALLEY

Conference: Western Athletic.
Mailing Address: 800 W University Pkwy, Orem, UT 84058. **Website:** www.gouvu.com.
Head Coach: Eddie Smith. **Baseball SID:** James Warnick. **Telephone:** (801) 863-6231.
Assistant Coaches: Nate Rasmussen, Grant Kukuk.
Home Field: UCCU Ballpark. **Seating Capacity:** 5,000. **Outfield Dimension: LF**—306, **CF**—426, **RF**—309.

VALPARAISO

Conference: Missouri Valley.
Address: 1700 Chapel Drive, Valparaiso, IN. 46383. **Website:** valpoathletics.com.
Head Coach: Brian Schmack. **Telephone:** 219-464-6117.
Baseball SID: Brandon Vickrey. **Assistant Coaches:** Kory Winter*.
Home Field: Emory G. Bauer Field. **Capacity:** 1,000. **Outfield Dimensions:** LF-330 CF-400 RF-330.

VANDERBILT

Conference: Southeastern.
Mailing Address: 2601 Jess Neely Drive, Nashville,TN 37212. **Website:** www.vucommodores.com.
Head Coach: Tim Corbin. **Telephone:** (615) 322-3716. **Baseball SID:** Josh Foster. **Telephone:** (615) 322-3716.
Assistant Coaches: Scott Brown, Mike Baxter, Tyler Shewmaker. **Telephone:** (615) 322-3716.
Home Field: Hawkins Field. **Seating Capacity:** 3,700. **Outfield Dimension: LF**—310, **CF**—400, **RF**—330.

VILLANOVA

Conference: Big East.
Mailing Address: 800 Lancaster Avenue, Villanova, PA 19085. **Website:** www.villanova.com.
Head Coach: Kevin Mulvey. **Baseball SID:** Drew McDonald.
Assistant Coaches: Eddie Brown, Jabin Weaver.
Home Field: Villanova Ballpark at Plymouth. **Seating Capacity:** 750. **Outfield Dimension: LF**—320, **CF**—400, **RF**—320.

VIRGINIA

Conference: ACC.
Address: Disharoon Park - Po Box 400839 - Charlottesville,Va, 22904-4839. **Website:** virginiasports.com.
Head Coach: Brian O'Connor. **Telephone:** (434) 982-5129.
Baseball Sid: Scott Fitzgerald. **Assistant Coaches:** Kevin Mcmullan*, Matt Kirby.
Home Field: Disharoon Park. **Capacity:** 5,919. **Outfield Dimension: LF**—332, **CF**—404, **RF**—332.

VIRGINIA COMMONWEALTH

Conference: Atlantic 10.
Mailing Address: 1300 W. Broad St. Box 842003 Richmond, Va. 23284. **Website:** www.vcuathletics.com.
Head Coach: Bradley LeCroy. **Baseball SID:** Andy Lohman.
Assistant Coaches: Andrew Cox, Tanner Gordon.
Home Field: The Diamond. **Seating Capacity:** 9,560. **Outfield Dimension: LF**—330, **CF**—402, **RF**—330.

COLLEGE

VIRGINIA MILITARY INSTITUTE

Conference: Southern.
Mailing Address: 401 N Main Street Lexington, VA 24450. **Website:** www.vmikeydets.com.
Head Coach: Sam Roberts. **Telephone:** (540) 464-7601. **Baseball SID:** Mike Carpenter. **Telephone:** (540) 464-7015. **Assistant Coaches:** Aaron Lesiak, Ray Noe, Tyler Cox. **Telephone:** (540) 464-7605.
Home Field: Gray-Minor Stadium. **Seating Capacity:** 1,400. **Outfield Dimension: LF**—320, **CF**—380, **RF**—330.

VIRGINIA TECH

Conference: ACC.
Address: 260 Duck Pond Dr Blacksburg, VA 24060.
Website: hokiesports.com.
Head Coach: John Szefc.
Baseball SID: Michael Skovan. **Assistant Coaches:** Kurt A Elbin*, Ryan Fecteau.
Home Field: English Field at Atlantic Union Bank Park. **Seating Capacity:** 4,000. **Outfield Dimension: LF**—330, **CF**—400, **RF**—330.

WAGNER

Conference: Northeast.
Mailing Address: One Campus Road, Staten Island, NY, 10301. **Website:** www.wagnerathletics.com.
Head Coach: Craig Noto. **Telephone:** (718) 420-4121. **Baseball SID:** Kamaili O'Brian.
Assistant Coaches: Devin Burke.
Home Field: Richmond County Bank Ballpark.
Seating Capacity: 6,500. **Outfield Dimension: LF**—318, **CF**—390, **RF**—322.

WAKE FOREST

Conference: Atlantic Coast.
Mailing Address: 1834 Wake Forest Rd., Winston-Salem, N.C. 27106. **Website:** www.godeacs.com.
Head Coach: Tom Walter. **Baseball SID:** Ryan Sosic.
Assistant Coaches: Bill Cilento, Corey Muscara.
Home Field: David F. Couch Ballpark. **Seating Capacity:** 3,823. **Outfield Dimension: LF**—310, **CF**—400, **RF**—300.

WASHINGTON

Conference: Pac-12.
Mailing Address: Box 354070, Graves Building, Seattle, WA 98195. **Website:** www.gohuskies.com.
Head Coach: Jason Kelly. **Telephone:** (206) 616-4335. **Baseball SID:** Mike Bruscas. **Telephone:** (908) 447-0783.
Assistant Coaches: Jake Silverman*, Billy Boyer.
Home Field: Husky Ballpark. **Seating Capacity:** 2,200.
Outfield Dimension: LF—327, **CF**—395, **RF**—317.

WASHINGTON STATE

Conference: Pac-12.
Mailing Address: Cougar Baseball Complex, Pullman, WA, 99163. **Website:** www.wsucougars.com.
Head Coach: Brian Green. **Telephone:** (509) 335-0250. **Baseball SID:** Bobby Alworth. **Telephone:** (509) 335-5785.
Assistant Coaches: Jake Valentine, Anthony Claggett. **Telephone:** (509) 335-0211.
Home Field: Bailey-Brayton Field. **Seating Capacity:** 3,500. **Outfield Dimension: LF**—335, **CF**—400, **RF**—335.

WEST VIRGINIA

Conference: Big 12.
Mailing Address: 1 Waterfront Place, Morgantown, WV 26501. **Website:** www.wvusports.com.
Head Coach: Randy Mazey. **Baseball SID:** Adam Grossman.
Assistant Coaches: Steve Sabins, Mark Ginther.
Home Field: Wagener Field at Monongalia County Ballpark. **Seating Capacity:** 3,500. **Outfield Dimension: LF**—325, **CF**—400, **RF**—325.

WESTERN CAROLINA

Conference: Southern.
Mailing Address: Ramsey Center - Athletics; 92 Catamount Road, Cullowhee, N.C. 28723. **Website:** www.catamountsport.com.
Head Coach: Alan Beck. **Telephone:** (828) 227-2021. **Baseball SID:** Daniel Hooker. **Telephone:** (828) 227-2339.
Assistant Coaches: Jeff Korte, Derek Beasley. **Telephone:** (828) 227-2022.
Home Field: Ronnie G. Childress Field at Hennon Stadium. **Seating Capacity:** 1,500. **Outfield Dimension: LF**—325, **CF**—395, **RF**—325.

WESTERN ILLINOIS

Conference: Summit League.
Mailing Address: 1 University Circle Macomb, Illinois 61455. **Website:** www.goleathernecks.com.
Head Coach: Taylor Sheriff. **Baseball SID:** Keion Robinson. **Telephone:** (309) 298-1133.
Assistant Coaches: Michael Keeran*, Mike Snyder, Chasen Claus. **Telephone:** (814) 525-8881.
Home Field: Alfred D. Boyer Stadium. **Seating Capacity:** 500. **Outfield Dimension: LF**—330, **CF**—400, **RF**—330.

WESTERN KENTUCKY

Conference: Conference USA.
Mailing Address: 1605 Champions Ave, Bowling Green, KY 42101. **Website:** www.wkusports.com.
Head Coach: Mark Rardin. **Baseball SID:**Jack Todd.
Assistant Coaches: Rob Fournier, Dillon Napoleon.
Home Field: Nick Denes Field. **Seating Capacity:** 1,500. **Outfield Dimension: LF**—330, **CF**—400, **RF**—330.

WESTERN MICHIGAN

Conference: Mid-American.
Mailing Address: 1903 W. Michigan Ave, Kalamazoo, MI 49008. **Website:** www.wmubroncos.com.
Head Coach: Billy Gernon. **Baseball SID:** Rob Low. **Telephone:** (269) 387-4122.
Assistant Coaches: Cory Mee, Jordan Keur.
Home Field: Robert J. Bobb Stadium at Hyames Field. **Seating Capacity:** 2,500. **Outfield Dimension: LF**—310, **CF**—395, **RF**—335.

WICHITA STATE

Conference: American Athletic.
Mailing Address: 1845 Fairmount Street, Wichita, KS, 67260. **Website:** www.goshockers.com.
Head Coach: Loren Hibbs. **Telephone:** (316) 978-3636. **Baseball SID:** Denning Gerig. **Telephone:** (316) 978-5461.
Assistant Coaches: Mike Sirianni*, Mike Pelfrey. **Telephone:** (316) 978-3636.
Home Field: Eck Stadium. **Seating Capacity:** 8,153.
Outfield Dimension: LF—330, **CF**—390, **RF**—330.

COLLEGE

WILLIAM & MARY

Conference: Colonial.
Address: Williamsburg, VA. **Website:** .
Head Coach: Mike McRae.
Baseball SID:: John Moyer. **Assistant Coaches:** Paul Panik*, Dan Sweeney.
Home Field: Plumeri Park. **Capacity:** . **Outfield Dimensions: LF**—330, **CF**—400, **RF**—330.

WINTHROP

Conference: Big South.
Address: 1162 Eden Terrace Rock Hill , SC 29733.
Website: www.winthropeagles.com.
Head Coach: Tom Riginos. **Telephone:** 864-903-9796.
Baseball SID: Brett Redden. **Assistant Coach:** Austin Hill .
Home Field: Winthrop Ballpark. **Capacity:** 1900.
Outfield Dimensions: LF—325, **CF**—400, **RF**—325.

WISCONSIN-MILWAUKEE

Conference: Horizon.
Address: 3409 N Downer Ave Milwaukee, WI 53211.
Website: mkepanthers.com.
Head Coach: Scott Doffek.
Baseball SID: Cody Bohl. **Assistant Coaches:** Shaun Wegner*, Cory Bigler.
Home Field: Franklin Field. **Capacity:** 4,000. **Outfield Dimensions: LF**—330, **CF**—408, **RF**—330.

WOFFORD

Conference: SoCon.
Address: 429 N church St Spartanburg SC 29303.
Website: woffordterriers.com.
Head Coach: Todd Interdonato. **Telephone:** 864597.
Baseball SID: Wyatt Streett. **Assistant Coaches:** Josh Schulman*, JJ Edwards.
Home Field: Russell C King. **Capacity:** 980. **Outfield Dimensions: LF**—315, **CF**—390, **RF**—330.

WRIGHT STATE

Conference: Horizon League.
Mailing Address: 3640 Colonel Glenn Hwy, Dayton, OH 45435. **Website:** www.wsuraiders.com.
Head Coach: Alex Sogard. **Baseball SID:** Nick Phillips.
Assistant Coaches: Nate Metzger,* Chase Stone.
Home Field: Nischwitz Stadium. **Seating Capacity:** 1,500. **Outfield Dimension: LF**—330, **CF**—400, **RF**—330.

XAVIER

Conference: Big East.
Mailing Address: 3800 Victory Pkwy Cincinnati OH 45207. **Website:** www.goxavier.com.
Head Coach: Billy O'Conner. **Telephone:** (513) 745-2890. **Baseball SID:** Hayley Schletker.
Assistant Coaches: Doug Willey, Joey Bellini.
Home Field: Hayden Field. **Seating Capacity:** 500.
Outfield Dimension: LF—310, **CF**—380, **RF**—310.

YALE

Conference: Ivy League.
Address: 20 Tower Parkway, New Haven, CT 06511.
Website: yalebulldogs.com.
Head Coach: Brian Hamm.
Baseball SID: Ernie Bertothy. **Assistant Coaches:** Chris Wojick*, Corey Keane.
Home Field: George H.W. Bush '48 Field. **Capacity:** 5400. **Outfield Dimensions: LF**—330, **CF**—405, **RF**—330

YOUNGSTOWN STATE

Conference: Horizon League.
Mailing Address: 1 University Plaza, Youngstown, Ohio 44555. **Website:** www.ysusports.com.
Head Coach: Dan Bertolini. **Baseball SID:** Drae Smith.
Telephone: (330) 941-8359.
Assistant Coaches: Eric Bunnell, Shane Davis*.
Home Field: Eastwood Field. **Seating Capacity:** 6,000.
Outfield Dimension: LF—335, **CF**—405, **RF**—335.

AMATEUR & YOUTH

AMATEUR/YOUTH

INTERNATIONAL ORGANIZATIONS

WORLD BASEBALL SOFTBALL CONFEDERATION

Headquarters: Maison du Sport International—54, Avenue de Rhodanie, 1007 Lausanne, Switzerland. **Telephone:** (+41-21) 318-82-40. **Fax:** (41-21) 318-82-41.

Website: www.wbsc.org. **E-Mail:** office@wbsc.org. **Year Founded:** 1938.

President: Riccardo Fraccari. **Secretary General:** Beng Choo Low. **Vice Presidents:** Willi Kaltschmitt, Beatrice Allen, Luís Rafael Mejía Oviedo. **Executive Vice President, Baseball:** Jeffrey Jr. Koo. **Executive Vice President, Softball:** Craig Cress. **Treasurer:** Angelo Vicini.

Members At-Large, Baseball: Paul Seiler, Ron Finlay. **Member At-Large, Softball:** Taeko Utsugi, Gabriel Waage. **Athlete Representatives For Baseball:** Ayako Rokkaku, Randolph Oduber. **Athlete Representatives for Softball:** Monica Abbott, Cole Vans. **Global Ambassadors:** Andrés Manuel López Obrador, Antonio Castro, Melitón Sánchez.

Executive Director: Michael Schmidt. **Assistant To The President:** Victor Isola. **Anti-Doping Manager:** Victor Isola. **Media and Communications Director:** Richard Baker. **Membership Manager:** Francesca Fabretto. **Events Manager:** Joan Garcia. **Accounting Manager:** Laetitia Barbey.

CONTINENTAL ASSOCIATIONS

CONFEDERATION PAN AMERICANA DE BEISBOL (COPABE)

Mailing Address: Calle 3, Francisco Filos, Vista Hermosa, Edificio 74, Planta Baja Local No. 1, Panama City, Panama. **Telephone:** (507) 229-8684. **Website:** wbscamericas.com/en. **E-Mail:** emayorgab@yahoo.com

Chairman: Eduardo De Bello (Panama). **Secretary General:** Hector Pereyra (Dominican Republic).

AFRICA BASEBALL SOFTBALL ASSOCIATION (ABSA)

Office Address: Paiko Road, Chanchaga, Minna, Niger State, Nigeria.

Mailing Address: P.M.B. 150, Minna, Niger State, Nigeria.

Telephone: (234) 8037188491. **Website:** wbscafrica. org. **E-mail:** absasecretariat@yahoo.com

President: Sabeur Jlajla. **Vice President Baseball:** Etienne N'Guessan. **Vice President Softball:** Fridah Shiroya. **Secretary General:** Ibrahim N'Diaye. **Treasurer:** Moira Dempsey. **Executive Director:** Lieutenant Colonel (rtd) Friday Ichide. **Deputy Executive Director:** Francoise Kameni-Lele.

BASEBALL FEDERATION OF ASIA

Mailing Address: 9F. -3, No. 288, Sec 6 Civic Blvd., Xinyi Dist., Taipei City, Taiwan (R.O.C.). **Telephone:** 886-227910336. **Website:** wbscasia.org/en.

E-Mail Address: bfa@baseballasia.org

Presidents: Tom Peng, Beng Choo Low. **Vice Presidents:** Suzuki Yoshinobu, Chen Xu, Susan Zhang Xuan. **Secretary General:** Hua-Wei Lin, Sallw Lim Swee Gaik. **Members At Large:** Allan Mak, Alfonso Martin Eizmendi, Pervaiz Shah Khawar. **Directors:** Richard Lin, Yi Chuan Pan, Kazuhiro Tawa, Chang Chia Hsing.

EUROPEAN BASEBALL CONFEDERATION

Mailing Address: Savska cesta 137, 10 000 Zagreb, Croatia. **Telephone:** 43-17744114. **E-Mail Address:** office@wbsceurope.org . **Website:** www.wbsceurope.org/en

Presidents: Didier Seminel (France), Gabriel Waage (Czech Republic). **Secretary General:** Krunoslav Karin. **Treasurer:** Eddy Van Straelen. **Members At Large:** Petr Ditrich, Marco Manucci, Roderick Balk, Youri Alkalay, Kristian Palvia, Mette Nissen Jakobsen.

BASEBALL CONFEDERATION OF OCEANIA

Mailing Address: 48 Partridge Way, Mooroolbark, Victoria 3138, Australia. **Telephone:** +61-394170022. **E-Mail Address:** office@wbscoceania.org

Secretary General: Chet Gray. **Vice Presidents:** Laurent Cassier, Rex Capil. **Members At Large:** Inoke Niubalavu, Ralph Tarasomo, Hynes David, Vaughan Wyber.

ISG BASEBALL

Mailing Address: 3829 S Oakbrook Dr. Greenfield, WI 53228. **Telephone:** 414-704-5467. **E-Mail Address:** isgbaseball14@gmail.com. **Website:** isgbaseball.com. **President:** Tom O'Connell. **Vice President:** Peter Caliendo. **Secretary/Treasurer:** Randy Town. **Board Members:** Jim Jones, John Casey, Ron Maestri, Pat Doyle, John Vodenlich.

230 · Baseball America 2023 Directory

BaseballAmerica.com

AMATEUR/YOUTH

NATIONAL ORGANIZATIONS

USA BASEBALL

Mailing Address, Corporate Headquarters: 2933 South Miami Blvd, Suite 119, Durham, NC 27703. **Telephone**: (919) 474-8721. **E-mail Address**: info@usa-baseball.com. **Media Inquiries**: mediarelations@usabase-ball.com. **Website**: usabaseball.com.

BOARD OF DIRECTORS
Mike Gaski (President), Jason Dobis (Treasurer), Elliot Hopkins (Secretary), Veronica Alvarez, Willie Bloomquist, Jenny Dalton-Hill, John Gall, George Grande, Steve Keener, Abe Key, Chris Marinak, Jacob May, Tony Reagins, Derek Topik, Ernie Young.

NATIONAL MEMBER ORGANIZATIONS
American Amateur Baseball Congress (AABC), American Baseball Coaches Association (ABCA), American Legion Baseball, DYB, Inc., Little League Baseball, National Amateur Baseball Federation (NABF), National Assocaition of Intercollegiate Athletics (NAIA), National Collegiate Athletic Association (NCAA), National Federation of State High School Athletic Associations (NFHS), National High School Baseball Coaches Associatin (BCA), National Junior College Athletic Association (NJCAA), PONY Baseball

STAFF
Executive Director/CEO: Paul Seiler. **Chief Operating Officer:** David Perkins. **Chief Financial Officer:** Ray Darwin. **Coordinator, Sport Performance:** Jake Barnes. **Director, Coaching Development:** Andrew Bartman. **Director, 12U National Team Program:** Cole Beeker. **General Manager, National Teams:** Ashley Bratcher. **Director, Athlete Safety:** Lisa Braxton. **General Manager, Collegiate & Professional National Teams:** Eric Campbell. **Coordinator, Athlete Safety:** Taylor Clayton. **Director, Youth Programs:** Tyler Collins. **Director, 18U National Team Program:** Brett Curll. **Coordinator, Social Media:** Ira Dorin. **Coordinator, Baseball Operations:** Jeff Feltman. **General Manager, USA Baseball Sports Properties:** Jimmy Frush. **Director, Baseball Administration:** Allison Gupton. **Senior Director, Technology:** Russell Hartford. **Director, Communications:** Lizzie Hattrich. **Assistant Director, Creative Services:** Jenna Hiscock. **Director, Creative Services:** Mark Jenkins. **Director, Brand:** Kevin Jones. **Director, 15U National Team Program:** Ben Kelley. **Coordinator, Baseball Administration:** Makenzie Kelly. **Director, Player Development:** Jim Koerner. **Coordinator, Athlete Safety and Education:** Paris LaPoint. **Director, Accounting & Finance:** Cicely McLaughlin. **Director, Social Media:** Alex Nash. **Senior Director, Retail:** Carrington Nicholson. **Scouting Director:** Mark O'Sullivan. **Assistant Director, Creative Services:** Colin Pelosi. **Coordinator, National Training Complex Operations:** Dylan Pfingst. **Senior Director, Athlete Safety and Education:** Lauren Rhyne. **Director, Baseball Operations:** Ann Claire Roberson. **Coordinator, Retail Operations:** Tracy Sewell. **Assistant Director, Communications:** Josh Spitz. **Coordinator, Baseball Technology:** Mariah Vargas. **Senior Director, National Training Complex Operations:** James Vick. **Assistant Director, Education:** Sarah Wood. **Senior Director, Communications:** Brad Young.

BASEBALL CANADA

Mailing Address: 2212 Gladwin Cres., Suite A7, Ottawa, Ontario K1B 5N1. **Telephone:** (613) 748-5606. **Fax:** (613) 748-5767. **E-mail Address:** info@baseball.ca. **Website:** baseball.ca.
President & CEO: Jason Dickson. **Head Coach/Director, National Teams:** Greg Hamilton. **Business/Sport Development Director/Women's National Team Manager:** Andre Lachance. **Media/PR Coordinator:** Adam Morissette. **Project Coordinator/Safe Sport Liaison:** June Sterling. **Administrative Assistant:** Penny Baba. **Coach & Umpire Service Coordinator:** Michel Landriault. **Administrative Coordinator, Men's National Teams:** Nancy Dunbar.

NATIONAL BASEBALL CONGRESS

Mailing Address: 300 N. Mead, Ste 109 Wichita, KS 67202. **Telephone:** (316) 265-6236. **Website:** nbcbase-ball.com.
Year Founded: 1931.

ATHLETES IN ACTION

Mailing Address: 651 Taylor Dr., Xenia, OH 45385. **Telephone:** (937) 352-1000. **E-mail Address:** baseball@athletesinaction.org. **Website:** aiabaseball.org. **Baseball Director of Operations/GM:** Chris Beck. **Xenia Scouts Program Director:** Dave Gnau. **International Teams Director:** John McLaughlin. **Baseball Staff:** Jason Lester.

BaseballAmerica.com

Baseball America 2023 Directory • **231**

AMATEUR/YOUTH

SUMMER COLLEGE LEAGUES

NATIONAL ALLIANCE OF COLLEGE SUMMER BASEBALL

Telephone: (321) 696-6995. **E-Mail Address:** sfoggi@FloridaLeague.com. **Website:** nacsb.pointstreaksites.com

Executive Director: Stefano Foggi (Florida League). **Assistant Executive Director:** Bobby Bennett (Sunbelt Baseball League), Jeff Carter (Southern Collegiate Baseball League). **Treasurer:** Jason Woodward (Cal Ripken Collegiate Baseball League). **Director, Public Relations:** Henry Bramwell (Hamptons Collegiate Baseball League). **Compliance Officer:** Sean McGrath (New England Collegiate Baseball League).

Member Leagues: Atlantic Collegiate Baseball League, California Collegiate League, Cal Ripken Collegiate Baseball League, Cape Cod Baseball League, Florida Collegiate Summer League, Great Lakes Summer Collegiate League, New England Collegiate Baseball League, New York Collegiate Baseball League, Southern Collegiate Baseball League, Sunbelt Baseball League, Valley Baseball League, Hamptons Collegiate Baseball League.

ALASKA BASEBALL LEAGUE

League Mailing Address: P.O. Box 2690 Palmer, AK 99645. **Commissioner:** Chip Dill. **Email:** chipfd@gmail.com.

MAT-SU MINERS

General Manager: Pete Christopher. **Mailing Address:** P.O. Box 2690 Palmer, AK 99645. **Telephone:** 907-746-4914/907-745-6401. **Fax:** 907-746-5068. **E-Mail:** gmminers@gci.net. **Fax:** 907-561-2920. **Website:** matsuminers.org. **Head Coach:** Tyler LeBrun **Field:** Hermon Brothers, Grass, No Lights.

ANCHORAGE BUCS

General Manager: Shawn Maltby **Mailing Address:** 435 W. 10th Avenue Suite B, Anchorage, AK 99501. **Office:** 907-561-2827. **Fax:** 561-2920. **E-Mail:** shawn@anchoragebucs.com. **Website:** anchoragebucs.com **Head Coach:** Ken Hokuf **Field:** Mulcahy Field—Turf Infield, Grass Outfield, Lights

ANCHORAGE GLACIER PILOTS

General Manager: Mike Hinshaw **Mailing Address:** 435 W. 10th Avenue, Suite A, Anchorage, Alaska 99501. **Office:** 907-274-3627. **Fax:** 907-274-3628. **E-Mail:** gpilots@alaska.net. **Website:** glacierpilots.com. **Head Coach:** Dave Serrano. **Field:** Mulcahy Field—Turf Infield, Grass Outfield, Lights

CHUGIAK-EAGLE RIVER CHINOOKS

General Manager: Tim Cole. **Mailing Address:** 651 Taylor Drive, Xenia, Ohio 45385. **Office:** 937-352-1000. **Fax:** 937-352-1001. **E-Mail:** timothy.cole@athletesinaction.org. **Website:** cerchinooks.com. **Head Coach:** Tim Cole. **Field:** Lee Jordan Field-Turf Infield, Grass Outfield, No Lights

PENINSULA OILERS

General Manager: Larry McCann. **Mailing Address:** 601 S. Main St., Kenai, Alaska 99611. **Office:** 907-283-7133. **Fax:** 907-283-3390. **E-Mail:** lmccann@oilersbaseball.com. **Website:** oilersbaseball.com. **Head Coach:** Larry McCann. **Field:** Coral Seymour Memorial Park-Grass , No Lights

APPALACHIAN LEAGUE

E-Mail Address: frank@appyleague.com. **Website:** www.appyleague.com.

Executive Director: Brian Graham. **Director, Player Personnel:** Justin Morgenstern. **Manager, Baseball Administration:** Frank La Sala. **Umpire Evaluator:** Thomas Newsom.

Division Structure: East—Bluefield, Burlington, Danville, Princeton, Pulaski.

West—Bristol, Elizabethton, Greeneville, Johnson City, Kingsport.

Regular Season: 48 games. **2023 Opening Date:** June 6. **Closing Date:** July 31. **All-Star Game:** July 25. **Roster Limit:** 32 active.

BLUEFIELD RIDGE RUNNERS

Office Address: 2003 Stadium Dr. Bluefield WV 24701. **Mailing Address:** P.O. Box 356 Bluefield WV. 24701. **Telephone:** 304-324-1326. Fax 304-324-1318. **Email address:** bluefieldridgerunners@gmail.com. **Website:** www.bluefieldridgerunners.com.

Ownership/Management: Bluefield Baseball Club **President:** George McGonagle. **General Manager:** Rocky Malamisura

Manager: Mike Weatherford. **Hitting Coach:** Mike White. **Pitching Coach:** Garrett Schilling. **Bench Coach:** Cristian Crespo. **Head Groundskeeper:** Mike White.

Stadium Name: Bowen Field. **Location:** I-77 to Bluefield exit 1, Route 290 to Route 460 West, fourth light right onto Leatherwood Lane, left at first light, past Hometown Shell station and turn right, stadium quarter-mile on left. **Ticket Price Range:** $6.

BRISTOL STATE LINERS

Office Address: 1501 Euclid Ave, Bristol, VA 24201. **Mailing Address:** PO Box 1434, Bristol, VA 24203. **Telephone:** (276) 206-9946. **Fax:** (423)-968-2636. **E-Mail Address:** gm@bristolbaseball.com. **Website:** www.bristolstateliners.com.

Owned by: Bristol Baseball Inc. **Operated by:** Bristol Baseball Inc. **President/General Manager:** Mahlon Luttrell. **Assistant General Manager:** Craig Adams. **VP Community Relations:** Mark Young. **Treasurer:** Jean Luttrell. **Secretary:** Connie Kinkead. **Head Groundskeeper:** Michael Adams.

Manager: Bill Kinneberg. **Hitting Coach:** TBA. **Pitching Coach:** TBA. **Athletic Trainer:** TBA. **Strength & Conditioning Coach:** TBA.

Stadium: DeVault Memorial Stadium. **Standard Game Times:** Mon.-Sat., 7 pm, Sun., 6 pm. **Ticket Price Range:** $4-$8.

232 · Baseball America 2023 Directory

BaseballAmerica.com

AMATEUR/YOUTH

BURLINGTON SOCK PUPPETS

Office Address: 1450 Graham St, Burlington, NC 27217. **Mailing Address:** PO Box 1143, Burlington, NC 27216. **Telephone:** (336) 222-0223. **E-Mail Address:** info@gosockpuppets.com. **Website:** www.gosockpuppets.com

Owner: Knuckleball Entertainment, LLC. **President:** Ryan Keur. **General Manager:** Anderson Rathbun. **Director of Sockville:** Sam Santos. **Director of Ticket Sales:** Matthew Hydock. Promotions & **Experience Manager:** Zach Kunar.

Manager: Anthony Essien.

Stadium: Burlington Athletic Stadium. **Standard Game Time:** 7:00 pm. **Ticket Price Range:** $8-15.

DANVILLE OTTERBOTS

Office Address: Dan Daniel Memorial Park, 302 River Park Dr, Danville, VA 24540. **Mailing Address:** PO Box 330, Danville, VA 24543. **Telephone:** (434) 554-4487. **E-Mail Address:** danvillebaseball21@gmail.com. **Website:** www.mlb.com/appalachian-league/danville.

Operated by: Danville Baseball Club LLC. **Owners:** Ryan Keur. **General Manager:** Austin Scher. **Assistant General Manager:** Jacob Lemanowicz. **Coordinator of Fun:** Wyatt Sutton.

Manager: Desi Relaford. **Hitting Coach:** Angel Berroa. **Pitching Coach:** TBA. **Bench Coach:** TBA. **Athletic Trainer:** TBA. **Strength & Conditioning Coach:** TBA.

Stadium: American Legion Post 325 Field at Dan Daniel Memorial Park. **Standard Game Times:** Mon.-Sat., 7:00 pm, Sun. 5:00 pm. **Ticket Price Range:** $5-11.

ELIZABETHTON RIVER RIDERS

Address: 804 Holly Lane, Elizabethton, TN 37643. **Telephone:** (423) 547-6443.

Owned/Operated by: Randy and Jenny Boyd. **CEO:** Doug Kirchhofer. **President:** Chris Allen. **Vice President:** Jeremy Boler. **General Manager:** Kiva Fuller. **Ticket Sales Account Executive:** Bobby Lewis.

Manager: Jeremy Owens. **Hitting Coach:** Jeremy Owens. **Pitching Coach:** TBD. **Athletic Trainer:** TBD. **Strength & Conditioning Coach:** TBD

Stadium: Northeast Community Credit Union Ballpark. **Standard Game Times:** 7:00 pm. **Ticket Price Range:** $5-7.

GREENEVILLE FLYBOYS

Address: 135 Shiloh Road, Greeneville, TN 37745. **Telephone:** (423) 609-7400. **E-Mail Address:** contact@flyboysbaseball.com. **Website:** https://www.mlb.com/appalachian-league/greeneville.

Owned/Operated by: Randy and Jenny Boyd. **CEO:** Doug Kirchhofer. **President:** Chris Allen. **Vice President:** Jeremy Boler. **General Manager:** Brandon Bouschart. **Account Executive:** Matthew White.

Manager: Dennis Cook. **Hitting Coach:** TBD. **Pitching Coach/Assistant to the Pitching Coordinator:** TBD. **Bench Coach:** TBD. **Athletic Trainer:** TBD. **Strength & Conditioning Coach:** TBD

Stadium: Pioneer Park. **Standard Game Time:** Mon-Sat., 7:00 pm, Sun., 5:30 pm. **Ticket Price Range:** $5 group discount, $7 reserved, $8 premium.

JOHNSON CITY DOUGHBOYS

Office Address: 510 Bert St., Johnson City, TN 37601. **Mailing Address:** PO Box 179, Johnson City, TN 37605.

Telephone: (423) 461-4866. **E-Mail Address:** zclark@jcdoughboys.com. **Website:** www.jcdoughboys.com.

Owned/Operated by: Randy and Jenny Boyd. **CEO:** Doug Kirchhofer. **President:** Chris Allen. **Vice President:** Jeremy Boler. **General Manager:** Patrick Ennis. **Account Executive:** Styles Martin.

Manager: Kevin Mahoney.

Stadium: TVA Credit Union Ballpark. **Standard Game Time:** Mon.-Sat. 7 pm, Sun. 5:30 pm. **Ticket Price Range:** $6-$9.

KINGSPORT AXMEN

Address: 800 Granby Rd, Kingsport, TN 37660. **Telephone:** (423) 224-2626. **Fax:** (423) 224-2625. **Website:** www.kingsportaxmen.com

Owned/Operated by: Randy and Jenny Boyd. **CEO:** Doug Kirchhofer. **President:** Chris Allen. **Vice President:** Jeremy Boler. **Assistant General Manager:** Jarrod Bowen. **Account Executive:** Mollie Allen.

Manager: Mike Guinn. **Hitting Coach:** TBD. **Pitching Coach:** TBD. **Bench Coach:** TBD. **Athletic Trainer:** TBD. **Performance Coach:** TBD

Stadium: Hunter Wright Stadium. **Standard Game Times:** Mon-Sat., 7pm, Sun., 5:30pm. **Doubleheaders—** Mon-Sat. TBD, Sun: TBD. **Ticket Price Range:** $6 -$8.

PRINCETON WHISTLEPIGS

Office Address: 345 Old Bluefield Road, Princeton, WV 24739. **Mailing Address:** PO Box 5646, Princeton, WV 24740. **Telephone:** 304-487-2000. **Email Address:** gm@whistlepigsbaseball.com. **Website:** www.whistlepigs-baseball.com

Operated By: Princeton Baseball Association, Inc. **President:** Dewey Russell. **General Manager:** Danny Shingleton. **Director Stadium Operations:** Adam Sarver, Rusty Sarver. **Executive Assistant:** Courtney Longworth. **Field Manager:** TBD.

Stadium: Hunnicutt Field. **Standard Game Time:** Mon.-Sat., 7 pm, Sun., 6 pm. **Ticket Price Range:** $5-8.

PULASKI RIVER TURTLES

Office Address: 529 Pierce Avenue, Pulaski, VA 24301. **Mailing Address:** PO Box 852, Pulaski, VA 24301. **Telephone:** (540) 980-1070. **Email Address:** info@pulaskiriverturtles.com

Operated By: Calfee Park Baseball Inc..

Field Manager: Clark Crist.

Stadium: Historic Calfee Park. **Ticket Price Range:** $5-11

ATLANTIC COLLEGIATE BASEBALL LEAGUE

Mailing Address: 8 Millbrook Drive, Middletown, NJ 07748.

Telephone: (215) 536-5777. **Fax:** (215) 536-5777.

Website: acbl-online.com.

Year Founded: 1967.

Commissioner: Angelo Fiore. **President:** Joe Mazza. **Secretary:** Mike Kalb. **Vice President:** Brian Casey. **Treasurer:** Bob Hoffman.

ACBL Kaiser Division: Atlantic Whitecaps, East Coast Sandhogs, Hitters Club Hawkeyes, Old Town Road Patriots, Nassau Collegians, New York Crush, New York Valor, LIB Neptunes.

ACBL Wolff Division: Bergen Metros, Jersey Pilots, Jersey Shore Stallions, New Brunswick Matrix, New York Phenoms, Ocean Ospreys, South Jersey Kings, Trenton Generals.

AMATEUR/YOUTH

CALIFORNIA COLLEGIATE LEAGUE

Mailing Address: 11756 Chestnut Ridge Street, Moorpark, CA 93021. **Telephone:** (805) 680-1047. **Fax:** (805) 684-8596. **E-Mail Address:** aaron@calsummerball.com. **Website:** calsummerball.com.
Founded: 1993. **Executive Director:** Aaron Milam.

ACADEMY BARONS

Address: 901 E. Artesia Blvd, Compton, CA 90221. **Telephone:** (310) 763-3479. **Website:** calsummerball.com/academy-barons-roster. **E-Mail Address:** Yano.alvin@mlb.com. com. **Baseball Operations:** Yano Alvin. **Field manager:** Kenny Landreaux.

ARROYO SECO SAINTS

Telephone: (626) 695-6903. **Website:** arroyosecosaints.com. **E-mail Address:** amilam@arroyosecobaseball.com. **General Manager:** Aaron Milam/Nicholas Gorman. **Field Manager:** Aaron Milam.

CONEJO OAKS

Address: 1710 N. Moorpark Rd., #106, Thousand Oaks, CA 91360. **Telephone:** 805-304-0126. **Website:** calsummerball.com/conejo-oaks-roster/.com. **E-Mail Address:** oaksbaseball@yahoo.com. **Field Manager:** David Soliz. **General Manager:** Randy Riley.

HEALDSBURG PRUNE PACKERS

Address: Rec Park 515 Piper St. Healdsburg, Calif. 95448. **Mailing Address:** PO Box 1543 Healdsburg CA 95448. **Telephone:** 707-280-6693. **Email Address:** JGG21@aol.com. **GM/Field Manager:** Joey Gomes.

LINCOLN POTTERS

Address: 436 Lincoln Blvd., Ste. 104, Lincoln, CA 95648. **Telephone:** (916) 752-8986. **Website:** lincolnpotters.com. **E-Mail Address:** ryan.stevens@slugger.com. **Field Manager:** Ryan Stevens. **General Manager:** Matt Lundgren.

ORANGE COUNTY RIPTIDE

Address: 14 Calendula Rancho, Santa Margarita, CA 92688. **Telephone:** (949) 228-7676. **Website:** ocriptide.com. **E-Mail Address:** ocriptidebaseball@gmail.com. **General Manager:** Moe Geohegan.

SAN LUIS OBISPO BLUES

Address: 3195 McMillan Ave, Ste. B2, San Luis Obispo, CA 93401. **Telephone:** 805-704-4388. **Website:** bluesbaseball.com. **E-Mail Address:** adam@bluesbaseball.com. **GM:** Adam Stowe. **Field Manager:** Bob Miller.

SANTA BARBARA FORESTERS

Address: 4299 Carpinteria Ave., Suite 201, Carpinteria, CA 93013. **Telephone:** (805) 684-0657. **Website:** sbforesters.org. **E-Mail Address:** pintard@earthlink.net. **General Manager and Field Manager:** Bill Pintard.

SOLANO MUDCATS

Address: 508 Stonewood Dr., Vacaville, CA 95687. **Website:** solanomudcats.org. **E-mail Address (GM):** solanomudcats@gmail.com. **General Manager:** Ben Crombie.

SONOMA STOMPERS

Address: 117 W. Napa St., Suite A, Sonoma, CA 95476. **Website:** stompersbaseball.com. **E-mail Address:** info@stompersbaseball.com.

WALNUT CREEK CRAWDADS

Address: 1630 Challenge Dr., Concord, CA 94607. **Website:** crawdadsbaseball.com. **E-mail Address (GM):** bcummings@walnutcreekcrawdads.com. **Field Manager:** Brant Cummings.

CAL RIPKEN SR. COLLEGIATE LEAGUE

Address: 24219 Hawkins Landing Drive, Gaithersburg, MD 20882. **Telephone:** (301) 693-2577. **E-Mail:** jason_d_woodward@mcpsmd.org. **Website:** calripkenleague.org.
Year Founded: 2005.
Commissioner: Jason Woodward. **League President:** Brad Rifkin. **Director of Operations:** Chris Rogers
Regular Season: 36 games. **Playoff Format:** Top two teams from each division plus the two remaining teams with the best records qualify. Teams play the best of three series, winners advance to the best of three series for the league championship. **Roster Limit:** 40 (college-eligible players). 22 and under).

ALEXANDRIA ACES

Address: 221 9th Street, S.E. Washington, DC 20003. **Telephone:** (202) 255-1683. **E-Mail:** cberset21@gmail.com. **Website:** alexandriaaces.org. **Chairman/CEO:** Frank Fannon. **General Manager:** TBD. **Head Coach:** Chris Berset. **Ballpark:** Frank Mann Field at Four Mile Run Park.

BETHESDA BIG TRAIN

Address: 6400 Goldsboro Road Suite 220 Bethesda, MD 20817. **Telephone:** 301-229-1854. **Fax:** 301-229-8362. **E-Mail:** faninfo@bigtrain.org **Website:** bigtrain.org. **General Manager:** Michael Michaud. **Head Coach:** Sal Colangelo. **Ballpark:** Shirley Povich Field.

D.C. GRAYS

Address: 1800 M Street NW, 500 South Tower, Washington, DC 20036. **Telephone:** (202) 492-6226. **Website:** dcgrays.com. **E-Mail Address:** barbera@acg-consultants.com. **President:** Mike Barbera. **General Manager:** Chris Spera. **Head Coach:** TBD. **Ballpark:** Washington Nationals Youth Academy.

METRO SOUTH COUNTY BRAVES

Address: 8925 Leesburg Pike, Vienna, VA 22182. **Telephone:** (702) 909-2750. **Fax:** (703) 783-1319. **E-Mail:** cawarren90@gmail.com. **Website:** fcabraves.com. **President/General Manager:** TBD. **Head Coach:** Chris Warren. **Ballpark:** Annandale High School.

GAITHERSBURG GIANTS

Address: 18221A Flower Hill Way, Gaithersburg, MD 20879. **Telephone:** (240) 793-3367. **E-Mail:** gaithersburggiants@gmail.com. **Website:** gaithersburggiants.org. **General Manager:** Matt Cangas. **Head Coach:** TJ Brockway. **Ballpark:** Criswell Automotive Field.

AMATEUR/YOUTH

SILVER SPRING-TAKOMA THUNDERBOLTS

Address: 906 Glaizewood Court, Takoma Park, MD 20912. **Telephone:** 301-983-1358. **E-Mail:** tboltsbaseball@gmail.com. **Website:** tbolts.org. **General Manager:** Richard O'Connor. **Head Coach:** Brock Hunter. **Ballpark:** Blair Stadium at Montgomery Blair High School

CAPE COD BASEBALL LEAGUE

Mailing Address: PO Box 266, Harwich Port, MA 02646. **Telephone:** (508) 432-6909. **E-Mail:** info@capecodbaseball.org.
Website: capecodbaseball.org.
Year Founded: 1885.
Commissioner: Eric Zmuda. **President:** Andrew Lang. **Treasurer:** Paul Logan. **Secretary:** Ashley Hansen Kilgallon. **Senior VP:** Tom Gay, **VP:** Mary Henderson, Steve West. **Senior Deputy Commissioner:** Peter Hall. **Deputy Commissioner:** Steve Faucher, Ben Layton, Mike Carrier. **Director Public Relations:** Michael Lane. **Director Broadcasting:** John Garner. **Director Communications:** Shawn McBride. **Division Structure:** East—Brewster, Chatham, Harwich, Orleans, Yarmouth-Dennis. **West—Bourne, Cotuit, Falmouth, Hyannis, Wareham.**
Regular Season: 44 games. **All-Star Game and Home Run Contest:** July 22. **Playoff Format:** Top four teams in each division qualify for three rounds of best-of-three series.

BOURNE BRAVES

Mailing Address: PO Box 895, Monument Beach, MA 02553. **Telephone:** (508) 868-8378. **E-Mail Address:** nnorkevicius@yahoo.com. **Website:** bournebraves.org.
President: Nicole Norkevicius. **General Manager:** Darin Weeks. **Head Coach:** Scott Landers.

BREWSTER WHITECAPS

Mailing Address: PO Box 2349, Brewster, MA 02631. **Telephone:** (508) 896-8500, ext. 147. **Fax:** (508) 896-9845. **E-Mail Address:** ckenney@brewsterwhitecaps.com.
Website: brewsterwhitecaps.com.
President: Bob Graczewski. **General Manager:** Ned Monthie. **Head Coach:** Jamie Shevchik.

CHATHAM ANGLERS

Mailing Address: PO Box 428, Chatham, MA 02633. **Website:** chathamas.com. **President:** Steve West. **General Manager:** Mike Geylin. **Email:** mgeylin@kgpr.com. **Head Coach:** Tom Holliday.

COTUIT KETTLEERS

Mailing Address: PO Box 411, Cotuit, MA 02635. **Telephone:** (508) 428-3358. **E-Mail Address:** bmurpf cape@aol.com. **Website:** kettleers.org. **President:** Terry Moran. **General Manager:** Bruce Murphy. **Head Coach:** Mike Roberts.

FALMOUTH COMMODORES

Mailing Address: PO Box 808 Falmouth, MA 02541. **Telephone:** (508) 566-4988. **Website:** falmouthcommodores.org. **President:** Bob Curtis. **General Manager:** Chris Fitzgerald. **Head Coach:** Jeff Trundy.

HARWICH MARINERS

Mailing Address: PO Box 201, Harwich Port, MA 02646. **Telephone:** (508) 432-2000. **Fax:** (508) 432-5357. **E-Mail Address:** mehendy@comcast.net. **Website:** harwichmariners.org.
President: Mary Henderson. **General Manager:** Ben Layton. **Head Coach:** Steve Englert.

HYANNIS HARBOR HAWKS

Mailing Address: PO Box 832, West Hyannis Port, MA 02672. **Telephone:** (508) 737-5890. **Fax:** (877) 822-2703. **E-Mail Address:** brpfeifer@aol.com. **Website:** harborhawks.org.
President: Dan Johnson. **General Manager:** Nick Johnson. **Head Coach:** Eric Beattie.

ORLEANS FIREBIRDS

Mailing Address: PO Box 504, Orleans, MA 02653. **Telephone:** (508) 255-0793. **Fax:** (508) 255-2237. **E-Mail Address:** bodonnell15@gmail.com. **Website:** orleansfirebirds.com. **President:** Bob O'Donnell. **General Manager:** Sue Horton. **Head Coach:** Kelly Nicholson.

WAREHAM GATEMEN

Mailing Address: PO Box 287, Wareham, MA 02571. **Telephone:** (508) 748-0287. **Fax:** (508) 880-2602. **E-Mail Address:** alang.gatemen@gmail.com.
Website: gatemen.org. **President:** Andrew Lang. **General Manager:** Bob Prince. **Head Coach:** Harvey Shapiro.

YARMOUTH-DENNIS RED SOX

Mailing Address: PO Box 78 Yarmouth Port, MA 02675. **Telephone:** (508) 889-8721. **E-Mail Address:** sfaucher64@gmail.com. **Website:** ydredsox.org. **President:** Paul Izzo. **General Manager:** Terry Hisey. **Head Coach:** Scott Pickler.

COASTAL PLAIN LEAGUE

Mailing Address: 117 Thomas Mill Road, Holly Springs, NC 27540. **Telephone:** (919) 852-1960. **Email Address:** justins@coastalplain.com. **Website:** coastalplain.com. **Year Founded:** 1997. **Owner:** Capitol Broadcasting Company Inc. **Commissioner:** Chip Allen. **Deputy Commisioner:** Justin Sellers. **Founder/Commisioner Emeritus:** Pete Bock.

ASHEBORO ZOOKEEPERS

Mailing Address: P.O. Box 4036, Asheboro, N.C. 27204. **Telephone:** (336) 460-7018. **Email Address:** info@zookeepersbaseball.com
Owners: Doug Pugh, Ronnie Pugh, Steve Pugh, Mike Pugh. **General Manager/Director of Baseball Operations:** Melissa Godwin.
Head Coach: Korey Dunbar. **Assistant Coach:** Josh Pike.
Ballpark: McCrary Park. **Game Start Times:** Monday-Saturday, 7 p.m./Sunday, 6 p.m.

BOONE BIGFOOTS

Address: 982 Jakes Mountain Rd, Deep Gap, N.C. 28618. **Telephone:** (909) 935-7470. **Email Address:** bigfootsbaseball@gmail.com.

BaseballAmerica.com

Baseball America 2023 Directory • **235**

AMATEUR/YOUTH

Owner: Robert Wilson. **General Manager:** Julia Williams

Head Coach: Randall Ortiz. **Assistant Coaches:** Hayden Cross, Jacob Whitley

Ballpark: Jim and Bettie Smith Stadium. **Game Start Times:** Monday-Saturday, 6:30 p.m./Sunday, 4 p.m.

FLORENCE FLAMINGOS

Address: 1951 Pisgah Road, Florence, S.C. 29501. **Telephone:** (843) 629-0700.

Email Address: info@florenceflamingos.com

Majority Partner: Steve DeLay. **Partner:** Brandon Raphael. **Minority Partner:** Kevin Barth. **President:** Mitchell Lister. **Director of Marketing & Business Analytics:** Anna Spinks. **Director of Stadium Operations, F&B, Merchandise:** Tyler Gibson. **Manager, Digital Marketing, Game Entertainment & Sponsorship Activation:** Austin Altenau. **Manager, Group Sales:** Katie Cook. **Manager, Premium Seating:** A.J. Alston. **Director of Ticket Operations & Inside Sales:** Matt Downing

Head Coach: Lane Harvey. **Assistant Coaches:** Lex Tuten, Benton Schweinfurth.

Ballpark: Carolina Bank Field. **Game Start Times:** All games, 7.00 p.m.

FOREST CITY OWLS

Mailing Address: P.O. Box 1062, Forest City, N.C. 28043. **Telephone:** (828) 245-0000. **Email Address:** sblatnicky@forestcitybaseball.com.

Owners: Phil and Becky Dangel. **Minority Owner:** Rob Frost. **Director of Ballpark Operations:** Stephanie Blatnicky. **Assistant Director of Ballpark Operations:** Jason Alvis.

Head Coach: Connor Dailey.

Ballpark: McNair Field. **Game Start Times:** All games, 7:05 p.m.

HP-THOMASVILLE HITOMS

Address: 7003 Ballpark Road, Thomasville, N.C. 27360. **Telephone:** (336) 472-8667. **Email Address:** info@hitoms.com.

Owner/President: Greg Suire. **Assistant General Manager:** Zach Davis. **Player Personnel Consultant:** Scott Davis.

Ballpark: Finch Field. **Game Start Times:** Monday-Friday, 6:30 p.m./Saturday, 6 p.m./Sunday, 5 p.m.

HOLLY SPRING SALAMANDERS

Address: 101 Tennis Court, Holly Springs, N.C. **27540.** **Telephone:** (919) 249-7322. **Email Address:** info@salamandersbaseball.com.

Owner: Capitol Broadcasting Company

Vice President: Mike Birling. **General Manager:** Shari Massengill. **Ticket Sales Manager:** Thomas Phelps. **Director of Corporate Partnerships:** Amanda Gillis.

Head Coach: Brian Rountree. **Assistant Coaches:** Mike Valder, Derek Roy

Ballpark: Ting Stadium at Ting Park. **Game Start Times:** Monday-Friday, 7 p.m./Saturday, 6:30 p.m./Sunday, 5:40 p.m.

LEXINGTON COUNTY BLOWFISH

Address: 474 Ballpark Road, Lexington, S.C. **29072.** **Telephone:** (803) 254-3474. **Email Address:** info@blowfishbaseball.com.

Owners: Shanahan and Company Sports Management (Bill & Vicki Shanahan)

President: Bill Shanahan. **General Manager:** Tony Baldwin. **Director of Operations:** Matt Jinnette. **Director of Stadium & Field Operations:** Robbie Hardy. **Ticket Sales Coordinator:** Jacob Miller. **Group Sales/Asst. Director Stadium Ops:** Thomas Flor.

Head Coach: KC Brown.

Ballpark: Lexington County Baseball Stadium. **Game Start Times:** All games, 7:05 p.m.

MACON BACON

Address: 225 Willie Smokey Glover Drive, Macon, GA 31201. **Telephone:** 478-803-1795. **Email Address:** info@maconbaconbaseball.com.

Owner: Steve DeLay. **President:** Brandon Raphael. **Director of Marketing:** Anna Spinks. **Director of F&B & Ballpark Operations:** Lisa Williams. **Director of Ticket Sales & Operations:** Austin Karp. **Manager, Digital Marketing:** Harrison Tarr. **Group Account Executive:** Noah Schramm.

Head Coach: Kevin Soine

Ballpark: Luther Williams Field. **Game Start Times:** All games, 7 p.m.

MARTINSVILLE MUSTANGS

Address: 450 Commonwealth Blvd. E, Martinsville, VA, 24112. **Telephone:** (276) 403-5250. **Email Address:** info@martinsvillemustangs.com

Owner: City of Martinsville. **Managing Partner:** Next P.L.A.N. Athletics. **General Manager:** Connor Akeman.

Head Coach: Kregg Snook.

Ballpark: Hooker Field. **Game Start Times:** All games, 7 p.m.

MOREHEAD CITY MARLINS

Address: 1208 Mizzelle Dr., **Morehead City, NC 28557.** **Telephone:** (252) 269-9767. **Email Address:** mcmarlins@gmail.com.

Owner: Buddy Bengel. **Executive VP:** Rich Mackesy. **Executive VP & Interim GM:** Dave Lipay.

General Manager: TBD. **Assistant General Manager:** Jackson Chladek. **Director of Broadcasting & Media Relations:** Erich Back. **Assistant, Broadcasting & Media Relations:** Trey Redfield. **Head Coach:** Sam Carel

Ballpark: Puck O'Neal Field at Big Rock Stadium. **Game Start Times:** All games, 7 p.m.

PENNINSULA PILOTS

Mailing Address: P.O. Box 7376, Hampton, VA 23666. **Telephone:** (757) 245-2222. **Email Address:** info@peninsulapilots.com

Owner/Caretaker: Henry Morgan. **Vice President and Head Coach:** Hank Morgan. **General Manager:** Matt Mitchell. **Associate Head Coach:** David Mitchell

Ballpark: War Memorial Stadium. **Game Start Times:** All games, 7 p.m.

TRI-CITY CHILI PEPPERS

Address: 901 Meridian Ave, Colonial Heights, VA 23834. **Telephone:** (804) 499-3104. **Email Address:** HaveFun@chilipeppersbaseball.com

Owners: Chris Martin & Byron Wurderman. **Director of Operations & Group Outings:** Austin Sizemore. **Director of Operations & Account Executive for Group Outings:** Rob Perez. **Host Family Coordinator:** Brent Ellenburg.

AMATEUR/YOUTH

Head Coach: James Bierlein.
Ballpark: Shepherd Stadium. **Game Start Times:** Monday-Saturday, 7 p.m./Sunday, 5:45 p.m.

WILMINGTON SHARKS

Mailing Address: P.O. Box 15233, Wilmington, N.C. 28412. **Telephone:** (910) 343-5621. **Email Address:** info@wilmingtonsharks.com
Owner: NSS Sports (Matt Perry and Bill Davidson). **Owner/President:** Matt Perry. **Owner/Managing Member:** Bill Davidson. **General Manager:** John Hunt. **Director of Ticketing:** Michael Magnanti. **Director of Community Relations:** Tom Lamont.
Head Coach: Russ Burroughs.
Ballpark: Buck Hardee Field. **Game Start Times:** All games, 7:05 p.m.

WILSON TOBS

Address: 300 Stadium Street, Wilson, N.C. 27893. **Telephone:** (252) 291-8627. **Email Address:** mike@wilsontobs.com
Owner & CFO: Richard Holland. **President:** Greg Suire. **General Manager:** Mike Bell. **Assistant General Manager:** Drew MacKinnon. **Community Outreach & Digital Media Coordinator:** Griffin Meyers.
Head Coach: Tony Rosselli.
Ballpark: Historic Fleming Stadium. **Game Start Times:** Monday-Saturday, 7 p.m./Sunday, 6 p.m.

FLORIDA COLLEGIATE SUMMER LEAGUE

Mailing Address: 477 Commerce Way, Suite 115, Longwood, FL 32750. **Telephone:** (321) 206-9174. **E-Mail Address:** info@floridaleague.com.
Website: floridaleague.com.
Year Founded: 2004.
President: Stefano Foggi. **Commisioner:** Rob Sitz.

DELAND SUNS

Operated by the league office.
E-Mail Address: suns@floridaleague.com.

LEESBURG LIGHTNING

E-Mail Address: lightning@floridaleague.com.

SANFORD RIVER RATS

Operated by the league office.
E-Mail Address: rats@floridaleague.com.

SEMINOLE COUNTY SCORPIONS

Operated by the league office.
E-Mail Address: scorpions@floridaleague.com.

WINTER GARDEN SQUEEZE

Operated by the league office.
Email Address: squeeze@floridaleague.com.

WINTER PARK DIAMOND DAWGS

E-Mail Address: dawgs@floridaleague.com.

THE FUTURES LEAGUE

Mailing Address: P.O. Box 458, Weymouth, MA 02190. **Telephone:** (339) 440-3417. **E-Mail Address:** administrator@thefuturesleague.com.

Website: thefuturesleague.com.
Year Founded: 2010.
Commissioner: Joe Paolucci. **Director of Media Relations & League Administrator:** Joshua Kummins.
Teams (Contact): Brockton Rox (**Tom Tracey:** ttracey@brocktonrox.com); Nashua Silver Knights (**Cam Cook:** cam@nashuasilverknights.com); New Britain Bees (**Bret DeRosa:** bderosa@nbbees.com); Norwich Sea Unicorns (**Lee Walter:** lee@goseaunicorns.com); Pittsfield Suns (**Sander Stotland:** sander@pittsfieldsuns.com); Vermont Lake Monsters (**CJ Knudsen:** cjk@vermontlakemonsters.com); Westfield Starfires (**Chris Thompson:** ct@westfieldstarfires.com); Worcester Bravehearts (**Dave Peterson:** dave@worcesterbravehearts.com).
Regular Season: 64 games. Extra-inning games are determined by Home Run Derby. **Playoff Format:** Four teams qualify. Best-of-three semifinal series (1 seed vs. 4 seed and 2 seed vs. 3 seed) followed by best-of-three championship series between the two remaining teams.
Roster Limit: 40. At least 10 must be from New England or play collegiately at a New England college.

GREAT LAKES SUMMER COLLEGIATE LEAGUE

Mailing Address: PO Box 666, Troy, OH 45373. **Telephone:** (937) 308-1536. **E-mail:** glsclcommish@gmail.com.
Website: pointstreaksites.com/view/greatlakesleague/home. **Year Founded:** 1986.
President: Darrel Grissom. **Commissioner:** Deron Brown. **Vice-President:** Tim Clark. **Treasurer:** Tony Brumfield.
Regular Season: 42 games. **Playoff Format:** Top six teams meet in playoffs. **Roster Limit:** 30 (college-eligible players only).
Teams: (15 Teams)—Cincinnati Steam (Cincinnati, OH); Grand Lake Mariners (Celina, OH); Grand River Loggers (Grand Haven, MI); Hamilton Joes (Hamilton, OH); Jet Box (Sterling Heights, MI); Flat Rock, MI); Licking County Settlers (Newark, OH); Lima Locos (Lima, OH); Muskegon Clippers (Muskegon, MI); Richmond Jazz (Richmond, IN); Royals Oak Leprechaus (Royal Oak, MI); Sandusky Bay Ice Haulers (Sandusky, OH); Southern Ohio Copperheads (Athens, OH); Xenia Scouts (Xenia, OH).

METROPOLITAN COLLEGIATE BASEBALL LEAGUE

Mailing Address: 78 Knollwood Drive, Paramus NJ 07652
President: Brian Casey 374-545-1991
Website: metropolitanbaseball.com
Email: info@metropolitanbaseball.com

M.I.N.K. LEAGUE

(Missouri, Iowa, Nebraska, Kansas)
Telephone: 816-581-1430. **Email Address:** kcbb14@hotmail.com. **Website:** minkleaguebaseball.com
Year Founded: 1995.
Commissioner: Ron Rodriguez. **President:** Ky Turner. **Vice President:** Chris Whitaker. **Secretary:** Edwina Rains.
Regular season: 44 games.

CARROLL MERCHANTS

Stadium: Carroll Merchants Park, Vine St., Carroll, Iowa. **Telephone:** 712-830-7176. **E-Mail Address:** carrollmerchantsbaseball@gmail.com. **Website:** merchantsbaseball.com. **Managers:** Chris Whitaker and Rod Berg.

AMATEUR/YOUTH

CHILLICOTHE MUDCATS

Stadium: June Shaffer Memorial Park. **Telephone:** (660) 752-6253. **E-Mail Address:** caitlyncothern@gmail. com. **Website:** chillicothemudcats.com. **General Manager:** Caitlyn Cothern. **Head Coach:** Tyler Hudlow.

CLARINDA A'S

Stadium: Clarinda Municipal Stadium. **Telephone:** (712) 542-7638. **E-Mail Address:** m.everly@mchsi.com. **Website:** clarindaiowa-as-baseball.org.
General Managers: Ryan Eberly, Rodney J. Eberly. **Head Coach:** Ryan Eberly.

DES MOINES PEAK PROSPECTS

Stadium: Memorial Park, 2001 Boone St., Boone, Iowa. **Telephone:** 641-226-2952. **E-Mail Address:** dmpeak-prosmink@gmail.com. **Website:** peakperformancebase-ballclub.com.
General Manager: Eric Evans.

JEFFERSON CITY RENEGADES

Stadium: Vivion Field, Washington Park, 1201 Washington Park Dr., Jefferson City, MO. **Telephone:** 630-781-7247 **E-Mail Address:** jcrenegades@gmail.com. **Website:** jeffcityrenenegades.com. **President/General Manager:** Steve Dullard. **Head Coach:** Mike DeMilia and Rusty Creed.

JOPLIN OUTLAWS

Stadium: Joe Becker Stadium., 4th and High Streets, Jolpin, Mo. **Telephone:** (417) 825-4218. **E-Mail Address:** mark@joplinoutlaws.com. **Website:** joplinoutlaws.com. **President/General Manager:** Mark Rains.

NEVADA GRIFFONS

Stadium: Lyons Stadium, Nevada, MO. **Telephone:** (417) 667-6159. **E-Mail Address:** gwodell@mmm.com. **Website:** nevadagriffons.org. **Manager:** Greg O'Dell

SEDALIA BOMBERS

Stadium: Liberty Park Stadium, Sedalia, MO 65301. **Telephone:** (660) 287-4722. **E-Mail Address:** sedbomb-ers@gmail.com. **Website:** sedaliabombers .com. **President/General Manager:** Jud Kindle. **Manager:** Craig McAndrews.

ST. JOSEPH MUSTANGS

Stadium: Phil Welch Stadium, St. Joseph, MO. **Telephone:** (816) 244-8045. **Website:** stjoemustangs. com. **Manager:** Johnny Coy.

MLB DRAFT LEAGUE

Website: www.mlbdraftleague.com.
Email: draftleague@prepbaseballreport.com.
Founded: 2021.
Operated By: Prep Baseball Report.
President, Draft League: Sean Campbell.
2023 Master Schedule: 80 games. **Start Date:** June 1. **Closing Date:** Sept. 2. **Playoffs:** Championship game, Sept. 4.
Amateur Schedule: 30 games. **Start Date:** June 1. **Closing Date:** July 4
Professional Schedule: 50 games. **Start Date:** July

7. **Closing Date:** Sept. 2. **Playoffs:** Championship Game, Sept. 4.

FREDERICK KEYS

Mailing Address: 21 Stadium Drive, Frederick, MD 21703. **Email:** info@frederickkeys.com. **Telephone:** 301-662-0013. **Website:** https://www.mlbdraftleague.com/frederick
General Manager: Andrew Klein.

MAHONING VALLEY SCRAPPERS

Address: 111 Eastwood Mall Blvd., Niles, OH 44446-1357. **Email:** info@mvscrappers.com. **Telephone:** (330) 505-0000. **Website:** www.mlbdraftleague.com/mahoning-valley
General Manager: Heather Sahli.

STATE COLLEGE SPIKES

Address: 112 Medlar Field at Lubrano Park, University Park, PA 16802. **Email:** frontoffice@statecollegespikes. com. **Telephone:** (814) 272-1711. **Website:** www.mlb-draftleague.com/state-college
General Manager: Scott Walker.

TRENTON THUNDER

Mailing Address: 1 Thunder Road, Trenton, N.J. 08611. **Email:** fun@trentonthunder.com. **Telephone:** 609-394-3300. **Website:** www.mlbdraftleague.com/trenton
General Manager: Jeff Hurley.

WEST VIRGINIA BLACK BEARS

Address: 2040 Gyorko Drive, Granville, WV 26534. **Telephone:** (304) 293-7910. **Website:** www.mlb-draftleague.com/west-virginia
General Manager: Leighann Sainato.

WILLIAMSPORT CROSSCUTTERS

Address: 1700 West Fourth St, Williamsport, PA 17701. **Telephone:** (570) 326-3389. **Website:** www.mlb-draftleague.com/williamsport
General Manager: Doug Estes.

NEW ENGLAND COLLEGIATE LEAGUE

Mailing Address: 122 Mass Moca Way, North Adams, MA 01247. **Telephone:** (413) 652-1031. **Fax:** (413) 473-0012. **E-Mail Address:** smcgrath@necbl.com. **Website:** necbl.com. **Year founded:** 1993. **President:** John DeRosa. **Commissioner:** Sean McGrath. **Deputy Commissioner:** Gregg Hunt. **Secretary:** Max Pinto. **Treasurer:** Paul Morgan.

BRISTOL BLUES

Stadium Address: Muzzy Field, Muzzy Street, Bristol, CT 06010. **Telephone:** (203) 981-8331. **E-Mail Address:** jordan.bristolblues@gmail.com. **Website:** bristolblues-baseball.com. **General Manager:** Jordy Scheiner. **Manager:** Tim Binkowski.

DANBURY WESTERNERS

Stadium Address: Rogers Park, 21 Memorial Dr., Danbury, CT 06810. **Telephone:** (203) 502-9167. **E-Mail Address:** jspitser@msn.com. **Website:** danburywestern-ers.com. **President:** Jon Pitser. **General Manager:** Chris Nathanson. **Field Manager:** Ian Ratchford.

AMATEUR/YOUTH

KEENE SWAMP BATS

Stadium: Alumni Field, 77 Arch St., Keene, NH 03431. **Telephone:** 603-731-5240. **E-Mail Address:** kwatterson@ghousen.com. **Website:** keeneswampbats.com. **President:** Kevin Watterson. **Manager:** Shaun McKenna.

MARTHA'S VINEYARD SHARKS

Stadium: MRV High School, 100 Edgartown Vineyard Haven Rd, Oak Bluffs, Martha's Vineyard. **Telephone:** 508-813-0380. **E-Mail Address:** russ.curran@mvsharks.com. **Website:** mvsharks.com. **General Manager:** Russ Curran. **Field Manager:** Jay Mendez.

MYSTIC SCHOONERS

Stadium: Dodd Stadium, 14 Stott Ave., Norwich, CT 06360. **Telephone:** (860) 333-4771. **E-Mail Address:** don@mysticbaseball.org. **Website:** schoonersbaseball. com. **Executive Director:** Don Benoit. **General Manager:** Dennis Long. **Field Manager:** Phil Orbe.

NEWPORT GULLS

Stadium: Cardines Field, Americas Cup Ave., Newport, RI 02840. **Telephone:** (401) 845-6832. **E-Mail Address:** gm@newportgulls.com. **Website:** newportgulls.com. **President/General Manager:** Chuck Paiva. **Field Manager:** Frank Holbrook.

NORTH ADAMS STEEPLECATS

Stadium: Joe Wolfe Field, 310 State St., North Adams MA 01247. **Telephone:** 413-841-5590. **E-Mail Address:** paul.procopio@steeplecats.org. **Website:** steeplecats. org. **General Manager:** Paul Procopio. **Field Manager:** Austin Straub.

NORTH SHORE NAVIGATORS

Stadium: Fraser Field, 365 Western Ave., Lynn, MA 01904. **Telephone:** 781-316-6656. **E-Mail Address:** dj@nsnavs.com. **Website:** nsnavs.com. **General Manager:** Derek January. **Manager:** Bob Macaluso.

OCEAN STATE WAVES

Stadium: Old Mountain Field, 875 Kingston Rd, S. Kingston, RI 02879. **Telephone:** (516-317-0803. **E-Mail Address:** eric@oceanstatewaves.com. **Website:** oceanstatewaves.com. **President/General Manager:** Eric Hirschbein-Bodnar. **Field Manager:** Eric Hirschbein-Bodnar.

SANFORD MARINERS

Stadium: Goodall Park, 38 Roberts Street, Sanford, ME 04073. **Telephone:** (207) 650-1902. **E-Mail:** aizaryk@bridgtonacademy.org. **General Manager:** Aaron Izaryk. **Field Manager:** Nic Lops.

UPPER VALLEY NIGHTHAWKS

Mailing Address: 134 Stevens Road Lebanon, NH 03766. **Telephone:** 864-380-2873 **E-Mail Address:** noah@uppervalleynighthawks.com. **Website:** upper uppervalleynighthawks.com. **General Manager:** Noah Crane. **Field Manager:** Justin Devoid.

VALLEY BLUE SOX

Stadium: MacKenzie Stadium, 500 Beach St.

Holoyoke, MA 01040. **Telephone:** 860-930-9257. **E-Mail Address:** mattd@valleybluesox.com. **Website:** valleybluesox.com. **President:** Matt Drury. **Manager:** Pedro Randolph.

VERMONT MOUNTAINEERS

Stadium: Montpelier Recreation Field, Elm St., Montpelier, VT 05601. **Telephone:** (802) 272-8728. **E-Mail Address:** gmvtm@comcast.net. **Website:** thevermont mountaineers.com. **General Manager:** Brian Gallagher. **Field Manager:** Mitch Holmes.

NEW YORK COLLEGIATE BASEBALL LEAGUE

Mailing Address: 398 East Dyke St. Wellsville, NY 14895. **Telephone:** (585) 455-2345. **Website:** nycbl. com. **Year founded:** 1978. **President:** Bill McConnell. **Commissioner:** Joe Brown. **Email Address:** joebrown. nycbl@gmail.com. **Vice President:** Brian McConnell Jr. **Deputy Commissioner:** Dave Meluni. **Treasurer:** Dennis Duffy. **Secretary:** Steven Ackley. **Franchises: Eastern Division:** Cortland Crush, Rochester Ridgemen., Sherrill Silversmiths, Syracuse Salt Cats, Syracuse Spartans. **Western Division:** Dansville Gliders, Genesee Rapids, Hornell Steamers, Horesheads Hitmen, Olean Oilers. **Schedule:** 42 games. **All-Star Game:** July 10. **Roster Limit:** Unlimited (college-eligible players only).

CORTLAND CRUSH

Mailing Address: 2745 Summer Ridge Rd, LaFayette, NY 13084. **Telephone:** 315-391-8167. **Email Address:** wmmac4@aol.com. **Website:** cortlandcrush.com. **Vice President:** Matt DeHart. **President/Field Manager:** Bill McConnell.

DANSVILLE GLIDERS

Mailing Address: P.O. Box 553, Dansville, NY 14437. **Telephone:** 585-596-9523. **Email Address:** glidersb21@gmail.com. **Owner/GM:** Steven Ackley. **Field Manager:** Steve Bowley.

GENESEE RAPIDS

Address: 9726 Rte 19, Houghton, NY 14744. **Telephone:** (716-969-0688. **E-Mail Address:** gm@hornelldodgers.com. **Website:** geneseerapidsbaseball.com. **Owner/General Manager:** Ralph P. Kerr. **Field Manager:** Beach Harmon.

HORNELL STEAMERS

Mailing Address: PO Box 235, Hornell, NY 14843. **Telephone:** (607) 661-4173. **Fax:** (607) 661-4173. **Website:** hornellsteamersbaseball.com. **General Manager:** Paul Welker. **Field Manager:** Mike Gibson.

HORSEHEADS HITMEN

Mailing Address: P.O. Box 634, Horesheads, NY, 14845. **Telephone:** (570) 335-9575. **Website:** www.hh-hitmen. com. **President/General Manager:** Larry Gill. **Field Manager:** Brian Hill.

OLEAN OILERS

Address: 122 North Barry St., Olean, NY 14760. **Email:** oleanoilers@gmail.com. **Website:** oleanoilersbaseball. com.

Baseball America 2023 Directory • **239**

AMATEUR/YOUTH

ROCHESTER RIDGEMEN

Mailing Address: 651 Taylor Dr, Xenia, OH 45385. **Telephone:** (937) 352-1000. **E-Mail Address:** baseball @athletesinaction.org. **Website:** rochesterridgemen .org. **President:** Jason Jipson. **Field Manager:** John Byington.

SHERRILL SILVERSMITHS

Address: 139 E. Hamilton Ave., Sherrill, NY 13461. **Telephone:** (401) 935-1352. **E-Mail Address:** silver-smithsbaseball@gmail.com. **President:** Dennis Duffy & Mike Sherlock. **Field Manager:** Tim Bailey.

SYRACUSE SALT CATS

Mailing Address: 208 Lakeland Ave, Syracuse, NY 13209. **Telephone:** (315) 727-9220. **Fax:** (315) 488-1750. **E-Mail Address:** Syracusesaltcats@gmail.com. **Website:** saltcats.sportingin.com/home. **President:** Mike Martinez. **Field Manager:** Mike Martinez.

SYRACUSE SPARTANS

Mailing Address: 208 Lakeland Ave, Syracuse, NY 13209. **Telephone:** (315) 727-4251. **E-Mail Address:** mmarti6044@yahoo.com. **Director:** Dean Panos. **President:** JJ Potrikus. **Field Manager:** Paul Ludden

NORTHWOODS LEAGUE

Office Address: 2900 4th St SW, Rochester, MN 55902. **Telephone:** (507) 536-4579. **Fax:** (507) 536-4597. **E-Mail Address:** info@northwoodsleague.com. **Website:** northwoodsleague.com. **Year Founded:** 1994. **Chairman:** Dick Radatz, Jr. **Corporate Secretary:** Robert D. Finnell. **Treasurer:** Kathy Radatz. **League Affiliates Representative:** Rob Zerjav.

DIVISIONS: Great Plains West--Bismarck Larks, Mankato MoonDogs, Minnesota Mud Puppies, Minot Hot Tots, St. Cloud Rox, Willmar Stingers. **Great Plains East**--Duluth Huskies, Eau Claire Express, La Crosse Loggers, Rochester Honkers, Thunder Bay Border Cats, Waterloo Bucks. **Great Lakes West**—Fond Du Lac Dock Spiders, Green Bay Rockers, Lakeshore Chinooks, Madison Mallards, Wausau Woodchucks, Wisconsin Rapids Rafters, **Great Lakes East**--Battle Creek Battle Jacks, Kalamazoo Growlers, Kenosha Kingfish, Kokomo Jackrabbits, Rockford Rivets, Traverse City Pit Spitters.

BATTLE CREEK BATTLEJACKS

Mailing Address: 189 Bridge Street, Battle Creek, MI 49017. **Telephone:** (269) 962-0735. **Fax:** (269) 962-0741. **Email Address:** info@battlecreekbombers.com. **Website:** battlecreekbombers.com. **Owner:** Brian Colopy. **General Manager:** Denny Smith. **Director of Operations:** Steven Laws. **Director of Digital Content:** Evan Brown. **Fan Experience Director:** Alex Kuehl.
Field Manager: Chris Clark.
Field: C.O. Brown Stadium.

BISMARCK LARKS

Mailing Address: 300 N 4th Street, Suite 103, Bismarck, ND 58501. **Telephone:** (701) 557-7600. **Email Address:** info@larksbaseball.com. **Website:** larksbaseball.com. **Founder/Majority Owner:** John Bollinger. **Chief Experience Officer:** Kaitlyn Mack. **VP, Operations:**

Nathan Maddox. **VP, Ticket Sales and Experience:** Aaron Guerrero. **Sponsorship Experience Director:** Cody Nielson. **Creative Director:** Kayla Rimer. **Marketing Director:** Isaac Bugarin. **Entertainment Director:** Joe Zollo.
Field Manager: Will Flynt. **Assistant Coaches:** Jack Schaffer, Joey Rosenblum.
Field: Bismarck Municipal.

DULUTH HUSKIES

Mailing Address: PO Box 16231, Duluth, MN 55816. **Telephone:** (218) 786-9909.
Fax: (218) 786-9001. **E-Mail Address:** huskies@duluth-huskies.com. **Website:** duluthhuskies.com.
Owner: Michael Rosenzweig. **General Manager:** Greg Culver.
Field Manager: Marcus Pointer. **Hitting Coaches:** Jeff Chapuran, Chris Miguel. **Pitching Coach:** Will Peterson.
Field: Wade Stadium.

EAU CLAIRE EXPRESS

Mailing Address: 108 E Grand Ave, Eau Claire, WI 54701. **Telephone:** (715) 839-7788. **Fax:** (715) 839-7676. **E-Mail Address:** info@eauclaireexpress.com. **Website:** eauclaireexpress.com.
Owner: Craig Toycen. **General Manager:** Sammi Costello. **Director of Food and Beverage:** Ben Teske. **Director of Marketing:** Michelle Hofacker.
Director of Operations/Field Manager: Dale Varsho.
Field: Carson Park.

FOND DU LAC DOCK SPIDERS

Mailing Address: 980 E Division St., **Fond du Lac, WI 54935. Telephone:** (920) 907-9833. **Email Address:** info@dockspiders.com. **Website:** dockspiders.com.
President: Rob Zerjav. **General Manager:** Jim Musudek. **Assistant General Manager:** Tate Tranel. **Ticket Manager:** TJ Draves.
Field Manager: Douglas Coe.
Field: Herr-Baker Field

GREEN BAY ROCKERS

Mailing Address: 2325 Holgren Way Suite, Green Bay, WI 54303. **Telephone:** (920) 497-7225. **Fax:** (920) 437-3551. **Email Address:** info@greenbayrockers.com Website: northwoodsleague.com/green-bay-rockers
Owner: Mark Skogen. **Vice President:** Brian Stenzel. **VP and General Manager:** John Fanta. **Director of Partnerships:** Brian Kuklinski. **Director of Ticket Sales:** Andrew Johnson. **Facility Director:** Kevin Leisgang. **Event Manager:** Kelly Hawkins. **Graphic Design:** Alex Dozek. **Inside Sales Coordinator:** Trevor Amerson.
Field Manager: Chris Krepline. **Hitting Coach:** Cody Hartman. **Assistant Coach:** Michael Ruggiero.
Field: Capital Credit Union Park.

KALAMAZOO GROWLERS

Mailing Address: 251 Mills St, Kalamazoo, MI 49048. **Telephone:** (269) 492-9966.
Website: growlersbaseball.com.
Owner: Brian Colopy. **General Manager:** Kevin Timmer. **Assistant GM:** Nick Stoglin. **Director of Buisness Relations:** Kendall Soto. **Director of Stadium Operations:** Tom Olds. **Food and Beverage Director:** Avery Cleveland. **Director of Media and Entertainment:** Dean Thomas. **Director of Business Relations:** Justin Zeldes. **Partnership Activation Director:** Michaila

240 · Baseball America 2023 Directory

BaseballAmerica.com

AMATEUR/YOUTH

Hanley. **Office Manager:** Tonya Byers.
Field Manager: Cody Piechocki. **Pitching Coach:** Ben Harley. **Field:** Homer Stryker Field.

KENOSHA KINGFISH

Mailing Address: 7817 Sheridan Rd, Kenosha, WI 53143. **Telephone:** (262) 653-0900. **Website:** kingfish-baseball.com.
Owner: Bill Fanning. **General Manager:** Ryne Goralski. **Marketing Manager:** Justin Dade. **Community Engagement Manager:** Delaine Candela. **Ticket Sales Manager:** Spencer Roberts. **Ticket Sales:** Andrew Curtis.
Field Manager: JT Scara.
Field: Simmons Field.

KOKOMO JACKRABBITS

Address: 400 S Union St, Kokomo, IN 46901.
Telephone: (765) 457-5000. **Website:** northwoods-league.com/kokomo-jackrabbits
General Manager: Nathan Martin. **Assistant GM:** Connor Carey. **Ticket Sales Representative:** Tanner McBride.
Field Manager: Johnston Hobbs.
Field: Kokomo Municipal Stadium.

LA CROSSE LOGGERS

Mailing Address: 1225 Caledonia St, La Crosse, WI 54603. **Telephone:** (608) 796-9553. **Fax:** (608) 796-9032. **E-Mail Address:** info@lacrosseloggers.com. **Website:** lacrosseloggers.com.
Owner: Dan and Ruth Kapanke. **President:** Chris Gooddell. **General Manager:** Ben Kapanke. **Director of Group Sales:** Magann Dykema.Field Manager: Brian Lewis. **Field:** Copeland Park.
Field Manager: Josh Frye.
Field: Copeland Park.

LAKESHORE CHINOOKS

Mailing Address: 983 Badger Circle, Grafton, WI 53024. **Telephone:** (262) 618-4659. **Fax:** (262) 618-4362. **E-Mail Address:** info@lakeshorechinooks.com. **Website:** lakeshorechinooks.com.
Owner: Jim Kacmarcik. **General Manager:** Eric Snodgrass. **Assistant General Manager:** Robert Rothe. **Director of Partnerships. David Christensen. Director of Hospitality:** Brie Bartz. **Media Manager:** David Koler.
Field: Kapco Park.

MADISON MALLARDS

Mailing Address: 2920 N Sherman Ave, Madison, WI 53704. **Telephone:** (608) 246-4277. **Fax:** (608) 246-4163. **E-Mail Address:** info@mallardsbaseball.com. **Website:** mallardsbaseball.com. **Owner:** Steve Schmitt. **President:** Vern Stenman. **Owner:** Steve Schmitt. **President:** Vern Stenman. **COO:** Conor Caloia. **VP of Finance:** Molly Schicantek. **General Manager:** Samantha Rubin. **Director of Merchandising:** Chase Eagan. **VP of Corporate Ticket Sales: Monica Wagner: Corporate Account Managers:** Scott Preimesberger and Ashlea Klootwyk. **Director of Ticket Operations:** Ashley Kouba. **Assistant GM of Inside Ticket Sales:** Brett Tornow. **Inside Ticket Sales:** Andrew Wirtzfeld, Zach Parr, Brady Quinn, Logan McNames. **Marketing Director:** Kyle Chisholm. **Director of Operations:** Sean Brandhorst. **HR Director:** Nathan Diehl.
Field Manager: Donnie Scott.
Field: Warner Park.

MANKATO MOONDOGS

Mailing Address: 1221 Caledonia Street, Mankato, MN 56001. **Telephone:** (507) 625-7047. **Fax:** (507) 625-7059. **E-Mail Address:** office@mankatomoondogs.com. **Website:** mankatomoondogs.com.
President: Chris Gooddell. **General Manager:** Tyler Kuch. **Director of Ticket Sales:** Walker Regier.
Field: Franklin Rogers Park.

MINNESOTA MUD PUPPIES

Travel team that is operated by the league.

MINOT HOT TOTS

Address: 1905 2nd St SE, Suite S4, Minot, ND 58701. **Telephone:** (701) 838-8687. **Website:** northwoods-league.com/minot-hot-tots/
General Manager: Monica Blake. **Director of Ticket Sales:** John Armstrong. **Partnership Marketing Manager:** Hannah Ekwall. **Content Media Manager:** Emily Love. **Ballpark Operations Manager:** Daniel Schuetz.
Field Manager: Mitchell Gallagher.
Field: Corbett Field.

ROCHESTER HONKERS

Mailing Address: 307 E Center St, Rochester, MN 55904. **Telephone:** (507) 289-1170. **Fax:** (507) 289-1866. **E-Mail Address:** honkersbaseball@gmail.com. **Website:** rochesterhonkers.com.
General Manager: Jeremy Aagard. **Assistant GM:** Clint Narramore. **Team President:** Chris Goodell.
Field Manager: Andrew Urbistondo. **Pitching Coach:** Mark Reardanz.
Field: Mayo Field.

ROCKFORD RIVETS

Mailing Address: 4503 Interstate Blvd., Loves Park, IL 61111. **Telephone:** 815-240-4159. **E-Mail Address:** info@rockfordrivets.com Website: rockfordrivets.com.
General Manager: Chad Bauer.
Director of Ticket Sales: Bryan Fish.
Field: Rivets Stadium.

ST. CLOUD ROX

Mailing Address: 5001 8th St N, St. Cloud, MN 56303. **Telephone:** (320) 240-9798. **Fax:** (320) 255-5228. **E-Mail Address:** info@stcloudrox.com. **Website:** stcloudrox.com. **President:** Gary Posch. **Vice President:** Scott Schreiner. **General Manager:** Mike Johnson. **Field Manager:** Augie Rodriguez. **Field:** Joe Faber Field.

THUNDER BAY BORDER CATS

Mailing Address: PO Box 29105 Thunder Bay, Ontario P7B 6P9. **Telephone:** (807) 766-2287.
President: David Valente. **VP:** Bryan Graham. **Treasurer:** Dan Nucci. **Secretary:** Dean Woloschuk. **Clubhouse Manager:** Taylor Metzger. **Concession Manager:** Sherry Archer.
Field Manager: JM Kelly.
Field: Port Arthur Stadium.

TRAVERSE CITY PIT SPITTERS

Address: 333 Stadium Dr., Traverse City, MI 49685. **Telephone:** (231) 943-0100. **E-Mail Address:** info@tra-

AMATEUR/YOUTH

versecitybaseball.com. **Website:** northwoodsleague.com/traverse-city-pit-spitters/

CEO/Managing Member: Joe Chamberlin. **General Manager:** Jacqueline Holm. **Assistant GM:** Sam Connell. **Ticket Sales Manager:** Ian Williamson. **Operations Manager:** Kendall Patrick. **Food and Beverage Manager:** Katie Johnson.

Field Manager: Josh Rebandt.

WASAU WOODCHUCKS

Address: 2401 N 3rd St, Wausau, WI 54403. **Telephone:** (715) 845-5055.

Owner: Mark Macdonald. **President/GM:** Ryan Trey. **Assistant GM:** Traci Wisz. **Manager of Operations:** Brianne Barta. **Marketing and Creative Services Manager:** Ryan Malone. **Ticket Sales:** Kaitlyn Pedersen.

Manager: Brock Moss.

Field: Athletic Park.

WATERLOO BUCKS

Mailing Address: PO Box 4124, Waterloo, IA 50704. **Telephone:** (319) 232-0500. **Fax:** (319) 232-0700. **E-Mail Address:** waterloobucks@waterloobucks.com. **Website:** waterloobucks.com.

General Manager: Dan Corbin.

Assistant GM: Jake Horan.

Field Manager: Darrell Handelsman.

Field: Riverfront Stadium.

WILLMAR STINGERS

Mailing Address: PO Box 201, Willmar, MN, 56201. **Telephone:** (320) 222-2010. **E-Mail Address:** ryan@willmarstingers.com. **Website:** willmarstingers.com.

Owners: Marc Jerzak, Ryan Voz. **VP of Operations (Ticketing):** Jordan Yessak. **VP of Operations (Sales):** Hunter Rommes. **VP of Operations (Video):** Jaydon Simonson.

Field Manager: Freddy Smith. **Pitching Coach:** Michael Newstrom. **Assistant Coach:** Mason Rapp.

Field: Taunton Stadium.

WISCONSIN RAPIDS RAFTERS

Mailing Address: 521 Lincoln St, Wisconsin Rapids, WI 54494. **Telephone:** (715) 424-5400. **E-Mail Address:** info@raftersbaseball.com. **Website:** raftersbaseball.com.

Owner: Joe and Vince Fonti. **Inside Sales and Video Production Manager:** Tyler Miller.

Field Manager: Kirk Shrider. **Associate Head Coach:** John Halama. **Infield Coach:** Sean Grebeck.

Field: Witter Field.

PERFECT GAME COLLEGIATE LEAGUE

Mailing Address: 8 Michaels Lane, Old Brookville, NY 11545. **Telephone:** (516) 521-0206. **Fax:** (516) 801-0818. **E-Mail Address:** valkun@aol.com.

Website: pgcbl.com.

Year Founded: 2010.

President: Jeffrey Kunion.

Director of Communications: Travis Larner

Executive Committee: Bob Ohmann (Newark Pilots), Paul Samulski (Albany Dutchmen). Robbie Nichols (Elmira Pioneers), George Deak (Utica Blue Sox), Kevin Hinchey (Saugerties Stallions)

ALBANY DUTCHMEN

Stadium Address: 4702 Hurst Rd, Altamont, NY

12009. **Phone:** 518-210-8383. **Email:** jbrinkma@gmail.com. **Website:** dutchmenbaseball.com

President/Partner: Paul Samulski. **Partner:** Alan Bignall. **General Manager/Vice President:** Jason Brinkman.

Head Coach: Nick Davey

AMSTERDAM MOHAWKS

Stadium Address: 65 Crescent Avenue, Amsterdam, N.Y. 12010. **Mailing Address:** P.O. Box 334, Amsterdam, N.Y. 12010. **Phone:** 607-222-4086. **Email:** gm@amsterdammohawks.com. **Website:** amsterdammohawks.com

President: Brian Spagnola. **Vice President:** Dave Dittman.

Head Coach: Keith Griffin.

AUBURN DOUBLEDAYS

Address: 130 North Division Street, Auburn, N.Y. 13021. **Phone:** (315) 255-2489. **Website:** auburndoubledays.com

Owners: Bob Ohmann, Don Lewis. **Operations Manager:** Sam Shedden.

Head Coach: Ben Julian

BATAVIA MUCKDOGS

Address: 252B State Street Batavia NY 14020. **Phone:** (585) 524-2260. **Website:** canusamuckdogs.com

Owner: Robbie Nichols. **General Manager:** Marc Witt.

Head Coach: Joey Martinez

BOONVILLE LUMBERJACKS

Stadium Address: 220 Line Drive, Boonville, N.Y. 13303. **Email:** boonvillelumberjacks@gmail.com. **Website:** boonvillelumberjacks.com

Owner: Butch Russo

ELMIRA PIONEERS

Stadium Address: 546 Luce Street, Elmira, N.Y. 14904. **Phone:** 607-734-2690. **Email:** donspioneers@gmail.com. **Website:** theelmirapioneers.com

Owners: Nellie Franco-Nichols and Robbie Nichols

Head Coach: Andy Drum

GENEVA RED WINGS

Stadium Address: 180 Lyceum Street, Geneva, N.Y. **Phone:** 919-422-4323. **Email:** info@genevaredwings.com. **Website:** genevaredwings.com

Owner: Bob Ohmann, Leslie Ohmann, Dave Herbst. **General Manager:** John Salone

Head Coach: Dan Munn

GLENS FALLS DRAGONS

Stadium Address: 175 Dix Avenue, Glens Falls, N.Y. 12801. **Phone:** 518-361-5316. **Email:** benbernard1@yahoo.com. **Website:** gfdragons.pointstreaksites.com/view/gfdragons. **President:** Ben Bernard

Head Coach: Jon Mueller

JAMESTOWN TARP SKUNKS

Stadium Address: 485 Falconer Street, Jamestown, N.Y. 14701. **Phone:** 716-705-5600. **Email:** jacob@tarpskunks.com. **Website:** tarpskunks.com/

Owner: Mike Zimmerman. **Chairman:** Russ Diethrick. **Director of Business Operations:** Jacob Kindberg.

Head Coach: Jordan Basile

AMATEUR/YOUTH

MOHAWK VALLEY DIAMONDDAWGS

Stadium Address: Burwell Street, Little Falls, N.Y. 13365. **Phone:** 315-985-0692. **Email:** travis@mvdiamonddawgs.com. **Owner:** Travis Heiser. **Website:** mvdiamonddawgs.com
Head Coach: Steve Luby

NEWARK PILOTS

Stadium Address: 1160 East Union Street, Newark, N.Y. 14513. **Mailing Address:** 65 Williams Street, Lyons, N.Y. 14489. **Phone:** 315-576-6710. **Fax:** 315-573-7190. **Email:** newarkpilots@gmail.com. **Website:** newarkpilots.com.
Owner: Bob Ohmann, Don Lewis
Head Coach: Brian Greisman

NIAGARA POWER

Address: 1201 Hyde Park Blvd Niagara Falls NY 14301. **Phone Number:** 716-286-8653. **Email:** john.m.dicarlo@gmail.com. **Website:** niagarapowerbaseball.com
Owner: John DiCarlo

ONEONTA OUTLAWS

Stadium Address: 15 James Georgeson Avenue, Oneonta, N.Y. 13820. **Mailing Address:** 291 Chestnut Street, Oneonta, N.Y. 13820. **Phone:** 607-432-6326. **Email:** joehughes@oneontaoutlaws.com. **Website:** oneontaoutlaws.com.
Owner: Gary Laing. **General Manager:** Joe Hughes
Head Coach: John Boland

SAUGERTIES STALLIONS

Stadium Address: Washington Avenue Extension Saugerties, N.Y. 12477. **Phone:** 845-707-0265. **Email:** thesaugertiesstallions@gmail.com. **Website:** saugertiesstallions.com. **Owner:** Kevin Hinchey
Head Coach: Collin Martin.
Director of Baseball Operations: Justin Whittaker

UTICA BLUE SOX

Stadium Address: 898 Rose Place, Utica, N.Y. 13502. **Mailing Address:** PO Box 7, Marcy, N.Y. 13403. **Telephone:** 315-855-5013. **Email:** george@globalgraphicsny.com. **Website:** uticabluesox.net.
Owner: George Deak. **General Manager:** Juliano Macera. **Director of Communications:** Jack Angelucci.
Head Coach: Doug Delett.
Assistant Coach: Chris Amaya

WATERTOWN RAPIDS

Stadium Address: 970 Coffeen St., Watertown, N.Y. 13601. **Mailing Address:** PO Box 6250, Watertown, N.Y. 13601. **Phone:** 315-836-1545. **Email:** rapidsgm@gmail.com. **Website:** watertown-rapids.com
Owner: Michael Schell and Paul Velte.
General Manager: Nick Czerow.
Head Coach: Mike Kogut.

PROSPECT LEAGUE

Mailing Address: PO Box 1156, Mahomet, IL 61853. **E-Mail Address:** commissioner@prospectleague.com. **Website:** prospectleague.com.
Year Founded: 1963 as Central Illinois Collegiate League; known as Prospect League since 2009.

Commissioner: David Brauer
Deputy Commissioner: Lisa Bastien. **Director of Media & Technology:** Jacob Wise

ALTON RIVER DRAGONS

Stadium: Lloyd Hopkins Field
Mailing Address: 4550 College Avenue, Alton, IL 62002
Telephone: (618) 433-3665
E-Mail Address: alton@prospectleague.com
Website: altonbaseball.com
General Manager: Dallas Martz
Field Manager: Scotty Scott

BURLINGTON BEES

Stadium: Community Field
Mailing Address: 2712 Mt. Pleasant St., Burlington, IA 52601
Telephone: (319) 754-5705
E-Mail Address: Jill@gobees.com
Website: gobees.com
General Manager: Tad Lowary. **Assistant General Manager:** Jill Mason. **Director of Media Relations:** Ted Guzman. **Director of Stadium Operations:** RJ Larson
Field Manager: Owen Oreskovich.

CAPE CATFISH

Stadium: Capaha Field
Mailing Address: 1400 Broadway St., Cape Girardeau, MO 63701
Telephone: 573-803-3103
E-Mail Address: info@capecatfish.com
Website: capecatfish.com
General Manager: Mark Hogan.
Assistant General Manager: Cindy Gannon.

CHAMPION CITY KINGS

Stadium: Carleton Davidson Stadium
Mailing Address: 1301 Mitchell Blvd., Springfield, OH 45503
Telephone: (937) 342-0320
E-Mail Address: cckings@gmail.com
Website: championcitykings.com
General Manager: Ginger Fulton.
Field Manager: Gavin Murphy.
Baseball Operations: Mark Lucas

CHILLICOTHE PAINTS

Stadium: VA Memorial Stadium
Mailing Address: 11 East 2nd St., Chillicothe, OH 45601. **Telephone:** (740) 773-8326
E-Mail Address: paints@bright.net
Website: chillicothepaints.com
General Manager: Bryan Wickline. **Director of Media & Broadcasting:** Jacob Wise. **Director of Stadium Operations:** Tyler Hart

CLINTON LUMBERKINGS

Stadium: NelsonCorp Field
Mailing Address: 537 Ballpark Drive, Clinton, IA 52732
Telephone: (563) 242-0727
E-Mail Address: lumberkings@lumberkings.com
Website: lumberkings.com
General Manager: Ted Tornow. **Director of Merchandise:** Scott Damhoff. **Director of Operations:** Jake Fratzke. **Head Groundskeeper:** Matthew Troxel.
Field Manager: Jack Dahm

BaseballAmerica.com

Baseball America 2023 Directory • **243**

AMATEUR/YOUTH

DANVILLE DANS

Stadium: Danville Stadium
Mailing Address: 4 Maywood, Danville, IL 61832
Telephone: (217) 918-3401
Fax: (217) 446-9995
E-Mail Address: danvilledans@comcast.net
Website: danvilledans.com
League Director: Jeanie Cooke.
General Manager: Jeanie Cooke.
Field Manager: Eric Coleman.

ILLINOIS VALLEY PISTOL SHRIMP

Stadium: Schweickert Stadium at Veterans Memorial Park
Mailing Address: 3210 Anton Dr., Aurora, IL 60504
E-Mail Address: info@pistolshrimpbaseball.com
Telephone: (630) 708-2416
Owner & Field Manager: John Jakiemiec
General Manager: June Kelly. **Assistant General Manager & Play-by-Play Voice:** Lucas Burris.
Operations Supervisor: Katie McCumber. **Digital Support Administrator:** Anthony DiSerio. **Sales and Hospitality:** Sarah Kaminsky

JACKSON ROCKABILLYS

Stadium: The Jackson Baseball Stadium
Mailing Address: 4 Fun Place, Jackson, TN 38308
Telephone: (731) 574-9300
E-Mail Address: info@rockabillysbaseball.com
Website: rockabillysbaseball.com
President & CEO: Dennis Bastien. Executive Vice President, **Operations:** Lisa Bastien. **Vice President & General Manager:** Steve DeSalvo. **Marketing & Social Media Coordinator:** Camryn Martz.
Field Manager: Matt Franco

JOHNSTOWN MILL RATS

Stadium: Sargent's Stadium at the Point
Mailing Address: P.O .Box 522, Johnstown, PA 15907
Telephone: (814) 535-1305
E-Mail Address: tickets@millrats.com
Website: millrats.com
Assistant General Manager: Sarah Rex.
Director of Partnerships: Lisa Downey.
Media Relations & Broadcaster: George Lucas.

LAFAYETTE AVIATORS

Stadium: Loeb Stadium
Mailing Address: 1915 Scott St, Lafayette, IN 47904
Telephone: (765) 464-6810
E-Mail Address: tickets@lafayettebaseball.com
Website: lafayettebaseball.com
General Manager: David Krakower. **Director of Community Engagement:** Gabbie Bush. **Director of Ticket Sales:** Hunter Roush. **Director of Marketing:** Cass Clark.

NORMAL CORNBELTERS

Stadium: The CornCrib
Mailing Address: 1000 W Raab Rd, Normal, IL 61701
Telephone: (309) 454-2255
Email Address: info@cornbeltersbaseball.com
Website: cornbeltersbaseball.com
President of Operations: Matt Stembridge. **Assistant General Manager:** Gavin Legett. **Director of Facilities:** Brad Yochum. **Director of Sales:** Jarrett Rodgers.

O'FALLON HOOTS

Stadium: CarShield Field
Mailing Address: 100 North Main St., O'Fallon, MO 63366
Telephone: (636) 741-4668
Email Address: ofallon@prospectleague.com
General Manager: David Schmoll. **Director of Corporate Sponsorships:** Matthew Lyday. **Director of Ticketing:** Mackenzie Scott.

QUINCY GEMS

Stadium: QU Stadium
Mailing Address: 1400 N. 30th St., Suite 1, Quincy, IL 62301
Telephone: (217) 214-7436
E-Mail Address: quincygems@yahoo.com
Website: quincygems.com
Team Owners: Jimmie and Julie Louthan
General Manager: Jacob Hollensteiner
Field Manager: Brad Gyorkos

REX BASFRALL

Stadium: Bob Warn Field at Sycamore Stadium
Mailing Address: 1111 North 3rd St, Terre Haute, IN 47807
Telephone: (812) 478-3817
E-mail Address: frontoffice@rexbaseball.com
Website: rexbaseball.com
League Director/General Manager: Bruce Rosselli
Field Manager: Harry Markotay

SOUTHERN ILLINOIS

Stadium: Rent One Park
Mailing Address: 1000 Miners Drive, Marion, IL 62959
Telephone: (618) 998-8499
E-Mail Address: info@marionstadium.com
General Manager: David Kost
Field Manager: Ralph Santana

SPRINGFIELD LUCKY HORSESHOES

Stadium: Robin Roberts Stadium at Lanphier Park
Mailing Address: 1415 North Grand Avenue East, Suite B, Springfield, IL 62702
Telephone: (217) 679-3511
E-Mail Address: fun@shoesbaseball.com
Website: shoesbaseball.com
Chief Storyteller: Jamie Toole.
Director of Swag & Events: Melissa Gaynor.
Emperor of Engagement: Andrew Miller.
Field Manager: Chris Holke

SOUTHERN COLLEGIATE BASEBALL LEAGUE

Mailing Address: 9723 Northcross Center Court, Huntersville, NC 28078. **Cell:** (704) 604-8298
E-Mail Address: jbillings@scbl.org. **Website:** scbl.org
Year Founded: 1999.
Chairman: Bill Capps, **Commissioner:** Jamie Billings. **President:** Jeff Carter. **Treasurer:** Brenda Templin.
Umpire in Chief: Gary Swanson.
Regular Season: 30 games. **Playoff Format:** Six-team single-elimination tournament with best of three championship series between final two teams.
Roster Limit: 40 (College-eligible players only).

244 · Baseball America 2023 Directory

BaseballAmerica.com

AMATEUR/YOUTH

CONCORD ATHLETICS

Mailing Address: 366 George Lyles Parkway, Suite 125, Concord, NC 28027.
Telephone: (704) 786-2255.
Email Address: playconcordathletics@gmail.com.
General Manager: Jeremy Teeter
Head Coach: John Edwards

LAKE NORMAN COPPERHEADS

Mailing Address: 2158 Killian Creek Dr, Denver, NC 28937. **Telephone:** (704) 604-8298. **Email Address:** jbillings@scbl.org
General Manager: Jamie Billings. **Head Coach:** Noah Jarrett

QUEEN CITY CORNDOGS

Mailing Address: 12104 Copper Way, Suite 200, Charlotte NC 28277. **Telephone:** 980-256-5346.
E-Mail Address: bnichols@tprsolutions.com
General Manager: Blaine Nichols.
Head Coach: Brice Davis

STATESVILLE OWLS

Owner: Reece Honeycutt
Telephone: 704-880-8674
Email: Fifteensports@yahoo.com

MOORSVILLE SPINNERS

Mailing Address: 2643 N Hwy 16 Denver, NC 28037.
Telephone: (704) 491-4112.
E-Mail Address: ploftin@mooresvillespinners.com.
General Manager: Phillip Loftin.

REGULATORS BASEBALL CLUB

Mailing address: 1805 Mt Isle Harbor Dr, Charlotte, NC 28214. **Email:** info@regulatorsbaseball.com.
Telephone: 980-213-1889
General Manager: Ben Teague

TEXAS COLLEGIATE LEAGUE

Mailing Address: 405 Mitchell Street, Bryan, TX 77801. **Telephone:** 979-977-4825.
E-Mail Address: info@tclbaseball.com.
Website: texascollegeleague.com.
Year Founded: 2004.
President: Uri Geva.
Roster Limit: 30 (College-eligible players only)

ACADIANA CANE CUTTERS

Mailing Address: 221 La Neuville, Youngsville, LA 70592. **Telephone:** (337) 451-6582.
E-Mail Address: info@canecuttersbaseball.com.
Website: canecuttersbaseball.com.
Owners: Richard Chalmers, Sandi Chalmers.

BATON ROUGE ROUGAROU

Mailing Address: 1113 Range Ave. Suite 110 #165 Denham Springs, LA 70726. **Telephone:** (225) 802-6040.
E-Mail Address: ronnie@brrougarou.com. **Website:** brrougarou.com. **Owner:** Ronnie Rantz.

SEGUIN RIVER MONSTERS

Mailing Address: 950 S Austin StSeguin, TX 78155.
Telephone: (210) 281-1628. **E-Mail Address:** seguinrivermonsters@gmail.com. **Website:** www.seguinrivermonsters.com. **Owner:** Mike Gigliotti.
General Manager: Scott Barry

BRAZOS VALLEY BOMBERS

Mailing Address: 405 Mitchell St, Bryan, TX 77801.
Telephone: (979) 799-7529. 8. **E-Mail Address:** info@bvbombers.com. **Website:** bvbombers.com. **Owners:** Uri Geva, Chris Clark. **Field Manager:** James Dillard.

VICTORIA GENERALS

Mailing Address: 1307 E Airline Road, Suite H, Victoria, TX 77901. **Telephone:** (361) 485-9522. **Fax:** (361) 485-0936. **E-Mail Address:** info@baseballinvictoria.com, tkyoung@victoriagenerals.com. **Website:** victoriagenerals.com. **President:** Tracy Young. **VP/General Manager:** Mike Yokum.

VALLEY BASEBALL LEAGUE

Mailing Address: Valley Baseball League, PO Box 1127, New Market, VA 22844. **Telephone:** (540) 810-9194. **Fax:** (540) 435-8453. **E-Mail Address:** cbalger@shentel.net. **Website:** valleyleaguebaseball.com.
Year Founded: 1897. **President/Commissioner:** R.W. Bowman. **Senior Vice President:** Lance Mauck. **Executive Vice President:** Jay Neal. **Secretary:** Megan Shepard. **Treasurer:** Ed Yoder. **Media Relations Director:** Ridge Fuller. **Director of Umpires:** Tim Detweller. **Regular Season:** 42 games. **Playoff Format:** Eight teams qualify; play three rounds of best of three series. **Roster Limit:** 30 (college-eligible only)

CHARLOTTESVILLE TOM SOX

Mailing Address: PO Box 4836, Charlottesville, VA 22905. **E-Mail Address:** info@tomsox.org. **Website:** www.tomsox.com. **President:** John Raymond. **Vice President:** Chesley Mullins.

COVINGTON LUMBERJACKS

Mailing Address: PO Box 30, Covington, VA 24426.
Telephone: (540) 962-1155. **E-Mail Address:** vblcov@gmail.com. **Website:** www.covingtonlumberjacks.com.
President: Dizzy Garten and Tommy Garten.
General Manager: Mike Pifer.

CULPEPER CAVALIERS

Mailing Address: 25023 Algonquin Trail, Culpeper, VA 22701. **Telephone:** (703) 216-2952. **E-Mail Address:** info@culpepercavaliers.org. **Website:** www.culpepercavaliers.org. **President:** Troy Ralston.

FRONT ROYAL CARDINALS

Mailing Address: 382 Morgans Ridge Road, Front Royal, VA 22630. **Telephone:** (703) 244-6662. **E-Mail Address:** DonnaSettle@centurylink.net. **Website:** www.frontroyalcardinals.com. **President:** Donna Settle.

HARRISONBURG TURKS

Mailing Address: 1489 S Main St, Harrisonburg, VA 22801. **Telephone:** (540) 290-2929.
E-Mail Address: hbturksbaseball@gmail.com.
Website: harrisonburgturks.com.

BaseballAmerica.com

Baseball America 2023 Directory • **245**

AMATEUR/YOUTH

NEW MARKET REBELS

Mailing Address: PO Box 902, New Market, VA 22844. **Telephone:** (540) 435-8453. **Fax:** (540) 740-9486. **E-Mail Address:** nmrebels@shentel.net. **Website:** new marketrebels.com. **President/General Manager:** Mike Jones.

PURCELLVILLE CANNONS

Mailing Address: P.O. Box 114, Purcellville, VA 20132. **Telephone:** (540) 327-4276. **E-Mail Address:** PurcellvilleCannons@gmail.com. **Website:** purcellvillecannons.com.

STAUNTON BRAVES

Mailing Address: PO Box 428, Stuarts Draft, VA 24447. **Telephone:** (443) 250-2657. **E-Mail Address:** stauntonbraves@gmail.com. **Website:** stauntonbravesbaseball. com. **President:** Lance Mauk. **General Manager:** Steve Cox.

STRASBURG EXPRESS

Mailing Address: PO Box 417, Strasburg, VA 22657 **Telephone:** (540) 325-5677, (540) 459-4041. **Fax:** (540) 459-3398. **E-Mail Address:** neallaw@shentel.net, strasburgxpress@gmail.com. **Website:** strasburg express.com. **President:** Jay Neal. **General Manager:** Parker Neal.

WAYNESBORO GENERALS

Mailing Address: 1562 Jefferson Highway, Fisherville, VA 22939. **Telephone:** (540) 241-0065. **E-Mail Address:** waynerborogenerals1@gmail.com. **Website:** waynesborogenerals.com. **General Manager:** Stacy Lotts.

WINCHESTER ROYALS

Mailing Address: PO Box 2485, Winchester, VA 22604. **Telephone:** (540) 974-4104, (540) 664-3978. **Fax:** (540) 662-1434. **E-Mail Addresses:** info@winchesterroyals.org. **Website:** winchesterroyals.com. **President:** Mitch Rode. **General Manager:** Brian Burke. **Coach:** Mike Smith.

WOODSTOCK RIVER BANDITS

Mailing Address: P.O. Box 227, Woodstock, VA 22664. **Telephone:** (540) 335-5434. **E-Mail Address:** banditsbaseball200910@yahoo.com. **Website:** woodstockriverbandits.org. **General Manager:** R.W. Bowman III. **Head Coach:** Mike Bocock.

WEST COAST LEAGUE

Mailing Address: PO Box 10771, Portland OR 97296. **Telephone:** 503-233-2490. **E-Mail Address:** info@westcoastleague.com. **Website:** westcoastleague.com.

Year Founded: 2005. **Commissioner:** Rob Neyer. **President:** Tony Bonacci. **Vice President:** Glenn Kirkpatrick. **Secretary:** Jose Oglesby. **Treasurer:** Dan Segel. **Supervisor, Umpires:** John White. **Division Structure: South**—Bend Elks, Corvallis Knights, Cowlitz Black Bears, Portland Pickles, Ridgefield Raptors, Springfield Drifters, Walla Walla Sweets, Yakima Valley Pippins. **North**—Bellingham Bells, Edmonton Riverhawks, Kamloops NorthPaws, Kelowna Falcons, Nanaimo NightOwls, Port Angeles Lefties, Victoria Harbourcats, Wenatchee Applesox, Yakima Valley Pippins. **2023 Opening Date:** June 2. **Closing Date:** August 6. **Playoff Format:** Eight-team tournament. **Roster Limit:** 35 (college-eligible players only).

BELLINGHAM BELLS

Mailing Address: 1221 Potter Street, Bellingham, WA 98229. **Telephone:** (360) 527-1035. **E-Mail Address:** stephanie@bellinghambells.com. **Website:** bellinghambells.com.

Owner: Glenn Kirkpatrick. **General Manager:** Stephanie Morrell. **Head Coach:** Jim Clem.

Field: Joe Martin Field.

BEND ELKS

Mailing Address: 70 SW Century Dr Suite 100-373 Bend, Oregon 97702. **Telephone:** (541) 312-9259. **Website:** bendelks.com. **Owners:** John and Tami Marick. **Marketing and Sales:** Kelsie Hirko. **General Manager:** Michael Hirko. **Head Coach:** Joey Wong.

Field: Vince Genna Stadium.

CORVALLIS KNIGHTS

Mailing Address: PO Box 1356, Corvallis, OR 97339. **Telephone:** (541) 752-5656. **E-Mail Address:** dan.segel@ corvallisknights.com. **Website:** corvallisknights.com.

General Manager: Jennifer Beaumont. **Head Coach:** Brooke Knight.

Field: Goss Stadium.

COWLITZ BLACK BEARS

Mailing Address: PO Box 1255, Longview, WA 98632. **Telephone:** (360) 703-3195. **Website:** cowlitzblac kbears.com. **Owner/President:** Tony Bonacci. **General Manager:** Gus Farah.

Head Coach: Kelly Stinnett.

Field: David Story Field.

EDMONTON RIVERHAWKS

Address: RE/MAX Field, 10233 96 Ave, Edmonton, Alberta. **Telephone:** (587) 802-2244. **E-Mail Address:** admin@gohawks.ca. **Website:** gohawks.ca.

General Manager: Steve Hogle. **Operations Manager:** Ryan Gregg.

Head Coach: Jake Lanferman.

Field: RE/MAX Field.

KAMLOOPS NORTHPAWS

Address: 1500 Island Pkwy, Kamloops, BC. **Owners:** Norman Daley, Neal Perry, Jon Pankuch. **General Manager:** Jenna Forter.

Head Coach: Brian Anderson.

Field: Norbrock Stadium.

KELOWNA FALCONS

Mailing Address: 201-1014 Glenmore Dr, Kelowna, BC, V1Y 4P2. **Telephone:** (250) 763-4100. **Website:** kelownafalcons.com. **Owner:** Dan Nonis. **General Manager:** Mark Nonis.

Head Coach: Doug Noce.

Field: Elks Stadium.

NANAIMO NIGHTHAWKS

Address: PO Box 39084, Nanaimo, BC V9R 7B7. **Website:** nanaimonightowls.com.

Director/GM: Jim Swanson.

Head Coach: Greg Frady.

Field: Serauxmen Staidum

246 · Baseball America 2023 Directory

BaseballAmerica.com

AMATEUR/YOUTH

PORT ANGELES LEFTIES

Mailing Address: PO Box 2204, Port Angeles, WA 98362. **Phone:** (360) 701-1087. **Website:** lefties baseball.com. **E-Mail Address:** matt@leftiesbaseball.com. **Owners:** Matt Acker, Jacob Oppelt, Eric Traut, Connor Traut. **General Manager:** Matt Acker.
Head Coach: TBD
Field: Civic Field.

PORTLAND PICKLES

Address: 5308 SE 92nd Ave. Portland, OR 97266. **Phone:** (503)775-3080. **Owners:** Alan Miller, Jon Ryan, Scott Barchus. **GM:** Parker Huffman.
Head Coach: Mark Magdaleno.
Field: Walker Stadium.

RIDGEFIELD RAPTORS

Owner: Tony Bonacci. **Partner:** Wade Siegel. **E-Mail Address:** info@ridgefieldraptors.com. **General Manager:** Gus Farah.
Head Coach: Chris Cota.
Field: Ridgefield Outfield Recreation Center.

SPRINGFIELD DRIFTERS

Owners: Ike Olsson and Kelly Richardson. **Assistant GM:** Kyle Whitty. **Head Coach:** Tommy Richards.
Field: Hamlin Sports Complex.

VICTORIA HARBOURCATS

Mailing Address: 101-1814 Vancouver Street, Victoria, BC, Canada, V8T 5E3. **Telephone:** (778) 265-0327. **Website:** harbourcats.com. **General Manager:** Christian Stewart. **Head Coach:** Todd Haney
Field: Royal Athletic Park.

WALLA WALLA SWEETS

Mailing Address: 109 E Main Street, Walla Walla, WA 99362. **Telephone:** (509) 522-2255. **E-Mail Address:** info@wallawallasweets.com. **Website:** wallawalla sweets.com. **General Manager:** Cody Miller. **Head Coach:** Jarrod Molna.
Field: Borleske Stadium.

WENATCHEE APPLESOX

Mailing Address: 610 N. Mission St. #204, Wenatchee, WA 98801. **Telephone:** (509) 665-6900. **E-Mail Address:** info@applesox.com. **Website:** applesox.com.
General Manager: Allie Schank. **Head Coach:** Mitch Darlington.
Field: Paul Thomas Sr. Field.

YAKIMA VALLEY PIPPINS

Mailing Address: PO Box 2397, Yakima, WA 98907. **Telephone:** (509) 575-4487. **E-Mail Address:** info@pippinsbaseball.com. **Website:** pippinsbaseball.com.
General Manager: Jeff Garretson. **Head Coach:** Kyle Krustangel.
Field: Yakima County Stadium.

HIGH SCHOOL BASEBALL

NATIONAL FEDERATION OF STATE HIGH SCHOOL ASSOCIATIONS

Mailing Address: PO Box 690, Indianapolis, IN 46206. **Telephone:** (317) 972-6900. **E-Mail Address:** baseball@nfhs.org. **Website:** nfhs.org.
Executive Director: Karissa Niehoff. **Chief Operating Officer:** Davis Whitfield. **Chief Financial Officer:** JoAnne Bennett. **Chief Marketing Officer:** Mark Koski. **Chief Talent Officer:** Mautrice Meriweather. **Director of Sports:** Julie Cochran, Sandy Searcy. **Director of Sports and Sports Medicine:** Bob Colgate. **Director of Sports, Sanctioning and Student Services:** B. Elliot Hopkins. **Director, Publications/Communications:** Bruce Howard. **Coordinator of Social Media and Communications:** Olivia Jennings. **Director of Information Technology:** Alex Shaw.
NFHS Board of Directors: Sally Marquez (president), Tom Keating (president-elect), Mike Burnham, Bob

Lombardi, Eddie Bonine, Dan Swartos, Ron Nocetti, Ty Jones, David Frazier, Kim Wilbanks, Tommy Cox, Amanda Kaus.

NATIONAL HIGH SCHOOL BASEBALL COACHES ASSOCIATION

Mailing Address: PO Box 1038, Dublin, OH 43017. **Telephone:** (614) 578-1864. **E-Mail Address:** tsaunders@baseballcoaches.org. **Website:** baseballcoaches.org.
Executive Director: Tim Saunders (Dublin Coffman HS, Ohio). **Assistant Executive Director:** Ty Whittaker (Eastern Technical HS, Md.). **Associate Executive Director:** Ray Benjamin (St. Charles HS, Ohio). **Associate Exectuive Director:** Paul Twenge (Minnetonka HS, Minn.). **Executive Secretary:** Robert Colburn. **President:** Tony Perkins (Francis Howell HS, Mo.). **1st VP:** Tim Bordenet (Lafayette Central Catholic HS, Ind.). **2nd VP:** Scott Manahan (Bishop Watterson HS, Ohio).

BaseballAmerica.com

Baseball America 2023 Directory • **247**

AMATEUR/YOUTH

YOUTH BASEBALL

ALL AMERICAN AMATEUR BASEBALL ASSOCIATION
E-Mail Address: bming23@aol.com.
Website: aaabajohnstown.org
President/Executive Director: Bob Mingo
2023 Events: aaabajohnstown.org/tournaments/

AMATEUR ATHLETIC UNION OF THE UNITED STATES, INC.
Mailing Address: P.O. Box 22409, Lake Buena Vista, FL 32830. **Telephone:** (407) 828-3459. **Fax:** (407) 934-7242. **E-mail Address:** oldpro77@msn.com. **Website:** aaubaseball.org.
Year Founded: 1982. **National Baseball Chairperson:** Ed Skovron.

AMERICAN AMATEUR BASEBALL CONGRESS
National Headquarters: 100 West Broadway, Farmington, NM 87401. **Telephone:** (505) 327-3120. **Fax:** (505) 327-3132. **E-mail Address:** info@aabc.us. **Website:** aabc.us.
Year Founded: 1935.
President: Richard Neely.

AMERICAN AMATEUR YOUTH BASEBALL ALLIANCE
Mailing Address: 3851 Iris Lane, Bonne Terre, MO 63628. **Telephone:** (314) 803-7222. **E-mail Address:** presidentbusinessoperations@aayba.com. **Website:** aayba.com.
President, Business Operations: Greg Moore.

AMERICAN LEGION BASEBALL
National Headquarters: American Legion Baseball, 700 N Pennsylvania St., Indianapolis, IN 46204. **Telephone:** (317) 630-1213. **Fax:** (317) 630-1369. **E-mail Address:** baseball@legion.org. **Website:** legion.org/baseball.
Year Founded: 1925.
2023 World Series (19 and under): americanlegion. sportngin.com/2023

BABE RUTH LEAGUE
International Headquarters: 1670 Whitehorse-Mercerville Rd., Hamilton, NJ 08619. **Telephone:** (800) 880-3142. **E-mail Address:** info@baberuthleague.org. **Website:** baberuthleague.org.
Year Founded: 1951.
President/Chief Executive Officer: Steven Tellefsen.

BASEBALL FOR ALL
Mailing Address: 30745 Pacific Coast Hwy #328 Los Angeles, CA 90265. **E-mail Address:** girlsbaseball@baseballforall.com. **Website:** BaseballForAll.com
Providing baseball programming for girls.

CALIFORNIA COMPETITIVE YOUTH BASEBALL
Mailing Address: P.O. Box 338, Placentia, CA 92870. **Telephone:** (714) 993-2838. **E-mail Address:** ccybnet@ gmail.com. **Website:** ccyb.net.
Tournament Director: Todd Rogers.

CONTINENTAL AMATEUR BASEBALL ASSOCIATION
Mailing Address: P.O. Box 1684 Mt. Pleasant, SC 29465. **Telephone:** (843) 860-1568. **E-mail Address:** Diamonddevils@aol.com. **Website:** cababaseball.com.
Year Founded: 1984.
Chief Executive Officer: Larry Redwine. **President/COO:** John Rhodes. **Executive Vice President:** Fran Pell.

COOPERSTOWN BASEBALL WORLD
Mailing Address: P.O. Box 646, Allenwood, NJ 08720. **Telephone:** (888) CBW-8750. **Fax:** (888) CBW-8720. **E-mail:** cbw@cooperstownbaseballworld.com.
Website: cooperstownbaseballworld.com.
Complex Address: Cooperstown Baseball World, SUNY-Oneonta, Ravine Parkway, Oneonta, NY 13820.
President: Debra Sirianni.
2023 Tournaments (15 Teams Per Week): Open to 12U, 13U, 14U, 15U, 16U

COOPERSTOWN DREAMS PARK
Mailing Address: 330 S. Main St., Salisbury, NC 28144. **Telephone:** (704) 630-0050. **Fax:** (704) 630-0737. **E-mail Address:** info@cooperstowndreamspark.com. **Website:** cooperstowndreamspark.com.
Complex Address: 4550 State Highway 28, Milford, NY 13807.

COOPERSTOWN ALL STAR VILLAGE
Mailing Address: P.O. Box 670, Cooperstown, NY 13326. **Telephone:** (800) 327-6790. **E-mail Address:** info@cooperstown.com. **Website:** cooperstown.com.

DIXIE YOUTH BASEBALL
Mailing Address: P.O. Box 877, Marshall, TX 75671. **Telephone:** (903) 927-2255. **E-mail Address:** dyb@dixie. org. **Website:** youth.dixie.org. **Year Founded:** 1955.
Commissioner: William Wade.

DIXIE BOYS BASEBALL
Mailing Address: P.O. Box 8263, Dothan, AL 36304. **Telephone:** (334) 793-3331. **E-mail Address:** jjones29@ sw.rr.com. **Website:** baseball.dixie.org.
Commissioner/Chief Executive Officer: Sandy Jones.

DIZZY DEAN BASEBALL
Mailing Address: P.O. Box 856, Hernando, MS 38632. **Telephone:** (662) 429-4365. **E-mail Address:** dannyphillips637@gmail.com. **Website:** dizzydeanbbinc.org.
Year Founded: 1962.
Commissioner: Danny Phillips. **President:** Joe Chandler. **VP:** Brent Frey. **Secretary:** John Gravet. **Treasurer:** Jim Dunn.

LITTLE LEAGUE BASEBALL
International Headquarters: 539 US Route 15 Hwy, P.O. Box 3485, Williamsport, PA 17701-0485. **Telephone:** (570) 326-1921. **Fax:** (570) 326-1074. **E-mail Address:** media@littleleague.org. **Website:** littleleague.org.
Year Founded: 1939.
Chairman: Steven P. Johnson. **Vice Chariman:**

248 · Baseball America 2023 Directory

BaseballAmerica.com

Jon Litner. **President and Chief Executive Officer:** Stephen D. Keener. **Senior Vice President and Chief Financial Officer:** David Houseknecht. **Chief Operating Officer:** Patrick Wilson. **Senior Vice President and Chief Marketing Officer:** Elizabeth Brown. **Senior Vice President and Chief Legal Officer:** Joy Renolds McCoy. **Treasurer:** Melissa Singer.

NATIONAL AMATEUR BASEBALL FEDERATION

Mailing Address: P.O. Box 4099 Brandon, MS 29047. **Telephone:** 769-251-5158.

E-mail Address: nabfexecdirector@gmail.com. **Website:** nabf.com. **Year Founded:** 1914.

Executive Director: Derek J. Topik. **President:** Paul Wolf. **Vice Presidents:** Robert Chiara, Fred LeSage, William Bellinger.

SENIOR BASEBALL

MEN'S SENIOR BASEBALL LEAGUE

(18+, 25+, 35+, 45+, 55+, 65+)

Mailing Address: One Huntington Quadrangle, Suite 3N07, Melville, NY 11747. **Telephone:** (631) 753-6725.

President: Steve Sigler. **Vice President:** Gary D'Ambrisi.

E-Mail Address: info@msblnational.com. **Website:** msblnational.com.

NATIONAL ADULT BASEBALL ASSOCIATION

Mailing Address: 5944 S. Kipling St., Suite 200, Littleton, CO 80127. **Telephone:** (800) 621-6479. **E-Mail:** nabanational@aol.com. **Website:** dugout.org.

President: Shane Fugita. **Vice President:** Joe Collins. **Office Manager:** Stacy Fugita.

NATIONAL AMATEUR BASEBALL FEDERATION

Mailing Address: P.O. Box 4099 Brandon, MS 29047. **Telephone:** 769-251-5158.

E-mail Address: nabfexecdirector@gmail.com. **Website:** nabf.com. **Year Founded:** 1914.

Executive Director: Derek J. Topik. **President:** Paul Wolf. **Vice Presidents:** Robert Chiara, Fred LeSage, William Bellinger.

ROY HOBBS BASEBALL

Veterans (30 or 35 and Over), Masters (45 and Over), Legends (53 and Over); Classics (60 and Over), Vintage (65 and Over), Timeless (70 and Over), Forever Young (75 and Over).

Mailing Address: 4301-100 Edison Ave., Fort Myers, FL 33916. **Telephone:** (239) 689-8550. **E-Mail Address:** teammatesupport@royhobbs.com.

Website: royhobbs.com.

INDEX

INDEX

MAJOR LEAGUE TEAMS

Team	Page
Arizona Diamondbacks	14
Atlanta Braves	16
Baltimore Orioles	18
Boston Red Sox	20
Chicago Cubs	22
Chicago White Sox	24
Cincinnati Reds	26
Cleveland Guardians	28
Colorado Rockies	30
Detroit Tigers	32
Houston Astros	34
Kansas City Royals	36
Los Angeles Angels	38
Los Angeles Dodgers	40
Miami Marlins	42
Milwaukee Brewers	44
Minnesota Twins	46
New York Mets	48
New York Yankees	50
Oakland Athletics	52
Philadelphia Phillies	54
Pittsburgh Pirates	56
St. Louis Cardinals	58
San Diego Padres	60
San Francisco Giants	62
Seattle Mariners	64
Tampa Bay Rays	66
Texas Rangers	68
Toronto Blue Jays	70
Washington Nationals	72

MINOR LEAGUE TEAMS

Team (League)	Page
Aberdeen (South Atlantic League)	122
Akron (Eastern League)	101
Albuquerque (Pacific Coast League)	95
Altoona (Eastern League)	101
Amarillo (Texas League)	111
Arkansas (Texas League)	111
Asheville (South Atlantic League)	122
Augusta (Carolina League)	134
Beloit (Midwest League)	116
Biloxi (Southern League)	107
Binghamton (Eastern League)	102
Birmingham (Southern League)	107
Bowie (Eastern League)	102
Bowling Green (South Atlantic League)	123
Bradenton (Florida State League)	139
Brooklyn (South Atlantic League)	123
Buffalo (International League)	85
Carolina (Carolina League)	134
Cedar Rapids (Midwest League)	116
Charleston (Carolina League)	135
Charlotte (International League)	85
Chattanooga (Southern League)	108
Clearwater (Florida State League)	139
Columbia (Carolina League)	135
Columbus (International League)	86
Corpus Christi (Texas League)	112
Dayton (Midwest League)	117
Daytona (Florida State League)	140
Delmarva (Carolina League)	136
Down East (Carolina League)	136
Dunedin (Florida State League)	140
Durham (International League)	87
El Paso (Pacific Coast League)	95
Erie (Eastern League)	103
Eugene (Northwest League)	127
Everett (Northwest League)	127
Fayetteville (Carolina League)	136
Fort Myers (Florida State League)	140
Fort Wayne (Midwest League)	117
Fredericksburg (Carolina League)	137
Fresno (California League)	130
Frisco (Texas League)	112
Great Lakes (Midwest League)	118
Greensboro (South Atlantic League)	123
Greenville (South Atlantic League)	124
Gwinnett (International League)	87
Harrisburg (Eastern League)	103
Hartford (Eastern League)	103
Hickory (South Atlantic League)	125

INDEX

Scranton/Wilkes-Barre (International League)	93
Somerset (Eastern League)	106
South Bend (Midwest League)	120
Spokane (Northwest League)	128
Springfield (Texas League)	114
St. Lucie (Florida State League)	142
St. Paul (International League)	92
Stockton (California League)	132
Sugar Land (Pacific Coast League)	99
Syracuse (International League)	93
Tacoma (Pacific Coast League)	99
Tampa (Florida State League)	142
Tennessee (Southern League)	110
Toledo (International League)	94
Tri-City (Northwest League)	128
Tulsa (Texas League)	114
Vancouver (Northwest League)	129
Visalia (California League)	133
West Michigan (Midwest League)	120
Wichita (Texas League)	115
Wilmington (South Atlantic League)	126
Winston-Salem (South Atlantic League)	126
Wisconsin (Midwest League)	121
Worcester (International League)	94

MLB PARTNER TEAMS

Team (League)	Page
Billings (Pioneer)	189
Boise (Pioneer)	189
Charleston (Atlantic)	180
Chicago (American)	176
Cleburne (American)	176
Evansville (Frontier)	184
Fargo-Moorhead (American)	177
Florence (Frontier)	184
Frederick (Atlantic)	181
Gary Southshore (American)	177
Gastonia (Atlantic)	180
Gateway (Frontier)	185
Glacier Range (Pioneer)	190
Grand Junction (Pioneer)	190
Great Falls (Pioneer)	190
High Point (Atlantic)	181
Idaho Falls (Pioneer)	190
Joliet (Frontier)	185
Kane County (American)	177
Kansas City (American)	178
Lake Country (American)	178
Lake Erie (Frontier)	185
Lancaster (Atlantic)	181
Lexington (Atlantic)	181
Lincoln (American)	178
Long Island (Atlantic)	182
Milwaukee (American)	179
Missoula (Pioneer)	191
New Jersey (Frontier)	185
New York (Frontier)	186

Team (League)	Page
Northern Colorado (Pioneer)	191
Ogden (Pioneer)	191
Ottawa (Frontier)	186
Quebec (Frontier)	186
Rocky Mountain (Pioneer)	192
Schaumburg (Frontier)	186
Sioux City (American)	179
Sioux Falls (American)	179
Southern Maryland (Atlantic)	182
Staten Island (Atlantic)	182
Sussex County (Frontier)	187
Tri-City (Frontier)	187
Trois-Rivieres (Frontier)	187
Washington (Frontier)	188
Windy City (Frontier)	188
Winnipeg (American)	179
York (Atlantic)	182

Hillsboro (Northwest League)	127
Hudson Valley (South Atlantic League)	124
Indianapolis (International League)	87
Inland Empire (California League)	130
Iowa (International League)	88
Jacksonville (International League)	89
Jersey Shore (South Atlantic League)	125
Jupiter (Florida State League)	141
Kannapolis (Carolina League)	137
Lake County (Midwest League)	118
Lake Elsinore (California League)	130
Lakeland (Florida State League)	141
Lansing (Midwest League)	119
Las Vegas (Pacific Coast League)	96
Lehigh Valley (International League)	89
Louisville (International League)	90
Lynchburg (Carolina League)	138
Memphis (International League)	90
Midland (Texas League)	113
Mississippi (Southern League)	108
Modesto (California League)	131
Montgomery (Southern League)	108
Myrtle Beach (Carolina League)	138
Nashville (International League)	90
New Hampshire (Eastern League)	104
Norfolk (International League)	91
Northwest Arkansas (Texas League)	113
Oklahoma City (Pacific Coast League)	96
Omaha (International League)	91
Palm Beach (Florida State League)	142
Pensacola (Southern League)	109
Peoria (Midwest League)	119
Portland (Eastern League)	104
Quad Cities (Midwest League)	119
Rancho Cucamonga (California League)	131
Reading (Eastern League)	105
Reno (Pacific Coast League)	97
Richmond (Eastern League)	105
Rochester (International League)	92
Rocket City (Southern League)	109
Rome (South Atlantic League)	125
Round Rock (Pacific Coast League)	97
Sacramento (Pacific Coast League)	98
Salem (Carolina League)	138
Salt Lake (Pacific Coast League)	99
San Antonio (Texas League)	114
San Jose (California League)	132

252 • Baseball America 2023 Directory

OTHER ORGANIZATIONS

Organization	Page
Africa Baseball/Softball Association	230
Alaska Baseball League	232
America East Conference	201
American Baseball Coaches Association	200
American Athletic Conference	201
American Legion	248
Appalachian League	232
Arizona Fall League	198
Athletes In Action	231
Atlantic Coast Conference	201

Organization	Page
Atlantic Collegiate Baseball League	233
Atlantic Sun Conference	201
Atlantic 10 Conference	201
Australian Baseball League	198
Babe Ruth League	248
Baseball Assistance Team	78
Baseball Canada	231
Baseball Chapel	78
Baseball Confederation of Oceania	230
Baseball Federation of Asia	230
Baseball Winter Meetings	78

Organization	Page
Big East Conference	201
Big South Conference	201
Big Ten Conference	201
Big 12 Conference	201
Big West Conference	201
Cal Ripken Collegiate League	234
California Collegiate League	234
California Community College Athletic Association	200
Cape Cod League	235
Catholic Athletes For Christ	78
Coastal Plain League	235
Colonial Athletic Association	202
Confederation Pan Americana De Beisbol	230
Conference USA	202
Dominican League	197
Dominican Summer League	195
Dutch Major League	197
European Baseball Confederation	230
Florida Collegiate Summer League	237
Futures Collegiate League of New England	237
Great Lakes Summer Collegiate League	237
Horizon League	202
International Sports Group	230
Italian Baseball League	197
Ivy League	202
Korea Baseball Organization	196

	Page
Little League Baseball	249
MLB Players Alumni Association	77
MLB Draft League	238
Metro Atlantic Athletic Conference	202
Metropolitan Collegiate Baseball League	237
Mexican League	194
Mexican Pacific League	198
Mexican Academy	194
Mid-American Conference	202
M.I.N.K. League	237
Missouri Valley Conference	202
Mountain West Conference	202
National Alliance of College Summer Baseball	232
National Baseball Congress	231
National Baseball Hall of Fame	77
National Collegiate Athletic Association	200
National Federation of State High School Associations	247
National High School Baseball Coaches Association	247
National Junior College Athletic Association	200
Negro Leagues Baseball Museum	77
New England Collegiate League	238
New York Collegiate Baseball League	239
Nippon Professional Baseball	195
Northeast Conference	202
Northwoods League	240
Ohio Valley Conference	202
Pacific-12 Conference	203
Patriot League	203
Pecos League	192
Perfect Game Collegiate Baseball League	242
Prospect League	243
Puerto Rican League	198
Reviving Baseball in Inner Cities	78
Senior Baseball	249
Society for American Baseball Research	77
Southeastern Conference	203
Southern Collegiate Baseball League	244
Southern Conference	203
Southland Conference	203
Southwestern Athletic Conference	203
Summit League	203
Sun Belt Conference	203
Texas Collegiate League	245
United Shore Professional Baseball League	192
USA Baseball	231
Valley Baseball League	245
Venezuelan League	198
West Coast Conference	203
West Coast League	246
Western Athletic Conference	203
World Baseball Softball Confederation	230